Personal Finance for Canadians

for Canadians

Ninth Edition

Elliott J. Currie
University of Guelph

Thomas F. Chambers

Kathleen H. Brown

PEARSON
Prentice
Hall

Toronto

To our wives, Ann and Heather, for caring enough to help in order to enjoy the fruits of our labours.

Library and Archives Canada has catalogued this publication as follows:

Currie, Elliott J.
    Personal finance for Canadians/Elliott J. Currie, Thomas F. Chambers, Kathleen H. Brown.

Triennial.
8th ed.–
Continues: Brown, Kathleen H. (Kathleen Helen), 1926– Personal finance for Canadians.
ISSN: 1202-9386
ISBN: 978-0-13-228675-6 (9th edition)

1. Finance, Personal—Canada–Periodicals. 2. Consumer credit—Canada—Periodicals. 3. Financial security—Periodicals. I. Chambers, Tom, 1940– II. Brown, Kathleen H. (Kathleen Helen), 1926– III. Title.

HG179.B76   332.024'005   C2004-901688-1

ISBN-13: 978-0-13-228675-6
ISBN-10:   0-13-228675-0

Editor-in-Chief: Gary Bennett
Executive Editor: Samantha Scully
Marketing Manager: Eileen Lasswell
Developmental Editor: Rema Celio
Production Editor: Laura Neves
Copy Editor: Martin Townsend
Proofreader: Ron Jacques
Production Coordinator: Christine Kwan
Composition: Integra
Art Director: Julia Hall
Cover Design: Chris Tsintziras
Interior Design: Chris Tsintziras
Cover Image: Veer

For permission to reproduce copyrighted material, the publisher gratefully acknowledges the copyright holders listed on pages throughout the text, which are considered extensions of this copyright page.

Statistics Canada information is used with the permission of Statistics Canada. Users are forbidden to copy the data and redisseminate them, in an original or modified form, for commercial purposes, without permission from Statistics Canada. Information on the availability of the wide range of data from Statistics Canada can be obtained from Statistics Canada's Regional Offices, its World Wide Web site at **http://www.statcan.ca**, and its toll-free access number 1-800-263-1136.

1 2 3 4 5   12 11 10 09 08

Printed and bound in the United States of America.

Brief Contents

Contents

Chapter 8   Saving and Investing   222

Chapter 9   Debt Securities   265

Chapter 10   Stocks, Mutual Funds, and Other Investments   296

Chapter 14 Credit, Debt, and Bankruptcy   479

Preface

In the not-too-distant past the world of personal finance, for most people, was uncomplicated and easy to understand. A person worked, received his or her pay by cheque, deposited this cheque in a bank account in person and then wrote personal cheques to cover expenses. If this person owned a home or rented an apartment, a regular monthly expense was the mortgage or rent payment, also paid by cheque. If there was any extra money left over and this person wanted to invest, he or she might have done so by purchasing Canada Savings Bonds or bonds and stock in Canadian companies (there were no mutual funds, and few of the other investment choices available today). Then he or she would have deposited the certificates for these investments in a safety deposit box, in person.

In a very short time much of this system has changed. For one thing, in today's financial world, very little paper changes hands at all. Most financial transactions are done electronically. Salaries are deposited in this way. While cheques still exist, few are used; most bills are paid via the computer or by telephone. Money may be deposited and withdrawn from bank machines almost anywhere in the world using a bank card. Many of our routine purchases are also made with plastic. Money, in the form of cash, is therefore used much less as a medium of exchange. Stocks and bonds are now held in street form (by account number only) at an investment dealer. Certificates of such securities are no longer needed. As a result of changes in technology, many basic financial transactions have therefore become both simpler and faster in a very short space of time.

Technology has allowed us to access our bank accounts 24 hours a day, seven days a week, but we have, in the process, become more dependent on this technology. Who has not experienced the complete helplessness of our banks, and in fact our whole financial and commercial system, because "the computer is down"? When this happens, you can't get money, pay your bills, or shop. Retail outlets—and indeed, commerce—cannot function when the system breaks down.

While technology, when it works (which is most of the time), allows us easier access to our money and instant records of our accounts and financial transactions, it has forced us to memorize numbers in ways unheard of a short while ago. How many PIN numbers and ID numbers must the ordinary person learn? Some people therefore find that using technology can be very frustrating and yearn for the simpler, less complicated, and very recent past.

In addition to basic financial transactions, other aspects of personal finance have also quickly changed beyond recognition. Day traders, discount brokers, and electronic stock exchanges are a few examples. Proliferating mutual funds, hedge funds, segregated funds, and dot-com companies are a few others. While technology has helped investors, these other changes have made the world of personal finance far more challenging and confusing. There is a much greater array of investment vehicles to choose from than ever before, and there are many more questions that need to be asked. What, for example, does one invest in to get the best returns? What is meant by due diligence? Who should one turn to for advice? How can one tell if the received advice is sound? How does one become a day trader, invest in a hedge fund, invest abroad, etc., etc.?

Other areas of personal finance have also changed beyond recognition. Life insurance, for example, used to be quite a simple thing to buy. If people wanted insurance, they chose between term or whole life, depending on their personal situations. Now, a variety of different policies are available: critical illness insurance, disability insurance, and universal life policies. Any one of these will make a major difference to a person's financial affairs. Such variety, however, poses new challenges. Just which, if any, of such policies does a person need? Insurance salespeople can make an excellent case for each of their products, but not everyone needs them.

Life and death used to be simple matters, too. In preparation for the latter, a person wrote a will detailing how his or her estate should be settled. This should still happen, but now, long before a person dies, it is recommended that everyone appoint a power of attorney for personal care and a continuing power of attorney for property. The former gives someone (usually a close family member) the right to make decisions about a person's physical and mental health when that person is unable to do so. The latter allows the person named to make financial decisions for the signer of the power of attorney. In an age when the longevity of Canadians is constantly increasing, along with the variety of illnesses that can plague the elderly (and not so elderly), the need for such powers has never been greater. Without them, decisions might be taken that are not really in the individual's best interests.

Now, as well as having last will and testaments, many people have written "living wills" in which they indicate what medical treatment they wish to receive if they become incapable of communicating. This could happen, for example, as a result of a car accident that leaves the person hospitalized and on life support.

The purpose of this book is to throw some light on all aspects of personal finance and to help people plan their financial affairs with knowledge and confidence. It discusses the basic financial topics and tools and how they may be used to provide financial security. The book also gives a warning that is rarely mentioned in the financial press. No one knows what tomorrow will bring. Financial planning requires that decisions about the near and the far term be made. But all such decisions can become meaningless in the uncertain world in which we live. The global economy can affect the local economy very quickly and can change what once seemed like wise decisions into very poor ones. Negative events of whatever kind, whether of human or natural causes, can seriously harm an economy and the investments that are dependent upon it. The book explains how the ruinous nature of such events can be moderated. Likewise, uncertainty can prove some financial decisions, once questionable, to have been very wise indeed.

Content and Organization

Part 1: Financial Planning includes chapters on *Financial Planning; Introduction to Personal Income Tax;* and *Economic Risks and Financial Security. Part 2: Financial Security* includes chapters on *General Insurance; Life and Health Insurance; Retirement Income; Interest; Saving and Investing; Debt Securities; Stocks, Mutual Funds, and Other Investments;* and *Wills and Powers of Attorney.* In *Part 3: Credit,* the chapter sequence has changed. The chapter on *Home Mortgages* now comes before the chapter on *Consumer Credit and Loans* and the last chapter to round out the book is *Credit, Debt, and Bankruptcy.*

The book is intended to serve as an introduction to personal finance. The content is as current and up-to-date as is possible in a book. Some material has been rewritten. New material has been added. Reading the text and doing the problems should provide those new to the subject with a greater understanding of this fascinating topic. This book is not intended to serve as the final word and will hopefully encourage readers to learn more by turning to other sources, such as the financial press, and to seek advice from professionals about their own financial situations.

New to This Edition

- New material has been added to broaden the scope of the book.
- Many of the Personal Finance in Action boxes have been changed.
- The Women Take Charge boxes have been rewritten and are now more expansive.
- Many of the end-of-chapter problems have been updated.
- New Internet-based exercises have been added to each chapter. Previous examples, which proved popular, have been kept.
- New Legal Issues boxes have been introduced to this edition. The purpose of these boxes is to raise awareness of legal issues in financial planning and offer practical advice.
- The weblinks and reference lists have been completely revised and updated.

Features

- Each chapter begins with a set of **Learning Objectives.**
- **Key Terms** are highlighted where they are defined.
- A large number of **Personal Finance in Action** boxes appear throughout the book, illustrating financial concepts and making the contents more real to the reader.
- Each chapter also contains a **Women Take Charge** box, presenting scenarios where women are faced with decisions regarding their financial future.
- Each chapter concludes with a point-form **Summary.**
- An extensive number of **Problems** are included in each chapter. These allow the reader to apply the material discussed in the text. The inclusion of **Internet problems** shows the reader how valuable the internet is as a tool in personal finance.
- **References** at the end of each chapter direct the reader to other useful sources of information.
- Each chapter has a **Personal Finance on the Web** section, which allows the reader to learn more as well as to keep up to date—a definite bonus in a world that is constantly changing.

Supplements

The following supplements accompany this edition.

- An **Instructor's Resource Manual** includes answers to the end-of-chapter problems and an overview of the chapter contents. It also contains Financial Planning Worksheets, which are downloadable from the website.
- A computerized **TestGen** contains multiple-choice questions, true-false questions, and problems for each chapter. These are classified according to their level of difficulty (easy, moderate, or challenging).
- **PowerPoint® Presentations** are available for each chapter, which highlight the main concepts of the chapter.
- A **Companion Website** (**www.pearsoned.ca/currie**) contains self-test material (multiple-choice, true-false, and short essay questions) for students, links to other relevant websites, and Excel files containing financial worksheets for downloading. PowerPoint presentations with figures and tables from the text can also be downloaded from the website.

Acknowledgments

This book could not have been written without the help of other people and their organizations. We would like to thank the following for their help:

W. Douglas Newlands and Andy Maggisano, BMO Nesbitt Burns, Private Client Division, Toronto; Professor Ken Deck, North Bay; Lloyd Burke, KPMG, North Bay; Rob Seguin, Deputy Manager, Bank of Montreal, North Bay; and Jeff Keay, TD Canada Trust, Toronto.

We would like to thank Judy Palm of Malaspina University-College for her help in preparing the Women Take Charge boxes. Our thanks also to executive editor Samantha Scully and associate editor Rema Celio for their suggestions and help with this edition, as well as production editor Laura Neves, production coordinator Christine Kwan, copy editor Martin Townsend, and the rest of the team at Pearson Education Canada for all their hard work on this edition.

Finally, we would like to thank the following reviewers whose comments helped develop this ninth edition:

Derek Cook, Okanagan College

Hardeep Gill, Northern Alberta Institute of Technology

Robert Symmons, George Brown College

Joel Ender, Fanshawe College

Judith Palm, Malaspina University-College

Allan Riding, University of Ottawa

Eric Wang, Athabasca University

Geoffrey Prince, Centennial College

Donald Wheeler, College of the North Atlantic

Larry Stubbs, British Columbia Institute of Technology

Janice Seto, Nunavut Arctic College

Elliott Currie   *Tom Chambers*

A Great Way to Learn and Instruct Online

The Pearson Education Canada Companion Website is easy to navigate and is organized to correspond to the chapters in this textbook. Whether you are a student in the classroom or a distance learner you will discover helpful resources for in-depth study and research that empower you in your quest for greater knowledge and maximize your potential for success in the course.

[www.pearsoned.ca/currie]

Enter

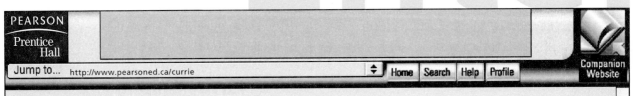

PEARSON
Prentice
Hall

Jump to... http://www.pearsoned.ca/currie   Home Search Help Profile

Companion Website

Home >

Companion Website

Personal Finance for Canadians, Ninth Edition
by Currie, Chambers, Brown

Student Resources

- Online Study Guide
  Featuring True/False, Multiple Choice, and Essay questions
- Reference Material
  Web Destinations: provide a directory of websites relevant to the subject matter in each chapter
  NetSearch: simplifies key term search using Internet search engines
- **Excel Templates:** Let students apply what they have learned

Instructor Resources

- **Syllabus Builder:** provides instructors with the option to create online classes and construct an online syllabus linked to specific modules in the Companion Website
- **Additional Teaching Tools:** include downloadable PowerPoint presentations and an Instructor's Resource Manual

Part 1

Financial Planning

Current interest in financial planning has generated increasing numbers of books and articles on the subject and a developing profession dedicated to helping people address their financial issues. But what is financial planning? It can be whatever you want it to be: a tax plan, an investment strategy, a life insurance needs assessment, or a comprehensive financial appraisal. Analyzing or forecasting almost any personal financial activity may be labelled financial planning; consequently, the results can range in scope from a very specific tax plan to a complete strategy covering all personal financial affairs.

In Chapter 1 we explain the general process of making financial plans, including why future cash flow projections should be based on identification of future goals and knowledge of present resources. Most financial planning involves some understanding of basic tax concepts, which are outlined in Chapter 2. After this introduction to the topic, income tax will come up again in later chapters dealing with retirement income, savings, investments, and estate plannings.

chapter 1

Financial Planning

"If you don't know where you're going you'll probably end up somewhere else."

Yogi Berra,
New York Yankees baseball player and manager

Learning Objectives

Knowledge of the material in this chapter should make the concept of financial planning more meaningful.

After studying this chapter, you should be able to:

1. Explain how the use of economic resources can be improved by financial planning.

2. Examine reasons for taking a lifetime perspective in personal financial planning.

3. Demonstrate how a financial plan can influence decisions about spending, income tax, insurance, and investments.

4. Explain the basic principles of financial planning.

5. Identify the functions of net worth statements, expenditure records, and budgets in the planning process.

6. Evaluate a net worth statement.

7. Distinguish between income and wealth.

8. Evaluate various methods of controlling expenditures and identify obstacles to successful control.

9. Identify behaviours with a psychological or social origin that may interfere with successful implementation of a financial plan.

10. Examine the costs and benefits of various models for handling finances in a two-income family.

11. Identify reasons why women face greater economic risks than do men.

12. Examine the status of the financial planning industry.

Introduction

We live in a very materialistic world. Money and the quantity of possessions one can acquire with it are important to many people. Even those for whom money is not an obsession are forced to pay attention to it. We depend on it to acquire the goods and services we need. We need it to maintain our standard of living. Our place in the world is based on our monetary resources, our ability to earn money, and our attitude toward money.

How we think about money and how we use it are determined by our cultural and family values and by our personalities. The wants and desires of many Canadians exceed their financial resources. This gap has led to an enormous amount of consumer debt and financial insolvency, as well as to serious social problems.

This text is written from an economic and financial perspective. It realizes, however, that subjective influences also determine how people manage their affairs. People may fully comprehend the importance of budgeting and financial planning, but they may be unable to implement their ideas because of personal or family problems. A list of books dealing with the psychology of money is included at the end of this chapter to help readers understand their own financial behaviour.

Women in particular have a large need to plan their financial affairs, as they can expect to live longer than men, frequently earn less than men, and, for the large part, are the heads of single-parent households.

Even though a financial plan makes sense, few people have one. One reason for not having such a document is the complexity of the financial industry and the many choices available. Often, people just don't know where to start. Another reason may be that financial planning requires discipline and a commitment many people lack. The result is a failure to begin financial planning, along with a serious shortfall of financial resources when one is older. This chapter discusses how to start a financial plan and some of the psychological concerns involved.

Financial decisions may be made with long-term goals in mind, or they may be made with no plan at all. Without a plan of some sort, it is difficult for most of us to achieve the financial security advertised on television and in the press. With a plan in mind to guide us and the discipline to carry out the plan, we can improve our quality of life. Financial security is within the grasp of everyone, no matter how limited his or her resources.

Need for Financial Plans

What Is a Financial Plan?

To create a **financial plan**, as with any other kind of plan, begin with goals that indicate what you want to achieve. Then, after you have identified and assessed available resources, allocate them to the desired objectives. Finally, develop a strategy to ensure that you can reach your desired goals. Although the procedure for making a plan is straightforward, implementing it is quite another matter, especially if some change in behaviour is required.

Financial plans come in many degrees of completeness and complexity. A small plan might be devised to control spending on entertainment and recreation; such a plan would include specific goals, a set limit for this category, and some ways to ensure that you do not overspend. At the other extreme, a very comprehensive financial plan can include all aspects of a person's financial affairs, starting with financial objectives and including current spending and saving projections, investment strategies, income tax plans, estate plans, and schemes for financing such specific goals as retirement. In most cases, people make financial plans that fall somewhere between these two extremes of complexity. Several examples of financial plans are included later in this chapter.

Why Plan Financial Affairs?

Planning makes it possible for you to live within your income, save money for short-term and long-term goals, and reduce financial worries and stresses in the household. Do you hope to purchase expensive goods, take a big trip, buy a house, send your children to university, or just make ends meet? Do you want to achieve financial independence and have a comfortable retirement? Do you wish to leave your dependents well provided for if something should happen to you? A financial plan will help you to take control of your finances and attain these goals.

There are both non-economic and economic reasons for making financial plans. Taking control of your finances can reduce anxiety, raise self-confidence, and increase satisfaction. In addition to helping you feel much better about yourself and your finances, planning can help you accomplish a number of economic goals:

(a) balancing cash flows,
(b) accumulating funds for special goals,
(c) adjusting lifetime earnings to expenses and saving for retirement,
(d) meeting the needs of dependents in case of death or disability,
(e) minimizing income taxes,
(f) maximizing investment returns.

Balance Cash Flows Everyone faces the necessity of ensuring that current income is adequate to cover expenses, a task otherwise known as making ends meet. Those with financial plans are in a better position to balance receipts and expenditures because of their overall view of the situation. Some non-planners go through cycles of feast and famine, spending money when they have it and doing without when it is gone. Others have a sufficient margin between income and expenses so that such problems do not arise. Taking control of current cash flows leads to peace of mind and greater success in achieving financial goals.

Special Goals We all dream of things we would like to do or buy but know the cost is too much to handle on our current income. We have a choice: to wait until we have saved enough or to do it now and pay later. Each option has costs and benefits. Is it better to submit to the discipline of waiting and saving or to pay the extra costs of using credit? (See Personal Finance in Action Box 1.1, "The Credit Trap," for an example of a family facing this challenge.) If the expenditure can be postponed, there is much to be said for selecting a savings target and gradually accumulating the needed funds. This way, you earn interest while waiting instead of paying it to someone else as a credit charge. Good money managers try to receive interest, not pay it. It is usually worthwhile to save before buying a house because a large down payment substantially reduces interest costs. The key point is that your goals will be more easily reached if you have a plan for achieving them.

Lifetime Perspective A planner has a long time horizon, looking ahead to future years and not just this month or year. For instance, most people can expect the relation between their income and expenses to vary over their lifespan: generally, living expenses will be more stable than employment earnings. Living costs tend to rise somewhat as our expectations increase—and they definitely expand when children join the family. Earnings, on the other hand, may be very small or non-existent for a student, take a jump when the student joins

Personal FINANCE in action 1.1

The Credit Trap

Sean and Melanie married shortly after graduating from college. Student life had been good, and their government-sponsored student loans enabled them to attend college. Sean and Melanie like having a car, so despite their tight budget, they purchased one with a graduation package offered by an automobile manufacturer.

Shopping for their new apartment became a virtual hobby for them; in fact, shopping online with their new computer has become one of their favourite pastimes. Sean is now working for a large foreign-owned manufacturing firm, and Melanie works in the hospitality industry.

Their finances are always tight, especially now that they are making payments on their student loans. Even with the maximum time allowed to repay the loans, the payments for the car, rent, and insurance make money very tight. Unable to pay off their credit card balance every month, they are only paying the minimum. Consequently, they have a large amount owing and are paying a very high rate of interest. Fortunately, the car is less than a year old, but with no money in the bank for emergencies, they are beginning to worry: there are rumours that the foreign company that Sean works for is going to rationalize its worldwide operations. If this happens, Sean's department may be closed, with the possible consequence that he may be transferred, and with Melanie possibly losing her job.

the labour force, increase gradually as the student who has become the worker gains experience, be interrupted by unemployment or a return to school, and reach a peak just before terminating at retirement. Some people elect to continue to work past retirement for economic or personal reasons.

In the early stages of family formation, it is not unusual to find expenses exceeding income, with a consequent dependence on consumer credit. In middle age, as the children leave home and earnings are reaching a peak, opportunities to save may be particularly good. At retirement, there may be income from deferred earnings in the form of pensions, but often this is inadequate to support one's accustomed lifestyle. At this stage, investment income can make life much more comfortable. In summary, an important planning task is to develop a way of distributing resources to support a fairly stable consumption level throughout the lifespan. A lifetime perspective on income and expenses is suggested in the diagram in Figure 1.1.

Needs of Dependents If you have dependents, you will want to consider the economic consequences if you should die unexpectedly or become seriously ill. Would there be enough money to support your dependents for as long as needed? Young families, who usually lack enough wealth to cope with such situations, buy life insurance and disability insurance to fill the gap. Critical illness insurance is also gaining popularity in this day of AIDS and cancer. Another aspect of planning is to make a will to ensure that funds will be distributed as you intend after your death.

Minimize Income Tax The income tax system has become very complex. While there are ways to minimize your tax bill, the responsibility is yours to know and take advantage of all the possibilities. By tax-filing time in April, it is usually too late to implement most tax-saving strategies. Plans must be made well in advance.

FIGURE 1.1   INCOME AND LIVING COSTS: AVERAGE LIFETIME PROFILE

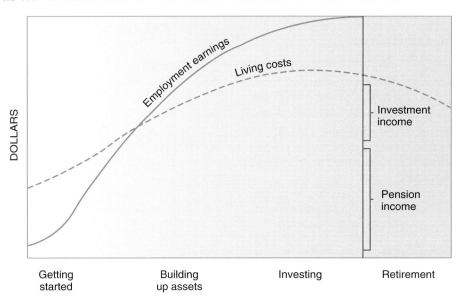

STAGES IN THE FINANCIAL LIFE CYCLE

Maximize Investment Income   Some people who are good savers have no idea how to go about investing. They find the subject of investments so overwhelming that they leave too much money in low-yielding securities. If increasing wealth is one of your goals, you must not only save but also invest prudently.

When to Start Planning

Planning is best not postponed on the assumption that there will be more money in the future. Start right now to make the best use of what you have. You can achieve financial independence if you are determined to do so. Achieving financial independence means taking deliberate control of your own financial affairs, rather than delaying decisions, letting things drift, and becoming a victim of circumstances. Many opportunities have been missed by those who considered financial matters beyond their control. Many people have retired with insufficient funds for a comfortable life because they did not save and invest during their working years.

Reaching Financial Independence

The way to financial independence is to spend less than you earn and to invest the savings. As your wealth gradually grows, you will be able to achieve more of your financial goals and perhaps even retire earlier. The key is to increase your wealth steadily so that eventually investment income can replace or augment your employment income. Naturally, it helps to have a high income, but many highly paid people spend their money as quickly as they get it. The sooner you begin to plan, save, and invest, the more time the money will have to grow. It is not how much you make, but how much you save and invest.

Life Cycle Differences

Although there are individual differences, most of us will go through a series of phases in our lifetimes. Sociologists call these "**life cycle stages**." In terms of financial management, they could be designated as follows:

(a) getting started (to mid-thirties),
(b) building up assets (mid-thirties to fifties),
(c) investing (fifties to retirement),
(d) retirement.

Financial planning is dynamic. Expect your plans to change as you move through the life cycle.

Getting Started Students are naturally concerned with educational and living costs and with obtaining a job in a chosen field. It is wise to invest money saved from summer employment in secure short-term deposits (savings account, term deposit, Canada Savings Bonds) that will generate as much interest as possible. Careful spending plans can be helpful in ensuring that funds last until the end of term. Perhaps you have noticed that for some students, the money ends before the term does. Others manage to put themselves through college or university and still have a nest egg at the end of it all. Why the difference? Could it be planning?

After graduation, high priority will be given to career advancement, saving for an emergency fund, paying off student debt, perhaps buying a house, and starting a modest investment portfolio. If you are raising a family, life insurance may be needed to cover the risk that you might die while supporting dependents. The funds available to do all these things will usually come from earnings, since you have not yet had time to build up wealth that will generate investment income.

Building Up Assets The middle years are the time to concentrate on paying off the mortgage on the house, increasing savings and investments, and giving some thought to retirement planning. (See Personal Finance in Action Box 1.2, "When to Start Saving for Retirement.")

Investing In middle age, most people have the best opportunity to save and to acquire a variety of assets. Obligations to children usually diminish, the house becomes mortgage-free, and income is at or near its peak. This is the time to give a high priority to increasing assets in a way that will provide an adequate retirement income.

Retirement After retirement, your opportunities to increase wealth will be much diminished. Your attention will be focused on sound management of previously acquired assets and on changing the mix of assets to emphasize income and security rather than growth.

This review of changes in financial management as one moves through the life cycle demonstrates that long-term planning is essential. People who make even small investments that are left to grow for many years will be able to take advantage of the beneficial effects of compounding interest over time, but those who wait until age 55 to start saving for retirement will have to save more to compensate for the shorter time for growth in investments. To achieve financial independence, we must be willing to pay the price in time, effort, and self-discipline.

When to Start Saving for Retirement

Yolanda and Dan were debating when they should start saving for their retirement. Yolanda thought that if they put away $2000 each year for the next 30 years, they would have a useful sum when they turned 65. Dan, however, argued that with a young family it would be too hard for them to do without $2000 each year for the next few years. He said that if he started in 20 years at age 55 and saved $6000 a year, he would be just as far ahead as Yolanda at retirement. Either way, they would have saved the same amount—$60 000. To support her position, Yolanda decided to calculate the value of her investment, using compound interest tables. Assuming an average return of 8 percent compounded annually, she found that in 30 years her savings would grow to $246 692. With 10 years of investment, Dan's $60 000 would become only $99 873. The results are shown in Figure 1.2.

The Financial Planning Process

Financial planning is the currently popular name for an age-old process, usually known as "budgeting." However, financial planning sometimes means a more comprehensive plan than the traditional budget. A word here about terminology: the word "budget," which has a strict technical meaning, is often misused. A **budget** is a plan for using financial resources, that is, a projection for the future. It is not a record of what was spent last year. Very often

FIGURE 1.2 VALUE OF ANNUAL DEPOSITS OF $2000 PER YEAR FROM AGE 35 TO 65 AND $6000 FROM AGE 55 TO 65

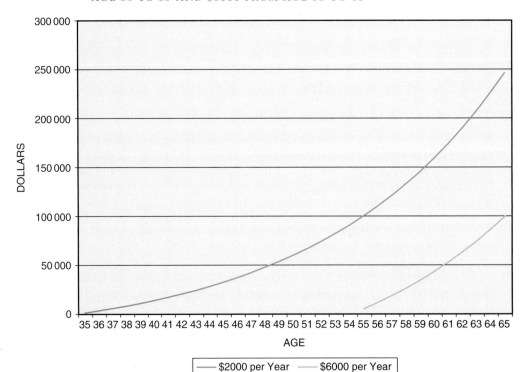

FIGURE 1.3 STEPS IN THE FINANCIAL PLANNING PROCESS

| 5. EVALUATE PROGRESS |
| 4. DEVELOP IMPLEMENTATION & CONTROL STRATEGIES |
| 3. BALANCE FUTURE CASH FLOWS |
| 2. ASSESS RESOURCES |
| 1. IDENTIFY GOALS & SET PRIORITIES |

"budget" is used to imply thrift, scrimping, or lower quality. This book adheres to the technical definition of a budget.

The basic principles of management apply just as much to handling financial affairs as to any other kind of activity. In this section, a general overview of the financial planning process will be followed by more detailed discussion of each component. The time span used for financial planning is entirely personal, but for simplicity we will assume that the planning period is one year. During that time, most kinds of expenses and income will have occurred at least once.

The first principle of financial management—as with any other type of management—is that goals must be identified before they can be achieved. Because it is usual to have more objectives than financial resources, priorities must be attached to goals to reflect their relative importance. The second principle is that an analysis of present financial resources is basic to future planning. Assemble all records of income and expenses for the past year, as well as a list of your assets and debts.

The third principle is that successful planning requires balanced cash flows. Refer to past spending records as a basis for estimating the cost of accomplishing your objectives. Draw up a plan or forecast for a specific period, perhaps a year, which includes a statement of your anticipated financial resources and their allocation; this plan is called a budget.

Fourth, strategies for the implementation and control of the plan are essential. A plan is intended to direct some action so that you can manage changes as they occur. The fifth and final principle is that effective financial management requires the ongoing evaluation of plans and implementation strategies to keep the plan relevant and effective. A summary of the process is shown in Figure 1.3.

Identify Values, Goals, and Priorities

All people have personal goals, whether they are aware of them or not. To some, a major goal may be to have a comfortable life; for others, it may be to travel or to own a Maserati. Perhaps the goals may be to raise a family, to have vacation property, or to retire comfortably. Every person's goals are different and incorporate different time frames. A financial goal is usually the quantitative portion and concrete measurement that coincides with the personal goal. If the desire is to have a comfortable lifestyle, then the household must determine the level of comfort. The Maserati has a price tag and can easily be measured. It is, therefore, also a financial goal; it merely lacks another aspect of financial planning—timing. When does the individual want the car, the house, or the vacation? When does the family want children, and how much will it cost to send each child to college or university? Now the goals have financial aspects, which are the major focus of this book.

It is imperative to set goals for the household to ensure that the household is attaining what it desires. Knowing where we want to go, when we want to get there, and how much it will cost are the fundamental building blocks of financial planning and goal setting. Starting the whole planning process with where you want to end up will help with the actual planning by providing a measuring stick for determining progress as well as a regular re-evaluation of the goals. The financial elements of goals are easier to quantify and discuss and are the primary focus of this book.

Three major areas in which many people have goals with financial elements are (i) level of living, (ii) financial security, and (iii) estate planning. In allocating financial resources, each individual creates his or her own balance among desires for comforts and amenities in the present, the need to develop a reserve of funds to be used in emergencies and on retirement, and the wish to amass an estate that can be bequeathed to others.

Establishing financial goals is a very personal matter. A counsellor or advisor can ask questions to help you identify goals and the priorities you place on them, but cannot and should not attempt to decide what your goals are. Once you have identified your goals and their priorities, a financial advisor can help you learn the management process necessary to reach those goals.

Conflicts in Goals and Values

Unfortunately, it is a common family problem that people who share economic resources do not always share financial goals. For example, one partner may want to save as much as possible for a down payment on a house, while the other has a strong desire to pursue an expensive hobby or other recreation. With limited resources, such a couple will have difficulty in reaching both goals. Furthermore, they will likely have problems in their relationship until they settle their differences. Recognizing that a difference in values is at the root of their problem is an essential first step in resolving these difficulties. In this era of dual-income households, the tasks of goal setting and following through on the plan become even more complex, with both parties contributing and deciding on goals.

Financial management may sound easy, but it can be difficult to accomplish because conflicts in attitudes, beliefs, and values continually intrude. As you would expect, the greater the number of individuals involved in the financial management of a common set of resources, the greater the potential for conflict. One might think, though, that a person who lives alone and who does not have to share resources or co-operate with others in determining goals would have no problems. Not so. Single individuals often experience financial difficulties because of a lack of clarity in goals, unresolved conflicts in priorities, lack of self-discipline, and poor methods of control. You may wish to do further reading about clarifying values and handling interpersonal conflicts; here it is emphasized that attitudes, values, and motivation are probably the most important components in the financial management process. Books, courses, and financial advisors can tell you how to manage your money, but only you can decide whether to act and what to act toward.

Assess Resources

Once you are clear about goals and priorities, the next step is to take an inventory of the resources you either have or can expect to receive that may be used to achieve these goals. There are two components to this resource assessment: (i) an inventory of assets, called a net worth statement, and (ii) an income statement. The distinction between income and wealth is important. A net worth statement shows your assets and liabilities at a specific time—that is, your net **wealth**. **Income**, which is not an asset but a flow of resources over a period of time, is usually expressed as an amount per week, per month, or per year. An analogy may help to clarify this point. Think of income as the rate at which water flows into a pond, and net wealth, or worth, as the amount of water in the pond. Think of expenses as the rate at which water flows out of the pond. (See Figure 1.4.) Those people who do not let some water stay in their ponds will find that their net worth fails to grow.

FIGURE 1.4 ECONOMIC RESOURCES OF THE HOUSEHOLD: FLOWS AND STOCK

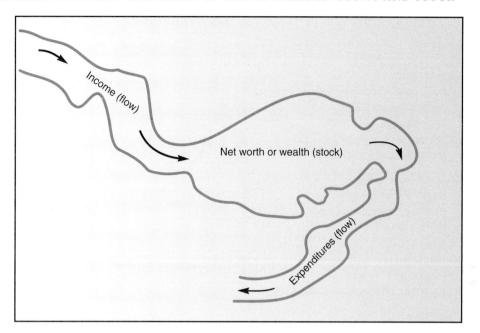

Net Worth

An essential requirement for financial planning is knowledge of exactly what you own and what you owe. Begin by making a list of all your assets and liabilities, or a net worth statement. Subtract the liabilities from the assets to find your actual **net worth**, or wealth. Those who make a wealth inventory are usually surprised by what they find. They may have more assets than they thought, or more debts than they imagined, or they may find that their assets are not sufficiently diversified.

Measure of Economic Progress If your goal is to increase wealth for financial security and independence, you must have some way to measure your progress. A series of annual net worth statements will reveal the rate at which your wealth is growing and will indicate whether you should make changes in your saving or investing practices. Think of a net worth statement as a snapshot of wealth on a given day; since it may be larger or smaller at another time, it should always be dated.

Net Worth Statement When making a net worth statement, list all your assets at their current value and the total amounts currently outstanding on all existing liabilities, as shown in Table 1.1. Assets that are not fully paid for, such as a house or car, are listed at their present market value in the asset column, and the amount owing is listed under liabilities.

Total each column, and find the difference between the two. If your assets exceed your liabilities, you have a positive net worth. Many people start their working lives with a negative net worth, but expect a growing positive net worth as middle age nears. In summary:

$$\text{Net worth} = \text{total assets} - \text{total liabilities}$$

Use the sample net worth statement in Table 1.1 or download the worksheet from our Companion Website, **www.pearsoned.ca/currie**, as a guide in preparing your own. A couple

TABLE 1.1 NET WORTH STATEMENT

ASSETS	SELF OR JOINT		SPOUSE	
	Amount	% of Total	Amount	% of Total
Liquid Assets				
Cash, bank accounts (savings & chequing)	$ 500	0.10%	$ 950	0.33%
Canada Savings Bonds	$ 5 000	0.98%	$ 500	0.17%
Term deposits	$ 8 000	1.56%	$ 5 000	1.75%
Life insurance cash surrender value	$ 1 750	0.34%	$ –	0.00%
(A) TOTAL LIQUID ASSETS	$ 15 250	2.98%	$ 6 450	2.26%
Other Financial Assets				
Stocks and equity mutual funds	$ 12 000	2.34%	$ 15 000	5.25%
Bonds and bond mutual funds	$ 7 500	1.47%	$ 20 000	6.99%
Loans to others	$ –	0.00%	$ –	
GICs	$ 2 500	0.49%	$ 5,000	1.75%
RRSPs	$ 24 500	4.79%	$ 12 500	4.37%
Pension plan credits	$ 8 000	1.56%	$ 32 500	11.37%
(B) TOTAL OTHER FINANCIAL ASSETS	$ 54 500	10.65%	$ 85 000	29.73%
Real Estate				
Home (market value)	$ 285 000	55.69%	$ –	0.00%
Other real estate	$ –	0.00%	$ 55 000	19.23%
(C) TOTAL REAL ESTATE	$ 285 000	55.69%	$ 55 000	19.23%
Personal Property				
Vehicles	$ 32 500	6.35%	$ 27 000	9.44%
Artwork, collectibles, jewellery, etc.	$ 4 500	0.88%	$ 12 500	4.37%
Furnishings, stereos, etc.	$ 45 000	8.79%	$ 25 000	8.74%
(D) TOTAL PERSONAL PROPERTY	$ 82 000	16.02%	$ 64 500	22.56%
(E) BUSINESS EQUITY	$ 75 000	14.66%	$ 75 000	26.23%
(F) TOTAL ASSETS (A+B+C+D+E)	$ 511 750	100.00%	$ 285 950	100.00%
LIABILITIES				
Short-Term Debt				
Loans, student loans, leases	$ 25 000	14.75%	$ 15 000	21.90%
Credit card debts	$ 4 500	2.65%	$ 3 500	5.11%
Life insurance loans	$ –	0.00%	$ –	0.00%
Long-Term Debt				
Mortgages	$ 115 000	67.85%	$ 25 000	36.50%
Other debts, tuition, business, etc.	$ 25 000	14.75%	$ 25 000	36.50%
(G) TOTAL LIABILITIES	$ 169 500	100.00%	$ 68 500	100.00%
TOTAL ASSETS (F)	$ 511 750		$ 285 950	
ASSETS(F)–LIABILITIES(G) = NET WORTH	$ 342 250		$ 217 450	
COMBINED NET WORTH OF SELF AND SPOUSE		$ 559 700		

DATE: August 25, 2006

is advised to make individual net worth statements as well as a joint one. Since Canadians prepare individual tax returns, it is helpful for tax planning to be able to analyze the assets of each partner separately. For instance, a family might decide that the spouse with the lower income will own those assets that generate the most income. For later analysis, calculate what proportion of the total is represented by each asset.

What to Include   What you include in a net worth statement will depend on how you intend to use it. Be consistent in your choice of items for measuring economic progress so that you can compare your results from year to year. You may decide that household furnishings and clothing are fairly constant and can be excluded. On the other hand, if you need to monitor the growth in your personal household capital goods, you may decide to include specific items. When an estate is being settled, a very detailed net worth statement may be required that includes all the personal possessions of the deceased. For loan applications, the credit manager might ask questions to estimate the borrower's net worth, with emphasis mainly on liquid assets and real property. When preparing a net worth statement for retirement planning, focus on assets that have income-producing potential.

Valuing Assets and Liabilities   Setting a value on the assets you own can be a very complicated process, especially when considering personal property. Certified individuals can appraise your collectibles, such as artwork or jewellery; this may help establish the required levels of insurance coverage, but is frequently beyond what is needed for a net worth statement. Financial assets can be easily valued from recent statements, but when it comes to real estate, it is advisable to use a recent selling price for a similar house in your neighbourhood. For vehicles, check newspaper ads for the selling prices of similar vehicles. As stated above, your personal property may be excluded, but should it be of significant value, include it either at what you consider a reasonable value or at its appraised value. Debts can be easily valued from your most recent statements or by calling your financial institution for a current amount.

Applying the Net Worth Statement   In what way can you use your net worth statement, other than to measure economic progress, obtain a loan, or settle an estate? An analysis of assets and debts can help determine whether the asset mix is appropriate and whether the debt-asset ratio is satisfactory. When making plans for retirement, you will want to know what wealth you have available to generate future investment income. Should you need to quickly draw on net worth in a time of crisis, it will help if you have a clear idea of the extent of your resources. If you are trying to decide whether you need life insurance, the net worth statement can be examined to see whether there is a gap between the resources your dependents would need and what the family already has. See the boxed feature "Women Take Charge 1.1" for an example of how one family utilized a net worth statement to plan for the future.

Analyze Net Worth   Once you make a net worth statement, make sure to analyze it, not just file it. Use Table 1.2 and the following questions as a guide for evaluating net worth.

(a) **Has your net worth grown faster than inflation in the past year?**
   If not, assets have been losing purchasing power. Look for a minimum long-term growth of about 3 percent after inflation. For instance, if net worth increased 8 percent in a year

Women take CHARGE 1.1

Eleanor noticed the challenges that a recently divorced friend had faced in handling family finances for the first time. She decided to become financially literate and more involved in her own family's financial affairs. As a first step, Eleanor and her husband, Jon, sat down together to take an inventory of their assets and set up a net worth statement. The net worth statement revealed that most of the family wealth came from their house. Liquid assets were low and insufficient to tide the family over for more than two months in the event of an emergency.

Eleanor suggested developing a budget to help them keep expenditures under control and build up savings. During the budgeting process, she noted that some of the expenses were optional and could perhaps be reduced or eliminated. The process also forced them to think about financial goals. They defined joint goals of paying off the mortgage, educating the children, providing for retirement, and giving Eleanor the opportunity to complete her university degree.

Eleanor discovers that taxes take a big portion of Jon's earnings. Wanting to learn how to fill out an income tax return, she suggests that Jon sit down and explain each step of his latest return to her. She also consults books in the local library on personal taxation. She notices that Jon's marginal tax rate is quite high and that certain investments, such as capital gains and dividends, have lower rates of taxation than interest income. Eleanor would like to get more involved in researching tax-efficient investments and serving as a volunteer tax preparer in the community.

Because Eleanor stays at home to raise the children, she is concerned about her side of the retirement picture. Has Jon arranged his pension so that she will continue to receive pension benefits after his death? Perhaps some of Jon's RRSP contribution room could be used to set up a spousal RRSP for Eleanor. This splitting of RRSP income could prove to have tax advantages on retirement. Jon and Eleanor will draw up wills and look into the feasibility of putting certain assets into joint tenancy.

Jon has life insurance through his job and is covered by an additional personal term insurance policy. It would be very expensive to replace all of the services in the home provided by Eleanor, so she suggests purchasing an affordable term insurance policy for her as well.

When the children get older, Eleanor plans to return to university to study more about finance and launch a career in financial planning. Her tuition and education amounts can be transferred to Jon, thus resulting in tax savings. After commencing work, she would like to put some of their savings into a registered education savings plan (RESP) for their children. With the team effort of both spouses in managing finances, Eleanor and Jon have an excellent chance of achieving their goals.

when inflation was 5 percent, there would be a net change of 3 percent after inflation, also known as the **real rate of return**. Next, check to see whether all the growth has been in the value of your home. If so, this increase may be overshadowing a lack of growth in other assets. However, in today's stock market and at today's interest rates, it can vary across all assets.

(b) **What is the ratio of liquid assets to total assets?**

In order to answer this question, you need to know that **liquid assets** are those that can readily be converted to cash without loss of principal, such as bank deposits or Canada Savings Bonds. Too much or too little liquidity can be unwise, as will be discussed in the chapter on investments. Some liquid assets, perhaps the equivalent of three months' wages, may be reserved for emergencies. However, since liquid assets tend to earn less

TABLE 1.2 ANALYSIS OF NET WORTH

1. ANNUAL GROWTH IN NET WORTH

Present net worth	$ 559 700
Previous net worth	$ 467 500
Change in net worth	$ 92 200
Percentage change in net worth	19.7%
Inflation rate for same period	2.8%
Net change after inflation (real rate of growth)	16.9%

2. LIQUIDITY

Total liquid assets	$ 21 700
Total assets	$ 559 700
Liquid assets/total assets ratio	3.9%

3. DEBT RATIOS

Total short-term debt	$ 48 000
Liquid assets	$ 21 700
Short-term debt/liquid asset ratio	2.21
Total assets in property and other investments	$ 776 000
Total debts for property and other investments	$ 190 000
Investment asset/debt ratio	4.08
Total short-term debt	$ 48 000
Total long-term debt	$ 190 000
Short-term/long-term debt ratio	0.25

4. DIVERSITY

Deposits and other debt securities	$ 26 000
Total liquid assets	$ 21 700
Total RRSPs	$ 37 000
Bonds and bond mutual funds	$ 27 500
Other loans (you are the lender)	$ –
Total debt securities	$ 112 200
Total stocks and equity mutual funds	$ 27 000
Total equity in property	$ 200 000
Total business equity	$ 100 000
Total equity securities	$ 327 000
Debt securities/equity securities ratio	0.34

DATE: August 25, 2006

than other investments, an overemphasis would mean a loss of potential income. Many people have too large a proportion of their assets in liquid form.

(c) **What is the ratio of short-term debt to liquid assets?**

A high ratio indicates a precarious position if anything should happen to income. Is the ratio appropriate for your stage in the life cycle? Normally, the debt/asset ratio will decrease with age.

(d) **What is the ratio of investment assets to investment debt?**

Just after you purchase a house with a large mortgage, this ratio may be low, but with time, it should increase.

(e) **What is the ratio of short-term to long-term liabilities?**

Short-term debt should not be greater than long-term debt. Are you using most of the long-term debt to acquire assets? Is your short-term debt for living expenses? Borrowing to buy assets such as property makes sense, but too much dependence on credit for day-to-day living costs is a drain on resources and impedes the growth of wealth.

(f) **How diversified are the assets?**

Add up all the assets that are deposits, bonds, or investment certificates, also referred to as debt securities. These assets are usually low risk, and pay interest income.

Compare this total with the total of the assets that you own, such as property, mutual funds, or stocks. These are called equity securities. What is the ratio of debt securities to equity securities? Are the various kinds of risks balanced? What might happen to the assets' purchasing power over a period of high inflation? What country or region or industry are you invested in? Generally, debt securities lose purchasing power in periods of inflation, and equity securities are more likely to appreciate. How much is exposed to market risk, as in a business or the stock market? Different types of risks are explained in Chapter 8.

Income

The second task in assessing financial resources is to predict your income for the planning period by examining past income records. Use either Table 1.3 or download the spreadsheet at our Companion Website, **www.pearsoned.ca/currie**, to record your income for the last calendar year. Income tax records can be helpful for this task. Enter your gross income before any deductions, not your take-home pay. All deductions, including income tax, will be shown in the expenditure record.

Other Resources Include in the income statement any other resources you used last year to cover living expenses, such as savings, credit, or gifts, if you expect to use those resources again in the next planning period.

Expenditures

Estimate Living Costs Before making plans for next year, it is best to have the most complete information possible about current living costs. Being able to access past records will be a great advantage here. Otherwise, make the best and most detailed estimates possible of your costs for the past year by using Table 1.4 or the spreadsheet on our Companion Website, **www.pearsoned.ca/currie**, as a guide. Try to reconstruct the outward cash flow, using cheque stubs, receipts, and any records available. Anyone who feels overwhelmed by the detail required in Table 1.4 can skip to the end and use only the summary part. If you use the spreadsheet, the summary will be automatically calculated based on your input. This approach may be quicker, but you will recognize that these estimates may not be as accurate.

Note that in Table 1.4 a check mark is placed beside each expense that is considered fixed. It is helpful in planning to distinguish between **flexible expenses** (which can be altered if needed) and **fixed expenses** (which are difficult to change in the short term). In the long run, of course, all expenses can be altered. Whenever quick adjustments are required, changes will probably have to be made in the flexible expenses. Enter expenses by week or month as convenient, and then convert them all to annual amounts.

TABLE 1.3   ESTIMATED ANNUAL INCOME

SOURCE	SELF	SPOUSE
Employment		
Gross Income from employment	$ 52 000	$ 78 000
Other (bonuses, etc.)	$ 2 500	$ 2 500
(A) TOTAL EMPLOYMENT INCOME	$ 54 500	$ 80 500
Government Payments		
Employment Insurance	$ –	$ –
Workers' Compensation	$ –	$ –
Pensions (veteran, CPP, OAS, other)	$ –	$ –
Welfare, family benefits	$ 250	$ 750
(B) TOTAL GOVERNMENT PAYMENTS	$ 250	$ 750
Investment		
Interest	$ 152	$ 345
Dividends	$ 350	$ 750
Rent (net income)	$ –	$ –
Capital Gains	$ 365	$ 3 500
Profit	$ –	$ –
Annuities	$ –	$ –
Other	$ –	$ –
(C) TOTAL INVESTMENT INCOME	$ 867	$ 4 595
Other Income		
Self-Employment	$ 5 600	$ –
Other	$ –	$ 250
(D) TOTAL OTHER INCOME	$ 5 600	$ 250
Total Annual Income (A+B+C+D)	$ 61 217	$ 86 095
Total Family Income	$ 147 312	
Other Resources Used		
Savings spent	$ 5 000	$ –
Money borrowed	$ 25 000	$ 15 000
Gifts received	$ 500	$ 500
Total other resources	$ 30 500	$ 15 500

DATE: August 25, 2006

Analyze Expense Record Review the expense record to discover whether there is consistency between the way money has been spent and the statement of goals and priorities. Quite often we say one thing but do another. Identify spending categories that may need better methods of control. Is debt repayment too large a proportion of expenses? Will next year's expenses be about the same as those for last year, or are changes expected?

Saving What percentage of income was saved last year? Is this satisfactory, or could it be increased? A discussion of savings strategies may be found in Chapter 8.

TABLE 1.4   ESTIMATED ANNUAL EXPENSES

EXPENSE ITEM	Per Wk.	Biweekly	Per Mo.	Per Yr.	Fixed Expenses
Deductions from Pay					
Income tax included with security and taxes at the end					
Canada Pension Plan	$ –	$ 147.00	$ –	$ 3 822.00	✓
Employment Insurance	$ –	$ 57.00	$ –	$ 1 482.00	✓
Parking	$ –	$ –	$ 22.50	$ 270.00	✓
Company pension	$ –	$ 305.65	$ –	$ 7 946.90	✓
Association/union dues	$ –	$ –	$ 35.00	$ 420.00	✓
Health insurance	$ –	$ 25.46	$ –	$ 661.96	✓
Group life insurance	$ –	$ 20.00	$ –	$ 520.00	✓
Long-term disability insurance	$ –	$ –	$ 27.56	$ 330.72	✓
Dental plan	$ –	$ –	$ 23.86	$ 286.32	✓
Extended health insurance	$ –	$ –	$ 3.45	$ 41.40	✓
Other	$ –	$ –	$ –	$ –	
TOTAL DEDUCTIONS	$ –	$ 555.11	$ 112.37	$ 15 781.30	
Food					
Groceries	$ –	$ 250.00	$ –	$ 6 500.00	
Dining out	$ 25.00	$ –	$ –	$ 1 300.00	
TOTAL FOOD	$ 25.00	$ 250.00	$	$ 7 800.00	
Housing					
Rent or mortgage	$ –	$ –	$ 872.00	$ 10 464.00	✓
Real estate taxes	$ –	$ –	$ 247.00	$ 2 964.00	✓
Hydro, water	$ –	$ –	$ 78.00	$ 936.00	✓
Heat	$ –	$ –	$ 89.00	$ 1 068.00	✓
Telephone	$ –	$ –	$ 125.00	$ 1 500.00	✓
Cable TV	$ –	$ –	$ 56.00	$ 672.00	✓
Household operation and help	$ –	$ –	$ 150.00	$ 1 800.00	
Home maintenance	$ –	$ 60.00	$ 50.00	$ 2 160.00	
Purchase of furniture and appliances	$ –	$ –	$ 150.00	$ 1 800.00	
Home insurance	$ –	$ –	$ 38.35	$ 460.20	✓
TOTAL HOUSING	$ –	$ 60.00	$ 1 855.35	$ 23 824.20	

continued

TABLE 1.4   ESTIMATED ANNUAL EXPENSES (CONTINUED)

EXPENSE ITEM	Per Wk.	Biweekly	Per Mo.	Per Yr.	Fixed Expenses
Medical					
Insurance premiums	$ –	$ –	$ –	$ –	✓
Dental	$ –	$ –	$ –	$ –	✓
Drugs	$ –	$ –	$ –	$ –	
Optical (annual coverage)	$ –	$ –	$ –	$ –	
Other	$ –	$ –	$ –	$ –	
TOTAL MEDICAL	$ –	$ –	$ –	$ –	
Transportation					
Vehicle payments	$ –	$ –	$ 369.00	$ 4 428.00	✓
Vehicle purchase	$ –	$ –	$ –	$30 000.00	
Vehicle insurance	$ –	$ –	$ 157.00	$ 1 884.00	✓
Operation (gas, oil, licence & parking)	$ –	$ –	$ 250.00	$ 3 000.00	✓
Vehicle maintenance	$ –	$ –	$ 50.00	$ 600.00	✓
Travel and public transportation	$ –	$ 75.00	$ –	$ 1 950.00	✓
TOTAL TRANSPORTATION	$ –	$ 75.00	$ 826.00	$41 862.00	
Personal Needs					
Pocket money	$ 100.00	$ –	$ –	$ 5 200.00	
Personal care	$ –	$ –	$ 75.00	$ 900.00	
TOTAL PERSONAL NEEDS	$ 100.00	$ –	$ 75.00	$ 6 100.00	
Gifts and Donations					
Gifts	$ –	$ –	$ 300.00	$ 3 600.00	
Charitable donations	$ –	$ –	$ 50.00	$ 600.00	
Religious contributions	$ 15.00	$ –	$ –	$ 780.00	
TOTAL GIFTS AND DONATIONS	$ 15.00	$ –	$ 350.00	$ 4 980.00	
Clothing					
Spouse	$ –	$ –	$ 200.00	$ 2 400.00	
Spouse	$ –	$ –	$ 200.00	$ 2 400.00	
Other family members	$ –	$ –	$ 200.00	$ 2 400.00	
Laundry and cleaning	$ 15.00	$ –	$ –	$ 780.00	
TOTAL CLOTHING	$ 15.00	$ –	$ 600.00	$ 7 980.00	

continued

TABLE 1.4   ESTIMATED ANNUAL EXPENSES (CONTINUED)

EXPENSE ITEM	Per Wk.	Biweekly	Per Mo.	Per Yr.	Fixed Expenses
Recreation and Entertainment					
Hobbies	$ –	$ –	$ 50.00	$ 600.00	
Liquor and tobacco	$ –	$ –	$ 50.00	$ 600.00	
Books and subscriptions	$ –	$ –	$ 25.00	$ 300.00	
CDs, DVDs, etc.	$ –	$ –	$ 50.00	$ 600.00	
Other (i.e., travel)	$ –	$ –	$ 100.00	$ 1 200.00	
TOTAL RECREATION	$ –	$ –	$ 275.00	$ 3 300.00	
Security and Taxes					
Life insurance	$ –	$ –	$ 68.00	$ 816.00	✓
Annuities, RRSPs	$ –	$ –	$ 500.00	$ 6 000.00	
Regular savings	$ –	$ –	$ 300.00	$ 3 600.00	
Income tax (from deductions)	$ –	$ 815.00	$ –	$ 21 190.00	✓
TOTAL SECURITY AND TAXES	$ –	$ 815.00	$ 868.00	$ 31 606.00	
Other Expenses	$ –	$ –	$ –	$ –	
TOTAL OTHER EXPENSES	$ –	$ –	$ –	$ –	
Debt Repayment (excluding mortgage)	$ –	$ –	$ 369.00	$ 4 428.00	
TOTAL DEBT REPAYMENT	$ –	$ –	$ 369.00	$ 4 428.00	

Expense Summary

Expense Item	Per Year	
1. Deductions	$ 15 781.30	
2. Food	$ 7 800.00	
3. Housing	$ 23 824.20	
4. Medical	$ –	
5. Transportation	$ 41 862.00	
6. Personal needs	$ 6 100.00	
7. Gifts and donations	$ 4 980.00	
8. Clothing	$ 7 980.00	
9. Recreation & entertainment	$ 3 300.00	
10. Security and taxes	$ 31 606.00	
11. Debt repayment	$ 4 428.00	
12. Other	$ –	
TOTAL EXPENSES	$ 147 661.50	
TOTAL FIXED EXPENSES	$ 67 713.50	
TOTAL SAVINGS	$ 4 078.50	2.8% of Income

Balance Future Cash Flows

Income

Based on the data you have assembled, estimate your income for next year. If you are at all unsure whether you will receive some income, do not include it. There will be fewer unpleasant surprises if you are conservative in predicting income, but generous in estimating expenses. Enter the amounts in Table 1.4. You can download this table from our Companion Website at **www.pearsoned.ca/currie**.

Irregular Income When income is irregular or seasonal, it is harder to make a forecast unless there are adequate records from past years. Make the best estimate possible of next year's income, but be restrained. Since expenses are likely to be more regular than income, divide total expenses by 12 and allocate this amount for monthly living expenses.

Other Resources

If you expect that your income will not be high enough to cover your expenses, list the other resources that you will use, such as savings, borrowed funds, and gifts from others. Such resources may be needed by students, the unemployed, or the retired if they have insufficient income to support their living costs. At other times in the life cycle, it should be possible to add to savings rather than use them. It has been observed, however, that those who have been good savers all their lives are often reluctant to use these assets to support their lifestyle when they are old. They have saved for a rainy day, and they are concerned that things may be worse in the future. Sometimes it is difficult to decide when you have arrived at a rainy day!

Savings

Plan your savings for the year first; don't just hope that some money will be left over. How much must be saved to meet various long-term and short-term objectives? For instance, if you are planning a large purchase in four years, determine how much you must save each year. Is there enough in the emergency fund? What part of the savings is going toward a retirement fund? Keeping in mind goals and annual resources, decide how much would be realistic to save for the year. This subject is explored in more detail in Chapter 8.

Living Expenses

How much does it cost to run a household, to clothe and feed family members, to take an annual holiday? How much will be needed for those desired expensive items or for the down payment on a house? Past records of expenditures will be helpful in predicting regular costs.

 If you lack adequate records, or expect that next year will be very different from the last, it may be difficult to make realistic projections. Allow for flexibility in your plan. Estimate your total expenses for the year to come using a table similar to the summary part of Table 1.4, and enter total predicted expenses in Table 1.5. If you use the spreadsheet available on our Companion Website at **www.pearsoned.ca/currie**, these numbers, excluding savings, will be automatically calculated from your earlier input.

TABLE 1.5   THE BUDGET

Planning period from	January 1, 2006	to	December 31, 2006	
Available Resources				
Income			$ 147 312.00	
Savings			$ 5 000.00	
Borrowing			$ 40 000.00	
TOTAL RESOURCES AVAILABLE				$ 192 312.00
Allocation of Resources Savings				
Emergency funds	$ 6 500.00			
Short-term goals	$ 3 900.00			
Long-term goals	$ 7 800.00			
TOTAL SAVINGS			$ 18 200.00	
Expenses				
TOTAL EXPENSES			$ 147 661.50	
TOTAL SAVINGS AND EXPENSES				$ 165 861.50
Difference between Total Resources				
and Total Savings and Expenses				$ 26 450.50

Personal Allowances   Designate a sum of money for each individual in the family for personal expenditures. Each person should not have to account for how he or she spends this allowance. This will simplify record-keeping and also enhance family harmony. Obviously, you will need to reach some agreement about what sorts of expenditures will be covered by these personal allowances.

Balance Income and Expenses

Use Table 1.5 as a guide for comparing total budget figures. Will the financial resources you expect to have available during the budget period cover predicted saving and spending? It is not unusual at this stage to find that there is not enough money for everything and that adjustments are therefore needed. To balance the budget, you have the choice of increasing resources, reducing wants, or doing some of both. This balancing step is critical in financial management because goals, priorities, and the total expected financial situation for a year (or other period) are being taken into consideration. A calm look at the overall plans will lead to a more careful and rational allocation of resources than will hasty *ad hoc* decisions made while shopping.

When trying to make a budget balance, review estimates to ensure that they are as accurate as possible. Has uncertain income been included? Are the expenditure estimates inflated? What has been included that is not essential or important? Could better use be made of the money?

Develop Implementation and Control Strategies

A critical part of the planning process is controlling the plan. Many splendid budgets have been prepared and filed away by their creators, who thought the task was finished. In fact, a plan for any type of activity is ineffective until it is put into action. Once the saving and spending estimates have been balanced with expected resources, consider how you can make the plan work.

The following generalizations summarize key points about controlling financial plans:

(a) All those handling the money share a commitment to the plan.
(b) The control system is compatible with an individual's personality and habits.
(c) Controlling a plan requires that someone know where the money is going.
(d) The funds for major groups of expenditures are segregated in some way to prevent overspending.

Shared Commitment

All those who are sharing income and expenses and have a common budget must not only be informed about the budget but also be committed to it. Any plan not supported by all those concerned is doomed from the outset. For instance, a family argument may result in one person using money to punish the other by running up large bills on a spending spree. Such a family relations problem must be dealt with before any budget can be effective. Ideally, all those in the spending unit will work together in preparing the financial plan, taking time to resolve conflicts in values as they arise and achieving their joint goals.

A System to Suit Your Personality

It is impossible to prescribe a system of control for another person's financial affairs; we can only suggest possible alternatives. People differ too widely in their styles of handling money and in their willingness to maintain written records. Consider your own habits and personality, and develop ways to ensure that your money will be spent or saved as planned. If money burns holes in your pockets, you will need to do something to curb your impulsiveness.

Know Where the Money Is Going

In order to keep track of expenses, you will need to do some kind of record-keeping, but make the system simple enough that it does not become onerous and thus neglected. (See Personal Finance in Action Box 1.3, "Simple Record-Keeping and Control.") Decide how much detail is needed or wanted, and proceed accordingly. Often the very act of recording expenditures serves as a control on spending because having to write down what you spend tends to encourage reflection on your financial habits. There are numerous reasonably priced software packages to help in this area. Quicken from Intuit is the most popular. Money from Microsoft is second in popularity.

Control the Allocations

There are several ways to control allocations. The simplest method is to operate strictly on a cash basis, putting the allocated amounts in envelopes, purses, sugar bowls, or bank accounts. During a specific period, restrict spending to the sum in each container. This system is not practical for many people, both because of the danger of theft and loss and because of the inconvenience of handling complex affairs this way. However, this concrete approach is useful for people who have difficulty with abstract thinking. At the opposite extreme is the completely abstract method of control by double-entry bookkeeping, which can be very effective if you are committed to the system and well trained in accounting.

A possible compromise is to establish several levels of control by opening a number of savings and chequing accounts. For example, you could have one account for long-term savings, one for short-term goals, one for irregular expenditures, and one for regular living expenses. These accounts serve the same function as the envelopes or sugar bowls mentioned above. Decide which expenditures can be handled by the same account, and deposit the planned amount each time a paycheque is received. To make certain that this system will work, cheques or debits must be taken from the appropriate account and records kept up to date. If you have a joint account, each user must inform the other of deposits and withdrawals.

Actions or Events That Jeopardize Plans

Unexpected Expenses   As many will attest, unexpected expenses occur just about every month, so you may as well plan for them. Add such a category to the budget to prevent frustration when the unforeseen occurs. It is virtually impossible to plan spending exactly to the last dollar, but approximating how much to allow for the unexpected becomes easier with experience.

Use of Credit   How does using credit cards affect the control system? If you pay for purchases with a credit card because it is convenient and you pay off the total bill monthly, you can treat credit card bills in the same way as other bills. However, if you are susceptible to the impulse buying that credit cards encourage, you will need to develop restrictions on having or carrying credit cards. If your charge account balances are growing because you pay only a portion of the total each month, consider how much you are spending on costly credit charges and also whether you have a tendency to overspend.

Irregular Expenses   Everyone has irregular large bills that cannot be paid from the monthly allocation without planning for them. Using last year's records as a guide, find the annual total of expenses such as insurance, taxes, auto licence and maintenance, and income tax. Divide the total by the number of paydays, and deposit the appropriate amount in the account earmarked for these bills.

Unrealistic Plans   If your plans never seem to materialize, it could be because they are unrealistic. The first time you make a budget, lack of experience and inaccurate records may result in poor plans. Do not give up, but do expect to make adjustments to your plans. Remember that you can change the plan at any time, and that as time goes on, your plans will become more realistic.

A budget may be most needed just when predictions are most difficult to make. For instance, when there is a change in living arrangements or in household composition, or a drop in income, it is evident that things are going to be different but it is hard to know how different. A couple establishing a new household will have no past records to refer to. They will have to make the best estimates they can for a few months, and then review those estimates and make a better plan. Likewise, the arrival of a child will add to costs and potentially decrease family income, but new parents lack sufficient data to make accurate forecasts.

Inflexible Plans   Do not consider plans to be unchangeable. A plan is a device to help achieve goals, not a straitjacket. If it becomes inappropriate for some reason, it can be revised. Consider plans to be your servants, not your masters.

Personal FINANCE in action 1.3

Simple Record-Keeping and Control

Ann works for a large financial institution as an analyst/manager and is also working toward an accounting designation. Because of her training, she has become aware that she needs to manage the household funds through budgeting and a system of controls. Ann and her husband, Francis, believe they can achieve financial freedom through financial management. The problem is, after Ann's two-hour commute and studying for the accounting program, she feels too exhausted to set up a system for managing their money.

Francis now manages their money, while running his commercial artist service from their home. They have two bank accounts: one joint and one for Francis's business. All bills are paid from the joint account. Francis keeps track of their expenses and inflows on his computer. The expenses are broken down into categories such as household expenses; utilities; telephone; savings; education; business; emergencies; food; pocket money; and gifts. He records all paycheques in these spreadsheets as well as the receipts from his business.

He records each expense and allocates the inflows to the different accounts, with a proportional share from the business for tax reasons and to ensure that the business pays for its particular expenses. Francis pays all of their bills at night on his computer; this saves money on postage and frees his time during the day for his business.

Too Much Precision Expected Decide how precise financial plans and records must be to achieve the desired goals, and proceed accordingly. Do not make the mistake of embarking on a first financial plan with unrealistic notions of how much record-keeping will be done and how precisely the actual expenses must match the budgeted amount.

Using a Financial Plan to Reform Behaviour If you are feeling guilty about the way you are now spending money, you might want to make a plan on the assumption that certain vices will be cut out. How successful will that plan be? Reforming yourself may be a good idea, but it would be best to separate that goal from financial planning. We need to accept the fact that changing behaviour, even our own, is difficult. Anyone who intends to change his or her spending habits, record-keeping practices, or savings goal must plan for a series of small changes, not a large one. Success with each small change achieved will provide the motivation for undertaking another modification. Attempts to make too big a change usually result in failure.

Evaluate Progress

Since the purpose of making a budget is to have a blueprint that will guide financial decisions, there must be a mechanism for measuring progress. Periodically, compare the plan with what is actually happening. Are goals being met? If what is happening does not correspond very well with the plan, ask why. Was the plan unrealistic, perhaps because it was based on wrong assumptions or on incomplete data? Is the problem with the methods of control? Do not expect a perfect match between the actual and the budgeted amounts for each category of spending. Rather, look for a balance in overall cash flow, and check whether any particular category is out of line.

Develop some system for simplifying comparisons between the amounts budgeted and actual cash flow, and check on this often enough to prevent things from getting out of control. An annual review of changes in net worth should be adequate, but allocations for savings and living expenses need a closer watch—perhaps monthly, or at least quarterly. Successful monitoring and review of budgets requires a system of records.

Financial Records

Cash Flow Control Worksheet There are three steps in this record-keeping task:

(a) collecting the data,

(b) summarizing or finding monthly and annual totals,

(c) analyzing the results.

Some may get stuck at the first step because they have no system for recording what they have spent. It may help to begin by concentrating on regular, fixed expenses, which are usually well-known or are recorded in cheque books. Once all the information on the fixed expenses has been obtained, the flexible expenses can be added.

Develop a method that suits you and that provides enough information for your purposes. Do not attempt a scheme that is too ambitious; such a system may be neglected because it is too time-consuming. Some people use a ledger book, or ruled loose-leaf pages, with columns for all the expense categories. Enter each expense, as it occurs, under the appropriate column. Others carry a small notebook to record expenditures as they occur, and later transfer the information to a ledger.

Analyze the results by comparing the actual monthly totals with the budgeted amounts. This can be done on another summary sheet that has space for 12 months.

A computer can be helpful for record-keeping. A number of commercial software programs have been developed for this purpose. Although they do not eliminate the task of collecting the data, such programs do other tasks well, making it much easier for you to categorize entries, create totals, and calculate percentages so that you can summarize and analyze the data and do some basic planning and projections. If you find working with a computer more fun than working with pencil and paper, use it for your record-keeping and analysis. Most programs will interact with your bank to pay bills and balance accounts. Take a look at Quicken or Money. They will also help prepare your taxes and manage investments.

Strategies for Two-Income Households

Changing Family Patterns

Among the many dramatic changes in family structure we have witnessed in recent decades, the increasing number of women in the labour force is one that has had an impact on many households' finances. In the late 1960s, women with young children or with high-earning husbands tended not to take paid employment, but that is no longer true. It is clear that nowadays dual-earner families have become the most common type, even when the husband receives a high income.

By 1994, the number of two-earner households had increased to 3.3 million versus 1.9 million single-earner households. This trend has almost exactly reversed the situation of 20 years earlier. The presence of children—even preschoolers—in the home has had almost no impact on the incidence of two-earner households. This significant shift has had major implications for the way household finances are managed. A strategy that may have been reasonable for a one-earner family, such as pooling all resources, may be less appropriate when there are two earners. Some models used by dual-income families to organize their finances are outlined below.

(a) *Pooled funds.* All income is combined, and expenses are paid from this pool. This approach requires frequent discussion to achieve shared values and goals.

(b) *Equal split.* Each partner puts the same amount into a common pool to cover specified joint expenses. They also have separate personal and savings accounts. This system works best if both partners earn about the same amount.

(c) *Proportionate contributions.* When one partner earns more than the other, their contributions to the common pool are based on agreed proportions of their incomes to make it more equitable.

(d) *Dividing the bills.* Instead of pooling funds, each person agrees to handle certain expenses.

When deciding what model to try, couples should take stock of their personalities and values. (See Personal Finance in Action Box 1.4, "A Plan That Works for Them.") Some systems require more discussion and agreement than others do. The pooled fund system works best if both people share values and attitudes toward money. When one partner is a spendthrift and the other a tightwad, it might work better to have each individual handle more of his or her money on a personal basis.

Personal FINANCE in action 1.4

A Plan That Works for Them

Ilona and Pierre belong to the ranks of people who don't like to keep a regular record of their expenses and who prefer to plan their budget in their heads. However, now that their children have reached university age, they find that they need to maintain a reserve fund to cover some of the children's expenses. Also, they want to be able to finance the family's hobbies of cycling and skiing, both of which are becoming more expensive with each new high-technology development. To find the least demanding and least tiresome method of financial planning, they attended a one-day workshop that also included information about planning for retirement.

After deliberating briefly, they decided that the best method for them was to create a budget based on their current spending habits. To start, they needed to estimate their expenses for the coming year. This involved figuring out how much they would spend on three major categories: (i) the house (e.g., mortgage, utilities, taxes, insurance, telephone, landscaping, repairs, and mainte-

nance); (ii) personal/discretionary (e.g., groceries, drugstore, cosmetics, clothes, medical, non-essentials for the house, gifts, books, ski and bicycle accessories, race fees, and boots), and (iii) savings and investment (e.g., RRSPs, mutual funds, savings account).

Their paycheques, with combined earnings of $83 000 per year, are deposited into their personal chequing account. Automatic monthly transfers of funds have been arranged for RRSPs, investments, life insurance, mortgage payments, and savings. To avoid recording detailed grocery expenditures, they set aside $850 per month ($180 a week) for this purpose.

Once a month, Ilona and Pierre spend a few hours recording the previous month's cash flows. They use a transaction log to record deposits, automatic transfers, cheques, cash withdrawals (from automatic tellers), and any other transactions. From credit card statements and chequebook records, they are able to categorize all expenses according to their two major categories: personal/discretionary and

continued

A Plan That Works for Them (continued)

house. Next, the amounts for each category are totalled and entered on the monthly budget page and also on a year-to-date statement.

Like everyone else, they find that there are times when they have overspent in one or more categories. They are then able to bring the budget in line over the next several months either by spending less in each category or by skipping a category (for example, buying no new cycling outfits, or renting videos instead of going to the movies).

By choosing a budget method that suits their personalities, Ilona and Pierre have been able to gain control over their expenses without drastically changing their lifestyle and without feeling bound by too stringent a system. In their case, flexibility and ease of administration were the key factors that made their financial planning successful.

In summary,

(a) Inflow/Outflow

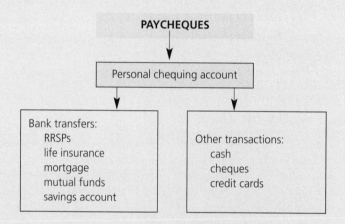

(b) Monthly Budget Control Sequence and Records

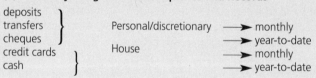

(c) Categories and Items

HOUSE	PERSONAL/ DISCRETIONARY		SAVINGS/ INVESTMENT
mortgage	groceries	race fees	RRSPs
utilities	clothes	books	mutual funds
taxes	car	magazines	Canada Savings Bonds
insurance	cosmetics	medical	savings account
telephone	gifts	entertainment	
landscaping	ski & bicycle accessories	donations	
repairs	travel	miscellaneous	
maintenance			
furnishings			

Reasons for Not Making Plans

Although almost anyone will tell you that it is a good idea to make a financial plan, fewer people actually do much planning. Why the discrepancy? Making and using a financial plan requires motivation, knowledge, time, effort, and, finally, self-discipline and persistence. Planning is easily postponed in favour of more interesting or more pressing activities. This chapter, like other sections of this book, is intended to increase your motivation for taking control of your personal financial affairs and to show you how to do it, but only you can provide the other necessary components.

Those who think they ought to do some financial planning, but don't, should ask themselves what obstacles are preventing them from taking greater control of their finances. Is it lack of motivation or lack of a reason for getting involved? Is it not knowing how to get started? Is it a perceived lack of time? Or is it a general distaste for financial matters? Once the reason for not doing more planning has been identified, steps can be taken to improve matters. You may choose to learn how, to delegate planning to someone else in the family, or to hire assistance.

People have a variety of reasons for not making financial plans. Some people say that their income and expenses are too unpredictable to plan anything; others feel that plans are much too confining or that planning takes all the fun out of spending. Discouragement with a plan that has not worked effectively may be the result either of unrealistic estimates or of inadequate methods of controlling the plan. It would be better to try again than to abandon all plans.

Women and Finance

In order to take the initiative in acquiring and managing their own assets, women need to build a foundation of knowledge that will form the basis for a lifelong learning process as they pass through the various stages of the financial life cycle.

In getting started, many women today consider buying a house or condominium on their own. Thus, it is crucial that the female homebuyer understands the responsibilities and costs involved in securing a home mortgage. Senior women living on their own may consider a reverse mortgage to help improve their financial condition.

As women play a greater role in the workforce and secure better working conditions for themselves, they frequently have discretionary income to invest, and thus they form an important market for the securities and investment industries. All women should be active participants in family investment decision-making.

The federal *Income Tax Act* provides opportunities for spouses to work together to minimize the tax burden. One example involves the transfer of unused education, age, pension income, and disability credits from one spouse to another. Husbands and wives must understand the taxation implication of various investment alternatives when making investing decisions.

Since many families are now dependent on two incomes and women perform many necessary unpaid services in the home, insurance issues for women are becoming as crucial as those for male wage earners. As well, since women have a longer average life expectancy than do men, it is vital that women get involved in the estate-planning process.

Because many women and men find themselves in low-paying jobs and managing as single parents, they may be faced with difficult debt burdens. The wise use of credit then becomes an important financial issue.

As women go through the various stages of the life cycle, it would be ideal to look forward to a comfortable retirement. A knowledge of the many areas of financial planning would be helpful in achieving this goal.

Employment Opportunities in Financial Planning

Job opportunities are available to women as well as men in the financial planning area. Many planners help customers with financial planning issues in the banking and insurance industries, and some serve as securities traders and mutual fund representatives. A thorough knowledge of the many aspects of financial planning is necessary to pass the professional examinations, which are often a prerequisite for such employment.

Professional Financial Advisors

Professional advice on personal financial affairs has long been available to certain segments of society. The wealthy pay investment counsellors for advice on investments and tax planning. The overindebted go to publicly and privately supported credit counsellors, who suggest ways of coping with too much debt. Where do the rest of us go for advice? There is no shortage of people who *want* to advise us—to invest in term deposits, guaranteed investment certificates, Canada Savings Bonds, mortgages, real estate, stocks, bonds, mutual funds, or limited partnerships, or to buy insurance. Each advisor has a special interest in promoting ways to invest our spare cash, and each is knowledgeable in a special area. Since many of these salespeople depend on sales commissions, their advice may not be unbiased.

The various kinds of financial advisors may be categorized as follows:

(a) investment counsellors,
(b) credit counsellors,
(c) officers and sales representatives of financial institutions (e.g., bankers, trust company officers, life insurance agents, brokers, mutual fund agents),
(d) financial planners,

— fees only
— commissions only (may be the same as item c above)
— mixture of commissions and fees.

Investment Counsellors

For years, professional **investment counsellors** have advised the wealthy on how to handle their finances, with special attention to minimizing income tax and maximizing investment return. Many investment counsellors will invest funds and handle all the day-to-day decisions for their clients, although some are not interested in clients with less than $200 000 or even $500 000. For ongoing investment services, the management fee is usually based on a percentage of assets. Clearly the assistance of an investment counsellor is beyond the reach of most families. Some, however, will work with groups of people with assets totalling in the millions.

Credit Counsellors

At the other end of the financial spectrum are the overindebted—people who often, although not always, have low incomes, or who buy too much on short-term credit. When facing a debt crisis, they may turn to **credit counsellors** for help in reducing the pressure from creditors and debt collectors. Such counsellors make every effort to find ways to help families and individuals cope with such a crisis. People who are not yet overindebted may also go to a credit counsellor for information and assistance in financial management. These services, now available in most major communities, may or may not be free to clients. There is more about credit counselling in Chapter 14.

Financial Advice for the Majority

The majority of citizens, who are neither very wealthy nor overindebted, generally lack independent financial counsellors to turn to for help. If they want to know more about financial management, they must read books, take courses, or consult those who sell various financial products. The high cost of providing advice, and people's reluctance to pay for this kind of service, means that independent financial advisors have not been widely available to the middle class.

In the 1980s, both the availability of microcomputers and greater family affluence (partly the result of an increase in the number of two-earner households) caused some changes. As the sums of money being handled by families increased and the services and products offered by financial institutions became ever more complex, the demand for information about and help with financial management grew. This need was recognized by publishers, who rapidly expanded the number of books, magazines, and newsletters about personal finance, and by companies selling such products as mutual funds, stocks, life insurance, annuities, and RRSPs. The offer of financial planning became a new marketing tool for a variety of companies. Large financial institutions, such as banks and trust companies, began to offer financial planning without charge, to entice customers. Computers made the planning process quicker and cheaper.

Financial Planners

Financial planners may be categorized in three groups, based on the source of their remuneration. Many people who call themselves financial planners actually sell financial products, such as mutual funds, guaranteed investment certificates, life insurance, bonds, and stocks; they gain their incomes from sales commissions. A much smaller number are fee-only planners, whose incomes depend solely on client fees and who sell no financial products. The third group consists of planners who combine characteristics of the other two: they charge fees for financial planning and also receive commissions on any products they sell.

A big issue is the potential conflict of interest that arises when a financial advisor does not charge for advice but gains his or her income from product commissions. It would be natural for such a planner to find that a client's solutions included some of the products he or she is particularly well informed about and is licensed to sell.

Financial planning, a rapidly growing business in Canada, may soon become an accepted profession. In the meantime, though, efforts are being made to reduce the confusion resulting from its rapid expansion. This activity has been largely unregulated to date, but it is under review by securities branches in several provinces. Establishing standards for education, liability insurance coverage, and ethics are current issues. In 1989, Quebec became the first province to pass legislation linking the use of the term "financial planner" with specific educational criteria and mandatory registration. Other provinces are studying the matter; some are expected to take similar action soon. Until then, anyone can call him- or herself a financial planner, financial consultant, or financial advisor.

The Canadian Association of Financial Planners (CAFP), founded in 1983, is eager to solve the problems of educational requirements and certification. People with two years' experience who complete six correspondence courses become "Chartered Financial Planners (CFPs)." In September 2002, the CAFP and the Canadian Association of Insurance and Financial Advisors (CAIFA) voted to merge and became Advocis. Advocis operates to better serve their members and their clients through training and maintaining a set of standards and advocacy for their members.

The Financial Planners' Standards Council (FPSC) has established standards with input from accountants, the insurance industry, the credit unions, and international organizations.

The FPSC in turn has licensed many organizations such as Advocis to train and certify practitioners as CFPs.

Computer Programs for Financial Planners Since it may take a financial planner up to 40 hours to create a comprehensive financial plan for a family, and cost as much as $3000 or $4000, a way was needed to deliver financial planning to clients more cheaply. The solution was found in computers. By inputting selective client data into a computer program, a financial planner can generate a financial plan for a client fairly inexpensively. The programs vary widely in the extent to which the user can make adjustments for personal habits and preferences, as well as in the assumptions upon which they are based. The expansion of financial planning coincided with the availability of microcomputers and suitable programs, and most financial planners now depend heavily on computers.

Choosing a Financial Advisor

It is wise to make some inquiries before entrusting your financial affairs to an unknown advisor.

(a) Find out how the financial planner is paid. Is his or her income based only on fees, on fees and commissions, or only on commissions?

(b) Ask about the planner's qualifications. What educational background, experience, and licences does the person have? Does he or she have any recognized certificates?

(c) Does this planner have certain areas of specialization?

(d) What sort of planning is he or she offering? Will you receive a very detailed, comprehensive plan or the solution to a specific problem? Will there be a written report with recommendations? Does the planner have a sample plan to show you?

(e) Will the planner provide an analysis of the costs and benefits of the various alternatives suggested?

(f) What will the plan cost?

(g) Has the planner ever been sued by a client?

(h) How does the planner keep up to date on financial and legal matters?

(i) What institutes is the planner affiliated with?

(j) Does the planner issue regular newsletters?

Review the relationship regularly.

Summary

- Financial plans assist people in ordering their lives. Financial planners sell financial products, or work for fees to help establish financial plans, or both.
- Life cycle stages are the various phases of our lifetimes, of which there are generally many.
- A budget is a plan for financial resources.
- Income is the total of all sources of financial resources received. Net worth (wealth) is the value of your assets less your liabilities.
- Real rate of return is actual change in the value of an asset after accounting for inflation.
- Liquid assets are those assets that may be quickly converted into cash.

- Fixed expenses are those expenses that are difficult to change in the short term. Flexible expenses can be altered in the short term.
- Investment counsellors advise persons on how to handle their finances, in particular their investments. Credit counsellors assist debtors in facing credit crises.

Financial planning is a growing and evolving profession. Financial planners offer advice on personal financial affairs, sometimes for a fee. Those who do not charge fees for their advice depend on commissions from the sale of financial products, such as mutual funds, life insurance, stocks, bonds, annuities, and RRSPs.

Key Terms

budget *(p. 8)*

credit counsellors *(p. 30)*

financial plan *(p. 3)*

financial planners *(p. 31)*

fixed expenses *(p. 16)*

flexible expenses *(p. 16)*

income *(p. 10)*

investment counsellors *(p. 30)*

life cycle stages *(p. 7)*

liquid assets *(p. 14)*

net worth *(p. 11)*

real rate of return *(p. 14)*

wealth *(p. 10)*

Problems

1. Where Does All the Money Go?

   Jan and Dave, a couple in their early thirties, have recently purchased a new house in Vegreville, Alberta. The purchase price of $145 000 was a little more than they had anticipated, but they love the life in this small town. Dave is able to commute to his office in Edmonton, where he works as a sales manager for a scientific supply company. Jan, an elementary schoolteacher, is just getting back into the workforce now that eight-year-old Brent and six-year-old Karen are both attending school. Since she is working as a substitute teacher until a full-time position becomes available, her income is quite uncertain and irregular.

   With a down payment of $49 000 from the sale of their old home, the mortgage of $96 000, to be paid off in 25 years, costs them $621.24 a month. In the excitement of buying the new house, however, they forgot to allow for legal bills, moving costs, and the need for new draperies, so they had to get a $3000 personal loan with a two-year term. Recently, they purchased a new car for Jan, costing $12 500, financed with a $10 000 loan on which the monthly payments are $295.

   They have $1500 in Canada Savings Bonds (a gift from Jan's grandmother), $355 in Jan's savings account, and about $456 in their joint chequing account. Last year they received about $82.50 in interest from Canada Savings Bonds. Except for a pension plan refund put into an RRSP a few years ago (when Dave transferred from another company), which is now worth about $3755, their only major asset is their home.

   When they married, Jan and Dave each bought a $100 000 life insurance policy. If they were to cash in these policies, each would have a cash surrender value of $2000.

   They rely on a line of credit from the bank for emergencies, but apart from this, they would have very little flexibility if Dave should be off work for any length of time. He does have insurance coverage at work that would pay about half his usual wages if he should become disabled for longer than three months. During the three-month waiting period, there would be an Employment Insurance benefit and a few days' sick leave with pay.

Dave's benefits at work include the use of a leased car and an expense account for lunches and the occasional dinner. He also has comprehensive dental, drug, and vision care plans, along with some group life insurance coverage, the value of which is equal to one year's salary.

Fortunately, their new house seems to need little maintenance work, but Jan and Dave would like to start fixing up the basement. They are hoping that Jan will get full-time work soon, so that they will be able to clear some debts and start on the basement.

Dave feels that with his relatively high income of $55 000 a year, including commissions, they should not have the money worries they are currently experiencing. He feels they should be in a better position to invest some funds in RRSPs to save for the future and take advantage of the tax saving, but at the moment he does not see how they can afford to do so.

Jan confesses that before the children came along they were used to spending quite freely, since both were earning good wages. Now, with no established management pattern, the money just seems to disappear.

Following is the list Jan and Dave made of their monthly income and expenses. They do not keep records, so these are their best estimates. The income figures are net of deductions at the source, such as income tax, Canada Pension Plan and Employment Insurance premiums, and registered pension plan contributions.

Income per month

Dave's take-home pay	$2 909.00
Jan's average salary	1 400.00
TOTAL	$4 309.00

Short-term debt repayment

Bank loan for car	$295.00
Bank loan	135.00
TOTAL	$ 430.00

Expenses

Mortgage	$ 622.00
Heating	140.00
Electricity and water	135.00
Telephone	68.00
Home insurance	35.00
Property taxes	185.00
Food	650.00
Entertainment	150.00
Clothes	400.00
Babysitter	40.00
Books, magazines, CDs	35.00
Gifts	150.00
Life insurance	110.00
Transportation (Jan's car)	200.00
Miscellaneous	300.00
TOTAL	$3 220.00

(a) Prepare a net worth statement for this couple. Analyze their net worth position and make a list of issues you would raise in a discussion with them if you were their financial counsellor.

(b) Make a summary cash flow statement for Jan and Dave, noting which expenditures are fixed and which are flexible. Analyze their cash flow situation. Do any expense categories seem to be missing?

(c) Evaluate this couple's financial security. How well-prepared are they for a financial emergency?

(d) Do you think this couple ought to be saving more? What do you suggest? What future difficulties do you foresee for them if they continue as at present?

(e) Evaluate this couple's financial management strategies in terms of the basic steps of financial planning. If they were really motivated to make a change, where might they begin?

2. Decide whether you AGREE or DISAGREE with each of the following statements:

(a) Making and sticking to a financial plan is easier if some rewards are built into the system.

(b) A budget takes all the fun out of spending.

(c) Financial planning makes more sense for people with a good income; for people who are poor, planning is impossible.

(d) If you and your spouse cannot agree on some financial goals, perhaps the solution is to handle your money separately instead of pooling it.

(e) If your financial affairs have been stable for some years and you have reached a comfortable agreement with your spouse about who pays for what and how much to spend on various things, your need for detailed budget analysis may be less than that of a recently married couple.

(f) Students can't really make spending plans because they have no regular income.

(g) If your income is very irregular, your spending must necessarily be adjusted to the fluctuations of your income.

(h) It is impossible to make a budget work because of all the unexpected expenses that occur.

(i) The reason more people believe in the value of budgets than actually draft them is the amount of paperwork involved.

3. Referring to Figure 1.1, "Income and Living Costs: Average Lifetime Profile," describe what you consider to be the greatest financial challenges for the following stages in a person's or a couple's life:

(a) recent graduate from college or university

(b) newlyweds

(c) new parents

(d) newly separated single parent

(e) a family with two teenage children

(f) a couple in their mid-fifties

(g) a newly retired couple

(h) a widowed senior

4. Julie was taught that responsible financial management requires that a record be kept of every penny she spends. She has kept such records throughout her life. She keeps them in a running diary, without any expenditure categories, and never totals the figures or does any analysis. What value does this record-keeping probably have for Julie? What is your opinion of its usefulness?

5. How important is it to have an emergency fund when you do not know whether you will ever need it and you feel that you could always borrow in a pinch?

6. (a) List some internal factors that may cause people to become financially distraught.

   (b) What external factors may cause people to become financially distraught?

7. Refer to Personal Finance in Action Box 1.1, "The Credit Trap." Why do you think this couple got caught in this trap? Is this a problem mostly for low-income families?

8. What appears to be the major financial planning method of your classmates?

9. What easily implemented processes could college or university students engage to better manage their finances?

10. Ask your classmates if they balance their chequing accounts monthly. If they do not, ask them why not. What would motivate them to do so?

11. Refer to Figure 1.2. Why did Yolanda's $60 000 grow to a larger sum than Dan's?

12. For Darryl and Ilana, life was progressing well, but not the way they wanted it to progress. Darryl's career challenges and opportunities were limited in his current position. Consequently, they were exploring the possibility of Darryl returning to school to complete an MBA. This would require both Darryl and Ilana to quit their jobs and move to a larger city. Ilana would then have to find another job, thus putting her career on hold for Darryl's two-year MBA. After his graduation, they would likely have to move again to whatever job he might get.

    Both agreed to this arrangement, but once they had moved, Ilana could not find a job. Darryl felt he was too busy to work as a teaching assistant. Meanwhile, the bills continued to roll in. The savings they had set aside for Darryl's MBA only proved adequate for tuition and books; living expenses became the sole responsibility of Ilana. Employment insurance proved inadequate as only Ilana could collect it. The situation was extremely stressful for the two of them, so they went to the graduate student counsellor for advice.

    As their advisor, what advice would you give this couple?

13. Lucy called a financial advisor, saying that she did not know how to cope with her financial affairs. She had never had to give money much thought before her recent divorce from a well-to-do businessman. When she decided to look for work, she found herself at a disadvantage without previous work experience. However, she did land a job in a women's clothing store, where she enjoyed selling clothes and getting things for herself at a discount. She loves clothes and always dresses well. Her two children are grown and independent, and she owns a spacious condominium apartment in a good part of town.

    Lucy had initially tried to maintain her accustomed level of living, but she had lately begun to dip into her divorce settlement funds to make ends meet. Also, she was having trouble with a trust company over the way her money was being handled and was quite confused about what kinds of accounts she had. Now in her early fifties, Lucy has been too absorbed in recent family crises to think about her own future. She does not feel very enthusiastic about the advisor's suggestion that they make a long-term financial plan for her. She had wanted an immediate solution and freedom from financial stress.

(a) If you were in Lucy's shoes, what would you do now?

(b) Identify the factors that have created Lucy's current problems.

(c) What sources of income will Lucy probably have when she turns 65?

 14. By accessing the Financial Planners Standards Council's website at **www.cfp-ca.org**, determine the steps a financial planner is expected to proceed through compared with the five steps outlined in Figure 1.3. What are the differences and what are the similarities between the two? Which entails the most work, and is the planner's work and time worth the $3000 to $4000 mentioned in this textbook?

References

BOOKS AND ARTICLES

Akright, Carol. *Funding Your Dreams Generation to Generation: Intergenerational Financial Planning to Ensure Your Family's Health, Wealth and Personal Values.* New York: Dearborn Trade, 2001.

Bamber, Lori M. *The Complete Idiot's Guide to Personal Finance for Canadians.* Scarborough: Pearson Education Canada, 2001. Part of the popular "Complete Idiot's Guide" series, which presents clear, understandable information about difficult topics (the kind that make many intelligent adults feel like complete idiots—hence the series' title). Numerous complementary titles are also available.

Bamber, Lori M. *Financial Serenity: Successful Financial and Investment Planning for Women,* Scarborough: Pearson Education Canada, 1999.

Chakrapani, Chuck. *Financial Freedom on Five Dollars a Day.* Sixth edition. Vancouver: Self-Counsel Press, 1994. A frugal perspective on financial independence.

Chun, Anne, and Patricia Jermey. *Planning Your Financial Future: A Guide for Canadians.* Toronto: ITP Nelson, 1997. A how-to book on the topic of planning.

Deloitte and Touche. *Canadian Guide to Personal Financial Management 2000.* Scarborough: Prentice Hall Canada, annual. A team of accountants provides guidance on a broad range of topics, including planning finances, estimating insurance needs, managing risk, and determining investment needs. Instructions and the necessary forms for making plans are also included.

Douglas, Ann. *Family Finance: The Essential Guide for Canadian Parents.* Scarborough: Pearson Education Canada, 2000. An excellent methodology for managing finances for your family.

Epstein, Lita. *Streetwise Retirement Planning: Saving Strategies and Practical Advice for a Secure Financial Future.* Avon, MA: Adams Media Corporation, 2003.

Personal Finance on the Web

Each of the following websites provides high-quality links to many other internet resources.

Canada WealthNet
www.nucleus.com/wealthnet An index of Canadian financial and investment news and a list of advisors accessible via the net. Extensive investment information.

Canadian Financial Network
www.canadianfinance.com Provides solid information about finance for Canadians, along with extensive links to other relevant sites and a window on Canada for global investors.

Canadian Women's Business Network
www.cdnbizwomen.com This website is relevant for women who are operating businesses, but it is also relevant to financial planning.

Financial Planners Standards Council
www.cfp-ca.org The home site for the Canadian branch of the international designation Certified Financial Planner.

The Financial Advisors Association of Canada
www.advocis.ca The website for the national organization representing the CAFP and the CAIFA. Good for professional development and finding an advisor.

MochaSofa: Women Connecting for Solutions
www.mochasofa.ca/Mochasofa/client/en/Work/Home.asp This website covers a variety of topics of interest to women, but the work and money sections contain information that is highly relevant to women and finances.

Quicken Financial Network
www.quicken.com A Canadian site provided by the developers of the popular software programs Quicken and QuickTax that encompasses a financial fitness test, expert advice and analysis, investment tracking, and other financial help.

chapter **2**

Introduction to Personal Income Tax

"Income tax has made more liars out of American people than golf."
Will Rogers, The Illiterate Digest (1924)

"The avoidance of taxes is the only pursuit that still carries any reward."

John Maynard Keynes

Learning Objectives

Understanding the concepts discussed in this chapter should help you become a wiser manager.

After studying this chapter, you should be able to:

1. Provide a basic introduction to and overview of the Canadian personal income tax system.

2. Distinguish between the following pairs of concepts: gross income, taxable income, and net income; average tax rate and marginal tax rate; progressive tax rate and marginal tax rate; wealth and capital gain; before-tax and after-tax dollars; tax-exempt income and tax-sheltered income; tax avoidance and tax

evasion; income exemption and tax credit; capital gain and taxable capital gain; refundable and non-refundable tax credit; RRSP, RRIF, and RESP; and tax avoidance and tax deferment.

3. Outline at least three approaches to tax planning, including income deferment, income splitting, and transfer of tax credits.

4. Explain the principle of attribution.

Introduction

The intent of this chapter is to provide an overview of the personal income tax system, rather than an in-depth treatment of what is a very large and complex topic. The explanations of basic terminology offered here, along with a simplified framework that shows the relationships among a few key concepts, should make it easier for you to understand the many articles and books available on personal income tax. In addition to the discussion in this chapter, you will find income tax mentioned elsewhere in the book in relation to other topics, especially retirement income and investments.

In the late 1980s, Canada's federal government made major revisions to the income tax system, reducing the kinds of allowable deductions, increasing tax credits, changing tax rates, and shifting some taxation from income to expenditures. To keep up to date with the details of our ever-changing tax rules, it is necessary to follow the financial press or read some of the regularly revised tax guides. These are especially important with all the recent tax changes and cuts.

Such matters become even more important for people who are self-employed or who own their own business. The tax laws vary considerably, depending on whether you are an employee or are responsible for calculating and remitting your own taxes. Self-employed people and small business owners are eligible for tax deductions that are not available to people who work for others. Some of these details will be discussed both in this chapter and in later chapters.

The Tax Burden

Personal income tax has become an increasing burden. In 2005, Canadians paid $155 billion in income taxes to federal and provincial governments; that works out to about $4808 for each man, woman, and child in the country. Since 1961, Canadians' income tax burden has been steadily increasing, as shown by the per capita data in Figure 2.1. These data have been adjusted for the effects of inflation by converting all values to 1986 dollars using the Consumer Price Index. Thus, it is possible to see the trend in the income tax burden while holding population and inflation constant. The percentage of income paid in income taxes to both federal and provincial governments has also grown over this period, as shown in Figure 2.2. The rate has increased from over 7 percent of income in 1961 to just over 15 percent of the average annual income in Canada of over $32 000 in 2005. The percentage has dropped almost 2 percent since 1998.

Income tax was introduced in 1917 as a temporary measure to help pay the costs of World War I. It has been continued ever since to meet governments' ever-increasing need for funds. Canadians have become accustomed to a wide variety of government-provided and government-funded services and comprehensive income security programs such as Old Age Security, supported by large amounts of public funds. So it is not surprising to find that we are paying increasing amounts of income tax to fund these programs.

The Personal Income Tax System

Who Pays Income Tax?

All Canadian residents with incomes above a certain level are taxed on their Canadian income as well as on any income received from outside the country. Each of us must file an individual income tax return; spouses must file individually, not jointly, as they do in the United States. Contrary to popular belief, members of the First Nations do pay income tax. Should they live off the reserve, they pay tax like any other Canadian resident. Even those living on the reserves

FIGURE 2.1 AVERAGE INCOME AND INCOME TAXES PER CAPITA 1961–2005

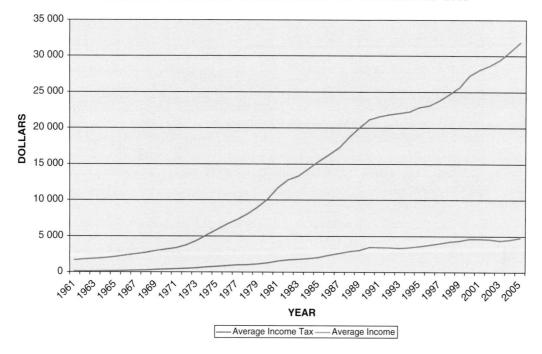

SOURCE: Statistics Canada, Canadian Economic Observer, Historical Supplement, 2005, Catalogue No. 11-210, Table 3, p. 13 and Table 6, p. 24 (July 17, 2006).

pay income tax on earnings from off the reserve if the earnings exceed 10 percent of their income. The rules are complex and worth investigating for First Nations people.

Federal Income Tax Rates

In Canada, we use a **progressive tax rate** system, which means that as taxable income increases, the tax rate increases. Taxable income is calculated by subtracting certain deductions from gross income (more about this later). The diagram below illustrates the progressive nature of federal income tax (using taxable income and 2006 tax rates).

Under this system, a taxable income of $36 378 or less is taxed at 15.25 percent. If your taxable income is higher than that, the next $36 378 is taxed at 22 percent; income over $72 756 but less than $118 285 is taxed at 26 percent; anything beyond $118 285 is taxed at 29 percent.

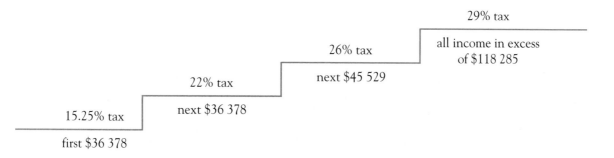

FIGURE 2.2   PERCENTAGE INCOME PAID IN INCOME TAXES 1961–2005

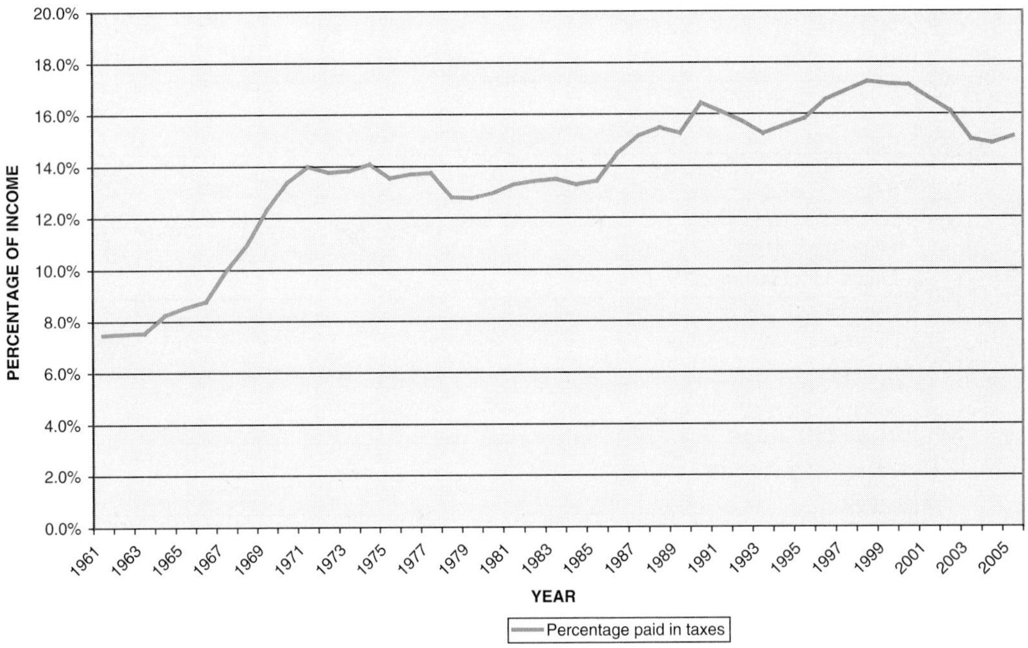

SOURCE: Statistics Canada, Canadian Economic Observer, Historical Supplement, 2005, Catalogue No.
11–210, Table 3, p. 13 and Table 6, p. 24 (July 17, 2006).

The highest rate that you personally pay on taxable income is referred to as your **marginal tax rate** (that is, 15.25 percent, or 22 percent, or 26 percent, or 29 percent, as illustrated in the diagram on the previous page). Understanding this concept is basic to understanding the significance of tax shelters and to choosing investment alternatives. For example, if you are now paying 22 percent as your highest federal tax rate, that would be your federal marginal rate: each extra dollar of taxable income you receive will be taxed at this rate. Obviously, if your taxable income increases enough, you will move to the next step: your marginal tax rate will become 26 percent. In other words, your marginal tax rate is the rate of taxes that you pay on the last dollar earned.

Your **average tax rate** is the percentage of your gross income that you actually pay in income tax. Generally, this concept is less useful in tax planning than the marginal tax rate, although occasionally there may be a need to know what proportion of your income was paid in taxes.

Provincial Income Tax Rates

Although all Canadian provinces and territories levy income taxes in addition to those imposed by the federal government, all except Quebec have arranged for the Canada Revenue Agency (CRA) to collect this tax for them. This approach makes life simpler for most of Canada's taxpayers, who must complete only one combined tax return. (Quebec residents file separate provincial returns.) The provincial rates provided in this book are for planning purposes only and do not reflect the actual tax one would have to pay. Most provinces actually charge a percentage of the federal taxable income (see Table 2.1, the line reading "Provincial Tax"), but the rates vary for each province and change regularly with each new government and provincial budget. Check with your provincial finance ministry for the rate charged in your province. For approximate 2006 provincial rates, see Table 2.1.

TABLE 2.1   ESTIMATE YOUR INCOME TAX BILL

Year 2006

Income

Employment income	$62 000.00
Pension income	$ —
Employment Insurance benefits	$ —
Dividends (125% of amount received)	$ 1 250.00
Other investment income	$ —
Rental income (or loss)	$ —
Business or self-employed income (or loss)	$ —
1/2 of capital gains	$ 500.00
Other income	$ —
Total Income	**$63 750.00**

Less Deductions

RRSP or RPP contributions	$ 3 750.00
Union or professional dues	$ 450.00
Eligible child- and attendant-care expenses	$ 3 500.00
Allowable business investment losses	$ —
Moving expenses	$ —
Alimony and maintenance expenses	$ —
Other deductions	$ 375.00
Clawback of OAS	$ —
Non-capital losses from previous years	$ —
Net capital losses from previous years (only against capital gains)	$ 125.00
Capital gains deductions	$ —
Other deductions (EI, CPP, etc.)	$ 2 639.70
Total Deductions	**$ 10 839.70**
Total Taxable Income	**$ 52 910.30**

Income Tax

Federal Tax:

15.25% of first $36 378 taxable income (maximum income tax of $5 548)	$ 5 548.00
22% of next $36 378 taxable income (maximum income tax of $8 003)	$ 3 637.00
26% of next $45 529 taxable income (maximum income tax of $10 473)	$ —
29% of taxable income in Excess of $118 285	$ —
Total Federal Tax	**$ 9 185.00**

Less Tax Credits

Personal tax credits *	$ 1 382.82
Dividend tax credit, 13.33% of grossed-up dividends (in Quebec use 8.897%)	$ 166.63
Total Tax Credits	**$ 1 549.45**

continued

TABLE 2.1   ESTIMATE YOUR INCOME TAX BILL (CONTINUED)

Basic Federal Tax (Total Tax Less Tax Credits)	$ 7 634.66
Plus	
CPP or QPP Contributions (maximum $1 910.70 or $3 821.40 if self-employed)	$1 910.70
Employment Insurance Contributions (maximum $729; zero if self-employed)	$ 729.00
Total	$ 2 639.70
Net Federal Income Tax	$10 274.36
Provincial Tax	
See table below for tax rates to use.	$ 4 709.59
Total Income Tax Payable	$ 14 983.95

Provincial Income Tax Rates for 2005

	Income	Rate		Income	Rate
British Columbia	first 33 755	6.05%	**Alberta**	all levels	10.00%
	next 33 756	9.15%	**Manitoba**	first 30 544	10.90%
	next 10 000	11.70%		next 34 456	14.90%
	next 16 610	13.70%		over 65 000	17.40%
	over 94 121	14.70%	**Northwest**	first 34 555	5.90%
Saskatchewan	first 37 579	11.00%	**Territories**	next 34 555	8.60%
	next 69 788	13.00%		next 43 248	12.20%
	over 107 367	15.00%		over 112 358	14.05%
Yukon	first 36 378	7.04%	**Nunavut**	first 36 378	4.00%
	next 36 378	9.68%		next 36 378	7.00%
	next 45 529	11.44%		next 45 529	9.00%
	over 118 285	12.76%		over 118 285	11.50%
Ontario	first 34 758	6.05%	**Quebec**	first 28 303	16.00%
	next 34 759	9.15%		next 28 040	20.00%
	over 69 517	11.16%		over 56 070	24.00%
New Brunswick	first 33 450	9.68%	**Prince Edward**	first 30 754	9.80%
	next 33 452	14.82%	**Island**	next 30 755	13.80%
	next 41 866	16.52%		over 61 509	16.70%
	over 108 768	17.84%	**Newfoundland &**	first 29 590	10.57%
Nova Scotia	first 29 590	8.79%	**Labrador**	next 29 590	16.16%
	next 29 590	14.95%		over 59 180	18.02%
	next 33 820	16.67%			
	over 93 000	17.50%			

*** Personal Tax Credits**

Individual Credit	**$1 318.82**
Spousal Credit: if spouse's income is less than $735, claim	$1 232.05
Spousal Credit: if spouse's income is more than $735 and is less than $8 079, reduce claim from $1 232 by 15.25% of the income	
Equivalent to Married (supporting a child)	$1 232.05
Child Tax Credits are included under child-care expenses and claimed by spouse with lower income	calculated

After calculating the amount of your federal tax, you must add the appropriate provincial tax.

Quebec tax rates, including the federal tax, are included in Table 2.1 for reference only and are not inclusive of all situations, such as an individual with dependents. The Quebec tax system is provincially administered and in 2006 exceeds 24 percent of taxable income over $56 070.

Combined Marginal Tax Rate

To find your **combined marginal tax rate**, multiply your federal marginal tax rate by the provincial rate, and then add the result of that calculation to the federal rate. Assume, for example, that you have a federal marginal tax rate of 22 percent and that your provincial rate is 45 percent of your federal tax. Your combined marginal tax rate would be $22 + (0.45 \times 22) = 31.9$ percent.

How Much Tax to Pay

Stripped of detail, the process of calculating how much federal income tax you need to pay annually can be summarized in three steps:

(a) Total relevant income $-$ Deductions $=$ Taxable income
(b) Taxable income $\times$ Tax rate $=$ Total tax
(c) Total tax $-$ Tax credits $=$ Tax payable

If you analyze the articles on income tax in the financial press, you will find that much of their content has to do with these three issues:

(a) What is counted as relevant income for tax purposes?
(b) Which deductions can be used to reduce taxable income?
(c) How can a person make the most effective use of tax credits?

The following sections will examine each of these topics in turn.

What Is Income?

Gross, Net, and Taxable Income

Gross income is all the income you received before anything was subtracted. Wage rates are usually quoted as gross income. **Net income** is harder to define: it simply refers to your income after something has been subtracted. Any use of this term should therefore be accompanied by information about what the income is "net *of*." For instance, it may be "net of deductions by the employer" or "net of income tax" or "net of expenses related to generating self-employed earnings."

Legislative Concept of Income

Income can be quite difficult to define. In economic terms, **income** is a flow of economic resources over a specified time period, usually expressed as a rate per hour, per day, per week, per month, or per year (for example, you might say that your new job pays "$35 000 a year"). The *Income Tax Act* uses a legislative concept of income for the purposes of taxation, and thus does not necessarily define income in the way economists do. Therefore, we find that as a result, some types of income are currently subject to income tax, and some are not. Here is an abbreviated list of some forms of income that are taxable and some that are not:

Income Subject to Tax	Income Exempt from Tax
Income from employment	
• wages, salaries, commissions, bonuses	
• net income from self-employment (after expenses)	
• value of employment benefits	
Pensions and social security	*Income support payments*
• Canada/Quebec Pension Plan	• Guaranteed Income Supplement
• Old Age Security	• Spouse's Allowance
• Employment Insurance	• Workers' Compensation
• employment-related retirement pensions	• welfare
• income from an annuity bought with RRSP funds	
• withdrawals from a RRIF	
Investment income	
• interest	
• dividends	
• rent	
• net profit	
• withdrawals from RRSPs	

Employment Benefits In addition to income, employees may receive taxable benefits: the value of these benefits must be added to your income for tax purposes. Some examples are employee loans, personal use of a company car, medical care plans, and travel benefits. Some benefits—such as employers' contributions to employee pension plans or group insurance—are exempt from taxation until you have actually received them.

Capital Gains

In addition to taxing income, governments may tax changes in wealth. In the past, Canada's governments have taxed estates, inheritances, and gifts, but these taxes have all been discontinued. Currently, however, Canadians do pay taxes on capital gains. A **capital gain** is not income; it is a change in wealth—that is, the windfall accruing to an owner because property or possessions have increased in value. In simple terms, a capital gain is the difference between an asset's original cost and its selling price. The income tax literature makes a distinction between capital gains and **taxable capital gains** because only a portion of any capital gain (currently 50 percent) is taxable.

Deductions from Income

Once income and the changes in wealth that are subject to tax have been identified and listed, the next step is to examine what deductions may be used to reduce taxable income. (Although technically there is a difference between an exemption and a deduction, both serve to reduce taxable income, and the terms are often used interchangeably.) The exact nature and amounts of deductions allowed may change whenever the federal government amends the *Income Tax Act*. Deductions from income may be classified in the following three categories, with the specific examples changing from time to time. In many cases, there are limits on the amounts that may be deducted.

(a) Contributions to retirement pension plans
- registered pension plans (RPPs)
- registered retirement savings plans (RRSPs)

(b) Specified expenditures associated with any of the following activities:
- earning a living, such as self-employed earnings or commissioned sales income
  - union and professional dues
  - moving expenses
  - child care
  - travel expenses
  - home office
- investing (excluding RRSPs)
  - interest on money borrowed to invest
  - rent for safety deposit box
  - accounting fees
  - investment counsel fees
- paying child support under an arrangement dated before May 1, 1997
- paying alimony and spousal support

(c) Capital gains exemption for small businesses and farm property
- net capital gains

Contributions to Retirement Plans

Since the 1950s, encouraging Canadians to save for retirement has been a matter of public policy implemented through the income tax system. Contributions to employer-sponsored registered pension plans (RPPs) and to registered retirement savings plans (RRSPs) have been exempt from tax, within limits. Since money goes into these plans tax-free, while any return generated within the plan is also not taxed, such plans are known as **tax-sheltered funds**. Only when the money is no longer sheltered, that is, withdrawn or turned into a retirement pension, does the money become fully taxable. A major reason for putting money in a tax shelter is to defer taxes until a time (such as retirement) when you expect to have a lower marginal tax rate.

Specified Expenditures

Within limits, a few types of expenditures are deductible for tax purposes, including some associated with earning a living, investing, and family support. Some examples are listed above, in the introduction to this section.

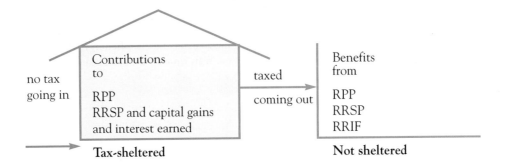

Capital Gains Exemption

The opportunity to make a capital gain is always associated with the possibility of having a capital loss. For tax purposes, capital losses are therefore subtracted from capital gains, to get **net taxable capital gains**. These terms and relationships are summarized in the following calculations:

Sale price	−	Purchase price	=	Capital gain (or loss)
Capital gain	−	Capital loss	=	Net Capital gain
Net capital gain	×	0.50	=	Net taxable capital gain

Primary Residence Any capital gain realized on the sale of your home is not subject to tax, but there are limits on this exemption: you (and your spouse) can have only one primary residence at any given time. This means that any capital gains on the sale of the family cottage would be taxable, but selling the family's primary home would not generate taxable capital gains. This matter can be of significant concern to some families and will therefore be discussed in more detail in later chapters. (Income properties—properties that are owned by you but rented or leased to others—are considered investment properties; capital gains on such properties are automatically taxed.)

Lifetime Exemption For a while (from 1985 until the February 1994 federal budget), all Canadian taxpayers were allowed up to $100 000 in tax-exempt capital gains during their lifetime. This general personal exemption has now been eliminated, but the federal government has left two exemptions still available: the small business corporation shares exemption and the exemption for family farms. Under the first of these categories, an individual who owns shares in a start-up corporation that conducts (or conducted) the majority of its business in Canada can deduct up to $500 000 of any capital gain from the sale of those shares. In the second instance, the owners of a family farm or farm quotas are entitled to a tax exemption up to the same $500 000 limit per person.

Non-Taxable Changes in Wealth If you receive an inheritance, win a lottery, or make a gain from another form of gambling, these increases in your wealth are not subject to income tax. In the case of an inheritance, any taxes owing on the estate of the deceased will have been paid before the estate was distributed. Life insurance is not taxed and is paid directly to the beneficiary unless there is foul play. Insurance is paid for with after-tax dollars, and hence has already been taxed.

Tax Credits

After calculating your total federal income tax, determine your eligibility for certain tax reductions, called tax credits. A **tax credit** is subtracted after total tax has been determined. Because, as we will see shortly, deductions tend to be of the greatest benefit to those with higher incomes, many income deductions were replaced with tax credits in the 1988 tax reforms. To see how tax credits make the tax burden more equitable, consider this example: under the previous rules, a person with a combined marginal tax rate of 48 percent and a $1000 deduction would have saved $480 in taxes, while someone with a marginal rate of 22 percent and the same deduction would have saved only $220. If both persons were instead eligible for the same tax credit, each would receive the same benefit, regardless of his or her income.

Most tax credits are not refundable, which means that they are useful only if you have some taxable income. Suppose, for example, you calculate that your federal tax will be $5000 and your tax credits will be $1000; the tax credits reduce your federal tax to $4000. But if your taxable income is so low that you owe no tax, that non-refundable tax credit does you no good: your tax is still zero. (If, on the other hand, the tax credit were refundable, you would get a $1000 "tax refund" from the government, even though you paid no taxes into the system. See the next section for more details.)

Some tax credits—for example, the basic personal amount that every taxpayer is allowed to claim, and the married amount—are indexed; that is, they are adjusted to reflect the annual change in the Consumer Price Index. If the price index rose 3 percent in the previous year, these credits would be increased by the same 3 percent. For instance, an annual inflation rate of 5.5 percent would mean an increase of 5.5 percent in certain tax credits. (For another example of indexations, see Personal Finance in Action Box 2.1, "Indexation of Pensions.")

Refundable Tax Credits Sometimes the federal income tax system also includes **refundable tax credits**. If you are eligible for such a tax credit, whether you receive it will depend on whether or not you have taxable income. If you have no taxable income, you can claim the tax credit anyway; the government will issue it to you by cheque. If you have a taxable income, you can use a refundable tax credit to reduce the taxes you owe. One example of a refundable tax credit is the GST tax credit. Designed to provide benefits for low-income individuals, it is negatively related to taxable income. This means that the more you earn, the smaller the credit you receive, and vice versa.

Non-Refundable Tax Credits Most tax credits fall into this category. Here is a partial list of the types of **non-refundable tax credits** available to qualified taxpayers in 2006:

Basic personal amount	Age amount
Spouse amount	Dependent children
Pension income	Disability
Tuition fees	Medical expenses
Charitable donations	Donations to political parties
Dividend	Employment Insurance contributions
Canada or Quebec Pension contributions	Textbook fees

Because the specifics of each of these tax credits (how much, who is eligible, and so on) can and do change, we will not discuss them in further detail here; to learn more about the credits currently available, consult a recent income tax guide. The dividend tax credit, because of its significance for investment planning, will be explained in detail in Chapter 10. Some of these

Indexation of Pensions

Marina's CPP retirement pension, which was $540 a month last year, will be revised in January to take account of the inflation rate. Since prices rose an average of 4 percent the previous year, her pension will be increased by 4 percent: $540 + (540 × 0.04) = $561.60. This is an example of **full indexation**.

Unfortunately for her, the pension from her previous employment is only partially indexed, with adjustments made for inflation greater than 3 percent. Under **partial indexation**, a pension of $750 a month would be adjusted as follows: $750 + (750 × (0.04 − 0.03)) = $757.50.

credits, such as tuition and charitable donations, can be transferred from one family member to another; again, refer to current tax books for specific details.

Table 2.1 presents a simple form for calculating your income tax, with a particular view to planning for the current year or the upcoming year. You can download a spreadsheet, which is almost identical to Table 2.1, from our Companion Website at **www.pearsoned.ca/currie.** Basic information on exemptions and tax deductions are included at the end of this table. For final definitive rates check the Canada Revenue Agency website at **cra-arc.gc.ca.**

Tax Planning

The aim of personal tax planning is to pay no more taxes than necessary at present and, whenever possible, to defer tax to a future time when your marginal rate may be lower. Tax planning cannot be done effectively if you leave it until April, when you are completing your tax return; instead, it should be an ongoing process. Most tax planning possibilities may be classified as either (i) tax avoidance or (ii) tax deferment. A few examples to be discussed here include avoiding tax by income splitting and by transferring deductions or credits, and deferring tax with registered retirement savings plans or registered education savings plans.

Tax Avoidance

Arranging one's affairs to minimize income tax is considered perfectly acceptable and is called **tax avoidance**. Many Canadians pay more tax than necessary through ignorance of the tax rules and failing to report deductions or tax credits for which they are eligible. Such errors are quite understandable, given the increasing complexity of our income tax system. The solution is either to become knowledgeable yourself by following the financial press, or to obtain advice from a tax accountant.

Deliberate **tax evasion**, on the other hand, is a violation of the law. Our system depends on voluntary compliance, which is encouraged by unannounced audits of a sample of taxpayers each year. During an audit, the Canada Revenue Agency examines records, receipts, cancelled cheques, bank statements, and other background documents. It is in your own interest to keep your records in good order. Less complex than a tax audit is a tax *reassessment*. The CRA may conduct a reassessment of your taxes for any year within the past three; this process typically involves a request for more information to support your claims.

Income Splitting A family unit, which pools income and expenses, may have one or more members who earn a great deal more than the other family member(s); nevertheless, each person in the family must file an individual tax return. Tax planning aims to shift some of the income from high earners to low earners, who have lower marginal tax rates, thus reducing the family's total income tax. Income splitting is a complicated matter and is best attempted only after seeking professional advice.

A basic principle to be considered when contemplating intrafamilial transfers of funds is that of **attribution of income** (see Personal Finance in Action Box 2.2, "Attribution of Income"). Under income tax legislation, all reported income must be identified with a specific earner. In most cases, the person who earned the income also received it. However, if Person A earns revenue but arranges for that revenue to be received by Person B, that income is generally "attributed" to the person who earned it (A), who is liable for the tax on it. Attribution rules are designed to discourage income splitting.

With professional advice, some income splitting can be achieved. For instance, attribution rules do not generally apply to business income earned by a spouse or child from funds lent or transferred to them. Funds may be contributed to a spouse's RRSP, which will be discussed further in Chapter 6. As a gift, the higher-income spouse may pay the income tax of the lower-income spouse as a way of transferring funds. Or, if one spouse has more income than the other, the higher-income earner can pay as many of the family expenses as possible, leaving the other to invest his or her personal income. For example, if Joan has a higher income than John does, she could pay more than her share of expenses. John would then invest much of his income. The family's investment income would thus be reported by the lower-income spouse, thereby attracting less tax. A common practice is for a spouse or child to be paid an income for work performed in the family's business or for a self-employed parent or spouse.

Transfer of Tax Credits If your spouse cannot use all the tax credits for which he or she is eligible, those credits can be transferred to you. For instance, if one spouse is eligible for but cannot use tax credits, such as the age amount, the pension income amount, or the allowance for charitable donations, the credits may be transferred to the other spouse. If a student cannot use all of his or her education tax credit, it may be transferred to a parent or spouse. See Personal Finance in Action Box 2.2, "Attribution of Income."

Personal FINANCE in action 2.2

Attribution of Income

Matt and Stephanie want to provide all the best for their son Peter—especially the opportunity to go to university, something they did not get a chance to do. So to help Peter pay for his education, they saved money for him, putting $2000 a year, every year, into Canada Savings Bonds. When Peter was 16, Matt and Stephanie gave him the money, which now totalled $45 000. The plan was that Peter would now receive the interest in his name and hence reduce the taxes owed on the annual interest earned on the CSBs.

Unfortunately, Matt and Stephanie did not understand the laws regarding the transfer of wealth to family members. Although this money was a gift, the laws of attribution apply, and Matt and Stephanie must still pay taxes on the interest earned on the CSBs. However, any earnings that Peter keeps and reinvests will then be his, and the earnings on his new investments will be taxable in his hands. It is best if Matt and Stephanie keep the earnings on the CSBs in a separate account. This will more easily allow them to keep track of the earnings and Peter's taxable income.

Income Tax Disputes

Should an individual not agree with the assessment that he or she received from the Canada Revenue Agency, there is a procedure to follow to attempt to resolve the issue.

Initially, the CRA requests that it be contacted to try to resolve any misunderstanding. If there is no resolution, the person must file the objection to the Appeals Division of the CRA either within 90 days of the assessment's mailing date or one year after the deadline for filing the return, whichever is later. Specific information must be included, such as name, Social Insurance Number, facts and reasons for the objection, and supporting documentation.

The Chief of Appeals then reviews the appeal and, if he or she agrees or partially agrees with it, orders a further reassessment. The filing deadline may be extended if there are extenuating circumstances.

If the individual does not agree with the decision, he or she may appeal within 90 days of receipt of the decision to the Tax Court of Canada, choosing either an informal procedure of review—providing the amount in fines and tax in dispute is less than $12 000, the loss amount is less than $24 000, or only federal tax and penalties are in dispute—or the General Procedure. There is no form, but the appeal must be in writing. Of course, one must send a filing fee of $100 as well. The court must respond within set time limits. There are no set court procedures in this method of appeal, but in the General Procedure normal rules of evidence and examinations are in place.

Proceed to the Canada Revenue Agency website, **www.cra-arc.gc.ca**, to answer the following questions:

1. If your appeal is for more than $12 000, what is the maximum fee for your filing?

2. Who can be considered liable for the total legal fees? Who decides?

3. To whom may one appeal their ruling? To whom may one then appeal as last resort?

4. During the appeal procedure, what happens to the stated amount of money owed? Is this appropriate? Are you innocent till proven guilty?

Tax Deferment

With careful planning, you may be able to defer income tax by arranging for some income not to come into your hands until a later time, such as retirement, when you expect to have a lower marginal tax rate.

Registered Retirement Savings Plans RRSPs are good examples of tax-deferment vehicles. While you are earning wages, you can shift some funds into an RRSP or into another type of tax shelter without paying any tax. The money you have invested in such a plan will grow, sheltered from tax (that is, you will not be required to pay tax on any income generated within the plan—such as interest income or dividend income), until you "deregister" the plan. Of course, when you take funds out of an RRSP, you must pay income tax on those funds, but if you choose to withdraw the funds during a year when you have a lower-than-usual income, the funds will be taxed at a lower rate. Even if your marginal tax rate is not expected to be lower in the future, funds held in a tax shelter will grow faster than unsheltered funds. (This point is illustrated in Personal Finance in Action Box 2.3, "Should She Use a Tax Shelter?")

Whenever you have income that you do not currently need—for example, when you receive a pension plan refund after changing jobs, or when you receive an allowance for taking early retirement—give some thought to ways of deferring the payment of tax on that income. You may be able to transfer these types of funds directly from your employer into your RRSP. Best to check with a professional tax planner.

Registered Education Savings Plans To create a fund to support a child's post-secondary education or your own and to defer tax on investment income, you might enroll in an **RESP**. The money put into an RESP is not tax-deductible, but the money earned while it is in the plan is tax-sheltered. If the beneficiary pursues a post-secondary education, the money will be paid to the student and the interest will be taxed in his or her hands, presumably at a lower student-based marginal rate. For parents, there may be a disadvantage in such a plan, in that if the child does not continue past the secondary level of education, and no other children in the family continue either, the money earned in the fund may be forfeited; only the invested capital would be refunded to the parents. In some cases, the interest may be transferred to the parents' RRSP. However, some plans permit the funds to be paid to almost any designate attending a post-secondary educational program. See the Women Take Charge feature for one woman's experience with an RESP for her child.

The two main types of RESPs are individual plans or group plans. Group plans operate similarly to a pension plan, investing on behalf of the contributors. Individual RESPs, like RRSPs, can be invested in mutual funds. However, they are not limited to foreign content.

Women take CHARGE 2.1

Miriam has been reading about the rising cost of post-secondary education. She wants to ensure that her daughter, Jill, is financially able to pursue higher education. Although Jill is only five years old, Miriam wants to take advantage of the earnings generated by long-term, tax-sheltered compounding. She can do this by subscribing to a registered education savings plan (RESP) with Jill as the beneficiary.

Miriam initiates the plan by getting a social insurance number for Jill and contributing $2500, which is within the $4000 annual limit on contributions to an RESP. Miriam can contribute up to $42 000 over the years. As an added bonus, the contribution is entitled to the Canadian Education Savings Grant (CESG) paid by the Government of Canada. The yearly maximum for the grant is 20 percent of the contribution or $400. Recent legislation has provided for an additional grant in the year of contribution equal to 20 percent or 10 percent of the first $500 contributed to the plan. The percentage applied is determined by family income. Miriam's family income is such that Jill will

receive 10 percent of $500, or $50, in addition to the $400. The $2000 grant room can be carried forward if Miriam is unable to make a contribution during a future year. The plan can accumulate up to $7200 in CESG money.

Some suitable investments for the RESP are savings accounts, guaranteed investment certificates, and mutual funds. Whereas the contribution to an RRSP is tax-deductible, the contribution to an RESP is not tax-deductible. However, the income earned by the investments within an RESP is tax-sheltered until the income is withdrawn, thus providing for more growth than would be generated by a non-sheltered investment.

If Jill attends a qualifying educational institution, she can start withdrawing the income and grant money from the plan in the form of an educational assistance payment. As a student, she will be in a low tax bracket, and very little or no tax would have to be paid on the withdrawal. Miriam could decide to give her original contributions to Jill for educational purposes. The original contributions are not taxed on withdrawal because they are made with after-tax dollars.

continued

Women take Charge (continued)

Miriam hopes that Jill will complete a degree. If Jill decides not to pursue a post-secondary education, Miriam can name a new beneficiary for the plan, donate the funds to an educational institution, or transfer the income to her own RRSP if she has sufficient contribution room. The current limit on an RRSP transfer is $50 000. If Miriam decides to withdraw the income from the plan, she may be subject to an additional 20 percent tax, and the grant money will have to be paid back.

Personal FINANCE in action 2.3

Should She Use a Tax Shelter?

Maya has $1000 (before tax) to invest and is wondering whether to put the money in a five-year guaranteed investment certificate inside her RRSP or in a GIC outside her RRSP. Maya's combined marginal tax rate is 39 percent. She can obtain 5 percent interest on a certificate. A comparison of the two alternatives is shown below.

Year 1	Alternative 1, RRSP	Alternative 2, No Shelter
Investment	$1 000.00	$1 000.00
Income tax	0.00	390.00
Net investment	1 000.00	610.00
Interest earned @ 5%	50.00	30.50
Income tax @ 39%	0.00	11.90
Balance	$1 050.00	$ 628.60
Year 2		
Interest	$ 52.50	$ 31.43
Income tax @ 39%	0.00	12.26
Balance	$1 102.50	$ 647.77
Year 3		
Interest	$ 55.13	$ 32.39
Income tax @ 39%	0.00	12.63
Balance	$1 157.63	$ 667.53
Year 4		
Interest	$ 57.88	$ 33.38
Income tax @ 39%	0.00	13.02
Balance	$1 215.51	$ 687.89
Year 5		
Interest	$ 60.78	$ 34.39
Income tax @ 39%	0.00	13.41
Balance	1 276.29	708.87
Income tax @ 39%	497.75	0.00
Balance	$ 778.54	$ 708.87
Total interest earned	$ 276.29	$ 162.09
Total income tax paid	$ 497.75	$ 453.22
After-tax value, year 5	$ 778.54	$ 708.87

It is apparent that deferring the payment of taxes represents a "win" for the investor, the investment community, and the government, based on the amount of taxes paid and on the amount of money invested in the Canadian economy. In this example, if the individual retired

continued

and was then taxed at the lower combined marginal tax rate of 25.5 percent, then she would pay only $325.45 in taxes and would be able to keep $950.84.

Another valuable perspective regarding before- and after-tax dollars can be acquired by calculating the actual values of the two kinds of money. If a person needs $1000 to purchase a new stereo, this money is considered after-tax dollars. But how many before-tax dollars does this person need to earn, and pay tax on, in order to be left with $1000? Using the same tax rates as above, $1000 after tax equals × before tax times (1 minus the marginal tax rate); to put this another way, × before tax equals $1000 after tax divided by (1 minus 39 percent). Maya would therefore have to earn $1639.34 in before-tax dollars in order to have the equivalent of $1000 in after-tax dollars.

Before-Tax and After-Tax Dollars

Articles on tax planning or investing often mention the terms "before-tax dollars" and "after-tax dollars." It is important to make a distinction between money on which income tax has already been paid, or **after-tax dollars**, and money that has been received but on which no tax has yet been paid, or **before-tax dollars**. Personal Finance in Action Box 2.3 ("Should She Use a Tax Shelter?") illustrates the difference.

Summary

- Progressive tax rate means that as taxable income increases, so does the tax rate owing. Average tax rate is the percentage of an individual's total monies that are paid in taxes. Marginal tax rate is the highest rate paid in taxes on taxable income. Combined marginal tax rate is the combination of the federal and provincial or territorial income tax on the last dollar earned.

- Income is a flow of resources over a period of time. Gross income is all the income received prior to any deductions. Net income is income after deductions.

- A capital gain is a change in wealth but not income. Taxable capital gains are that portion of capital gains upon which taxes are due. Net taxable capital gains is the difference between capital gains and losses reduced by 50 percent. Tax-sheltered funds are investment programs that defer tax payment on the investment and earnings till the monies are withdrawn.

- A tax credit is a mandated tax deduction from taxes owing. Non-refundable tax credits are not paid to the taxpayer unless income is earned. Refundable tax credits are credits, such as the GST tax credit, that are paid out to those making the least income.

- Full indexation is the increasing of income equal to the rate of inflation. Partial indexation generally revises income to compensate for only part of the inflation.

- Tax evasion is the deliberate and illegal process of evading tax. Tax avoidance is a management process to reduce tax paid. Attribution of income allocates earnings to the person who earned the money.

- RESPs (Registered Education Savings Plans) are a tax-sheltered investment program for post-secondary education. RRSPs (Registered Retirement Savings Plans) are a tax-sheltered investment program for retirement income. RRIFs (Registered Retirement Income Funds) are one tax-sheltered means to manage RRSPs after the age of 69.

- After-tax dollars have had taxes paid on them; before-tax dollars are those dollars yet to be taxed.

Key Terms

after-tax dollars *(p. 55)*	non-refundable tax credits *(p. 49)*
attribution of income *(p. 51)*	partial indexation *(p. 50)*
average tax rate *(p. 42)*	progressive tax rate *(p. 41)*
before-tax dollars *(p. 55)*	refundable tax credits *(p. 49)*
capital gain *(p. 46)*	RESP *(p. 53)*
combined marginal tax rate *(p. 45)*	RRSPs *(p. 52)*
full indexation *(p. 50)*	taxable capital gains *(p. 46)*
gross income *(p. 45)*	tax avoidance *(p. 50)*
income *(p. 45)*	tax credit *(p. 49)*
marginal tax rate *(p. 42)*	tax evasion *(p. 50)*
net income *(p. 45)*	tax-sheltered funds *(p. 47)*
net taxable capital gains *(p. 48)*	

Problems

1. If you received any of the following, should they be reported as income on your tax return?

   (a) an inheritance from your grandfather's estate

   (b) a lottery winning

   (c) the Old Age Security pension

   (d) a capital gain from selling your primary residence

   (e) Employment Insurance benefits

2. If you have dependent children, can you claim a deduction for them, a tax credit, or both? Explain.

3. Decide whether you AGREE or DISAGREE with each of the following statements:

   (a) The money put into a tax shelter would be classified as after-tax dollars.

   (b) The proportion of taxable income on which tax is paid is called the marginal tax rate.

   (c) To find your taxable income, you would deduct from gross income any applicable tax credits.

   (d) Capital gain is a change in wealth rather than a kind of income.

   (e) Persons over the age of 65 are allowed special tax credits.

   (f) On a per capita basis, the federal income tax burden has not changed significantly over the past 25 years.

   (g) Spouses have a choice regarding whether to file individual or joint income-tax returns.

   (h) Interest income is deductible from gross income.

   (i) Capital loss is deducted from capital gain before determining net taxable capital gain.

   (j) RRSPs are tax shelters because the funds put into these plans are not taxed, even though the income gained while in the shelter is taxed.

4. Jean, who lives in Manitoba, has determined that she owes $8997 in federal income tax. How much provincial tax does she owe? Find the current tax rate for Manitoba, or use the rates given in this chapter. What would the tax benefit be if she lived in Alberta, Ontario, British Columbia, or Nova Scotia?

5. Assume that you have a mortgage at 6 percent and also have $6000 that can be used either to reduce the mortgage or to invest at 5 percent. Should you (i) reduce your mortgage by $6000 and borrow money to invest, or (ii) simply invest the money?

   Assumptions: the mortgage company will not charge a penalty if you decide to reduce your mortgage; your combined federal and provincial marginal tax rate is 39 percent; if you borrow money to invest, the interest will be a tax deduction, but the interest paid on your mortgage is not deductible.

6. Obtain a current income tax form and complete it for Karen, aged 40, who lives in Vancouver, is employed full-time, and has **one dependent**. She has never before reported any capital gains. The information she provides is as follows:

Employment income	$48 500.00
Interest income	950.00
Net capital gain from selling property(not her home)	8 500.00
Contributions to	
Employment Insurance	729.00
Canada Pension Plan	1 910.70
RRSP	2 500.00
registered pension plan	3 000.00
professional dues	500.00
Charitable donations	750.00
Rent on safety deposit box	25.00
Accountant's fee	250.00
Donation to the Green Party	250.00
Income tax remitted/withheld	8 100.00

   (a) Find Karen's
     — taxable income
     — federal tax
     — provincial tax
   (b) What is her federal marginal tax rate?
   (c) Does Karen have any tax credits? If so, which ones? How much?
   (d) How much income tax does she owe or will she receive back?

7. Suggest some ways of reducing a family's income tax. For each approach, indicate whether it would be considered tax avoidance or tax evasion.

8. Using Table 2.1, determine the province or territory with the second lowest income tax payable for a Canadian who earns
   (a) $30 000
   (b) $50 000
   (c) $75 000
   (d) $110 000

9. Proceed to the Canada Revenue Agency's website or an accountant's website such as the one listed at the end of the chapter. Then determine the income tax for your province and a province next to it that should be paid by a single parent who is earning $40 000 and supporting two children.

References

BOOKS AND ARTICLES

Beach, Wayne, and Lyle R. Hepburn. *Are You Paying Too Much Tax?* Toronto: McGraw-Hill Ryerson, annual. A tax-planning guide for the general reader that discusses capital gains, RRSPs, and investment income.

Cestnick, Tim. *Winning the Tax Game 2006.* Toronto: Prentice Hall Canada, 2005, annual. A non-technical book to assist those interested in keeping more of the money they earn. Helps in building a solid tax plan no matter what stage in life you're in.

Deloitte and Touche. *Canadian Guide to Personal Financial Management.* Scarborough: Prentice-Hall Canada, annual. A team of accountants provides guidance on a broad range of topics, including planning finances, estimating insurance needs, managing risk, and determining investment needs. Instructions and the necessary forms for making plans are also included.

Deloitte and Touche. *How to Reduce the Tax You Pay.* Toronto: Key Porter Books, annual. A non-technical guide, prepared by tax accountants, that explains the basics of personal income tax.

Hogg, R.D. *Preparing Your Income Tax Returns.* Toronto: CCH Canadian, annual. A complete and technical guide to income tax preparation.

Jacks, Evelyn. *Jacks on Tax Savings.* Toronto: McGraw-Hill Ryerson, annual. Explains the current tax rules and demonstrates how to prepare a tax return.

PERIODICALS

Drache, Arthur B.C., editor. *The Canadian Taxpayer.* Toronto: Richard De Boo Publishers, bi-monthly. A newsletter with up-to-date income tax information. Includes articles on tax cases, relevant political events, recent changes to regulations, and other topics of interest related to tax planning.

————, editor. *Canada Tax Planning Service.* Toronto: Richard De Boo Publishers, subscription service (four-volume looseleaf set). A detailed professional reference that is kept up to date through regular mailings of replacement pages.

The National Post. Daily. 300–1450 Don Mills Rd, Toronto, ON M3B 3R5. Current information on business, economics, income tax, and investments.

Report on Business. Daily. A section of *The Globe and Mail.* Important source of information on the financial markets.

Personal Finance on the Web

Each of the following websites provides high-quality links to many other internet resources.

Canadian Taxpayers Federation
   www.taxpayer.com A taxpayers' advocacy group with extensive commentary on the tax system in Canada. This site offers numerous links to political parties and right-wing money groups.

Ernst & Young

    www.ey.com/ca One of Canada's large accounting firms; provides information on taxes and other accounting concerns. Significant current information available. Sponsor of Canada's Entrepreneur-of-the-Year Award.

Grant Thornton

    www.GrantThornton.ca A major accounting firm in Canada, specializing in small- and medium-size firms and individuals. Readily accessible information on tax and other financial matters.

KPMG

    www.kpmg.ca/tax One of Canada's largest accounting firms; keeps up to date with tax laws and can provide significant information for those interested in assistance. Still, you may need to see an accountant and pay for professional advice.

Canada Revenue Agency

    www.cra-arc.gc.ca You might as well go to the horse's mouth for information. This site contains information, brochures, and forms; you can even get some questions answered here. Recent changes are posted for up-to-date information as well.

The WaterStreet Group

    www.waterstreet.ca Tim Cestnick writes extensively on tax and appears in *The Globe and Mail's* 'Report on Business' and CBC 'Newsworld.' The site updates current tax rates and other tax topics of interest.

Quicken/Intuit

    www.intuit.ca The QuickTax section contains current computerized tax forms. Individuals with low income can use these forms for free.

Financial Security

The processes of making financial plans to maximize the use of resources during one's lifetime and afterward, along with a few basic tools, were the focus of Part One. An integral part of financial planning involves ensuring financial security for oneself and one's dependents. The objective of Part Two is to examine in some depth a variety of ways to protect financial security, such as buying insurance or increasing net worth.

Before becoming too involved with specific information about insurance, pensions, annuities, bonds, and stocks, it is essential to reflect on the necessity for any of them. Part Two therefore begins with an introductory chapter, which explains financial security and identifies economic risks. The rest of the chapters in this section are concerned with ways of enhancing financial security by reducing risk. Two chapters explain the risks that can be handled by general and life and health insurance. Next, retirement income, an important aspect of financial security, is explored: both social security programs and private savings—including pensions, annuities, and registered retirement savings plans—are discussed. The section's three final chapters are concerned with the area of credit loans, mortgages, and laws governing this area.

chapter 3

Economic Risks and Financial Security

"Money differs from an automobile, a mistress or cancer, in being equally important to those who have it and those who do not."

John Kenneth Galbraith

Learning Objectives

Understanding the concepts discussed in this chapter should help you become aware of economic risk.

After studying this chapter, you should be able to:

1. *Define financial security.*

2. *Explain how the need for financial security affects decisions about the use of economic resources—e.g., saving for the future or selecting insurance.*

3. *Identify events that pose economic risks for individuals or families.*

4. *Differentiate between assuming risk and sharing risk.*

5. *Distinguish between the steps an individual can take to enhance financial security and the means provided by society to do so.*

6. *Identify the threats to financial security that are posed by a serious disability, and two ways to alleviate the consequences of disability.*

7. *Analyze the meaning of disability as defined by various insurers.*

8. *Identify important features in disability insurance coverage.*

9. *Identify the threats posed by critical illness and the important features of critical illness insurance.*

Introduction

Maintaining a feeling of financial security, or assurance that we can cope with whatever may happen, is of prime concern to everyone. This feeling of security can be enhanced if we know what our economic risks are and if we can take steps to reduce their consequences. Life is full of economic risk, but sometimes we fail to recognize the particular risks that most threaten our economic well-being. Perhaps that explains why some people buy life insurance whether or not they need it, and why some others who really need such protection fail to buy it. This chapter first helps to identify the economic risks that pose the greatest threats to personal welfare and then suggests ways to minimize those risks. Certain risks, such as the untimely death of a person with dependents, or theft of or damage to personal property, may be shared through the purchase of insurance. Canada has social programs (e.g., Old Age Security, the Canada/Quebec Pension Plan, Employment Insurance, Social Assistance) to minimize the effects of some events, such as loss of income. The risk of becoming disabled or seriously ill, with the consequence of being unable to earn a living, is too often ignored.

The chapters that follow this one consider in some detail several important ways to reduce economic risk, such as insuring your possessions or your life, planning for retirement income, and saving and investing to build up your net worth.

Financial Security

What do we mean by financial security? You will experience a feeling of **financial security** if you are confident that you will have the economic means to meet your needs in the present and in the future. Just as there are many conceptions regarding what is needed for a satisfactory level of living, so are there many notions of what constitutes financial security. Your feelings about risk, as well as your economic situation, will have much to do with the nature of your concerns about financial security. For instance, a family living on Social Assistance may well consider that having enough money to pay the current bills for food, shelter, and clothing represents financial security for them, while a family living in affluent circumstances may have much more expansive ideas about what is required to maintain their financial security. The latter may feel economically threatened if they have to give up a vacation home, regular holidays, or restaurant meals.

If you feel financially secure, it may be assumed that you feel confident that you will be able to handle the following needs: (i) maintaining your accustomed level of living, (ii) coping with financial emergencies or unusual expenses, and (iii) making provisions for replacing income lost because of illness, unemployment, retirement, aging, or disability. When you know that you are protected from financial threats, you can feel reasonably secure about the future. But is such peace of mind possible for many of us? Who among us can be certain of what our future needs will be or of what resources we will have as we move through the various stages in our life cycle?

As individuals and as a society, we have taken an increasing interest in ensuring financial security. For one thing, we have become used to a complex level of living with more to protect. For another, our society has changed within a few generations to feature less economic self-sufficiency and more economic interdependence. In an agrarian society, many families can supply more of their needs outside the market than is possible in a society like ours. We rely, for the most part, on money income rather than on household production to support our desired lifestyle; anything that interrupts or halts the flow of income is therefore a serious threat. In response to social changes, government-sponsored programs have been instituted to provide partial financial security for the young, the old, the disabled, the unemployed, and the poor. Since most of us want more than partial financial security, we must take further steps to protect ourselves against a variety of economic risks.

Economic Risks

Before we can make any plans to enhance our financial security, we must first identify what events pose economic risks for us. The list of risks will not be identical for everyone, nor will it be the same at all stages of our lives. If you do not own a house, you do not face the risk, for example, of having it burn down; if you do not have dependent children, you need not worry about the risk of being unable to support them; if you do not own a car, damage to it is not one of your risks. It is essential to remember that economic risks and our ideas about financial security will change constantly as our lives change. Most of our economic risks can be categorized as follows:

(a) loss of income
  — destruction of earning capacity
  — loss of market for your services

(b) unexpected large expenses
  — destruction or loss of property
  — illness and death
  — personal liability

(c) loss in value of capital
  — drop in market value
  — inflation

Loss of Income

Anything that causes the income stream to stop poses a very serious threat to economic security. As long as your income continues, there is some possibility of coping with unexpected expenses or with a loss of capital; but without a regular income, it is difficult to obtain enough resources. The reason for termination of income is usually either the destruction of your earning capacity or the disappearance of the market for your services.

Destruction of Earning Capacity The ability to earn income may be lost temporarily (through illness) or permanently (through chronic illness, disability, aging, or death—to see how the *Journal of the American Medical Association* assesses the risk of death for people in their fifties and older, see Personal Finance in Action 3.1, "The Odds of Dying."). Of these possibilities, permanent disability presents a particularly serious risk. Not only would you be unable to work, you would have to be supported and might also need expensive care. Social mechanisms for coping with this financial burden have not developed as fully as those for coping with aging or death, perhaps because we all expect to get older and eventually to die, but few people expect to be disabled.

It is estimated that the average 20-year-old male in Canada is three times more likely to be disabled for more than four months before he reaches 65 than he is to die by that age. Women at age 35 have a likelihood of being disabled that is seven times that of dying before they are 65. This is not the side issue so many of us think it is.

Personal FINANCE in action 3.1

The Odds of Dying

In February 2006 there was much publicity about a study released in the *Journal of the American Medical Association* that claimed to be 81 percent accurate in evaluating the risk of those over 50 years of age of dying in the near future. In the spirit of "less is better," here is the questionnaire and evaluation process.

1. Age
   (a) 50–59 years old—0 points;
   (b) 60–64 years old—1 point;
   (c) 65–69 years old—2 points;
   (d) 70–74 years old—3 points;
   (e) 75–79 years old—4 points;
   (f) 80–84 years old—5 points;
   (g) 85 and older—7 points.
2. Male—2 points.
3. Body-Mass Index: less than 25 (normal weight or less)—1 point. Calculated by multiplying height in inches by itself and dividing weight in pounds by that total and then multiplying the total by 703.
4. Diabetes—2 points.
5. Cancer (excluding minor skin cancers)—2 points.
6. Chronic lung disease that limits activities and requires oxygen use at home—2 points.
7. Congestive heart failure—2 points.
8. Cigarette smoking in the past week—2 points.
9. Difficulty bathing/showering because of a health or memory problem—2 points.
10. Difficulty managing money, paying bills, keeping track of expenses because of a health or memory problem—2 points.
11. Difficulty walking several blocks because of a health problem—2 points.
12. Difficulty pushing or pulling large objects like a living room chair because of a health problem—1 point.

Score:
0–5 points: less than a 4 percent risk of dying;
6–9 points: 15 percent risk of dying;
10–13 points: 42 percent risk of dying;
14 or more points: 64 percent risk of dying.

SOURCES:
www.theglobeandmail.com/servlet/story/ RTGAM20060214.wdeath0214/BNPrint/s . . . Accessed February 16, 2006.
Simple Quiz Can Predict Your Fate, Sharon Kirkey, *National Post*, Wednesday, February 15, 2006, Page A18.

Loss of Market for Your Services People who are self-employed must consider the possibility that the market for their goods or services may disappear, leaving them without income. Under such circumstances, they will need to change what they produce if possible. People who are employees may find that their services are no longer needed because the demand for particular skills has fallen, because economic conditions have reduced economic activity, because a change in technology has made their skills obsolete, or because of many other reasons. The ever-increasing globalization of our economy may raise this spectre for even the most confident earner. So employees, like the self-employed, may have to acquire new skills to fit into the labour market again.

Unexpected Large Expenses

Many kinds of unexpected large expenses may threaten financial security, but only three will be discussed here:

(a) destruction or loss of personal property,

(b) illness and death,

(c) personal liability.

Destruction of Property The more we own, the greater is the risk that our possessions may be lost or destroyed. Loss can be the result of many factors, including theft, fire, or severe weather. Should a family lose their house and all the contents through fire, they would probably be unable to replace everything by using only their own resources (e.g., savings); for this reason, they buy home insurance.

Illness and Death Here in Canada, many, but not all, of the large expenses associated with illness and death have for decades been shared through our health insurance program. But caring at home for a person who is ill for a long time can be very expensive, and some or all of this expense may have to be borne by the family. Therefore, some personal resources may be needed in addition to health insurance and other social programs. In this age of AIDS and other long-term illnesses, some insurance companies have started to introduce **critical illness insurance** to cover just such instances. This type of policy generally pays a lump sum of money if you survive over 30 days. A critical illness insurance policy is three to four times more expensive than a general life insurance, as we have a higher likelihood of getting ill than dying. The money paid out can be used for any purpose, ranging from therapy to wigs, to a vacation home, to daycare for the children, and more. These policies generally cover cancer, heart disease, organ transplants, multiple sclerosis, paralysis, and other serious illnesses or diseases. Some plans focus on particular illnesses such as breast cancer. Individuals should examine their family medical history to determine risk. This chapter's Women Take Charge feature considers this type of insurance.

Just as caring for an ill person can be emotionally and physically draining, the financial cost of proceeding through the process of a death, the funeral, burial, and legal and court costs may be also quite large. This matter will be covered in more detail in the chapter on wills and estates. But it is still a risk that all of us must face whether we wish to or not.

Personal Liability Any one of us could face a very large unexpected expense if we were to be found liable for damage or injury because of negligence. We are probably most aware of this possibility in relation to our cars because of the potential for destruction and death from a moment's inattention while driving. This concept will be more fully developed in the chapter on general insurance.

Women take CHARGE 3.1

Clarissa has been working for 10 years and has decided to review her financial plan, as she is concerned about medical expenses not covered by the provincial health care plan. She wants to avoid having to withdraw funds from her RRSP, a central part of her retirement resources, to pay additional medical expenses. Moreover, Clarissa still has a mortgage to pay off on her condominium.

Clarissa's financial advisor has suggested that she investigate critical illness insurance. Critical illness insurance provides a one-time lump sum payment when the holder of the policy contracts an illness that is covered by the policy. The illness must be certified by a medical professional, and to receive payment the patient must survive for a certain time period such as 30 days after the official diagnosis. Critical illness insurance differs from life insurance in that you get paid while you are living. There is also mortgage critical illness insurance, which will pay off a mortgage if the purchaser contracts a covered disease.

The recipient can decide how to use the funds delivered by the policy. The funds could be used to cover treatment expenses not covered by the provincial plan, out-of-country medical attention, home care, mortgage payments, debts, or even a vacation to deal with the stress.

continued

In searching for an appropriate policy, Clarissa will note which illnesses are specifically covered. Common illnesses specified are cancer, heart attacks, bypass surgery, and strokes. Some policies cover more than 20 different illnesses.

The amount of the benefit is another important issue. Policies can pay $25 000 or more. Clarissa will inquire if the policy will repay premiums or a portion of premiums to a named beneficiary if she never uses it during her lifetime.

Clarissa should not delay purchasing a critical illness policy because she may not be able to purchase it after age 55. She should note the length of coverage. For example, will she be covered up to age 75 or beyond?

Age, gender, medical history, smoking habits, number of illnesses covered, and size of the benefit all play a role in determining the premium cost. Her financial advisor, who specializes in critical illness insurance, can furnish quotes for various policies. Clarissa might also explore the possibility of critical illness insurance in combination with a term or universal life insurance plan.

Loss in Value of Capital

Things that you own can lose value because of a reduction in the demand for them. If a highway is built close to your house, if interest in a certain artist wanes, or if no one wants your mining stocks, your capital—in the form of a house, a painting, or shares, respectively—diminishes through no action of yours.

Inflation affects various assets differently: some lose value, while others gain it. The value of money saved in deposits tends to suffer substantial loss during inflationary times. For instance, a dollar earned in 1980 and saved under your mattress until 2006 would buy only 39 percent of what it would have purchased 26 years earlier. Another way to look at it: to buy the same $100 of goods from 1980 would cost $255.67 in March 2006. That is why it should have been invested to earn a return equal to or greater than the rate of inflation. To do so, your annual return would have to be 4 percent after taxes to maintain your buying power over the 26 years. Real estate, on the other hand, appreciated significantly during the same period.

What Are Your Economic Risks?

Make a list of economic risks that could threaten your financial security this year. Which events might cause a loss of income, even temporarily? What are some unexpected large expenses that would create hardship? How much of your net worth is at risk from price changes? Next, assign priorities to your list so that you can make plans to handle these risks.

Second, make a list of future economic risks—issues that are not concerns currently but may become important at another time—such as insufficient retirement income and inability to support children or other relatives.

Need for Savings

Even if you are fortunate enough to go through life without experiencing a disability, a major illness, or unemployment, you will probably retire sometime. When you do, your employment income will stop, and you will become dependent on pensions and investment earnings. Unless you spend your entire working life with the same employer, you may find that your work pension will not support you in the style you would wish. Public pensions will help, but many people find retirement much more comfortable if they also have private investment income. However, before you get any investment income, you must first save some money and then invest it.

Handling Risks

Once you have identified your economic risks, the next step is to decide what to do about them. Essentially, there are three possibilities:

(a) try to prevent the event from happening,

(b) assume the risk yourself,

(c) share the risk with others.

The task of thinking of ways to reduce or prevent risks is left to you. Some possibilities for assuming and sharing risk are outlined here, but the concept will be more fully developed in subsequent chapters on general insurance, life insurance, and annuities.

Assuming Risk

If you have enough financial resources, you can assume your own risks; that is, you can handle unfortunate events without jeopardizing your level of living. You can expect to have the funds to cope with unemployment, an unexpected large expense, illness, or retirement. Accumulating net worth is clearly one way of preparing to handle whatever risks come your way. That is why all sound advice on financial planning stresses the importance of saving three months of take-home pay for unforeseen needs, emergencies, and retirement.

Another way a family can assume risk is to expect individuals to help each other. When one earner is unable to work, someone else in the family may be able to support the household. Two-income families have spread the risk of having something happen to the income stream. Still, most of us are unable to assume all potential risks; usually, we must depend on some risk-sharing.

Sharing Risk

When a risk is too much for individuals or families to bear alone, it can be shared, either through private insurance or through social income-security programs. Collecting small contributions from many people allows for the creation of a fund that will be sufficient to compensate those few people who experience an unfortunate event. For example, all car owners contribute to car insurance, but only those who have accidents draw on the fund. Participating in a risk-sharing program enhances financial security by providing the knowledge that compensation would be available if the insured people required it.

Private Efforts General insurance allows us to share the risks that our personal property may be lost or damaged, as well as the risk that we may be held personally liable for injury to another person or damage to another person's property. Life insurance is designed to protect against the financial risk of the premature death of a person with dependents. Annuities, by turning capital into an income stream guaranteed for life, protect against the risk of living so long that there are no savings left.

Public Programs Canada's public income-security programs are based on risk sharing, one way or another. The Canada and Quebec Pension Plans, along with Employment Insurance, are social insurance programs to which employed people make contributions; your eligibility for benefits under these programs depends on your having been a contributor. Such programs offer protection against the risks of becoming unemployed or disabled, of aging, and of dying. Canadians fund several other programs, such as Old Age Security and social welfare, through taxes rather than by direct contributions. In this way, those in the labour force provide support for those who are old or are unable to work.

In addition to these income-security programs, society takes other steps to help us plan for our own financial security. Canada's income tax system encourages retirement planning by offering tax deductions for people who invest in RRSPs or contribute to employment-related pension plans.

Disability: A Serious Risk

In this chapter, brief mention will be made of personal disability, a very significant economic risk that people too often ignore. A common hazard is the potential loss of one's ability to earn a living because of temporary or permanent disability due to an accident or an illness. The case study in Personal Finance in Action Box 3.2, "His Life Was Changed by a Fall"—which is based on a real situation—illustrates the disastrous effect that permanent disability can have on a family's financial security.

For people under the age of 65, the probability of suffering a disability is greater than that of dying. Yet people of any age are more likely to have life insurance than to have disability insurance. The gender differences in the probability of being disabled for more than six months between the ages of 25 and 55 are illustrated in Figure 3.1. Females in this age group face a significantly greater risk of being disabled than of dying, but have a lower mortality rate than males of the same age. Studies have shown that anyone who is disabled for more than three months will probably still be disabled five years later. The risk of becoming disabled is one that few of us are financially able to assume alone. How many people have enough savings to support themselves for a year or more?

To protect ourselves against the risk of becoming disabled, we can purchase **disability insurance** (sometimes called income replacement insurance). Without such protection, we would have to depend on others—our families or the social welfare system—to support us.

FIGURE 3.1 PROBABILITY OF DEATH OR LONG-TERM DISABILITY (OVER SIX MONTHS) OCCURRING WITHIN A YEAR, BY GENDER

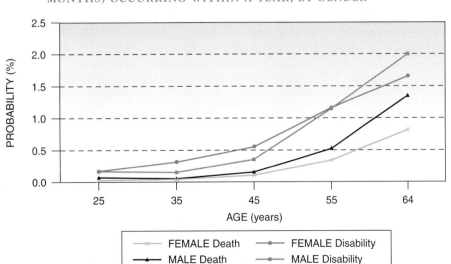

SOURCE: Clarica's group insurance data. Reproduced with the permission of Clarica of Canada.

Disability Insurance

Disability insurance may be purchased either privately (the more expensive of the two options) or through a group policy (which is a less-expensive approach). When an insurance company insures a group of people in one policy, each person's coverage is less costly than if he or she had bought it separately. Many people have some group disability insurance through their place of work. It is critical, however, to find out exactly what coverage you have. Policies vary in many ways: the waiting period before benefits start may be shorter or longer, the definition of disability may be broader or narrower, the amount of benefits may be higher or lower, the benefit period may be shorter or longer, and other options may also differ. The cost of the coverage typically depends on what features are included; better benefits cost more. Cost may also vary due to the rate of claims, especially for group plans.

Waiting Period When assessing your coverage, it is important to know how long you would need to be considered unable to work before disability payments would begin. If you have sick-leave coverage at your place of work, that might or might not be enough to cover you until the income replacement benefits begin. Either way, you could have to wait several months before receiving any payments. Policies can have waiting periods as short as one week or as long as four months. Consider how long you could survive without any income; then, to keep the cost of your premiums down, choose the longest waiting period you could manage.

Definition of Disability How disabled must you be in order to become eligible for benefits? It is essential that you read this part of a policy very carefully; many people who become disabled have been surprised to find that, although they have insurance, the policy's definition of disability excludes them. A distinction is usually made between partial and total disability; as well, benefits may be withheld if the insurance company deems you capable of working part-time or working at an occupation other than your usual one. By paying more, you can get a policy that provides benefits until you are able to return to your usual occupation. For instance, consider a teacher who has suffered some voice impairment. He might be

Personal FINANCE in action 3.2

His Life Was Changed by a Fall

Simon, a self-employed mason, fell 15 metres from a scaffold, injuring himself so badly that despite having spent months in the hospital, he still lives in constant pain and walks with difficulty. He can't lift or carry anything. Fortunately, he was covered by Workers' Compensation, which provides him with a small pension, but he was inexplicably classified as only 25 percent disabled. Two years after the accident, Simon is still negotiating with Canada Pension about the extent of his disability. His first application was rejected because of the possibility that he might be able to return to work. He has now applied again.

At 40, Simon is unable to work to support his wife and three teenage children. He has given up his business and sold the family's home; they lived on their savings as long as they lasted. The monthly Workers' Compensation cheque, though not taxed, is just large enough to pay the rent on a subsidized apartment. The small additional amount that Simon gets from welfare is insufficient to buy the family's food. Applying for disability benefits involves considerable red tape and waiting, as Simon has discovered. Simon's fall drastically changed life for him and for his family.

unable to continue teaching but able to do a clerical job. Since he would not be considered totally disabled, some disability policies would provide partial or no support for him because he appears able to handle certain types of work—just not the career he has chosen and trained for. Personal Finance in Action Box 3.3, "Collecting Disability Benefits Can Be Difficult," illustrates a similar scenario.

Amount of Benefits Even if you obtain the most coverage you can afford, at best the benefits will probably amount to only 60 to 70 percent of your usual income. Depending on the policy's payment process, this amount may or may not be tax-free. If it is tax-free (and most are), it may prove adequate at the present time. No insurance company will offer a policy that would make it profitable for anyone to become disabled. For an additional premium, it is sometimes possible to have a policy that would index benefits to inflation.

Benefit Period What limits the benefit period? Policies may restrict benefits to a few weeks, one year, five years, or until you reach age 65. Again, you will want the longest benefit period you can afford.

Renewability Is there a clause in the policy that guarantees that it is non-cancellable or renewable? You would not want to find, as you get older, that the company will not renew your policy. Should you develop a medical condition, such as a heart ailment, some policies may not renew due to your high risk, even though you currently can work.

Social Support for the Disabled

Are there social programs for which you might be eligible if you became disabled? You may only be eligible if you have previously contributed to the specific social program or if you become disabled as a result of an injury sustained either on the job or during military service. Here is a list of the major social supports for disabled people in Canada:

(a) **Employment Insurance**—a federal program that provides short-term benefits to contributors.
(b) **The Canada and Quebec Pension Plans**—a disability pension for contributors with a severe or prolonged disability, and for their dependents and survivors.

Personal FINANCE in action 3.3

Collecting Disability Benefits Can Be Difficult

A decade ago, Ken was happily employed as a nursing assistant in a Nova Scotia hospital. Then disaster struck: while he was lifting a heavy patient, he had a heart attack that left him with a poorly functioning heart. Various medications and treatments added to his miseries and disability. At age 45, after a 23-year career, Ken was no longer able to work as a nursing assistant.

He applied for benefits under his group income replacement insurance. To his surprise, the insurance company refused his claim, on the grounds that he did not qualify as totally and permanently disabled, since he would be able to work at some occupation, though not necessarily nursing. He took his case to court and eventually received a partial settlement. Still, at 45 years of age he is starting over, with no insurance.

(c) **Workers' Compensation**—provincial plans that offer medical, financial, and rehabilitative assistance to workers who become disabled by accidents or illness related to their jobs.

(d) **Short-term or Long-term Welfare**—municipal and provincial programs for those with few other resources.

Summary

- Financial security occurs when a person is confident in his or her ability to meet current and future financial needs.

- Critical illness insurance assists in covering expenses arising from severe illnesses such as AIDS or cancer.

- Disability insurance (income replacement insurance) helps to replace income should one become disabled.

Key Terms

critical illness insurance *(p. 66)*   financial security *(p. 63)*

disability insurance *(p. 69)*

Problems

1. When Disaster Struck

    Six months ago, Luke and Vera never imagined that they would find themselves in such dire financial straits that they would have to apply for welfare. He was a self-employed, skilled construction worker who was making a good income when suddenly he developed a heart condition that required open-heart surgery. Complications ensued; after an extended hospitalization, Luke went home but was not well enough to work. His doctor advised him that any physical activity could cause a coronary.

    The stress of Luke's illness, the financial problems, and having to look after the home and children on her own caused a gastric condition that made Vera miserable and not well enough to go out to work. And even if she had been able to do so, who would have looked after the children at the time (a five-year-old, a four-year-old, and a ten-month-old)?

    When Luke stopped working, the couple had $8000 in the bank and had built up equity amounting to about $75 000 in the semi-detached home they owned. They did not apply for welfare immediately because they were afraid they would have to sell their house and car; instead, they lived on their savings as long as they could. Because he was self-employed, Luke was not covered by Employment Insurance, but he had been paying into the Canada Pension Plan. He had once thought about disability insurance but had decided against purchasing it because of the high premiums. Besides their regular living expenses, costly drugs were needed for Luke, along with a special formula for the baby, who was allergic to milk.

    Finally this family became so desperate that they called Social Services. They were immediately granted short-term welfare, which included a waiver of their health insurance premium, free prescription drugs and dental care, and an allowance for the baby's special diet. They were advised to see their bank about the mortgage payment (which was one month in arrears) to ask that it be deferred and that the mortgage be extended a month. They discovered to their surprise that welfare recipients are allowed to have a car and a few assets, and that if they had applied sooner, they could have kept their savings in the bank.

    (a) Can you think of anything this family could have done to be better prepared for such an economic disaster?

    (b) Should they be applying for disability benefits from the Canada Pension Plan?

    (c) Do you have any other suggestions for ways they could obtain more resources?

2.   If possible, interview your parents and grandparents about financial security. Determine what financial security means to them.

3.   At what stage in the life cycle do you think economic risks are most threatening?

4.   Make a list of the five major economic risks you will face after you graduate. What major risks are you likely to face 15 years from now?

5.   What features would you like to see in a disability insurance policy? What other major health risks are not covered by disability insurance or life insurance for which it would be advisable to be covered? Hint: Go to **www.statscan.ca**.

6.   What major factors cause people to ignore the need for a) life insurance, b) disability insurance, and c) critical illness insurance?

7.   In this chapter, we have mentioned a variety of economic risks and suggested various ways to minimize the effects of encountering each. As an aid in summarizing this information, complete the following chart. In addition to the material in this chapter, you should be able to draw on your general knowledge. The first and last lines have been filled in as examples.

| | | Ways to Handle Economic Risks | | |
Economic risks		As an individual or family member	As an employee	As a citizen
A.	LOSS OF INCOME			
1.	Earning capacity destroyed (a) temporarily (e.g., illness)	*Use savings. Income of another family member*	*Sick leave with pay*	*Health insurance*
	(b) permanently —disability			
	—illness			
	—aging			
	—death			
2.	Market for earner's services destroyed			
	(a) unemployment			
	(b) fall in profits for self-employed			
B.	UNEXPECTED LARGE EXPENSES			
	1. Destruction or loss of personal property			
	2. Illness, death			
	3. Personal liability			

C.   LOSS OF VALUE OF CAPITAL

1. Drop in market value (e.g., house, stock)	*Diversify assets*	*n/a*	*n/a*
2. Price changes (e.g., inflation)	*Diversify assets*	*n/a*	*n/a*

8. Evaluate the following long-term disability plan, which covers one group of employees. How effective do you think it will be in meeting the needs of employees who become disabled?

    Benefits: 66⅔ percent of basic monthly earnings, to a maximum of $3500. This will be reduced by any amount to which you are entitled from Workers' Compensation or Canada Pension (benefits for dependents are excluded). The employer will supplement this at 13⅓ percent of the basic salary for a period of four months, to a maximum of 80 percent of your basic earnings.

    Waiting Period: Benefits begin on the 91st consecutive day of total disability.

    Benefit Period: Until age 65 for total disability; two years for a temporary disability that prevents you from performing the duties of your occupation. Benefits are payable beyond two years if you are disabled to such an extent that you cannot engage in any occupation for which you are or could reasonably become qualified as determined by your doctor.

9. Try to find the cost of buying disability insurance privately for employed 25-year-old males and females. If possible, compare this amount with the cost of group protection.

10. Explore the website of Statistics Canada at **www.statcan.ca**. Find the Health area. Determine your personal expectations of illness or disability. Now do the same for your other family members. How significant are these risks?

11. Find any one of the major life and health insurance websites and examine their offerings for disability and critical illness insurance. How do they define these terms and what do they offer? Is this individual or group coverage? Suggested companies: Manulife, Sun Life, and Great West Life.

12. Explore the Bank of Canada's website at **www.bank-banque-canada.ca**. In the Inflation Calculator section, determine how much $100 in the year of your birth would be worth today.

13. Refer to the Personal Finance in Action Box 3.1, "The Odds of Dying." If you are less than 50 years of age, apply the calculation to a family member or close friend who is 50 or older. What would you suggest that he or she do to reduce the risk of dying in the near future (less than four years)? If you apply the calculation to yourself, what are you going to do to reduce the risk?

References

BOOKS AND ARTICLES

Praskey, Sally, and Helena Moncrieff. *The Insurance Book.* Toronto: Prentice-Hall, 1999. A thorough and plain examination of the insurance field for consumers and endorsed by the Consumers Council of Canada.

Wyatt, Elaine. *The Money Companion: How to Manage Your Money and Achieve Financial Freedom.* Toronto: Penguin, 1997. A guide to personal financial management that focuses on planning, investment strategy, and retirement needs.

Personal Finance on the Web

Statistics Canada

www.statcan.ca The Health section (which can be accessed through the site index) contains some illuminating data that can help you determine how much risk you face depending on your gender, age, profession, or place of residence.

Insurance Bureau of Canada

www.iicc.ca An industry website with significant reference material on property and casualty insurance information.

Canadian Life and Health Insurance Association Inc.

www.clhia.ca An industry body representing the 100 life and health insurance companies in Canada. An overview of the industry and the role it plays as well as the self-established rules of the industry.

Insurance-Canada.ca

www.insurance-canada.ca A consumer-focused site with information regarding the needs and intricacies of the industry. It is co-sponsored by the Consumers Council of Canada and the Consumers Association of Canada.

Bank of Canada

www.bank-banque-canada.ca The website for the central bank of Canada, with some inflation and investing/saving calculators.

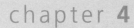

chapter 4

General Insurance

"Insurance, n. An ingenious modern game of chance in which the player is permitted to enjoy the comfortable conviction that he is beating the man who keeps the table."

Ambrose Bierce

Learning Objectives

Understanding the concepts discussed in this chapter should help you understand basic insurance.

After studying this chapter, you should be able to:

1. *Identify two major financial risks associated with owning a house and its contents, personal possessions, or an automobile, and also, the appropriate type of insurance coverage for each risk.*

2. *Understand and demonstrate applications of the following basic insurance principles: sharing risk, indemnification, subrogation, and co-insurance.*

3. *Distinguish between the following terms: pure cost of insurance and loading charge; premium and policy; insurable interest and insurable risk; insured and insurer; actual cash value and replacement value; deductible and policy limits; scheduled property rider and clause covering possessions taken from home; and named-peril coverage and all-risks coverage.*

4. *Explain the different functions of the following: an actuary, an insurance agent, an insurance broker, an adjuster, and a claims department.*

5. *Determine, from an insurance policy, the risks that the policy covers and the risks that it excludes.*

6. *Identify at least two factors that insurers consider when settling claims.*

7. *Explain how the concept of negligence affects insurance claims.*

8. *Explain the following terms: depreciation, rider or endorsement, short rate, and accident benefits.*

9. *Introduce the concept of no-fault insurance.*

Introduction

The analysis of financial security in Chapter 3 led to the conclusion that some risks can be minimized by purchasing insurance. This chapter identifies economic risks that are of concern to anyone who owns real property or personal possessions, explains the basic concepts and principles of general insurance, and examines in detail three types of general insurance: property insurance, personal liability insurance, and automobile insurance. Life insurance and health insurance, which are not considered types of general insurance, are discussed in the next chapter.

The Economic Risks of Ownership

Two types of risk are associated with ownership: (i) the property itself may be damaged, destroyed, or lost, and (ii) people may be held responsible for injury to others or for damage to others' possessions because of what they do or own. Fire and theft are examples of the first type of risk. The second type of risk is known as a personal liability risk, and is perhaps less easily understood than the former. A person may have a financial responsibility (or liability) if his or her car, dog, or broken steps causes damage or injury, although it is usually necessary for those making the claim to prove that there was negligence involved. Moreover, liability risks need not be related to ownership; careless behaviour can also create liability.

Damage to or Loss of Property

Both tenants and homeowners must consider the risk that their furnishings and other possessions could be damaged by fire or stolen; homeowners must also consider the possibility that their house could burn down. Damage to, or loss of, a car are other risks to consider, but these are less serious than the risk of being responsible for injury to other people. At the very worst with respect to the irretrievable damage or loss of a car, one would be left without a car, although perhaps burdened with a monstrous debt for many years.

Liability for Damages

Being found responsible, because of negligence, for damage to the lives or property of others is one of the risks that anyone may be exposed to. Here we are speaking not about damage to you or your possessions, but about claims against you by others for their losses. A tenant may be held responsible for damage to rented premises. If, for instance, the tenant's careless smoking or forgetfulness in using a cooking or heating appliance were to cause an apartment fire, the landlord's insurer would reimburse the landlord for the damage to the building, but would probably bill the tenant for the cost of the repairs. The extent of the tenant's liability would depend on the circumstances. Other tenants may also be reimbursed for damage to their contents from smoke, fire, or water.

A homeowner faces the risk that his or her walks, yards, trees, and so on could cause injury. A tree could fall on the neighbour's car, or someone could fall on the homeowner's broken or ice-covered steps. An automobile owner faces the serious risk of being held liable for a death or an injury, with potentially enormous financial consequences. Recent Canadian settlements for personal injury in automobile accidents have been as high as several million dollars. Driving can also lead to damage of other people's cars or property, but claims involving such incidents are usually lower than those related to personal injury.

Most of us consider the risks outlined above to be too great to accept entirely on our own, so we buy insurance in order to share the risks with others. In fact, society considers the liability risks associated with car ownership so serious that liability insurance coverage is mandatory in most jurisdictions. Before we examine the various types of insurance, it is necessary to review and understand a few basic insurance concepts and principles.

Basic Concepts and Principles

The Insurance Principle

Since a major fire or auto accident can financially cripple an individual or a family, methods have been devised that allow people to spread the risk of these events. If a large number of people who face a common risk decide to pool their money, the result will be a fund that is intended to be sufficient to compensate the few who actually experience the disaster in question. This idea of sharing or **pooling risk** is the basic principle on which all types of insurance are based. But because this approach depends on the law of large numbers, it will not work for a small group. The insurance companies that collect, manage, and disperse the pooled funds employ specialized mathematicians called **actuaries** to predict the probability that a particular event will occur among a group of 1000 people in a 12-month period. Such predictions can be fairly accurate when large numbers of people or events are involved, but actuaries cannot, of course, identify which persons will be affected in a particular year. The amount that each person must contribute to the insurance pool or fund depends on several factors:

(a) the probability (according to actuarial estimates) that the event will occur,

(b) the amount that compensation can be expected to cost,

(c) the number of people sharing the risk.

The simplified example in Personal Finance in Action Box 4.1, "Sharing the Risk," illustrates this principle.

Personal FINANCE in action 4.1

Sharing the Risk

In the town of Bayfield there are 1000 houses, all wooden and of approximately equal value. Past records reveal that, on average, one house burns down each year, and the cost of rebuilding a house is approximately $100 000. (It is not necessary to take into account the value of the land on which the house stands because fire does not destroy the lot.)

The loss of a house is such a serious disaster that the community does not expect the affected family to cope with it alone. In nineteenth-century North America, it was customary for neighbours to come to the rescue, providing temporary shelter for the homeless family while they felled logs and sawed boards to construct a new house. Now, the scarcity of trees and the complexity of house construction has caused the house-building "bee" to be abandoned in favour of property insurance.

How large a fund will be needed in Bayfield to cover the potential fire losses to houses?

Number of homeowners
  sharing the risk: 1000
Probability of fire: . . . . 1 per 1000/year
Cost of compensation: $100 000/house

If each owner contributes $100 per year, there will be a fund of $100 000. At the end of a typical year, with one claim for $100 000, the fund will be exhausted.

To summarize, the principle of sharing risk works when a large number of people are willing to pay a regular fee that is certain in exchange for protection against a hazard that is uncertain. The people in this group who experience a loss will be compensated from the pooled funds, and those who are fortunate enough not to have had a loss will not need to claim anything from the insurance fund. Nevertheless, all participants will have enhanced their financial security by having insurance.

Factors Affecting Cost

The cost of property insurance, as we have said, depends on the probability that a particular peril will occur, the cost of compensation, and the number of people sharing the risk. In practice, actuaries take into consideration many more complex factors than those in the above example. The probability of fire and the extent of damage are affected by the availability of fire-fighting facilities and hydrants, the proximity of hazards such as paint factories or oil storage tanks, and the flammability of the house. The cost of compensation depends on the value of the property that would need to be repaired or replaced, which can, of course, vary considerably in the case of houses.

Once the probability that the event will occur has been established and the cost of compensation estimated, an actuary can determine the cost of covering this risk, which is called the **pure cost of insurance**. To this amount will be added a **loading charge,** which covers the costs that the insurance company incurs in collecting and managing the insurance funds, settling the claims, and returning profits to the company's shareholders. Not surprisingly, the estimates of all these costs vary from company to company. The cost of insuring a property, called a **premium**, is paid at regular intervals to keep the insurance in force and is reviewed at least annually by the insurance company.

Risk Management

Insurable Interest It is impossible to buy insurance against a risk unless it can be shown that the buyer has an **insurable interest** in the risk in question. In other words, would the buyer suffer a financial loss if the event occurred? A property owner has an insurable interest in the possibility of the property being stolen or destroyed, but a relative or friend who has no legal relation to the property cannot insure it. This principle applies to all types of insurance, including life insurance.

Insurable Risks Insurance is concerned with only **insurable risks**; such risks result from chance events and are not caused by deliberate action on the part of the person insured. A fire that starts because of lightning is a chance event, but a house fire started by the property owner is a deliberate action. Insurance companies must be certain about the cause of the damage before settling the claim.

Handling Risk As noted earlier, there are three possible ways of dealing with insurable risks:

(a) taking steps to eliminate or reduce the risk,
(b) preparing to handle the loss oneself,
(c) sharing the risk with others.

An example of reducing the risk of injury or damage from fire would be to install monitored smoke detectors or a sprinkler system in one's home. The risk of theft could be reduced by improving the locks on the doors and windows or installing an alarm system. Some people decide to handle some risks themselves when the risk is not too high and their financial resources are adequate. A person who decides not to buy collision coverage (which, unlike liability coverage, is a matter of choice rather than a legal requirement for car owners unless required by a financing company) on an old car is accepting the risk that the car could be destroyed in the event of a collision instead of sharing that risk by buying insurance. Sharing risks through insurance is prudent whenever the possible loss would be too heavy to handle alone. In planning for financial security, it may be wise to use a combination of these three options. Most people probably need some insurance, but they may be able to reduce the cost of that insurance by taking steps to minimize the risk and by assuming some portion of the risk themselves.

The Insurance Contract

A person who decides to buy insurance may contact an **agent** (someone who represents a single insurance company) or a **broker** (someone who represents several companies). The broker can do comparison shopping for the client among the several companies that he or she represents to find the most economical and most appropriate coverage.

Someone who wants to buy insurance will need to complete an application form, and an agent or broker can explain the policy. Generally, purchasers are more likely to be given a complete copy of a home insurance policy than an automobile policy, perhaps because, in some provinces, there is a standard car insurance policy for the whole province, irrespective of insurance company.

The legal contract or agreement between the person buying insurance (called the **insured**) and the insurance company (called the **insurer**) is known as a **policy**. Traditionally, policies have been written in legal language that is difficult to understand, but some insurers are now writing their policies in a more simplified form. Refer to your home insurance policy, or to the sample policy in Appendix 4A, for an example. A policy will seem less daunting if you begin by identifying the following main components:

(a) the preamble or declaration sheet,
(b) the insuring agreement,
(c) the statutory and policy conditions,
(d) any endorsements or riders.

Declaration Sheet The preamble, or declaration sheet, is a separate page that is filled in for each insurance policy holder, and lists the names of the insurer and the insured, the dates the insurance will be in effect, the amounts paid, and the risks to be covered in the agreement. Without this sheet, it is impossible to know what coverage the insured has bought. This page can be easily identified because the spaces in it have been filled in by writing or typing.

The rest of the policy consists of several printed pages that the company routinely uses for all similar risks. For instance, the company may have a standard fire insurance policy that can be adjusted to fit the individual requirements of each policy holder. If the space beside a risk on the declaration sheet is not filled in, that risk is not covered in that particular agreement. The declaration sheet outlines specific coverage of risks. When reading a policy, first determine what coverage is in force by examining the declaration sheet, and then locate the relevant sections of the policy's printed portion.

Insuring Agreement The printed part of the policy will contain an insuring agreement that sets out which kinds of property are covered, which perils are insured against, the

---

Insurance Terminology

Insured—the person whose risks are covered by the insurance, usually the purchaser
Insurer—the insurance company
Policy—the contract between the insured and the insurer that specifies the terms of the agreement
Premium—the regular payment made by the insured for insurance coverage
Peril—a risk of some damage or injury
Endorsement or rider—a statement appended to an insurance policy that may specify additional coverage and a change in ownership or in risk

---

exclusions (situations not covered by the policy), and the circumstances under which insurance settlements will be made.

Policy Conditions Statutory and policy conditions include statements about the responsibilities of the insurer and the insured, including the duty to avoid misrepresentation; why and how the policy may be terminated; the actions required after a loss; and the consequences of fraud.

Endorsements Insurance policies may be modified by attaching to the contract a statement known as an **endorsement** or **rider**. Riders may address a change in the ownership of the property, a change in the risk situation of the property owner, or additional coverage for such things as artwork, antiques, jewellery, firearms, or electronics.

Cancellation The insured may cancel a policy at any time, but if this occurs, the insurer may choose to retain a portion of the premium calculated at the **short rate**. This means that the insurer keeps more than just the prorated share of the premium. For instance, if a one-year policy is cancelled after six months, the refund will be less than half of the premium paid. The difference is to reimburse both the insurance company and the agent or broker for the work in setting up the policy and undertaking the risk.

Insurance Settlements

Claims Process After a loss has occurred, it is the insured's responsibility to provide proof of the loss. Specialists called **adjusters**, who may either be on the regular staff of the insurance company or be working independently for a number of companies, go to the scene of the misfortune to begin estimating the extent of the damage. They report their results to the insurance company's claims department, which negotiates a settlement. Agents and brokers have little, if any, part in the claims procedure. Police, on the other hand, have to be called if the loss is as a result of any criminal act or other relevant law. The police report may be used in the insurance investigation or any lawsuit that may arise later.

There are two approaches to determining the amount of an insurance settlement: (i) actual cash value (indemnification) and (ii) replacement value. Traditionally, most claims were settled on the basis of cash value or indemnification, but in recent years, insurers have offered replacement value coverage. Actual cash value coverage will be considered first.

Actual Cash Value Property insurance, unlike life insurance, is based on the principle of indemnifying the insured for a loss. **Indemnification** is defined as compensating the insured at such a level that the insured will be returned to approximately the same financial position

---

How to Read a Policy

Examine the sample home insurance policy in Appendix 4A to find the answers to the following questions:

1. What property is covered?
2. What are the financial limits of the coverage?

3. What is the total premium?
Your instructor may have other questions about the rest of the policy.

---

enjoyed before the loss (since it is not intended that anyone should profit from an insurance settlement). The concept of indemnification may sound simple. But in practice it may not be easy to determine exactly what the previous financial position of the insured was with regard to the lost or damaged property.

Some property insurance policies promise to indemnify on the basis of the **actual cash value** of the property at the date of the loss—that is, the cost of replacing it less the estimated value of the "wear and tear" on the property. Therefore, the cash value when the loss occurred is the significant value, not the value of the property either when it was bought or when it was insured.

There are various methods of arriving at the actual cash value, but a common one is to determine the **replacement value** of the loss and then deduct any accumulated depreciation. The replacement value of a house is the cost of rebuilding it, not the amount it might have sold for. The replacement value of a household possession is the cost of buying a similar new one. **Depreciation** is the monetary value that has been used up since the item was new. Different objects wear out at different rates because of the object's characteristics or the way it is used or cared for. Insurance companies have tables of standard rates of depreciation for many household goods. Adjusters may adapt these rates somewhat to allow either for especially good care or for very hard usage. The well-established depreciation rates for cars are found in tables possessed by most automobile dealers. The way to calculate actual cash value is shown in the Personal Finance in Action Box 4.2, "Actual Cash Value."

The insurer has the option of offering the following:

(a) a cash settlement,

(b) a similar article as a replacement for the damaged one,

(c) the repair of the damaged article.

If the repair results in an improvement of the property, the value of the betterment is charged to the insured. In addition to the factors mentioned, the condition of the property and the standard of maintenance also affect the estimated cash value. In the case of a building that has been destroyed or damaged, the insurer usually settles by paying for the repair or rebuilding, but does not take possession of the property.

In cases of partial loss, the insured might be reimbursed for a total loss, but any **salvage value** of the damaged property subsequently belongs to the insurance company. For instance,

Actual Cash Value

A fire in Nathan's kitchen damaged his appliances beyond repair as well as the cabinetry and some of the contents. The insurance company adjuster adequately accounted for the repairs to the house, but Nathan was quite upset about the amount of money he was to receive for the appliances he purchased three years earlier for $4000. The adjuster advised that since Nathan had purchased the least expensive policy, he was only covered for the cash value of the appliances, which equals the replacement cost less depreciation. The settlement was calculated as follows with depreciation being estimated at 10 percent per year, or 30 percent in total for the three years:

$$\text{Actual Cash Value} = \text{Replacement Cost} - \text{Depreciation}$$
$$= \$5000 - (0.30 \times \$4000)$$
$$= \$5000 - \$1200$$
$$= \$3800$$

Nathan was very upset, as this money would barely cover the loan to the furniture store that sold the appliances on their delayed-payment program. Now Nathan would have to go out and buy new appliances all over again. From now on, Nathan would review his policy and purchase full replacement coverage, not just indemnification for a loss.

if a heavily damaged car is replaced by the insurer, the owner has no claim on the remnants of the smashed car; the wreck would belong to the insurance company as salvage. To retain the salvage value, the owner must pay the insurer and buy the car back.

Replacement Value Insurance In recent years insurers have begun offering replacement value insurance—that is, they may now agree to replace used possessions with similar new ones. This practice increases the cost of compensation and consequently raises the premium that must be paid. Replacement value insurance does not follow the classic principle of indemnification of losses because replacing used furniture with new may leave the insured in a better position than before the loss. Replacement value insurance is now very popular, and some companies report that it predominates over actual cash value coverage. Claimants, pleased to receive settlements that enable them to replace lost articles without considering depreciation, have proved willing to pay the higher premiums.

Insurer's Liability The insured is entitled to compensation for personal loss, but this amount can never be greater than the **policy limits** purchased. An $80 000 fire insurance policy limits the insurer's liability on this contract to $80 000. For any claim, the insurer will pay the least of the policy limits, the actual cash value of the loss, or the cost of repairs. If a replacement value policy has been purchased, the insurer will pay the lesser of the policy limits or the replacement value. A claimant who has had a loss valued at $7000 but has a policy limit of $5000 will receive only $5000. In the case of automobiles, the insurer's liability is the lesser of the actual cash value or the cost of repairs.

Since small claims are expensive for an insurance company to handle, it is customary to offer the insured the opportunity to pay a lower premium and carry a certain amount of the risk personally. If the insured agrees to assume responsibility for the first $200 of damages, the contract is said to have a **deductible clause** of $200. The higher the deductible, the lower the premium.

Subrogation When an insurer indemnifies a claimant for a loss, the insurer is entitled to attempt to recover damages from any other persons who may have been responsible for the loss—a procedure called **subrogation**. For instance, if a tenant is responsible for fire damage in an apartment, the building's insurer may indemnify the landlord and then, by subrogation, attempt to collect from the tenant who caused the damage. This may extend to other tenants who also may have experienced a loss from the same fire. They or their insurance company may attempt to collect from the person(s) who caused the damage.

Property Insurance

In the interests of clarity, this discussion of property insurance will be limited to coverage of personal possessions, houses, and liability, and we will look at each type separately. However, in practice, coverage for several risks is often combined in one policy—as, for example, is common in the case of homeowners' or tenants' policies.

The Risks

The many perils that may befall a house (or apartment) or its contents can be categorized as either (i) accidental or (ii) the result of criminal actions. Such perils as fire, smoke, water, windstorms, and falling objects represent accidental damage; vandalism and stealing are examples of criminal actions. Defining perils and specifying exclusions (situations not covered in the contract) can be quite complex. For instance, stealing is subdivided into theft, burglary, or robbery. Theft means the loss of property by stealing without either violence against persons or forced entry. Burglary involves theft accompanied by forcible entry that leaves visible marks on the premises. Robbery is theft accompanied by violence or the threat of violence to a person.

Coverage

Most insurance companies sell two types of homeowner coverage: (i) **named-peril coverage**, which provides protection from losses that may arise from any of a list of perils named in the contract, or (ii) **all-risks coverage**, which covers all risks except for any that may be specifically excluded. The more comprehensive coverage may be limited to the house, while the contents of the house are covered for named perils only. All-risks insurance is also more expensive than the more basic named-peril policies.

It is possible to insure only certain possessions against all risks by having an endorsement or rider added to the policy. Such added coverage includes all the kinds of risks associated with direct physical loss or damage, and such coverage is limited only by any exclusions that may be listed. It is usually specified that the extra coverage applies only to accidental damage and not to damage that is due to the nature of the property itself (for example, rust or age). When all-risks coverage is bought for such items as electronics, furs, jewellery, and collections, these items are listed as scheduled property. It is prudent to update your list from time to time, especially after a wedding, a major birthday, or an inheritance.

A **scheduled property rider**, also called a **valued contract endorsement**, lists the items covered, along with their value, and also includes identifying information such as descriptions and serial numbers. To confirm the value, the insurer will require either a bill of sale (if the item was recently acquired) or an official appraisal (if the item was previously purchased, is a gift, or is a collectible). In the event of loss or damage, the insurer's maximum liability is the value placed on the property when it was insured. Such contracts are generally used to insure items whose true value is difficult to determine after a loss, such as jewellery, works of historic or artistic value, antiques, and stamp and coin collections. Unfortunately, in periods of rapid inflation, the maximum liability established when the insurance was bought can become outdated quickly. Unless the insurance company offers automatic adjustment for inflation, the owner should have new appraisals done periodically. (See Personal Finance in Action Box 4.3, "Scheduled Property Rider.")

Personal Property Taken Away from Home Policies often contain a personal property clause that covers personal items when they are taken away from home temporarily. The key word here is *temporarily*: possessions taken on a trip, to a summer cottage for a few weeks, or by a student to a college residence would be considered temporarily away. The amount of coverage for possessions under such circumstances varies with the policy. For instance, if the policy states that possessions taken away from home are covered for 10 percent of the total coverage on all personal possessions, and if the household contents are insured for $30 000, there would be coverage of $3000. Read the policy to find out the extent of the coverage.

Co-insurance

Actuaries base the premium structure for property insurance on the assumption that property owners will carry sufficient insurance to cover a total loss of the building. In fact, however, most buildings do not burn completely; thus, most claims involve damage costing only a few thousand dollars. Knowing this, the insured might decide to buy a policy with very low limits. If many insured people were to take this approach, the pooled insurance funds would be insufficient to provide compensation for all claims. To prevent such under-insurance, many companies include a co-insurance clause in each policy; such clauses apply to the building, but not to its contents.

A **co-insurance** clause states that the insured must carry policy limits to a level considered adequate by the company. An adequate level might be defined, for example, as 80 percent or 100 percent of the building's replacement value. If the owner fails to carry sufficient

---

Personal FINANCE in action 4.3

Scheduled Property Rider

Emil and Anne had built up quite an art collection over the years, primarily from artwork that was created by artists whom they had known as friends at university. Paintings hung all over their apartment and carvings and crafts were everywhere. In many ways, the art proved to be a good investment; a few of the pieces were purchased from artists who later became quite famous. Some of their creations were worth over $10 000 each. To protect their investment, Emil and Anne had an artist friend appraise their collection for insurance purposes.

Five years later, their apartment was burglarized and three of the artworks were stolen. The insurance company offered them $7500 for the three works based on the appraisal their friend had done five years earlier. This amount was not even a quarter of the value of one of the paintings alone. If Emil and Anne had wanted to be fully insured, they should have had the artwork appraised more frequently and by an expert, at least whenever the coverage limits of their policy changed.

insurance, any claims made for damage to the building will be prorated. For instance, if the policy's limits are only half of what is considered adequate, the claim for damages from a small fire will be reduced by half. Personal Finance in Action Box 4.4, "Under-Insured," illustrates how a claim is prorated if the insured has not been carrying sufficient insurance. The purpose of the co-insurance clause is to encourage the purchase of adequate limits. Those who choose not to do so must share the risk with the insurance company—hence the term "co-insurance." In the event that the house has a mortgage on it, the lender usually requires full insurance coverage and a certificate to that effect. The lender is frequently named in the insurance policy as co-insured.

Property Insurance and Mortgages

Property insurance may include a mortgage clause; such a clause recognizes that there is a mortgage on the property and it specifies the rights and obligations of both the lender and the insurer. This clause in effect expresses an agreement between the mortgage lender and the insurer that is independent of the agreement between the insured and the insurer, even though this clause is attached to the insured's policy.

The lender has the right to share in any insurance settlement on the property as long as the insured still has an outstanding balance owing. Once the mortgage is completely repaid, the mortgage lender no longer has a claim. The mortgage clause entitles the lender to receive a loss payment regardless of any act or neglect on the part of the homeowner or borrower. For example, the insured could breach a condition of the contract with the insurance company, making the insured's claim for damages void; even so, the lender would still be entitled to compensation. Thus, an insured who commits arson cannot collect insurance on the burned property, but the lender can.

The mortgage lender is obliged to inform the insurer of any factors that may change the risk situation. If the risk should increase, and the insured does not pay the additional amount

---

Personal FINANCE in action 4.4

Under-Insured

The Wongs bought a policy on their house with limits of $150 000. A few years later they had a bad fire, which resulted in damage calculated at $80 000. At that time, their house was estimated to have a replacement value of $250 000. Their policy had a co-insurance clause requiring that they have coverage for 80 percent of the replacement value.

Policy limits . . . . = $150 000
Replacement value . . . . . . = $250 000
Adequate coverage . . . . . . = 80% of
                                  replacement
                                  value
. . . . = 0.80 × $250 000
. . . . = $200 000
Claim . . . . = $80 000

The insurance settlement was calculated as follows:

$$\frac{\text{Policy limits they had}}{\text{Policy limits they should have had}} \times \text{Claim} = \text{Settlement}$$

$$\frac{\$150\ 000}{\$250\ 000} \times \$80\ 000 = \$48\ 000$$

Although their loss was estimated at $80 000, they received a settlement of only $48 000 because they were under-insured.

required, the lender is responsible for this amount. The determination of the lender's rights in an insurance settlement would take into account the amount still owing on the property at that time. Conversely, if the insured/borrower fails to make a premium payment, the insurer notifies the lender, who in turn ensures that the premium does get paid.

The Inventory

When someone experiences a loss, this person must produce proof of what was lost. In some instances, enough evidence may remain for the adjusters to see what sorts of possessions the insured had; at other times, though, very little if anything may be left. It is therefore best to be prepared by keeping an up-to-date inventory of possessions in a secure place away from the house—for example, in a safety-deposit box at a bank. An inventory will not be of much help if it burns up along with the possessions it lists.

For those who feel that creating a written inventory is too tedious, a camera, video camera, tape recorder, or some combination of these devices can be used. With a video camera or a tape recorder, someone can go through the house describing all that is seen, including the contents of cupboards. These records should be supplemented with sales receipts, lists of serial numbers, and any other relevant information, especially for major items.

Preparing a detailed inventory and attaching current values to each item will also help you determine how much insurance coverage you require. Consideration should be given to the need for additional coverage for such items as jewellery, special collections, or antiques. Preparing this inventory will not be a one-time event; your list of possessions will change, and some of what is listed may increase in value over time. Regular valuation of possessions is therefore recommended. Generally, though, insurance companies estimate the value of a house's contents to be 30 percent of the value of the house, excluding land. Once again, an insured may be under-insured if the valuation is inaccurate.

Inflation

If the insurance company does not automatically adjust policy limits in relation to changes in general price levels, the policyholder may have to review his or her coverage regularly. Replacement costs tend to increase during periods of inflation, leaving policy limits too low to cover a total loss. For this reason, many homeowners' policies now contain an automatic inflation clause, particularly for the coverage that applies to the building. Of course as inflation increases so does the premium charged.

Personal Liability Insurance
The Risks

Anyone's financial security may be jeopardized if he or she should be found responsible either for damage to someone else's property or for an injury to another person. However, in order to succeed with such a liability claim, the person seeking damages must prove that the loss or damage was caused by negligence. Negligence is defined as either (i) failing to do what a reasonable and prudent person would do in a similar situation, or (ii) doing what a prudent person would *not* do in a similar situation. Everyone lives under the legal requirements of (1) not to harm others or their property and (2) to take reasonable steps to preserve the safety of others. Besides being held liable for their own negligent acts, employers are also legally responsible for their employees' work-related actions. Each of us is responsible for any losses that may be caused by our animals and, to some extent, for our children's carelessness and, in some provinces, criminal acts. The examples in Personal Finance in Action Box 4.5, "Personal Liability Insurance Claims," illustrate some types of personal liability claims that were successful.

Coverage

Liability insurance (sometimes called legal liability) covers the risk of being found responsible for damage caused by your own negligence or by the negligence of your family members, employees, animals, and so on. Such policies are known as **third-party insurance** because they involve not only the insured and the insurer but also some third party who is seeking compensation for a loss. The need to establish who is at fault makes liability insurance claims more involved with legal matters than other kinds of insurance are.

Under liability insurance coverage, the insurer agrees to pay for damages attributed to the policy holder, including the costs of a court defence, interest, and reimbursement for some immediate expenses. Because the insurance company defends the insured in a liability suit, it is important that there be no admission of liability or offer to make payments because such actions or statements could prejudice the defence. In some situations, there must be a court case to prove negligence; in others, an out-of-court settlement may be reached. Before the

Personal FINANCE in action 4.5

Personal Liability Insurance Claims

1. Ten-year-old Rosa, whose broken leg was in a cast, was sitting in an ice-cream parlour with her friends when an elderly woman who was walking down the aisle tripped and fell over Rosa's cast. The woman broke her leg and claimed $10 000 for damages. Rosa's father's insurance company investigated the circumstances; finding that the woman's companion, who had preceded her down the aisle, had maneuvered safely around the cast, the insurer subsequently decided that the case for finding Rosa negligent was not strong. Rather than go through the expense of defending itself against a suit, however, the company paid the woman $2000 *ex gratia,* that is, without admitting any liability. The settlement was made under Rosa's father's personal liability insurance.

2. Larry's children broke the windshield of the car next door while playing baseball. Larry's insurance company paid to replace the windshield.

3. A child who was visiting the Duval family was attacked by their dog and required stitches and plastic surgery. The Duvals' insurer paid the extra medical bills.

4. At a campground, a young woman broke her neck by diving into water that was only 1.2 metres deep. She eventually recovered with only a 20 percent disability. Because she had earned various Red Cross swimming certificates, it was established that she was 25 percent at fault for not having investigated the water's depth before diving; the campground owner was held to be 75 percent at fault. His insurer paid the woman $50 000.

5. Mr. Nielsen, a self-employed handyperson, was called to a commercial building to check the plumbing. He proceeded to thaw frozen pipes with a blowtorch and succeeded in igniting the whole building, resulting in a total claim that exceeded $2 000 000. His liability coverage was only $1 000 000, leaving him responsible for the difference.

insurance company will settle a liability claim, however, it must be satisfied (i) that the insured was indeed legally liable in this instance and (ii) that the policy covers this particular liability.

Liability insurance may be bought separately or, more commonly, as a part of another policy, such as home or auto insurance. A homeowners' or tenants' policy that includes comprehensive personal liability may cover damage to property or injury to people as a result of the use or maintenance of the insured property, the personal acts of the insured, the ownership of animals, the ownership of boats, and children's carelessness. It may cover the insured's legal liability for fire, explosion, and smoke in rented premises. In addition, some policies include a small amount of coverage for damage caused by the insured without reference to negligence. Subject to a list of exclusions, personal liability coverage applies wherever the insured is engaged in normal activities as a private individual; business pursuits are commonly excluded from personal liability policies. Personal liability insurance is an inexpensive way to protect yourself against risks that may have a low probability of occurring but can be extraordinarily costly if they do happen.

People who operate home-based businesses must be sure to examine any household policy that is in force to determine whether it covers "business use of the home." If, as may very well be the case, the policy does not cover the business, then additional liability coverage should be acquired to apply to any visitors to the home and any assets that are at the home and used in the business. Computers and software are usually covered but rarely are data. Similar consideration should be given to the family automobile: if the car is used for business, you need to have business insurance for it. In most instances, the increase in coverage for a home-based business will have only a minimal impact on your premiums for both the home and auto insurance.

Whether to include liability insurance coverage is one issue addressed in this chapter's Women Take Charge box.

Women take CHARGE 4.1

Now that Jan has bought her first house, she is in the market for a home insurance policy to protect what will probably be the largest investment in her life. An insurance broker can put her in touch with a number of different companies and their various policies. Jan wants to be sure she understands the policy terminology, provisions, and fine print before signing. Jan hopes never to have to use the policy, but she will be more comfortable knowing she is protected from costly losses. The premiums paid by many policyholders can be used to recompense the few who make claims.

The home insurance policy will cover both the house and contents. Comprehensive policies that cover all risks or perils are more expensive than policies that cover just a few, specifically named perils. Jan has decided to take comprehensive coverage on the house and "named perils coverage" on the contents. She is especially concerned about water damage and will make a specific inquiry as to what type of water damage is covered. Jan has read about natural disasters involving flooding, hurricanes, and earthquakes and will ask about coverage for these perils.

With respect to insuring the contents, Jan has a choice between actual cash value insurance, which takes depreciation into consideration, and replacement insurance, which does not. Because she does not have a lot of money invested in the contents of the house, Jan has decided to take out actual cash value insurance because she can spend the reimbursement as she wishes. Replacement cost insurance may put restrictions on how the money is spent. Jan plans on taking a deductible to keep the premium more affordable. If the policy offers a "no-claim" discount, this will give Jan the incentive to handle small losses herself.

Jan will carry a large amount of personal liability insurance to cover claims of individuals who may be injured on her property. She will note whether the policy covers her worldwide for personal liability claims.

continued

Jan wants to review her policy over the years. It may be necessary to increase the policy limits to provide for inflation and to keep the limits high enough to meet co-insurance requirements. She will keep an up-to-date inventory of the contents as well. Now that related risks are covered, Jan is set to enjoy home ownership.

Automobile Insurance

The intent of this section is to outline the basic principles and concepts associated with auto insurance, not to supply the details of coverage available in each province or territory, because there is too much variation across Canada. The social and financial risks associated with automobiles are widely considered too significant to be left to people's personal discretion with regard to insurance. So, to some degree, Canadians are protected by minimum insurance laws in each jurisdiction. We will identify three major categories of risk and explain the relevant types of insurance protection associated with each category. With this basic knowledge, you will be prepared to investigate the specific arrangements for auto insurance that apply where you live.

Two important distinguishing features of the various provincial/territorial arrangements for automobile insurance relate to (i) who supplies the insurance coverage (a public body, private companies, or a combination of public and private resources), and (ii) how fault is handled. We will discuss fault after identifying the risks associated with car ownership and explaining the basic types of insurance protection.

Insurance Providers

In British Columbia, Manitoba, and Saskatchewan, basic automobile insurance coverage is provided by the provincial government, with extra insurance available from private insurers. Quebec splits auto insurance coverage between government and private companies, and the other provinces and territories leave the provision of auto insurance to private companies. Wherever auto insurance is publicly provided, there is just one price for coverage and one place to get it; where insurance is offered by private enterprise, there may be many competing suppliers, and prices may vary. Some factors to consider are the kind of coverage desired and the level of service required. If your home and auto insurance are bundled there is frequently a discount. Selecting a car with a lower cost of coverage is also a way to lower costs, as well as the option of raising deductibles and removing collision coverage on an older vehicle.

The Risks

As noted earlier, car ownership poses such a significant threat to society as well as to the financial security of individuals that it is mandatory for car owners to carry a minimum amount of public liability and accident benefits coverage. The three major types of financial risks that a car owner assumes, along with the basic types of protection against those risks, are outlined below:

Risk	Insurance Coverage
1. Liability to others for injury, death, or property damage	Public liability (third-party)
2. Injury to or death of self or passengers	Accident benefits
3. Damage to insured's vehicle	Physical damage (e.g., collision, comprehensive)

Liability to Others

Anyone who owns or drives a car faces the risk that, because of negligence, he or she could be held financially responsible for injuries caused to others or for damage to their property. When assessing your own liability risk, reflect on the high probability of being involved in a car accident at some time, simply because of the large number of vehicles on our roads. Despite our best intentions, a little mistake can cause a serious accident. The consequences of severely injuring one or more persons could be financially disastrous; courts have been awarding increasingly large settlements—sometimes as high as several million dollars—in successful negligence suits. The rising costs of car repair, medical care, and income replacement for killed or injured persons have increased settlements to the point where some insurers are now advising their customers to have at least $1 000 000 in liability coverage. The legal requirement for liability insurance is $50 000 in Quebec and $200 000 elsewhere in Canada.

Policy Limits As with most types of insurance, the liability policy limits determine the maximum that the insurer will pay on a claim. However, a court can order that an accident victim be awarded a settlement that exceeds the policy limits. The insured is then responsible for paying the difference, unless the policy includes specific coverage for such situations.

Negligence Public liability insurance does not apply either to damage to your car or to injury to you; instead, it is limited to situations where others suffer loss due to your negligence. Because liability claims depend on proving negligence, it is important to give some thought to the legal concept of negligence. Sometimes distinctions are made between ordinary negligence and gross negligence. Ordinary negligence involves either failing to do what a reasonable person would do in similar circumstances or doing what a reasonable person would not do. Gross negligence, on the other hand, constitutes reckless, wanton, and willful misconduct in which someone fails by a wide margin to exercise due care, thereby reflecting an indifference to the probable consequences of his or her actions.

A basic rule in our society is that each of us has the duty to take proper care no matter what we are doing, and to take responsibility for any injury caused by our carelessness. Motorists can be held negligent for not keeping a proper lookout or for failing to have their vehicles under complete control at all times. Icy roads or storms are not an excuse; drivers are expected to adjust their driving to suit the conditions. In some jurisdictions, a car owner is also held responsible for the consequences of any negligence on the part of anyone who is driving his or her car with consent. When your friend borrows your car and has an accident with it, liability or collision claims may be handled by your insurance. It is wise, therefore, to know the terms of the policy when lending your car or borrowing someone else's car. If you as the car owner are liable, the claim will be submitted to your insurer, who in turn might raise future premiums if your friend is found to be at fault.

Highway Traffic Act Where a highway accident involves an infraction of a regulation under the *Highway Traffic Act*, the insurer may take that into account when determining negligence. However, being found not guilty of a traffic offence does not necessarily mean absolution of negligence as far as the insurance company is concerned, or in a civil court.

Proving Fault A serious problem for insurance companies is the difficulty of proving negligence in auto accidents, where events happen very fast and there may be no witnesses. If there is uncertainty about who was at fault, the issue can be decided in court; alternatively, the two insurers may reach an out-of-court agreement in which the responsibility for the accident is divided between them. For instance, a 60/40 split would mean that 60 percent of all the damages resulting from the accident would be assessed to one driver and 40 percent to the other; both drivers would in turn refer these claims to their respective insurance companies as third-party liability claims. High legal costs, prolonged court processes, and the difficulty of determining fault have created so many problems that some measures have been devised to expedite certain types of claims by not requiring that fault be established. In a later section, we will examine so-called no-fault auto insurance, but first we will consider the two other types of risks faced by motorists.

Personal Injury or Death

The second major risk is that the car's driver or passengers will be injured in an accident. Medical insurance or accident benefits coverage is designed to provide benefits in case of bodily injury to the occupants of a vehicle or to anyone struck by the vehicle. Note that the term **accident benefits** refers to insurance coverage for personal injury or death. Payment of claims for accident benefits occurs without reference to fault, and claims are made to the policyholder's insurance company. All provinces except Newfoundland and Labrador require compulsory accident benefits coverage as part of auto insurance. There is some variation by province, but essentially, accident benefits cover (to defined limits) such things as medical and rehabilitation costs in excess of provincial health plan

---

Questions to Ask about Your Liability Coverage

1. **Who is covered by this part of the policy and in which situations?**

   There should be protection for you (the car owner), and for anyone who drives the vehicle with your consent, if the driver's negligence causes injury, death, or property damage to others. Find out whether you are covered when driving cars that you do not own or use regularly, such as temporary substitute cars or uninsured cars. Whose insurance would cover you if you were found negligent in an accident while driving a friend's car? Also, does your liability coverage protect you if family or passengers sue you for negligence?

2. **How much liability coverage do you need?**

   Inquire about the size of recent liability settlements to get an idea of the amount of coverage you need.

3. **What is not covered by your liability insurance?**

   Liability insurance does not cover injuries sustained by you, and it does not cover your death. Additionally, it does not cover damage to your own car or to property that is being carried in or on it.

4. **What other things does your insurer agree to do?**

   Besides paying claims that result from your negligence, the insurer may cover the costs of investigating the accident, negotiating a settlement, settling a claim, and defending you in court. Also, the insurer may reimburse you for out-of-pocket costs for immediate expenses associated with the accident, and pay court costs and interest on the insured portion of settlements charged to you. Such costs are paid even where they exceed your policy's liability limit.

5. **Does the insurer cover business use of your car?**

   Even if you are an employee who is reimbursed for mileage, this condition should be explained to the insurance company to ensure that you are covered when travelling for work.

coverage, disability income, death payments, and funeral expenses. Find out what the accident benefits are where you live.

Damage to Your Vehicle

The least serious risk faced by car owners is that their vehicle may be stolen or damaged. Insurance coverage is generally not mandatory for this risk (with the exception of Saskatchewan and Manitoba). Physical damage coverage does not have a dollar limit but is based on the car's actual cash value at the time of the loss. Because of the rapid rate at which cars depreciate, it is best to review physical damage insurance from time to time; you might drop the coverage when the premium becomes too high in relation to the size of the risk being covered. For instance, if an old car has an actual cash value of only a few hundred dollars, that value would also be the maximum settlement in the event of a total loss of the car. Is protecting the small amount of capital in the car worth the cost of the annual premiums?

Coverage for physical damage to a car is often subject to some deductible amount. The deductible is the amount of each claim that the insured pays; for instance, if you purchase collision coverage with a $500 deductible, you will take responsibility for paying the first $500 in damages. By sharing the risk with the company, you lower your insurance costs.

Most insurance companies will offer a choice of physical damage coverage, such as (i) all-perils, (ii) specified-perils, (iii) collision, or (iv) comprehensive. All-perils coverage is the broadest, encompassing everything that is included in the other three categories and possibly more. Such a policy should be examined to find out what is excluded because everything else will be covered. By contrast, specified-perils coverage includes only named risks. The two other types of coverage, collision and comprehensive, are common.

Collision Coverage Collision coverage applies when a car collides with another object. Usually a collision involves the car's striking or being struck by another car, but it also includes one-vehicle accidents (those in which the car strikes a tree, a guard rail, another object, or the surface of the ground).

If a collision is caused by the negligence of another person, the car owner's insurer will pay the damage claim if it is greater than the deductible; then, by the right of subrogation, the insurer will endeavour to collect from the person responsible for the accident. The insurer has agreed to indemnify the owner under the collision coverage whether or not the driver was at fault. If the insurer is successful in collecting from the third party, the policy holder will be reimbursed for the deductible amount.

Comprehensive Coverage To be protected against perils other than collision that may happen to a car, you need comprehensive coverage. The distinction between collision and comprehensive coverage can seem confusing. If a specific type of loss is excluded under your collision coverage, it may be included under your comprehensive coverage. Some of the perils included in comprehensive coverage are theft, vandalism, fire, lightning, windstorm, hail, and falling or flying objects. Such coverage is usually subject to a deductible amount, but the deductible may not apply in certain situations—for example, when the entire auto is stolen.

Mandatory Provincial Coverage

A summary of how auto insurance is provided and what coverage is mandated in various provinces and territories is presented in Table 4.1.

TABLE 4.1   AUTOMOBILE INSURANCE PROVIDERS AND MANDATED COVERAGE
BY PROVINCE, CANADA, 2003

PROVINCE/ TERRITORY	PUBLIC LIABILITY MINIMUM	MANDATORY ACCIDENT BENEFITS	MANDATORY COLLISION COVERAGE
Public Insurer			
BC	$200 000	X	
Sask.	$200 000	X	X
Man.	$200 000	X	X
Public & Private Insurers			
Que.	$50 000*	X	
Private Insurers			
Alta.	$200 000	X	
Ont.	$200 000	X	
NB	$200 000	X	
NS	$200 000	X	
PEI	$200 000	X	
Nfld.	$200 000		
Yukon	$200 000	X	
NWT/Nunavut	$200 000	X	

* Quebec residents are compensated for injury without regard to fault. Liability limits are $50 000 for property damage claims within Quebec, and for personal injury and property damage claims outside the province.

SOURCE: Data from Insurance Bureau of Canada website, www.ibc.ca. Accessed August 2003.

Factors Affecting Insurance Rates

Usually we pay more to insure our cars than we do to insure our houses—even though a house is much more valuable—because cars pose a greater risk to financial security. The number of accidents and the rising cost of settlements have caused car insurance premiums to escalate. These factors plus investment losses experienced by insurance companies have also contributed to serious rate increases recently. Auto insurance premiums reflect not only the coverage requested, but often a number of other factors as well. These factors can be grouped according to (i) the personal characteristics of the insured, (ii) the type of car, (iii) the use that is made of the car, and (iv) the region where the insured lives.

Personal Characteristics   Traditionally, auto insurance premium rates are based on statistics that link accident frequency to car drivers' personal characteristics (for example, age, gender, and marital status). Although eliminating these criteria has been discussed, not all provinces have yet done so. The risk-according-to-age method may be modified in the case of young people who have had driver training, since they are expected to present less risk to the insurer. Likewise, a driver who has had no accidents for several years is considered a much better risk than one with a record of accidents or traffic violations. After an accident, insurers reassess the insured's risk classification and usually increase the premium if the insured is deemed to have been at fault.

Type of Car   The type of car will have an obvious effect on the cost of collision and comprehensive coverage because of the variations in repair costs. In addition, insurers often increase liability and accident benefits premiums for powerful cars because of their potential for causing substantial damage.

Use of Car The number of kilometres driven in a year and the number of people who normally drive a particular car also affect the risk situation. The more a car is driven, the more it is exposed to risk. Whether or not the car is used for driving to work is also a consideration, as is the distance driven to work. A vehicle that is to be used for business purposes, as mentioned earlier, will also require a revised risk assessment. (For the insurance options that are typically available to people who rent a car, see Personal Finance in Action Box 4.6, "Damage to Rental Cars.")

Region More accidents occur in certain regions of the country, usually either because of population density or because of adverse driving conditions due to weather.

Provincial/Territorial Differences Premium rates are different across Canada. Quebec, for instance, has a set premium for a given class of vehicle, regardless of the risk presented by the individual. In Manitoba, rates are based on the make and model of the vehicle, how it is used, geographical location, and the insured's driving record, with no discrimination based on age, sex, or marital status. British Columbia drivers pay premiums determined by the value of the vehicle, its use, geography, and the driver's claims record.

Personal FINANCE in action 4.6

Damage to Rental Cars

Denise and her friend plan to rent a car for two weeks while they are on holiday. A friend has pointed out to them that they will be expected to sign a rental agreement stating they are responsible for returning the car in the same condition as it was when they took it, meaning that they bear the risk of any damage. When Denise inquired about supplementary insurance for rented cars, she found three alternatives. The first option was to buy the extra coverage offered by whichever rental company they choose. One firm offers a damage waiver for about $10 a day that protects customers against damage to the vehicle from just about any cause, including collision, vandalism, falling trees, etc., with no deductible. Another company offers a waiver that covers damage only if it is caused by a collision. Clearly, it is important to read a car rental contract before signing it.

Next, Denise checked her own car insurance policy to see whether it had a clause regarding rental cars. She found that she can buy additional coverage for the duration of her holiday for a small fee ($15 to $20), but that her own deductible amounts would apply if she submits a claim. Furthermore, if she decides to have her own insurance company protect her against damage to a rented car, she will be required by the rental company to provide written documentation of that coverage.

Denise's third option is to use her premium credit card to pay for the car rental. The card, which costs her over $100 a year for a variety of services, provides the same protection as that sold by the first rental company—broad damage coverage with no deductible.

Since circumstances vary with the individual, each person must make his or her own decision in such situations. It is also of concern when travelling outside Canada or one's home province. Coverage from an individual's insurance company may not be available or adequate.

Insurance for High-Risk Drivers

There are some drivers whose accident records or other characteristics make them very high risks and thus unacceptable to insurers. However, if they are able to get a driver's licence, and if car insurance is mandatory where they live, there must be some way to insure them in order to protect society as well as to protect them. The insurance industry has solved this problem by creating an arrangement whereby insurers pool the high risks, which makes it possible to cover all licensed drivers and registered owners. The high-risk driver applies for auto insurance the same way that anyone else does, but the policy is then transferred to the insurance pool—which in turn assigns these high-risk cases to companies in proportion to their share of auto insurance in each province. Thus, no single company receives more than its fair share of bad risks, and all those who want insurance can obtain it. Naturally, the premiums paid by high-risk drivers are very high. Claims made on these policies, however, are handled in the usual way by the insurer concerned.

Comparison Shopping for Insurance

If you want to find the best rates for car or home insurance, you have several choices. You can get prices from a number of agents, an approach that can be time-consuming. Or you can consult an insurance broker, who, by definition, represents a number of companies.

However, a broker who subscribes to a computerized rating service will give you access to the broadest rate comparison. Both insurance brokers and insurance agents (who represent only one insurance company) are listed in your telephone book.

Responsibility of the Insured

The agreement with the insurer requires the policyholder to give the company written notice of an accident as soon as possible after the event occurs. The notice should include important details. At the scene of an accident, information about the other driver (including his or her name and address, the name and address of his or her insurance company, and the licence-plate number of his or her car) should be collected. Names and addresses of passengers and other witnesses may also prove useful later. At the time of the accident, the driver should not say anything to suggest assuming any obligation or accepting any responsibility for the accident, nor should the driver offer or make any payments to the victim or victims.

After the accident, the car owner must co-operate with the insurer by providing information as needed; forwarding all summonses, notices of suit, and other correspondence received; and appearing in court if required. The victim is making a claim against the car owner, not against the insurer. If a victim named Smith brings a case to court concerning an accident involving a car that Jones was driving, the court case will be labelled *Smith v. Jones*, not *Smith v. Jones's Insurer*. The insurer is responsible only for helping to resolve the problem, not for taking it over entirely.

No-Fault Automobile Insurance

The Fault System

Under the law of torts, which has descended to us from the English common-law system, each person has a basic duty to take care not to harm other people or damage other people's property, either intentionally or unintentionally. When applied to car accidents, this system often creates problems because in many instances it is difficult to clearly establish fault. Besides driving errors, accidents may be caused by adverse road or weather conditions, or by cars or pedestrians who are not involved in the crash. Naturally, the more extensive the injuries and damage, the greater is the need to establish fault in order to receive compensation, but such cases often take years to settle because of long delays in getting court hearings. Some accident victims are never compensated because no one can be shown to have been negligent. Still, fault is frequently assigned by the police through the assessment of moving violations and is used to reassess insurance premiums. In the event the police do not find fault under the *Criminal Code*, the *Highway Traffic Act* or the *Insurance Act*, the insurance companies still follow a means, as determined by law, to allocate the degree of fault to each driver.

No-Fault Insurance

Claims under accident benefits and claims for physical damage to one's own car have usually been paid without regard to fault. Much of the controversy that has occasionally surrounded the introduction of no-fault insurance has been in relation to third-party liability claims. In a pure no-fault system, proof of fault would not be required in order to settle claims for injuries and damages resulting from car accidents. Instead, each person would claim damages from his or her own insurer, thus saving litigation costs and considerable time, while also ensuring that all claims are paid. However, this simple idea raises some important questions. Should the insurance premium be raised because the policyholder was paid a large settlement for damages caused by another? Should a consistently bad driver continue driving without penalty? Should those who have been seriously injured be deprived of the right to sue for damages?

Because so many attempts have been made to change the basic no-fault approach in a number of provinces and in the United States, we have now reached a state of terminological confusion. The term "no-fault" has been applied to so many versions of the basic idea that it is no longer meaningful. For example, a partial no-fault scheme may pay claims without regard to fault up to some maximum amount but permit claimants to sue for further damages in court.

Examples of No-Fault Insurance

Quebec and Manitoba have no-fault insurance programs that have eliminated the option of making claims entirely. Instead, the injured party can take his or her case to a tribunal and press for compensation to the injured party. In Ontario, a partial no-fault insurance system permits injured parties to sue in situations involving serious injury or death. By instituting such plans, all three provinces are attempting to speed the payment of claims for minor injuries and to prevent all but the most serious cases from involving the time and expense of a court case. These programs are constantly evolving and operate differently in each province as they are revised by the different governments. It is vital for residents of any province that permits lawsuits to ensure for themselves that they carry adequate liability insurance, preferably above the prescribed minimum coverage.

Summary

- Actuaries are mathematically trained individuals who calculate the risk of a loss. Pooling risk is where a large enough group of people share the financial loss of the few who do encounter a loss. Pure cost of insurance is the actuarial cost of covering the risk of a loss.

Loading charge is the additional cost of insurance to cover administration and sales charges. The premium is the regular payment made by the insured for insurance.

■ The idea of insurable interest is that an individual is eligible to buy insurance only when he or she would suffer a financial loss if a detrimental event occurred. Insurable risks are those chance events that cause a financial loss.

■ An agent sells insurance for only one company; a broker is a person who sells insurance for many insurance companies. The insured is the person whose risks are covered by insurance; the insurer is the insurance company. The policy is the contract between the insured and insurer that specifies the terms of the agreement.

■ Adjusters are professionals who review a loss and estimate the loss incurred. Indemnification is the compensation such that the insured would return to the approximate same financial position as before the loss. Actual cash value is the indemnification for the replacement value less depreciation. Replacement value is the cost of fully replacing the loss at present values. Depreciation is the monetary value of the asset that has been used up since acquisition. Salvage value is the residual value of an asset after damage.

■ Policy limits state the maximum amount of compensation. A deductible clause is the initial risk faced by the insured to reduce the premium. Subrogation is the ability of the insurer to attempt to recover the compensation paid to the insured from a third party who may be responsible.

■ Named-peril coverage lists the events for which the insured would be compensated. All-risks coverage covers all risks but the specified exclusions. A scheduled property rider (valued contract endorsement) is a list of items to be covered in the insurance.

■ Co-insurance is a clause requiring that the insured carry a policy to an adequate level according to the insurer.

■ Liability insurance (third-party insurance) covers the risk of being found responsible for damage caused by one's own negligence or that of family members, employees, etc.

■ Short rate is an adjusted rate of reimbursement for a cancelled insurance policy to compensate for administration and sales expenses.

■ Endorsement (rider) is a statement appended to an insurance policy that may specify additional coverage and a change in ownership or in risk.

■ Accident benefits are insurance coverage for personal injury or death.

Key Terms

accident benefits (p. 92)	deductible clause (p. 83)
actual cash value (p. 82)	depreciation (p. 82)
actuaries (p. 78)	endorsement (rider) (p. 81)
adjusters (p. 81)	indemnification (p. 82)
agent (p. 80)	insurable interest (p. 79)
all-risks coverage (p. 84)	insurable risks (p. 79)
broker (p. 80)	insured (p. 80)
co-insurance (p. 85)	insurer (p. 80)

liability insurance (third-party insurance) *(p. 88)*	pure cost of insurance *(p. 79)*
loading charge *(p. 79)*	replacement value *(p. 82)*
named-peril coverage *(p. 84)*	salvage value *(p. 82)*
policy *(p. 80)*	scheduled property rider (valued contract endorsement) *(p. 84)*
policy limits *(p. 83)*	short rate *(p. 81)*
pooling risk *(p. 78)*	subrogation *(p. 84)*
premium *(p. 79)*	

Problems

1. To answer this question, you need to refer to Appendix 4A.

   (a) Look for the answers to the questions posed in the box "How to Read a Policy" on page 82.

   (b) Is there any automatic inflation adjustment of the policy limits? If so, does it apply to both the house and the contents?

   (c) How much coverage is there for personal property taken away from home?

   (d) Does the policy include coverage for personal liability? If so, what is the liability limit?

   (e) If the owner of this policy were to lose all of his or her personal possessions in a fire, would the maximum settlement represent the actual cash value of the loss or the policy limits?

   (f) Would this policy cover a theft that occurred while the family was away?

   (g) Are there any riders or endorsements attached to the policy?

   (h) Is this an all-risks policy or a named-perils policy?

   (i) Is there a co-insurance clause? If so, what is the policyholder's responsibility?

   (j) Is there coverage for property away from home?

2. The Bates returned home to find their townhouse under the fire department's careful watch for a fire recently extinguished. A candle left burning while they went for a walk had probably started the fire. The townhouse was seriously damaged. The walls and ceilings were heavily damaged by smoke, and there was extensive water damage throughout. The condominium company was claiming damages to the property; as well, the neighbours on either side were claiming damage to their properties. The contents portion of the Bates' insurance policy provides for replacement coverage with $500 000 personal liability coverage.

   (a) Who pays for what in this case?

   (b) Would the Bates receive a settlement large enough to replace their damaged furniture? How would the insurance company account for the depreciation of the furniture and the inflation in the cost of the furniture and appliances?

   (c) Would the insurance company pay for the lost computer and its contents for the home business?

3. The MacDonalds have bought their first house for $220 000. The building itself is estimated to have a replacement cost of $150 000.

    (a) How much insurance do they require?

    (b) Who else will likely be listed on the policy?

    (c) The co-insurance clause of their insurance policy requires that they cover 80 percent of the replacement value of the property. During a windstorm they lost their roof, a number of pieces of outdoor furniture, and the garden shed. They had insured for $125 000, as that was the amount of their mortgage. Calculate the amount of the settlement, if the damages totalled $12 000 in value.

4. (a) What are the pros and cons of buying a replacement value insurance policy on your household effects?

    (b) How does replacement value insurance alter the basic principle of indemnification?

    (c) What should you do on a regular basis to maintain adequate coverage?

5. Obtain an automobile insurance policy, and examine it to find answers to the following questions:

    (a) If you or your passengers should be injured in an accident and as a result become unable to work, would there be any income replacement payments? How much? For how long?

    (b) If one of your passengers were to be killed, would there be any compensation for funeral costs?

    (c) If your injuries included some that were not covered by the provincial health insurance, would the accident benefits portion of your car insurance policy provide some help? Is there any limit on the amount?

    (d) Do you have collision coverage? What is the deductible amount?

    (e) Is there a deductible amount on the comprehensive coverage?

    (f) Are there any exclusions to the coverage for damage to the insured's automobile?

    (g) Is there a no-fault rider?

    (h) If so, what can you still sue for?

    (i) What is your coverage outside your province? Outside Canada?

6. When Dave Hill's father was buying a new car, he found that his old one was valued at only $1900 as a trade-in. He offered it to 19-year-old Dave, on the condition that Dave would handle all the operating costs and insure it. Dave was delighted—he would have his own car at last. The insurance agent was happy to help him arrange suitable coverage for the car, but Dave was dismayed to find that the premium would be higher than the value of the car. To economize, he decided that he could cut down on some parts of the insurance. He told the agent that he would take collision coverage but drop the third-party liability because the car was getting old; however, he definitely wanted coverage for theft and fire.

Consider each of the following statements in relation to Dave's case, and decide whether you AGREE or DISAGREE, and explain why.

    (a) If Dave does not buy public liability coverage, he will not be able to register his car.

    (b) If Dave buys an automobile insurance policy, he is required to have at least $200 000 in public liability coverage.

    (c) In Dave's case, it is probably a good idea for him to skip the public liability coverage because it would not be a great disaster if the old car were wrecked.

(d) If Dave takes out a policy with collision coverage that has a $500 deductible and then later runs into a bridge, completely demolishing his car, he will have to pay the first $500 of damages, but his insurance company will pay him $1400 to buy another car.

(e) Dave is wise to insist on coverage for fire and theft even if he must do without some other coverage in order to afford it.

(f) Because of the province's mandatory no-fault accident benefits insurance coverage, Dave would not be held accountable if he injured another person in an auto accident.

7. Analyze the following complaints from car owners regarding insurance claims, and note how you would explain the situation to each.

(a) Sam writes, "Under conditions of icy roads and high winds, our car was blown off the road. When I presented a claim for damage to my car, I was told that my policy did not include collision coverage. On reading the policy, I find that we are covered for windstorm damage. The company still insists that it has no responsibility for paying my car repairs."

(b) The summer before last, Bob was in a head-on collision with a car that suddenly appeared on his side of the road. Because he had no collision coverage, he was advised to settle on a 50/50 basis, since it would cost too much to prove that he was in the right. His lawyer will not take the case; she says that it will cost more to fight the case than the car is worth. Bob wonders what to do.

(c) Until recently, Sophie considered her car insurance quite adequate: she has collision, comprehensive, and public liability coverage. Then an unknown driver damaged her car when it was parked legally on the street. She assumed that such damage would be covered under the comprehensive clause (which had only a $100 deductible) because she believed that collision would, by definition, mean that her car had collided with another vehicle or with some object. The insurer, however, says that since her car was hit by another car, rather than by, for example, a stone, the accident is indeed classified as a collision. To Sophie, this seems impossible: she was not even in the car, and the car was not moving. She thinks that collision coverage should pay for damage caused by her own carelessness, not someone else's. She says that comprehensive ought to cover this event, since it covers vandalism. But the insurer wants her to pay for the damage in full because it amounted to less than the deductible amount that applies to her collision coverage. Is this right?

8. What is the extent of no-fault auto insurance coverage where you live? To what extent may a victim or his or her family sue for loss or damages?

9. **One Man Dead, Another Paralyzed in Two-Car Crash**

The foggy wet weather and poor driving conditions on Saturday evening accounted for a head-on collision involving cars driven by Richard Chaney and Russell Talcott. Police reports indicate that Chaney's car went out of control in the northbound lane and crossed the slippery pavement into the southbound lane, where it collided with the vehicle driven by Talcott. On arrival at the General Hospital, Russell Talcott was pronounced dead. He is survived by his wife, Mary, and their young son, Jason. At present Richard Chaney is reported to be in critical condition as a result of a serious spinal injury. No charges were laid in this case.

Assume the following information about the insurance and other security plans of these men:

	Chaney	Talcott
Health insurance	covered	covered
Canada/Quebec Pension	contributor	contributor
Group life insurance	$25 000	$50 000
Personal life insurance	$175 000	$150 000
Disability insurance	none	pays 1/2 salary
Auto insurance:		
Collision	none	$300 deductible
Comprehensive	none	$50 deductible
Accident benefits	yes	yes
Public liability	$500 000	$1 000 000

(a) In the chart below, identify by check marks the areas of probable financial need for each man's family as a result of this accident.

	Chaney	Talcott
Personal injury		
Funeral expenses		
Property damage		
Liability to others		
Loss of income		
Other		

(b) Using the chart below, note the resources that these families could call on and what each resource would cover.

	Chaney	Talcott
Health insurance		
Canada/Quebec Pension		
Group insurance		
Personal life insurance		
Disability insurance		
Auto insurance:		
Collision		
Comprehensive		
Public liability		

Note: When answering the following questions, assume that the accident happened in your province.

(c) Will Chaney's insurer immediately authorize repairs to his car and look after the bill? Would you expect Talcott's company to do this? Explain.

(d) Both of these drivers had third-party liability. Explain how claims against this portion of their coverage would proceed. Would the case necessarily have to go to court? What would the claims be for?

(e) If the case does go to court and if Chaney is declared to be more than 50 percent responsible for the accident, will Chaney receive any compensation for his disability from Talcott's insurer?

(f) From the information provided, which of the two families seems to be in the worst financial position as a result of this accident? Why?

(g) Does the fact that the police did not press charges under the province's *Highway Traffic Act* mean that the insurer will not make any settlement under the liability coverage?

10. Explore the Insurance Bureau of Canada's website at **www.ibc.ca** and determine the process recommended for an accident claim and report.

(a) How should you act when asked questions at the scene of an automobile accident?

(b) What rights do pedestrians have if struck by a car?

(c) Under whose policy are the accident benefits paid if the pedestrian also is an insured driver?

(d) How much mandatory funeral expense coverage is in force in your province?

11. At the Insurance Bureau of Canada's website (**www.ibc.ca**), proceed to the Publications section and complete the Home Security Audit (13 pages).

(a) At your home (house or apartment), what issues should be remedied as soon as possible?

(b) Do you undertake the efforts outlined for extended leaves such as vacations?

(c) What different issues are faced by apartment dwellers (as opposed to house dwellers)?

(d) What different issues would be faced by rural and urban dwellers?

(e) What particular risks do cottage owners face and how can they mitigate the risks?

12. Examine the website **InsuranceHotline.com.** Obtain an insurance quote for you to commute 30 km daily to work driving the Honda Civic Si hatchback and the four-cylinder Toyota Camry. Proceed through the same exercise but now as someone of the other gender. Now what are the rates? Is this fair? Why or why not? What do you suggest for someone your age when considering purchasing a car? What kind of automobile are you planning to purchase next?

References

BOOKS AND ARTICLES

Deloitte and Touche. *Canadian Guide to Personal Financial Management*. Toronto: Prentice-Hall Canada, annual. A team of accountants provides guidance on a broad range of topics, including planning finances, estimating insurance needs, managing risk, and determining investment needs. Instructions and the necessary forms for making plans are also included.

Insurance Bureau of Canada. *Facts*. Toronto: Insurance Bureau of Canada, annual. An annual summary of industry statistics.

Insurance Bureau of Canada. *Home Insurance Explained*. Toronto: Insurance Bureau of Canada. A thorough pamphlet offering tips on insurance for homes, tenants, and condominiums.

Praskey, Sally, and Helena Moncrieff. *The Insurance Book: What Canadians Really Need to Know Before Buying Insurance*. Toronto: Pearson Education Canada Inc., 2000. A straightforward book with information and answers to various questions for Canadians at all stages of their lives. The focus is on making informed decisions on insurance.

Personal Finance on the Web

Insurance Bureau of Canada

www.ibc.ca An overview of the industry, with extensive coverage of the legal aspects of property and casualty insurance. Many links are provided to the member companies. Available in both English and French, but does not cover life and health insurance. Some excellent references.

Insurance-Canada.ca

www.insurance-canada.ca A consumer-focused site with information regarding the needs and intricacies of the industry. Co-sponsored by the Consumers Council of Canada and the Consumers Association of Canada.

InsuranceHotline.com.

www.insurancehotline.com A website with the full range of insurance quotes available and numerous industry sources of information.

Appendix 4A

Excerpt from a Home Insurance Policy

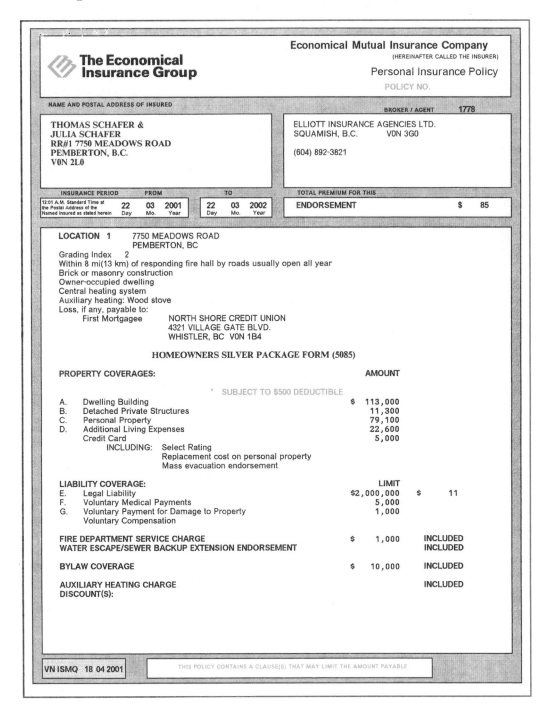

continued

5085 (05/2001) BC

PRINCIPAL AND SEASONAL RESIDENCE

HOMEOWNERS
SILVER PACKAGE FORM

AGREEMENT

We provide the insurance described in this policy in return for payment of the premium as stated on the Policy Declaration Page and subject to the terms and conditions set out. This form consists of two sections.

SECTION I describes the insurance for your property.

SECTION II describes the insurance for your legal liability to others because of bodily injury and property damage, and provides for certain voluntary payments.

SECTION I -- PROPERTY COVERAGES

DEFINITIONS (Applicable to Section I)

"You" or **"Your"** refers to the insured.

"Insured" means the person(s) named as insured on the Coverage Summary page and, while living in the same household:

> his or her spouse

> the relatives of either, and

> any person under 21 in their care

Spouse includes either of two persons who are living together in a conjugal relationship outside marriage and have so lived together continuously for a period of 3 years or, if they are the natural or adoptive parents of a child, for a period of 1 year.

In addition, a student who is enrolled in and actually attends a school, college or university and who is dependent on the Named Insured or his or her spouse for support and maintenance is also insured even if temporarily residing away from the principal residence stated on the Coverage Summary page.

Only the person(s) named on the Coverage Summary page may take legal action against us.

"We" or **"Us"** means the Company or Insurer providing this insurance.

"Dwelling" means the building described on the Coverage Summary page, wholly or partially occupied by you as a private residence.

"Premises" -- means the land contained within the lot lines on which the dwelling is situated.

"Residence Employee" means a person employed by you to perform duties in connection with the maintenance or use of the insured premises. This includes persons who perform household or domestic services or duties of a similar nature for you. This does not include persons while performing duties in connection with your business.

"Occupancy" means the presence of the insured or a representative in the described seasonal dwelling. A seasonal dwelling will be considered occupied if an interior and exterior inspection is carried out by a competent adult at least once every 60 days.

"Unoccupied" means the dwelling is uninhabited.

Seasonal Dwelling only - "unoccupied" means the absence of the insured or a representative in the described furnished seasonal dwelling. A seasonal dwelling will not be considered unoccupied if an interior and exterior inspection is carried out by a competent adult at least once every 60 days.

"Vacant" refers to the circumstance where, regardless of the presence of furnishings: all occupants have moved out with no intention of returning and no new occupant has taken up residence; or in the case of a newly constructed house, no occupant has yet taken up residence.

"Ground water" means water in the soil beneath the surface of the ground including but not limited to water in wells and in underground streams, and in percolating waters.

"Surface waters" means, but it is not limited to, water on the surface of the ground where water does not usually accumulate in ordinary watercourses, lakes or ponds.

"Domestic appliance" means a device or apparatus for personal use on the premises for containing, heating, chilling or dispensing water.

Coverages

The amounts of insurance are shown on the Policy Declaration Page. These include the cost of removing debris of the insured property, or the debris that damaged the property, as a result of an insured Peril.

If you must remove insured property from your premises to protect it from loss or damage, it is insured by this form for 30 days or until your policy term ends - whichever occurs first. The amount of insurance will be divided in the proportions that the value of the property removed bears to the value of all property at the time of loss.

COVERAGE A -- Dwelling Building

We insure:

1. The dwelling and attached structures.
2. Permanently installed outdoor equipment on the premises.
3. Outdoor swimming pool and attached equipment on the premises.
4. Materials and supplies located on or adjacent to the premises intended for use in construction, alteration or repair of your dwelling or private structures on the premises. The peril of theft applies only when dwelling is occupied or completed and ready to be occupied.

continued

5085 (05/2001) BC

Tear Out

If any walls, ceilings or other parts of insured buildings or structures must be torn apart before water damage from a plumbing, heating, air conditioning or sprinkler system or domestic appliance can be repaired we will pay the cost of such repairs. The cost of tearing out and replacing property to repair damage related to outdoor swimming pools or public watermains is not insured.

Building Fixtures and Fittings

You may apply up to 10% of the amount of insurance on your dwelling to insure building fixtures and fittings temporarily removed from the premises for repair or seasonal storage.

Outdoor Trees, Lawns, Shrubs and Plants

You may apply up to 5% in all of the amount of insurance on your dwelling to trees, lawns, plants and shrubs on your premises. We will not pay more than $500 for any one tree, plant or shrub including debris removal expenses. We will also reimburse you for up to $500 in total for removal of trees due to a peril not covered.

We insure these items against loss caused by fire, lightning, explosion, theft, impact by aircraft or land vehicle, riot, vandalism and malicious acts, as described under Insured Perils.

We do not insure lawns or items grown for commercial purposes.

COVERAGE B -- Detached Private Structures

We insure structures or buildings separated from the dwelling by a clear space, on your premises but not insured under Coveage A. If they are connected to the dwelling by a fence, utility line or similar connection only, they are considered to be detached structures.

COVERAGE C -- Personal Property

1.   We insure the contents of your dwelling and other personal property you own, wear or use, while on your premises, which is usual to the ownership or maintenance of a dwelling.

   If you wish, we will include uninsured personal property of others while it is on that portion of your premises which you occupy but we do not insure property of roomers or boarders who are not related to you.

   We do not insure loss or damage to motorized vehicles, trailers and aircraft or their equipment (except watercraft, wheelchairs, lawn mowers, gardening equipment or snow blowers). Equipment includes audio, visual, recording or transmitting equipment powered by the electical system of a motor vehicle or aircraft.

2.   We insure your personal property while it is temporarily removed from your premises anywhere in the world. We also insure newly acquired personal property in situations where there has not been an opportunity to take such property to your premises. If you wish, we will include personal property belonging to others while it is in your possession or belonging to a residence employee travelling for you.

   The coverage is extended to cover personal property normally kept in a land recreation vehicle you own.

   This coverage is extended to insure the personal property of students insured by this policy while temporarily residing away from home and in full time attendance at school.

   Personal property kept at any other location you own, rent, lease or occupy, except while you are temporarily living there, is not insured. Personal property stored in a warehouse is only insured for 30 days unless loss or damage is caused by theft. To extend cover in storage for a further period we must be notified in writing and endorse your policy as required.

3.   We insure your personal property damaged by change of temperature resulting from physical damage to your dwelling or equipment by an Insured Peril. This only applies to personal property kept in the dwelling.

4.   If the insurance is governed by the law of Quebec, the words "Personal Property" shall, subject to the coverages, exclusions and conditions of this insurance, mean corporeal, moveable property other than the right to property.

5.   We insure your personal property that is being moved to another location within Canada which is to be occupied by you as your principal dwelling, the limit insurance for personal property will be divided between the premises, in transit, and at the new location on the basis of the percentage of the total value of the property at your premises, in transit and at the new location. This coverage applies only for a period of 30 days from the date you commenced removal.

6.   We insure your personal property up to $500 in all, normally kept at your place of business.

7.   We agree to insure the personal property of a named insured or a parent who is dependent on the named insured or his or her spouse for support and maintenance if residing in a nursing home for up to a total of $10,000.

Special Limits of Insurance

We insure:

(1)   Books, tools and instruments pertaining to a business, profession or occupation for an amount up to $2,000 in all, but only while on your premises. Other business property, including samples and goods held for sale, is not insured;
(2)   Securities up to $2,000 in all;
(3)   Money, bank notes, bullion, gold other than goldware, silver other than silverware, platinum, coins, medals and medallions up to $300 in all;
(4)   Watercraft, their furnishings, equipment, accessories and motors up to $1,000 in all;
(5)   Computer software up to $1,000 in all. We do not insure the cost of gathering or assembling information or data;
(6)   Garden type tractors including attachments and accessories up to $5,000 in all.

The following special limits of insurance apply if the items described below are stolen:

(7)   Jewellery, watches, gems, fur garments and garments trimmed with fur up to $3,000 in all;
(8)   Numismatic property (coin collections) up to $300 in all;
(9)   Manuscripts, stamps and philatelic property (such as stamp collections) up to $1,000 in all;
(10)   Silverware, silver-plated ware, goldware, gold- plated ware and pewterware up to $10,000 in all;

continued

5085 (05/2001) BC

(11) Sound and electronic communication equipment, including radios, tape players/decks, compact disc players, telephones, cellular telephones, CB radios, ham radios, televisions, facsimile machines, computers and items of a similar nature including their tapes, discs and compact discs, up to $500 in all if stolen from an automobile;
(12) Bicycles, including their parts, equipment and accessories, for not more than $500 any one bicycle;
(13) Collectible cards, sports memorabilia and comic collectibles up to $250 any one item with a maximum of $2,000 in all.

Specified Perils

Subject to the exclusions and conditions in this policy, Specified Perils means:

1. fire;
2. lightning;
3. explosion;
4. smoke due to a sudden, unusual and faulty operation of any heating or cooking unit in or on the premises;
5. falling object which strikes the exterior of the building;
6. impact by aircraft or land vehicle;
7. riot;
8. vandalism or malicious acts, not including loss or damage caused by theft or attempted theft;
9. freezing of any part of a plumbing, heating, sprinkler or air conditioning system or domestic appliance;
10. rupture of a heating, plumbing, sprinkler or air conditioning system or escape of water from such a system, or from a swimming pool or equipment attached, or from a public watermain; or damage caused by melting of ice and snow and resulting interior water damage from the roof;
11. windstorm or hail;
12. transportation meaning loss or damage caused by collision, upset, overturn, derailment, stranding or sinking of any automobile or attached trailer in which the insured property is being carried. This would also apply to any conveyance of a common carrier.

COVERAGE D -- Additional Living Expenses The amount of insurance for Coverage D is the total amount payable for any one or a combination of the following coverages. The periods of time stated below are not limited by the expiration of the policy.

1. **Additional Living Expense**: If an Insured Peril makes your dwelling unfit for occupancy, or you have to move out while repairs are being made, we insure any necessary increase in living expenses, including moving expenses incurred by you, so that your household can maintain its normal standard of living. Payment shall be for the reasonable time required to repair or rebuild your dwelling or, if you permanently relocate, the reasonable time required for your household to settle elsewhere.

2. **Fair Rental Value**: If an Insured Peril makes that part of the dwelling or detached private structures rented to others or held for rental by you unfit for occupancy, we insure its Fair Rental Value. Payment shall be for the reasonable time required to repair or replace that part of the dwelling or detached private structure rented or held for rental. Fair Rental Value shall not include any expense that does not continue while that part of the dwelling or detached private structure rented or held for rental is unfit for occupancy.

If a civil authority prohibits access to your dwelling as a direct result of damage to neighbouring premises by an Insured Peril under this form, we insure any resulting Additional Living Expense and Fair Rental Value loss for a period not exceeding two weeks.

We do not insure the cancellation of a lease or agreement.

FIRE DEPARTMENT SERVICE CHARGE

We will pay up to $1,000 for your liability assumed by contract or agreement for fire department changes incurred when the fire department is called to save or protect your property from an Insured Peril.

Any deductible specified in the policy does not apply to these charges.

LOCK REPLACEMENT

We will pay up to $500 to replace or re-key, at our option, the locks on your principal residence if the keys are stolen during a burglary, robbery or in conjunction with theft of other property.

Any deductible specified in the policy does not apply to this coverage.

REWARD COVERAGE

We will pay up to $500 to any individual or organization for information leading to the arrest and conviction of any person(s) who robs, steals, or burglarizes any covered personal property from any insured. We will also pay $1,000 for information which leads to a conviction for arson in connection with a fire loss to property insured by this form. This coverage may increase the amount otherwise applicable, however, the $500 or $1,000 limit will not be increased regardless of the number of persons providing information. This coverage is not subject to a deductible.

INFLATION PROTECTION

During the term of this policy, we will automatically increase the limit of insurance on your Dwelling Building (Coverage A) by an amount which is solely attributable to the inflation increase since the inception date of this policy or the latest renewal or anniversary date.

We will also automatically increase the limits of insurance on your Detached Private Structures (Coverage B), Personal Property (Coverage C) and Additional Living Expenses (Coverage D) by the same proportion.

On renewal date, we will automatically increase the limits of insurance shown on the Policy Declaration Page in the same way and adjust the premium.

If, at your request, we change the limit of insurance on your Dwelling Building (Coverage A) shown on the Policy Declaration Page, we will apply this Inflation Protection on the changed limits of insurance from the date the change is made.

continued

5085 (05/2001) BC

We will pay for the cost of supplying or renewing artificial limbs or braces, made necessary by the accident, for up to 52 weeks after the accident, subject to a maximum of $5,000.

We do not insure you for costs recoverable from other insurance plans.

All other items and conditions of the policy to which this rider applies remain unchanged.

SPECIAL LIMITATIONS

Watercraft -- Watercraft You Own: You are insured against claims arising out of your ownership, use or operation of watercraft equipped with an outboard motor or motors of not more than 18kW (24 HP) in total when used with or on a single watercraft. You are also insured if your watercraft has an inboard or an inboard-outboard motor of not more than 38kW (50 HP) or for any other type of watercraft not more than 8 metres (26 feet) in length. We do not insure damage to the watercraft itself.

If you own any motors or watercraft larger than those stated above, you are insured only if they are shown on the Policy. If they are acquired after the effective date of the policy, you will be insured automatically for a period of thirty days only from the date of their acquisition.

Watercraft You Do Not Own. You are insured against claims arising out of of your use or operation of watercraft which you do not own, provided:

1. the watercraft is being used or operated with the owner's consent;
2. the watercraft is not owned by anyone included in the definition of "you" or "your" in Section II of this form.

You are not insured for damage to the watercraft itself.

Vehicles You Own. You are insured against claims arising out of your ownership, use or operation of the following including their trailers or attachments:

1. self-propelled lawn mowers, snow blowers, garden-type tractors, of not more than 19kW (25 H.P.), used or operated mainly on your property, provided they are not used for compensation or hire;
2. motorized golf carts while in use on a golf course;
3. motorized wheelchairs, including motorized scooters having more than two wheels and specifically designed for the carriage of a person who has a physical disability.

Vehicles You Do Not Own. You are insured against claims arising out of your use or operation of any self-propelled land vehicle, amphibious vehicle or air cushion vehicle including their trailers, which you do not own, provided that:

1. the vehicle is not licensed and is designed primarily for use off public roads;
2. you are not using it for business or organized racing;
3. the vehicle is being used or operated with the owner's consent;
4. the vehicle is not owned by anyone included in the definition of "you" or "your" in Section II of this form.

You are not insured for damage to the vehicle itself

Trailers: You are insured against claims arising out of your ownership, use or operation of any trailer or its equipment used for private pleasure purposes, providing that such trailer is not being towed by, attached to or carried on a motorized vehicle.

Business and Business Property. You are insured against claims arising out of:

1. your work for someone else as a sales representative, collector, messenger or clerk provided that the claim does not involve injury to a fellow employee;
2. your work as a teacher, provided the claim does not involve physical disciplinary action to a student or injury to a fellow employee;
3. the occasional rental of your residence to others; rental to others of a one or two-family dwelling usually occupied in part by you as a residence, provided no family unit includes more than 2 roomers or boarders;
4. the rental of space in your residence to others for incidental office, school or studio occupancy;
5. the rental to others, or holding for rent, of not more than 3 car spaces or stalls in garages or stables;
6. activities during the course of your trade, profession or occupation which are ordinarily considered to be non-business pursuits;
7. the temporary or part time business pursuits of an insured person under the age of 21 years.

Claims arising from the following business pursuits are insured only if the properties or operations are declared on the Policy Declaration page:

1. the rental of residential buildings containing not more than 6 dwelling units;
2. the use of part of your residence by you for incidental office, school, or studio occupancy.

LOSS OR DAMAGE NOT INSURED

You are not insured for claims arising from:

(1) war, invasion, act of a foreign enemy, declared or undeclared hostilities, civil war, rebellion, revolution, insurrection or military power;
(2) (a) loss or damage caused directly or indirectly by any nuclear incident as defined in the Nuclear Liability Act or any other nuclear liability act, law or statute, or any law amendatory thereof or nuclear explosion, except for ensuing loss or damage which results directly from fire, lightning or explosion of natural, coal or manufactured gas;
     (b) loss or damage caused directly or indirectly by contamination by radioactive material.
(3) your business or any business use of your premises except as specified in this policy;
(4) the rendering or failure to render any professional service;
(5) bodily injury or property damage caused by any intentional or criminal act or failure to act by:
     (a) any person insured by this policy; or
     (b) any other person at the direction of any person insured by this policy;
(6) the ownership, use or operation of any aircraft or premises used as an airport or landing strip, and all necessary or incidental operations;
(7) the ownership, use or operation of any motorized vehicle, trailer or watercraft except those for which coverage is provided in this form;
(8) the transmission of communicable disease by any person insured by this policy.
(9) (a) sexual, physical, psychological or emotional abuse, molestation or harassment, including corporal punishment by, at the direction of, or with the knowledge of any person insured by this policy; or
     (b) failure of any person insured by this policy to take steps to prevent sexual, physical, psychological or emotional abuse, molestation or harassment or corporal punishment;

continued

5109 (08/90)

RENT AND RENTAL VALUE ENDORSEMENT

If this coverage is shown on the Policy Declaration Page, we insure Rent and Rental Value of the dwelling building indicated in the Schedule of Additional Coverages and/or Endorsements in accordance with the terms and conditions of this endorsement.

We will not pay more than the amount shown in the Policy Declaration Page for this coverage at each location indicated.

COVERAGES

We insure the reduction in "gross rent and rental value" which is a direct result of the dwelling building being unfit for occupancy as a result of damage caused by an Insured Peril. Payment shall be for the reasonable time required to repair or replace the dwelling building but not exceeding twelve (12) months from the date of damage. The insurance shall not include any expense that does not continue while the dwelling building held for rental is unfit for occupancy.

"Gross Rent and Rental Value" is defined as:

(1)   the actual total annual gross rent or rental value of the occupied portion(s) of the dwelling building.
(2)   the estimated annual rental value of the unoccupied portion(s) of the dwelling building; and
(3)   a fair rental value of any portion of the dwelling building occupied by the insured.

If a civil authority prohibits access to the dwelling building as a direct result of damage to neighboring premises by an Insured Peril, we insure any resulting Rent and Rental Value loss for a period not exceeding two weeks.

Co-Insurance Clause: In return for the rate of premium charged for this endorsement, you are required to maintain insurance similar in form and wording to a limit of at least 100% of the annual "gross rent and rental value" (as defined) of the building(s) to which this insurance applies. Failing this, you will only be entitled to recover the portion of any loss that the amount of insurance in force bears to the amount of insurance required by this clause.

This clause applies separately to each location where a separate amount of insurance is shown in the Policy Declaration Page.

LOSS OR DAMAGE NOT INSURED

We do not insure:

(1)   loss or damage as stated in the "Loss or Damage Not Insured" Clause under Section 1 of the Homeowners Form or the "Loss or Damage Not Insured" Clause under the Residential Building and/or Contents Rider (AB).
(2)   any increase of loss due to interference at the location(s) specified in the Policy Declaration Page by strikers or other persons with rebuilding, repairing or replacing the property.
(3)   loss due to the suspension, lapse or cancellation of any lease or license or contract which may affect your gross rent and rental value after the period following any loss during which indemnity is payable.

BASIS OF CLAIM PAYMENT

Any loss hereunder shall not reduce the amount(s) of insurance provided by this endorsement.

Subrogation: We will be entitled to assume all your rights of recovery against others and may bring action in your name to enforce these rights when we make payment or assume liability under this endorsement. Your right to recover from us is not affected by any release from liability entered into by you prior to loss.

Insurance Under More Than One Policy: Our policy will pay its rateable portion of the loss.

All other terms and conditions of the policy to which this endorsement applies remain unchanged.

SOURCE: Economical Mutual Insurance Company. Reprinted with permission.

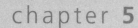

chapter **5**

Life and Health Insurance

"When you don't have money, the problem is food. When you have money, it's sex. When you have both it's health."

S.P. Dreleavy, American novelist

Learning Objectives

Understanding the concepts discussed in this chapter should help you to mitigate additional risks.

After studying this chapter, you should be able to:

1. *Explain the function of life and health insurance in enhancing financial security.*

2. *Relate the need for life insurance to changing life cycle requirements.*

3. *Evaluate the use of life insurance as a savings vehicle.*

4. *Explain the following principles: pooling risk, the pure cost of life insurance, the level premium, term insurance, whole life insurance, and universal life insurance.*

5. *Demonstrate how the two basic types of life insurance policies differ with respect to policy reserves, duration of insurance protection, and insurer's liability.*

6. *Explain how the following policy variations serve specific needs: decreasing term, limited-payment life, family policy, family income policy, and universal life.*

7. *Assess the merits of renewability, convertibility, waiver of premium, guaranteed insurability, accidental death benefit, cash surrender value, dividends, and mortgage insurance.*

8. *Ascertain from an insurance policy the main features of the agreement.*

9. *Explain the functions of long-term disability insurance, critical illness insurance, and travel insurance.*

Introduction

The intent of this chapter is to help you take control of another aspect of your financial affairs. Most Canadians believe they ought to have some life insurance, but many are bewildered by the process of making a choice. Besides experiencing a natural reluctance to think about their own mortality, many people are dubious about insurance agents and feel unable to evaluate the sales presentation. Their perplexity stems from a lack of understanding of life insurance principles and concepts and is compounded by the sometimes confusing terminology used within the industry. Since a standard nomenclature for life insurance policies does not exist, companies adorn their offerings with a wide variety of names. Much of the confusion felt by buyers can be traced not only to the naming of policies but also to the existence of various financing methods and renewal provisions. In fact, there are only two fundamental types of life insurance. The confusion arises because of the numerous modifications and combinations of the basic types, which companies describe as they see fit. By gaining an understanding of basic principles and terms, you will put yourself in a better position to determine your own life insurance requirements and to make rational choices about these matters.

Ultimately, though, far fewer people die before retirement than become unable to earn the living that they previously enjoyed because of illness or disability. The health insurance field has many alternative services available, and Canadians' needs may be increasing as we travel more and the health care system of Canada undergoes regular review and increasing costs. Long-term disability insurance, health insurance in its many offerings, and dental insurance—services many of us expect—are also brought into view in this chapter to assist you in gathering control of your financial life and addressing the risks you face.

The Economic Risk of Dying Too Soon

If you died tomorrow, would your death create economic hardship for anyone? If the answer to that question is yes, you will want to consider insuring your life as one way of improving financial security for your dependents. If, as far as you can foresee, the answer is no, you probably do not need life insurance. The primary purpose of life insurance is to protect an income stream for dependents should a breadwinner die prematurely. Another reason for getting life insurance, important in certain cases, is to provide liquidity for an estate at death. When ready cash is needed by the survivors, but most of the assets are tied up in property or securities that take time to sell, a lump-sum insurance settlement can be helpful. This chapter concentrates on protecting a family's income stream through life insurance. At the same time, there are many complicating factors should one become ill. Not only is the cost of health care constantly rising, there is the concern for lost income, a loss that may not be alleviated by savings or government programs. Critical illness insurance is one topic covered to address this issue.

Financial Responsibility of Parents

Raising children creates a financial risk that peaks on the day the last one is born; at that time, the family has its maximum number of children with the longest period of dependence ahead. (See Personal Finance in Action Box 5.1, "When Insurance Is Needed.") As the children grow and the time left to support them decreases, this economic risk lessens. That is, the amount of money that would be needed to support children until they become independent becomes less each year. This changing risk is represented in Figure 5.1 by a hypothetical curve; for comparison, the profiles of an average family income and wealth over the life cycle are superimposed.

Personal FINANCE in action 5.1

When Insurance Is Needed

Neither Tara nor Ravi had any life insurance when they married, but after baby Daphne's arrival, they became aware of their responsibility to support her for at least 18 years. Since both were employed, they decided that each should have some life insurance coverage, and they bought two policies. The birth of Adam two years later increased their financial commitments. Now that they were responsible for supporting Daphne for at least 16 more years and Adam for 18, or the equivalent of 34 child-years in total, they needed to increase their insurance coverage.

Will Tara and Ravi need to carry the same amount of life insurance throughout their lives? Assuming that they have no more children, the economic risk of parenthood will decline each year, going from the peak of 34 child-years to 32 at the end of the next year, then to 30, and so on to zero, when they stop supporting the children. After the child support years and before their retirement, they should be building their net worth in anticipation of their non-earning years while also reducing debt. Thus, their need for life insurance may slowly decline, eventually reaching a point where they need very little or even none.

For many families, the financial risk associated with parenthood does not correspond very well with their economic resources. Their financial risk tends to peak before their income or assets reach their highest levels. On average, parents can expect their income to increase until at least middle age and their assets to grow until retirement or after, with the period of greatest wealth occurring after the children have left home. This discrepancy, which can pose a significant threat to the financial security of young families, may be minimized by life insurance.

FIGURE 5.1 RESOURCES AND ECONOMIC RISKS OF PARENTHOOD BY LIFE CYCLE STAGE

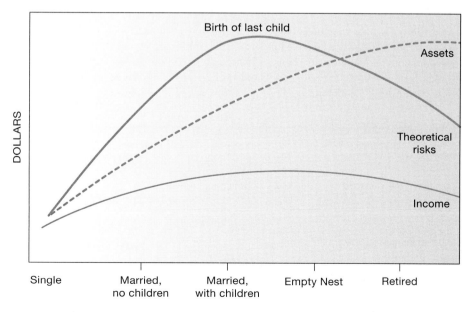

Basic Concepts and Principles

Terminology

When you buy life insurance, the company provides an agreement or contract, called a **policy**, that states which risks the company has agreed to assume. The policy specifies in detail all aspects of the agreement, including the maximum liability that the company will assume, known as the face amount or face value. A policy with a **face amount** of $100 000 is an agreement that the insurance company will pay your beneficiary $100 000 upon your death, usually tax-free. In other words, the **beneficiary** is the person, as stated in the policy, who will receive the proceeds under the terms of the contract. There may be more than one beneficiary. The regular payments that are required to keep the policy in force are called **premiums**. Insurance premiums may be paid monthly, semi-annually, or annually, depending on the arrangement with the company, and are generally paid throughout the period during which the coverage is in force.

As with any type of insurance, a policy cannot be purchased unless there is an **insurable interest**, or a relationship between the insured and the event being insured against. You do not have an insurable interest in the life of another person unless that person's death would have a financial impact on you. Usually, a person is considered to have an insurable interest in his or her own life and in the life of a spouse, parent, child, grandchild, employee, or any person on whom he or she may be wholly or partially dependent. For example, a creditor has an insurable interest in the lives of his or her debtors.

Basic Principles

Three basic principles of life insurance will be discussed here:

(a) pooling risk,
(b) the pure cost of life insurance,
(c) the level premium.

Pooling Risk Life insurance, like general insurance, is a method of pooling small contributions from many people to create a fund that will be able to compensate those who experience a loss. Actuaries refer to mortality tables, which are based on the information in death records collected over many years, to predict the number of persons of any given age who can be expected to die within the year. These predictions, although quite accurate for large numbers, cannot

---

Pooling the Risk

Population of men aged 30 . . . . 200 000
Amount to be paid per deceased $50 000
Mortality rate for males aged 30 . . . . 2.13/1000

Number of deaths expected in the year in this population:

$$200\ 000 \times \frac{2.13}{1000} = 426$$

Fund for dependents:

$426 \times \$50\ 000 = \$21\ 300\ 000$

Cost per man:

$$\frac{21\ 300\ 000}{200\ 000} = \$106.50 \text{ for the year}$$

At the end of the year, the fund would be exhausted; more contributions would then be needed.

include which persons will die in a given year—only how many. Once the number of expected deaths is known for a specific population, as well as how much money is to be given to the dependents of each person in the fund, it is possible to determine the size of fund required to make the payments. The simplified example in the box "Pooling the Risk" illustrates this point.

The Pure Cost of Life Insurance As you can see from Figure 5.2, the one-year mortality rate rises with age and is higher at any given age for males than females. The cost of insuring a life for one year is based on the mortality rate for persons of the same age and gender and is called the pure cost of life insurance. Therefore, the **pure cost of life insurance** follows the mortality curve, becoming more expensive each year as one ages, but is less costly for females.

The Level Premium In response to resistance from buyers, who dislike having to pay higher premiums each year, insurance companies have devised the level premium. Rather than charge enough to cover the pure cost of insurance each year, they establish a constant or **level premium** when a life insurance policy is bought; the policyholder pays this amount regularly for the duration of the policy, whether that is 5 years or 50 years. If we superimpose

FIGURE 5.2 PROBABILITY OF DYING WITHIN THE YEAR BY AGE AND GENDER

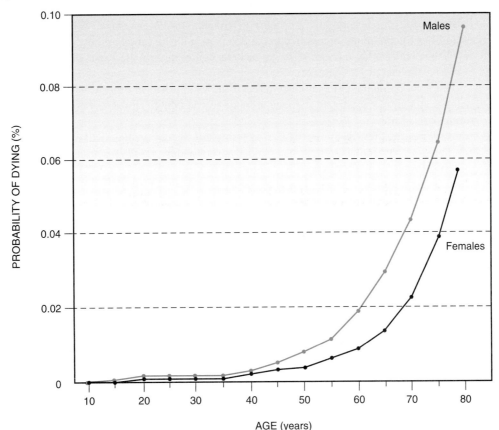

SOURCE: Adapted from the Statistics Canada publication *Selected Mortality Statistics, Canada, 1921–1990*, Catalogue 82–548, March 1994, Table 5, pages 59–60.

FIGURE 5.3   OVERPAYMENT AND UNDERPAYMENT TO SUSTAIN A LEVEL PREMIUM

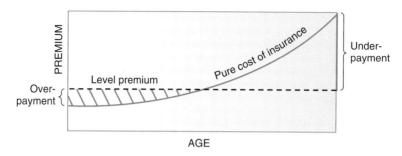

the amount of the level premium on the curve of risk, or the pure cost of insurance, it is obvious that in the early years of the contract the premium is higher than the pure cost, but in later years it is lower (Figure 5.3). The reserve accumulated from the overpayment at the beginning, together with the interest generated by that reserve, helps to meet the higher cost of coverage in the later period.

When an insurer writes an insurance policy to cover an individual for his or her entire life, the insurer assumes a liability that is certain. In other words, the insurer has promised to pay a specific sum when the insured person dies—a situation with 100-percent probability; this is an important feature distinguishing life insurance from other forms of insurance. Many policies on homes, cars, and personal liability do not result in claims, and of those that do, few require payment of the maximum coverage. When an insurer establishes the premium for a policy to cover a person for life, the premium must be set at a level that will enable enough reserves to be accumulated in the early years so that the certain claim can be paid later on.

The level premium and the policy reserves are established in order to ensure that there will be enough money to pay the face amount to the beneficiary or beneficiaries at some future date. However, if the policyholder decides to cancel the policy, the insurance company is relieved of the promise to pay the face amount, and the reserve fund will not be needed; it can therefore be refunded to the policyholder or retained by the life insurance company.

Unfortunately, much of the life insurance literature (and sales pitch) refers to policy reserves as the savings feature. The policy reserves are available to the policyholder only if the policy is cancelled or the coverage reduced; it is impossible to have both full life insurance coverage and access to the policy reserves at the same time. (See Personal Finance in Action Box 5.2, "Alec and Katrina Cancel Their Policies.") Life insurance will be easier to understand if you remember that a policy's cash value is the reserve required to cover the certain liability that the company has assumed.

Factors Affecting Cost

A number of factors affect the cost of life insurance, including mortality rate, loading charges, the frequency of premium payments, whether or not it is a participating policy, and the type of policy.

Mortality Rate

Mortality rate is the primary determinant of the price you will pay for life insurance. To estimate your mortality risk, an actuary would need to know your age and gender, the

Alec and Katrina Cancel Their Policies

When Alec and Katrina first got married they followed the advice of her father and purchased whole life insurance policies on both their lives. (See "Whole Life Insurance" later in the chapter for more details.) The face values were $150 000 each, and they paid premiums of $64 and $62 a month each.

By the time Alec and Katrina were 48, they had paid off their mortgage and their two daughters had moved out. With no other dependents and no debts, they decided to cancel the policies and use the money they paid monthly for life insurance for saving for their retirement. They informed the insurance company of their plan, and the policy reserves of $8650 and $7950 were returned to them tax-free. When Alec and Katrina cancelled their policies, their life insurance company had no further liability to them. Both of them did, however, have life insurance policies through their employers, more monthly income, and some cash as well.

state of your health, your and your family's medical history, and whether you engage in any hazardous activities. Your cost will be raised by anything that increases the risk of death (for instance, smoking or skydiving). If the insurance company considers the probability of your dying soon to be too high, the company will not insure your life. Fortunately, the proportion of applicants who are rejected is very small (only about 2 percent), but people who are classified as higher-than-average risks do sometimes have to pay larger premiums. Consider your life expectancy based on the chart presented as Table 5.1. Are you a good risk?

TABLE 5.1 LIFE EXPECTANCY, BY AGE GROUP AND SEX, CANADA, 1996 AND 2002

	1996	2002	DIFFERENCE
Men			
0	75.5	77.2	1.8
1–4	74.9	76.7	1.8
5–9	71.0	72.8	1.7
10–14	66.1	67.8	1.7
15–19	61.2	62.9	1.7
20–24	56.4	58.1	1.7
25–29	51.6	53.3	1.6
30–34	46.9	48.5	1.6
35–39	42.2	43.7	1.5
40–44	37.5	38.9	1.5
45–49	32.9	34.3	1.4
50–54	28.3	29.7	1.4
55–59	24.0	25.3	1.3
60–64	19.9	21.1	1.2
65–69	16.1	17.2	1.1
70–74	12.7	13.7	1.0
75–79	9.8	10.5	0.8
80–84	7.3	7.9	0.6
85–89	5.4	5.6	0.3
90+	3.9	4.1	0.2

continued

TABLE 5.1   LIFE EXPECTANCY, BY AGE GROUP AND SEX, CANADA,
1996 AND 2002 (CONTINUED)

	1996	2002	DIFFERENCE
Women			
O	81.2	82.1	0.9
1–4	80.6	81.5	0.9
5–9	76.7	77.6	0.9
10–14	71.8	72.6	0.8
15–19	66.8	67.7	0.8
20–24	61.9	62.8	0.8
25–29	57.0	57.9	0.8
30–34	52.1	53.0	0.8
35–39	47.3	48.1	0.8
40–44	42.4	43.3	0.8
45–49	37.7	38.5	0.8
50–54	33.0	33.8	0.8
55–59	28.5	29.2	0.7
60–64	24.1	24.8	0.7
65–69	20.0	20.6	0.6
70–74	16.1	16.7	0.6
75–79	12.5	13.0	0.5
80–84	9.4	9.8	0.4
85–89	6.8	7.0	0.2
90+	4.8	5.0	0.1

SOURCE: Statistics Canada, Catalogue 82–003, Health Reports, Vol. 17, No. 1, November 2005.

Loading Charges

In addition to the pure cost of insuring a life, an amount called the loading charge is included in the premium. The company's **loading charge** includes administrative costs, commissions to salespeople, and profit for shareholders. The largest component of a loading charge is the commission to life insurance agents, which may range from 13 percent to 110 percent of the first year's premium. The commission on renewals may range from 2 percent to 15 percent. Individual life insurance policies are sold by sales agents who depend on commissions for income and who must therefore search energetically for clients, a very expensive method of selling. Other financial institutions—especially banks—are also involved in selling insurance. With the recent collaboration among banks and life insurance companies, such as CIBC with Great-West Life and TD with Sun Life, in the areas of joint marketing loan insurance, it will be interesting to see the future landscape of the insurance industry.

Offsetting these loading costs to some extent is the income that may be earned on the pooled funds, which the company can invest until claims are made. Life insurance companies, as managers of the pooled insurance funds, usually collect more than they expect to pay out in claims, not just to establish policy reserves, but also to set up special reserve funds in case their estimates are too low.

Frequency of Premium Payments

Your total cost per year will vary slightly, depending on how frequently you pay the premiums. If you pay annually, the total cost is lower than if you were to pay either semi-annually or monthly. These differences reflect the amount of income the company knows that it can obtain by investing the premium funds.

Participating and Non-Participating Policies

The difference between participating and non-participating policies lies in the way the premiums are calculated. Premiums for **non-participating policies** are estimated as accurately as possible and cannot be increased by the company. If the company turns out to have underestimated or overestimated the cost, the difference is met from the company's funds or by changing the premium rates on policies sold in the future. For **participating policies**, the premiums are usually set somewhat higher than for non-participating ones, but the policyholder will receive a refund on any excess. These refunds are called **dividends**; but the term is confusing since, unlike stock dividends, these are not a form of income. Because they are refunds, they are not subject to income tax. In other words, insurance dividends are a return of after-tax dollars.

In any one year, the dividend amount will depend on such factors as the company's efficiency, its return on investments, the amount that has been paid out in claims, and the number of policies that have been cancelled. Dividends may be taken in cash, used to pay the next premium, used to buy more insurance, or left on deposit to earn interest. Although the dividends themselves are not considered taxable income, any income they generate will be taxable.

Basic Types of Life Insurance

Distinguishing Features

A life insurance policy, however it may be labelled to interest prospective buyers, is almost always one of two types of policy—term or whole life—or a combination of the two. The variety of labels has led to unnecessary confusion. Despite the lack of uniform terminology, you may identify the fundamental policy type if you have a good understanding of the distinguishing features of each. Two important characteristics to consider are whether or not

(a) the coverage is for life,

(b) the policy accumulates a cash value.

Term insurance is coverage for a specific period, without cash value, while whole life provides lifelong protection, with cash value.

Term Insurance

Like fire or auto insurance, **term insurance** provides protection against a specified risk for a definite period of time. At the end of that time, or term, the insurance lapses unless it is renewed. The important characteristic of term insurance is that it represents protection for a designated period—not for life. Term insurance may be purchased for periods of various lengths; periods of one year, five years, and ten years are common. It is also possible to buy term to age 65, or even to age 100. A product called "term to 100" adds to the confusion by offering coverage for life with no cash value.

Because most buyers of term insurance have a fairly low probability of dying in the near future—they are usually under 65 years of age—and because the company does not assume coverage for life, the cost of term insurance is lower than that for other types. The premium is made level for the term of the policy; any reserves accumulated are relatively small and will

FIGURE 5.4   PREMIUM LEVELS FOR FIVE-YEAR RENEWABLE TERM INSURANCE
BY GENDER AND AGE

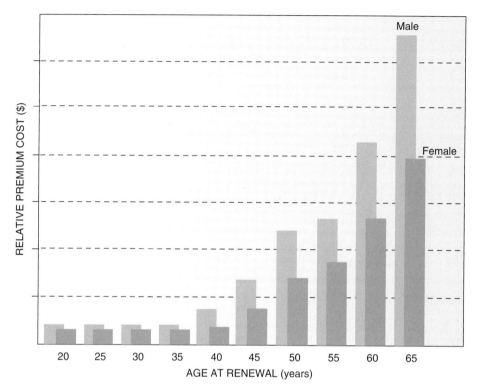

be used up during the term. For these reasons, no cash value is available to the policyholder. As with all life insurance, the face value will be paid to the beneficiary or beneficiaries if the insured dies while the policy is in force. However, from the insurer's point of view, the probability of paying claims on term insurance is low; the insurer has not taken on the certain liability that it assumes for policies with lifelong coverage.

Although the premium for term insurance is level for the specified term, at the next renewal the premium must necessarily be raised, since the insured has aged and the probability of his or her dying has therefore increased. Figure 5.4 illustrates the changes in premium at each renewal as the pure cost of life insurance rises. By age 65, the pure cost of life insurance becomes very high, and few term policies are offered because of the limited market at that price.

Term insurance offers the most face value per premium dollar of any type of life insurance because it does not give protection at advanced ages (when the cost of insurance is high). As illustrated in Figure 5.5, for every $100 that you can afford to spend each year on life insurance, you will obtain more face amount (life insurance coverage) with term insurance than with other types of policies. Although this is a useful comparison, there are two caveats. First, the insurer's liability is not the same with each type of policy shown, where the policies vary from five years to life. Second, the premiums shown in this comparison have been made level for different periods, involving varying amounts of reserve funds. Looked at in another way, for a given amount of life insurance, the annual cost will be lowest for term coverage.

Decreasing Term Insurance
Thus far we have discussed term insurance with a face amount that is constant throughout the term. However, it is also possible to buy

FIGURE 5.5   FACE AMOUNT BY POLICY TYPE FOR A GIVEN PREMIUM

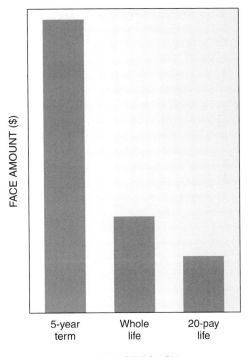

term insurance with a decreasing face amount. This option is useful when the risk being covered is expected to diminish. It is often used as mortgage insurance by people who wish to leave their dependents a debt-free home in the event of their death. At the outset, the policy's face amount is equal to the outstanding debt on the house, but the face amount decreases at a rate roughly equal to that at which the debt is expected to be reduced. If the insured dies during the term, the policy's face amount at that time should be adequate to pay the outstanding balance on the mortgage. The beneficiary is, of course, under no obligation to use the death benefit for this purpose. It is simply a life insurance policy that will pay a certain sum to the beneficiary when the insured dies. One may argue that special mortgage insurance is unnecessary if overall life insurance coverage is adequate.

Decreasing term insurance can also provide income protection for a young family. Many people feel that it is wise to arrange their insurance coverage to match the period of highest financial risk, so that coverage is at a maximum when the children are very young. As the children grow, the risk decreases, and so may the need for life insurance. While decreasing term insurance is appropriate for such a situation, the impact of inflation requires consideration.

The face amount of a decreasing term policy falls to zero at the end of the term, with downward adjustments monthly or annually. Premiums, however, are level for the term, probably to discourage policyholders from cancelling the policy when the coverage becomes low. Some companies set a level premium for a period shorter than the entire term; for instance, the premiums on a 20-year decreasing term policy might be paid up in 16 years. Term insurance and decreasing term insurance are compared in Figure 5.6.

FIGURE 5.6   TERM AND DECREASING TERM INSURANCE

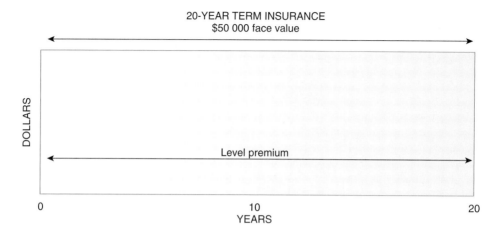

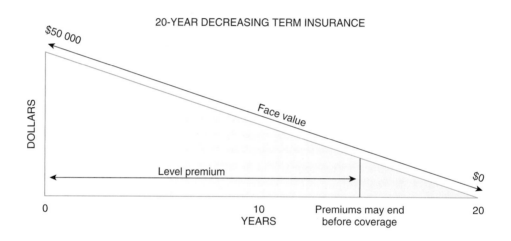

Group Life Insurance   Life insurance may be purchased by individuals or groups. In its most common form, group insurance is bought by employers to cover the lives of a large group of employees. Payment for this insurance may be shared by employer and employee; alternatively, one or the other may pay the entire amount. In either event, one policy covers a group of lives. Usually no medical examinations are required as evidence of insurability, but there are some rules. These rules are intended to avoid a selection of risks that might be adverse to the insurance company. For instance, all employees may be required to join the group plan; or, if there is a choice, employees may be required to join at a specific time, perhaps when they begin employment. In any case, such a plan will be arranged so that most employees cannot avoid being insured. The amount of coverage will also depend on a rule: the face amount may be some multiple of the employee's annual salary, or all employees may be covered for the same amount. There may be an option to purchase more coverage.

Group insurance is most often based on a one-year renewable term, but it can be converted to whole life insurance. Since employees of all ages pay the same premium or rate, group coverage can be a bargain for the older worker. The coverage usually ends whenever an employee terminates employment, but the option of converting, within a month of retiring, from the group policy to individual term or whole life may exist. The premiums for group policies are usually lower than those for similar insurance bought individually because selling and administration costs are decreased when a single policy covers a large group of lives. The employer collects the premiums and pays the insurer for the group.

Credit Life Insurance   A specialized version of group term insurance, known as **credit life insurance**, is purchased by lenders to cover the lives of a group of borrowers. If a borrower should die with a debt still outstanding, the insurer will reimburse the creditor for the balance owing. Ultimately, the cost of such insurance is borne by the borrower, who may or may not be given a choice about having the loan life-insured. This type of insurance is certainly of interest to creditors, who are not keen to see debt repayments cease when a borrower dies; it can also be useful to anyone who is anxious not to leave a debt that must be paid out of his or her estate.

Homeowners frequently purchase from their lending institution a common form of group term insurance—that is, **mortgage insurance**. As the principal owing on the mortgage decreases, so too does the amount that would be paid to the lending institution should one of the homeowners die prematurely. This is an easy method of insuring your mortgage but may be more expensive than buying a straight term policy; it definitely offers less flexibility for the survivors, who may need more coverage than merely having the mortgage paid off or may not wish to pay off a low-rate mortgage.

Women take CHARGE 5.1

Irene, a single mother with two children, is reviewing her financial plan with regard to insurance needs. Even though she is launched on a successful career with an agency that provides a life insurance package as a benefit, Irene would like to obtain additional insurance independent of her employment since she is the sole support of her children and has a mortgage to pay off.

She would like a policy that would continue even after she retires. The children would be the named beneficiaries on the policy. Since children do not receive the same privileges as spouses in estate planning, the insurance would provide liquidity for her estate. The insurance could be used to pay the taxes on "deemed distribution" of the capital gains on assets held in the estate without the children having to sell the assets. The insurance proceeds could be used to pay other debts as well.

A term insurance policy would provide more insurance for the premium, but there would be issues with renewals and premium increases over the years.

On the other hand, whole life or permanent insurance would be more expensive but would provide for the creation of a cash reserve where savings accumulate, tax-sheltered. The cash reserve could be used to take out a policy loan or pay premiums when resources were low. The premium would stay the same over the years.

Irene has decided to take out a term-100 policy for $400 000. Being healthy and a non-smoker will help in minimizing the cost of the premium. The savings in premium costs over whole life insurance will enable her to look at critical illness and long-term insurance.

Critical illness and long-term care insurance provide coverage when you are alive. The long-term care insurance would pay benefits if she needed long-term institutional or home care. The critical illness policy would provide benefits if she came down with a serious illness covered by the policy. Irene and the children always take out travel insurance when they travel outside Canada to cover any unexpected medical costs. All of these opportunities for handling risk should be considered in a family's financial plan.

Critical Illness Insurance Many lenders are also offering, in conjunction with life insurance companies, **critical illness insurance,** as discussed in earlier chapters. This insurance, more expensive than life insurance, offers coverage for major illnesses that may occur. Different from mortgage insurance mentioned above, critical illness insurance is more flexible for the insured about what can be done with the benefits, but at the same time it is priced as a group program and may be available at a premium rate that would be accessible to the individual. Generally if the individual is diagnosed with cancer, heart attack, or stroke there is a one-time lump-sum payment to the beneficiary that will likely ease financial worries, enabling the stricken person to focus on getting well. (Critical illness insurance is part of the insurance package envisioned by one single mother in this chapter's Women Take Charge.)

Whole Life Insurance

A type of insurance commonly bought by individuals is **whole life insurance** (also called straight life or ordinary life). It provides insurance protection from the time of purchase until death (Figure 5.7). To maintain this lifelong coverage, premiums must be paid each year as long as the insured lives—unless the premiums are prepaid. Some companies terminate the

FIGURE 5.7   TYPES OF LIFE INSURANCE

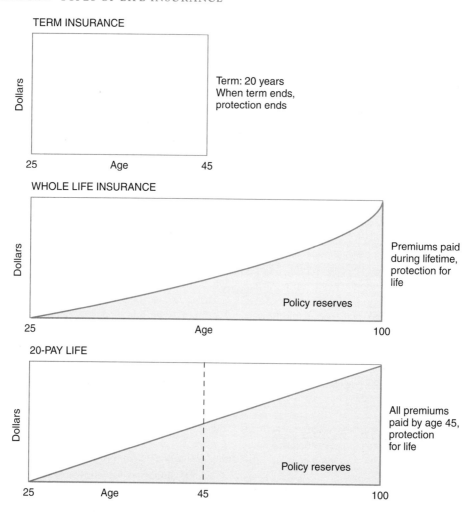

policies before the policyholders reach a very advanced age, such as 95, and pay the policy-holder the face amount at that time. The premium, which is established at the time of purchase, is level for life.

In addition to its long duration, another distinguishing feature of whole life insurance is the accumulation of policy reserves, also known as **cash reserves** or **cash surrender value**. From Figure 5.3, you will recall that in order to have a level premium, the policyholder in effect overpays during the early years and underpays later. Because the early payments exceed the pure cost of insurance, they create a reserve that in turn grows over time as more premiums are paid and the reserve funds earn interest.

Any cash reserves created in the first year or two help to pay the company's selling and issue expenses, including commissions, and therefore the policy has no cash value at first. A sample whole life policy is reproduced in Appendix 5A. This policy has a table (of guaranteed values) showing a cash value for each year that the insurance is in force. To read the table, find the Age column (which represents the policyholder's age at the time of purchase), which in this case is 30. Assume that you wish to know the cash value five years later. This policy was for $50 000; therefore, the cash value after five years would be $715. The reserves continue to grow each year until around age 100, when the cash value will equal the face amount (Figure 5.7).

It is impossible to use the cash reserves while also maintaining full insurance coverage. The policy states that if Mr. Hill (the insured person) dies, the policy's full face amount will be paid to the beneficiary. Whenever that happens, the policy terminates—and so does the cash value. However, during Hill's lifetime, he can use the cash reserves if he is willing to diminish the coverage accordingly. A number of uses for the cash reserves will be outlined under "Uses for the Cash Reserves," later in this chapter.

Limited Payment Life Insurance A variation on whole life insurance is the **limited payment policy**, which, as the name indicates, is completely paid for during a specified period. Instead of paying premiums for life, the insured pays higher premiums for a shorter time, usually 20 years or to age 65. After it is paid up, the policy remains in force for the rest of the insured's life. This type of policy is selected when the insured expects to be able to pay for insurance more readily early in life, and thus may be appropriate for people who expect high incomes for a short time, such as professional athletes. However, for most families this type of policy cannot provide sufficient coverage when it is most needed.

The more rapid rate of payment with limited payment insurance causes the cash surrender value of such a policy to increase faster than with whole life. After the payment period ends, the cash surrender value continues to grow (Figure 5.7). Except for the shorter payment period, limited-pay life is similar in most respects to whole life insurance; the cash surrender value can also be used in the same ways.

Combination Policies

There are too many variations and combinations of the two basic types of life insurance to consider them all here. As well, the industry is constantly inventing new versions. We will discuss three combination types: universal life, family income policy, and family policy.

Universal Life Insurance

The rigidity of having to face a fixed premium for life with an inflexible face amount to be paid many years later has not always been attractive to insurance buyers. For instance, in inflationary periods, insurance coverage once thought to be sufficient to provide for dependents may become inadequate because of lost purchasing power. If you want to invest your savings with an insurance company, you may prefer to keep insurance coverage and savings separate. **Universal life insurance**, invented to offer buyers such flexibility, is a combination of term insurance and a savings account.

The distinctive features of universal life are (i) the flexibility in payments, (ii) the opportunity to withdraw funds, (iii) the freedom to alter the amount of insurance coverage at any time, and (iv) the regular disclosure of fees, interest earned, and other information. These features contrast with those of traditional policies, where the buyer does not know (i) how the premiums are divided among the pure cost of insurance, the policy reserves, and the loading charges, or (ii) what rate of interest is being credited on the reserves.

Flexible Payments

The payment of money into a universal life policy is voluntary within prescribed limits. The money is used to create a fund from which the company deducts the cost of insurance protection—which is rather like term coverage—and a loading charge. The balance is credited with interest and treated as a sort of investment fund from which the policyholder may make withdrawals. The policyholder can choose how much to put in each year, but if he or she does not make any payments for a time, the insurance cost will be deducted from the fund. If the company deducts the pure cost of insurance each year, this deduction will increase as the policyholder grows older.

Withdrawal Privileges

The funds in the cash account are available for you to withdraw from or borrow against as you wish. If you leave the money in the account, you will draw interest at current rates. A minimum rate may be guaranteed for a year.

Flexible Coverage

Changing your coverage may be possible, within limits, as your needs change. However, the flexibility in premiums sometimes leads buyers to forget payments, with consequent loss of coverage.

Regular Statements

You will receive regular statements showing all the transactions in your account. These statements will keep you informed about your coverage and its cost, the loading charges, and the return on the cash account.

Caveats for Buyers

Prospective buyers of universal life insurance should be aware of all the possible charges—for example, one-time administrative fees, loading charges, and surrender charges. Buyers should also know how the loading charges will be distributed. Some companies deduct loading charges before depositing the premium in the account, while others first credit the premium and then deduct charges. Some may charge an initial fee and then add a loading charge of 5 percent to 10 percent, as well as a fee for each withdrawal. A loading charge may be a constant proportion of each premium, front-loaded, or back-loaded. If in the early years of the policy the loading charge is a larger share of the premium, the policy is referred to as **front-loaded**. When little is deducted from the premiums at the outset for loading charges, but a disproportionate share is added when a policy is surrendered, the policy is **back-loaded**. Some companies may impose very high surrender charges if the policy is cancelled within a few years. However, if the policy remains in force for some years, the surrender charges usually diminish.

Other aspects to investigate include the tax treatment of interest, buried fees, and the costs and benefits of having insurance coverage combined with a savings account, along with the payments to beneficiaries (with respect to tax treatment) and the nature of the various fees. It is also possible that some charges may be buried in changing rates for the "pure cost of insurance." Companies may use high interest rates to attract buyers, but decrease them later, or project unrealistic future interest rates. Thought should be given to the wisdom of combining a term life policy and an investment fund in one contract, instead of making separate arrangements for each.

Family Income Policy

Term and whole life insurance can be combined in various ways to make a **family income policy** (Figure 5.8). The insured person is usually the family's principal income earner. The whole life portion of the policy covers the insured for life, paying a specified amount on his or her death, whenever it may occur. The term portion provides coverage for a definite period—for example, 20 years. If the insured dies during the term, the policy will provide an income for dependents that will continue for the remainder of the term. If the insured lives more than 20 years after buying the policy, the term coverage will have expired, but the whole life coverage will continue.

Family Policy

Some insurers may offer a **family policy**, which is a package with separate coverage for the husband, the wife, and each present and future child. This policy may involve only term

FIGURE 5.8 FAMILY POLICY AND FAMILY INCOME POLICY

FAMILY POLICY

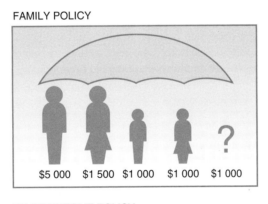

$5 000 $1 500 $1 000 $1 000 $1 000

FAMILY INCOME POLICY

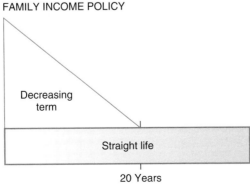

Decreasing term

Straight life

20 Years

insurance, or a combination of term and whole life. In the latter instance, the whole life coverage would probably be on the life of the principal earner. If any family member should die during the term of his or her coverage, the insurer will pay the coverage for that individual, but the package will continue to cover the lives of the survivors. The buyer should evaluate the risks to the family's economic situation of the death of each family member.

The Insurance Policy

A life insurance policy is a contract between the insuring company and the policyholder. Some aspects of this complex legal document will be outlined here. A life insurance contract is not a contract of indemnity—unlike property insurance, where the insured is to be indemnified, that is, returned to his or her financial position that existed before the loss occurred. With a life insurance policy, a predictable sum of money is payable by the insurer—an important distinction. For a sample whole life policy, see Appendix 5A.

Description of Policy

Near the beginning of the printed policy, there should be such basic information as the face amount, the type of policy, the name of the insured person, the insured's age, the date the coverage begins, the period during which the insurance is to be effective, and the amount of the premium.

Grace Period

The policyholder is usually given a **grace period** of one month after the date the premium is due, during which the insurance remains in force and the premium may be paid without penalty. If the insured should die during the grace period, the beneficiary or beneficiaries will receive the face value less the amount of the unpaid premium.

Dividends

The dividend clause in a participating policy covers the details of the company's payment of dividends and describes the various options available to the policyholder. The insured may take the dividends in cash, use them to reduce the premium, use them to reduce indebtedness, use them to purchase paid-up additions to the life insurance in force or one-year term additions, or leave them on deposit with the company to earn interest. The range of options available is determined by the company.

Incontestability

To protect themselves from future legal actions arising from alleged misrepresentations by the insured, life insurance companies have instituted an **incontestability clause**. This clause states that after the policy has been in force for two years, it cannot be invalidated by any nondisclosure or misrepresentation that may be discovered, with the exception of fraud. During these two years, the company can seek to be released from the contract if it discovers that the applicant made false statements.

Policy Loans

For any policy with cash reserves, the conditions under which policy loans are available will be stated somewhere in the policy. Related to these conditions is the automatic premium loan, which provides that if a policyholder fails to pay the premium or take certain other actions (such as requesting a grace period for delayed payments), the company will use the cash surrender value to pay the premium and will continue to do so as required until the cash value has been exhausted.

Ownership Rights and Assignment

The rights of the life insurance policy owner include the right to name and change the beneficiary or beneficiaries, to use the cash value, to receive any dividends, and to dispose of any of these rights. If one person holds all of these rights, that person is the sole owner of the policy; if the policy's ownership is shared with one or more other people, each becomes a part or joint owner. Usually the person insured and the owner are the same. Like other contracts, a life insurance policy is assignable—that is, its ownership may be transferred. For example, when a policy is used as collateral for a loan, the policy is assigned to the creditor.

Beneficiary

The beneficiary clause identifies the person(s) or organizations intended to receive the proceeds of the insurance in the event of the policyholder's death. In most cases, the insured may alter the designation of beneficiary by signing a declaration to be filed with the insurance company. Sometimes people forget to sign and file a declaration when family conditions change, leaving the insurance payable to an estranged, divorced, or deceased spouse. Insurance proceeds payable to a named beneficiary are not distributed through the deceased's will but go directly to the person designated, free from claims that creditors or others may have on the estate, including the Canada Revenue Agency (tax-free).

If the primary beneficiary dies before the person whose life has been insured, and no alternative (secondary) beneficiary has been named, the company may pay the proceeds to the estate of the deceased. Only rarely will a policyholder name a beneficiary irrevocably, which means that the designation of beneficiary cannot be changed without the consent of the beneficiary. In such instances, the policyholder cannot assign the cash surrender value of the policy to a third party without the consent of the named **irrevocable beneficiary**.

Settlement Options

The way in which the proceeds of a life insurance policy will be paid to the beneficiary may be settled by the insured, prior to death, or may be left to the beneficiary's discretion. There are several ways in which life insurance can be paid, other than as a lump sum. The interest option involves leaving the principal sum on deposit with the insurance company, where it will collect interest regularly. In the instalment option, the proceeds are paid in instalments over a selected period of time by various arrangements, all involving payment of principal and interest. The proceeds can also be used to purchase a single-payment annuity (life income), with payments to begin either immediately or at a later date; this is sometimes referred to as the life income option. (Annuities are explained in the chapter on retirement income.)

Viatical Settlements

Another, smaller but potentially growing area in the settlement of life insurance proceeds is **viatical settlements**. These settlements are sometimes arranged when a person is unable to acquire long-term disability insurance or critical illness insurance due to existing conditions, or when a person is entering a long-term care facility (such as a nursing home) and has limited resources to live on. In such cases, an opportunity may exist—though at the time of writing this is more an American trend than a Canadian one—to sell the current life insurance policy that is still in force. In these "viatical" arrangements the purchaser of the insurance policy becomes the new beneficiary. He or she continues to pay the premiums till the death of the named individual and then receives the value of the insurance policy. The amount of money that is paid for the policy varies but can be upwards of half the face value, depending on the life expectancy of the named person.

The Canadian life insurance industry has not adopted this practice as fully as in the USA, where viaticals are even considered a reasonable investment for some persons. The real benefit, however, is intended for the insured and his or her family, to help them meet their unanticipated financial needs. Viatical settlements should be very carefully thought out and treated as strictly financial transactions.

Uses for the Cash Reserves

The policy reserve, also known as the cash value or the cash surrender value, has a number of possible uses during the policyholder's lifetime; five of them will be reviewed here:

(a) Surrender of the policy

(b) Policy loan

(c) Automatic premium loan

(d) Collateral for a loan

(e) Paid-up policy

Surrender of the Policy

One obvious use of the cash value involves cancelling or surrendering the policy and taking the cash value, effectively terminating the insurance coverage. The table of cash values (or guaranteed values) in the policy shows how much the cash value is according to the number of years the policy has been in force (see Appendix 5A for an example).

Policy Loan

It is possible to arrange a **policy loan,** or to borrow from the cash surrender value, usually at an interest rate that is lower than the rate on loans from other sources. (See Personal Finance in Action Box 5.3, "Mimi Takes Out a Policy Loan.") There is no pressure to repay a policy loan, but in the meantime the interest continues to accumulate. If the insured should die before the loan is repaid, the unpaid balance and outstanding interest will be deducted from the face value of the policy before the proceeds are paid to the beneficiary or beneficiaries.

Personal FINANCE in action 5.3

Mimi Takes Out a Policy Loan

As she reviewed her finances in preparation for buying a new car, Mimi remembered that she had a whole life insurance policy, purchased 20 years previously. Since her children were now independent and her need for life insurance protection had therefore declined, it occurred to her that a policy loan might be appropriate. On calling her insurance agent, she discovered that the current rate on policy loans was 4 percent, with interest calculated annually on the policy's anniversary date. The maximum cash value available for a loan on this policy was $15 000.

Mimi decided to request a policy loan and to let the interest accumulate as a claim against the policy. Seven years later, when Mimi died, the insurance company paid her beneficiary the policy's face value minus the outstanding debt. The amount was determined as follows:

Face amount of policy: $50 000.00

Amount of loan: 15 000.00

Compound interest factor:
(1%, for 7 years) 1.32

Principal + interest due:
$15 000 × 1.32 = $19 800.00

Amount payable to beneficiary:
$50 000 − 19 800 = $30 200.00

Automatic Premium Loan

The cash surrender value may be used to pay the premiums if for some reason the policyholder does not do so. Such an arrangement is essentially the same as a policy loan because the face value will be reduced by the amount used for this purpose. However, for the **automatic premium loan**, the company will use the cash value to pay the premiums rather than let the policy lapse if the policyholder takes no action. Policyholders who have assumed that their policy has lapsed because they have stopped paying premiums might be surprised to learn how much longer their coverage extends. If the insured should die, the face amount would be diminished by the amount of any such loan.

Collateral for a Loan

The cash surrender value may also be used as collateral for a loan. To use the cash value this way, the insured must transfer the right to the cash surrender value to the creditor until the loan is repaid. If the insured defaults on the loan, the creditor can cash in the policy and retain whatever is owed. Such an event would effectively terminate the policy. Should the insured die during the term of the loan, the outstanding balance would have to be paid either from the insurance proceeds or from the estate.

Paid-Up Policy

Instead of cancelling the policy and taking the cash surrender value, the policyholder can use the cash value to purchase a **paid-up policy** with a smaller face value. (See Personal Finance in Action Box 5.4, "Choose a Paid-Up Policy.") This approach is, in effect, a single-premium purchase of life insurance. The amount of the face value will depend on the amount of the cash surrender value at that time. Policies usually include tables that show, for each year the policy is in force, the cash value in addition to the amount of paid-up insurance that the cash value will purchase. Alternatively, the policyholder could use the cash surrender value to purchase term insurance with a larger face value.

FIGURE 5.9 PERCENTAGE DISTRIBUTION OF INDIVIDUAL AND GROUP LIFE
INSURANCE OWNED, 1960–2004

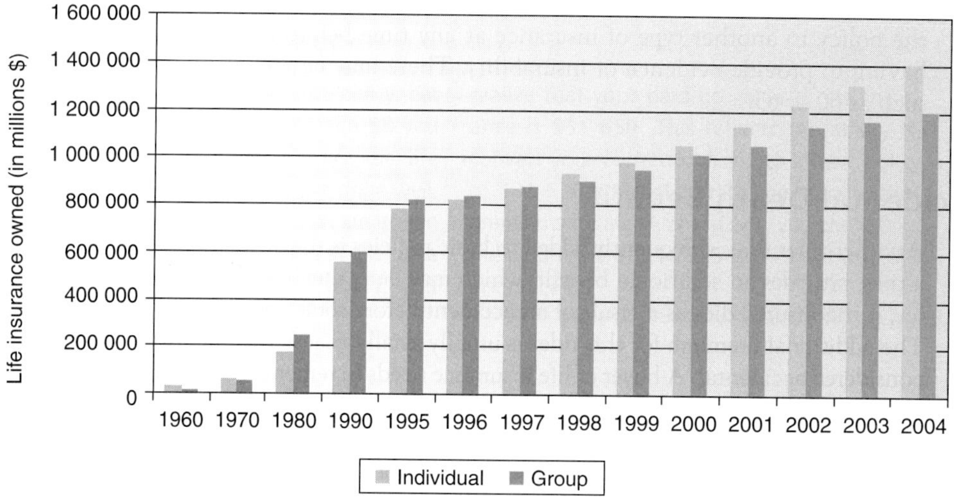

SOURCE: Reprinted from the "Canadian Life and Health Insurance Facts, 2004 edition," with the permission of the Canadian Life and Health Insurance Association Inc.

lives of the wrong people. The combination of uninformed buyers and high-pressure sales techniques can be disastrous for some families.

Individual or Group Policies   If you were to examine the total value of life insurance owned in Canada, you would see that the long-term trend, until recently, has been toward an increasing share for group insurance (Figure 5.9). Group insurance represented nearly 60 percent of all insurance owned in 1980, but that proportion had dropped somewhat by 2004 to 46 percent.

Characteristics of the Insured   The decision to buy life insurance is influenced by a number of variables, but most logically by the presence of dependents. The available industry data do not mention dependents but do include the insured's gender, age, and income. There is more coverage on the lives of males (68 percent) than on females (32 percent). With regard to age, the largest proportion of the coverage is on those over the age of 45. Buyers of life insurance tend to have incomes between $30 000 and $50 000. One might conclude, therefore, that over time mature males are the ones purchasing life insurance.

Type and Size of Policy   Although whole life policies have historically been the leading type sold to individuals (as opposed to groups), it is interesting to note that by 2004 whole life represented less than one-tenth of face value purchased individually. There was more term coverage (70 percent) than any other type, with the balance spread among universal life and various other combination policies. The average coverage purchased in 2004 was $199 900 each.

How Much to Buy

The following five steps provide a simplified way of estimating how much life insurance you may need. First, assume that your death could occur tomorrow. Who would need financial support and for how long? Refer to Table 5.2 for an example.

TABLE 5.2   CURRENT LIFE INSURANCE NEEDS

AS OF OCTOBER 10, 2006

1. **Available Assets**

Liquid Assets (Table 1.1 Subtotal A)	$ 15 250
Other Financial Assets, Including	
Pensions and RRSPs (Table 1.1 Subtotal B)	$ 179 900
Personal Assets to Be Liquidated	$ 37 500
Lump Sum Benefits (CPP, RPP, etc.)	$ 4 250
Group Life Insurance	$ 25 000
Mortgage Life Insurance	$ –
Personal Life Insurance	$ 250 000
Total Assets Available	$ 511 900 (A)

2. **Financial Expenses**

Funeral and Medical Expenses	$ 12 000
Debts, Excluding Mortgage	$ 54 500
Short-term Living Expenses (50% of Annual Salary)	$ 32 500
Income Taxes Due Including Capital Gains	$ 13 654
Mortgage Principal Outstanding	$ 125 000
Post-Secondary Education of Children	$ 120 000
Total Financial Assets Required	$ 357 654 (B)
Capital Available (Insurance Required) (A – B)	$ 154 246 (C)

3. **Annual Required Income**

Income Replacement (60% of Annual Salary		$ 48 750 (D)
if Mortgage is paid off or is covered elsewhere;		
otherwise 75% of Current Salary)		
Covered Elsewhere (yes = 1, no = 0)	0	
Annual Income or Value of Work Performed	$ 65 000	
Less EXTRA Annual Income from:		
Spouse's Income	$ –	
CPP/QPP pension	$ 4 236	
RPP	$ –	$ 4 236 (E)

Annual Required Income (D – E)	$ 44 514 (F)
4. **Capital Required to Generate Income (F / 0.10)**	$ 445 140 (G)
5. **Total Required Insurance (G – C)**	$ 290 894

1. Estimate your total available assets. Call this total A.
2. List the financial expenses that will need to be covered, including debts and future obligations (such as children's education). Call this total B.
3. The difference between A and B is the capital available, or C.
4. Calculate a percentage of your annual income or salary: 60 percent if your mortgage is paid off and 75 percent if it is not. If you are a stay-at-home parent who is the primary caregiver for a child or children, estimate the value of the services you provide (generally considered to be at least $20 000 per year) to cover the cost of housekeeping, daycare, and so on. This amount is D. Deduct from this amount the increase in income for the household from a spouse returning to work or from pension income such as CPP. This amount is E, and the difference between D and E is the annual increase in income that the household will need to generate from investments derived from life insurance; this increase is F.

5. Divide the net amount of annual income required, F, by a discount figure, expressed as a percent, to determine the gross amount of money that will be needed to generate that annual income. Table 5.1 uses 10 percent as a discount, to account for the declining need for money over time as dependents mature and leave the home and to generate the sum of additional or unneeded insurance; the result is G.

6. Deduct the total required insurance for immediate needs (C) from the total required for long-term needs (G) in the final calculation. This number is the starting point for discussion and for determining whether you have adequate coverage to maintain the lifestyle that the household would require and prefer should the breadwinner(s) die prematurely and leave dependents.

Selecting a Policy

Potential buyers of life insurance are advised to first define their needs and then obtain quotations from several companies. (See Personal Finance in Action Box 5.5 "Term or Whole Life?"). It may be difficult to make meaningful comparisons because different companies offer dissimilar insurance packages that protect against different risks. The more clearly you can specify your requirements before approaching an insurance agent, the greater the probability of getting comparable quotations.

Selling Methods

Individual life insurance policies are sold by salespeople who depend on commissions for their livelihood, thus creating a possible conflict of interest when they act as advisors to buyers. When companies pay higher commissions on certain types of policies, salespeople may attempt to sell those kinds rather than others. Generally, it has been possible to earn higher commissions by selling cash value policies than by selling term policies. A recent development is that agents are presenting themselves more as general financial planners than as insurance agents. If the planner's remuneration comes from commissions rather than from fees, conflicts of interest are bound to arise.

Another difficulty for consumers is the rapid turnover among life insurance salespeople; after three years, only 20 percent of agents remain in the business. Although some do make a career in insurance sales, the large number of new entrants lowers the overall knowledge and skill level. This situation, combined with the pressure on agents to sell, makes it essential that prospective buyers of life insurance be as well-informed as possible.

Protection for Buyers

Although there have been few instances of life insurance companies that have gone out of business and left policyholders unprotected, the industry has set up a compensation fund called Assuris to provide for such a contingency. For holders of segregated mutual funds, Assuris protects 85 percent of the value over $60 000 and 100 percent under $60 000. The Canadian Deposit Insurance Corporation insures up to $100 000 on deposits at banks, trust companies, and credit unions. Any accumulated values in a life insurance policy are fully protected up to $100 000, and cash values are fully guaranteed up to $60 000 and 85 percent above that threshold. This plan is similar to an insurance plan initiated by the general insurance companies in the event that one of their members were to go out of business.

Personal FINANCE in action 5.5

Term or Whole Life?

Rich, who is 30 years old and has two dependents, has decided that he requires $150 000 of life insurance coverage, but he wonders which type of policy to buy. With the information he has collected from agents, he plotted the annual premium costs (Figure 5.10). He was surprised to find that five-year term insurance, although much cheaper than whole life initially, would increase in cost at each renewal. This graph clarified for him the difference between the level premium for whole life and the increasing premiums for term. It also illustrated that until he turns 55, even the increasing premiums for term coverage will be significantly less than those for whole life. He now realizes that since his children should be independent in 15 years, he does not need whole life coverage. He has decided to buy five-year renewable term insurance.

FIGURE 5.10 ANNUAL PREMIUMS FOR FIVE-YEAR RENEWABLE TERM AND WHOLE LIFE INSURANCE, BY AGE

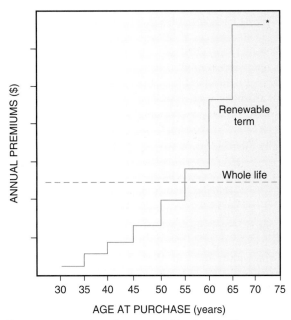

* Five-year renewable term insurance is no longer available after age 65.

Health Insurance

Like critical illness insurance, **health insurance** can support individuals and families through the financial fallout from a severe health crisis. Health insurance comes in many forms across Canada. As Canadians we are all covered by government programs that pay for hospital and doctor services as well as some other services, such as physiotherapy and home care. Still, many people are also covered by supplemental health insurance programs from their employers and pension plans that assist in paying for additional services. These programs generally cover one of three areas: long-term disability, extended health care, and dental care.

In 2004 over nine million workers were covered by **long-term disability insurance** that generally paid up to 70 percent of the normal pay of the insured, with payments usually commencing 90, 120, or 180 days after the diagnosis of disability. This money is usually tax-free, and hence the beneficiary of such policies is generally no better or worse off financially than before the disability. The benefits can be complex in their determination by the insurance company because of the various levels of disability and the opportunity of some of the disabled to return to some level of employment. The benefits usually terminate after a stated term or at a stipulated age such as 65. Frequently this form of coverage is part of a benefit package provided by an employer, so those who are self-employed need to pay particular attention to this kind of coverage. The argument for long-term disability insurance is especially compelling when we consider that 20-year-old males have a three-times greater chance of being disabled during their working life than dying, and women have a seven-times greater chance between the ages of 35 and 65. We may all consider life insurance, but disability insurance is even more likely to be needed.

Almost 20 million Canadians are enrolled in an **extended health care** plan that covers such items as semi-private or private hospital rooms, prescription drugs, special duty nursing, paramedical services such as chiropractors and naturopaths, ambulance services, artificial limbs, prostheses and medical appliances, wheelchair rentals, and vision care. These various forms of coverage have become especially important as government programs have rationalized the services they pay for and the insurance companies have expanded their coverage to those delisted services. Frequently, though, these kinds of services require a deductible to be paid by the insured, after which the insurance company covers the rest of the expenses to an agreed-upon limit.

Dental care coverage is another form of frequently acquired insurance, currently covering almost 11 million Canadians. Generally these programs cover preventive and maintenance procedures such as root canals and cleanings, and sometimes restorative procedures such as crowns, dentures, and braces, to name a few. Again there is likely to be a limit on some procedures, especially the restorative ones.

Another form of extended coverage provided by the life and health insurance industry is what is frequently referred to as travel insurance. **Travel insurance** may actually be included in your extended health care plan at work, but check to see the limitations of the coverage. These plans are there to help cover expenses should a traveller become ill while away and require treatment abroad or a return trip to Canada for treatment. They may also include interruption insurance, should the trip be cut short for any one of many reasons, such as a death or illness in the family, and cancellation insurance, in case the insured has to cancel the trip because of work, health, or family issues. These types of coverage may be purchased through travel agents, banks, and trust companies, and sometimes they are available through the use of bank or trust company "gold" cards and other credit cards. Once again, it is wise to confirm the kinds of coverage offered and the conditions upon which they come into effect. Remember, these policies are for emergencies, not routine procedures, and some of these emergencies can cost $20 000 to $30 000 per day. Also, if you are also planning an extended stay within Canada but outside your home province, it is wise to notify your provincial health insurance office for advice. There is even health insurance coverage available for visitors to Canada.

Summary

- The life insurance policy's face amount (face value) is the maximum value the company is liable for. The beneficiary is the person stated in the policy to be the eventual recipient of the proceeds of the contract. Insurable interest is when an individual would face a financial loss if the event occurred or is related to the individual. The pure cost of life insurance is the upward-curving cost of life insurance as the insured ages. A level premium is an agreed premium for life insurance that does not change during the term of the policy.

■ Non-participating policies do not have fluctuating premiums regardless if there were incorrect calculations of the premium. Participating policies generally have higher premiums than non-participating but refund any excess premiums. Dividends are refunds of excess premiums.

■ Term insurance provides a specified coverage for a set time. Credit life insurance is purchased by a lender to cover any loss should a creditor die. Mortgage insurance is a form of life insurance with the lender as the beneficiary and usually the agent as well. Whole life insurance provides life insurance till death at a set rate. Cash reserves (cash surrender value) are the monies that have accrued in excess of the premiums necessary for the pure cost of life insurance.

■ Universal life insurance is a combination of a term insurance policy and a savings account. Front-loaded policies have the loading charge paid from the early premiums. Back-loaded policies are policies that, when surrendered, have the loading charge deducted from the surrender value.

■ A grace period is usually a one-month period in which the insured may pay delinquent premiums while keeping the policy in force. Incontestability clauses permit the insurance company to withdraw from policies where there is misrepresentation; they usually expire after two years. An irrevocable beneficiary is one who may not be removed as beneficiary without his or her approval. A viatical settlement is when an insured, generally one who is terminally ill, sells his or her life insurance policy to another for a portion of the face amount.

■ A policy loan is where the insured borrows the cash reserves of his or her policy at a previously contracted rate. In an automatic premium loan, the cash reserves of the policy are drawn on to continue payment of the insurance premiums. A paid-up policy is where the insured uses the cash value of his or her policy to purchase another policy of lesser value.

■ Endorsements (riders) are modifications to a policy, expressed in supplements, that specify additional coverage or reductions.

■ Critical illness insurance pays the insured a flexible amount of money should he or she develop an illness preventing the earning of a living. Health insurance assists in providing coverage for those medical expenses not covered under the public health programs. Long-term disability insurance covers loss of income due to a disability. Extended health care covers additional health care items such as prescriptions, nursing, semi-private hospital rooms, etc. Dental care is coverage for various levels of dentistry procedures, both preventive and maintenance. Travel insurance covers many items while the insured is away from home, including emergency health care and return airfare costs.

Key Terms

automatic premium loan (p. 131)	dental care (p. 138)
back-loaded (p. 126)	dividends (p. 119)
beneficiary (p. 114)	endorsements (riders) (p. 132)
cash reserves (cash surrender value) (p. 125)	extended health care plan (p. 138)
	face amount (face value) (p. 114)
credit life insurance (p. 123)	family income policy (p. 127)
critical illness insurance (p. 124)	family policy (p. 127)

front-loaded *(p. 126)*	non-participating policies *(p. 119)*
grace period *(p. 128)*	paid-up policy *(p. 131)*
health insurance *(p. 137)*	participating policies *(p. 119)*
incontestability clause *(p. 128)*	policy *(p. 114)*
insurable interest *(p. 114)*	policy loan *(p. 130)*
irrevocable beneficiary *(p. 129)*	premiums *(p. 114)*
level premium *(p. 115)*	pure cost of life insurance *(p. 115)*
limited payment policy *(p. 125)*	term insurance *(p. 119)*
loading charge *(p. 118)*	travel insurance *(p. 138)*
long-term disability insurances *(p. 138)*	universal life insurance *(p. 126)*
	viatical settlement *(p. 130)*
mortgage insurance *(p. 123)*	whole life insurance *(p. 124)*

Problems

1. Bert, a 33-year-old marketing representative, is wondering whether he has enough life insurance, especially since a second child is due to arrive in a few months. His wife, Mira, who is 32, is busy looking after young Jake, the couple's first-born, and does not work outside the home. Reviewing his financial situation has led Bert to estimate that if he should die tomorrow, he would need to leave a sum of $300 000 in his estate to support his children until they become independent, and to support his wife for her lifetime. His list of assets and debts is as follows:

Life insurance, five-year renewable term	$100 000
Deposits in bank	2 700
Equity in home	25 000
Registered Pension Plan	9 000
Mutual funds	3 500
Consumer debts	12 400
Funeral expenses	4 500
RRSPs	15 500

    (a) If Bert were to die tomorrow, what would be the net worth of his estate? Would it be sufficient to provide the support he desires for his family? Should the equity in the house be included in this analysis? Give your reasons.

    (b) What recommendation would you make to Bert regarding the amount and type of life insurance?

    (c) Assuming that Bert could purchase five-year renewable term insurance for $2.40 per $1000 and whole life for $6.50 per $1000, how much would your recommendation cost him per year?

    (d) Assume that Mira acquires a full-time job. Should she have life insurance also? Would this change Bert's need for life insurance?

    (e) Assume that Mira stays home. Should she have life insurance? Would this change Bert's need for life insurance?

2. Henry (40) and Maureen (39) own their own small tool-and-die company located in a small town close to a major automotive town. Henry has become involved in supporting local sports teams on top of being the operations designer and manager of the company. Maureen manages the office of the company and is involved part-time as a volunteer in the schools that their two sons, aged 11 and 14, attend. Henry and Maureen have placed the majority of their savings into the business and have recently paid off their mortgage, so they have virtually no debts. They do not carry any life insurance at this time as Henry believes, in the event of his death, the business would be either sold or Maureen could continue to operate it at a reasonable income with the assistance of the foreperson, and in the future, one or both of their sons.

   (a) Do you think Henry and Maureen require life insurance?
   (b) If so, why?
   (c) What measures should they take?
   (d) If you recommend life insurance, how much coverage and what kind of policy should they purchase, either individually or as a family?

3. When you bought the policy shown in Appendix 5A, you had been convinced that whole life insurance was the correct way to go. You had researched the alternatives, consulted various advisors, and considered the future you face in your current job and family situation. When applying for the policy, your agent required that you complete a detailed application form that requested information about your job, finances, family health history, your own health history, hobbies, and lifestyle, among other concerns.

   (a) Why does the life insurance company need the information?
   (b) How does each kind of information affect your policy or premium?

4. Decide whether you AGREE or DISAGREE with the following statements:

   (a) If Phil and Melanie applied to the same company for the same type of life insurance policy and both were accepted, they would pay the same annual premiums.
   (b) If they chose whole life, both would pay level premiums for life, or until they reached an age limit such as 85.
   (c) If Phil purchases decreasing term insurance, his premiums will decrease each year during the term of the contract.
   (d) If Melanie changes her job, her present group insurance coverage will continue as long as she pays the premiums.
   (e) If Phil chooses a participating policy, he can expect to receive dividends.
   (f) Five-year renewable term insurance means that the contract can be renewed at the same premium after five years.
   (g) If Phil's health deteriorates, his term policy premium would increase.
   (h) A dividend may be regarded as interest earned by the money you paid the insurance company.
   (i) A group policy is the same as a participating policy.

5. In the case of a couple where one of the spouses stays home, should both spouses be insured? Why? And what factors would warrant the different treatment?

6. In the distribution of property after the death of a policyholder whose life insurance is payable to her estate rather than to a named beneficiary, what difference does it make if (a) she dies intestate or (b) she leaves a will?

7. Analyze each of the following situations and decide whether you AGREE or DIS-AGREE with the conclusions, explaining why.

   (a) A single woman of 35, without dependents, who has $35 000 of group insurance in association with her employment, has been called on by a life insurance agent. He encourages her to take out a whole life policy of $100 000. His arguments are as follows: (i) the premium will increase if she postpones buying insurance and (ii) she should have permanent insurance and not depend on the group policy, which covers her only as long as she stays with that employer. She decides that he is right.

   (b) A woman who is widowed at 35 returns to work as a professional librarian to support her four school-age children because her husband's estate was small. She asks an insurance agent for a renewable term policy. The agent recommends that she buy permanent whole life insurance instead, so that she will have something for her old age. She tells the agent that she doesn't want a small amount of permanent life insurance, but a large amount right now.

   (c) A young couple with three small children wonders what kind of life insurance to buy. He earns $45 000 a year, and she stays at home to look after the children, while working part-time for another $12 000 per year. They are thinking of taking out a family policy that would put $10 000 on his life, $3000 on hers and $4000 on the life of each child. That way, the couple would cover the major risks.

   (d) A retired couple of 75 and 73, who have a whole life policy for $25 000 on the husband's life, wonder whether to keep paying the annual premium of $175, or to cash in the policy and take the cash surrender value of $12 200. They are living on Old Age Security, Canada Pension, an employer's pension, and the income from their modest investments. They decide not to cash in the policy now but to keep it for the wife's protection in case she should be widowed.

8. Review the life insurance policy in Appendix 5A and decide whether you AGREE or DISAGREE with each of the following:

   (a) It is a limited-pay whole life policy.

   (b) The insured should have requested an accidental death rider as better protection for the insured's family.

   (c) It is a participating policy.

   (d) If the insured decided to cancel the policy one year after purchasing it, the insured would receive a cash value.

   (e) If the insured decided to surrender the policy 10 years after purchase, the insured could apply for the cash value plus accumulated dividends.

   (f) The insured could buy a paid-up policy if the insured surrendered this policy after 10 years.

   (g) If the insured could not make a payment, the policy would be cancelled.

   (h) The insured should select a lump-sum settlement option for the beneficiary, because this will leave the insured free to select the settlement option that best suits the situation at the time.

   (i) Who selects how the proceeds are to be paid?

   (j) If the policy is cancelled, can it be reinstated? If so, under what terms?

9. Examine the following statements, and identify those that are myths or that involve faulty reasoning. Explain the error.

    (a) Buying life insurance is a good way to build up savings.

    (b) A policyholder's savings in a whole life insurance policy drop to zero when the policyholder dies.

    (c) You should buy life insurance while you are young, when the premiums are lower.

    (d) The cash surrender value of a whole life policy is your own money, and the company should not charge interest when you borrow your own money.

    (e) Term insurance is not a good buy because the coverage is temporary but the problem is permanent.

    (f) At your death, your beneficiary should receive your policy's cash value as well as its face value.

    (g) Only wage earners need life insurance.

10. Why is it said that "life insurance is sold but not bought"?

11. At retirement, a person needs to review his or her insurance coverage in the light of future needs. What are some reasons for either (a) cashing in or cancelling all life insurance, (b) retaining some coverage, or (c) buying more life insurance?

12. Proceed to the Canadian Life and Health Insurance Association's website, **www.clhia.ca**, and determine the code of conduct for members when dealing with consumers. What would you expect the typical insurance salesperson to do to help you with buying insurance? What other concerns would you want addressed? What else can a life insurance agent do for you?

13. What are the pros and cons of purchasing credit life insurance? What do you recommend? Why?

14. Review Table 5.1, "Life Expectancy by Age Group and Sex."

    (a) Should you purchase life insurance?

    (b) What is your life expectancy?

    (c) What is the life expectancy of the rest of the members of your family?

    (d) Is there adequate coverage for your family?

15. Walter and June are nearing 50 years of age. For almost all of their 25-plus years of marriage, they have lived in the cozy one-and-a-half-storey house that they purchased shortly after marriage, the home they have raised their teenage daughter in and have been planning to retire in as well. Now, faced with June's rapidly declining health, they are considering the use of their life insurance policy to finance her dream: building the house she always wanted to and decorating and furnishing it the way that she would like to do. They have life insurance of $250 000 on each life and are considering selling June's policy for $150 000 and then using their savings and mortgaging their current house to realize June's dream. Assuming that June has a maximum of one year to live, that Walter and their daughter will be financially taken care of by his income and pension, and that the remaining debts can be eliminated by the sale of one of the houses, what arguments would you make for and against June and Walter's entering into a viatical arrangement with June's insurance policy?

References

BOOKS AND ARTICLES

Baldwin, Ben. *The Complete Book of Insurance: The Consumer's Guide to Insuring Your Life, Health, Property and Income*. Revised Edition. Toronto: Irwin Professional Publishing, 1996. A guide that helps you explore and determine your actual insurance needs and costs for all facets of your life.

Canadian Life and Health Insurance Association Inc. *Canadian Life and Health Insurance Facts*. Toronto: Canadian Life and Health Insurance Association, annual. A booklet that provides industry data on purchases and ownership of life insurance, health insurance, and annuities. 1 Queen Street East, Suite 1700, Toronto, ON M5C 2X9.

Canadian Life and Health Insurance Association Inc. *Health Insurance for Travellers*. Toronto: Canadian Life and Health Insurance Association. A booklet describing and advising on the need for and the types of travel insurance available for travellers from and to Canada. 1 Queen Street East, Suite 1700, Toronto, ON M5C 2X9.

Deloitte and Touche. *Canadian Guide to Personal Financial Management*. Scarborough: Prentice Hall Canada, annual. A team of accountants provides guidance on a broad range of topics, including planning finances, estimating insurance needs, managing risk, and determining investment needs. Instructions and the necessary forms for making plans are also included.

Praskey, Sally, and Helena Moncrieff. *The Insurance Book: What Canadians Really Need to Know Before Buying Insurance*. Toronto: Pearson Education Canada Inc., 2000. A thorough coverage of all the insurance options available to Canadians.

Personal Finance on the Web

Canadian Life and Health Insurance Association Inc.
www.clhia.ca An industry body representing the 100 life and health insurance companies in Canada. This site provides an overview of the industry and the role it plays as well as the self-established rules of the industry.

InsuranceCanada.ca
www.insurance-canada.ca A consumer-focused site with information regarding the needs and intricacies of the industry. It is co-sponsored by the Consumers Council of Canada and the Consumers Association of Canada.

Manulife Financial
www.coverme.com. This site is another internet resource that provides information regarding benefits, needs assessment, and quotes.

Appendix 5A
Sample Life Insurance Policy

SAMPLE

Basic insurance benefit

London Life will pay $50,000 on the death of the life insured.

Premiums

The agreements made by London Life are conditional on payment of premiums as shown in the policy summary. The first premium is payable on February 12, 2001.

Premiums are payable monthly under London Life's Pre-authorized payment agreement (PPA). If the agreement stops and is either re-started or a different method of paying premiums is selected, increased premiums may become payable due to higher administration charges then in effect.

If any premium other than the first is not paid within thirty-one days after it is due, the contract ceases to be in force, except as provided in Premium loans. If proceeds become payable within the thirty-one days, unpaid premiums will be deducted.

If any premium is paid by cheque or other promise to pay which is not honoured, the premium will be considered unpaid.

Premium Vacation
Premium Vacation is an arrangement that permits the policyowner to apply available dividends and/or existing values (dividend acquired values) to pay part or all of each premium due under the contract, as described in the Use of dividends provision, for a selected period of time. The policy does not become paid-up if Premium Vacation is chosen.

Dividends are not guaranteed and may vary from time to time. Changes in the dividends credited or actions by the policyowner, such as taking a policy loan, may cause the dividends credited and/or existing values (dividend acquired values) to be insufficient to pay the amount selected for Premium Vacation. In that event, other arrangements must be made to pay that part of the premium which can no longer be paid under Premium Vacation. Payment of the full premium, regardless of payment method selected, remains at all times the responsibility of the policyowner.

The policyowner may discontinue Premium Vacation at any time by notifying London Life, though income tax considerations may restrict flexibility when making other premium payment arrangements. London Life may also discontinue Premium Vacation at any time.

Guaranteed values

The guaranteed values at certain dates are shown in the policy summary. Values at other dates will be calculated by London Life on the same basis. There are no values before the first date for which an amount greater than zero is shown.

Dividends

Dividends apportioned by the directors of London Life will be credited to the contract at each anniversary of February 12, 2001. A dividend will not be credited at the first anniversary unless the premium then due is paid.

Policy number - B000030-3   London Life   12 Feb 01   page 1

SOURCE: London Life Insurance Company, London, Canada.

continued

SAMPLE

Econolife

Dividends credited provide an Econolife insurance benefit, subject to the Use of dividends provision. The Econolife insurance amount is guaranteed not to be less than $50,000, provided no part of the Econolife insurance benefit is surrendered under the Use of dividends provision. The Econolife insurance benefit will be paid in the same event and subject to the same terms as the basic insurance benefit.

Use of dividends

Part or all of the Econolife insurance benefit may be surrendered for its cash value less any indebtedness. On written request and with the agreement of the policyowner and London Life, part of the dividends credited, and/or part or all of the cash value of the Econolife insurance benefit may be

- applied towards payment of premiums (Premium Vacation),
- applied to reduce any indebtedness, or
- paid in cash.

These uses of dividends may result in decreases to the Econolife insurance amount.

If part of the dividends credited are used for purposes other than purchasing the Econolife insurance benefit, and/or part or all of the Econolife insurance benefit is surrendered, the Econolife insurance amount of $50,000 will no longer be guaranteed.

Conversion

The policyowner may exchange the Econolife insurance benefit for

- paid-up additions under this contract, plus
- a new contract on the life insured

by giving written notice to London Life not later than thirty-one days after February 12, 2036 and paying the first premium under the new contract. The total amount of paid-up insurance under this contract after the exchange plus the basic insurance amount of the new contract will be equal to the death benefit under this Econolife insurance benefit.

The application for the new contract includes the application for this contract and any application for change or reinstatement of this contract received before the new contract is made.

New contract after conversion

The policy date will be the date of exchange. The plan of insurance, subject to London Life's issue limits, may be any plan issued by London Life at the date of exchange, other than term insurance.

The premium will be determined according to

- the plan and amount of insurance,
- additional insurance benefits included in the new contract,
- the attained age of the life insured at the date of exchange, and
- the class of risk applicable to this Econolife insurance benefit.

Subject to London Life's issue limits and evidence of insurability satisfactory to London Life, additional insurance benefits issued by London Life at the date of exchange may be included in the new contract.

The beneficiary under the new contract will be the beneficiary under this contract. The policyowner may change or revoke the beneficiary as permitted by law.

page 2   12 Feb 01   London Life   Policy number - B000030-3

continued

SAMPLE

Use of policy values

The cash value of the contract is the cash value of the basic insurance benefit plus the cash value of the Econolife insurance benefit.

Premium loans

If any premium is not paid, and if the contract has a cash value, London Life will keep the contract in force until the indebtedness exceeds the cash value of the contract. Unpaid premiums become indebtedness. The policyowner may start paying premiums again at any time while the contract is in force.

Cash loans

If the basic insurance benefit has a cash value, on written request London Life will make a loan on the security of the contract. The maximum loan available at any time will be

- the cash value of the contract at the next anniversary of the policy date, discounted to the date of the loan at the interest rate then applicable to the loan
- less existing indebtedness at the time of the loan.

The loan will be made within ninety days after receipt of the request for the loan.

Indebtedness

The indebtedness at any time is

- premium loans plus cash loans,
- less payments made to reduce indebtedness
- with interest to that time.

London Life sets the rate of interest and the times when interest is compounded, and may change them. Payments to reduce indebtedness may be made at any time while the contract is in force.

If the indebtedness becomes greater than the cash value of the contract, the contract will cease to be in force.

Indebtedness will be deducted in determining the proceeds under the contract.

Paid-up insurance

On written request to London Life, this contract will be changed to a paid-up contract. If there is indebtedness, it is first deducted from the cash value of the Econolife insurance benefit. Any remaining cash value of the Econolife insurance benefit will continue to provide an Econolife insurance benefit. The amount of the Econolife insurance benefit will be determined by London Life according to its rules at that time. Any remaining indebtedness is deducted from the cash value of the basic insurance benefit. The amount of paid-up insurance will be

- the amount of paid-up insurance determined from the table of guaranteed values in the policy summary for the date the contract is changed to paid-up (values for dates not shown will be calculated by London Life on the same basis),
- multiplied by the cash value of the basic insurance benefit after deducting any indebtedness, as described above, and
- divided by the cash value of the basic insurance benefit before deducting any indebtedness.

There will be no other benefits in the paid-up contract.

continued

Surrender for cash

On written request, London Life will pay

SAMPLE

- the cash value of the contract
- less any indebtedness.

Payment will be made within ninety days after surrender of all rights under the contract.

Claims

Death claim

London Life must be provided with proof of death. London Life may also require proof of the truth of the information in the application for the contract and for any amendment or reinstatement of the contract.

Exceptions

Suicide

If the life insured commits suicide, while sane or insane, the amount of proceeds payable with respect to that portion of any insurance benefit that has been continuously in force with respect to that life insured, for less than two years immediately before the death of that life insured, will be limited to the greater of the cash value of that portion and the sum of the premiums paid for that portion during that period.

Settlement options

The payee may elect to have any proceeds that are payable under the contract in one sum applied to provide one or more of the following, subject to the rules and rates London Life is using at that time:

- a deposit account earning interest,
- periodic payments for a selected number of years up to 30,
- periodic payments for life, with payments guaranteed 10, 15 or 20 years as selected,
- periodic payments as long as either of two persons lives, with payments guaranteed 10, 15 or 20 years as selected, and
- any other settlement option London Life is issuing at that time.

London Life will issue a new policy if the proceeds are applied to provide periodic payments.

General provisions

Contract

The contract is the agreement between the policyowner and London Life. It consists of

- this policy,
- any amendment to the contract, and
- the application for the contract and for any amendment or reinstatement of the contract.

page 4   12 Feb 01   London Life   Policy number - B000030-3

continued

London Life

SAMPLE

The contract comes into force if

- the first premium has been paid,
- the policy has been delivered to the policyowner or the beneficiary, and
- there has been no change in the insurability of the life insured since the application was completed.

The contract ceases to be in force when the basic insurance benefit ceases to be in force.

The signature of a London Life registrar is required to amend the contract or to waive any of its terms.

Giving facts to London Life

London Life makes the contract on the basis of facts disclosed in the written application for

- the contract,
- any amendment to the contract, and
- any reinstatement of the contract.

It is not sufficient that an agent, employee or medical examiner has knowledge of a fact. If a fact that is material to the insurance benefits was not disclosed in the written application, the contract may be declared void.

Proof of birth date

If the date of birth of the life insured was not correctly disclosed, London Life may

- adjust the amount of the insurance benefits for the correct date of birth,
- adjust any starting and expiry date of the insurance benefits and the date to which premiums are payable, and
- cancel any insurance benefit not available because of age.

Beneficiary

The policyowner may designate a beneficiary to receive the proceeds and may revoke or change the designation as permitted by law.

Reinstatement

London Life will put the contract back into force if

- application for reinstatement is made within two years after the contract ceased to be in force,
- the good health and insurability of the life insured are proved to the satisfaction of London Life,
- overdue premiums with interest at a rate determined by London Life are paid, and
- indebtedness is paid to London Life.

Place of payment and currency

All payments to or by London Life will be made in Canada in lawful money of Canada.

Policy number - B000030-3   London Life   12 Feb 01   (last page) 5

continued

SAMPLE

Secretary's Office - Terminal 467

Information about your voting privileges

As the owner of one or more London Life participating policies or one or more policies to which voting rights are attached, you are entitled to attend and vote at meetings of the company. This includes the right to vote for policyholder directors. Your right to vote can be exercised either in person or by proxy.

If you complete and return the *Request for meeting notification* form below, you will receive notices of, and forms of proxy that may be used to appoint a proxyholder for, meetings of policyholders and shareholders of the company during the three-year period commencing on the date the form is received by the Corporate Secretary of London Life.

The Request for meeting notification form should be mailed to:

> The Corporate Secretary, Terminal 467
> London Life Insurance Company
> Head Office, 255 Dufferin Avenue
> London, Ontario, Canada, N6A 4K1

Request for meeting notification (completion is optional)

I am the owner of one or more London Life participating policies or one or more policies to which voting rights are attached. I request London Life to send me notice of the time and place of, and a form of proxy that may be used to appoint a proxyholder for, each meeting of policyholders and shareholders of the company held or begun during the three-year period commencing on the date the Corporate Secretary of London Life receives this request. I understand that notice will be sent not later than twenty-one days and not earlier than fifty days before any meeting is held.

Month   Day   Year   Signature of   LIFE INSURED 30

Policy number	Policyholder's name
B000030-3	LIFE INSURED 30

continued

SAMPLE

Premiums

The total premium payable on the 12th day of each month consists of the following benefit premiums:

Benefit	Premium	Prior to
Basic insurance	$82.98	February 12, 2071

Mode of payment is monthly (PPA).

Guaranteed values

Basic insurance benefit

Date	Age	Cash value - $	Paid-up value - $
Feb 12, 2001	30	0.00	00
Feb 12, 2002	31	0.00	00
Feb 12, 2003	32	50.00	250
Feb 12, 2004	33	100.00	400
Feb 12, 2005	34	170.00	700
Feb 12, 2006	35	715.00	2,700
Feb 12, 2007	36	1,285.00	4,700
Feb 12, 2008	37	1,870.00	6,700
Feb 12, 2009	38	2,470.00	8,600
Feb 12, 2010	39	3,090.00	10,500
Feb 12, 2011	40	3,730.00	12,350
Feb 12, 2012	41	4,385.00	14,100
Feb 12, 2016	45	7,190.00	20,750
Feb 12, 2021	50	10,650.00	26,850
Feb 12, 2026	55	14,375.00	31,650
Feb 12, 2031	60	18,480.00	35,750
Feb 12, 2036	65	22,845.00	39,100
Feb 12, 2041	70	27,370.00	41,900
Feb 12, 2046	75	31,720.00	44,050
Feb 12, 2051	80	35,610.00	45,650
Feb 12, 2056	85	38,945.00	46,850
Feb 12, 2061	90	41,715.00	47,750
Feb 12, 2066	95	44,015.00	48,400
Feb 12, 2071	100	50,000.00	50,000

The guaranteed cash values shown above apply to the basic insurance benefit only. Total value at any time includes the guaranteed cash value plus any dividend acquired values.

continued

London Life

Policy summary

SAMPLE

Data

Life insured	David Gerald Hill
Insuring age	30
Policyowner	David Gerald Hill, the life insured
Beneficiary	BENEFICIARY 30
Plan	Jubilee Whole Life with annual dividends
Dividend option	Econolife
Policy number	B000030-3
Policy date	February 12, 2001

Benefits

On death of the life insured

Basic insurance	$50,000
Econolife insurance	$50,000 initially
Total basic plus Econolife	$100,000 initially

chapter **6**

Retirement Income

> "In retirement, will you enjoy the Golden Pond? Or be up the creek
> without a paddle? Planning should start as early as possible—or at the
> latest in your early 40s—and build as you near the big day. Too many
> people leave it until their late 50s. That's too late, considering the
> sums and lifestyle decisions required."
>
> Bruce Cohen, The Money Adviser

Learning Objectives

Knowledge of the material in this chapter should make the concept of
retirement more meaningful.

After studying this chapter, you should be able to:

1. Outline the three basic sources of retirement income.

2. Define the terms used with the Canada and Quebec Pension Plans: year's basic exemption, year's maximum pensionable earnings, and contributory earnings.

3. Define the terms used with private pension plans: defined contributions, defined benefits, portability, and indexing.

4. Define the annuity principle and the terms used with annuities.

5. Differentiate between the various types of annuities.

6. Outline the costs of buying an annuity.

7. Show how an RRSP can help to provide for a financially secure retirement.

8. Understand the various options available when selecting an RRSP.

9. Define the following terms associated with RRSPs: spousal plan, contribution limits, and maturity date.

10. Define segregated funds, RRIFs, and LIFs.

11. Understand the costs and benefits of universal life policies as a means of creating an estate.

Introduction

Retirement is not likely to be on the minds of students as they select courses and make plans for their future careers. Neither is it an important priority for many working people, who put the thought of retirement, like that of death itself, out of their minds. This head-in-the-sand approach is foolish, however, because without a plan for one's retirement, what are popularly called the "golden years" can be very grey indeed. The purpose of this chapter is to raise your awareness of the importance of financial planning for retirement and to emphasize that the earlier this planning starts, the better off you'll be.

Everyone faces two questions when planning for retirement:

(a) Where will I find the money for my retirement?
(b) Will I have enough to live comfortably?

The biggest financial change facing newly retired people is the replacement of their employment income with income from pensions and investments. The level of both types of replacement income depends on investment decisions made many years earlier. Retirees may have no control over employment-related pensions, but they do have control over their own investments and RRSPs. It is important that they pay careful attention to these private investments in order to best meet their retirement needs. While determining these needs may be very difficult when you are young, failing to think about them can have serious consequences. References (to websites) given at the end of the chapter outline methods of estimating your retirement needs.

Techniques for saving and investing to meet your retirement needs will be discussed in Chapters 8 through 10. In this chapter, we will identify sources of retirement income, discuss private and public pensions, and examine annuities, segregated funds, RRSPs, RRIFs, and LIFs.

Financial Planning for Retirement

Retirement planning requires a long-term perspective on personal finances. As explained in Chapter 1 (under the heading "Lifetime Perspective"), over a lifetime your income is likely to be more variable than your living costs, and the positive gap between your income and expenditures will probably be largest during your middle years (see Chapter 1, Figure 1.1). When you retire, your earnings cease; from then on, pensions and investments will be your main sources of income. What you do about pensions and investments during your working years will have a significant bearing on the amount of retirement income available to you.

The basic rule in planning for retirement income is to begin saving early. To achieve financial independence and be able to maintain your preferred lifestyle in retirement, you must ensure that your net worth grows steadily during your working years. It is truly amazing how, due to the magic of compounding, small amounts saved regularly over a long period of time can result in a substantial sum (see Chapter 8, Figure 8.1). Generally, saving gradually in this way is preferable to attempting to save a great deal during the last few years of your working life (see Chapter 1, Figure 1.2). Since it is difficult to predict the exact time you will retire (illness or a decision to retire early could affect the event's timing), it can be unwise to leave saving for retirement until your last few working years.

Sources of Retirement Income

There are three sources of retirement or pension income in Canada. The first of these, the government income support program, is composed of the Old Age Security (OAS) and the Guaranteed Income Supplement (GIS). The second source is the Canada Pension Plan

(CPP) or the Quebec Pension Plan (QPP). The third source is made up of private pensions and investment income. These include registered retirement savings plans (RRSPs) and employer pension plans.

Government Income Support Programs
    Old Age Security (OAS)
    Guaranteed Income Supplement (GIS)

Public Pensions
    Canada Pension Plan (CPP)
    Quebec Pension Plan (QPP)

Private Pensions
    Registered retirement savings plans (RRSPs)
    Defined benefits and defined contribution pension plans
    Income from private investments

To qualify for the **OAS**, you must be over 65 and a Canadian citizen or a legal resident of Canada on the day prior to the approval of your application. You must also have lived in Canada for at least 10 years after turning 18. Those who have lived in the country for 40 years after turning 18 qualify for the full pension. Anyone who does not qualify for a full pension may do so for a partial pension. A partial pension is determined at the rate of one fortieth of the full pension for each year lived in Canada after the eighteenth birthday.

In July 2006, the maximum OAS benefit was $487.54 per month. This amount was *clawed back* (repaid or taken back) for anyone who had a net income higher than $62 144. It was completely clawed back for anyone earning $101 031.

Canadians of age 65 or older who have left the country but lived in Canada for 20 years after turning 18 also qualify.

There is an allowance for spouses or common-law partners whose partner has died, who are Canadians or legal residents, are between the ages of 60 to 64, and have lived in Canada for 10 years after their eighteenth birthday.

As for the **GIS**, only those with incomes of $14 352 annually, or lower, are eligible. The spouse of a recipient is eligible if his or her annual income is less than $34 560. The maximum payment for a single person in July 2006 was $597.53 per month. The spouse of someone receiving the GIS received a maximum GIS of $392.01.[1]

Income Patterns

The income sources for Canadians over 60 are shown in Table 6.1. As one would expect, income from employment gradually decreases as people age, while income from investments and pensions increases. The decline in employment income is compensated, to a certain degree, by money received from the CPP/QPP, and for those with the lowest income, by the OAS/GIS.

The number of elderly Canadians living at Statistics Canada's "low-income cutoff rate" declined between 1996 and 2002. In 2002, the number of women over 65 living at the low-income cutoff rate was 9 percent, and for men, 4.4 percent. Single seniors have not fared as

---

[1]Government support programs are meant for lower-income Canadians.

TABLE 6.1   INCOME SOURCES OF PERSONS 60 AND OVER

SOURCES	60–64	65–69	70–74	75+
Employment/all sources	43.39%	16.12%	7.24%	2.52%
Investment	10.97%	13.63%	13.77%	20.79%
CPP/QPP	9.08%	17.19%	18.20%	18.89%
Other pensions + RRSPs	21.42%	26.58%	31.77%	27.82%
OAS/GIS		15.33%	17.67%	19.69%
Other	15.14%	11.15%	11.35%	10.29%

Investment includes rental income. All income sources not included in the above categories are included in Other.

SOURCE: Canada Revenue Agency, Income Statistics 2004, Interim Basic Table 4-Universe Data. Reproduced with permission of the Minister of Public Works and Government Services Canada, 2005.

well as couples or those living with their families. In 2002, 20 percent of elderly women were considered low-income, compared with 14 percent for men.[2]

"Low-income cutoffs," a term used by Statistics Canada, is a subjective evaluation of wealth and varies according to the size of one's community. It is higher in urban than rural areas. A single person in a city of 500 000 earning $20 100, for example, is considered poor, while in a rural area, a person is not considered poor unless he or she is earning $13 982 or less.[3]

The Financial Health of Seniors

In 2000, seniors made up 12.5 percent of the Canadian population. By 2021, it is expected that this figure will have increased to 18 percent.[4] While studies indicate that the financial health of seniors has improved, many cannot be considered affluent by any stretch of the imagination. The poorest senior citizens tend to be those living on their own, women over 80, visible minorities, and immigrants. The poor status of these seniors is expected to increase.

Nearly 7 percent—over 250 000—of Canada's seniors have incomes below the low income cut-off (LICO) that the National Council on Welfare considers the poverty level.[5] Of this figure, 154 000 are single women.[6] They have fared worse than men because, frequently, even for similar occupations, their incomes were lower. They also tend to live longer than men and often run out of savings.

There is considerable inequality in the amount of retirement savings Canadians have at their disposal. In 2001, the latest year for which figures are available, 25 percent of retirees owned 84 percent of retirement savings.[7] A major reason for this is that some seniors with low levels of savings did not prepare well for their retirement, did not start to save soon enough, and did not invest. For those with low incomes it is often difficult just making ends meet without thinking about saving for investment. In addition, some may have been affected by layoffs and economic problems beyond their control and were therefore unable to save.

Related to the poor retirement savings of retirees is the fact that many baby boomers have a fear of investing. The investment world, to many, is a great big mystery. Almost 50 percent think that making investment decisions has grown more complicated over the past 10 years.

[2]Statistics Canada: Analysis of Income in Canada. Chapter 8: Low Income.
[3]National Council on Welfare Fact Sheet: 2004 Poverty Lines Estimates.
[4]National Advisory Council on Aging (NACA).
[5]This use of the LICO is quite controversial and by no means accepted by all who deal with and study seniors.
[6]National Advisory Council on Aging, Aging in Poverty in Canada, 2005.
[7]NACA.

A recent report indicates that over half of boomers are not saving enough to have a financially worry-free retirement. Serious problems for them are that they lack an understanding of the investment options available and have little experience in investing. This means that many must turn to an advisor for professional help but are not sure whom to turn to. Ignorance is bliss, it seems. A significant number rated spending time on personal finance ninth behind such important activities as sleeping and leisure activities.[8]

How much money do retirees need? This depends, of course, on individual lifestyles, but after retirement people usually need less. Any children should have left the home, and the mortgage should be paid off. Therefore, even if retirees are on pensions, most need less than previously. Regardless of past needs, it has long been assumed that a person can retire comfortably on a retirement income equal to 70 percent on his or her salary. A major consulting company concerned with retirement feels that 50 percent is an adequate amount.[9] The key to having golden years worth living for is finding the right amount of income to meet one's needs, be they gardening and going for long walks or taking Adriatic cruises.

Until recently, unless one was self-employed, the mandatory retirement age in all parts of Canada was 65. This is no longer the case. Ottawa and most of the provinces have recently decided to end this requirement because it discriminates against the elderly.

The chance to work beyond 65 changes the dynamics of financial planning for retirement and will be of great benefit to those who started saving late in life, or not at all. Many of those still employed will be earning at the top end of their salary scales, able to invest for longer periods before requiring income from their investments, and therefore, if both wise and lucky, able to accumulate larger estates. They will be able to make larger contributions to RRSPs. The accumulation period for pensions generally will be longer, the pensions larger. Payouts from the CPP will be for a shorter period.

Public Pensions

The federal, provincial, and municipal governments provide a variety of social security programs, some of which are intended to provide benefits for older or retired persons. Federal programs are the major source of public retirement pensions, but most provinces and the territories provide income supplements for people who are in financial need.

Public Retirement Pensions

Federal	Eligibility Criteria
Old Age Security	age, residence, need
Guaranteed Income Supplement	age, residence, need
Spouse's Allowance	age, residence, need
Canada Pension Plan	age, contributions
Provincial	
QPP for Quebec residents	age, contributions
Income support programs	need

---

[8] "56% of Boomers Admit to Not Saving Enough for Retirement and Lack of Financial Confidence," **www.MoneySense.ca,** October 25, 2005.

[9] Mercer Human Resources Consulting.

Canada Pension Plan (CPP)

This federal plan was established in 1966 to provide a measure of economic security for three categories of people: the retired, the disabled, and the dependent survivors of contributors. The Province of Quebec decided not to participate in the Canada Pension Plan, setting up the companion Quebec Pension Plan (QPP) instead. There is complete portability between the two plans for those who move into or out of Quebec.

Contributions Employees and employers are both required to contribute to either the CPP or the QPP. On retirement, the employee will receive a lifetime pension. The amount of the pension depends on the length of time the employee spent in the labour force and on the amount contributed to the plan. The information that follows applies to the Canada Pension Plan; those who live in Quebec are advised to investigate the specific details of the Quebec Pension Plan.

Employers must match their employees' contributions. Self-employed people must make both contributions themselves. To calculate contributions, earnings are divided into three parts. The first part, known as the **year's basic exemption**, is excluded from the calculations. In 2006, this amount was $3500. The second part, the portion on which the employee's contribution rate is based, is called **contributory earnings** and includes any income between $3500 and $38 600. The third part, which is also exempt from the calculations, is any income above the year's **maximum pensionable earnings** ($42 100 in 2006). See Figure 6.1 for a graphic summary of these terms.

The maximum pensionable earnings figure has been increasing annually in recent years. Using 2003 figures, the Personal Finance in Action Box 6.1, "Contributions to the CPP," shows how an employee's contributions are calculated.

In 1996, the federal government indicated that unless changes were made to CPP funding, the fund would be exhausted by 2015. In order to prevent a financial calamity and a major political embarrassment, the government proposed some major funding changes. The 1997 contribution rate was 5.85 percent of contributory earnings, with half of that amount paid by the employer and half by the employee. In 1998, Parliament passed legislation (Bill C-2) to gradually increase the contribution rate until it reached a combined rate of 9.9 percent. It reached 9.9 percent in 2003.

Another change was the creation by Parliament in 1997 of the **CPP Investment Board**. This board began investing CPP contributions in bonds in 1999 and in equities in 2001. As of March 2006, assets in the CPP were worth $98 000 000 000. Of this amount 27.7 percent

FIGURE 6.1 TERMINOLOGY ASSOCIATED WITH CPP/QPP CONTRIBUTIONS (2006 AMOUNTS)

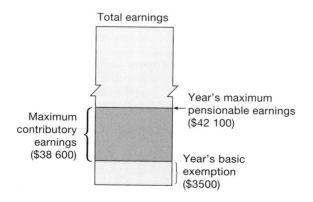

Contributions to the CPP

Yusef's earnings in 2006	$44 000
The year's basic exemption	3 500
2006's maximum pensionable earnings	$42 100
Yusef's contributory earnings ($42 100 – $3500)	$38 600

In 2006, Yusef paid 4.95 percent of $38 600, or $1910.70, into the CPP, and his employer paid the same amount.

was invested in bonds, 58.50 percent in equities, and 4.00 percent in real return bonds, those indexed for inflation.

Benefits In 2006, the average CPP retirement pension was $463.95 per month and the maximum was $844.58. These benefits are indexed for inflation and are taxable. The maximum OAS benefit for those who qualified was $487.54 per month. See Personal Finance in Action Box 6.2, "The Arbenzes and the Retirement Hoax," for an example of life on CPP and OAS.

There is also a survivor's benefit of $341.65 for those under 65 and $278.13 for those over 65. Disabled pensioners receive $758.86 per month and children of disabled pensioners receive $195.96 per month.

The Arbenzes and the Retirement Hoax

Julio and Bianca Arbenz had come to Canada from Spain in the 1980s. They lived in a mid-sized Ontario city where they did contract work. Fearing retirement, they worked until forced to retire at 65. Now retired, they had no idea how they would manage financially. They had read in newspapers and magazines that it was advisable for those wishing to retire to have investments of at least $1 000 000. Over the years they had saved nothing. Any extra cash they earned was spent on their two sons, Felipé and José. Now their only income was the $828.75 and $476.97 per month each received from the CPP and OAS. Combined, their incomes totalled $31 337.28 a year. Could they manage on this small sum, or would they need to ask their children for help? Thankfully, they owned their own home. They also had a large fruit and vegetable garden, which saved them a lot in groceries. To find out if their government support payments were enough, they wrote down exactly what their expenses were.

Groceries: $80 per week	$ 4 160
Property taxes	$ 2 000
Hydro: $300 per month	$ 3 600
Water: flat rate of $40 per month	$ 480
Car: loan @ 0% interest of $400 per month	$ 4 800
Gardening: seeds, fertilizer, supplies, etc.	$ 200
Holidays: two-week cottage rental @ $600 per week	$ 1 200
	$16 440

It seemed from this that they could live quite comfortably, with cash to spare, without $1 000 000 in investments. The figure of $1 000 000 is often referred to as an essential sum, but such a figure is meaningless. How much people need depends on how they live.

Long-Term Viability of the CPP

In 2000 there was considerable concern about whether or not the CPP would be able to meet its long-term obligations. It was reported widely in the news media that the ratio of working taxpayers to pensioners was declining. Public worry over this issue caused the government to increase CPP employee/employer contributions to 9.9 percent of contributory earnings to provide a larger pool of funds.

Worry increased even more after the CPP Investment Board was created and began to invest in equities. Equities are considered dangerous investments by many because of the tendency of the stock market to decline, and even crash, periodically. If this happened, the retirement of Canadians who depended on receiving a CPP pension could be bleak indeed.

Such concern seemed justified when the board's portfolio suffered a $4 billion loss in 2002. However, John MacNaughton, CPP Investment Board President, believes pensioners need not worry. There is a risk associated with every investment. While there was a drop in the Investment Board equity assets of $4 billion, this was compensated for, to a certain extent, by a $2.5-billion gain in the board's bond portfolio. The net loss of $1.5 billion only represented 2.2 percent of the total portfolio, and this loss happened as a result of one of the worst periods for stock markets in the past 100 years.

Ever cognizant of public concerns, the CPP Investment Board continues to try to reassure retirees. In October 2004, Mr. MacNaughton reported that the assets administered by the Investment Board were expected to grow to $190 billion by 2014, more than enough to satisfy the CPP's obligations. Previously, the chief federal actuary went much further, forecasting that the assets would likely be in the vicinity of $1.6 trillion by 2050.[10]

The majority of the Investment Board's funds are invested in equities because "they have historically delivered higher returns over the long term than bonds."[11] The Investment Board would invest in what it considers will provide the greatest return. This position led the New Democratic Party to introduce a motion in Parliament that, if passed, would have prohibited the Investment Board "from investing in companies and enterprises that manufacture and trade in military arms and weapons, have records of poor environmental and labour practices or whose conduct and practices are contrary to Canadian values."[12]

The motion prompted the following comment from Fred Ketchen, Scotia Macleod's managing director of equities: "I know that it's tough for those people who may think that some of their Canada Pension Plan money is being invested in God knows what—Rothmans or Molsons or Lockheed Martin or Boeing—but I thought the Canada Pension Plan was supposed to represent all Canadians."[13] His statement accurately represents the Investment Board's point of view.

The CPP Investment Board has 12 directors with extensive backgrounds in economics, business, investments, and financial planning. Chairwoman Gail Cook-Bennett has a Ph.D. in economics and is well-qualified to assess macroeconomic trends. The Investment Board's policy regarding its decisions and the performance of investments is expressed by the following: "Canadians have a right to know why, how, and where we invest their Canada Pension Plan money, who makes the investment decisions, what assets are owned on their behalf, and how the investments are performing. We provide as much information as we can, to tell our story, so that you can judge for yourself."[14]

---

[10]Bruce Cohen, Pension Tension. **www.50plus.com**.

[11]CPP Investment Board.

[12]Anthony Edwards, CPP Investment Board Comes Under Fire, Ethical Investing: An Investment Advisor's Published Works. **www.ethicinvest.bc.ca/blog/2004/03/cpp-investment-board-comes-under-fire.htm** (March 2, 2004).

[13]CPP Investment Board Comes Under Fire, ibid.

[14]CPP Investment Board, Keeping You Informed.

Private Pensions

Private retirement pensions may be arranged from personal savings, but generally when we speak of private pensions we mean employment-related ones. The following terms can be considered synonyms: registered pension plans (RPPs), company pension plans, private pension plans, and employer-sponsored pension plans. Essentially, private pension plans represent a way of deferring a portion of your wages until retirement. There is, however, no uniformity in the benefits provided by private pension plans, nor are all of Canada's paid workers covered by such a plan. Almost all medium and large companies have RPPs for their employees. Companies contribute and administer the funds. Employees are not obligated to contribute. Many workers are not members of private pension plans and will therefore have to depend on public pensions and on their own savings when they retire.

Defined Contributions or Defined Benefits

Contributory pension plans require employees to pay a percentage of their wages to the plan in addition to whatever the employer contributes. Some employers offer non-contributory plans—that is, plans in which the employer provides all funds.

There are two main types of private pension plans: defined contribution plans and defined benefits plans. A **defined contribution** (or money purchase) **pension plan** has rules about the amounts that can be contributed by the employer and employee, but it makes no promises about the size of the retirement pension. The contributions credited to an employee's pension account, plus interest, will be available at retirement to purchase an annuity. A **defined benefits pension plan**, by contrast, has a formula for calculating a retirement pension; the formula usually depends on the employee's years of service and on the average wages earned during the last five years of the employee's working life. With such a plan, the employer promises a certain level of retirement benefits. For the long-service employee, a defined benefits plan is usually preferable to a defined contribution plan. Not surprisingly, some employers prefer defined contribution plans because under such plans they have no pension liability to fund (as they would with a defined benefits plan); that is, they have not promised employees a certain level of pension income.

Although the majority of private pension plans have been of the defined-benefits type, the trend is changing. Some employers, finding the new pension regulations onerous, are shifting the risk to employees by setting up defined contribution plans or group RRSPs. Thus, contributions are made to a retirement fund for employees, but the employer does not promise any particular level of pension. The employer also has less of an obligation to compensate for the effects of future inflation rates or to maximize the yield from the invested pension funds.

The Crisis Facing Defined Benefits Plans

There could be a crisis in the near future facing Canadians expecting to receive a pension from a defined benefits plan. The Certified General Accountants Association of Canada reported that, as of December 31, 2003, 59 percent of defined benefits plans had deficits. The organization estimated that $160 billion, almost equal to the federal government's budget, will be required to eliminate the deficits and provide necessary funds for the future indexing of benefits.[15]

[15]Addressing the Pensions Dilemma in Canada, Certified General Accountants Association of Canada, June 9, 2004, updated May 30, 2005.

FIGURE 6.2

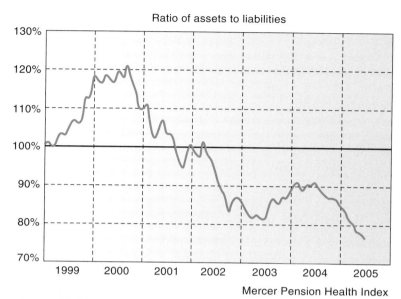

Ratio of assets to liabilities

Mercer Pension Health Index

SOURCE: Mercer Pension Health Index, July 2005, "Worse and Worse for Pensions," Mercer Human Resource Consulting Limited.

The deficits occurred because of the "pay as you go policy" whereby today's employees, of which there are fewer, fund today's retirees. Since most plans have a large part of their assets invested in stocks, the deficits were worsened by the decline in the stock market in the early years of the century. Even though the Canadian stock market became a bull market after 2003, the gains in stocks were not able to overcome the problem caused by lower than usual interest rates. In fact, the funding status of Canada's 100 largest defined-benefit pension plans continued to deteriorate in 2003 and 2004. The number of under-funded plans increased from 77 to 81.[16] Figure 6.2 shows in dramatic fashion the enormity of the problem.

Many plans offer generous early retirement benefits to their members. The shortage of skilled labour—and employees of all sorts, in many industries—and the expected shortfall in the future have put this policy in danger. This is shown dramatically in Table 6.2. It is no longer logical to offer such rich benefit plans when replacement workers are difficult, if not impossible, to find. The problem, arising from generous early retirement benefits, has caused a significant decline in the number of defined benefits plans. A considerable number of employers have collapsed their plans or prohibited the entrance of new employees. (Personal Finance in Action Box 6.3, "Maria and the Disappearing Pension," will give you an idea of the potential impact of these changes on unfortunate individuals.) As a result, the number of Canadians covered by such plans has declined by 5 percent since 1992.[17]

Two of the most publicized cases of companies with large deficits in their pension plans are Stelco and Air Canada. In Stelco's case, the deficit is $1.3 billion.[18] The problem, in most cases, was caused by the serious decline in the stock market between 2000 and 2002, a decline that also hurt the CPP. The poor performance was exacerbated by the very low interest rates in Canada at the time.

[16]Christine Wiedman and Heather Weir, Defined-Benefit Pension Plans: The Staying Power of Deficits, *Ivey Business Journal*, Sept/Oct 2005.

[17]Governor Dodge Discusses Efficiency and the Importance of Pension Plans, Bank of Canada, November 9, 2005.

[18]Ontario Rejects Stelco's Bid for Pension Plan Concessions, *CBC Business News*, August 8, 2005.

TABLE 6.2   WORKERS PER RETIRED PERSON

1991	3.8
2001	2.7
2011	1.8 (projected)

SOURCE: In Depth: Retirement, CBC News Online, February 11, 2005.

Pension Terminology

Important issues related to pensions involve vesting, portability, survivor benefits, and index-ation. We will examine each in turn.

Vesting   **Vesting** refers to the time when an employee becomes entitled to receive a pension upon retirement. The time required for vesting varies across the country but it is usually two years. If an employee changes employment before vesting has occurred, he or she will receive a refund of his or her contributions with interest but not the amount paid into the plan on the employee's behalf by his or her employer. If this person changes jobs after vesting has occurred, he or she will be given a choice, as explained in the next paragraph.

Portability   Formerly, employees who changed jobs could not take their pension credits with them. **Pension portability** is the right to transfer pension credits from one employer to another. The lack of portability in private pensions has long been a serious problem. Recent legislation has, however, brought about some improvement. Workers with vesting rights now have three options when they change jobs: they may (i) leave their pension credits with their former employer and receive a pension at retirement; (ii) transfer their credits to their new employer's pension plan if that plan permits such a transfer; or (iii) transfer their benefits to a locked-in registered retirement savings plan (RRSP). But if they do not stay long enough with an employer for vesting to kick in, all too often a change of job will cause a loss of pension rights and will require them to start over in another pension plan. Some of the options

Personal FINANCE in action 6.3

Maria and the Disappearing Pension

Maria had taught Spanish at a private girls' school since her arrival from Colombia. According to her last defined benefits pension statement, she would have a pension of $37 998.60 when she retired at 65. She was looking forward to retirement so she could again travel to South America and visit her friends. She had never married and believed she could easily manage on her school pension and the money she would get from the CPP. However, just before her sixty-fifth birthday she received a shocking letter from the fund manager. Instead of learning what her monthly pension would be, she was told that "due to serious under-funding and poor investment decisions," the fund was going bankrupt. She would receive a one-time payment of $10 000 but no pension. Maria had never saved much money and had no investments. Dismayed, she went to see an accountant friend who told her that the only money she could expect to get each month was $844.58 from the CPP, and since her income was so low, a combined payment of $1 085.07 from the OAS and GIS. Therefore, instead of getting her school pension, she would only get the princely sum of $22 965.84 a year. Her travel plans were shelved and she decided to find a new job.

listed above for handling the pension credits for those with vesting rights offer a partial solution to the portability problem. If you change jobs, analyze the costs and benefits of the various options to see which would make a better contribution to your retirement income.

Survivor Benefits When one member of a married couple dies, the surviving spouse, if he or she is 65 or older, will receive benefits equal to 60 percent of the calculated retirement pension. If the surviving spouse is disabled, the survivor's pension is equal to the above plus 37.5 percent of the calculated retirement pension. There are many private pension plans. The pension paid to surviving spouses aged 65 and older from such plans varies.

Indexation Although public pensions have been fully indexed, many occupational plans do not have either full or partial indexing. A **fully indexed** pension is adjusted regularly to reflect changes in the Consumer Price Index. **Partial indexation** means that the pension is adjusted for part of the change in the Consumer Price Index. There has been more partial or full indexation of pensions in the public sector than in the private sector. The limiting factor is the unknown cost. Employers have been reluctant to promise fully indexed pensions to retirees because of uncertainty about future pension liabilities. Many employees, who are often more oriented to the present than to the future, may also be reluctant to reduce their current take-home pay by making contributions to the pension plan that are large enough to cover future indexing. Those who have not yet retired often display a lack of awareness about the ways in which inflation can erode a fixed pension. For example, with inflation of only 4 percent per year, an unindexed pension will lose about a third of its purchasing power in 10 years, and about half its purchasing power in 18 years. If inflation is 6 percent, purchasing power will be reduced by half in only 12 years. However, at the low levels of inflation currently enjoyed in Canada, pension indexation has become less of a public issue than it once was.

Know Your Plan

An employee may not have much influence on the benefits offered by an employment-related pension plan. Nevertheless, it is in the employee's interest to be informed about the plan. Pension benefits vary so widely that it is wise to ask the following questions:

(a) Is the plan a defined benefits plan or a defined contribution plan?

(b) If it is a defined benefits plan, what formula will be used to calculate pension benefits?

(c) If it is a defined contribution plan, who makes the investment decisions, and what retirement options are offered?

(d) Are there provisions for early retirement?

(e) What happens if an employee should become disabled?

(f) What are the survivor's benefits?

(g) Will the employee's estate receive any of the employer's contributions?

(h) Is it possible to split pension credits in the case of marriage breakdown?

Life Annuities

At retirement, you may need to transform your life savings into an income stream. One way to do so involves purchasing an annuity. For instance, pension funds or RRSPs may be invested in annuities that will produce a monthly income for life. The following discussion of annuities will explain the basic annuity principle and the various ways in which annuities may be bought and paid out to the **annuitant**.

Because none of us knows how long we will live, retirees face the question of whether to use some of their capital for living expenses. If they do decide to use their capital, they must decide at what rate to spend it. If they spend too rapidly, they could outlive their resources; if they are too cautious, they could be forcing themselves to scrimp unnecessarily. So a method has been devised for ensuring that your savings last for a lifetime: a life annuity. Any system that involves liquidating a sum of money through a series of regular and equal payments is called an **annuity**. To annuitize a sum of money means to convert it into a monthly income. Annuity payments were originally made annually (hence the name *annuity*), but these days they are often made monthly or semi-annually instead. It is usually safe to assume that an annuity income payment will be made monthly, unless stated otherwise.

The Annuity Principle

There are two possible ways of protecting against the risk of outliving your savings: (i) acquiring sufficient net worth to support your desired lifestyle indefinitely, or (ii) buying a life annuity. Like insurance, a life annuity is a way of pooling resources with others to ensure that all members of the pool will be protected against a given risk—in this case, that of outliving the income generated by one's savings. Life insurance companies, the only financial institutions currently authorized to sell life annuities, accept the savings of many people; in return, the company promises each annuitant a life income. Those who live a very long time will receive more from the pooled funds than will those who die sooner, but each annuitant will receive an income for as long as he or she lives. As Figure 6.3 emphasizes, though, insurance companies do not promise annuitants that they will receive as much as they have contributed. A life annuity can be useful for a person with modest means who is concerned more about protecting his or her level of living than about

FIGURE 6.3 EXPERIENCES OF TWO LIFE ANNUITANTS

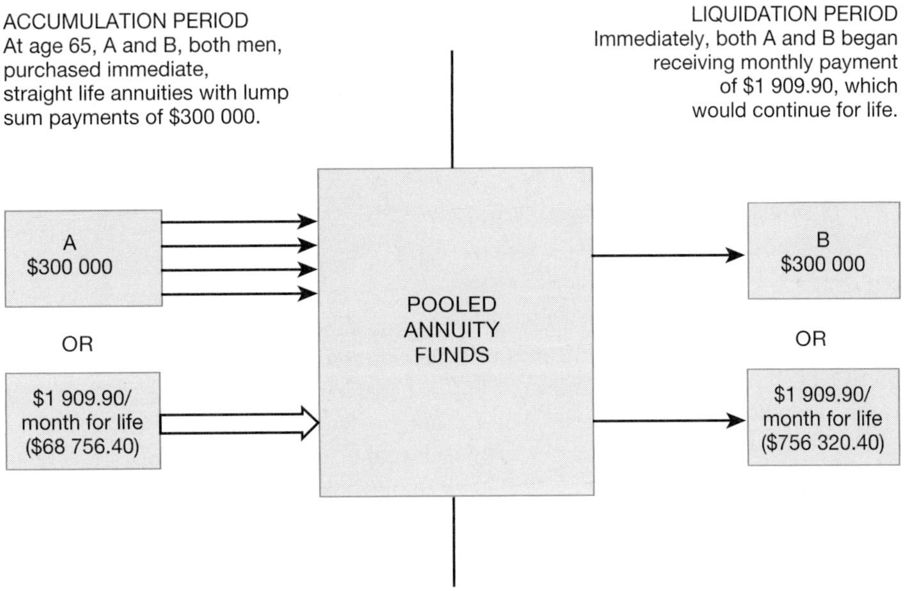

ACCUMULATION PERIOD
At age 65, A and B, both men, purchased immediate, straight life annuities with lump sum payments of $300 000.
LIQUIDATION PERIOD
Immediately, both A and B began receiving monthly payment of $1 909.90, which would continue for life.
A
$300 000
OR
$1 909.90/ month for life ($68 756.40)
POOLED ANNUITY FUNDS
B
$300 000
OR
$1 909.90/ month for life ($756 320.40)

A died at age 68 after receiving payments for three years, for a total of 36 x $1 909.90, or $68 756.40.

B died at age 98 after receiving payments for 33 years, for a total of (33 x 12) x $1909.90, or $756 320.40.

creating an estate for heirs. Some misconceptions about annuities stem from not understanding the annuity principle. Do not think of an annuity as a way of making money, but rather as a way of converting a sum of money into a lifetime income. This principle is at work in Personal Finance in Action Box 6.4, "Should He Use Some of His Capital?"

Characteristics of Annuities

Annuities have several important characteristics that should be clearly understood:

(a) the distinction between the accumulation period and the liquidation period,

(b) the method of paying the purchase price,

Personal FINANCE in action 6.4

Should He Use Some of His Capital?

You are a financial planner. Eric comes to you for advice. He will be retiring next month, when he turns 65. Over the course of his life, he has managed to save $500 000, and he wants to know what to do with this money. He is healthy and has never had a major illness. His wife, Ina, died recently. He has two grown-up children, both of whom are married and have good jobs; he also has three grandchildren.

You explain to Eric that what he ought to do with his money depends on his financial goals. Does he want to leave an estate for his heirs, or does he want to use up the capital himself? If he decides to protect the capital and thereby leave some money for his children and grandchildren, he has several options. You point out, however, that no investment can guarantee to protect the purchasing power of his money.

Eric decides that he would like to leave half of his money to his grandchildren but also to earn some money for himself by investing in something conservative. At his age he doesn't want to take risks. You suggest two conservative choices for him with the money divided equally between the two: GICs and preferred stock.

For the GIC you recommend that he put $250 000 in a Bank of Montreal RateRiser Max. The money will be locked in for five years, the interest increased each year and compounded annually. The rates for the five years are: 2.25 percent in year one, 2.5 percent in year two, 2.75 percent in year three, 3 percent in year 4, and 6.75 percent in year 5. After the five-year period is up, his GIC will have grown to $296 015.28.

For the balance you suggest the Bank of Commerce preferred CIBC Pfd. A Ser 27 with the ticker symbol CM.PR.E. While slightly more risky, it is still a conservative investment. It closed the day before at $26.31, yields 5.3 percent, and pays a dividend of $1.40 per share. He can afford to buy 9400 shares at $26.31. If he calls in his order or buys the shares online, the commission for any quantity of shares greater than 1000 is 0.03 per share at his investment dealers. Therefore, the shares will cost him

$$9400 \times \$26.31 = \$247\ 314$$
$$9400 \times 0.03 = \underline{\quad 282}$$
$$\$247\ 596$$

His dividend income from these shares will be $13 160 per year. When added to the income from his pension and the CPP, it will allow Eric to live quite comfortably.

You also tell Eric that, if he chooses not to leave an estate for his heirs, he can purchase a life annuity, which will guarantee him a good income for life. He will have no worries if he does but, you explain, there is one serious flaw or risk in making such a decision. This flaw is shown in Figure 6.3. If Eric should die prematurely, the insurance company that issued him the annuity will keep his capital. None will go to his heirs. Eric's options are shown in Figure 6.4.

FIGURE 6.4 OPTIONS FOR GENERATING RETIREMENT INCOME

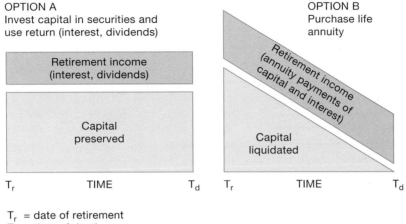

OPTION A
Invest capital in securities and
use return (interest, dividends)

Retirement income
(interest, dividends)

Capital
preserved

T_r TIME T_d

OPTION B
Purchase life
annuity

Retirement income
(annuity payments of
capital and interest)

Capital
liquidated

T_r TIME T_d

T_r = date of retirement
T_d = date of death

(c) when the liquidation period will start,
(d) the number of lives covered,
(e) the refund features.

Accumulation and Liquidation Periods Every life annuity comprises two stages: (i) the **accumulation period**—that is, the interval during which the annuitant pays the insurance company for the annuity; and (ii) the **liquidation period**—that is, the time span during which the insurer makes payments to the annuitant (see Figure 6.5). The accumulation period may last for many years if the annuity is bought by instalment; it may be very brief if the annuity is purchased with a lump sum. Regardless of the method chosen for buying an annuity, the accumulation period must be completed before the liquidation period may start.

Method of Paying If an annuity is purchased with a lump sum, it will be a **single-payment annuity.** The other alternative is to buy the annuity gradually, over a number of years, by making a series of regular instalment payments or premiums. The instalment method is useful for a person who finds saving difficult and therefore needs a contractual savings plan, but others may prefer the flexibility of accumulating capital on their own and then deciding later whether to buy an annuity. For an example of a single-payment annuity refer to Appendix 6A, Payout Annuity.

Starting the Liquidation Period The payout from an annuity may begin immediately after the annuity is purchased, or it may be deferred until a later date. An **immediate annuity** will start making regular payments to the annuitant at once. By definition, an immediate annuity must be bought with a single payment, since all payments for an annuity must be completed before the liquidation period begins. With a **deferred annuity**, the liquidation period begins some time after purchase, and the annuity may be bought either with a single payment or with a series of premiums. For instance, a young person who has inherited a sum of money could decide to buy a single-payment deferred annuity that will begin payments when he or she is older.

FIGURE 6.5 PAYMENT OPTIONS DURING THE ACCUMULATION AND LIQUIDATION PERIODS OF A LIFE ANNUITY

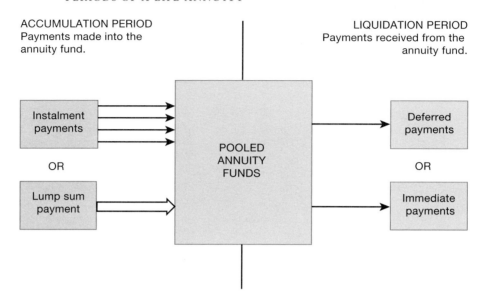

Number of Lives Covered The simplest and cheapest form of life annuity is the **straight life annuity**, which pays an income for the life of the annuitant and ceases at death, with no further payments to beneficiaries. But an annuity may also be designed to produce a life income for more than one person—commonly for two. A couple, for example, may buy a **joint-life-and-last-survivorship annuity**. The name of such an annuity is derived from "joint life," which pays as long as both are alive, and from "last survivor," meaning that the annuity will continue during the lifetime of the survivor. These points are illustrated in Figure 6.6.

Not surprisingly, a **joint-and-survivor annuity** (its abbreviated name) is the most expensive of all annuities. Table 6.3 illustrates the difference in cost between this option and a straight life annuity. The rate for a couple is based on the woman's age when the annuity is purchased because of her longer life expectancy and the possibility that she may

FIGURE 6.6 LIQUIDATION PAYMENTS BY NUMBER OF LIVES COVERED

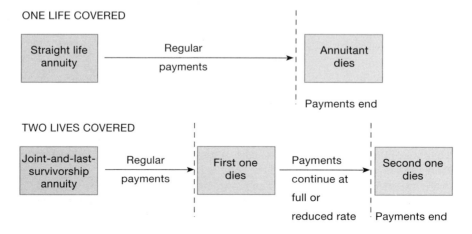

TABLE 6.3   TWO LIFE ANNUITY OPTIONS FOR A COUPLE

A.   STRAIGHT LIFE ANNUITY—15-year guarantee

Annuitant	*Purchase price*	*Income per month*
Husband, age 65	$750 693.37	$5000

B.   JOINT-LIFE-AND-LAST-SURVIVORSHIP ANNUITY—15-year guarantee
(Full income to survivor)

Annuitant	*Purchase price*	*Income per month*
Husband, age 65, and	$944 243.42	$5000
Wife, age 60, survivor		

be younger than her husband. The purchaser must decide whether, after the death of the first spouse, the survivor will continue to receive the full payment or will receive only some proportion of it, such as half or two-thirds. The cost of a joint-and-survivor annuity can be reduced if the payments are planned to decrease after the first death. Another possibility is to buy two separate life annuities, one on each life. Table 6.3 illustrates the costs of both alternatives.

Refund Features   An annuitant may be interested in the refund features available during either the accumulation period or the liquidation period of the annuity. If the annuitant should die during the accumulation period, or decide to discontinue payments, it would be desirable to have the amount that has already been paid, plus interest, refunded. Or, an annuitant who does not wish to continue payments may be given the option of converting to a smaller paid-up annuity.

Refund features during the liquidation period are very popular with buyers who worry that they may not live long enough to receive as much as they contributed. In response to this concern, life insurance companies have created annuity plans that include payments for a guaranteed length of time, or to a guaranteed minimum amount, regardless of whether the annuitant lives or dies. Because of these provisions, these plans are called **refund annuities.**

A very popular type of refund annuity is one with a minimum number of instalments guaranteed. A life annuity with 10 years "certain," for example, promises to make payments as long as the annuitant lives, but for a minimum of 10 years even if the annuitant dies during the 10-year period. If the annuitant should die within the first 10 years of the payout period, a named beneficiary will receive a lump sum equivalent to the balance of payments the annuitant would have received if he or she had lived until the end of the 10-year period. Note that the certain period refers to the minimum payment period, not the maximum. These ideas are summarized at the top of p. 170.

The Cost of an Annuity

Six factors influence the cost of an annuity:

(a) the size of the monthly payments desired,

(b) the annuitant's life expectancy (as influenced by age, gender, and health),

(c) interest rates,

(d) the length of the accumulation period,

(e) whether the annuity has either refund features or inflation protection features,

(f) the number of lives covered.

Refund Features During the Accumulation and Liquidation Periods of an Annuity

Situation	Refund
Accumulation Period:	
Annuitant decides to stop paying.	Contributions refunded.
Annuitant dies before completing purchase of annuity.	Contributions refunded.
Liquidation Period:	
Annuitant has policy with 10 years certain but dies before 10 years.	Sum equivalent to balance of payments remaining in the 10-year period is paid to the annuitant's beneficiary or to the annuitant's estate.

Size of Payments There are two ways to approach purchasing an annuity: either (i) put a certain amount of money into an annuity, and then accept the income it will generate; or (ii) determine the specific monthly income desired, and then pay the necessary amount to generate this. Most buyers of annuities fall into the first group; they buy as much monthly income as their limited funds permit, and they are well aware of the relationship between cost and expected income.

Life Expectancy Although an annuity's price is based on a number of factors, life expectancy is a critical one. Three variables commonly used to predict life expectancy are gender, age, and health. Since females, younger people, and healthy people are expected to live longer than are males, older people, or sickly people, the insurance company can expect to have to make annuity payments to someone who falls into one or more of the first three categories for a longer time. And because this situation is more costly for the insurance company, individuals in the former group will receive a smaller monthly income from a given amount that they put into an immediate life annuity. The difference gender makes is shown in Figure 6.7.

Interest Rates An annuity's cost is greatly influenced by the expected return that can be earned on the annuity's funds while they are held by the insurance company. When interest rates are high, the annuity income will also be higher, and when interest rates are low, the annuity income will also be lower. For this reason, financial advisors suggest carefully choosing the time when you will convert your capital into an annuity.

Length of Accumulation Period Compared with an immediate annuity, an annuity that is bought with instalments over many years will cost less because of the additional interest the insurance company earns during the longer time the premiums are on deposit. Table 6.4, which compares the total cost of two ways of buying a certain level of annuity income, shows that a single-payment, immediate annuity costs more than an instalment annuity that is bought over 30 years. Instalment annuities have largely been replaced by segregated funds. These are discussed later in this chapter.

Refund Features An annuity with a guaranteed period will cost you more because the guarantee changes the probable number of years the insurance company will have to make payments to you (see Table 6.5). The cost differences reflect the certainty of having to

FIGURE 6.7 MONTHLY ANNUITY INCOME BY AGE AT PURCHASE AND GENDER (SINGLE-PAYMENT, IMMEDIATE, STRAIGHT LIFE ANNUITY; ALL PURCHASES PAY THE SAME PRICE)

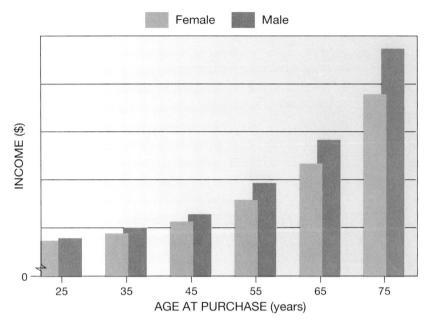

make payments for 10 years, regardless of the annuitant's life expectancy. Few insurance salespeople now sell annuities with no certain period.

Figure 6.8 makes the same point, showing that, in general, a lump sum that is used to buy an immediate annuity will produce a lower monthly income if the annuity has a refund feature (see also Personal Finance in Action Box 6.5, "Buying an Annuity"). However, if the annuity is bought before age 45, the difference is small.

Number of Lives Covered You will pay more to buy a life annuity that will provide an income for the lifetimes of two people than if the annuity must provide an income for just

TABLE 6.4 PURCHASE PRICE AND MONTHLY INCOME BY METHOD OF PAYMENT

METHOD OF PAYMENT	PURCHASE PRICE	MONTHLY INCOME
Single-payment, immediate annuity bought at age 65	$681 337.65	$4000.00
Instalment annuity, paid from age 30 to age 65*	$134 287.00**	$4000.00

*Straight-life Instalments earn 6%.

**Using present value and future value, we can determine the purchase price of an instalment annuity.

TABLE 6.5 PURCHASE PRICE BY GUARANTEED PERIOD

TYPE OF ANNUITY*	PURCHASE PRICE
Straight life; no certain period	$628 583.08
Life annuity; 10 years certain	$652 998.78

*Immediate annuity to provide a life income of $4000 per month for a male, aged 65.

FIGURE 6.8   ANNUITY INCOME BY AGE AT PURCHASE AND GUARANTEED PERIOD
(SINGLE-PAYMENT, IMMEDIATE LIFE ANNUITY)

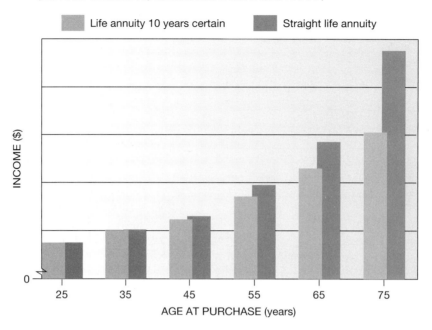

Personal FINANCE in action 6.5

Buying an Annuity

In preparation for her forthcoming retirement, Mrs. Alvarez is thinking of converting her three RRSPs to a life annuity to generate a dependable income. Because she has no dependents and has a distaste for investment management, she believes that an annuity is her best option. Her first thought is to ask her life insurance agent to make all the arrangements. But Mrs. Alvarez talks about her plans to several friends, who advise her to consult an insurance broker for help. An insurance broker can obtain quotations from many life insurance companies for a client, and since brokers get commissions from the companies that issue the annuities, the client is not normally charged for this service.

On talking to a broker, she discovers that there is more to buying an annuity than she has supposed. The broker first familiarizes himself with Mrs. Alvarez's financial situation, considering such aspects as other sources of

retirement income, her predicted marginal income tax rate, and the potential needs of any dependents. Then he presents several options for her consideration. He mentions that if a person's health is poor, she might, with the support of medical evidence, qualify for an impaired-health annuity, which would pay a higher income for the same premium. When Mrs. Alvarez asks why, the broker explains that the insurer's liability is reduced if the annuitant is not expected to live for a long time, making it possible for the company to pay a higher rate.

The broker presents Mrs. Alvarez with two potential ways of preserving purchasing power. She can investigate the escalating annuities offered by some insurance companies, or she can plan to buy a series of annuities in various years. The escalating annuity will initially pay a lower monthly income, but that income will be adjusted annually according to prevailing

continued

interest rates. Since an inflationary period normally causes interest rates to rise, she would therefore receive higher annuity payments to offset the inflation. If interest rates were to fall, the company would not lower payments but would instead increase them more slowly. Such escalating annuities are one example of the ways in which insurers have modified annuities to help preserve clients' purchasing power in inflationary times.

Some brokers suggest that a client buy a series of annuities in different years to take advantage of changing interest rates. The premiums for annuities are very sensitive to the interest rates that companies expect to receive on invested funds. Mrs. Alvarez could deregister one of her RRSPs to buy an annuity now, and do likewise with the other two in later years. (She must have all her RRSPs deregistered by the time she is 69 in order to comply with the income tax laws.) In a period of rising interest rates, buying a series of annuities could be

advantageous, but if rates were falling, the reverse could be true.

Mrs. Alvarez knows that she wants an immediate annuity, but she is undecided about the refund feature. She discovers that for a given premium, she can obtain a somewhat larger annual income with a straight life annuity than with one that has a 10-year guarantee. The broker asks her whether she would rather have (i) the higher income or (ii) the assurance that should she die before the 10 years elapse, her estate will receive payments for the balance of the decade.

The broker advises her to decide what kind of annuity she wants before he starts obtaining quotations for her, since annuity prices change rapidly—sometimes even daily. For this reason some companies will guarantee their quotations for only one to three days. Because rates vary not only from time to time but also among companies, the broker will seek quotations from quite a number of firms for Mrs. Alvarez.

one person. In the case of a couple, the cost is related to the gender and age of the younger partner. A woman is expected to outlive her husband even if they are the same age; a woman who is younger than her husband can be expected to live proportionately longer than he does.

Variable Annuities

Segregated funds have replaced variable annuities. This type of fund is discussed later in this chapter (see page 184).

Annuities and Income Tax

The income tax treatment of annuity payments depends on whether the annuity was bought with before-tax or after-tax dollars. Each payment includes both capital and interest, and these components may be treated separately for tax purposes. If the annuity was purchased with before-tax dollars (which would have been in a tax shelter, such as an RRSP), both the capital and the interest components of the income payments will now be exposed to income tax. But if the annuity was purchased with after-tax dollars (i.e., the annuity was not in a tax shelter), the capital portion is not taxable when received. The issuing company will provide the annuitant with annual statements that show the total capital and interest portions that he or she has received for each year. Income tax rules require that during the accumulation period of a deferred annuity, the annuitant report the accrued interest at least every three years.

Personal FINANCE in action 6.6

The Difference in Annuity Contract Premiums

Madu and his partner, Germaine, were born on the same day and were thus able to retire at 65 at the same time and receive full pensions. Both had saved vigorously for many years and had accumulated substantial assets. They had not invested in RRSPs. Rather than rely solely on the income from their investments, which, because they were mainly in GICs and Canada Savings Bonds, was very low as they neared retirement, they decided to look into annuities. What they found out surprised them.

Both wanted a single life annuity that would provide them with $1 000 each month, have an annual increase of 4 percent, and have a guaranteed period of 10 years. Madu was told that his annuity would require a total premium of $238 767. For the exact same annuity, Germaine was told that her premium would amount to $267 144. When she asked why, she was told, "You have a longer life expectancy." She thought this was a stupid reason because Madu played soccer on weekends and was extremely fit for his age.

The Annuity Market

In 2003, Canadians owned 3.4 million annuity contracts. During the year they paid annuity premiums of $20.9 billion. At the same time, Canadians received annuity payments totalling $20.1 billion. Of this sum, 10 percent was paid out in death benefits and 90 percent went to living annuitants.[19]

Whether to Buy an Annuity

Before deciding to buy an annuity, you should review the costs and benefits of various annuities. A major advantage of an annuity is that it provides a guaranteed, usually fixed, lifetime income without the concern of having to manage any investments. But by the same token, you lose the flexibility to manage your own money; once funds are put into an annuity, they are committed, and their management is out of your hands. If a more beneficial investment opportunity should arise, you will not be able to take advantage of it. Conversely, an annuity offers protection against a depressed investment climate. In an inflationary period, a fixed income loses purchasing power, but a fixed income would be an advantage if prices should fall. There is no way to guarantee that an annuitant will receive as much as or more than was paid into an annuity, but that should be of little concern. The annuitant will have a guaranteed life income, even if his or her heirs do not receive an estate. Of course, it is also possible to put only a portion of one's capital into an annuity, leaving part of it available to be bequeathed to others.

Annuities are not for everyone, but they are a useful way to make a small estate last for a lifetime. Those who are in poor health, those who want to leave an estate for heirs, and those who have the time and inclination to manage their own investments may all be wise to put their money elsewhere. But a deferred annuity is a reasonable option for anyone who needs a contractual savings plan to ensure that money is saved for his or her retirement. Please note that this discussion of annuities is intended only to illustrate the basic principles involved, not to describe all the possible variations of annuities that are or may become available. Financial institutions are quite inventive in constantly creating new services for consumers,

[19]*Canadian Life and Health Insurance Facts, 2004 Edition.* Canadian Life and Health Insurance Association.

so you will need to familiarize yourself with the options that are currently available before making your own decision.

Registered Retirement Savings Plans

What Is an RRSP?

A **registered retirement savings plan** (an RRSP) is one method for sheltering savings from income tax. When you invest savings outside a tax shelter, you are using after-tax dollars; any income earned by those investments, such as interest or dividends, is taxable. But if you put that same money into an RRSP, no tax is payable when the investment is made, nor is the yield taxable. Funds that go into an RRSP are referred to as before-tax dollars and tax must be paid when they are withdrawn. Chapter 2 contains a diagram that illustrates this point (see page 48). Note that having an RRSP does not mean that you need never pay tax on this income; sheltering money in an RRSP merely *defers* (postpones) having to pay tax on that money. All funds become taxable when they are removed from the tax shelter. The ideal strategy is to put money into an RRSP when you are being taxed at a high marginal tax rate, and then take it out later when your income (and therefore your tax rate) is lower—for example, after you have retired. An example in Chapter 2 (Personal Finance in Action Box 2.3, "Should She Use a Tax Shelter?") demonstrates how income tax may be deferred by putting money into an RRSP.

Two widely held misconceptions associated with RRSPs are (i) that everyone needs an RRSP and (ii) that an RRSP is a specific type of investment. Because Canadians are exposed to such energetic promotion of RRSPs, investors may forget that income tax deferment is a major reason for putting money into an RRSP. It is a way of sheltering savings from tax to allow them to grow at a faster rate than they otherwise would, and thus to accumulate a fund for retirement or for another purpose. If your financial circumstances are such that you already pay little or no income tax, you probably do not need an RRSP; you can invest your savings on your own without having to obey the restrictions imposed on RRSPs. *An RRSP is not a specific type of investment, but a way of registering one or more of a variety of types of investments in order to shelter the invested funds and to defer paying income tax both on the original funds and on any income generated by investing those funds.* As we will see, many kinds of investments may be put into an RRSP.

To repeat, the chief reason for putting money into an RRSP is to defer income tax. Your savings will grow faster inside a tax shelter than they could grow outside it, and when you take the money into income, or cash in the RRSP, in future years, when your marginal tax rate is lower, you may pay less income tax on it than you would have paid on the same amount had it been taxable the year in which you earned it. (Refer to Chapter 2, under "Federal Income Tax Rates," for an explanation of the marginal tax rate.) Remember, though, that the money in your RRSP will be taxable eventually, when you deregister the plan. Since RRSP funds are not quite as accessible as other savings, such plans may help some people build a retirement fund, especially those people who normally have a hard time holding onto their savings.

Putting money into an RRSP does involve investing, so you should take as much care in choosing an RRSP as you would in selecting any investment (as Ella does in this chapter's Women Take Charge). It can be a mistake to become so caught up in the prospect of deferring income tax that you pay little attention to the quality and appropriateness of your RRSP investments. The principles of investing that we will discuss in Chapters 8 through 10 apply equally well to RRSP decisions.

Ella has been working for several years and has built up her income as a financial planner. While pursuing her education, Ella worked part-time and accumulated unused RRSP contribution room. Even though she owed no taxes as a student, she filed a tax return each year to keep track of her unused RRSP contribution room. Now that Ella is in a higher marginal tax bracket, she would like to start an RRSP. Not only will she be able to reduce her tax bill and get a head start on retirement planning, but she will also be able to access her RRSP in the future to become a first-time homebuyer or to go back to university under the Lifelong Learning program, should the need arise.

Ella has done research on zero coupon or strip bonds, which do not make periodic interest payments but which are purchased at a discount. The bonds earn interest each year, which must be reported even though it is not actually paid. Since the interest is reported but not paid out,

Ella has decided to put the strip bond into her RRSP, where the interest will be tax-sheltered.

To supplement her RRSP, Ella will initiate a non-registered savings program outside an RRSP. She plans on purchasing some high-quality Canadian stocks that have a history of paying stable or growing dividends and that have a DRIP (dividend reinvestment program). The DRIP allows Ella to reinvest her dividends each year and buy additional shares at no extra cost. She will buy stock in Canadian companies that qualify for the dividend tax credit. The dividend tax credit is a tax break not given to interest income. The compounding effect of reinvested dividends helps build income for retirement.

Not only will Ella receive dividend income, but the shares could increase in value over the years. The capital gain on the increase in the value of the shares can be deferred until Ella decides to sell. Currently, only 50 percent of the net capital gain is included in taxable income, thus giving Ella another significant tax break.

Qualified RRSP Investments

The Canada Revenue Agency qualifies a considerable variety of investments as RRSP eligible. Not all of these are suitable for everyone. When putting investments into an RRSP, one needs to have the same concerns as when investing in non-registered investments. The only difference between investments inside an RRSP and investments outside a plan is that income and capital gains are not taxed inside a plan. Investment concerns are discussed in detail in Chapters 8 and 10. The most important consideration in selecting investments for an RRSP is the risk involved, since a major goal of such a plan is to help someone have a financially healthy retirement. Too-risky investments in the plan could put this in danger.

Every investment carries some risk. The investments listed in Table 6.6, below, are rated according to the risk involved. All such evaluations are subjective.

Popular RRSP Investment Choices

It is considered advisable to have investments inside a plan complement one's non-registered investments. Diversification and not duplication is advised to reduce the risk of loss.

GICs and Canada Savings Bonds While the principal sum is guaranteed (the investor gets the face value back), and interest is paid (this is guaranteed too with a CSB and

TABLE 6.6   QUALIFIED RRSP INVESTMENTS

LITTLE RISK	MODERATE RISK	HIGH RISK
Gold bullion	Silver bullion	Shares in venture capital corporations
Mortgages guaranteed by the federal or a provincial government	Gold and silver coins and bars	Shares in private corporations
Mortgages issued for real estate in Canada and administered by an approved lender	Gold and silver certificates	Shares in small businesses
Bonds guaranteed by the federal or a provincial government	Shares in publicly traded Canadian or foreign companies	Instalment receipts
Debentures guaranteed by the federal or a provincial government	Some mutual funds	Money in any currency
GICs issued by a Canadian company	Bonds and debentures issued by a publicly traded company, the shares of which are traded on a Canadian or foreign stock exchange (The quality of these can vary considerably.)	A mutual fund trust
Debentures with the same qualifications as bonds	Bonds issued by other countries that have an investment grade rating by a regular bond-rating agency	A Canadian unit trust
	Stripped bonds	A foreign stock exchange index trust
	Mortgages issued for real estate in Canada and administered by an approved lender	Call options
	Deposits with credit unions	Royalty units listed on an exchange that earn income from Canadian assets
	Savings accounts	
	Annuity contracts	
	Warrants and rights	
	Depository receipts listed on a Canadian or foreign stock exchange	
	Partnership assets listed on a stock exchange	

Source: Canada Revenue Agency IT-320R3.

is a virtual certainty with GICs), the interest is so low that the growth of the RRSP is also low. They are chosen because of their safety and because there is no tax on the interest as there would be if they were held in a non-registered account. Even without the GIC guarantee given by the banks, such funds are guaranteed up to $100 000 per institution, by the Canada Deposit Insurance Corporation, a federal crown corporation.

Canadian Mutual Funds Mutual funds will be dealt with extensively in Chapter 10. While sold throughout the year, they are most heavily marketed each winter during the RRSP season. They are often chosen for RRSPs by people with little investment experience as well as seasoned investors because they offer greater diversity than is possible for most investors selecting investments on their own. However, investors must be cautious when buying mutual funds. The quality of the funds varies considerably because the talents of the fund managers vary. If they are equity funds, they are also susceptible to the vagaries of the stock market that not even the most talented manager can predict or avoid. In the early years of the twenty-first century, some mutual funds turned in very poor performances. Before deciding on a mutual fund for an RRSP investors need to be very careful and find out as much as possible about the fund. This is sometimes not easy to do because the great volume of literature available (glossy brochures filled with colourful graphs and charts) is often not user-friendly. It sometimes seems created to confuse. Mutual funds also charge annual management fees, which are often quite steep, whether the fund does well or not. These reduce the growth in value of all funds and therefore reduce the money available for retirement.

Mutual funds are available from a variety of sources, including investment dealers, insurance companies, financial planners, and banks. Their ease of acquisition also helps to make them popular.

Corporate Bonds Canadian corporate bonds issued by well-run companies are in many RRSPs because they are not considered overly risky and pay higher interest than government bonds, CSBs, and GICs. Such interest is not taxed in registered accounts. This is called the tax advantage. GICs and CSBs have the same advantage. Outside such accounts bond interest is taxed more highly than either dividend income or capital gains, making bonds a less than exciting non-registered investment.

Shares in Publicly Traded Companies Also known as equities, these investments are in many accounts, but often investment advisors consider this to be foolish because shares are risky and putting them inside an RRSP could put someone's retirement at risk. It is considered wiser to put such investments in non-registered accounts where both the dividends they pay and the capital gains they might achieve have a tax advantage over bond interest. However, shares in good investment quality companies can do very well, providing both the dividend income and capital gains that can result in a healthy increase in the value of the RRSP.

Self-Administered Plans For those who have the time, interest, and enough money to make it worthwhile, a self-administered RRSP has the advantage of allowing the investor to make the investment decisions. A wider range of investment types may be held in a self-directed plan, such as Canada Savings Bonds, other bonds, stocks, treasury bills, or mortgages. You can shift funds from one form of investment to another as desired, and you can decide how much risk to assume. Institutions that handle self-directed RRSPs—which include investment dealers, banks, trust companies, and life insurance companies—usually charge an annual administration fee, as well as commissions on some transactions.

Group RRSPs Group RRSPs are offered to employees by their employers. Contributions are made through a payroll deduction plan and reduce the contributor's tax burden at once. This is the big advantage of such plans. Employees do not have to wait until the next income tax return to receive a refund. Investment managers administer the group account. Contributions are put into an employee's account and then invested according to his or her wishes.

Life Insurance Plans Besides offering guaranteed funds and mutual funds, life insurance companies provide a combination of life insurance coverage and retirement saving, whereby a policy's cash value is registered as an RRSP. Think carefully before tying your RRSP money to your life insurance coverage, though. The contract may require fixed annual payments that limit your flexibility in annual contributions and in moving RRSP money around. Since the fees and commissions tend to be heaviest in the early years of the (investment) contract, an investor who cancels such a contract after only a short time will lose money.

Various types of annuities available from life insurance companies are eligible as RRSP investments. The schedule of payments may be fixed or flexible. As with life insurance, there will be commissions payable in the early years.

Important RRSP Considerations

1. A major reason for opening an RRSP is to save tax. The exact amount of the RRSP tax savings will depend on your marginal tax rate. The higher the tax rate, the higher the savings.

2. Government policy regarding the contribution limit for RRSPs changes frequently. It has been 18 percent of earned income for some time and in 2005 the limits for the next five years were as follows:

2006	$18 000
2007	$19 000
2008	$20 000
2009	$21 000
2010	$22 000

If you are a member of a registered pension plan (RPP), you must subtract your *pension adjustment* from your contribution limit. This amount will be shown on your T4 slip for the previous year as well as on your Notice of Assessment.

3. Contribute early in the new year rather than later. This allows your contribution to grow more quickly.

4. A contribution is deductible in the year in which it is given or within 60 days of the new year, that is, up to March 1.

5. You are allowed to carry forward any unused contributions indefinitely. However, catching up can be very difficult for those who had difficulty making a contribution in the first place. Just how difficult can be seen from the fact that there was a 20 percent drop in RRSP contributions between 1997 and 2002.[20] As a result, Canadians had amassed an amazing $400 billion in unused contributions,[21] most of which is likely to stay that way.

[20]Hip Deep in Hock, *Maclean's Magazine*, December 6, 2004.
[21]Ian Davidson, Some Things to Think About, CA *Magazine*, June 2005.

6. Those with unused contribution room can always borrow the money. In December 2005, this was possible at the prime rate of 5 percent.[22] The cost of such a loan is less than one might expect because it allows an investor to take advantage of tax-deferred growth inside the RRSP. If the contribution results in a tax refund, this can be used to pay down the loan.

7. A key to good investing is diversification. This helps to spread risk and therefore to reduce it. The easiest way to diversify investments in an RRSP is to buy mutual funds since the size of contributions are generally too small to invest in board lots of stocks (see Chapter 10) or to buy a bond. Bond mutual funds are available that give the funds in the RRSP the tax advantage.

8. Prior to the spring of 2005, there was a foreign content rule for investing in RRSPs. Investors were only allowed to have 30 percent foreign content in their plans, thereby forcing them to rely on the small Canadian market. This restriction gave rise to a number of clone funds that evaded this restriction. Such a restriction no longer exists. The ability to add more foreign investments to one's portfolio allows for more diversification and if chosen wisely, less risk.

9. Self-directed RRSP fees range from $100 to $150. Fees for RRSPs managed by mutual fund representatives range from 1.5 to 2.5 percent of the value of the account. Pay any fees with funds outside the plan. Paying fees with money from inside the plan reduces the fund you are building for retirement.

10. The *top-up*. Once you have made your maximum contribution, you are allowed a $2000 top-up before being charged the penalty tax of 1 percent per month. This top-up allows your plan to grow more quickly. This over-contribution is not tax-deductible, but if it is withdrawn, the amount will be taxed as all other withdrawals would be.

11. Open a *spousal RRSP* if your spouse's income will be less than yours upon retirement. You can claim the deduction on your return, but when your spouse withdraws the funds, he or she will pay less tax. If the withdrawal is made within three years of the contribution, you will have to pay the tax.

12. Leave your RRSP to your spouse, not your estate. The RRSP will be included in your spouse's income and taxed, but your spouse can deposit up to the same amount into his or her RRSP and claim a deduction for the full amount. (See Personal Finance in Action Box 6.7, "Income Splitting on Retirement.")

Personal FINANCE in action 6.7

Income Splitting on Retirement

Omar will be retiring this year when he turns 65. Unlike many men his age, he is not worried about his financial future. He will have an excellent pension from his employer, the Ford Motor Company. He also has considerable income from his investments, and he will receive the Canada Pension.

Sarah, his wife, is 63 and has not worked outside their home since the birth of their first son, John, 30 years ago. As a result, she will get very little from the CPP, but she does have $200 000 in a spousal RRSP. Omar has contributed to this plan for many years in order to reduce his taxable income and to income-split with Sarah on his retirement. Since her taxable income will be less than his, they stand to realize considerable tax savings as a result of the spousal RRSP.

continued

[22]BMO ReadiLine Account, December 7, 2005.

Upon retirement, Omar and Sarah plan to travel, work in their garden, and pay more attention to their investments. Sarah has six years before she needs to close the spousal RRSP and wants to change the investments in the plan to significantly increase its value. She would like to have enough money once she turns 69 so that she is not dependent on Omar.

13. There is no limit to the number of RRSPs you can open, but having several makes the managing of a self-directed plan more difficult. You can also diversify more easily with a larger amount than with a number of smaller amounts.

14. *The Home Buyers' Plan*. First-time home buyers may borrow up to $20 000 from an RRSP in order to help buy or build a home. They may also borrow from their plans to buy a home for a disabled relative. The home must become the person's principal residence within one year. The money must be repaid to the RRSP over a 15-year period at the rate of one fifteenth of the original amount per year. Locked-in funds cannot be used.

15. *Lifelong Learning*. Up to $20 000 may be withdrawn from a plan, with a limit of $10 000 a year, to help finance the person's education or training as well as that for a spouse or common-law partner. The money must be repaid by the end of 10 years. Once the loan has been repaid, up to $20 000 may be borrowed again for the same purpose.

16. Funds transferred from a Registered Pension Plan to an RRSP are locked in and may not be withdrawn until retirement.

17. Any money withdrawn from a plan prior to age 69 is fully taxed. The funds, as explained below, must be removed from the tax shelter in the year the owner turns 69.

18. If the owner of an RRSP dies before reaching the age of 69, the money in the plan is refunded to the beneficiary. The beneficiary may transfer the amount to his or her own RRSP without having to pay tax. The beneficiary may also take the money and pay the tax. If no beneficiary is named, the full value of the RRSP is included as income in the estate's final tax return.

Who Needs an RRSP?

An RRSP is a good idea for anyone who has earned income and is paying a significant amount of income tax. On the other hand, if you have money to invest but pay very little income tax, you can forgo the restrictions of an RRSP. The financial press regularly publishes articles on RRSPs that emphasize the amount of tax deferred and the increase in savings possible with RRSPs. Whether these advantages will hold true for your particular case depends on your marginal tax rate and on the yield from your RRSP. (See Personal Finance in Action Boxes 6.8, "Is an RRSP Worthwhile?" and 6.9, "RRSPs and the Contrarian.")

Maturity Options

All of your RRSPs must be deregistered at some point before the end of the year in which you turn 69. Deregistering means changing from accumulating savings to either (i) removing the funds from the tax shelter and paying the required income tax on them, or (ii) initiating a liquidation plan to provide income. You can choose one or any combination of the following options:

RRSP Withdrawal Options

(a) Withdraw the money and pay tax on the full amount.

(b) Put the funds into a Registered Retirement Income Fund (RRIF).

Personal FINANCE in action 6.8

Is an RRSP Worthwhile?

Meena lives in Saskatchewan. She plans to save $3000 a year in anticipation of her retirement in 30 years' time. She decides to compare the results of putting her money inside a tax-sheltered RRSP with investing it outside a tax shelter. For comparison purposes, she makes the following assumptions:

Average interest rate 6%

Combined marginal tax rate 38.48%

After-tax interest rate

$6\% - (6\% \times .3848) = 3.69\%$

Annual investments for 30 years of

a) $3000 before-tax dollars in the RRSP

b) $1845.60 after-tax dollars outside an RRSP

$3000 - (3000 \times .3848) = 1845.60$

Using the formula for the "Future Value of a Series of Deposits," Meena learns why RRSPs are so popular. The $3000 inside the RRSP grows to $237 174 ($3000 × 79.058). Assuming that she pays the maximum tax rate upon withdrawing the funds, the tax would be

$237\ 174 \times 0.3848 = \$91\ 264.55$,

leaving her with $145 909.45. The $3000 invested outside the plan only grows to $98 399. Meena will therefore do much better if she invests her money inside an RRSP.

Personal FINANCE in action 6.9

RRSPs and the Contrarian

Tilda was 20 and had just landed her first full-time job. Her oldest friend, Lynne, told her that she should open an RRSP and start saving for her retirement. She had read that, even though it was hard to do, it was best to start saving as early as possible. As a result of compounding she would end up with far more money in the long run than if she waited until her thirties or forties to start saving.

Tilda wasn't sure what to do, so she went to see her Uncle Charles, who had recently retired from a bank. Her uncle said *there are good reasons for having an RRSP. You can easily find out what they are. I am going to be a contrarian and give you some good reasons why you shouldn't have one.*

(a) When you collapse your RRSP and put the money into a Registered Retirement Income Fund, the income you will receive may reduce what you receive in OAS payments. These may be clawed back.

(b) Your income is too low to justify having an RRSP.

(c) Investing in an RRSP may hurt your lifestyle. A young girl should have fun. This may not be possible if you invest the maximum 18 percent of your income.

(d) You would be better off saving up to put a down payment on a house. It will grow in value and will not be taxed when you sell it.

(c) Purchase a life annuity.

(d) Purchase an annuity spread over a number of years.

Withdraw the Funds The first of these options differs from the others in that you are moving funds from the RRSP tax shelter and into your control. Money taken out of an RRSP is always subject to tax in the year of its withdrawal. But once you have paid the tax, no more restrictions are imposed by the Canada Revenue Agency. Unfortunately, withdrawing all your RRSP funds at one time could result in an enormous tax bill. To minimize your tax burden, you can either make a series of withdrawals over a number of years or withdraw all the funds during a year in which your income is considerably lower than usual.

The other options represent various ways of converting RRSP funds into income gradually, over a number of years, thus spreading out your income tax liability. With any of these options, your RRSP funds do not come into your hands as a lump sum, but are instead transferred directly into an income plan. When an RRSP matures, there is no restriction in moving the funds to other firms, if desired. It is wise to do some comparison shopping before choosing an income plan and the company to handle it.

Life Annuity With a single-payment life annuity, your funds are transferred directly from your RRSP to a life annuity, which you can buy from a life insurance company. You can choose from among a variety of annuity products, some of which were described earlier in this chapter (under "Life Annuities"). An annuity converts funds into a lifetime income, with income tax payable each year only on the amount received in that year. This approach effectively spreads the tax burden over the annuitant's lifetime.

Fixed-Term Annuity Fixed-term annuities, which are available from life insurance companies and from trust companies, allow you to gradually convert your RRSP funds into income. A fixed-term annuity differs from a life annuity in that it is unrelated to life expectancy; it involves no pooling of funds with others. Your funds are simply converted into an income stream that will continue until you reach a specific age. But if you do not live that long, the balance in the account will be refunded either to your beneficiary or to your estate. Your monthly payment will depend on the term, the amount invested in the annuity, and interest rates. With life or fixed-term annuities, you have the option of cancelling the contract and taking the commuted value (see Chapter 7, under "Uniform Series of Payments Received") of the remaining payments. You can then take these amounts out of the tax shelter and pay the tax, or you can roll the amounts over into a RRIF.

Registered Retirement Income Fund A **registered retirement income fund** (a RRIF: the abbreviation is pronounced to rhyme with "stiff") is similar to a self-directed RRSP; with a RRIF, you can make your own investment decisions if you wish to do so. RRIFs may also be set up so that little management is required—by, for instance, investing all funds in fixed-income securities. The same firms that handle RRSPs also look after RRIFs, and RRIFs have the same investment options as RRSPs.

It is a good idea to do some comparison shopping when deregistering your RRSPs, in order to find a RRIF with the most suitable terms.

After you purchase a RRIF, income from the fund may start at any time. But the Canada Revenue Agency requires that you withdraw a minimum amount each year (there is no ceiling or maximum withdrawal). Your minimum withdrawal depends on your age. The formula for determining your minimum withdrawal until you turn 71 is as follows:

$$\frac{\text{RRIF balance at January 1}}{\text{90 minus age at January 1}} = \text{the minimum annual payment}$$

After you turn 71, your minimum withdrawal payments are based on a percentage of the fund's balance.

Since it is possible to have more than one RRIF, you can diversify your RRSP funds by using different firms or financial products. For instance, you could put some funds into bank deposits and others into equity mutual funds that are held elsewhere. You can transfer funds from one RRIF to another, but it would be wise to find out whether any restrictions or fees will be involved. The advantage of a RRIF over an annuity is that RRIFs leave you free to choose your preferred type of investment and to determine the amount you will withdraw beyond the required minimum each year.

There is also a serious disadvantage to purchasing a RRIF. The minimum withdrawal regulation may force people to take out more than they need and, as a result, require them to pay more in income tax than they expected. You may, in addition, make foolish investment choices that do considerable damage to your retirement plans. That, of course, is a risk when making any investment decision.

Figure 6.9 shows a sample RRIF contract. In this example, the RRIF was started by a 65-year-old man with an investment of $300 000 on October 12, 2000. A monthly payment of $2000 started on November 12, 2000. Payments are indexed at 3 percent and increase to age 90. If Mr. Average Canadian had purchased an annuity instead of a RRIF, it would have provided him with an income for life. The funds in this RRIF are invested in a segregated fund and are assumed to earn a return of 10 percent per year. This return is well within the historic return on such investments.

Life income funds (LIFs) are administered provincially and are available in all provinces except Prince Edward Island. They are purchased with funds from a registered pension plan and provide a retiree with an income up until the end of the year the person turns 80. Payments from a LIF cannot begin until 10 years before the normal retirement age of 65. The minimum withdrawal is the same as that for RRIFs. The Canada Revenue Agency requires the withdrawal of the minimum amount once a person reaches 65. The maximum amount is determined by provincial legislation. In British Columbia, for example, the amount that may be withdrawn is determined by the owner's age, current long-term interest rates, and the last year's investment returns for the LIF.

In most provinces, at the end of the year in which the owner turns 80, the balance in a LIF must be transferred to an annuity. In BC this rule no longer applies. In Manitoba, 50 percent of the balance may be transferred to a RRIF. Also Manitoba, like Ontario, Saskatchewan, and Alberta, allows the money to be transferred to an LRIF, or Locked-in Retirement Income Fund.[23]

Segregated funds, which have replaced the variable annuity, are pools of money available through insurance companies. They are purchased with a contract that specifies how much will be invested, for how long, and in what type of assets. They may be opened with little money. The purchaser may arrange for automatic monthly payments and may make minimum withdrawals. The assets in such funds are held separately from other insurance company products, hence the term "segregated." They have become popular with investors because the money in the funds is safer than in most other types of investment. If the money is invested for a minimum period, often 10 years, the contract guarantees that the owner will get back at least some of his or her money. The same guarantee applies upon the death of the investor. This guarantee is usually 75 percent, though some companies offer a 100 percent guarantee.

These funds also offer a unique feature not available in regular mutual funds. This is known as the reset option, which allows the investor to protect any capital gains earned by the fund, in addition to the original investment. In addition, because they are insurance

[23]An LRIF is similar to a RRIF but has a locked-in provision.

FIGURE 6.9 A SAMPLE RRIF CONTRACT

Annuitant: Mr. Average Canadian
Date of birth: Oct 15, 1935
Investment amount: $300 000.00
Source of funds: RRSP
Payment option: Increasing payment – 3.00%

Date of purchase: Oct 12, 2000
First payment date: Nov 12, 2000
Payment frequency: Monthly
Assumed interest rate: 10.00%

Year	Age	Jan. 1 fund value	Gross payment	Withholding tax	Net payment
2000	65	*$302 438	$2000	$200	$1800
2001	66	302 364	2060	105	1955
2002	67	306 632	2122	106	2016
2003	68	310 546	2185	106	2079
2004	69	314 048	2251	106	2145
2005	70	317 078	2319	106	2213
2006	71	319 556	2388	106	2282
2007	72	321 405	2460	48	2411
2008	73	322 536	2534	52	2481
2009	74	322 852	2610	57	2553
2010	75	322 239	2688	62	2626
2011	76	320 578	2768	67	2701
2012	77	317 734	2852	74	2778
2013	78	313 562	2937	81	2856
2014	79	307 891	3025	89	2936
2015	80	300 542	3116	98	3018
2016	81	291 314	3209	109	3101
2017	82	279 989	3306	121	3185
2018	83	266 313	3405	135	3270
2019	84	250 020	3507	151	3356
2020	85	230 809	3612	170	3442
2021	86	208 355	3721	193	3528
2022	87	182 286	3832	219	3613
2023	88	152 202	3947	251	3696
2024	89	117 661	4066	289	3776
2025	90	78 177	4188	336	3852
2026	91	33 298	2898	252	2646

Subject to the death benefit guarantee, any of the premium or other amount that is allocated to a segregated fund investment option is invested at the risk of the policy owner and may increase or decrease in value according to the fluctuations in the market value of the assets of the segregated fund.

* In the first year, fund value is shown at Nov 12, 2000, prior to payment.

products, money in a segregated fund does not become part of an investor's estate, if beneficiaries are named, and is therefore not subject to probate fees. It is also difficult for creditors to get any of the money in a segregated fund when the investor dies because it goes to the beneficiaries stated in the contract.

The downside to segregated funds is their expense. The management expense ratio (MER) may be one-half to a full percent higher than that for a mutual fund. This is a lot to pay for a guarantee that may not be worth it. While bonds, equities, and other investments come with no guarantees (except for GICs), investments can be protected to a certain extent by diversification. Also bonds, as well as GICs, held to maturity return the initial investment with interest. While stocks may decline, over an extended period the stock market does go up and has a history of outperforming other types of assets.

Universal Life Policies

Universal life policies, which have been available for over 20 years, have recently become popular with persons planning for their retirement. Unlike whole life policies, part of the universal life premium pays for life insurance, and part is invested to help provide for retirement. The amount a person may invest is determined by the size of the policy and his or her age. The investment part of the policy provides considerable choice. While some policies only allow investors to choose from a variety of mutual funds, others allow investing in stock market indices. Up to 75 percent of the investment portion may be lent tax-free to the policyholder. This can be used in a variety of ways, in addition to increasing retirement income, such as financing the purchase of a cottage, helping to pay for household renovations, funding children's education, or as a disability benefit.

Universal life policies have grown in popularity because the investment half of the policy is tax sheltered and can be used to create income upon retirement. While premiums for universal life are not tax deductible, as are RRSP contributions, the accumulated investment part of the policy, if paid to the beneficiary upon the death of the insured, is tax free, as is the insurance itself. The insurance component of the policy can be used to pay any capital gains generated upon the death of the policy holder and thereby preserve the value of the estate for the deceased's beneficiary or beneficiaries. (See Personal Finance in Action Box 6.10.)

Personal FINANCE in action 6.10

Investing Outside a Plan versus Investing in Universal Life to Create a Tax-Deferred Estate

Fernando has just turned 52. Chloe, his wife, is 48. They have three children ranging in age from 15 to 25. Like many baby boomers, they made a lot of money in the 1990s from their investments. Fernando works for one of Canada's leading telecommunications firms and earns a six-figure salary. Chloe, a trustee in bankruptcy with one of Canada's leading firms, earns even more. They have much more income than they need to maintain their lifestyle. Both are concerned about high taxes and what will happen to the value of their estates when they die. Their investment advisor suggests universal life to them as a means of protecting their wealth and leaving it to their children, tax-free. She shows them what will happen to money invested inside a universal life plan compared with the same money invested outside a universal life plan.

continued

A. $150 000 is invested each year for five years outside a plan. The income is not protected. Capital gains average 7 percent per year. One-third of the investments are realized each year, and taxes paid on all income are at the highest marginal tax rate. Rolling over portfolios every three years is typical behaviour for clients in their investment advisor's firm.

B. $150 000 is invested each year for five years. The money is used to purchase a joint universal last-to-die life policy of $4.3 million with benefits payable on the death of the last spouse. After 30 years, the insurance portion of their plan has grown to $7 540 717. No capital gains tax or probate is payable on the insurance left to their children.

A		B	
Annual Deposit	Value of Investment	Annual Investment	Cash Value
Year 1 $150 000	$ 157 875	$150 000	$ 87 728
Year 2 $150 000	$ 324 038	$150 000	$ 213 654
Year 3 $150 000	$ 498 925	$150 000	$ 334 905
Year 4 $150 000	$ 682 993	$150 000	$ 466 674
Year 5 $150 000	$ 876 724	$150 000	$ 642 483
	$ 922 751		$ 673 463
	$ 971 195		$ 735 789
	$1 022 182		$ 800 625
	$1 075 845		$ 868 161
	$1 132 326		$ 943 269
	$1 191 772		$ 993 085
	$1 254 339		$1 046 922
	$1 320 191		$1 105 103
	$1 389 500		$1 167 979
	$1 462 448		$1 235 930
	$1 539 225		$1 309 364
	$1 620 033		$1 388 724
	$1 705 083		$1 474 489
	$1 794 598		$1 567 175
	$1 888 813		$1 667 340
	$1 987 974		$1 775 589
	$2 092 341		$1 892 574
	$2 202 187		$2 018 999
	$2 317 800		$2 155 627
	$2 439 483		$2 303 280
	$2 567 553		$2 462 850
	$2 702 348		$2 635 296
	$2 844 219		$2 821 659
	$2 993 538		$3 023 062
	$3 150 696		$3 240 717

continued

As the table indicates, money invested inside a universal life plan performs slightly better than money invested outside a plan. There are several possible reasons for this. Money invested in such a plan is used to purchase units of index-based mutual funds. Money invested outside a plan faces no such restriction and may be subject to greater risk. As well, capital gains inside a plan are not subject to tax as are the funds outside a plan.

It should be pointed out that the management expense ratios or MERs are very high with universal life. These weaken the growth of the investments. It should also be stressed that a universal life policy is primarily a means of creating a tax-free estate for one's beneficiaries and only secondarily as an investment vehicle.

Such policies are sold by all insurance companies in Canada. Standard Life, one of the larger companies offering universal life, has 16 Index-Linked Funds. These allow the client to choose, for example, between conservative Canadian bond funds, the more speculative Science and Technology Equity Fund and EuroAsia Equity Fund, and a variety of other Canadian and US equity funds. It also has a number of asset allocation funds where deposits in the funds are divided between bonds and equities.

While basically the same, the policies of the different companies vary to a certain extent. Information on the universal life policies offered by some insurance companies in Canada may be found at the following companies' websites:

Canada Life: **www.canadalife.ca**
Great-West Life: **www.greatwestlife.com**
London Life: **www.londonlife.com/life/univ_f_e.htm**
Manulife Financial: **www.manulife.ca/Canada/ilc2.nsf/Public/ulinsurance**
Standard Life: **www.standardlife.ca/en/individual/insurance/universal/index.html**
Sun Life Financial Canada: **www.sunlife.ca/canada/cda/homepage_v2/0,11263,1-1-1,00.html**

Personal FINANCE in action 6.11

Madhu Seeks Retirement Advice

Madhu was 63. His wife had died three months ago, and as a result he had $300 000 from the term insurance she had taken out through her employer's extended health plan. He had expected to work until his sixty-fifth birthday, but since his wife's death he had lost interest in his job and everything associated with his married life. He wanted to retire but knew nothing about retirement and the financial steps he should take. What should he do with the money from Dini's insurance and the mutual funds she had invested in so carefully?

Seeking answers, he made an appointment to see a counsellor in his employer's human resources department. What he learned did not encourage him to take early retirement. The counsellor told him that she knew of three agencies that offered pre-retirement counselling: the Canadian Academy of Senior Advisors, the Canadian Initiative for Elder Planning Studies, and the Canadian Association of Pre-retirement Planners. To qualify with the first two organizations would-be planners need only take a three-day training course and pass an exam.

continued

No exam at all is required to earn the Professional Retirement Planner (PRP) designation offered by the third organization; one must only satisfy a group of PRP planners that one is committed to the concept of retirement. Upon learning how poorly qualified those versed in retirement planning are, he decided to delay his retirement until he had researched all angles of the retirement conundrum himself and felt confident about what he should do.

Summary

- The primary sources of retirement income are government income support programs, private pensions, and public pensions. The government programs are Old Age Security (a public pension program) and the Guaranteed Income Supplement (a public pension program for low-income seniors).

- In Canada, the public pensions are the Canada Pension Plan (CPP) and the Quebec Pension Plan (QPP). The Canada Pension Plan (CPP) is a retirement plan established by the federal government and funded by employers and employees. The Quebec Pension Plan (QPP) is Quebec's version of the CPP. Long-term viability of the CPP is now considered good, but the financial health of seniors is not. Many have not properly prepared financially.

- Private pensions are made up of employer pension plans, RRSPs, and private investment income. Defined contribution pension plans specify the amount employee and employer may give but do not define the amount of the pension. Defined benefits pension plans are offered and run by employers to provide retirees with an income. A crisis currently faces many defined benefits pension plans, many of which do not have enough money to meet their obligations.

- The formula for determining a pension is based on years of service and salary. Vesting refers to a period of time after which employee contributions to defined benefits plans may not be removed. Pension portability allows an employee to transfer his or her pension to another plan upon changing employment. Indexed pensions are adjusted to keep up with increases in the Consumer Price Index. Some are fully indexed, others only partially. Income splitting is a means whereby spouses can reduce tax and create an investment portfolio.

- Annuities are financial contracts that provide an income stream for a specified time period. The beneficiary of an annuity is called the annuitant. A single payment annuity is purchased with one payment. Joint-and-survivor annuities (taken out by a couple) pay as long as one of the annuitants survives. Refund annuities refund the payments should the annuitant cancel or die during the accumulation period.

- Life Income Funds (LIFs) allow retirees to transfer funds from a locked-in RRSP into a pension plan to provide regular income payments. Segregated funds are offered by insurance companies and guarantee a certain percentage of the funds invested.

- Registered Retirement Savings Plans (RRSPs) are a way to save for retirement and defer taxes at the same time. The individual's RRSP need depends on his or her income. The notice of assessment on tax returns tells the taxpayer how much may be contributed to an RRSP. The Canada Revenue Agency permits a great many RRSP investments to be held in such a plan. Group RRSPs are offered to employees by employers. The Homebuyer's Plan allows people to use money in an RRSP to buy a house. Lifelong Learning is a means by which funds may be withdrawn from an RRSP to help pay for education or training.

■ Registered Retirement Income Funds (RRIFs) are one choice available to those who must collapse their RRSPs at age 69. Universal life is an insurance policy with an investment component.

Key Terms

accumulation period (p. 167)

annuitant (p. 164)

annuity (p. 165)

contributory earnings (p. 158)

CPP Investment Board (p. 158)

deferred annuity (p. 167)

defined benefits pension plan
   (p. 161)

defined contribution pension plan
   (p. 161)

full indexation (p. 164)

Granteed Income Supplement
   (GIS) (p. 155)

immediate annuity (p. 167)

joint-life-and-last-survivorship
   annuity (joint-and-survivor
   annuity) (p. 168)

life income fund, or LIF (p. 184)

liquidation period (p. 167)

maximum pensionable earnings
   (p. 158)

Old Age Security (OAS) (p. 155)

partial indexation (p. 164)

pension portability (p. 163)

refund annuity (p. 169)

registered retirement income
   fund, or RRIF (p. 183)

registered retirement savings plan,
   or RRSP (p. 175)

segregated fund (p. 184)

single-payment annuity (p. 167)

straight life annuity (p. 168)

universal life (p. 186)

vesting (p. 163)

year's basic exemption (p. 158)

Problems

1. Go to **www.johnjordan.ca/annuity/insuredannuitytables.html** and click on Male or Female Insured Annuity Table. Complete the Table of Insured Annuity Rates by adding your marginal tax rate and whatever the current rate is for a five-year GIC. This can be determined by calling a chartered bank or by going to a bank's website such as **www.cibc.com/ca/gic/long-trm-gic.html**.

    (a) What will your gross annual interest income be?

    (b) What tax will you have to pay on this income?

    (c) How much will your after-tax income on the GIC be?

2. With reference to the retirement planning organizations available, discuss the sorry financial situation of many of Canada's seniors.

3. Why is there a crisis facing many defined benefits pension plans? How can this crisis be averted?

4. Should someone considering retirement start receiving the CPP at age 60 or 65? What are the pros and cons of each choice? To find out go to **www.investopedia.com/ask/answers/05/052705.asp**. If you start at 65, how long does it take you to catch up to someone who started receiving payments at 60? Who comes out ahead by age 90?

5. Louise is 23 and earns $40 000 per year. Assume that her income will rise by 3 percent each year. How much will she have invested in her RRSP if she contributes 18 percent of her income per year and earns a return of 5 percent in the plan?

6. You have finished your education and now have a full-time job. Will you open an RRSP? Explain your answer.

7. Discuss the NDP's motion in Parliament to restrict the CPP Investment Board from making certain types of investments. If you were a Member of Parliament, would you have voted in favour? If you were soon to be retired and expecting a CPP pension, would you have supported the motion? Is there merit in the idea from an investment point of view?

8. Hillary took early retirement when she turned 60. She decided to postpone getting the CPP until she turned 65. Her defined benefits pension is $42 635 a year. Her investment assets include $5000 in CSBs, which pay interest of 2 percent, $25 000 in GICs paying 3 percent per year, and the following shares:

    (a) 500 shares of Manulife Financial

    (b) 750 shares of Rothmans

    (c) 400 units of Canadian Oil Sands Trust

    Find out how much she will receive in dividends from these investments by going to **www.globeinvestor.com**. Calculate her total investment income. What percentage comes from each of her pension and her investments? Is this typical of seniors?

9. You had an RRSP worth $276 000 but when you were 69 collapsed it and put the money into a RRIF. You are now 70. What is the minimum amount that the Canada Revenue Agency says you must withdraw from the fund? If you live in Saskatchewan, are receiving the CPP, and have a pension of $34 700, what is your marginal tax rate?

10. True or false?

    (a) The OAS is funded by tax revenue, not premiums from Canadians.

    (b) You may collect the OAS if you live in the US but lived in Canada from birth until you were 18.

    (c) You must apply for the CPP.

    (d) The OAS is sent automatically to those 65 and older.

    (e) All seniors over 65 qualify for the GIS.

11. Referring to the income tax rates in Chapter 2, would it make sense for someone earning $35 000 to put the maximum eligible amount into an RRSP?

12. Go to **www.cppib.ca**, the website of the CPP Investment Board. Under Highlights, click on the November 15, 2005 announcement. Find out what is meant by a *middle market buyout fund of funds* and a *Canadian venture capital fund of funds*. Would you consider these funds to be low, moderate, or high-risk investments? Who will invest and manage the $400 million for the board?

13. Your contributory earnings are $37 600. How much will you have to contribute to the CPP?

14. You invested $100 000 in a segregated fund managed by a leading mutual fund company on January 1. The fund guarantees to repay you 75 percent of your investment.

It has a management expense ratio of 2.86 percent. By the end of the year your fund has increased by 13.7 percent.

(a) How much has the fund manager taken from your investment?

(b) How much is your investment worth on December 31?

(c) While your fund went up by 13.7 percent during the year, the S&P/TSX Composite gained 29.7 percent. Would you stay invested in this fund or withdraw your money?

15. Which of the following has the reset option: a) a RRIF, b) a segregated fund, or c) a LIF? Is this a valuable feature or simply a marketing tool?

16. Assess the Lifelong Learning feature of RRSPs.

17. You earn $44 000 a year but because of your lifestyle have no money available for investing in your RRSP. You decide to borrow the 18 percent you are allowed to add to your plan this year. Your bank manager suggests you put the money into a conservative Canadian bond fund because of the tax advantage bonds have in an RRSP. The bank will charge you 5 percent to borrow the money. The fund has a management expense ratio of 1.89 percent and yields 2.8 percent. Subtracting the cost of the loan from the amount you invested, how much will your investment in the fund be worth at the end of one year?

18. You made a first-time over-contribution to your RRSP last year of $2 000. You miscalculated again this year and made another over-contribution of $2 000. Your investments increased by 7 percent. After you have paid the penalty, was your over-contribution worth it?

19. Should you leave your RRSP to your estate or your spouse? Why?

20. By the time she reached 65, Laura had an investment portfolio worth more than $1 million, which she had actively managed. This she no longer wanted to do. Her brother and sister had died recently and she was unmarried. Should she purchase a universal life policy or an annuity? Why?

21. Which of the following would someone receiving the GIS be unlikely to have? Are such plans necessary for everyone?

(a) universal life

(b) a segregated fund

(c) a RRIF

(d) an RRSP

(e) a LIF

22. True or false?

(a) Canada's seniors seem very well-informed about their retirement needs.

(b) Annuities are an excellent way to preserve an estate.

(c) There is no risk in investing in a segregated fund.

(d) Defined benefits pension plans are usually vested.

(e) LIFs may not be purchased with funds taken from an RRSP when someone turns 69.

(f) The best choice for someone turning 69 is to collapse his or her RRSP and invest the money in the stock market.

(g) You can withdraw as much as you want from a RRIF.

(h) The Canada Revenue Agency does not care if you invest all of the money in your RRSP in foreign assets.

References

BOOKS AND ARTICLES

Bach, David. *The Automatic Millionaire: A Powerful One-Step Plan to Live and Finish Rich.* Toronto: Doubleday, 2003.

Bareham, Steve. *The Last Resort: A Retirement Vision for Canadians and How to Achieve It.* Toronto: HarperCollins, 1998.

Bond, David, and Diane Bond. *Future Perfect: Retirement Strategies for Productive People.* Vancouver: Douglas & McIntyre, 2003.

Canadian Bankers Association. *Planning for Retirement. A First Step Toward Securing Your Financial Future.* Toronto: CBA, 1998. An excellent guide, available free by calling toll-free 1-800-263-0231.

Canadian Life and Health Insurance Association. *Retirement As You Like It.* Toronto: Canadian Life and Health Insurance Association, 1994.

Cimoroni, Sandy, Beth Grudinski, and Patricia Lovett-Reid. *Retirement Strategies for Women: Turning Your Dreams into Reality.* Toronto: Key Porter Books, 1997.

Cohen, Bruce, and Brian Fitzgerald. *The Pension Puzzle: Your Complete Guide to Government Benefits, RRSPs and Employer Plans.* Toronto: John Wiley & Sons Canada Ltd., 2004.

Cohen, Dian. *The New Retirement: Financial Strategies for Life After Work.* Toronto: Doubleday Canada, 1999.

Dagys, Andrew. *The Ontario Retirement Handbook: A Guide to Programs and Services for Retirees.* Toronto: ECW Press, 1996.

Dagys, Andrew. *Financial Planner for 50+, The Complete Guide for Every Canadian over Fifty.* Toronto: Pearson, 1999.

Deloitte & Touche. *The Deloitte & Touche Guide to Retirement Planning.* Toronto: Key Porter, 1997.

Foster, Sandra E. *Make the Most of What You've Got: The Canadian Guide to Managing Retirement Income.* Toronto: John Wiley & Sons Ltd., 1999.

Foster, Sandra E. *You Can't Take It with You: The Common-Sense Guide to Estate Planning for Canadians.* Toronto: John Wiley & Sons Ltd., 2000.

Gallinger, Mary. *Strategies for Transition to Retirement.* 2nd Edition. Victoria: Trafford, 2002.

Gallinger, Mary. *107 Tips for Retirement.* Duncan, BC: Retirement Ready.net, 2005.

Human Resources Canada. *Canada's Retirement System. What's in It for You?* Ottawa, Human Resources Canada.

Kerr, Robert John. *The Only Retirement Guide You'll Ever Need.* Toronto: Nelson, 1998.

Laight, Gordon. *Offshore Advantage: A Canadian Guide to Wealth Creation, Asset Protection & Estate Planning.* Toronto: Prentice-Hall, 1998.

Little, Kenneth E. *The Pocket Guide to Investing in Annuities.* Toronto: Alpha (Penguin), 2005.

McCurdy, Diane. *How Much Is Enough? Balancing Today's Needs with Tomorrow's Retirement Goals*. Toronto: McGraw-Hill Ryerson, 2001.

McLean, Benjamin. *The Canadian Widow's Guide to Enjoying Your Retirement Dollars & Making Them Last*. Toronto: McGraw-Hill Ryerson, 2001.

Page, John A., Graham McWaters, and Jill L. O'Donnell. *The Canadian Handbook on Aging, Retirement, Caregiving and Health—How to Plan and Pay for It*. Toronto: Insomniac Press, 2004.

Pape, Gordon. *Retiring Wealthy in the 21st Century*. Toronto: Prentice-Hall, 2000.

Pape, Gordon. *Retirement Time Bomb: Achieving Financial Independence in a Changing World*. Toronto: Penguin, 2005.

Polson, Kirk, and George Brett. *Retire Right: The Practical Guide to RRIFs, Annuities and Pensions*. Toronto: Nelson, 1999.

Reynolds, John Lawrence with Charm Darby. *RRSPs & RRIFs for Dummies*. Toronto: CDG Books, 2000.

Tafler, David and Gordon Pape. *The Complete Guide to RRIFs and LIFs. How to Make the Best Investment Decisions for Retirement*. Toronto: Viking, 2003.

Trahair, David. *Smoke and Mirrors: Financial Myths That Will Ruin Your Retirement Dreams*. North Vancouver: Self-Counsel Press, 2005.

Wark, Kevin. *Everything You Need to Know About Estate Planning*. Toronto: Key Porter, 2001.

Watters, Gradydon G. *Financial Pursuit—Canada's Working Guide to Personal Wealth: How to Retire with Financial Dignity*. North York, Ontario: Financial Knowledge, 1999.

Personal Finance on the Web

Miscellaneous Retirement Sites

Advocis
www.advocis.ca This provides a list of financial planners across Canada.

American Association of Retired Persons
www.aarp.org AARP is the most important seniors' organization in the US.

Benefits Canada
www.benefitscanada.com A magazine published by Rogers Media for the pension industry.

A.M. Best Canada.
www.ambest.ca A.M. Best provides an insurance information service.

Canada Pension Plan
www.cpp-rpc.gc.ca Provides current information on the CPP.

Canadian Academy of Senior Advisors
www.certifiedsenioradvisors.ca This organization offers the Certified Senior Advisor (CSA) designation.

The Canadian Association of Pre-retirement Planners
www.retirementplanners.ca This organization offers the Professional Retirement Planner (PRP) designation.

Canadian Association of Retired Persons (CARP)
  www.carp.ca CARP covers many topics of interest to those over 50.

Canadian Initiative for Elder Planning Studies (CIEPS)
  www.cieps.com This organization offers the Elder Planning Counselor (EPC) designation.

Canadian Pension & Benefits Institute
  www.cpbi-icra.ca This is an association for those in the pension industry.

Capital Estate Planning Corporation
  www.capitalestateplanning.com Offers retirement planning advice.

Department of Finance Canada
  www.fin.gc.ca This site helps retirees by showing any taxation changes.

The Globe and Mail's mutual fund website
  www.globefund.com

Government of Canada
  http://canada.gc.ca This site provides information on federal government programs.

HR Canadian Reporter
  www.hrreporter.com/pensions The National Journal of Human Resource Management.

Human Resources and Social Development Canada
  www.hrsdc.gc.ca Information on the CPP and OAS/GIS can be found on this site.

Insurance-Canada.ca
  www.insurance-canada.ca This site has information on many insurance topics.

Diane McCurdy's Savings Calculator
  www.howmuchisenough.ca This site can help you determine whether you can afford to retire.

Office of the Superintendent of Financial Institutions
  www.osfi-bsif.gc.ca This office has a mandate to regulate pension plans.

CANADIAN LIFE INSURANCE COMPANIES

Canada Life
  www.canadalife.ca Canada Life has full range of insurance products.

Clarica
  www.clarica.com Clarica used to be Mutual Life.

Desjardins Financial Security
  www.dsf.dfs.com This site deals with the financial aspects of retirement.

Equitable Life of Canada
  www.equitable.ca Equitable offers a full range of insurance products.

Great-West Life & Annuity Insurance Company
  www.greatwest.com Canada's largest insurance company specializes in group and disability insurance.

London Life Insurance Company
  www.londonlife.com London Life offers individual and group insurance, retirement savings plans, and investment advice that focuses on mutual funds.

Manulife
www.manulife.com Manulife, formerly Manufacturers Life, is a major insurance company.

MetLife Canada
www.metlife.com A company that offers a full range of insurance services.

Standard Life
www.standardlife.ca Standard Life offers a full range of insurance products.

Sun Life Financial
www.sunlife.com Sun Life, a major insurance firm, runs many Canadian company benefit plans.

chapter 7

Interest

"At the most basic level, the time value of money demonstrates that, all things being equal, it is better to have money now rather than later."
Investopedia.com, http://www.investopedia.com

Learning Objectives

Knowledge of the material in this chapter should make the concept of interest more meaningful.

After studying this chapter, you should be able to:

1. Define the concept of interest and show how it relates to the time value of money.

2. Distinguish between simple and compound interest and demonstrate how to calculate each.

3. Distinguish between the nominal interest rate and the effective annual yield.

4. Outline the process of calculating a repayment schedule for a loan to be repaid in equal instalments, with each payment a blend of interest and principal.

5. Show how frequency of compounding interest affects the effective annual yield.

6. Show how the total interest charge on loan contracts for either simple or compound interest is determined.

7. List the five factors that influence the total interest charged on a loan.

8. Distinguish between the concepts of future value and present value.

9. Using either formulas or compound interest tables, compute the future and present values of a single payment.

10. Calculate the future and present values of an identical series of deposits made or an identical series of payments received.

11. Define the following terms: principal, maturity date, the term of a loan, blended payment, amortization, and net present value.

Introduction

Interest is important both to lenders and to borrowers. Contrary to popular belief, not all lenders are wealthy. When children open bank accounts with money they earn from paper routes or lawn-mowing jobs, they are actually lending money to the bank. In return, the bank pays them interest. This chapter discusses some basic principles of interest and the concept of the time value of money, and demonstrates a number of ways to calculate interest.

The Time Value of Money

An important concept in personal finance is the **time value of money.** An understanding of this concept is essential to an understanding of annuities, insurance, pensions, and investing in fixed income securities such as bonds. There are two aspects to the time value of money. One is the **future value of money** and the second is the **present value of money.**

We all have a basic understanding of the future value of money, probably without realizing it. It simply means what a sum of money will be worth at some point in the future based on a specific interest rate. Therefore, if someone asks you, "Do you want the $1000 I owe you today or next year?" there is no doubt that you would say, "Today," because you could spend or invest the money now and you know that next year the $1000 will buy you less than it will today. If you said instead, "Next year," you would therefore also want the person to pay you back not only the $1000 at the end of next year but also some interest to compensate you for the decline in the purchasing value of the money.

If money is lent or borrowed for longer periods, then we also want interest to be paid on the interest we have already received. Calculating interest on interest, known as compounding, is a key principle used in the lending and borrowing of money.

Present value refers to what a sum of money in the future is worth today, based upon a specific interest rate and a period of time. In other words, present value tells you how much you have to invest today at a certain rate to have so many dollars at a specific time in the future.

Knowledge of interest and the time value of money is important for a better understanding of the chapters on investments, credit, debt and bankruptcy, and mortgages. The ability to calculate compound interest, the future value of money, and the present value of money will help make you a better financial consumer and prepare you to face the financial world with all its many challenges.

Knowledge of the time value of money can also solve interesting historical problems. See Personal Finance in Action Boxes 7.2, "Who Was Richer?" and 7.3, "Were They Cheated?" for examples.

This chapter explains interest and defines basic terms associated with interest rate calculations. It outlines the difference between simple and compound interest and the frequency of compounding. It also shows how to calculate interest using formulas and gives examples of the time value of money.

The Concept of Interest

Interest, the payment for the use of someone else's money, is like rent. To the lender, interest is income; to the borrower, it is an expense. A loan allows a borrower to do today what he or she would otherwise have to postpone because of a lack of money. Interest compensates the lender for postponing the use of his or her money. Interest also pays the lender for the risk involved in lending and for the administrative costs associated with the loan.

The **interest rate** is defined as the ratio of the interest payable at the end of the year to the money owed at the start of the year. The boxed example "Annual Interest Rate" illustrates how to calculate the interest rate. This bare-bones definition will be clarified when the concepts of nominal rate and effective annual yield are explained. (Unless stated otherwise, when an interest rate is quoted in this chapter, it is assumed to be the annual rate.)

Annual Interest Rate

What is the interest rate on a $5000 debt, with interest of $500 payable annually?

$$\frac{500}{5000} = 0.10 \text{ (or 10\% per annum)}$$

A most important component of any loan transaction, the total interest charge, is the amount that must be repaid in addition to the **principal,** or the amount borrowed. The total interest charge represents the lender's total return and the borrower's total carrying cost. The five factors that determine the magnitude of the total interest charge are as follows: (i) rate of interest, (ii) frequency of compounding, (iii) term or length of time the loan is outstanding, (iv) principal, and (v) method of repayment. The effects of these factors will become apparent as various ways of calculating interest are explained in this chapter or illustrated in mortgage applications in Chapter 12.

Factors That Determine the Rate of Interest

A number of factors influence the rate of interest paid on deposits and that charged on loans. The most important is the Bank of Canada's "overnight rate": the rate of interest charged the chartered banks when they borrow from the Bank of Canada, Canada's central bank. This rate is part of the federal government's monetary policy. Once the rate changes, the banks will change their rates. The overnight rate will go up when the Bank of Canada is worried about inflation and wants to slow the economy down. The rate will go down when inflation is not a problem and the Bank wants to stimulate growth and employment. This was what happened from 2003 to 2006, when interest rates fell to their lowest level in over a generation and mortgage rates and interest on savings accounts dropped accordingly.

Other factors that influence interest rates are the market forces of supply and demand, the risk or credit rating of those wishing to borrow, the duration of the loan, the frequency of compounding, and how the loan is repaid.

Supply and demand have recently been at work in the auto industry as car makers have reduced their rates on loans to stimulate demand. In some cases, loans have been offered at 0 percent. These low rates have nothing to do with the Bank of Canada's policy but simply show the auto industry's desire to stimulate demand in an industry overstocked with product.

Credit card interest rates also have nothing to do with the central bank's policy. They are high because they are on unsecured loans and are riskier than bank loans. Of course, credit card customers do not need to borrow at such high rates if they pay their accounts in full.

For the saver, the more frequent the compounding, the higher the effective annual yield and the faster savings will grow. More frequent compounding also makes the cost of a loan greater. A loan that is repaid in blended payments of interest and principal will cost less than a loan where only interest is charged. One should assume that a large loan will have a higher rate of interest than a small one. The longer the duration of the loan, the higher the interest rate banks will charge because of the greater uncertainty. For example, in January 2006 the rate on a 10-year closed mortgage was 7.350 percent, while that on a five-year closed mortgage was 5.590 percent.

Simple Interest

Simple interest applies when the total principal and all interest due are to be repaid as a lump sum at a specified time. The date when a loan is due is called the **maturity date,** and the length of time during which the loan is outstanding is the **loan term.** The amount of interest due may be calculated with the following formula:

$$\text{Interest} = \text{principal} \times \text{annual rate} \times \text{time (in years)}$$

Simple Interest

Principal: $3000
Annual interest rate: 8%
Term of loan: 2 years
Interest = principal × rate × time
       = $3000 × 0.08 × 2
       = $480

At maturity, the borrower will pay the lender:
$3000   (principal returned)
  480   (total interest charge)
$3480   (total payment)

Compound Interest

Compound interest is paid on most savings accounts and charged on many loans, including home mortgages. **Compounding** simply means that at specified intervals, the accumulated interest is added to the principal. In other words, after the first period interest is earned on the new balance at the beginning of each successive period, where the new balance is the previous principal *and* the interest earned in the previous period. In this way, interest is reinvested to earn more interest. Compounding may be done daily, monthly, semi-annually, or annually. Naturally, the more frequent the rate of compounding, the faster the investment grows. Assuming that there is no repayment of principal or interest, calculating compound interest for each period is exactly like calculating simple interest, but for each calculation of compound interest, the new "principal" becomes larger with each compounding interval.

Compound interest is important to the saver because income (interest) is being reinvested regularly and begins earning additional interest. Banks calculate interest on savings accounts at different intervals, depending on the type of account. With a traditional savings account, interest may be calculated monthly on the minimum balance that was in the account during the month, but this interest is not added to the principal until the compounding date, which may be every six months. If you are planning to make a large withdrawal from such an account, consider doing so just after the end of a calendar month to avoid losing a month's interest. If you withdraw your money too soon, it will not earn any interest for that month.

With a daily interest account, interest is calculated daily on the minimum balance and then perhaps compounded monthly. Although the interest on such an account is usually slightly lower than that on the traditional savings account, a daily interest account can be worthwhile if you have a fluctuating balance in your account. Understandably, the interest rates paid by deposit institutions vary with the type of account: the interest rate may be depressed somewhat by chequing privileges, by having ready access to the deposit, or by compounding more frequently.

Daily Interest Rates

In January 2006, chartered banks were offering the following rates:

Amount	Annual Rate of Interest
Under $5000	.025
$5000 to $9999	.050
$10 000 to $24 999	.100
$25 000 to $59 999	.200
$60 000 to $74 999	.400
$75 000 to $99 999	.500
$100 000 and over	.500

Compound Interest

Principal: $3000
Interest rate: 8% compounded semi-annually
Term of loan: 2 years

(a) **At the end of the first six months,**
interest = principal × rate × time
= $3000 × 0.08 × 0.5
= $120.00
new balance = principal + interest
= $3000 + $120
= $3120.00

(b) **At end of the second six-month period,**
interest = principal × rate × time
= $3120.00 × 0.08 × 0.5
= $124.80
new balance = $3120.00 + $124.80
= $3244.80

To summarize compound interest calculations over the two-and-a-half-year period:

TIME PERIOD (MONTHS)	BALANCE OF PRINCIPAL AND INTEREST AT BEGINNING OF PERIOD	INTEREST AT END OF PERIOD	OUTSTANDING BALANCE AT END OF PERIOD
6	$3000.00	$120.00	$3120.00
12	3120.00	124.80	3244.80
18	3244.80	129.79	3374.59
24	3374.59	134.98	3509.58

At maturity, the borrower pays $3000.00 (principal returned)
+ 509.58 (total interest charge)
$3509.58 (total payment)

Rule of 72 If you would like to know approximately how fast your money will double under annual compounding, you can use the Rule of 72. Divide 72 by the compound interest rate, expressed as a decimal, to find the number of years it will take to double your money. Alternatively, you can estimate the compound interest rate by dividing 72 by the number of years that it will take to double your money.

Compounding and the Rule of 72 Compounding is frequently used to extol the virtues of fixed income investments. Safe and unglamorous, such investments such as Canada Savings Bonds and Guaranteed Investment Certificates appeal to investors who are afraid of investing in stocks because the stock market often seems like a roller coaster. They may not have much glamour, their supporters argue, but through the "miracle" of compounding they provide investors with sure and steady growth. Two figures from the past who believed in compounding were the multi-talented American Benjamin Franklin and nuclear scientist Albert Einstein. Franklin said, "Money makes money, and the money that money makes, makes more money."[1] Einstein, whose mind was usually concerned with theoretical physics, said, "The most powerful force in the universe is compound interest."[2]

While the Rule of 72 has been used to show the value of compounding, in recent years, with very low interest rates, it has not provided risk-averse investors with much joy. With the lowest rates in a generation, from 2002 to 2006, the results were less than sterling. As can be seen in Table 7.1, with rates quoted in January 2006 by Canada's banks, many people will have died before their money has doubled.

Those who still cherish the "rule" probably remember the heady days of the 1980s, when interest rates were exceptionally high. In the early years of that decade, interest on a CSB was 19 percent. At that rate, using the Rule of 72, a person's money doubled in less than four years. At the current interest of 2 percent earned on a CSB, it will take 36 years to double one's money.

Using Compound Interest Tables

What will be the value of $2000 in 20 years invested at 4 percent compounded annually? There are many tables on the internet. One such site can be found at **www.uic.edu/classes/ie/ie201/ discretecompoundinteresttables.html**.

From this table, we learn that the compound value of $1 at 4 percent for 20 years will be $2.19. The value of $2000 will therefore be $4380.

TABLE 7.1   THE RULE OF 72

AMOUNT	ANNUAL RATE OF INTEREST	YEARS TO DOUBLE
$5 000	.25 percent	288
$25 000 to $449 999	1.10 percent	65
$50 000 to $999 999 999.99	1.20 percent	60

[1] www.investmenttools.com/bonds.

[2] Thinkexist.com.

Compound Interest Tables To determine how much a sum of money will increase at various rates of interest, compounded annually, and left on deposit for various lengths of time, you may consult a compound interest table.

Frequency of Compounding and Yield Whenever you lend or invest money, you expect some return. This return, which is called **yield,** may be expressed as an annual rate or as the total dollar amount received over some time period. The rate of return or **effective annual yield** is not necessarily the same as the quoted interest rate or nominal rate. The **nominal interest rate** is an annual rate that does not take the compounding effect into account. The more frequently interest is compounded, the faster your savings will grow and the higher the effective annual yield will be.

Determining the interest for various compounding periods can become tiring because of the number of calculations required. It is much easier to use a formula such as the following, where f is the effective annual rate or annual percentage rate and n is the frequency of compounding at an interest rate of i. An example can be seen in Personal Finance in Action Box 7.1, "The Effective Rate of Interest."

$$f = (1 + i)^n - 1$$

The greater the frequency of compounding, the greater is the return. Which investment would you prefer,

(a) one paying 5.5% compounded monthly, or

(b) one paying 5.5% compounded semi-annually?

Which has the higher effective annual rate, or annual percentage rate (APR)?
Assume that $10 000 is invested for five years. First calculate the effective annual rate for each option.

Effective annual rate: $f = (1 + i)^n - 1$

(a) $i = \dfrac{0.055}{12} = 0.004\ 583$ $\quad f = (1.004\ 583)^{12} - 1 \quad = 0.05\ 640 \times 100 = 5.64$

(b) $i = \dfrac{0.055}{12} = 0.0275$ $\quad f = (1.0275)^2 - 1 \quad = 0.055\ 756 \times 100 = 5.5756$

Personal FINANCE in action 7.1

The Effective Rate of Interest

Atay and Behice had only been in Canada for two years. Neither knew much about personal finance and interest rates. They both had Visa cards and were paying 18.5 percent compounded monthly on the unpaid balance. At night school, their instructor told them that that was not what they were being charged annually. He said that they needed to find out the effective rate of interest to see what they

were really paying. To calculate this, he told them to use the following formula:

$$f = (1 + i)^n - 1 \qquad i = \dfrac{0.185}{12} = 0.0154$$

$$f = (1.0154)^{12} - 1$$
$$f = 0.201284597 \times 100 = 20.128 \text{ percent}$$

The effective rate of interest they were being charged was higher than either of them realized.

Then, using the formula S = P(1 + i)^n where S = the future value and P = the lump sum, we find at the end of five years

(a) S = P(1 + 0.0564)^5 = \$10 000 (1 +.0564)^5 = \$13 156.55
(b) S = P(1 + 0.055 765)^5 = \$10 000 (1 + 0.055 756)^5 = \$13 116.49

Therefore, we can see that a higher frequency of compounding results in a higher APR. More examples will be given later in the chapter.

Compound Interest on Instalment Loans

Blended Payments Loans are frequently repaid in equal monthly instalments that comprise both principal and interest. Each payment includes one month's interest on the outstanding principal, plus a return of some of the principal. As the loan is repaid each month, the principal gradually decreases, and the proportions of principal and interest in each payment change. Figure 7.1 illustrates this process graphically. Notice that the proportion of interest of the first payment is the largest of all the payments. As time goes on, the interest proportion declines, while the principal proportion increases. Such payments, which feature changing proportions of principal and interest, are called **blended payments.** The boxed example "Blended Payments" shows how the proportions of principal and interest are calculated, making the payments level.

Finally, there are a couple of points to note regarding compounding and compounding terminology. Although payments on instalment loans are remitted monthly, interest is typically compounded at some other interval—often semi-annually. You may encounter the

FIGURE 7.1   PROPORTIONS OF PRINCIPAL AND INTEREST IN EACH PAYMENT OF A 24-MONTH CONTRACT

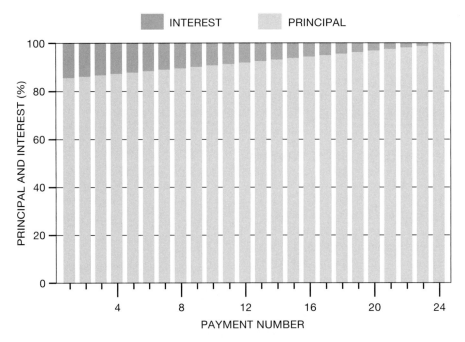

term **amortization,** which simply means repayment of a loan over a period of time. For instance, a loans officer might say that your loan will be amortized over three years, meaning that you will be required to repay the loan over three years.

To review, a loan that is amortized using blended payments, as in the boxed example "Excerpts from a Payment Schedule for a $3000 Loan," will include changing proportions of interest and principal in each payment. As you gradually reduce the principal that you owe, you gradually pay less interest each time and repay more of the principal. The relation between the interest and principal portions of each payment will vary with such factors as interest rates, the term of the loan, and the size of the monthly payment. Home mortgages work the same way, but the rate of principal repayment can be discouragingly slow at first if the loan is large, the payments are modest, and the term is 25 years or longer.

Total Interest Charge

In three of the boxed examples, we used the same principal, interest rate, and time, but the examples differed in the method of repayment and in whether or not interest was compounded. How do these two differences affect the total amount of interest paid? With an instalment loan that is repaid with blended payments, the total interest charge is less apparent than in the examples of simple and compound interest with a single repayment.

The total interest charge on each of the above examples is, respectively, as follows:

(a) simple interest $480.00
(b) compound interest $509.58
(c) compound interest, blended payments $252.24

Can you suggest reasons for the variation?

As indicated at the beginning of this chapter, the five factors that influence the total interest charge are as follows:

(a) rate of interest,
(b) frequency of compounding,
(c) term of the loan,
(d) principal borrowed,
(e) method of repayment.

It is fairly obvious that higher interest rates will increase the cost of borrowing (i.e., the total interest charge). On a short-term loan of modest size, small differences in the interest rate do not affect the cost very much. But when the principal is very large and the term is long, as is typically the case with a home mortgage, a difference of a quarter of a percentage point in the interest rate can make a substantial difference in the total interest charge.

The second factor, the frequency of compounding, is important for the borrower to keep in mind. If the interest on a mortgage is to be compounded quarterly instead of semiannually, the difference in the total interest charge will be significant. The effect of the third factor, the term of the loan or the amortization period, is also fairly obvious; the longer your loan is outstanding, the more total interest you will have to pay. Likewise, the larger the principal borrowed, the higher is the total interest charge.

Blended Payments

Principal: $3000
Annual interest rate: 8% compounded semi-annually
Amortization period: 2 years
Equal monthly blended payments

(a) How much will each monthly payment be?

The monthly payment on a loan of $3000, at 8%, for two years is $135.51.

(b) How much interest will be paid the first month?

Refer to a table of interest factors; such tools are used to calculate monthly interest on instalment loans. In this example, the appropriate interest factor is 0.006 558 1970.

$$\frac{\text{interest for}}{\text{1 month}} = \frac{\text{outstanding}}{\text{principal}} \times \frac{\text{appropriate}}{\text{interest factor}}$$
$$= \$3000 \quad \times \quad 0.006\ 558\ 1970$$
$$= \$19.67$$

(c) How much principal will be repaid the first month?

Interest for one month must come out of the payment; the balance of the payment will be applied against the principal.

$$\frac{\text{payment on}}{\text{principal}} = \frac{\text{monthly}}{\text{payment}} - \frac{\text{interest}}{\text{for 1 month}}$$
$$= \$135.51 \quad - \quad \$19.68$$
$$= \$115.83$$

(d) What will be the principal balance outstanding after the first payment has been made?

$$\frac{\text{principal}}{\text{still owing}} = \frac{\text{principal}}{\substack{\text{owing} \\ \text{before}}} - \frac{\text{payment}}{\text{on principal}}$$
$$= \$3000 \quad - \quad \$115.83$$
$$= \$2884.17$$

(e) How much interest will be paid the second month?

$$\frac{\text{interest for}}{\text{one month}} = \frac{\text{outstanding}}{\text{principal}} \times \frac{\text{appropriate}}{\substack{\text{interest} \\ \text{factor}}}$$
$$= \$2884.17 \quad \times \quad 0.006\ 558\ 1970$$
$$= \$18.91$$

The process of calculating the monthly interest and then determining the size of the repayment on the principal will continue each month until the principal has been reduced to zero, as illustrated in the boxed example "Excerpts from a Payment Schedule for a $3000 Loan." (You may note small discrepancies in amounts between the above calculations and the table in that boxed example because of differences in numbers of decimal points used in the calculations.)

(f) How much will the total interest be?

To find the total interest paid in a blended-payment contract, use the following formula:

$$\frac{\text{monthly}}{\text{payment}} \times \frac{\text{number of}}{\text{months}}$$
$$\$135.51 \times 24$$
$$= \frac{\text{total}}{\text{amount repaid}} - \frac{\text{borrowed}}{\text{principal}} = \frac{\text{total}}{\text{interest charge}}$$
$$= \$3252.24 \quad - \$3000 \quad = \$252.24$$

Finally, the method of repayment affects the total interest charge. If you do not repay any of the total principal for the whole term of the loan, you will have to pay more interest than if you start repaying the principal right away. Most mortgages and consumer loans are instalment loans with blended payments—payments that comprise both principal and interest. Since the very first payment includes some return of the principal to the lender, this approach will reduce the total interest charge. Essentially, the method of payment affects the amount of principal outstanding at various times during the term of the loan. Did you notice that the total interest charge was lowest for the boxed example that featured an instalment loan with blended payments? The reason is that the borrower repaid some of the total principal during the term. This chapter's Women Take Charge box looks at determining an appropriate repayment plan for a particular budget.

Excerpts from a Payment Schedule for a $3000 Loan (8% compounded annually for 2 years)

PAYMENT NUMBER	MONTHLY PAYMENT	PRINCIPAL OWING BEFORE PAYMENT MADE	INTEREST PAID PER MONTH	PRINCIPAL REPAID PER MONTH	PRINCIPAL OWING AFTER PAYMENT
1	$135.50	$3 000.00	$19.68	$115.82	$2 884.18
2	135.50	2 884.17	18.92	116.58	2 767.60
3	135.50	2 767.60	18.15	117.35	2 650.25
4	135.50	2 650.25	17.38	118.12	2 532.13
5	135.50	2 532.13	16.61	118.89	2 413.24
6	135.50	2 413.24	15.83	119.67	2 293.57
12	135.50	1 683.33	11.04	124.46	1 558.87
18	135.50	924.22	6.06	129.44	794.78
24	135.50	134.74	0.88	134.62	0.12

Women take CHARGE 7.1

Irene wants to buy her first home. After working for 10 years, she has saved funds for a substantial down payment. There is a lot of competition in the mortgage environment, and Irene is hoping to land a good rate. She is searching for a mortgage arrangement with a monthly payment within her budget range.

Irene is currently looking at a mortgage for $180 000. The interest rate on the mortgage is 6 percent compounded semi-annually, and the mortgage will be amortized over 25 years.

The present value of the payments required to pay off the mortgage is equal to the original amount of the loan. Since she plans to pay on a monthly basis, the quoted rate of 6 percent compounded semi-annually will have to be converted to an equivalent monthly rate, which we will designate as i.

The following equation can be set up to solve for i:

$$(1 + i)^{12} = (1 + .06/2)^2$$

$$i = .004\ 938\ 622$$

The following formula for the present value of an annuity can be used to solve for R.

$$A = P\ \frac{1-(1 + i)^{-n}}{i}$$

$$180\ 000 = P\ \frac{1-(1+.004\ 938\ 622)^{-360}}{.004\ 938\ 622}$$

For a 25-year term involving 300 monthly payments, the monthly payment is $1151.65. For a 30-year term involving 360 monthly payments, the payment can be calculated using the following formula:

$$180\ 000 = P\ \frac{1-(1+.004\ 938\ 622)^{-360}}{.004\ 938\ 622}$$

The monthly payment for a 30-year term is $1070.68. Irene decides to take out a 30-year mortgage to keep the monthly payment within her budget.

Future Values and Present Values

Investors frequently ask the following kinds of questions: How much will I have if I invest $5000 at 8 percent for five years? How much will I need to invest at 8 percent in order to have $5000 in five years? The first question deals with the **future value** of money—that is, what the total of principal and interest will be in five years. The second deals with the **present value** of money; in other words, how much will you have to invest *now* at 8 percent to have $5000 in five years?

The two questions above assumed that a lump sum would be invested and a single payment received at a later date. These are fairly simple situations. Sometimes, though, investments are made in a series of deposits, or money may be received in a series of payments, or "receipts," such as in an annuity. For instance, what is the future value at the end of 10 years if $500 is deposited once a year (at the end of each year) for 10 years? And what is the present value of an annuity that will pay $800 a month for seven years? For the sake of simplicity, we will examine instances of "lump sum" situations first, and will later explain how to determine future and present values when serial payments are involved.

Single Payments

Future Value of a Lump Sum What will a present sum of money (P) be worth in the future (FV, future value), if the money in a lump sum is deposited at an interest rate (i) for a period of years (n)?

$$FV = \text{unknown}$$
$$n\ = \text{known}$$
$$i\ = \text{known}$$
$$P\ = \text{known}$$

FV, the unknown sum, can be found using the following formula, where P is a single amount and the interest is compounded for n years.

$$FV = P(1 + i)^n$$

Therefore, assume you want to deposit $5000 and want to know what it will be worth in five years at 5 percent, compounded annually.

$$FV = \text{unknown}$$
$$n\ = 5$$
$$i\ = 0.05$$
$$P\ = \$5000$$

Using the formula $FV = P(1 + 0.05)^5$
$$FV = \$5000(1 + 0.05)^5$$
$$= \$6381.41$$

Present Value of a Lump Sum

In this case you want to know how much you will have to invest now to have a certain amount in the future. For example, you want to send your daughter to university in six years and would like to know how much you need to invest at current interest rates to be able to pay the expected $30 000 tuition. This can be determined by using the following formula:

$$PV = \text{unknown}$$
$$FV = \$30\,000$$
$$n\ = 6$$
$$i\ = 0.05$$

$$PV = \frac{FV}{(1 + i)^n} \qquad PV = \frac{\$30\,000}{(1 + .05)^6} \qquad PV = \$22\,386.46$$

Therefore, you will need to set aside $22 386.46 now to achieve your goal.

What a Lump Sum Was Worth in the Past

Inflation is a major concern in personal finance because it constantly erodes the value of money. If you want to know what $1000 was worth five years ago, if inflation has averaged 3 percent over this period, it can be done with the following formula:

$PV = \$1000$

$n \;\; = 5$

$i \;\;\; = 0.03$

$PV = \$1000(1.03)^{-5} = \$862.6087$

As can be seen, even at 3 percent, which is within the range accepted by the Bank of Canada, inflation can play havoc with one's finances.

Personal FINANCE in action 7.2

Who Was Richer?

In 1898, J. D. Rockefeller, who made his fortune in oil, was worth an estimated $800 000 000.

One hundred years later, Bill Gates, the founder of Microsoft, was worth an estimated $64 000 000 000.

To answer the question "Who was richer?" we need to use present value techniques to compare the two fortunes at the same point in time (1998). Using interest of 5 percent and the following formula:

$F = P\,(1 + i)^{100}$ or S = (Rockefeller's value in 1998 terms) = $800\,000\,000(1.05)^{100}$

$= \$105\,201\,006\,311$

A dollar was worth considerably more in 1898 than in 1998. Therefore, J. D. Rockefeller was worth considerably more than Bill Gates. This change in the value of money was caused by inflation, something everyone interested in personal finance should be aware of.

Personal FINANCE in action 7.3

Were They Cheated?

In 1626, the Dutch West-India Company purchased Manhattan Island from its native inhabitants with $24 worth of beads and blankets. This is often referred to as a steal. But was it? If $24 had been invested in 1626 at 6 percent interest compounded annually, the value by 2006 would have been

$FV = (1.06)^{380}$

$= \$99\,183\,639\,911$

It is therefore a moot point whether the natives were cheated or not.

Personal FINANCE in action 7.4

Saving for a Vacation Property

Hank and Gwen want to retire and buy a cottage in 10 years. Cottages on nearby lakes are now selling for between $75 000 and $125 000. They estimate that they should be able to buy one if they have $150 000 set aside. They live in a remote part of the province and property values there rise slowly. How much do they need to invest each year for ten years at an effective annual rate of 5 percent to achieve this goal?
Where

FV = known
n = known

i = known
PMT = unknown

$$FV = PMT \frac{(1 + i)^n - 1}{i}$$

$$\$150\ 000 = PMT \frac{(1 + .05)^{10} - 1}{.05}$$

$$\$150\ 000 = PMT \times 12.577\ 89 = \$11\ 925.69$$

Therefore, Hank and Gwen need to invest $11 925.69 a year for the next 10 years.

Uniform Series of Deposits

An interesting problem involves finding how much must be deposited on a regular basis (PMT) to reach a predetermined goal? This is illustrated in Personal Finance in Action Box 7.4, "Saving for a Vacation Property."

The formula used to determine this is

$$FV = PMT \frac{(1 + i)^n - 1}{i}$$

Present Value of a Series of Deposits Another interesting problem involves finding the present value of a series of deposits. What will be the present value PV of a series of deposits PMT for n years at an interest rate of i? An example is shown in Personal Finance in Action Box 7.5, "The Clearing House Prize."

PV = unknown
n = known
i = known
PMT = known

Uniform Series of Payments Received

The previous two examples involved the present and future values of a uniform series of deposits. Now we will consider the present and future value of a series of payments.

Commuted Value of a Series of Payments What is the present worth of a property that is now renting at a given rental rate (PMT) each year, at a given interest rate (i)? See Personal Finance in Action Box 7.6, "What Is the Value of a Future Sum of Money Today?"

Personal FINANCE in action 7.5

The Clearing House Prize

Helmut could not believe his good fortune. He had just been contacted by the Publishers Clearing House and told that this was his lucky day. He was the winner of their $10 000 000 Sweepstakes. He was given two options for receiving this money:

(a) He could take the whole amount now.

(b) He could receive a cheque for $83 333.33 every month for 10 years at 5 percent compounded monthly.

The clearing house told him that the latter option was probably the best choice for him because he would know what his income was and wouldn't need to worry about investing the money.

Why would the clearing house make this suggestion? To find out we use the formula

$$PV = PMT \frac{1 - (1 + i)^{-n}}{i}$$

$$PV = \$83\ 333.33 \frac{1 - (1.00416)^{-120}}{.00416}$$

$$PV = \$7\ 856\ 778.88$$

If Helmut agrees to receive the monthly payment, Publishers Clearing House only has to set aside $7 856 778.88, thereby saving it $2 143 221.12.

Personal FINANCE in action 7.6

What Is the Value of a Future Sum of Money Today?

Manfred owns a piece of property in the country. He no longer wants the property and decides to sell it for $35 000. Lars says that he will pay him $6000 per year for 7 years at interest of 6% compounded annually. Assume that the interest will be paid annually. Will Manfred be paid $35 000 in this way? To find out, we use the following formula:

$$\text{Present value} = \$6000 \frac{\left(1 - (1 + i)^{-n}\right)}{i}$$

$$= \$6000 \frac{\left(1 - (1.06)^{-7}\right)}{0.06}$$

$$= \$33\ 494$$

Therefore, it would be foolish for Manfred to accept Lars' offer. But since Lars really wants the property, Manfred tells him he can have it if he agrees to pay the realtor's fee.

$$
\begin{aligned}
PMT &= \text{known} \\
n &= \text{known} \\
i &= \text{known} \\
FV &= \text{unknown}
\end{aligned}
$$

The formula is $FV = PMT \dfrac{(1 + i)^n - 1}{i}$

Capital Recovery in a Uniform Series of Payments

How much can be withdrawn each year PMT from a capital fund that has a present value of PV if the capital fund is invested at interest rate i so that the fund will be exhausted in n years? See Personal Finance in Action Box 7.7, "Periodic Withdrawals," for an example.

Personal FINANCE in action 7.7

Periodic Withdrawals

Carmen has decided to retire. The accumulated value of her pension is $532 697.00. How much can she expect to receive annually (before taxes) starting in one year if the effective rate of return is 7 percent and her pension is to last for 25 years?

PV = known
n = known
i = known
PMT = unknown

$$PV = PMT \left(\frac{1 - (1 + i)^{-n}}{i} \right)$$

$$\$532\ 697 = PMT \left(\frac{1 - 1.07}{0.07} \right)^{-25}$$

$$\$532\ 697 = 11.653\ 583$$

PMT = $45 711.00

Carmen can expect to receive a pension of $45 711.01 per year.

PMT = unknown
n = known
i = known
PV   = known

The formula for this is

$$PV = PMT \frac{1-(1 + i)^{-n}}{i}$$

The Net Present Value Concept

The **net present value** of an investment is the amount (in current dollars) by which the economic value of the cash inflows exceeds the economic value of the cash outflows.

NPV = PVin − PVout

Personal Finance in Action Box 7.8, "The Growing Fast-Food Industry," provides an example of a problem related to this concept.

Personal FINANCE in action 7.8

The Growing Fast-Food Industry

Bill, who owns a doughnut shop, wants to increase his earnings. He is told by the consulting firm Campeau Inc. that if he sells pizza, as well as his doughnuts, he will make an extra $100 000 per year for the next five years. To achieve this goal he must do the following:

(a) Purchase two delivery vehicles at $17 000 each.

(b) Pay $1000 in maintenance for each vehicle per year.

(c) Buy and install five pizza ovens at $50 000 each.

He wants to make an extra 15 percent per year. Should he go ahead?

NPV = PVin − PVout

Cash inflows:

$$PVin = \$100\ 000\ \frac{1 - (1.15)^{-5}}{.15} = \$335\ 215$$

Cash outflows:

2 delivery vehicles @ $17 000 each = $34 000
5 pizza ovens @ $50 000 each = $250 000
$1000 maintenance per vehicle per year

$$PVout = \$2000\ \frac{1 - (1.15)^{-5}}{.15} = \$6704$$

$34 000 + $250 000 + $6704 = $290 704

Therefore, Bill should go ahead.

To Lease or to Buy, That is the Question

Ewart (a renowned English heart specialist, and his partner, Ros, have been enticed to move to Calgary where Ewart will teach in the University of Calgary's medical school. Ros wants a car and has convinced Ewart to look at an M3 Cabriolet, listed at $84 500. Should they lease or buy this car?

Option 1: Buy

$84 500 with 10 percent down and payments over 48 months at 4 percent, calculated monthly.

$$\$84\ 500 - \$8450 = \$76\ 050$$

$$\$76\ 050 = \text{PMT} \left(1 - \frac{1.0033333}{.0033333}\right)^{-48}$$

$$\$76\ 050 = 44.28923599 \times \text{PMT}$$

$$\text{PMT} = \$1717.14$$

Option 2: Lease

Deposit: $3000 down
Interest: 5 percent, calculated monthly
Residual or buy at the end of 48 months, 40 percent of list price.

$$\$84\ 500 - \$3000 = 81\ 500$$

$$\$81\ 500 = \text{PMT} \left(1 - \frac{1.005}{.005}\right)^{-48}$$

$$\$81\ 500 = \text{PMT}\ \frac{1-(1.005)^{-48}}{.005}$$

$$\$81\ 500 = \text{PMT}(42.500\ 317\ 78) + 40\% \text{ of } \$84\ 500$$

PMT = $1917.63 + 40% of $84 500. Therefore, they decide to buy at $1717.14 for 48 months because this is the least expensive of the two options.

Multiple Compounding Periods per Year

Thus far, we have explained how to calculate present and future values when interest is compounded annually, but very often interest is compounded more frequently. (See Personal Finance in Action Box 7.10, "The Effective Rate of Interest," for an example.) There is a simple way to adapt the formulas and procedures given in this chapter to accommodate various frequencies of compounding. Simply change the annual interest rate to the semi-annual rate (or the quarterly rate, or whatever rate is appropriate), and change the number of years to the number of compounding periods. For example, if the interest rate is 10 percent per year for six years, compounded quarterly, it will be expressed as 2.5 percent per quarter. The

The Effective Rate of Interest

José checks her credit card statement. It says that 2 percent will be charged on the unpaid balance monthly. She thinks this means that the annual rate is 2% × 12 = 24% until her girlfriend Sue, who works in a bank, tells her she needs to find the effective rate of interest, or APR. To find the APR, she needs to use the formula:

$$f = (1 + i)^n - 1 \quad i = 0.02$$

$$f = (1.02)^{12} - 1 \quad n = 12$$

$$= 1.268\ 241\ 795 - 1$$

$$= 0.268\ 241\ 795 \times 100$$

$$= 26.82\%$$

So the effective annual rate of interest is 26.82 percent.

Needless to say, after this lesson, José scaled back on her use of credit and managed to pay the balance owing on her credit card in full each month.

number of compounding periods will be 4 × 6 years = 24. When you are using the formula or tables, $i = 0.025$ and $n = 24$.

Frequency of Compounding

Why is it better to have your interest compounded more frequently if you are an investor and less frequently if you are a borrower? It is easy to figure out the worth of the investment, that is, the principal plus interest, when interest is compounded annually.

$1000 invested at 8% per year is worth $1080 at the end of the first year.

But how much is $1000 worth if the interest is compounded quarterly, monthly, weekly, and daily? To find out, use the following formula:

$$\text{Future value} = \$1000 \times \left(1 + \frac{i}{n}\right)^n$$

$$\text{Quarterly} = \$1000 \times \left(1 + \frac{0.08}{4}\right)^4 = \$1082.43$$

$$\text{Monthly} = \$1000 \times \left(1 + \frac{0.08}{12}\right)^{12} = \$1083.00$$

$$\text{Weekly} = \$1000 \times \left(1 + \frac{0.08}{52}\right)^{52} = \$1083.22$$

$$\text{Daily} = \$1000 \times \left(1 + \frac{0.08}{365}\right)^{365} = \$1083.27$$

Frequency of compounding increases the amount of the payment, but the amount of the increase declines as the frequency of compounding increases.

Many consumers in Canada owe money to retail stores, banks, and credit card companies. Such companies are required by law to state what interest they charge on outstanding accounts. However, usually this rate is stated on an annual basis and does not indicate the frequency of compounding. This is the case with major credit card companies. Consumers need to ask about the frequency of compounding, in addition to the annual rate when they are applying for credit. As has been shown, the greater the frequency, the greater the cost.

Construction Contracts and the Time Value of Money

Municipalities frequently contract out construction work. A knowledge of the time value of money is essential for those in the municipality's finance department if they are to get the best value on these contracts for ratepayers. One municipality decides that a number of bridges should be repaired. This municipality can afford to pay $102 000 for this repair work over a four-year period. A notice is placed in the local paper, asking for tenders to be submitted for the work. Two companies respond, as follows:

Cost to Repair Bridges for 2004–07

	2004	2005	2006	2007	Total
Vanguard Construction	$24 000	$24 000	$26 000	$26 000	$100 000
Central Construction	$96 000	$0	$0	$0	$96 000

What company should the city's Chief Financial Officer choose? He decides to apply the concept of the time value of money. How much will the municipality have in the bank when the work is completed if the bank pays interest of 5%, compounded annually? The results are as follows:

Vanguard Construction

	2003	2004	2005	2006	2007
Interest Earned		$5 100	$4 156	$3 162	$2 020
Costs to City		$24 000	$24 000	$26 000	$26 000
Bank Balance	$102 000	$83 100	$63 256	$40 418	$16 438

Central Construction

	2003	2004	2005	2006	2007
Interest Earned		$5 100	$556	$582	$612
Costs to City		$96 000	$0	$0	$0
Bank Balance	$102 000	$11 100	$11 656	$12 238	$12 850

When the Chief Financial Officer presented these figures to the Public Works Department, the staff were amazed. Everyone expected Central to get the job because of its low bid, but looking at the FO's calculations, they agreed that Vanguard should get the job because its bid actually cost the city less money. The reason for this, as the CFO explained, was based on the concept of the time value of money. What the municipality would have to pay in four years is less than what it had to pay today.

Summary

- The time value of money means that the money you have today is worth more than it will be in the future. The present value of money is what a sum of money in the future is worth today, based on a specific rate of interest and a specific period of time. The net present value is the difference between the present value of cash inflows and the present value of cash outflows. The future value of money involves compounding. How much will a sum of money increase in a time period at a specific interest rate?

- The maturity date is the date when a loan will mature. A term is the length of time a loan is outstanding. Interest is what you pay when you borrow money and what you earn if you lend it. Principal is the amount of money borrowed or the amount of money that is loaned. Factors that influence interest rates include the Bank of Canada's "overnight rate"; the supply of money; the demand for money; the lender's risk; and the duration of the loan. The real interest rate is adjusted for inflation. Simple interest, often paid annually, is the interest earned on the sum deposited and is not compounded.

■ Compounding is the adding of interest to the interest that was already added to the initial interest paid on a deposit or charged on a loan. The key to frequency of compounding is that the greater the frequency, the higher the effective annual rate.

■ Effective annual yield is the rate with compounding taken into account. Nominal interest rate is interest that is not adjusted for inflation.

■ Blended payments are a combination of interest and principal payments. Amortization refers to the paying off of a debt in regular interest payments over a period of time.

■ Commuted value, usually used in pensions, refers to the amount of money paid in a lump sum payment that is equal to the value of future pension payments.

Key Terms

amortization *(p. 205)*	loan term *(p. 200)*
blended payments *(p. 204)*	maturity date *(p. 200)*
commuted value *(p. 210)*	net present value *(p. 212)*
compounding *(p. 200)*	nominal interest rate *(p. 203)*
effective annual yield *(p. 203)*	present value *(p. 208)*
frequency of compounding *(p. 203)*	present value of money *(p. 198)*
	principal *(p. 199)*
future value *(p. 208)*	simple interest *(p. 200)*
future value of money *(p. 198)*	time value of money *(p. 198)*
interest rate *(p. 199)*	yield *(p. 203)*

Problems

1. Tony and Heather, a married couple, purchased their home in 1982 for $105 000. The house was appraised in 2006 for $321 000. What was the annual rate of appreciation in the home during this period?

2. Ken and his wife, also named Heather, bought out-of-town and paid $39 900 in 1978. Their home was appraised in 2006 for $157 000. What was the annual rate of inflation during this period?

3. Joe, a math graduate from the University of Waterloo, was hired by a community college in BC. His salary in 1972 was $6 800. When he retired in 2002, his salary was $82 000. At what compound annual rate did his salary increase during the 30-year period?

4. Miss Ellis bought her house in 1984 for $54 000. If she has to move into a retirement home in 2006, and inflation over this time has averaged 5.2 percent, what is the least amount she should sell her home for?

5. You wish to accumulate $75 000 so that your son will be able to go to college in 15 years. If you can earn 10 percent compounded annually, how much do you have to deposit into an account each year to achieve this goal?

6. Your finance professor has been given the following options when he retires:

   (a) Receive a lump sum of $200 000.

   (b) Receive an annuity of $25 500 each year for the next 10 years.

   Can you tell her, based on the information given in this chapter, which of the two choices she should take?

7. Visa quotes an annual interest of 18 percent. If the interest is to be charged monthly, calculate the effective interest rate.

8. A factory cost $8 000 000 to build. If your accountant tells you it will produce an inflow at 14 percent (after operating expenses) of $1 700 000 per year for 10 years, does this mean it will make $17 000 000? Net Present Value = PVin − PVout.

9. Jeff and Diane would like to buy a house. They have saved $35 000 for a down payment, and with their combined incomes they can afford $1200 in mortgage payments per month. What price range should they look for if money is worth 4 percent compounded monthly and they would like to pay the mortgage off in 15 years?

10. Hillary and Jack want to buy a house in 16 years. They deposit $1000 per year for 10 years in a trust company that pays 6 percent per annum. At the end of the 10-year period, they arrange for the money to be left in a savings account that earns 5.5 percent compounded semi-annually.

    (a) How much do they have in the bank at the end of 16 years?

    (b) How much interest has been earned?

11. Gaston bought a 52-inch TV on credit, signing a contract that required monthly payments of $55.25 per month for 36 months. The first payment was due one month after delivery of the set at 24 percent compounded monthly.

    (a) What was the cash price?

    (b) What will be the total sum paid?

    (c) What is the cost of financing the purchase?

12. The New York Americans fired their coach, J. C. Pronovost, at the end of year two of a five-year contract. He was paid $900 000 per year or $75 000 per month. How much must the owners pay to buy out the remaining three years of the contract if they use 6 percent compounded monthly as the value of a dollar at the time of firing?

13. You win Lotto 649, which has a value of $4 200 000. You want to use some of the money to pay off your mortgage. You have paid 10 years off on a mortgage of $202 000 at $1 500 per month at 8 percent compounded monthly. What do you still owe if the mortgage was for 20 years?

14. Dell offers online deals for its latest computer. Chris really needs a new one in order to enroll in the course he wants. His father, Ken, picks out a laptop at $750 and has it customized to suit Chris's needs. The total price, excluding shipping, is $1102. Since Ken has some serious financial problems and doesn't have the cash, Dell will sell him the computer at 14 percent monthly over three years. What is the monthly payment?

15. You are in the process of leasing a car for 60 months. The list price is $24 000 and the freight and PDI is $1 000. Interest is at 6.25 percent. The tax rate is 15 percent. You are making no down payment and have no trade-in.

    (a) What is the monthly payment?

    (b) What is the total amount to be financed?

    (c) What is the total interest charge?

16. Go to the Bank of Canada's website at **www.bankofcanada.ca/en**. Click on About the Bank, then FAQ, and then The Bank's Roles. What does it say about What We Do and Monetary Policy? Answer the following:

    (a) What is the Bank's monetary policy framework?

    (b) What is the Bank's inflation target range?

    (c) Should the Bank stick strictly to this target?

    To answer (c), assume that you have just bought a Canada Savings Bond, which has an interest rate of 2 percent, compounded annually.

    (1) What will this be worth in three years?

    (2) If inflation has stayed at 3 percent for the three years, what is your money really worth?

    (3) If inflation had only been 1 percent for the three years, what would your money be worth?

17. Go the website of Canadian Driver at **www.canadiandriver.com**. Click on Price Guide. Find the price for a 2006 Ford Escape with PDI added.

    (a) Click on Loan Calculator. Fill in these details:

    Down payment: $2000

    Term: 48 months

    Interest: 2.9 percent

    Province: Alberta

    (b) Click on Lease Calculator. Fill in these details:

    Lease amount: Purchase price − security deposit.

    Security deposit: $2000

    Province: Alberta

    No trade-in

    Residual Value: $9619.60

    Which will cost you less money?

References

BOOKS

There are fewer books dealing specifically with interest rates than most other topics covered in this book. Following is a list of some of the titles available.

Ballast, David Kent, Robert Rachlin, and Allen Sweeny. *Accounting and Financial Fundamentals for Nonfinancial Executives*. New York, NY: AMACON Div American Mgmt Assn, 1996.

Brigo, Damiano, and Fabio Mercurio. *Interest Rate Models: Theory and Practice*. Heidelberg: Springer Verlag, Winter/Spring 2006.

Christina, Robert A. *Compound Interest*. Visby, Sweden: Books On Demand.

Davis, Morton D. *The Math of Money*. Katlenburg-Landau, Germany: Copernicus Books, 2001.

Gray, Douglas A. *Mortgage Payments Made Easy: A Complete Canadian Guide*. Toronto: McGraw-Hill Ryerson, 1994. Out of print.

Guthrie, Gary, and Larry Lemon. *Mathematics of Interest Rates and Finance*. Toronto: Prentice Hall, 2003.

Homer, Sidney, and Richard Sylla. *A History of Interest Rates*. 4th Edition. Toronto: Wiley, 2005.

Paulos, John Allen. *A Mathematician Plays the Stock Market*. New York: Basic Books, 2003. A mathematical analysis of the stock market.

Rebonato, Riccardo. *Interest Rate Option Models*. Heidelberg: Springer Verlag, 2001. Quite theoretical.

Renn, Derek (Editor). *Life, Death and Money: Actuaries and the Creation of Financial Security*. Blackwell: London, 1998. Useful for dealing with the concept of annuities.

Ross, Sheldon M. *An Introduction to Mathematical Finance*. Cambridge, England: Cambridge University Press, 1999.

Sherman, Michael, and Delphi. *Comprehensive Compound Interest Tables*. New York: McGraw/Hill/Contemporary, 1986.

MAGAZINE AND JOURNAL ARTICLES

Journal of Insurance: Mathematics and Economics. St. Louis: Elsevier Publishing. 11830 Westline Industrial Drive, St. Louis, MO 63146. This journal has useful articles on pension funding and annuities.

Luchak, Andrew A. and Iann R. Gellatly. *What Kind of Commitment Does a Final-Earnings Pension Plan Elicit?* Oxford: Basil Blackwell. *Industrial Relations Journal*, Vol. 56, No. 2, 2001. The results of a study on the effects of an improved pension plan on employee commitment.

Journal of Pension Economics. New York: Cambridge University Press. 40 West 20th St., New York, NY 10011–4211. This journal has articles on pensions and retirement income.

Plus Magazine. (**http://plus.maths.org/index.html**) Published by mathematicians, this magazine has many useful articles on interest rates and related financial topics.

Woodward, Dustin. *The Power of Compounding: Discover the 8th Wonder of the World*. **http://mutualfunds.about.com/cs/mutualfunds101/a/compounding.htm**.

Personal Finance on the Web

Annuity.com
www.annuity.com

Bank of Canada
www.bankofcanada.ca

chapter 8

Saving and Investing

"First of all, you need savings. I used to think that the key to a fat investment port-folio was putting together the right mix of investments and selecting the best stocks, bonds and mutual funds; but the real key is good saving habits. The fact is, if you don't save a healthy amount each month and invest on an ongoing basis, it doesn't matter whether you earn 8 percent a year or 18 percent."

Sherry Cooper, Chief Economist, BMO Nesbitt Burns,
The Cooper Files

Learning Objectives

Understanding the concepts discussed in this chapter should help you become a wiser investor.

After studying this chapter, you should be able to:

1. *Distinguish between the following pairs of terms: saving and investing; investing and speculating; liquidity and marketability; debt and equity securities; income and capital gain; total and liquid assets; nominal and real interest rates; income and wealth.*

2. *Give four reasons for saving and explain how these reasons affect the choice of investments.*

3. *List three reasons why people find saving difficult and two reasons why they find investing overwhelming.*

4. *Examine the trends in the savings rate in Canada and analyze the effects of age and income on the amount that Canadians save.*

5. *Define the following terms: portfolio, term, and investment pyramid.*

6. *Distinguish among the different types of risks to which investments are exposed and give examples of the four types of risk associated with various kinds of investments.*

7. *Explain why there are trade-offs between risk and return, return and liquidity, term and return, and current income and capital gain.*

8. *Explain the principle of diversification and why it is important in investment planning.*

9. *Examine three ways of handling risk in an investment portfolio.*

10. *Identify conflicting investment objectives and explain how to make an investment plan.*

11. *Explain the differences between various investment theories.*

Introduction

One of the keys to successful financial planning is investing wisely. To invest, you first need to save. But investing and saving do not mean the same thing. A saver merely reduces spending and allows surplus funds to accumulate. An investor puts savings to work to generate income. This income is usually referred to as the yield. You are an investor if you have a savings account, a Canada Savings Bond (CSB), or a guaranteed investment certificate (GIC). If you simply keep your savings in a metal box in your desk, you are not.

The extensive range of investments available today can be quite confusing. Possible investment vehicles include everything from the simple savings account to the more complex mutual funds and derivatives. Each investment is chosen because it holds the promise of a gain. No one invests with the intention of losing money. Each investment also carries a risk. Generally, the greater the risk, the greater is the chance of a significant gain. There is little risk in a savings account, but also very little chance for gain. There is considerable risk in an emerging-markets mutual fund, but also the possibility of a large gain. Each investor must decide his or her own level of risk tolerance. How much risk you are comfortable tolerating will depend on your age, financial well-being, family circumstances, and investment objectives.

To become an investor, you must first become a saver. This chapter therefore begins by looking at ways to encourage saving and then introduces you to the world of investing. It also examines the characteristics of various investments, discusses investment objectives, and describes how to prepare an investment plan and create a portfolio of investments. Much of this information will be discussed in greater detail in Chapters 9 and 10.

Saving

Why Save?

As mentioned earlier, you must save before you can invest. Everyone with an income faces frequent decisions about whether to spend or save. In our market-driven economy, the desire to spend is often far greater than the desire to save. Spending, for many people, is exciting because it provides instant gratification. Saving, on the other hand, seems dull, since it provides no immediate reward. But unless you start saving at an early age, your retirement years could be very unpleasant.

To put the need for savings in perspective, it may be helpful to project income and economic needs over a lifespan (see Chapter 1, Figure 1.1). On average, earnings can be expected to increase until about age 55 or 60, after which they typically level off or start to decline. During your working years, your wages will probably increase to reflect your growing skills and experience as well as to accommodate price changes, but in late middle age your circumstances may shift: you may choose early retirement, or you may need to leave the labour force because of ill health or job loss. At retirement, which often occurs by age 65, earnings stop and must be replaced by pension and investment income. Whether you have investment income will depend on whether you first had some savings and then invested them wisely.

Your spending needs over a lifetime probably will not coincide with your level of income (see Chapter 1, Figure 1.1). Early in your working life, you may need more money than you are earning. But this imbalance will probably shift after you have been employed for some time. At that point, many people are well-established, own a house and other assets, and earn an income that exceeds their cost of living. Then, after retirement, incomes decline. Without some investment income, you may have difficulty maintaining the standard of living to which you have become accustomed.

It would certainly be more convenient if income increased gradually throughout a person's life and did not decline in later years. If this were a typical earning pattern, many people could maintain their financial independence relatively easily. But you can reach this goal by another route—that is, by creating a long-term financial plan with retirement in mind. To do so, you must invest some of your income on a regular basis, thereby creating an estate. Your estate can then be used when you retire to help you remain financially independent. You will also need some savings during your working years in order to meet short-term and emergency needs.

There are at least four important reasons to save. Funds are needed for (i) emergencies, (ii) liquidity, (iii) short-term goals, and (iv) long-term goals. We will consider each in turn.

Emergency Funds Since most people start out their working lives with very little net worth, the first need is to create an emergency fund—readily accessible money that can be used to handle the unexpected expenses that we all have. It is often suggested that several (perhaps three) months' take-home pay should be set aside as the emergency fund. Expect that you will need some time to achieve this goal. Emergency funds can be kept in a savings account, term deposits, Canada Savings Bonds, or any savings instrument that pays interest without locking in the money. In addition, you should give serious consideration to obtaining adequate insurance to cover risks to your property or dependents, as was discussed in Chapters 3 through 5.

Liquidity Needs You will need to have some funds available to cope with any unevenness in your cash flow and to pay for infrequent large expenses. Ready access to about one month's take-home pay may be adequate. Put these funds where they will earn as much interest as possible but remain easily accessible—for example, in an interest-bearing deposit account that permits chequing.

Short-Term Goals How can you distinguish a short-term goal from a long-term goal? When you review your financial goals, you will find some that can be accomplished within the next five years and others that will take longer. You can decide what time frame best fits your situation, but do distinguish between short-term and long-term goals. It is best to segregate the funds for short-term goals from those for longer-term goals, either on paper (in your accounting records) or by actually keeping the funds in separate accounts. The money being saved for next year's holiday should not get mixed with that being saved for retirement.

Short-term goals might include holidays and trips, vehicles, furniture, appliances, and education for you or your children. If your children are very young, planning for their post-secondary education will be a long-term goal. People who hope to own a home some day may want to start saving for a down payment; if you already have a house, you may want to reserve funds for mortgage prepayments.

Home ownership is the single most important investment for most Canadian families. In general, house prices change in response to both the prevailing inflation rate and the demand for housing. During periods of rapid inflation, the prices of houses tend to appreciate as much as or more than the inflation rate, making property an effective and tax-free storehouse of value. At other times, house prices may fall, to the disadvantage of people who must sell during those periods.

Despite some uncertainty about future house prices, home ownership has advantages. Any capital gain realized on your home is not taxed. From an investment perspective, buying a house is a form of forced saving. The discipline of regular mortgage payments results not only in a place to live now but also in the eventual ownership of an asset.

Depending on how soon you will need them, you may invest funds that you are saving for short-term goals in low-risk securities with appropriate maturities. The discussion that follows in this and later chapters should give you some ideas.

Long-Term Goals   Many people share the key long-term goal of increasing their net worth in such a way so that they will be able to enhance their financial security, achieve financial independence, and ensure financial support for their retirement years. To be certain of having a comfortable lifestyle during retirement, you must start planning early in your working years (for example, see Personal Finance in Action Box 8.1, "Saving with a Goal in Mind"). The magic of compounding will cause small amounts to grow to large sums if left invested for long periods. For instance, if you invest $1000 each year at an average annual compound rate of only 3 percent, your deposits of $30 000 will grow to $47 575 in 30 years. At 5 percent interest, your money will double in the same three decades, to $66 439; at 7 percent, it will triple, to $94 461 (see Figure 8.1). But if you put off saving for your retirement until you have only a few working years remaining, your savings will not have enough time to grow (see Chapter 1, Figure 1.2). Acquiring capital to fund your retirement is a long-term savings goal, and such funds can be invested with a longer-time horizon than those intended for short-term goals. That is, you can invest them in securities that, while not readily accessible, have prospects for long-term growth.

How to Save

Despite the widely held belief that everyone should save some money, many of us give these good intentions low priority. Saving can be hard to do, easy to postpone, and not much fun. To ensure success, you must have a firm commitment and definite plans. There will always be demands on your income that seem urgent and tempt you to postpone saving. You may reason that you will find saving easier at some later point, when you will have no unexpected expenses. But eventually you will discover that this pattern tends to become repetitious: no time ever seems to be the right time to save. The only solution is to set up an automatic savings plan now and follow it determinedly.

Personal FINANCE in action 8.1

Saving with a Goal in Mind

Horst was thirty years old. He had read a lot in the news about people retiring in their mid-fifties. No one he knew was even considering retirement. They had only been working for a few years and were getting on with their lives. Their financial decisions had to do with mortgages, raising children and just trying to make ends meet. But Horst was different. He had no interest in fitting into this pattern, which he found boring. He wanted to see the world, particularly out-of-the-way and unusual places like Mongolia and Nepal. He could not afford to do this yet but thought he could if he saved with discipline and invested wisely. Previously, he had spent all he earned on riotous living and had no idea where his money went. Now he decided that he would force himself to save 15 percent of every paycheque. This came to $200 every two weeks. If he started with his next paycheque and invested it in GICs for 40 years at an average of 5 percent compounded annually he would have over $650 000 to satisfy his wander lust. Of course, the final total would be much higher since his income would increase.

FIGURE 8.1   COMPOUND VALUE OF ANNUAL INVESTMENTS OF $1000, INVESTED AT 3%, 5%, AND 7%

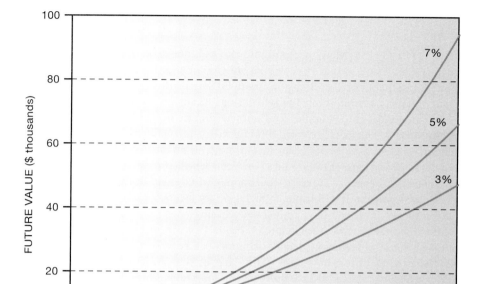

There are two basic approaches to saving—taking savings off the top of each paycheque before spending anything, or waiting to see what will be left at the end of the pay period. People who follow the first system will accumulate savings and will therefore have funds to invest; the others will never get around to it. Which approach will you take? The best plan is to establish a certain amount or percentage—e.g., 5 to 10 percent—that you will set aside from each pay.

When developing a savings strategy, be aware of your strengths and weaknesses. If you are an impulsive spender, you will need a system that makes your savings unavailable. Look into payroll savings plans and automatic saving methods at financial institutions; arrange for a certain portion of your income to be directed into such a plan before it ever reaches you. (See Personal Finance in Action Box 8.2, "An Automatic Savings Plan.") For example, each autumn Canada Savings Bonds become available by payroll deduction, some credit unions have automatic savings plans, and a number of mutual funds offer regular investment plans.

Rules for Saving   The three key rules for becoming a successful saver are as follows:

(a) Have a purpose or goal for which you are saving.

(b) Make a plan for accomplishing your goal.

(c) Save regularly.

You must be committed to a plan for increasing your net worth, or nothing will be accomplished. It would be ridiculous, of course, to go to the other extreme and become

Personal FINANCE in action 8.2

An Automatic Savings Plan

Peter finds saving very difficult. He always intends to bank whatever money is left at the end of the month—but more often than not, nothing is left. His friend Ayeesha, who belongs to a credit union, tells him about an automatic savings plan by which she saves $400 a month. She has authorized the credit union to deduct funds on each payday from the account into which her employer deposits her pay, and to transfer these funds to her savings account.

Peter decides that he will give this plan a try, but when he inquires at his bank, he finds that they have no such system in effect. An alternative, they suggest, is for Peter to write a year's supply of postdated cheques and, at the appropriate time, the bank will transfer funds from his chequing account to his savings account. Peter tries this method, and is very pleased at the end of the year to find that he has saved $4800.

a miser; letting saving become an end in itself is also a mistake. Your objective should be a balance between present and future consumption. Some financial experts suggest that if you save 10 percent of your salary throughout your working years and invest it carefully, you can become financially independent by the time you retire.

How Much Do Canadians Save?

The Importance of Saving

Savings are an essential part of financial planning. Without them a person cannot invest, nor can he or she effectively deal with the emergencies that invariably occur when least expected. Without saving, it is difficult for anyone to buy a car or a house, take a vacation, or more importantly, in the long run, live a care-free retirement. And, without savings, unless someone is very wealthy, life can be a constant struggle to make ends meet. Even the very wealthy need to be careful with their finances. If they are not, they may not be wealthy for long.

Frugality is the key to a successful savings plan, no matter the income level of the individual. This means that most ordinary Canadians must ignore the spending habits of their neighbours, including their new toys and expensive vacations. Authors Thomas J. Stanley and William D. Danko, in their very successful book *The Millionaire Next Door*, indicate that many wealthy people live frugal lives and do not appear to be wealthy. They do not spend lavishly but live in modest homes and drive older, moderately priced cars.

Envy is not a healthy emotion for smart savers-cum-investors to have. It prevents them from achieving their financial goals. And appearances can be deceiving. It is important to realize that many people who have an abundance of material goods may have borrowed the money to get them. Beautiful new cars may also be leased. However, as any honest car salesperson will explain, leasing is more expensive than buying. Beautiful houses may be mortgaged. It is common practice in Canada for a couple to use one spouse's income to pay off the mortgage. If downsizing or illness occur in a family that lives on credit, financial tragedy may ensue. This can also happen, of course, to those who are more prudent. An article in *MoneySense Magazine* claims that "the total net worth of the average Canadian family ticks in at a less-than staggering $125 000, including home ownership, RRSPs, bank accounts and company pension."[1] Therefore, anyone who does not have the latest SUV or snowmobile, or annual vacation in Cancun, need not feel bad. Many of those who do are probably living way beyond their means.

The value of savings to your long-term financial health cannot be overemphasized. It is far more important than the transitory pleasure one feels when buying a shiny new car. Those who spend less and save more will have longer-lasting pleasure eventually, when the pleasure really counts. We all grow old in the end. Does anyone want to spend his or her old age in poverty? The easiest way to prevent this is to save regularly and invest wisely. Yet many people do not seem to have received or understood the message. Keith Ambachtsheer, President of the Association of Canadian Pension Management, has said, "3.5 million family units out of a total of 12.2 million have no private pension or retirement savings at all."[2] One wonders how such people will care for themselves in their golden years.

Most things lose value as time passes. Even the prices houses command may not always increase. In spite of this, the only thing it makes sense to go into debt for is a house. Few people can afford the total cost of buying a house outright, and so most must finance the purchase with a mortgage. Such debt is beneficial because one day the person with a mortgage will own the house, which will, with luck, have risen in value over the years. A house is also a good investment because the gain in value, unlike that for stocks, is not taxed when the property is sold.

The savings rate of Canadians, or lack of it, has recently become a matter of public debate. For a number of reasons, most noticeably consumerism and the pull of the market economy, it has dropped seriously. In the 20-year period from 1973 to 1993 the savings rate was in double digits. In 1985, for example, it was 15.8 percent.[3] Between 1997 and 2003 it averaged a healthy 4.2 percent per year. By 2003 it had plunged to 1.4 percent, and in 2004 the average Canadian savings rate stood at zero.[4] The idea of saving has not dropped off the radar completely, however. One in five Canadians expect to save $100 000 or less for retirement and one in three plan to save $250 000 or less,[5] rates that show a complete lack of financial realism.

Realizing the importance of saving, the federal government provides a tax incentive to anyone who opens an RRSP. The main purpose of an RRSP is to encourage saving for retirement. RRSP funds can also accumulate tax-free. This "tax shelter" has become extremely popular with some Canadians but not with everyone. There are two good reasons for opening an RRSP. Besides sheltering investments from taxation, an RRSP allows a contributor to receive a tax deduction. In spite of these strong incentives, strangely enough, only one-third of those who can make a contribution do so.[6]

The one-third who do, contribute about $35 billion annually. At the same time, however, roughly the same amount is withdrawn each year, some of it to help to purchase new houses, another form of saving. In addition, Canadians have unused RRSP contribution room of $400 billion, a remarkable sum when one realizes that the total amount invested in such plans only amounts to $600 billion. While unused contributions can be made up, this is not an easy thing to do.[7] Highlighting concern over the poor savings habits of Canadians, a study

[1] Bruce Gillespie, "How to get financially fit at any age," *Money Sense Magazine*. Accessed at **www.moneysense.ca/magazine/article.jsp?content=850844** on October 31, 2003, this is the latest data available.

[2] Keith Ambachtsheer. "Pensions Need Reforms as Much as Health Care," *National Post*. January 2, 2003.

[3] Hip Deep In Hock, *Maclean's*, December 6, 2004.

[4] Geoffrey Hale, "Are Canadian Savings Rates a Problem?", *Policy.ca*, March 29, 2005.

[5] David Bach, *Start Late, Finish Rich, Canadian Edition*, Toronto, Doubleday Canada, 2005.

[6] Ian Davidson, "Some Things to Think About," *CAmagazine*. June 2005.

[7] Ian Davidson, op. cit.

by the Vanier Institute found that contributions to RRSPs had dropped by an average of 20 percent between 1997 and 2002.[8]

It used to be that one of the most controversial aspects of RRSPs was the limit on foreign investments. The 2005 federal budget eliminated all restrictions on foreign content. Because of the small size of the Canadian market this was thought to be a good thing by many investment advisors. The change opened the door to greater diversity and the potential for greater returns. It also, of course, opened the door to greater risk and the possibility of loss.

It is interesting to see who contributes to RRSPs. As one would assume, higher-income individuals are the most likely to contribute. They have the most to lose by not doing so. In 2000, those with the highest incomes paid 51 percent of the total income tax collected. Not to put money into such a tax haven would be very foolish for many people.[9] In addition to high-income earners, younger Canadians between 25 and 34, rather than older ones, usually contribute. Among single people, younger people in all income brackets contribute more than older people do. Single women are also more likely than single men to make RRSP contributions. The self-employed make greater contributions than those who work for someone else. Since self-employed income is unpredictable from year to year, self-employed people may cash in RRSP funds in lean years when their taxable incomes are low. People who contribute to their employer's pension plan are more likely to open an RRSP than those who do not have access to such plans. Married couples tend to make more RRSP contributions than those in common-law relationships.[10]

The amount a person saves will depend on a number of things. These include age, occupation, marital status, and the number of their dependents. The amount saved will also depend on a person's level of income as well as interest rates. Little research has been done recently on the savings habits of Canadians. However, with the baby boomers fast approaching retirement, it would be realistic to assume that at least some Canadians are saving a larger proportion of their incomes than in the past. If to the baby boomers we add the growing number of people who are self-employed and forced to provide for their own pensions, then the savings rate of Canadians should soon start to increase.

Investing

Why Invest?

The main reason for saving is to have money available for investing. It is only through investing wisely that you can reach your financial goals. Another reason is the entertainment it can bring. Interest in investing has become a hobby, not just for those of advanced years, but also for many who want to see their net worth grow. Tracking your investments and learning about the financial world is now much easier with the internet. These activities can easily become a full-time occupation for those with the available time.

Some people may be good savers but have little idea how to invest. As a result of the way in which much of the financial news is reported, many people have a fear of investing. The drama in the media that accompanies a sharp drop in the stock market is enough to make even the most experienced investor worried. And it can cause investors to become overly cautious. As a

---

[8]Hip Deep In Hock, *Maclean's*, December 6, 2004.

[9]Statistics Canada, "2000 Income: An Overview—Perspectives on Labour and Income" (January 2003), Vol. 4, No.1, Page 35.

[10]Statistics Canada, "Profiling RRSP Contributors, Perspectives on Labour and Income," (January 2003), Vol. 4, No.1.

result, they may only invest their savings in a bank account or buy Canada Savings Bonds and GICs, all of which are considered safe and risk-free. This approach may be comfortable but it exposes the investor to the risk of inflation and results in higher taxes than are necessary.

Investing Versus Speculating

Assuming that you have been successful at saving, what can you do to make your net worth grow? First, you must have (or cultivate) patience. Wise investing does not involve speculating or gambling. You do not want to risk your hard-earned savings: rather, you want them to increase gradually. Although many people erroneously believe that investing involves putting your money in a safe place, while speculating involves buying stocks, **investing** can be defined as committing funds in a way that minimizes risk yet at the same time protects capital, while also earning a return that is satisfactory for the degree of risk. You can achieve this combination of aims in a variety of ways.

Investors are not in a hurry; speculators, on the other hand, look for large profits from a small layout of funds within a short time. **Speculation** tends to be based on a shorter time horizon and to involve more risk than investing. Speculators invest money with the expectation of capital gain through a change in market value and are primarily motivated by short-term gains.

Unless you have several hundred thousand dollars in assets and can afford to hire an investment counsellor, you will have to manage your own investments. The choices are either to become knowledgeable and devote some time to monitoring your portfolio, or to choose investments that require minimal attention. Having a portfolio may sound very grand, but a **portfolio** is simply a list or collection of assets. If you would rather not have to deal with financial matters, put your savings into less risky investments that require little attention, such as guaranteed investment certificates or Canada Savings Bonds (as Jenny does in this chapter's Women Take Charge box). Most of the discussion that follows is based on the assumption that you are interested in learning more about investing.

When you have finished reading this book, you will have been introduced to the basics of investing and should have a vocabulary that allows you to understand the articles in the

Women take CHARGE 8.1

Jenny graduated from university with a degree in business a year ago. She wants to start a savings program as soon as possible because she has "time on her side" in which to take advantage of the compounding effect.

Jenny's goal is to build a secure nest egg to handle any possible emergencies before moving on to higher-yielding, more speculative investments. As a framework for judging an investing strategy, she will look at alternatives with respect to liquidity, marketability, term, management effort, tax treatment, and risk.

Canada Savings Bonds appeal to Jenny. She must decide whether to invest in the Regular bond, which currently pays 2 percent a year and can be cashed in at any time without loss of principal, or the Premium bond. The Premium bond pays 2.5 percent in the first year, 3.25 percent in the second year, and 4 percent in the third year, and can be cashed in on each anniversary date.

The Regular savings bond is more liquid but carries a lower rate as a tradeoff. However, the rate is higher than on her bank account. If interest rates were to rise during the year, the Regular bond could be cashed in to take advantage of a higher rate instead of having to wait until an anniversary date. With the Premium savings bond, if interest rates were

continued

to fall, Jenny would be guaranteed a rate of 2.5 percent, 3.25 percent, and 4.0 percent for the first, second, and third years, respectively.

There would be little management effort involved with the bonds, and safety of principal. The interest would be taxed at Jenny's combined marginal tax rate, which is fairly low since she is just starting her career. The interest must be reported each year for both the Regular and Compound bonds as well as the Premium bond.

Jenny has decided to put half of her savings into a Regular bond and the other half into a Premium bond, to provide liquidity and some interest rate protection.

financial press that you need to read to keep up to date. As mentioned before, lack of knowledge and fear of the unknown deter many people from making wise investment decisions. Since you need an understanding of the basic characteristics of investments before you can make a personal investment plan, these will be examined next.

LEGAL ISSUES

Investment Fraud

Circus promoter P. T. Barnum is reputed to have said, "There's a sucker born every minute." In the matter of investments, this often seems to be the case, as regulatory agencies report a significant increase in the number of people hurt by investment fraud. In 2003 an estimated $5 billion was stolen in this fashion.* The victims, often the elderly, are unsuspecting people who may have set funds aside for retirement that they cannot afford to lose.

A common scam involves making phone calls or sending letters and CDs to prospective targets, inviting them to participate in a "guaranteed" investment. Solicitations routinely promise amazing investment returns. This, in itself, should act as a danger sign. No legitimate returns of great magnitude are, or ever can be, guaranteed. Also, proper securities firms do not solicit customers in this fashion. To become a client of one, an individual must first contact the firm. He or she will then be sent a questionnaire, which will determine the person's investment knowledge, goals, and tolerance for risk.

To add an air of legitimacy, the rogue broker who makes the solicitation may claim an affiliation with an international organization such as the International Monetary Fund. Legitimate-sounding financial terms are often used. The ruse may lure victims with the suggestion that taxes may be evaded by investing in a tax haven.

Those who grab the bait may actually receive a gain on their initial investment. This is done to encourage them to part with more of their money. The rogue broker may then suggest that victims tell their close friends and relatives about their good fortune to lure them into the scheme.

The RCMP warns that those who practise investment fraud look and sound legitimate. They may have offices that are staffed with "investment professionals." However, once enough victims have been parted from their money, the bogus brokers disappear. Phone numbers are no longer in service. Offices are empty. The police cannot help. Once the money is gone, it is gone forever. The crooks are rarely caught.

*"Top Ten Investment Scams," Jennifer Walker, *50Plus.com.*

continued

Questions

1. **Discussion** One legitimate (not bogus) Canadian investment dealer who defrauded clients of $7 million received a five-year prison term, of which he served 10 months. Sentences for fraud of smaller amounts are often for less than two years, which means that the convicted criminals do not have to serve time in a federal penitentiary.

   (a) Why do you think the sentences are so lenient?

   (b) Would stronger sentences reduce the incidence of fraud?

2. **Discussion** All investors need to practise due diligence before deciding to invest. How should this idea be conveyed to investors to reduce the numbers who are hurt by investment fraud?

3. **Discussion** Describe the typical investor who would be a victim of such a scam.

4. **Research** Go to the Investment Dealers Association of Canada website, **www.ida.ca**.

   Click on Consumer Protection, select your province, and then click on Investment Dealer.

   (a) What plan does the industry have to protect the investor?

   (b) Does this plan help those who have been hurt by bogus investment dealers?

   (c) What help exists for the unsuspecting victims of the kinds of phony investment schemes described above?

Investment Theories

There are numerous investment theories, some good, some bad.[11] One of the most successful is called **value investing**. The concept was developed by British economist Benjamin Graham (1894–1976). Those who follow his approach look for well-managed companies with good products or services for which there is strong demand. They must also have healthy balance sheets and share prices that have been beaten down by the market. In other words, value investors look for bargains. By going against the market, a hard thing for many investors to do, they may also be considered **contrarians**. Contrarians believe that undervalued shares will eventually rise in price and they will one day be rewarded. Once the market has recognized this value, it will be too late to buy the shares.

Value investors often use **fundamental analysis** in choosing stocks. They look at a company's market value (the price determined by the market) and whether or not it is above, or at a discount to, book value (the asset value of the stock on the company's books). The book value is the price investors will receive if the company is wound up and, if it is higher than the market value, the stock is considered a buy.

---

[11]It is worth remembering that all theories look good in a bull market when anyone can pick winners. The ones to follow are those that make money in a bear market as well.

Two of the most successful value investors are Sir John Templeton and Warren Buffet.[12] Templeton started the Templeton Growth Fund in 1954. It is an equity fund with assets of $7 billion that invests in value stocks wherever they can be found, in any market. At the time of writing, it had an enviable record of providing investors with annual returns averaging 13 percent.

Buffet, one of North America's most successful investors, is the CEO of Berkshire Hathaway Inc., a holding company that owns and operates over three dozen companies. Shares in Berkshire Hathaway (BRK) are traded on the New York Stock Exchange. Those who buy them have the equivalent of units in a mutual fund company, without the management expense ratio, that invests in insurance businesses, apparel, building products, flight products, and financial services.

Buffet has a reputation, like Templeton, for picking winners. He also believes in the **buy and hold** theory of investing. According to this theory, unless something very bad happens to a company, its shares, once bought, are kept for a long time. He stays away from cyclicals, concentrating instead on high-quality consumer growth stocks. Proof that this works can be found in the performance of Berkshire stock. At the time of writing on July 11, 2006, one share of the A stock was worth $91 000. On February 12, 1990, the same share was worth $7220.

Realizing that, even at $7000, the shares were too expensive for most investors, Berkshire created B shares. Issued on May 9, 1996, at $1160, the B share was worth $3033 on July 11, 2006.

Followers of the buy and hold theory do not worry a great deal about the ups and downs of the market. They realize that it is impossible to time the market and believe that it is better to be in it than out. By holding stocks for a long time, they also avoid paying the commissions that those who try and time the market, trading frequently, must pay. Those who think they can determine the best time to buy stocks often miss out on the gains. Stock markets have a habit of not reacting as many investment analysts predict. They are, in fact, unpredictable.

A Canadian with an outstanding investment track record is Stephen Jarislowsky of Jarislowsky Fraser in Montreal. He follows the Buffet approach to investing and also stresses that investing need not be complicated. "First of all, don't complicate things with a lot of variables that you will have to keep track of. Keep it simple. Avoid frequent trading, develop long-term rather than short-term policies, don't try to guess the length of cycles, and forget strategies that require a lot of knowledge or constant research. . . . The game, I suggest, is not very complicated and it works."[13]

Technical analysts study statistics generated by a stock's historical performance (prices, volume, market activity) to try and determine future performance. Historical performance is charted, and buy and sell recommendations are made based on past trends. While some tech analysts are highly regarded, the market is too unpredictable for such analysis to always be an accurate guide.

Momentum investing is another popular theory. Its proponents seek out companies that are improving but are undervalued by the market. They are therefore somewhat like contrarians. Momentum investors believe that the stocks they buy have an upward

---

[12]Many investment theories tend to make investing more complicated and confusing than it needs to be. Values on the stock market are determined by fear and greed. If the market says a stock is worth $20.00 then that is what investors must pay for it, whether an analysis of the fundamentals or a technical analyst's report agrees or not. Even seasoned investment professionals know that it is better to be in the market than out of it. They also know that when the tide is coming in (a bull market), most stocks tend to rise, some a greater percentage than others, and when the tide goes out, the reverse can happen, but over the long haul, good stocks will gain in value. Therefore, a simple approach to investing, such as that followed by Warren Buffet, is often the best. Trading frequently results in more commissions, and when gains are made, more of the investor's money for Canada Revenue Agency.

[13]Stephen A. Jarislowsky, *The Investment Zoo: Taming the Bulls and the Bears*. Jarislowsky has over 50 years of investment experience and his firm manages assets of over $50 billion.

momentum, which has yet to be realized. This may be caused by higher revenues, improved earnings, or other positive corporate news such as a change in management or the introduction of a new product. Momentum investors do not hold stocks for a long time. Once the momentum has been realized or the stock begins to falter the investor sells. One never knows, however, when a stock has reached its highest potential, and such frequent trading often only benefits the investment dealer and the Canada Revenue Agency.

Two other ideas that have many followers are **growth investing** and **income investing**. Growth investors buy the shares of companies that are growing quickly by taking over or merging with other companies. They believe that when this happens a corporation's bottom line will improve and its stock price will rise. In fact, this may or may not happen, depending on the costs of the action taken to grow the company and whether the new additions have products or services for which there is strong demand.

Income investing is a concept popular with seniors who need a steady stream of income now. While some growth is also important to enable people to keep ahead of increases in the cost of living, income is a senior's main concern. Income investing involves buying investments that pay out a lot of regular income. These may be high-yielding common stocks, income trusts, preferred shares, or bonds. Companies that pay large dividends are usually older ones in established businesses and are often less risky. Growth stocks tend to plow earnings back into the company rather than pay them out to shareholders. Income trusts have become very popular with older investors because of their high yield, and the fact that many pay dividends monthly. As a result they have replaced the once popular preferred share. Bonds, too, are out of favour because of the poor tax treatment of interest by the Canada Revenue Agency.

Instead of looking at individual stocks to determine their suitability for a portfolio, **Modern Portfolio Theory** focuses instead on the overall risk or reward of a whole portfolio. Risk-averse investors will only include what are considered blue chip, or more secure, stocks in their portfolios, while those who can tolerate more risk, and its potential for gain, fill their portfolios with riskier stocks.

The problem with Modern Portfolio Theory, as with all investment theories, is that humanity has yet to learn how to foretell the future. As discussed in Random Events, unexpected events can help or hurt any portfolio. A recent example concerns the Canadian Imperial Bank of Commerce (CIBC), which along with other bank stocks, is normally considered one of the least risky investments. In August 2005 it was announced that the bank had agreed to pay US $2.4 billion to settle a class action lawsuit launched by shareholders of bankrupt Enron Corp. because of the bank's involvement with that company. Enron, a leading energy, natural gas, and electric utility company, filed for bankruptcy in December 2001. This turned out to be the largest bankruptcy in US history and an example of massive corporate fraud. The settlement meant that CIBC had a loss for 2005 of $1.9 billion and caused the bank's share price to drop 13 percent. A portfolio of bank stocks suddenly seemed less risk-averse than usual, and many investors changed the makeup of their portfolios.

The **Dogs of the Dow** strategy simply says that investors should buy the 10 highest-paying dividend stocks of the Dow Jones Industrial Average in January and adjust the portfolio the next January, deleting and adding when appropriate. This is a conservative and easy way to invest. One problem with it is that a stock's yield increases as the price of the stock falls, and investors may find that their portfolio suffers a capital loss if they stick with the highest-paying dividend stocks. Another concern is the commissions one must pay. The Dogs theory, however, has worked for most of the past 20 years. Table 8.1 shows what happened in 2004 to the top dividend-paying stocks.

TABLE 8.1   THE DOGS OF THE DOW STRATEGY IN 2004

COMPANY	SHARE PRICE JAN. 2, 2004	SHARE PRICE DEC. 31, 2004
General Motors	$54.63	$40.60
SBC Communications	$26.14	$25.77
Merck	$47.05	$32.14
Verizon	$35.25	$40.51
Altria	$54.65	$61.10
Citigroup	$49.00	$48.18
JPMorgan Chase	$36.62	$39.01
DuPont	$45.51	$49.05
Pfizer	$35.55	$26.89
General Electric	$31.12	$36.50

Dollar cost averaging is another popular way of investing. It involves investing the same amount of money in the same stock on a regular basis, no matter what has happened to the stock's price. When the price falls, more shares are purchased, and vice versa. The concept behind this idea is that the market cannot be timed. While it would be nice to be able to buy a stock when it falls in price, no one knows when this will happen, and waiting for it to do so can be costly. Investing through a dividend reinvestment plan is an example of dollar cost averaging.

Barclays Global Investors has developed a theory for lazy investors which consistently outperforms the TSX. The **Global Couch Potato Portfolio** invests in four different Barclays Exchange Traded Funds. The money is divided into fifths. One-fifth is invested in the i60c Fund, one-fifth in the 1500R Fund, one-fifth in the iINTR Fund, and two-fifths in the iBond Fund. The result is a portfolio that tracks markets in Australia, Europe, the Far East, and the Canadian bond market. The only trading required is whatever is necessary to maintain the above weightings and this is only done once a year.

Debt and Equity Investments

Debt Securities

There are two basic ways to invest: (i) by lending money or (ii) by acquiring ownership. Lenders become creditors and are said to possess **debt securities**. The income from debt instruments is called interest (see Chapter 7). The borrower promises to repay the principal with interest at some specified time. Perhaps you had not realized that you become a creditor whenever you deposit funds at a bank, trust company, or credit union. And did you know you are lending money to a government or a corporation whenever you buy a bond or a treasury bill? Deposit accounts, term deposits, guaranteed investment certificates, mortgages (when you are the lender), bonds, and treasury bills are types of debt securities. Their characteristics will be reviewed in the next chapter.

Equity Securities

You acquire **equity** when you own investments. A house is an investment; other types of investments include goods such as art, jewellery, and antiques for which there is a market.

FIGURE 8.2   AVERAGE ANNUAL RATES OF RETURN ON THREE-MONTH TREASURY
BILLS, 1975–2004

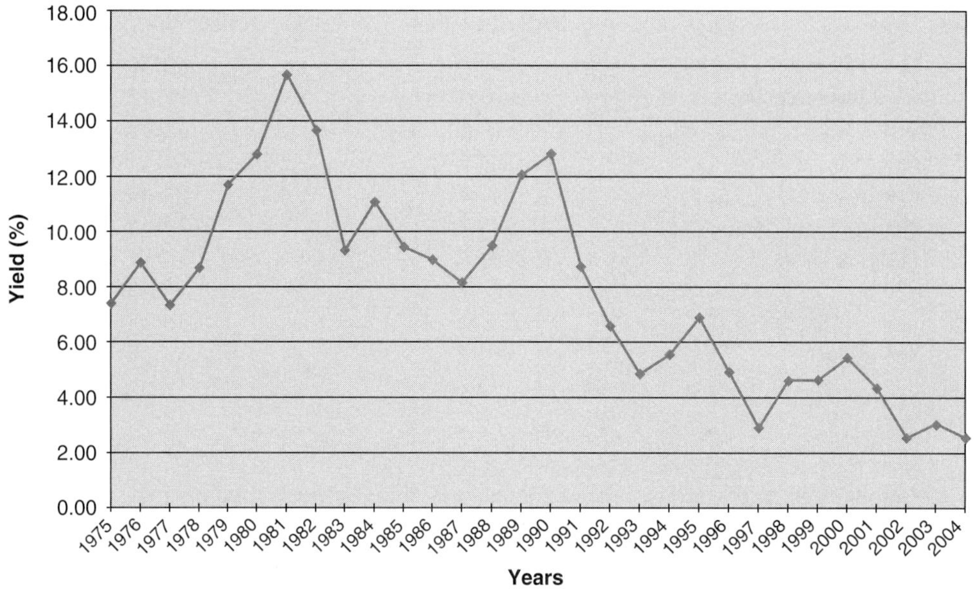

SOURCE: Bank of Canada Review (Jan. 1980, Jan. 1985, Jan. 1990, Aug. 1992, Summer 2005).

Investments may also include stocks, or shares, in publicly traded companies. Ownership gives you certain rights regarding the management of your equity but does not guarantee any gain or income because investment income depends on market forces over which you have no control. Equity securities are usually riskier than debt securities. A few equity securities, however, are less risky. Shares in telephone companies or chartered banks, for example, are less risky than mortgage loans to unreliable people. They are also often less risky than shares in many other types of companies. Shares in gold mining companies, for example, are usually quite speculative. Investors buy equities because of the expectation of a greater gain than they could obtain from debt securities.

Evidence that equity investments usually outperform debt securities is not hard to find. Between 1989 and 2005 the return on three Canadian mutual fund sectors was much better, for example, than that on three-month treasury bills. The best performance, with 11.2 percent annual growth, was turned in by the small-to-mid-cap equity funds. This was followed with the 10.2 percent gain of dividend funds and the 8.2 percent average annual growth of equity funds.[14] Compare this with the less-than-stellar returns on T-bills as shown in Figure 8.2. While treasury bills are a very conservative investment, many very conservative investors owned units in mutual funds included in these three sectors. More speculative investors are not as likely to have mutual funds since investment decisions are no longer in their hands.

More proof that equities usually outperform debt instruments can be found by turning to Figure 8.5 (on page 241), which shows the interest rates paid on Government of Canada bonds from 1975 to 2004.

[14]Where's the best growth? The Globe & Mail, February 14, 2005.

Investment Returns

Income The return on an investment may take one of two basic forms: (i) income (interest, dividends, rent, profit) or (ii) capital appreciation (capital gain). The type of return received will vary with the investment. Those who lend money expect interest; those who own shares in a business expect to earn dividends when the business makes a profit; and those who own property and rent it to others will receive rent. In addition to the income generated by ownership, the purchase itself (for example, the rental property) may increase in value, thereby generating capital gain.

Type of Investment	Form of Return
Debt investments	
Deposits, loans	interest
Mortgage loans	interest
Canada Savings Bonds	interest
Treasury bills	interest
Bonds	interest, capital gain (loss)
Equity investments	
Real property	rent, capital gain (loss)
Business	profit, capital gain (loss)
Stocks (shares)	dividends, capital gain (loss)
Gold, silver	capital gain (loss)

Capital Gain The difference between an asset's purchase price and the same asset's selling price represents capital gain or loss. For example, something purchased at $2700 and sold for $3500 would produce a capital gain of $800. **Capital gain** is the windfall that accrues to an investor, by virtue of the investor's ownership of the investment, during a change in prices that is caused by increased demand or inflation. Note that when you improve an asset (for example, when you renovate a house) and then sell it, the value added by the improvements does not count as capital gain. Remember, too, that the expectation of capital gain always carries with it the possibility of capital loss.

Current Income or Capital Gain?

Investments with a fixed yield, such as bonds and preferred shares, have little potential for a capital gain. If there is a gain, it is usually low. Bonds with a high yield will gain slightly in value if interest rates fall. Shares in growth-oriented companies that have potential for capital gain, on the other hand, have a very low yield. And they may not pay any dividends. If they do, the dividends are low. Instead, profit is reinvested in the company to fuel future growth. There is therefore an inverse relationship between the objectives of capital gain and high yield or current income. This is shown in Personal Finance in Action Box 8.3, "Income with Inflation Protection."

Investment Considerations

Investing always presents the individual with some difficult questions. Should I invest or not? If yes, what should I invest in? Every investment also comes with a risk, a risk the investor needs to consider carefully. Generally, the greater the risk, the greater is the investor's potential for reward (or loss). There is even a risk associated with what are often referred to as

Personal FINANCE in action 8.3

Income with Inflation Protection

Anwar owned a halal butcher shop. When he and his wife, Fatima, came to Canada from Egypt 15 years ago, they had few resources. At the suggestion of their neighbours, Anwar took out a life insurance policy after buying the butcher shop, naming Fatima as his beneficiary. Suddenly last March, Anwar was stricken by a heart attack and died almost immediately.

Now Fatima has $2 million from his life insurance but has no idea what to do with it. She is 45. Her son, Hosni, who is now running the shop, suggests she talk with their cousin who works for a discount broker.

The cousin explains some basic investment concepts such as risk/return, capital gains, and inflation. He points out, that while $2 million is a large sum of money, inflation could erode its value unless she invests in something with capital gains potential. Since Fatima also needs to live on the income from her investments, he recommends that her money be split between common and preferred shares in some of Canada's leading public companies. The combined after-tax return on her dividend income will be 4 percent, or $80 000. In the future, her cousin says that she could realize some of her capital gains and invest in high-yielding preferred shares to increase her income.

"risk-free" places to put your money. A savings account may seem risk-free because your money will always be there, but if it is left there for too long a period, you run the risk that it will purchase less than when it was deposited. Therefore, you have the choice of putting your money into "risky" investments and possibly seeing growth (or loss) or leaving it in a bank and seeing its value decline. As a result, making investment decisions is never easy.

The risk/return trade-off investors need to consider is shown in Figure 8.3. The lower the risk, the lower the return; the greater the risk, the greater the chance for a high return.

The investment considerations investors need to consider are as follows: liquidity/marketability, term, management effort required, tax treatment, and risk.

Marketability and Liquidity

These terms are often confused. A **liquid** asset is one that can be quickly converted to cash without a loss of capital. Strictly speaking, bank accounts, GICs, and Canada Savings Bonds are the only truly liquid assets. Other assets, such as stocks and bonds that can be sold at cost or above, are also liquid, at that time. Most, however, are not strictly liquid. They trade on markets on which prices fluctuate, and losses may occur as a result. They may not be liquid when you wish to dispose of them.

FIGURE 8.3 THE RISK/RETURN TRADE-OFF

Low					RETURN					High
0	1	2	3	4	5	6	7	8	9	10
10	9	8	7	6	5	4	3	2	1	0
High					LIQUIDITY					Low

Everything is marketable for a price, but not all marketable assets are liquid. Marketability refers to the ability of an asset to be bought or sold. A house close to a sewage treatment plant will not likely be marketable unless the price is very low. It certainly isn't liquid and would be a poor investment. The same house close to schools and parks should be very marketable. Recently in Canada, shares in resource-based companies were highly marketable and highly liquid. They will be much less so if the Chinese and Indian economies stop growing at the accelerated pace they reached in the early years of the twenty-first century.

Term

Investments that have a period of time, or **term**, before they can be turned into cash (the maturity date) are usually interest investments. Some, such as GICs, may not be redeemed before maturity. Others, such as Canada Savings Bonds, may be redeemed on any business day. All bonds have maturity dates or terms. Those with maturity dates far in the future will pay a higher rate of interest than those with a short term to maturity, unless there are major changes in government monetary policy. At the maturity date they can be redeemed for their face value. However, there is a bond market, and the prices of bonds fluctuate because of changes in interest rates. A 4 percent government bond will increase in value if new, similar bonds are issued at 3.5 percent. They will decline if the rate of new bonds is higher than 4 percent. Therefore, if you sell a bond before its maturity date, you may get more, or less, than you paid for it.

Management Effort

The amount of time an investor pays to his/her investments is often related to the investment theory the person is devoted to. If someone follows the Dogs of the Dow theory, little management effort is required. Those who follow the recommendations of technical analysts or believe in momentum investing will need to spend a considerably greater period of time managing their investments. The great investors like Warren Buffet and Stephen Jarislowsky spend very little time managing theirs. They believe in buying and holding high-quality stocks for which, hopefully, there will always be a market.

A careful investor who spends much of each day studying the market (managing his/her investments) and trading frequently on the ups and downs of the stock exchange will probably fare more poorly than those like Buffet who invest for the long term. No one can predict what will happen to his or her investments from day to day, or even during the day. If, like Jarislowsky, you buy high-quality, high-yielding dividend stocks, almost no management is required. Frequent managing can make a person a nervous wreck with no greater return.

Often busy investors decide to invest in mutual funds and let the fund managers manage their investments for them. This should work but is not a guarantee of success. If the stock market is bearish and in decline, most funds will suffer, and when the market is bullish all fund mangers look like geniuses. The point is that devoting a lot of time to managing investments is no guarantee of successful financial planning. It can also turn out to be very expensive if frequent selling and a lot of capital gains are involved.

Tax Considerations

When comparing the potential yield from two or more investments, you should think in terms of after-tax dollars because the various types of investment return are taxed differently: interest is taxed at a higher rate than dividends, and capital gains are taxed at a lower rate than both income and dividends for high-income investors. If you can defer income until a time when you expect to have a lower marginal tax rate, you may be able to gain two advantages. Not only will the total tax be less, but funds put in a tax shelter (an RRSP, for instance) grow faster, since the tax on the yield is also deferred. Later chapters will provide more information about income tax in connection with investments.

Investment Risks

Every investor wants maximum return with minimum risk, but unfortunately there are no risk-free investments. Every investment carries some risk: the possibility of (i) losing all or part of the principal, (ii) losing some of the principal's purchasing power, or (iii) receiving a return that is less than anticipated. Moreover, these risks are generally not insurable, though the Canada Deposit Insurance Corporation insures eligible deposits up to $100 000 at member institutions. You can attempt to reduce risk by being as well-informed as possible about investment alternatives and by building some diversity into your choice of assets, so that a single setback will not result in your losing everything. Since investments are not risk-free, it is essential to understand the different types of risks and to know which assets are most subject to which kinds of risks.

Types of Risks

Four classes of risk are associated with investments:

(a) **inflation risk**—the possibility that invested funds will lose purchasing power,
(b) **interest rate risk**—the likelihood that interest rates will fall, adversely affecting either the return or the price of the asset,
(c) **market risk**—the chance that the demand for the asset will drop, lowering its value,
(d) **business risk**—the possibility that the firm you invest in will do poorly or fail entirely.

Inflation is measured by the annual percentage change in the **Consumer Price Index**. Canada had very high inflation, by Canadian standards, in the early 1980s. To put this inflation in perspective, look at the trend in the inflation rate from 1981 to 2004 (see Figure 8.4). Inflation was over 12 percent in 1981 but by 1994 it had fallen to less than 2 percent annually. Therefore, in 1981, the **real rate of return** on Government of Canada Bonds was negative because the rate of inflation was greater than the rate of interest (see Figure 8.5). At that time, investors who owned these government bonds earned a **negative rate of return** on their investment. In other words, these investors lost money.

As can be seen, only looking at the interest earned on an investment can be quite misleading. The gains from interest may be illusory because of inflation. To be sure, one must look at the real rate of return and not just the nominal rate of interest. Another factor to consider is the taxation of interest income. This is higher than either the tax on dividend income or that from capital gains. Therefore, unless the rate of interest is very high, bonds are a poor form of investment.

Interest rates rise as a result of uncertainty in the economy. When this happens, neither businesses nor consumers have much interest in borrowing. When interest rates are low, confidence returns; businesses and consumers borrow and spend more, and the economy expands. (See Personal Finance in Action Box 8.4, "The Importance of Comparing Interest Rates," for an example of how interest rates have changed.) This sequence of events took place in 2002. Inflation was at its lowest level in a generation. This resulted in increased demand for new homes and cars.

FIGURE 8.4 THE RATE OF INFLATION, 1981–2004

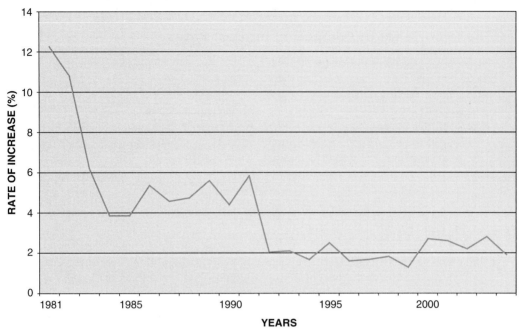

SOURCE: Adapted from Statistics Canada CANSIM database, Table 326-0002.

FIGURE 8.5 GOVERNMENT OF CANADA BONDS, REAL LONG-TERM INTEREST
RATES 1975–2004

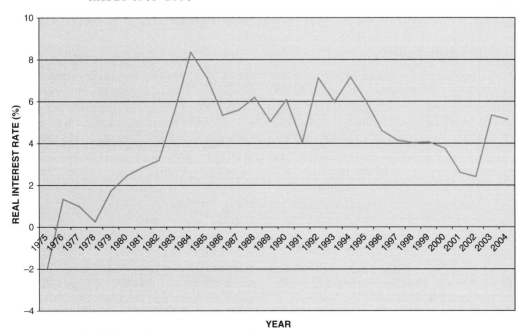

SOURCE: Bank of Canada.

Personal FINANCE in action 8.4

The Importance of Comparing Interest Rates

Mario, when hearing that Canada Premium Bonds carry an interest rate averaging 5.69 percent for the first three years, tells his grandson, Geno, of the good old days when he earned over 18 percent. "But Grandpa," says Geno, "wasn't your mortgage close to 25 percent? Now, I can find a variable rate mortgage for under 5 percent."

The flip side of this can be seen in the Personal Finance in Action Box 8.5, "Time and Money," where money is allowed to grow by compounding. While the $776 000 figure would seem to be a fortune in 2002, its real value is little more than his initial $100 000 was worth in 1960.

The Real Value of Money

Inflation's destructive effects can be seen in dramatic fashion if one compares what money will buy today with what it bought in the past. According to the Bank of Canada, what cost $10.00 in 1955 cost $75.12 in 2005, for an average annual decline in purchasing power of 4.12 percent.[15] Such declines must be a major consideration in financial planning. An example of the powerful effect inflation can have is seen in the price of SUVs, which cost more than many people paid for their homes in the 1970s. If inflation continues at this rate, what will cars cost in 30 years' time?

Interest Rate Risk Any change in interest rates can affect investments. The value of a long-term bond paying 6 percent will drop, for example, if interest rates rise. Under these

Personal FINANCE in action 8.5

Time and Money

In 1960, when Gerry was 20 years old, he inherited $100 000 from his grandfather. A busy man who knew little about investing, he put the whole sum into a five-year GIC and rolled the money over into a new GIC when the certificate matured. He used the interest he had earned to pay for skiing holidays and summer vacations. Spending the interest each year became his pattern over the next 42 years. After he retired in 2002, Gerry decided that it would be a good idea to increase the income from his investment. What had seemed like a lot of money in 1960 no longer went very far. But when he called an investment dealer for advice, he was surprised to learn just how far

interest rates had fallen. He had not paid much attention to financial matters over the years. The dealer told him to stay away from bonds and GICs since interest rates were low. Instead, she suggested some units in a new real estate investment trust her company was underwriting. These units would yield 9 percent, and tax on the income would be deferred for five years. She also told him that he should not have spent the interest from his GICs; instead, he should have reinvested it. If he had done so at an average of 5 percent, **compounding** would have made his $100 000 inheritance grow to over $776 000 by 2002, leaving him with fewer financial worries.

[15]Bank of Canada Inflation Calculator, **www.bankofcanada.ca/en/rates/inflation_calc.html**.

circumstances, investors will prefer to buy new bonds that pay higher interest. If you must sell the bond prior to maturity, you will sustain a capital loss. If you buy a five-year GIC paying 6 percent and interest rates rise, you will be unable to earn the higher rate if your money is locked in. If the interest you earn does not exceed the inflation rate, your investment's value declines. To protect yourself, you must therefore have debt securities in your portfolio with a broad range of maturities. (See Personal Finance in Action Box 8.6, "Ladder GICs: Spreading the Risk.")

Common stocks can also be influenced by changes in interest rates. A high rate will discourage business investment, encouraging investors to switch from stocks to bonds. Conversely, low rates stimulate the economy, causing investors to move from bonds to stocks.

Although interest rates and inflation do not follow each other exactly, they are linked. Generally, lenders require interest rates that are high enough to more than compensate for inflation. A lack of stability in interest rates complicates investing. When interest rates are volatile, it is difficult to make wise investment decisions because there is so much uncertainty about future rates. And when investors feel uncertain, they demand higher real interest rates as compensation.

Market Risk Economic conditions may cause the value of your assets to fall. During a period of robust economic activity, the demand for houses, and as a result, house prices, will be high. Suppose you buy a house during such a period; five years later, though—when you must sell because you are moving to another city—the economy is in the midst of a recession. Because workers are being laid off and factories closed, the demand for houses has fallen, and now you have to sell your house at a loss. Similarly, shares in many companies can fall in value when the investment climate turns bearish and stock prices start to decline. When such a sequence of events takes place, many investors will want to sell their shares and invest in something less risky.

Business Risk There is a risk to every business. The risk can range in seriousness from a bankruptcy and failure to a mere decline in earnings. Investors need to be aware of potential risk before they buy stocks or bonds. As an economy progresses through business cycles, company earnings rise and fall. Sometimes companies collapse, wiping out the investments of many people. But the most common risk that investors face is a decline in a company's earnings. When

Personal FINANCE in action 8.6

Ladder GICs: Spreading the Risk

When Jenny was in Grade 6, she asked her mother if she could get a paper route. The local paper was always advertising for more delivery girls and boys. Jenny was mature for her age and had good marks at school. Her mother thought a paper route would be a good experience and quickly agreed. Over the years Jenny put all of her earnings and all of her tips in the bank. When she was 15, her mother suggested she do something else with the money, which came to just over $5000. Jenny felt comfortable at her bank and one day asked to see the manager. The manager suggested that Jenny divide the money into five equal portions and put them into different GICs with maturity dates of from one to five years. As each matures, it will be rolled over into a new GIC at the current rate, thereby creating a **ladder GIC**. This will allow Jenny to take advantage of the higher interest rates that are expected,* without having all of her money locked in for the full five years.

*Of course, they might drop. If this happens Jenny would be forced to accept a lower rate. Her other GICs will still be at the higher rates.

this happens, the value of the company's shares may decline. Investors look for companies with either good prospects for growth or increased earnings, or both, and may sell shares in a company that does poorly. There is no insurance available for investors who suffer a capital loss.

Random Events

Nothing in life can be taken for granted. We do not know, with any certainty, what the future will bring. It is for this reason we make wills and buy life insurance to provide for our loved ones when we are unable to do so. This uncertainty makes investing fascinating or terrifying, depending on your point of view. The great unknown for investors (and for everyone else as well) can best be described as **random events** or **happenings**, the unexpected occurrences that can make stock prices rise or fall. These random events can be almost anything and can happen at any time. The death of a US president is one example. The devaluation of an important currency, such as the yen, is another. The announcement by a South American government that it can no longer service its debt load is a third. Such things happen all the time and may have a major influence on investments. They cannot be predicted with any degree of certainty. How many stock market pundits, for example, predicted accurately the collapse of technology companies, in particular the dot-coms, in 2000? Many knowledgeable people lost large amounts when shares in high-tech heavies like Cisco Systems and JDS Uniphase dropped. Others lost fortunes with the collapse of the hedge fund Long-Term Capital Management. Random events influence all four of the risk categories we have identified.

Negative random events usually cause stock prices to plummet initially, but as can be seen from Table 8.2, "Markets in Crisis," they usually recover. This initial reaction is caused by ignorance of the facts and unbridled panic. Once common sense returns, however, and the consequences of the event are fully considered, stock prices often rise, sometimes dramatically. The Iraqi invasion of Kuwait in 1990, resulting in the 1990–91 Gulf War, is but one example of how a random event can cause the market to react like a roller coaster. Even the terrible events of September 11, 2001, have had no lasting negative effect on the stock markets.

How to Reduce Risk

Uncertainty about the future creates investment risk, and the further into the future you try to predict the quality of an investment, the greater the uncertainty—hence, the greater the

TABLE 8.2 MARKETS IN CRISIS

EVENT	THE DOW JONES' INITIAL REACTION	CHANGE 6 MONTHS LATER
Japanese attack on Pearl Harbour	−6.5%	−9.6%
Assassination of President Kennedy	−2.9%	+15.1%
1987 financial panic	−34.2%	+15%
1990–91 Gulf War	−4.3%	+18.7%
1997 Asian stock market crisis	−12.4%	+25%
1998 Russian currency devaluation	−11.3%	+33.7%
September 11, 2001 terrorist attacks	−7.13%	+20.09%

SOURCE: Pioneer Investments, Boston, MA, "Crisis Events and the U.S. Stock Market," www.pioneerfunds.com/guide/classic/classiccrisis.jhtml. (Accessed on November 1, 2003.)

FIGURE 8.6   DEGREE OF RISK AND KNOWLEDGE ABOUT THE FUTURE

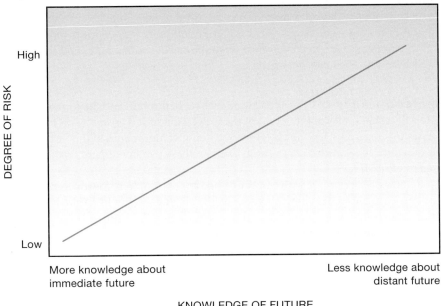

risk. Risk is thus related to both time and knowledge. This relationship is summarized in Figure 8.6, which shows that risk exposure increases as knowledge about the future decreases. The best defence against risk in your investment portfolio is an understanding of current economic conditions, knowledge of particular investments, and diversification.

Knowledge   There is a wide range of investment alternatives to consider, some of which will be discussed in later chapters.

FIGURE 8.7   EXPECTED RETURN AND ESTIMATED RISK OF SELECTED INVESTMENTS

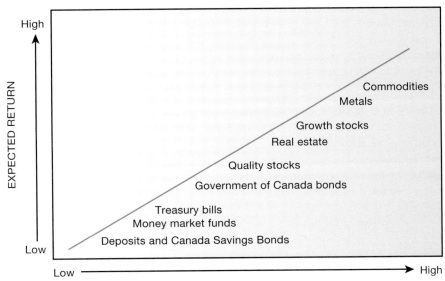

A successful investor should be well-informed about the securities he or she holds. Anyone who plans to invest in real estate must learn a great deal about the real estate market; to make money in the stock market, you will need to take an interest in the market in general and in some specific stocks in detail. Leaving money in deposits requires less learning on the investor's part. A compromise might be to buy mutual funds and then leave investment decisions to the funds' managers.

The Risk/Return Trade-off Everyone wants the highest return and the lowest risk, but most people will accept somewhat more risk if the expected return is greater. This fact brings up the risk/return trade-off. How much safety will you give up in anticipation of an additional unit of return? The inverse relationship between these two investment characteristics is illustrated in Figure 8.7.

Once you know your priorities with respect to risk and return, look for investments that provide the desired qualities. It is difficult to generalize about classes of investments and risk because there are always exceptions and qualifications. Figure 8.7 is intended as a general illustration of the relationship between risk and return.

Risk Management

What Are Your Risks?

Analyze the various kinds of assets you have, or might acquire, to identify which risks apply to them. Plan to avoid concentrating on investments that fall into one risk category. If most of your assets are fixed-income debt securities, you are more exposed to interest rate and inflation risks, but much less exposed to market and business risks. Try to diversify by choosing investments that expose you to different kinds of risks. A portfolio that reflects a balance between debt and equities should protect against a broad range of risks.

Balance Investment and Other Risks

Life Cycle and Risk The amount of risk that will be acceptable to you will likely vary with your life cycle stage. A young single person who has an adequate income and no dependents may be in a position to handle more risk than will be advisable a few years later, when the person is starting a family. The middle years, when income is typically more than enough to handle expenses, permit a higher proportion of risk than is wise to accept during retirement. A young person will have time to recoup a loss, but a retiree should not put her retirement income at risk unless her net worth is very large.

Income and Risk Some people have more risk associated with income than others. A civil service employee can usually count on more security than can either a self-employed person or someone who works in a cyclical industry that often lays off workers. Farmers and other self-employed people often invest in their businesses instead of in the stock market. To balance the high risk associated with their equity-based income, they may put some savings in very low-risk debt securities.

At this first level of diversification, look at your total net worth as well as at your income source or sources. If, for instance, your income depends on the real estate market, you will not want to put your savings into the same sector. Besides planning for a balance among a broad range of risks, you should also spread the risk within your investment portfolio by diversifying the types of assets you own.

Diversification

Diversification is considered the best way to reduce the risk associated with investing. Diversifying means that you should not put all of your investment money in the same type of investment but spread the money, and the risk, around. The most popular way to diversify is through *asset allocation* or having some of your assets in cash, some in fixed income investments, and some in stock. The exact split between the three depends on an investor's risk tolerance. The cash can be used to take advantage of opportunities that present themselves. Fixed income investments can be used to provide income and stocks the growth that is essential for long-term investing. Having investments in both of the latter categories allows investors to hedge their bets. Both fixed income investments and stocks are not likely to decline or rise in value at the same time.

Diversification can be extended by investing in different types of industries such as resources and consumer goods. The resource sector is quite cyclical and its success depends heavily on international markets. Demand for consumer goods is more dependent on such things as interest rates and inflation. All of this diversification can, of course, be done through investing in mutual funds. Funds allow investors to spread risk. They can also be used to spread the risk to other countries and regions of the world, which perhaps offer greater potential than the Canadian economy.

Investing Globally

As investors become more knowledgeable and experienced, they often search for opportunities outside Canada. Some prominent Canadian investment dealers, with many years' experience, feel that Canada only has about 20 investment-quality stocks. The number continues to diminish as a result of mergers and acquisitions—or consolidation, as it is often referred to. This process is continuing and has led to an increasing number of individual investors and fund managers investing outside of Canada. As a result, investors who think they are only invested in Canada may be surprised to learn that some seemingly Canadian mutual funds include foreign investments. In light of Canada's small market, some fund managers believe this is a prudent thing to do. Whether or not a fund has foreign content is not evident from its name but can only be determined by an examination of the prospectus, and even then the information may not be given. Examples of some of these funds follow:

- *Fidelity Canadian Disciplined Equity Fund* has 4.8 percent foreign content.
- *Altamira Canadian Value Fund* has 13.46 percent foreign content.
- *AGF Canadian Growth Equity Fund* has 6.5 percent invested in foreign markets, including the US, the Cayman Islands, South Africa, and the United Kingdom.
- *Mackenzie Select Managers Canadian Capital Class* has 10 percent invested in Japan and Brazil.
- *Trimark Income Growth (Canadian Income Balanced)* has 19 percent invested outside Canada, including Mexico, France, Japan, Norway, Germany, and Sweden.

The managers of these funds obviously believe that the foreign markets they have selected provide good opportunity. This is not being unpatriotic, just wise. The Canadian stock markets account for only about 2 percent of the world's total market capitalization. The US, on the other hand, accounts for roughly 50 percent. There is, therefore, much more opportunity for investors who wish to broaden their investment base south of the border.

The leading foreign market for Canadian investors has long been the United States. This made sense because many US companies, such as General Motors, Exxon (Esso), and McDonald's, are major presences in the Canadian economy, and we know and use their products. We also do much of our shopping in the Canadian subsidiaries of major US chains, such as Home Depot, Sears, and Wal-Mart. Many Canadians also travel frequently to the United States and are familiar with a variety of other US companies. But in 2004, most foreign stock markets did better than the American market. Many investment advisors therefore turned bearish toward the US at this time. Their concerns were justified, they believed, not only by the poor performance of many US equities, but also by that country's huge current account and fiscal deficits. It seemed to an increasing number as if the glory days of the American economy were coming to an end. Diversifying outside North America has thus become increasingly popular.

Canadian investors can easily find good investment opportunities beyond this continent. There are a number of simple ways to invest globally. The easiest is to invest in the shares of Canadian companies that do business outside Canada. Their financial performance is therefore not dependent on Canada. There are a number of well-known, investment-quality Canadian corporations that fit into this category. Topping the list is the communications giant, the Thomson Corporation, which has its head office in Canada but has businesses in 28 countries, including a large number in the United States. Thomson's shares should provide a hedge against most types of risk. Others include Alcan, CP Ships, Barrick, and Manulife Financial. Alcan, one of the world's leading manufacturers of aluminum, has facilities in North America, South America, Europe, Asia, and the Pacific. The freighters of CP Ships travel the world's oceans. Gold producer Barrick has mines in North America, South America, Australia, and Tanzania. The insurance company Manulife Financial does extensive business in Asia, including Hong Kong and Japan, and as a result of the takeover of the American firm John Hancock Financial Services in 2003, is now a major player in the US market.

If you wish to drop the Canadian connection altogether (and perhaps take on added risk), you can invest in the shares of companies that trade on any of the world's many stock exchanges. This can be done through a registered investment dealer. The share prices of companies traded in London, Paris, Hong Kong, and other leading exchanges are quoted in the financial pages of Canadian newspapers.[16] Prices of shares traded on smaller exchanges such as those in Malta and Tehran are not listed, but their prices may easily be found elsewhere.

Even greater international exposure is available by investing in the many US companies with global exposure. These include the thirty companies that make up the Dow Jones Industrial Average, such as Coca-Cola and pharmaceutical manufacturer Johnson & Johnson. Most of these companies are world leaders in their fields. This kind of high profile may, of course, be a liability if the forces of anti-globalization and anti-Americanism grow stronger, but these companies do conduct business around the world and satisfy the diversity requirement. Such diversity has helped keep them among the ranks of the world's most successful companies.

If investing directly in shares of such companies is not to an investor's liking, he or she can invest in mutual funds that invest globally. Each of the major Canadian fund companies has funds that invest in the American, Latin American, Asian, European, and emerging markets. (These are not like the funds mentioned above that invest mainly in Canada.) Investors who seek global diversity often find this route the easiest. Units of such funds are available directly from the fund companies or from investment dealers and unit prices are quoted in the financial press.

[16]*The Globe and Mail* has listings for companies traded on the Tokyo, Frankfurt, Brussels, Zurich, Amsterdam, Stockholm, Madrid, Sydney, and Mexico City stock markets, in addition to those listed above.

Another popular means of investing globally is to put money into SPDRS, WEBS, MSCIs, DIAMONDS, or ADRs. These are not viruses, bugs, or precious gems but *depository receipts and international indices.*

"SPDRS" refers to Standard & Poor's Depository Receipts, which are traded on the AMEX (American Exchange). SPDRS is an investment trust that holds shares in all the companies that make up the S&P 500 Composite Index. The price of a unit equals the current value of the S&P 500 divided by 10. Through SPDRS one gets an investment in much of the US economy.

DIAMONDS (DIA) also trade on the AMEX. The name stands for DIAMONDS Trust Series 1, a pooled investment trust created to provide investors with the results of the Dow 30 stocks. DIAMONDS had assets in the fall of 2005 of over US $7 billion and a three-year Beta (see Chapter 10) of 1.07. On September 13, 2005, a unit cost US $106.51, and DIAMONDS had a 52-week trading range of $97.27 to $109.83. Information on DIA and other depository receipts may be found online at **http://finance.yahoo.com** and **www.amex.com**.

American Depository Receipts (ADRs) allow you to invest in non-US stocks that are not traded in the United States. The shares of a foreign company are registered in the name of an American bank and held in trust. The bank then issues receipts against this stock. ADRs are traded on the NYSE, the AMEX, and the NASDAQ (National Association of Securities Dealers' Automated Quotations system). One example is Reuters Group PLC, the British business information provider, which trades on the NASDAQ under the symbol RTRSY.

Morgan Stanley, the American financial giant, has created another product that allows investors to gain international exposure. Morgan Stanley Capital International (MSCI) indexes are available for 17 countries and also for regions such as Latin America and Eastern Europe. WEBS (World Equity Benchmark Shares), are exchange-traded funds created by Morgan Stanley to track the MSCI country indexes and are traded on the NYSE. Morgan Stanley also offers closed-end mutual funds that are traded like shares on US exchanges. The Asia-Pacific Fund, which is traded on the NYSE under the symbol APF, is one example.

Investing globally does expose investors to other problems. Markets in most countries are not nearly as well-known, and in many cases not as well-regulated, as those in Canada and the United States. In addition, their countries' laws are different and their governments often untrustworthy. One possibility that is frequently mentioned is China. Because of its amazing economic growth, it is expected to one day bypass the United States and become the world's largest economy. In the first nine months of 2005, for example, the Chinese economy grew by 9.4 percent. This follows on the heels of over 9 percent growth in each of the previous two years. The government attempted to reduce this rapid rate by raising interest rates and increasing credit restrictions, all to no avail.

China, in spite of such rapid growth, must still be described as a developing economy. In 2005 it had a GDP per capita of only US $1462. Expressed in terms of US purchasing power parity, this became US $6513, still far below the equivalent figure for the Canadian economy of US $33 163.[17] A very small proportion of China's huge population has benefited from the country's economic growth. Most of the rural population still lives at close to a state of poverty. It is expected, therefore, that much of China's newfound wealth will have to be invested in basic infrastructure such as schools, hospitals, roads, and sanitary services to help improve everyone's standard of living. This will slow the economy down somewhat.

China does have stock markets. Its leading stock exchange is the Shanghai Stock Exchange. As of December 2004, it had 881 companies listed and 153 investment dealers. However, investing in China exposes investors to more risks than many advisors consider necessary, including the following: interest rate risk, equity risk, foreign investment risk,

---

[17] *The Economist.*

currency risk, and liquidity risk. At the present time, it is only advisable to look to China for diversification, if one can afford a substantial loss.

In spite of this, fund managers are betting that the Chinese economy is on the verge of greatness. One example of this enthusiasm was the sale in October 2005 of shares in the China Construction Bank, China's third-largest financial institution. US $8 billion worth of shares were offered and demand for almost 10 times that amount exceeded expectations.[18]

India is another Asian country experiencing rapid economic growth. While not as fast as the growth of the Chinese economy, at over 8 percent in 2005, it is still impressive. India also has stock exchanges. Founded in the nineteenth century, that in Mumbai, the Bombay Stock Exchange, is the oldest and largest. India's economy, of course, has a growth pattern similar to that of China's. Much of its population is rural and also lives in a state of poverty.

For an example, see Personal Finance in Action Box 8.8, "Investing Globally."

Summary of Investment Characteristics

Despite the difficulties of classifying investments by various characteristics, the summary in Table 8.3 is presented as a general guide.

TABLE 8.3   INVESTMENT CHARACTERISTICS BY ASSET CATEGORY

ASSET CATEGORY	SAFETY	LIQUIDITY	INCOME/ CAPITAL GAIN	INFLATION PROTECTION
Bank accounts, CSBs, term deposits	Nominal value guaranteed up to $100 000	Excellent	Little income, no gain	None
GICs	Nominal value guaranteed up to $100 000	Poor	Little income, no gain	None
Treasury bills, money market funds	Excellent	Good	Little income, no gain	None
High-quality bonds	Good if held to maturity, but nominal value declines	Varies	Income, perhaps some gain	Little
High-quality preferred stock	Varies	Varies	Some of both possible	Some
Common shares, equities	Varies; both gains and losses possible	Varies	Both possible	Good in the long run
Mutual funds	Often poor	Good	Both possible	Possible
Indexed funds	Good	Good	Both possible	Good
Depository receipts	Good	Good	Both possible	Good
Real estate	Varies	Poor	Both possible	Varies

Note: It is difficult to be dogmatic about the characteristics of investments. Much of this assessment has to do with conditions in the Canadian and international economies, which may change frequently. Therefore, these characteristics may change. What happens to real estate often depends on the local community as well as broad market forces.

[18]Chinese Lender Shines in IPO: Stock Offering Hits $8 Billion, The *Globe and Mail*, October 21, 2005.

Your Personal Investment Plan

Investment Objectives

Every investor hopes that his or her investment choices do well. (They may have different goals, however, as shown in Personal Finance in Action Box 8.7, "Diversity in Portfolios.")

Every investor wants to see a high yield or capital gains or some combination of both. No one wants to see his or her capital and income decline. Each investor must also understand the risk involved in every investment decision. The investor needs to learn how much risk is involved and must decide how much can be tolerated. This will determine the investment choices made. Characteristics of various assets are outlined in Table 8.3. It should be pointed out, however, that while GICs, treasury bills, and other fixed income securities are considered safe, this is true only with respect to nominal value. That is, $1000 invested in a GIC will still be $1000 in five years, but it will not buy what $1000 will buy today. If held for any length of time, the money in such investments declines in value. They provide no inflation protection and should only be held for a short time.

One must also be aware of the uncertainty that hangs, like a cloud, over investing of all types. No one knows what tomorrow will bring. A bond yielding 5 percent, for example, will

Personal FINANCE in action 8.7

Diversity in Portfolios

Three investors, Ann, Mohammed, and Carl, are at different stages in life and have different attitudes toward investments, as you can see from the following summary of their portfolios.

Investment	Ann	Mohammed	Carl
Canada Savings Bonds	0%	50%	15%
Guaranteed Investment Certificates	0%	25%	10%
Mutual fund (balanced)	0%	25%	30%
Corporate bonds	0%	0%	15%
Common stocks	60%	0%	25%
Gold	40%	0%	5%
TOTAL	**100%**	**100%**	**100%**

Which of the three investors is probably young, single, and not averse to risk? Who probably spends the least time looking after his or her portfolio? Who seems to have spread the risk most widely?

Mohammed, who appears to be the most conservative in this group (since three-quarters of his portfolio is in debt securities), is exposed to interest rate and inflation risks. But these are offset by the balanced mutual fund (invested in stocks and bonds), which offers some opportunity for growth and protection from inflation without very high risk. Perhaps

he is retired, has a lower marginal tax rate, and needs income-producing securities.

Ann, who owns no debt securities, has the most risk in her portfolio. She is very heavily exposed to market and business risks, but should be protected against inflation. Still, what will she use for emergency funds or short-term goals? If she happens to need funds when the market is low, she might be forced to take a capital loss.

Carl, the seasoned investor, may have the largest net worth. At any rate, he has diversified his holdings more than the others and has thereby protected his assets against a range of risks.

decline in value if new bonds yielding more than this are issued. The shares of many Canadian companies may fall if the economy of the United States, Canada's major export market, declines. Stock prices are based on fear and greed. Such emotions can, and do, wreak havoc with even the best investment plans.

One example of portfolio diversification made in September 2005 suggested the following:

Equities, or equity mutual funds	40 percent
Bonds	40 percent
Cash, or money market funds	20 percent

At this time, the bull market in Canadian equities had lasted for several years and more and more investment professionals were expecting a reversal, but no one could predict when, or how great, the reversal would be. In October, the S&P/ TSX composite index took a very large tumble[19]. A portfolio such as the one above would have helped to preserve the value of the person's assets. When the drop slowed, the cash could have been used to pick up some bargains.

Analyze Your Portfolio

Every investor must decide if his or her main goal is income or capital gain. While some investments can provide some of both, normally if the investor chooses only growth, he or she foregoes a high yield. And if the investor chooses only capital gain, he or she foregoes high yield. Other goals include liquidity, safety, and after-tax returns. These goals and how to achieve them are shown in Table 8.4.

You can analyze your investments by using Table 8.5. Other asset categories can be added. It should be stressed, however, that while one's objective in owning stocks and mutual funds may be capital gain, this may not be the only outcome of such an objective. In the first few years of the twenty-first century, both of these investments often provided only capital losses. Most objectives need to be long-term (over five years and preferably longer) if they are to be achieved. Investors must learn to be patient and not be overly influenced by negative financial news. Today's loss may turn out to be tomorrow's gain.

TABLE 8.4   INVESTMENT PRIORITIES AND INVESTMENTS TO MEET THEM

PRIORITIES	APPROPRIATE INVESTMENTS
Income	income trusts, high-yielding common stocks, preferred stocks, bonds
Capital gain	stocks, equity mutual funds, real estate (usually)
Liquidity	Canada Savings Bonds, chequing accounts shares in most publicly traded companies, mutual funds
Good after-tax returns	capital gains followed by dividends, gains from sale of real estate
Inflation protection	high-yielding common and preferred stocks, stocks with capital gains potential, high-yielding bonds (usually)
Little management required and preservation of face value	savings accounts, Canada Savings Bonds, GICs

[19]Referred to by the term "correction." This only seems to apply when markets decline, suggesting that declines are a good thing. When markets rise for an extended period of time, they are often called "overheated," implying that such increases are bad and that a correction is overdue.

TABLE 8.5   ANALYSIS OF PRESENT PORTFOLIO

PRESENT VALUE	% OF TOTAL	ANNUAL RATE OF RETURN	INVESTMENT OBJECTIVE
Savings account			
GIC			
Term deposits			
Canada Savings Bonds			
RRSPs			
Mutual funds			
Bonds			
Stocks			
Real estate			

It should be pointed out that in the first four years of the twenty-first century, interest rates were unusually low. This meant that the traditional "safe" places for conservative investors to put their money were not really safe at all. As a result of inflation and taxes, those investors' capital and purchasing power were both eroded. The lesson for investors today is that only small amounts of money should be left in savings accounts, Canada Savings Bonds, etc., and then only for a short period of time. More risk-tolerant investors should use their savings to purchase stocks or equity mutual funds when the prices of these investments are depressed. People buy goods like clothing and lawn mowers when they are on sale. Why not apply the same logic to stocks?

Draw an Investment Pyramid

A widely used guide to investment planning is the investment pyramid, which summarizes an individual's portfolio (for an example, see Figure 8.8). As the pyramid rises, so does the risk; the investments at the base of the pyramid carry the least risk. If you drew the figure to scale, each slice of the pyramid would represent the distribution within the portfolio of investments that fall into the various risk categories. The best order of priority is from bottom to top. First, ensure that you have put money aside for emergencies, liquidity needs, and short-term goals in secure but accessible investments. For those who choose home ownership, investment in a home property will be the next priority. After taking care of these needs, you can invest in good-quality securities with a view toward funding long-term goals. The pyramid's top slices contain high-risk securities: such investments should not represent a significant share of most portfolios and should be considered only when all other investment goals have been adequately funded.

Make a drawing of your own portfolio pyramid to see how well you have implemented your priorities. There is no one right way to divide the pyramid; the best arrangement will depend on your stage in the life cycle, your personal objectives, and your financial situation. People who are very young or very wealthy may be more aggressive than older or retired investors. Nevertheless, everyone needs a safety cushion of funds for short-term needs before moving into other types of investments. The pyramid exercise helps you become more aware of portfolio planning and to avoid haphazard investing, which is not usually the most effective way to achieve your financial goals.

FIGURE 8.8 THE INVESTMENT PYRAMID

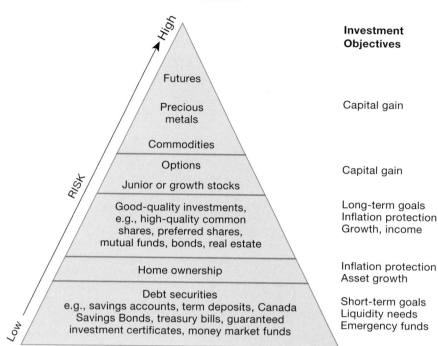

Investment Objectives

- Futures
- Precious metals — Capital gain
- Commodities
- Options — Capital gain
- Junior or growth stocks
- Good-quality investments, e.g., high-quality common shares, preferred shares, mutual funds, bonds, real estate — Long-term goals / Inflation protection / Growth, income
- Home ownership — Inflation protection / Asset growth
- Debt securities e.g., savings accounts, term deposits, Canada Savings Bonds, treasury bills, guaranteed investment certificates, money market funds — Short-term goals / Liquidity needs / Emergency funds

RISK — High / Low

Decide on Your Next Investment

Once you have a clear picture of your overall objectives, you will be in a position to determine the specific objectives of an additional investment. If your portfolio comprises largely low-risk, low-return fixed-income securities, you will probably want your next investment to offer more inflation protection, more return, and somewhat less safety.

Design an Investment Plan

A well-designed plan for saving and investing is crucial for setting you on the road to financial independence. As we saw in Chapter 3, financial security is the assurance that you can maintain your desired level of living now and in the future. Despite the existence of public income-security programs and personal insurance, a significant component of your financial security still depends on your individual net worth. If you hope to retire early from the labour force to pursue other interests, or to have a comfortable life after you reach the conventional retirement age, the size of your net worth will be a determining factor in whether you can achieve these goals. Furthermore, a saving and investment plan is a good defence against impulse spending or spending that is motivated by social pressure to buy things.

Earlier in this chapter, we discussed the need to save for emergency funds, liquidity needs, and short-term and long-term goals. This money should be invested in securities with appropriate maturities and with characteristics that match your priorities. Your investment plan will include a forecast of the total amount required, the amount to be saved each pay period, and indications as to how these savings will be invested.

Personal FINANCE in action   8.8

Investing Globally

Parvez's father had fled Iran after the overthrow of the Shah's regime in 1979. A high-ranking official in the Shah's government, he knew his life was in danger if he stayed. Like many of his friends, he had managed to transfer considerable funds out of the country. These had helped to educate Parvez and his sister, Beta, when they came to Canada. It had also left them with a substantial nest egg with which to establish a good life in their new country.

Now a university graduate with an MBA from Queen's University, Parvez decided to invest some of his money. His favourite course at Queen's had dealt with trends in global business. Knowing little about the Canadian economy or Canadian businesses, he therefore planned to take a global approach to investing. An easy way to do this, he had learned, was to buy American Depository Receipts (ADRs). First he looked at politically stable countries with healthy economies. Then he selected industries he thought should do well in an increasingly competitive world. The countries he decided to invest in were Finland, Ireland, and the United Kingdom. The companies he chose were Nokia, the cell phone company; Ryanair, the discount Irish airline; and the BG Group, a British gas company. He would have a diversified portfolio with companies that had good business models. In addition, both Nokia and Ryanair were not dependent on one market.

The Nokia ADR, symbol NOK, trades on the NYSE. It had increased in value by 4.15 percent in 2005. The Ryanair ADR, symbol RYAAY, trades on the NASDAQ. It had gone up in value by 18 percent in 2005. The BG Group ADR, symbol BRG, trades on the NYSE and it had gone up by 28.62 percent in 2005.

Banking and Financial Services

How Canadians handle their money has changed considerably in recent years. Much has been made in the press about how banking services have deteriorated. But contrary to what some newspapers have said about the decline in personal, or one-on-one, service with tellers, Canadians are obviously thrilled with the changes. According to the Canadian Bankers Association (CBA), only 15 percent of banking transactions are now done in banks with tellers. The remaining 85 percent of transactions are done via bank machines, over the telephone, or online. A survey done for the CBA in 2002 indicated that 76 percent of Canadians believe the new technology has made banking more convenient and 85 percent think future changes will add to this convenience. As evidence, Canadians made over 1.1 billion ABM transactions in 2004. We are the highest users of debit cards in the world, and one-quarter of us do all banking online. In spite of the increased use of technology, and contrary to what one would expect, the number of people working for banks has steadily increased from 221 400 in 1997 to 239 000 in 2004.[20]

Summary

- Setting financial goals is an important step every investor must take. The achievement of financial goals is difficult without investing, and no investing can take place unless funds are saved for that purpose.
- Real interest is the nominal rate of interest minus the rate of inflation.

[20]Canadian Bankers Association, Quick Facts, October 2005.

- Investing involves trying to buy investments that protect one's capital while at the same time providing a return; speculation, in contrast, is the purchase of an investment in the hopes of earning a quick reward and is more risky. Portfolio analysis involves studying your investments to determine if they satisfy your investment goals.

- Investment income comes in the form of dividends, interest, and capital gains. Capital gain is any amount an investment makes above the purchase price. Capital loss occurs when an investment is sold below the purchase price. Investment objectives are a good yield and capital gains, goals which may not be obtainable in the same investment. Basic characteristics of investments include their risk, their liquidity, and whether they provide dividend income, interest, or capital gains.

- Investment returns include interest on bonds and dividends and capital gains on equities. Equities are stocks in a company that give the buyer a share in the company's ownership.

- Investment considerations include the risk/reward trade-off as well as the marketability and liquidity of investments. Liquid assets are those that can be easily turned into cash. Marketability refers to things that can be sold.

- Investment risk is a concern with every investment, even the most conservative. Investment trade-offs are usually between income and capital gain. Generally, the greater the risk, the greater the chance for a capital gain or loss. With little risk, the trade-off is that there is little chance for capital gain. Investment pyramids analyze investments according to risk. The higher an investment's place on the pyramid, the greater is its risk.

- Risk comes in various forms. There can be the risk of inflation which lowers the value of money, interest rate risk which influences the price of stocks and bonds, market risk which lowers the value of an investment, and business risk caused by bad management or economic conditions. Risk reduction strategies include diversification and investing globally.

- Investment fraud is an attempt to separate gullible investors from their money.

- Debt securities include bonds and GICs where money is lent in return for the payment of interest. Term is the length of time to maturity of a fixed income investment. Creating ladder GICs refers to buying GICs with different maturity dates to take advantage of rising interest rates.

- Diversification is an attempt to reduce risk by investing in a variety of different types of investments. Investing globally is an attempt to minimize risk by investing outside Canada. Depository receipts are securities traded on US exchanges that allow an investor to own shares in foreign companies not traded in the country.

- Random events refer to unsuspected happenings that can have an effect on investments. Management effort will not protect a portfolio from unexpected events. To reduce worry the best advice is to follow the strategies of the most successful investors.

- Investment theories are many and varied as analysts try to determine the best way to be a successful investor. Value investing involves buying stocks in well-managed companies whose products are in demand and whose share prices are undervalued. Contrarians do the opposite of what the market does, buying stocks the market rejects and selling those it wants. Fundamental analysis involves looking at a company's market value to determine if its shares are above or below book value. Buy and hold is an investment theory whose supporters believe that one should buy good stocks and keep them for a long time unless something drastic happens to the company. Technical analysis involves looking at charts and graphs to try and determine the future performance of an investment. Momentum investing involves buying undervalued securities that should have upward momentum. Growth investing involves buying shares in companies that are growing by taking over other companies. Income investing means buying investments that provide the owner with a regular income. Modern Portfolio Theory focuses on the risk of a whole portfolio rather than individual investments. Dogs of the Dow is an investment theory that recommends buying the ten top-paying dividend stocks of the Dow Jones Industrial Average. Dollar cost averaging is an investment theory that recommends investing the same amount of money in the same stock on a regular basis. Global Couch Potato theory was developed by Barclays Global Investors as a means of spreading investment risk.

Key Terms

business risk *(p. 240)*	inflation risk *(p. 240)*
buy and hold *(p. 233)*	interest rate risk *(p. 240)*
capital gain *(p. 237)*	investing *(p. 230)*
compounding *(p. 242)*	ladder GICs *(p. 243)*
Consumer Price Index *(p. 240)*	liquid *(p. 238)*
contrarians *(p. 232)*	market risk *(p. 240)*
debt securities *(p. 235)*	Modern Portfolio Theory *(p. 234)*
diversification *(p. 247)*	momentum investing *(p. 233)*
Dogs of the Dow *(p. 234)*	negative rate of return *(p. 240)*
dollar cost averaging *(p. 235)*	portfolio *(p. 230)*
equity *(p. 235)*	random events (happenings) *(p. 244)*
fundamental analysis *(p. 232)*	real rate of return *(p. 240)*
Global Couch Potato Portfolio *(p. 235)*	speculation *(p. 230)*
	technical analyst *(p. 233)*
growth investing *(p. 234)*	term *(p. 239)*
income investing *(p. 234)*	value investing *(p. 232)*

Problems

1. **Inflation, Interest Income, and Taxes**

   An important concept for investors is what their after-tax income will be. This is not obvious from the simple interest rate paid on a bond or the dividend paid on a stock. Assume you have a taxable income of $50 000 and have $1000 invested in a Canada Savings Bond.

   Find out the rate of inflation for 2005 by going to **www.bankofcanada.ca**. Next, determine what interest you will earn on your CSB by going to **www2.csb.gc.ca/eng/bonds_rates.asp**. Reduce this by the amount of inflation. Now, figure out how much federal income tax you must pay on this interest by going to **www.walterharder.ca/MarginalTaxRateCalculator.html**.

   Was your decision to invest in a CSB a wise one?

2. Explain why investing outside Canada makes sound financial sense. Identify two ways of doing this without having to buy shares in a foreign equity market.

3. Discuss the savings habits of Canadians. How can the current trend be explained? What are the implications for those who have managed to reach the average savings rate? Is this a matter for policy-makers to be concerned with?

4. Do you approve or disapprove of the current policy regarding foreign investments in RRSPs? Explain your answer.

5. It is probably true to say that all investment advisors suggest diversification and the careful monitoring of one's portfolio as good ways of reducing investment risk. Why is it quite possible that even if these are done, and done well, an investor could still suffer serious loss?

6. Discuss the pros and cons of the Dogs of the Dow theory.

7. Explain the differences between the following investment theories: value investing; the contrarian approach; and fundamental analysis. Do they have anything in common?

8. Explain what is meant by the following investment theories:

   (a) Dollar cost averaging

   (b) Momentum investing

   (c) Buy and hold

   (d) Technical analysis

   (e) Growth investing

   Which best describes the investment philosophy of Warren Buffet, John Templeton, and Stephen Jarislowsky?

9. Why is the Dogs of the Dow theory popular with many investors? What is its fundamental weakness?

 10. Go to **www.berkshirehathaway.com**, the website for Berkshire Hathaway. Click on Links to Berkshire Subsidiary Companies. Would you describe Berkshire as a diversified or an undiversified company? What businesses are the subsidiaries in?

   Click on Owner's Manual. Describe the Owner-Related Business Principles mentioned here. Are these in the best interests of the shareholders or the principals of the company?

   Click on Annual Reports and then the report for the latest year. How much was the company worth at the end of this year? What were its net earnings?

   Go to **www.nyse.com**, the website for the NYSE. Find out what one share of Berkshire Hathaway is worth today. After realizing the scope of the company's business interests and its earnings, would you buy shares in the company if you could afford them?

11. "When the crisis is sudden and the future unknown, a long-term focus is paramount."[21] Discuss, with reference to the shares in energy companies and the hurricanes that devastated the southern United States and Central America in the fall of 2005.

12. **What Are His Investment Objectives?**

   Lee usually spends all of his income. He loves to shop and, until recently, had no reason to save. He is 28 and has worked as a welder-fitter since his graduation from a community college six years ago. For three years he has had a girlfriend, Tina; he wants to marry her as soon as he has a few thousand dollars in the bank. At Tina's suggestion, Lee recently bought a lottery ticket and won $100 000. Having learned about investments in an economics course he took at college, he has several goals for this money. He knows all about inflation and wants to invest this money so that it earns a capital gain. He also wants the money to be both secure and quite liquid.

---

[21]Paramount Investments.

Tina would like to buy a house, and Lee would like to be able to afford the one she has been admiring in a new subdivision.

(a) From this limited information, make a list of Lee's investment priorities.

(b) How would you suggest he should invest this money to achieve all of his goals?

(c) If you were Lee's investment advisor, what advice would you have for him?

13. **Investment Priorities**

Sid, a widower of 45, has two adult children who both have good full-time jobs. He owns a prosperous hardware store and recently paid off the mortgage on his house. He earns a good salary and has few expenses. Several years ago, he began to invest for his retirement: he owns a self-directed RRSP and a diversified portfolio of common stocks and bonds worth over $150 000. Recently he sold some shares in a high-tech stock and made a capital gain of $25 000. Yesterday his broker called with some suggestions for this money. Sid told him that income, capital gains, and security of the principal are his main priorities. He also said that liquidity and inflation protection are far less important. If he has another capital gain, he wants to invest in some mining stock and a second mortgage.

(a) Examine Sid's investment objectives in view of what you know about his financial situation.

(b) Identify any inconsistencies between his stated objectives and his plans.

(c) It is not uncommon to find such inconsistencies. Why is that?

14. **How Much Risk?**

Claude and Janet are in their mid-forties and live in Calgary. They have two teenage daughters and a large mortgage on their house. Claude is a multimedia developer who works for a very successful advertising agency; Janet is a high-school teacher. Their combined incomes total $105 000. The only investments they have are some Canada Savings Bonds and a $40 000 GIC. One recent night they were at a dinner party with their friends Frank and Chelsea. When the conversation turned to investing, Chelsea told them that she had invested in the shares of some Alberta energy companies. Recently these had appreciated considerably in value. She convinced Claude and Janet that they should also buy common stocks in energy companies with some of their savings. You are a financial planner. When they come to your office for some suggestions, you learn that their priority is inflation protection. They also want investments that require little attention and that have the potential for some capital gain. They are nervous about risk and want their investments to be quite liquid.

(a) What would you say to this couple about their investment goals?

(b) What kind of investment would you suggest for them?

 15. Go to **www.cannex.com** and select Canada. Under Products, click Term Deposits/GICs/GIAs. Under Non-registered, click on 1–6 Years. Compare the rate on five-year GICs issued by the following companies: *Achieva Financial, Bank of Nova Scotia, Citibank, DUCA Financial Services, Promutuel Capital,* and *Peoples Trust.* Why do you think the rates vary? What information is available on the internet about these companies? Try to find out the size of the assets under administration. While an investment in a GIC is guaranteed up to $100 000, would you buy one based solely on the amount of interest offered? Which company's or companies's GICs would you feel most comfortable buying?

16. Explain why going into debt to buy a house is not considered a bad thing.

17. How can investors shield themselves from the ravages of inflation?

18. (a) If you were to invest globally today, in which part of the world would you consider investing? Why do you think it is a better choice than Canada?

    (b) Referring to the investment choices mentioned in the section Investing Globally, which would you choose? Why?

    (c) Examine the businesses of the Thomson Corporation at **www.thomson.com**. Why do they make Thomson a good company in which to invest?

19. Examine the random events that caused the share prices of the following Canadian corporations to fall: Nortel, JDS Uniphase, Bre-X Minerals, Bombardier, and Canada 3000. Were any of these events predicted or predictable? What was the percentage drop in price in each case after the event? Which company or companies did not survive?

    For answers, try the following:

    For JDS go to **www.cbc.ca/news**. Type JDS in Search.

    For Bombardier and Canada 3000, also go to **www.cbc.ca/news**.

    For Nortel, do the same and read some of the links to get an idea of the history of this once-prominent Canadian company.

    How would you describe the financial health of Nortel and Bombardier today?

20. Two of the stocks that make up the Dow Jones Industrial Average are Coca-Cola and Johnson & Johnson. Go to **www.nyse.com** and make lists of the countries each does business in. What kind(s) of risk does ownership of these stocks help to avoid?

21. Create diversified portfolios of equities (by industry), bonds, GICs, and cash that should withstand the investment fall-out from each of the following random events:

    (a) A Taliban takeover of Saudi Arabia.

    (b) The election in Canada of an NDP government.

    (c) The spread of avian flu from poultry to humans before the development of the proper vaccine.

    (d) The discovery of a massive and easy-to-obtain supply of crude oil in northern Saskatchewan.

    (e) An attack on Taiwan by the armies of the People's Republic of China.

    (f) The discovery of an inexpensive cure for AIDS and the elimination of the virus from the African continent.

    (g) A continuation of the softwood lumber dispute between Canada and the US.

    (h) A jump in the Canadian inflation rate from 2 to 12 percent.

    (i) A major increase in the Bank of Canada's overnight rate (Bank Rate), as a result of this high inflation, to 15 percent.

    (j) The death in office of the US President.

22. The S&P/TSX Composite Index dropped drastically in October 2005. Assume that you are a contrarian investor. What kind of personality do you have in order to be able to invest in Canadian equities when the large majority of investors seem to be selling? In light of the recent rapid growth of both the Chinese and Indian economies, what kinds of equities will you buy?

23. Enron, once a huge American electricity, natural gas, and communications company went bankrupt in 2001. Its demise turned out to be the largest corporate bankruptcy in history and an example of a completely unexpected random event of epic proportions. If

you Google this topic, you will find close to 14 million sites dealing with Enron. Select as many as you need and write an essay explaining why this once-great company died.

24. A recent study indicated that three-quarters of Canadians have less than three months' worth of savings. Since other studies found that the rate of savings of Canadians has dropped to zero, the amount saved must be pitifully low. With that in mind, explain what financial goals and needs these Canadians have absolutely no chance of reaching.

25. A diagram in the text suggests that the more an investor knows about the future, the less risk he or she will have. Discuss what the average investor knows about the future and whether this is a help or a hindrance in making investment choices.

26. You meet a retired person at a neighbourhood party who tells you she spends at least eight hours every day managing her portfolio, which now amounts to almost $250 000. Is this a wise or foolish thing to do? Will this guarantee a healthy rate of return for her portfolio?

27. Identify at least six short-term financial goals that average Canadian families might reasonably hope to achieve. Suggest ways to invest their savings that offer a good chance that the money will be there when it is needed. What will they sacrifice if they follow your recommendations?

28. Apart from the fact that you can live in it, how does investing in a house differ from every other type of investment?

29. Managers of international equity funds search the markets of the world for bargains. Assume that you are the manager of a fund that has a mandate to invest in any market except the Canadian or American. What particular challenges do each of the following markets present: Nigeria, Russia, Venezuela, Turkey, Sri Lanka? For assistance go to **www.economist.com/index.html**. All have excellent potential in the minds of some managers. Would you invest any of the money in your fund in the industries in these countries?

30. You are the manager of an emerging markets fund that has invested all of the fund's money in Iran, Libya, Russia, the West African region, and Saudi Arabia, places many of your investors would never consider because of objections to their poor human rights records and the questionable legitimacy of their governments. Justify to those who have invested in the fund, and now question your judgment, why you have selected one of these places as a suitable location to invest their hard-earned money. For assistance, go to **www.emerging-markets.com/index.html**.

References

BOOKS AND ARTICLES

Ahrens, Dan. *Investing in Vice: The Recession-proof Portfolio of Booze, Bets, Bombs, and Butts.* New York: St. Martin's Press, 2004.

Anderson, Hugh. *Second Wave: Online Investing in the New Era for Canadians.* Toronto: Warwick, 2003.

Atkinson, Howard J., and Donna Green. *The New Investment Frontier III: A Guide to Exchange Traded Funds for Canadians.* Toronto: Insomniac Press, 2005.

Bach, David. *Smart Couples Finish Rich (Canadian Edition): 9 Steps to Creating a Rich Future for You and Your Partner.* Toronto: Random House, 2003.

Bach, David. *Start Late, Finish Rich.* Canadian Edition. Toronto: Doubleday Canada, 2005.

Carrick, Rob. *The Online Investor's Companion.* Toronto: John Wiley & Sons Canada Ltd., 2001.

Cooper, Sherry. *The Cooper Files: A Practical Guide to Your Financial Future.* Toronto: Key Porter Books, 1999.

Cooper, Sherry. *Ride The Wave: Take Control in the Acceleration Age.* Toronto: Prentice Hall, 2001.

Cork, Kevin. *The Money Book: A Survival Strategy for Canadians Under 35.* Toronto: Key Porter, 2002.

Coxe, Donald. *The New Reality of Wall Street: An Investor's Survival Guide to Triple Waterfalls and Other Stock Market Perils.* Toronto: McGraw-Hill, 2003.

Cruise, David, and Alison Griffiths. *The Portfolio Doctor: Your Prescription for Investment Health.* Toronto: Penguin Canada, 2004.

Dixon, Hugo. *The Penguin Guide to Finance.* Toronto: Penguin, 2000.

Dominguez, Joe, and Vicki Robin. *Your Money or Your Life: Transforming Your Relationship with Money and Achieving Financial Independence.* New York: Penguin, 1994.

Friedland, Seymour, and Steven G. Kelman. *Investment Strategies: How to Create Your Own and Make It Work for You.* Toronto: Penguin, 1996.

Gallander, Benj. *The Contrarian Investor's 13: How to Earn Superior Returns in the Stock Market.* Toronto: Penguin Canada, 2004.

Graham, Benjamin. *Intelligent Investor: The Classic Text on Value Investing.* Toronto: Harper Collins, 2005.

Jenks, Philip, and Stephen Eckett (Editors). *The Global-Investor Book of Investing Rules: Invaluable Advice from 150 Master Investors.* Upper Saddle River, New Jersey: Prentice-Hall, 2002.

Lynch, Peter, and John Rothchild. *Beating the Street.* New York: Simon & Schuster, 1993.

MacBeth, Hilliard. *Investment Traps and How to Avoid Them.* Toronto: Prentice-Hall, 1999.

Pape, Gordon, and Eric Kirzner. *Secrets of Successful Investing.* Toronto: Viking, 2003.

Pape, Gordon. *6 Steps to $1 Million: How to Achieve Your Financial Dreams.* Toronto: Viking, 2002.

Roseman, Ellen. *Money 101: Every Canadian's Guide to Personal Finance.* Toronto: John Wiley, 2003.

Stanley, Thomas J., and William D. Danko. *The Millionaire Next Door: The Surprising Secrets of America's Wealthy.* Atlanta: Longstreet Press, 2000.

Taleb, Nassim Nicholas. *Fooled by Randomness: The Hidden Role of Chance in the Markets and in Life.* New York: Texere LLC, 2001.

Vaz-Oxlade, Gail. *The Money Tree Myth: A Parent's Guide to Helping Kids Unravel the Mysteries of Money.* Toronto: Stoddart, 1996.

Waxler, Caroline. *Stocking Up on Sin: How to Crush the Market with Vice-Based Investing.* Toronto: John Wiley & Sons Canada Ltd., 2004.

Weir, Deborah. *Timing the Market: How to Profit on the Stock Market Using the Yield Curve, Technical Analysis and Cultural Indicators.* Toronto: John Wiley & Sons Canada Ltd., 2005.

Wyatt, Elaine. *The Money Companion: How to Manage Your Money and Achieve Financial Freedom.* Toronto: Penguin Canada, 1997.

Yih, Jim. *Seven Strategies to Guarantee Your Investments: Guide for the Conservative Investor.* Barrie, Ontario: The Federation of Canadian Independent Deposit Brokers, 2004.

Young, Duff. *The Money Companion: How to Manage Your Money and Achieve Financial Freedom.* Toronto: Penguin Canada, 2001.

Young, Duff. *Core and Explore. The Investing Rush without the Ruin.* Toronto: Prentice Hall, 2001.

Personal Finance on the Web

Advice for Investors. com
   www.fin-info.com

Bank of Montreal
   www.bmo.com

Bearmarket Central
   www.bearmarketcentral.com

Canada WealthNet
   www.nucleus.com/wealthnet

Canadian Business Online
   www.canadianbusiness.com/my_money/index.jsp

Canadian Financial Network
   www.canadianfinance.com

Canadian Investor Protection Fund
   www.cipf.ca

Canadian Western Bank Group
   www.cwbank.com

Contra the Heard
   www.contratheheard.com

E*Trade Canada
   www.canada.etrade.com

Fiend's SuperBear Page
   www.fiendbear.com

Financial Pipeline
   www.finpipe.com

Financial Sense Online
   www.financialsense.com

Fiscal Agents Financial Services Group
   www.fiscalagents.com

GloomBoomDoom
   www.gloomboomdoom.com

Howe Street
   www.howestreet.com

Hussman Funds
www.hussmanfunds.com

Lombardi Publishing
www.lombardipublishing.com

Merlea Investments
www.merlea.com.au/index.shtml

MSN Money
www.moneycentral.msn.com

PIMCO—"The Authority on Bonds"
www.pimco.com

Prudent Bear
www.prudentbear.com

RBC Royal Bank
www.royalbank.com

SafeHaven
www.safehaven.com

Scotiabank
www.scotiabank.com

TD Canada Trust
www.tdcanadatrust.com

TD Bank Financial Group
www.tdbank.com

TSX Group
www.tsx.com

chapter 9

Debt Securities

"Net of inflation and taxes, bond returns are very close to zero in most markets."

Stephen Jarislowsky, *The Investment Zoo*

Learning Objectives

Understanding the concepts discussed in this chapter should make the world of fixed income investments easier to understand.

After studying this chapter, you should be able to:

1. Understand the following features of debt securities: term, interest rate and frequency of compounding, minimum deposit, and accessibility of funds.

2. Explain the purpose of deposit insurance.

3. Define the following: term deposits, guaranteed investment certificates, commercial paper, treasury bills, money market funds, and mortgage-backed securities.

4. Outline the process of bringing a bond issue to market and determining interest rates on new issues.

5. Distinguish between the various types of bonds and the difference between a principal and an agent in the bond market.

6. Define the special feature of bonds.

7. Calculate the yield to maturity on a bond and show how the changing of a bond's price affects the yield.

8. Understand the accrual process.

9. Explain the different tax treatment of bond interest and capital gains.

10. Show why Canada Savings Bonds are more like savings certificates than bonds.

Introduction

This chapter is about debt securities, the kinds of investment in which the investor becomes a lender rather than an owner. As a result, there is generally less risk assumed and less management required. Five groups of debt securities will be discussed:

(a) deposits,

(b) money market securities,

(c) mortgage-backed securities,

(d) bonds and debentures,

(e) Canada Savings Bonds.

Most of these items are low-risk, very liquid investments, appropriate as a base for any portfolio. Deposits and Canada Savings Bonds are not transferable to other investors, but money market securities, mortgage-backed securities, and bonds may be traded in the financial markets. It is important to distinguish between Canada Savings Bonds, which are more like savings certificates, and other types of bonds.

This chapter introduces some of the basic principles and terminology associated with debt securities, but it does not address portfolio management strategies. To learn more about debt securities, you may wish to consult the other references and resources listed at the end of the chapter.

Deposits

The easiest and simplest way to invest is to lend capital to financial institutions by placing it in deposit securities. Savings accounts, term deposits, and guaranteed investment certificates are all examples of deposit securities. Although these savings vehicles may differ in interest rates, terms, minimum deposits, and accessibility, most involve a very low level of risk, pay interest regularly, and require minimal attention from the investor. The real return bond, another type of deposit security, is the subject of this chapter's Women Take Charge box on page 269.

Savings Accounts

Banks, trust companies, and credit unions (*caisses populaires* in Quebec) offer a great variety of accounts. Some permit chequing; others do not. These financial institutions pay a higher rate of interest on savings accounts where the money is left for long periods of time. If you do not need your money soon and you decide that you want such an account, look for one that pays a high interest rate and that compounds interest frequently. If you expect to use some of your money occasionally, consider a daily interest account instead. While the interest rate on such accounts is lower, it is paid on the daily balance and is compounded monthly. Interest on regular savings accounts is paid only on the minimum monthly balance and is compounded semi-annually. Competition for customers is so strong today that financial institutions make frequent changes to their account offerings, with a view to attracting and keeping customers. A wise consumer should therefore check with a number of institutions before opening an account. Some things to look for when comparing companies are shown in the boxed example "Comparing Banking Services."

Term Deposits

As the name implies, **term deposits** are deposits taken by a financial institution for a specified term at a guaranteed interest rate—and, in some cases, a minimum investment is required. Savings accounts, by contrast, have no guaranteed interest rate, no minimum deposit, and no set term during which the funds must stay on deposit. The rate of return on term deposits is usually higher than that on savings accounts, and although the money is invested for a specified term, funds can usually be withdrawn before maturity by sacrificing some interest. Since the frequency of interest payments affects the interest rate, you can expect a lower rate if interest is to be paid monthly.

Comparing Bank Services

When comparing banks, ask yourself these questions: What interest is paid on savings and chequing accounts? What balance is required?

All banks offer the following: low-fee accounts, senior's accounts, student accounts, youth accounts. How do the fees for these services compare?

To many consumers, the following things are equally important as the fees charged: hours of opening, location of branches, parking, availability of ATMs, and the knowledge and the friendliness of the staff.

Term deposits are no longer popular. They have largely been replaced by Guaranteed Investment Certificates. Two banks that still offer them are the Bank of Montreal and TD Canada Trust. Their deposits and rates are shown in Tables 9.1 and 9.2.

TABLE 9.1 BANK OF MONTREAL TERM DEPOSITS

TERM	$1000– $4999	$5000– $99 999	$100 000– $249 999	$250 000– $499 999	$500 000– $999 999
1–7 days	-	-	1.250%	1.350%	1.350%
8–15 days	-	-	1.250%	1.350%	1.350%
16–22 days	-	-	1.250%	1.350%	1.350%
23–29 days	-	-	1.250%	1.350%	1.350%
30–59 days	-	1.250%	1.250%	1.500%	1.500%
60–89 days	-	1.250%	1.350%	1.500%	1.500%
90–119 days	-	1.350%	1.450%	1.600%	1.600%
120–179 days	-	1.350%	1.450%	1.700%	1.700%
180–269 days	-	1.450%	1.550%	1.700%	1.700%
270 days–under 1 year	-	1.550%	1.650%	1.800%	1.800%
1 year–under 2 years	2.300%	2.300%	2.300%	2.300%	2.300%
2 years–under 3 years	2.500%	2.500%	2.500%	2.500%	2.500%
3 years–under 4 years	2.600%	2.600%	2.600%	2.600%	2.600%
4 years–under 5 years	2.700%	2.700%	2.700%	2.700%	2.700%
5 years exactly	2.850%	2.850%	2.850%	2.850%	2.850%

Redemptions are permitted anytime with interest paid after 30 days at predetermined rates. For deposits longer than one year, interest is compounded every six months. For shorter durations, interest is compounded at maturity.

SOURCE: www4.bmo.com/personal/0,2273,35649_36862,00.html (February 3, 2006).

TABLE 9.2   TD CANADA TRUST TERM DEPOSITS

LONG TERM	TERM	RATES	RSP RATES
	1 year	2.30%	N/A
	2 years	2.50%	N/A
	3 years	2.60%	N/A
	4 years	2.70%	N/A
	5 years	2.85%	N/A

Interest is paid semi-annually and at maturity. Short term deposits are also available.

With a minimum deposit of $5000, terms of from 30 to 364 days are possible. On deposits of 30 to 89 days, interest is paid monthly, while on deposits of 90 days or more, interest is paid at maturity.

SOURCE: **www.tdcanadatrust.com/GICs/GICTable.jsp** (February 3, 2006).

Guaranteed Investment Certificates (GICs)

Until quite recently, **GICs** were one of the most uninteresting investments. Money was locked in for a specific term and earned a very low rate of return. This has all changed. To compete with Canada Savings Bonds, which are redeemable on any business day and used to pay an attractive rate of interest, GICs with a number of new features are now available. They are available as either redeemable or non-redeemable, with fixed or variable rates of interest. Interest rate options are much more attractive than when GICs were simply competitive with Canada Savings Bonds. As with the latter, GICs may now be purchased (one-year term only) that are cashable at any time. On this particular option, interest is calculated daily. Another option (of special interest to younger investors), with a minimum of $1000, allows the investor to make pre-determined weekly, bi-weekly, or monthly contributions. Accelerated GICs with the interest rate increasing each year have also become very popular. In addition, certificates are available with terms ranging from 30 days to seven years.

As GIC investors try to protect themselves from the ravages of inflation, **ladder GICs** have grown in popularity. Investors purchase certificates with different maturity dates, perhaps five, with one maturing each year. As one matures it is reinvested for a new five-year term at current rates, thus allowing the investor to take advantage of any increase in rates that may have occurred. Of course, interest rates may also be lower. Now, instead of buying five different certificates, a ladder GIC may be purchased with one payment.

The most interesting features now available have gone a long way to shed the dull, boring reputation GICs had for so long. For the more risk-tolerant investor, certificates are available that are indexed to a stock market index such as the S&P/TSX 60 or the S&P 500. This allows the investor to participate in the increases in these indices, as well as the decreases.

CIBC has one of the most innovative of this new type of GIC. Called the Market-mix GIC, it has contributions invested in the following fashion:

■ 5 percent savings: three- to five-year CIBC GIC

■ 5 percent income: S&P/TSX Canadian Bond Index

■ 90 percent growth:

> 20 percent S&P/TSX 60
> 40 percent S&P 500
> 17 percent FTSE (London Stock Exchange) Eurotop 100
> 13 percent Nikkei (Tokyo Stock Exchange) 225

With this product the bank satisfies a number of important investment criteria: fixed income; growth; diversification; global investing. However, the Market-mix GIC is not a fixed-income investment since 90 percent of the funds contributed are invested in equities. It should also not be called a Guaranteed Investment Certificate because equities can go down in value as well as up. The same thing applies to any GIC indexed to a stock market index.

Women take CHARGE 9.1

Because Jean is a conservative investor concerned about inflation, she has decided to investigate real return bonds issued by the Government of Canada. A real return bond differs from a conventional bond in that the principal is adjusted periodically for changes in inflation. Interest is paid on June 1 and December 1. The base upon which the interest is calculated is adjusted for inflation. Consider a newly issued real return bond with a par value of $5000. If inflation had increased by 0.5 percent, the new base upon which interest is calculated would be $5025 (5000 × 1.005 = 5025). The interest payment would be determined by using $5025 as the base. The semi-annual interest payments would increase over time if the inflation rate increased because of the upward adjustment to the principal.

At maturity, a traditional bond generally returns the par value. If a real return bond is held to maturity, the principal plus the adjustments for inflation is returned, thereby protecting purchasing power. Real return bonds can be traded on the secondary market, but the market price of the bond will reflect the inflation adjustments.

The semi-annual interest payments are taxed each year. In addition, the annual inflation adjustments are taxed, even though the adjustments have not been received in cash. Tax is deferred if the investment is inside an RRSP.

Being a conservative investor, Jean inquires as to the risks involved with real return bond investments. Although the value of the bond may move up or down with changes in the interest rate environment, just as with other bonds, the inflation adjustment factor provides for less volatility. A downward shift in the Consumer Price Index would affect the inflation adjustment factor accordingly.

Jean has decided to include a few real return bonds in her diverse portfolio as a long-term investment for inflation protection. She can buy selected bonds through a broker or invest in a mutual fund specializing in real return bonds. The mutual fund's management expense ratio would diminish the return somewhat. Barclays Canada recently issued the iUnits Real Return Bond Index ETF, an exchange-traded fund with a low management expense ratio. The ETF trades like a stock and offers the associated advantages.

Deposit Insurance

Funds deposited in a bank, trust company, or credit union are insured against loss if the institution should become insolvent. In 1967, the federal government established the Canada Deposit Insurance Corporation (CDIC) as a Crown corporation to insure eligible deposits in member institutions. Signs indicating CDIC membership are often displayed in the windows of banks and trust companies.

The CDIC insures savings and chequing accounts, money orders, deposit receipts, guaranteed investment certificates, debentures, and other obligations issued by the member institutions. The maximum coverage is changed from time to time; currently, the limit is $100 000 per depositor for each institution (that is, the combined total of your deposits at all branches of a given institution must be $100 000 or less in order to be covered by CDIC). One restriction is that term deposits, to be insurable, must be redeemable no later than five years after deposit. Another restriction is that deposits must be in Canadian currency. Joint accounts are insured separately from individual accounts, meaning that it is possible to have both a personal account and a joint account in the same bank, with the maximum coverage of $100 000 on each account. Credit unions, through their provincial organizations, offer similar deposit insurance.

Money Market Securities

From time to time, governments and corporations need to borrow money. The federal government borrows money in a variety of ways. The best-known of these ways, and one that is also popular with many thousands of Canadians, is the Canada Savings Bond that is issued each October. The government also borrows money by selling treasury bills (often called T-bills) and Government of Canada bonds. Provincial and municipal governments raise money by selling bonds or debentures. Corporations often borrow from banks, of course, but they may also raise money by issuing bonds, debentures, and short-term commercial paper. The people who invest in these vehicles are lending their money to the corporation that issues them. These loans are classified as either short-term or long-term. Money market securities are short-term loans; bonds and debentures are long-term loans. This section examines money market securities, including T-bills, commercial paper, and money market funds.

The Money Market

A large pool of cash moves from lenders to borrowers for short periods through a mechanism known as the **money market**. The major actors in this market are banks, trust companies, investment dealers, corporations, governments, and the Bank of Canada. The lenders are usually corporations or institutions with spare cash that can be invested for a short period, and the borrowers are those who temporarily need extra funds. There is no physical site where money market transactions take place; the "market" consists only of a communication system. Money market funds are fully marketable. Because of the large minimum investment required, few individual investors are aware of all this money market activity.

The money market, as has been mentioned, deals strictly with short-term loans—mostly for periods of 30, 60, 90, or 365 days, but occasionally for as long as three to five years. Commercial paper and treasury bills are two of the money market's most widely used instruments. **Commercial paper** (discounted paper) is the name used for short-term loans or promissory notes. Instead of lending the borrower a principal sum and expecting the borrower to repay the principal and the accumulated interest at maturity, the lender may invest a discounted sum, expecting to receive at maturity an amount equivalent to the loan plus interest. For instance, a 30-day note for $50 000 might be purchased for $49 600 by the lender, who would receive $50 000 at maturity. The $400 difference between the amount invested and the amount received is the interest on the loan, which in this instance is 9.6 percent.

Other money market securities are bankers' acceptances, provincial treasury bills and Government of Canada money market strips.

Bankers' acceptances are short-term promissory notes issued by a corporation and fully guaranteed by a bank. When issued by a bank, they are known as **bearer-deposit notes** and offer a higher interest rate than T-bills. The minimum investment required for a period of three months to one year is $5000. The minimum required for one to two months is $25 000. There is no limit to how much may be invested.

Provincial treasury bills and promissory notes are fully guaranteed by the issuing province. The minimum investment required is $100 000. There is no limit.

Government of Canada money market strips are a little different. Interest coupons are separated from the bond, and both are sold separately at a discount to face value, in a similar fashion to T-bills as discussed below. The difference between the purchase price and the matured value is the interest earned. Again, there is no limit to the amount purchased.

Treasury Bills

Treasury bills are short-term promissory notes that are issued mainly by the federal government, but also by other levels of government. They are purchased by financial institutions (such as banks and trust companies) and have terms to maturity of 91, 182, or 364 days. Retail clients wishing to invest in high-quality, low-risk, very liquid securities often purchase T-bills from investment dealers. Each dealer has a specific minimum purchase requirement. T-bills do not have a specific interest rate; instead, they sell at a discount and mature at par. The yield on a T-bill, which is determined by the difference between its purchase price and its maturity value, is higher than savings account interest. Investors may sell T-bills before maturity, at a price determined by current interest rates.

Each Tuesday, Government of Canada treasury bills are auctioned in Ottawa by the Bank of Canada. Prior to the auction, the Bank of Canada announces the amounts and maturities of the bills to be auctioned, and interested investors (e.g., banks and investment dealers) submit bids. At the auction, bills are sold to the highest bidders. Most T-bills are bought by banks (to be kept as part of their reserves) or by investment dealers (who sell them on the secondary market).

Until recently the Bank of Canada could, in theory, announce a change in the Overnight Rate on any business day. In September 2000 it announced the introduction of a new system. Any changes to the Overnight Rate will now be made on eight pre-specified dates. Announcements will be made at 9 a.m. on either a Tuesday or Wednesday in specific weeks from January to December.

Investment dealers provide an active secondary market, offering outstanding T-bills with shorter maturities than the Bank's new issues. In recent years, some investment dealers have made T-bills available to small investors with a minimum purchase of $1000, in increments of $1000. Anyone who wishes to invest for the short term in a top-quality, low-risk, very liquid investment, might consider treasury bills (for example, see Personal Finance in Action Box 9.1, "Buying a T-Bill"). To buy treasury bills, you may need to open an account with a stockbroker. Usually treasury bills pay somewhat higher interest than do savings accounts or term deposits, as noted in Table 9.3.

Money Market Funds

Savings accounts are not the only low-risk, highly liquid way to earn interest with small sums. When you do not have enough money to buy treasury bills directly from a broker, you can still put your savings into the money market through a **money market fund**, which is a way of pooling contributions from many small investors. A money market mutual fund accepts small amounts from many people. A paid manager invests these funds in a portfolio of treasury bills and commercial paper. The return from money market funds, in the form of interest, may be received regularly by the investor or reinvested in additional shares of the fund. The investor's shares in a money market fund can be sold at any time.

Money market funds differ in selling practices and commission fees. Some funds are sold directly to customers, while others are available through brokers. Some funds

Personal FINANCE in action 9.1

Buying a T-Bill

When Ivan inherited $27 000, he needed a short-term investment until he made other plans. His broker offered him a 36-day treasury bill, quoted at a price of 99.627. Note that the quoted price is the amount he will pay for each $100 that he buys. The amount he invested was 270 × 99.627 = $26 899.29. When the T-bill matures, Ivan will receive $27 000, including interest of $100.71.

To calculate the yield on his T-bill, Ivan used the following formula:

$$\text{Yield} = \frac{100 - \text{price}}{\text{price}} \times \frac{365 \times 100}{\text{term}}$$

$$\text{Yield} = \frac{100 - 99.627}{99.627} \times \frac{365}{36}$$

$$\text{Yield} = \frac{0.373}{99.627} \times \frac{365}{36}$$

$$\text{Yield} = 0.003\ 743\ 965 \times 1013.888$$
$$= 3.8\%$$

If Ivan had needed to sell the treasury bill before it matured, the return would have been recalculated to reflect the current T-bill rate at the time of the sale.

TABLE 9.3   A COMPARISON OF SEVERAL WAYS TO EARN INTEREST INCOME FEBRUARY 3, 2006

METHOD	INTEREST RATE	FEATURES
Chequing account	0	Minimum monthly balance required, or fee charged
Premium rate savings account	2.60%	Up to $5000; money not locked in
Money market fund	2.30%	Slight risk; liquid
GIC, 1 year to 18 months	2.550% on $1000 to $99 999	Not liquid; minimum investment of $1000
Treasury bill (9 months)	3.49%	Liquid; minimum investment varies with investment dealer
Government of Canada Bonds (Canada Bonds), 1 to 30 years	3.97%	Liquid; guaranteed by Government of Canada; face value returned if held to maturity; $5 000 minimum

do not charge a fee, but require a large initial deposit; others charge an acquisition fee of 2 to 9 percent, depending on the size of the investment (the larger the deposit, the smaller the rate). Most money market funds charge annual management fees, which are deducted before any return is paid to the investor (see Personal Finance in Action Box 9.2, "Roberta's Lesson in Money Market Fund Investments"). In February 2006, there were 197 Canadian money market funds. These were issued by banks, mutual fund companies, and insurance companies. Fees for mutual funds will be discussed in detail in Chapter 10.

Roberta's Lesson in Money Market Fund Investments

One of Roberta's assignments for her securities course was to research the various money market funds offered by Canada's financial industry and to pick one that she would be happy to invest in. She was amazed at the number of such funds and the disparity in both management expense ratios (MER) and performance. She decided that she would put some money into a fund run by one of Canada's big banks because it had the lowest MER: 0.96 percent. It required an initial investment of $500, yielded 1.83 percent and made an income payment monthly. In addition, she was intrigued by where her money would be invested because some of the language used by the fund was strange to her ears, and she wanted to learn what the different investment terms meant. If she put $500 into this fund, her money would be invested as follows:

■ 45.7% in asset-backed securities
■ 24.7% in a bankers' acceptance
■ 17.8% in floating-rate notes

■ 7.9% in commercial paper
■ 1.8% in T-bills
■ 2.1% in cash

She had already learned about bankers' acceptances and treasury bills, but she knew nothing about the other investments. What she found out would be valuable when she started to work in the industry. With a little research, she learned, as we already have, that commercial paper is short-term debt issued by corporations to help meet such short-term needs as paying for accounts receivable and additions to inventories.

She also learned that **asset-backed securities** are bonds supported by a pool of assets. The assets are taken from a wide range of products, including computer lease agreements, auto loans, credit card receivables, residential mortgages, mutual fund fees, personal lines of credit, and equipment leases. **Floating-rate notes** are debt securities with interest rates that vary because they are tied to a money market index.

Mortgage-Backed Securities

Investing directly in home mortgages requires expertise, time, and willingness to accept risk. But you can overcome these difficulties by using **mortgage-backed securities**. When you buy mortgage-backed securities, you acquire a share in a large pool of residential mortgages that are secured by the Canada Mortgage and Housing Corporation (CMHC). Each pool of mortgages has its own interest rate and maturity date, which could be as short as six months. Mortgage-backed securities are available from stockbrokers in units of $5000 and are traded on the public market, where they may be sold before maturity. Generally, the yield on this investment vehicle is higher than that for treasury bills.

There are two types of mortgage-backed securities: open and closed (terms that will be more meaningful to you after you study Chapter 12, "Home Mortgages"). In essence, the terms mean that some mortgage pools permit home buyers to make prepayments in order to repay their mortgages faster. Investors in mortgage-backed securities are affected by this type of arrangement, because they may find their principal being repaid faster than they anticipated; investors must therefore reinvest their capital at a faster rate. But there may be a bonus of some extra money for investors because of penalties paid by those making prepayments.

Terms for mortgage-backed securities range from one to ten years. Each month, purchasers receive a share of the interest and principal payments made to the mortgage pool. Such investments appeal to many because of this and, as a result, mortgage-backed securities are often found in RRIFs.

Bonds

Bonds and Debentures

Debt securities with longer-term maturities include bonds and debentures, which may have terms of up to 25 years or more. Technically, there is a distinction between bonds and debentures, although the terms are often used interchangeably: **bonds** are secured with property, while **debentures** are unsecured loans. To further confuse matters, Government of Canada bonds are really debentures. In this chapter, "bonds" will be used as a generic term that includes both bonds and debentures. Bonds are issued by the federal, provincial, and municipal governments, by public utilities, and by private corporations when they need to borrow money. Those who buy their bonds become their creditors, receiving a promise that interest will be paid on specific dates and that the principal will be repaid at maturity.

How Bonds Are Issued

A government or corporation that wishes to float a new bond issue usually uses investment dealers as underwriters. The **underwriters** agree to purchase all of the bonds offered at a stated price, and then try to sell them at a slightly higher price. In the initial stages, the underwriters will be consulted for advice on terms (interest rate, maturity, etc.). Underwriters are involved in designing the terms of the issue as well as in its sale and distribution. The **par value** is the face value of the bond or other security, which is often $1000. Investment dealers advertise each new issue of bonds and sell them to buyers at a price that may be either at par or slightly below, depending on the market at the time.

A New Bond or Debenture Issue When a new bond or debenture is issued, a copy of a prospectus giving detailed information about the bond is sent to interested people. The first page of one such prospectus is shown in Figure 9.1. It shows the name of the issuer (Rogers Sugar Income Fund) and the value of the issue ($85 000 000) along with other relevant information. The debenture will pay 5.90 percent interest per year, payable semi-annually on June 29 and December 29, beginning on June 29, 2006, and ending on June 29, 2013. The debentures may be converted at the owner's option into units of the Rogers Sugar Income Fund at any time up until June 28, 2013. They may also be redeemed between June 29, 2009, and June 29, 2011.

Factors Affecting Interest Rates The three significant factors that affect the interest rate on a new bond issue are (i) the general level of interest rates in the country at the time, (ii) the length of time to maturity, and (iii) the issuer's credit rating. If general interest rates happen to be high, bond issuers will have to offer equivalent rates to attract investors. Recall from Chapter 7 that money has a time value. The longer the term, the more is the uncertainty about the future—and consequently, the higher is the rate needed to interest investors in very long-term bonds.

A bond issuer's credit rating depends on the issuer's financial status and revenue base. The federal government, which is considered to have the highest credit rating, can borrow more cheaply than the provinces can. Municipalities are considered to be in the third level of safety and must therefore pay somewhat more interest than the two senior levels of government do. Generally, corporations rank below all governments and must pay somewhat higher interest rates on their bonds. But corporations vary considerably in their credit ratings; some have a much better rating than others. Moreover, this ranking of credit status—from the federal government at the top to corporations at the bottom—is a useful generalization, but it does not cover all cases.

Bond Ratings

Before purchasing a bond, investors would be wise to find out the credit-worthiness of the issuing company and whether there is any risk that the company may not be able to make the expected interest payments. Ratings of this sort are done by the Dominion Bond Rating

FIGURE 9.1 ANNOUNCEMENT OF A BOND ISSUE

No securities regulatory authority has expressed an opinion about these securities and it is an offence to claim otherwise.

A copy of this preliminary short form prospectus has been filed with the securities regulatory authorities in each of the provinces of Canada but has not yet become final for the purpose of the sale of securities. Information contained in this preliminary short form prospectus may not be complete and may have to be amended. The securities may not be sold until a receipt for the short form prospectus is obtained from the securities regulatory authorities.

This short form prospectus constitutes a public offering of these securities only in those jurisdictions where they may be lawfully offered for sale and therein only by persons permitted to sell such securities. These securities have not been and will not be registered under the United States Securities Act of 1933, as amended. Accordingly, these securities may not be offered or sold within the United States of America and this short form prospectus does not constitute an offer to sell or a solicitation of an offer to buy any of these securities within the United States of America. **Information has been incorporated by reference in this short form prospectus from documents filed with securities commissions or similar authorities in Canada.** *Copies of the documents incorporated herein by reference may be obtained on request without charge from the Corporate Secretary of Lantic Sugar Limited, the administrator of the Fund, at 4026 Notre-Dame Street East, Montréal, Québec, H1W 2K3, telephone (514) 527-8686, and are also available electronically at www.sedar.com. For the purpose of the Province of Québec, this simplified prospectus contains information to be completed by consulting the permanent information record. A copy of the permanent information record may be obtained without charge from the Corporate Secretary of Lantic Sugar Limited at the above-mentioned address and telephone number and is also available electronically at www.sedar.com.*

Preliminary Short Form Prospectus

New Issue   February 7, 2006

ROGERS Sugar

ROGERS SUGAR INCOME FUND

$85,000,000

Third Series 5.90% Convertible Unsecured Subordinated Debentures

This short form prospectus qualifies the distribution (the "Offering") of $85,000,000 aggregate principal amount of Third Series 5.90% convertible unsecured subordinated debentures (the "Debentures") of Rogers Sugar Income Fund (the "Fund") due June 29, 2013 at a price of $1,000 per Debenture. The Debentures will bear interest at a rate of 5.90% per annum payable semi-annually on June 29 and December 29 in each year, commencing on June 29, 2006. Further particulars concerning the attributes of the Debentures are set out under "Description of the Debentures".

Each Debenture will be convertible into units of the Fund ("Trust Units") at the option of the holder at any time prior to 5:00 p.m. (Toronto time) on the earlier of June 29, 2013 and the business day immediately preceding the date specified by the Fund for redemption of the Debentures, at a conversion price of $5.10 per Trust Unit (the "Conversion Price"), being a conversion rate of 196.0784 Trust Units per $1,000 principal amount of Debentures, subject to adjustment in accordance with the terms of the trust indenture governing the terms of the Debentures. Further particulars concerning the conversion privilege, including provisions for the adjustment of the Conversion Price in certain events are set out under "Description of the Debentures — Conversion Privilege". **A holder of Debentures (a "Debentureholder") will not be entitled to deferred tax treatment on the conversion, redemption or repayment at maturity of such Debentures. See "Canadian Federal Income Tax Considerations".**

The Debentures are not redeemable prior to June 29, 2009. On or after June 29, 2009 and prior to June 29, 2011, the Debentures will be redeemable in whole or in part from time to time at the option of the Fund on not more than 60 days and not less than 30 days prior notice at a price equal to the principal amount thereof plus accrued and unpaid interest, provided that the weighted average trading price of the Trust Units on the Toronto Stock Exchange ("TSX") for the 20 consecutive trading days ending on the fifth trading day preceding the day prior to the date upon which the notice of redemption is given is at least 125% of the Conversion Price. On or after June 29, 2011 and prior to June 29, 2013, the Debentures may be redeemed in whole or in part from time to time at the option of the Fund on not more than 60 days and not less than 30 days prior notice at a price equal to the principal amount thereof plus accrued and unpaid interest.

On redemption or at maturity, the Fund may, at its option and subject to any required regulatory approvals, elect to satisfy its obligation to pay the principal amount of Debentures by issuing and delivering to the Debentureholders that number of Trust Units obtained by dividing the principal amount of the outstanding Debentures which are to be redeemed or have matured by 95% of the weighted average trading price of the Trust Units on the TSX for the 20 consecutive trading days ending on the fifth trading day preceding the date fixed for redemption or on maturity, as the case may be. See "Description of the Debentures — Payment Upon Redemption or Maturity".

There is currently no market through which the Debentures may be sold and purchasers may not be able to resell the Debentures. This may affect the pricing of the Debentures in the secondary market, the transparency and availability of trading prices,

continued

FIGURE 9.1 ANNOUNCEMENT OF A BOND ISSUE (CONTINUED)

the liquidity of the Debentures, and the extent of the Fund regulation. See "Risk Factors". The Fund has applied to have the Debentures and the Trust Units issuable upon conversion of the Debentures listed on the TSX. Listing will be subject to the Fund fulfilling all of the listing requirements of the TSX. The outstanding Trust Units are listed on the TSX under the symbol RSI.UN. On February 1, 2006, the last trading day prior to the announcement of the Offering, the closing price per Trust Unit on the TSX was $4.26.

No stability rating for the Debentures or the Trust Units (including the Trust Units issuable upon conversion of the Debentures) has been applied for or obtained from any rating agency.

A return on your investment in the Fund is not comparable to the return on an investment in a fixed-income security. The recovery of your initial investment is at risk, and the anticipated return on your investment is based on many performance assumptions. Although the Fund intends to make distributions of its available cash to holders of Trust Units ("Unitholders"), these cash distributions may be reduced or suspended. The ability of the Fund to make cash distributions and the actual amount distributed will depend on numerous factors, including the ability of Rogers Sugar Ltd. ("Rogers") and Lantic Sugar Limited ("Lantic") to pay their interest obligations under outstanding notes and to declare and pay dividends on or return capital in respect of their respective common shares, the debt covenants and obligations of the Fund, its working capital requirements and its future capital requirements. In addition, the market value of the Debentures may decline if the Fund is unable to meet its cash distribution targets in the future, and that decline may be significant.

An investment in the Debentures involves certain risks, including those that are described in the section entitled "Risk Factors" beginning on page 23. Prospective investors should consider such risks carefully prior to making an investment decision.

The after-tax return for any Trust Units acquired under the terms of a Debenture by Debentureholders which are subject to Canadian income tax and are Canadian residents will depend, in part, on the composition for tax purposes of distributions paid by the Fund (portions of which may be fully or partially taxable or may constitute tax deferred returns of capital). The adjusted cost base of Trust Units held by a Unitholder generally will be reduced by the non-taxable portion of distributions made to the Unitholder other than the portion thereof attributable to the non-taxable portion of certain capital gains. The composition for tax purposes of those distributions may change over time, thus affecting the after-tax return to Unitholders.

In the opinion of counsel, provided the Fund is a "mutual fund trust" within the meaning of the *Income Tax Act* (Canada) on the issue date, the Debentures will be qualified investments under the *Income Tax Act* (Canada) as at that date for certain deferred income plans. See "Canadian Federal Income Tax Considerations — Tax Exempt Unitholders" and "Eligibility for Investment".

Price: $1,000 per Debenture

	Price to the Public	Underwriters' Fee	Net Proceeds to the Fund[1]
Per Debenture	$ 1,000	$ 40	$ 960
Total Offering	$85,000,000	$ 3,400,000	$ 81,600,000

[1] Before deducting expenses of the Offering, estimated at $500,000.

Scotia Capital Inc., BMO Nesbitt Burns Inc., TD Securities Inc. and RBC Dominion Securities Inc. (collectively, the "Underwriters"), as principals, conditionally offer the Debentures for sale, subject to prior sale, if, as and when issued and delivered by the Fund and accepted by the Underwriters in accordance with the conditions contained in the Underwriting Agreement referred to under "Plan of Distribution" and subject to the approval of certain legal matters on behalf of the Fund by Davies Ward Phillips & Vineberg LLP and on behalf of the Underwriters by Osler, Hoskin & Harcourt LLP.

Subscriptions will be received subject to rejection or allotment in whole or in part and the right is reserved to close the subscription books at any time without notice. Book-entry only certificates representing the Debentures will be issued in registered form to the Canadian Depository for Securities Limited ("CDS") or its nominee as registered global securities and will be deposited with CDS on the closing of the Offering, which is expected to occur on or about March 7, 2006 or such later date as the Fund and the Underwriters may agree, but in any event not later than March 30, 2006. Debentureholders will not receive physical certificates representing their ownership of Debentures. See "Description of the Debentures — Book-Entry Delivery and Form".

Affiliates of two of the Underwriters are Canadian chartered banks which are lenders to or members of a syndicate of banks that have made credit facilities available to Rogers and/or Lantic. Consequently, the Fund may be considered to be a connected issuer of two of the Underwriters for the purposes of securities legislation in certain provinces. See "Plan of Distribution".

SOURCE: Rogers Sugar Ltd.

Service (DBRS), Standard & Poors (S&P), and Moody's Investors Services. The DBRS rating system is as follows:

- R-1 (high) is used to denote short-term debt of the highest quality.
- R-1 (middle) is used for short-term debt of a very high or superior credit quality.
- R-1 (low) is for short-term debt considered to have a satisfactory credit quality.
- R-2 (high) is used to describe debt at the upper end of adequate credit quality.

- R-2 (middle) is for credit quality that is only adequate.
- R-2 (low) is one step above speculative credit quality.
- R-3 (high), R-3 (middle), and R-3 (low) are considered to have speculative, or very poor, credit quality.
- D is very negative. This rating means that interest payments have not been met and will not be in the foreseeable future.

S&P uses a similar system but denotes credit quality by the letters AAA, A, BBB, BB, B, CCC, CC, and R. A bond with an AAA rating is risk-free. R is equivalent to the DBRS D. The Moody's system is the same as that used by S&P.

Examples of credit ratings follow:

- On February 7, 2006, DBRS rated Hudson's Bay Company Debentures Negative BB.
- On June 23, 2006, it rated Canadian Natural Resources Bonds BBB (high).
- Bonds issued by the federal government's Business Development Bank were given a credit rating of AAA, the highest possible.
- Bonds issued by municipalities usually have lower credit ratings than those issued by the two higher levels of government because of their more limited tax-raising ability. Thus bonds issued by both Calgary and Winnipeg have an R-1 rating.

Superficially, **junk bonds** resemble other bonds. They represent a loan made to the issuing company and a promise by the company to pay the lender interest until the bond matures, at which point the capital will be repaid. Where they differ is in the high interest the borrower must pay to attract investors. This is necessary because the borrower has a dreadful credit rating and its bonds are considered extremely risky. (One person's unexpected encounter with a junk bond is the subject of Personal Finance in Action Box 9.3.)

The Bond Market

There is no physical market for bonds as there is for stocks. Instead, there is an over-the-counter market, like that for unlisted stocks. Each investment dealer has a bond trading department that communicates with similar departments in other institutions. Trading in new issues begins once they have been sold. A record of all transactions is kept on the computer of the Canadian Depository for Securities. The same record will be on the investment dealer's computer.

Since there is no Toronto or Montreal bond exchange, the bond market is largely unknown in Canada. Even people who are not stockholders likely know of stock exchanges like the TSX and the NYSE. The operation of the bond market is known and understood by only a relative few, mainly investment professionals. Yet the size of the secondary bond market (after bonds have been issued) is very large. As of August 31, 2005, the market value of the S&P/TSX Canadian Bond Index of investment grade bonds was $638 million.[1] The value of shares traded on the TSX in 2005 was $99 605 million,[2] and Canada's GDP was worth $1 385 940 million.[3]

In the past everyone who purchased a bond received a certificate[4] stating the terms of the issue and the bond's par value or denomination. With the advent of computer technology,

[1]www.TSX.com/en/productsAndServices/marketData.
[2]www.statcan.ca.
[3]www.economist.com.
[4]There were two types of certificate, bearer and registered. **Bearer bonds** were unregistered and had no names on them. They no longer exist. Registered bonds, like stocks, have the owner's name on the certificate.

Personal FINANCE in action 9.3

Louisa and the Junk Bond

Louisa had been very close to her Uncle Fred, her grandfather's brother, often visiting him on her way home from school. Her aunt had died a number of years ago, and her uncle, who had done everything with his wife, lived alone and was lonely. Louisa's visits always cheered him up. When it was time for her to go to college, she decided on a nursing program that was only offered at a college 100 miles from her hometown. This would mean an end to her frequent visits to her uncle, but she told him that she would come home on weekends and would see him then. However, once she was settled into residence and made new friends, the number of visits home declined. Time passed, and after the Christmas break she received a phone call from her mother to say that Uncle Fred had died the night before and that the funeral would be in two days.

When Louisa got home, her mother told her, "Uncle Fred has left you something." Puzzled, she asked, "What is it?" Her mother said, "It's a small trunk I've put it in your bedroom." Louisa rushed up and saw the trunk on her dresser with a note, "For Louisa," on top. She opened it and saw that it was filled with old photographs and letters, but also a file marked "Investments." Excited, she opened the file and found it contained an automobile company bond for $5000.

Before she returned to college, Louisa took the bond to her father's investment advisor. She thought that if she could sell it, the money would help pay for her tuition. What she learned came as a bit of a shock. While the certificate said the bond was worth $5 000 and paid interest of 5 percent, the advisor told her this was no longer the case. Now, because of the problems facing the auto industry, her bond was only worth $3 750 and because the price was so much lower, it now yielded 15 percent. Normally, if she held the bond to maturity in 2010 she would get the face value for it, but the advisor said, "Since there is some doubt the company will still be around then, I recommend you sell it now while you can still get something for it. What you have is a junk bond that could easily become worthless."

this is no longer necessary. Bonds can now be held at an investment dealer just like stocks. This is much more convenient for the bond owner. Interest payments, like stock dividends, are deposited in the client's account and forwarded on a regular basis to the client's bank. Selling and redeeming bonds is also simpler since the client no longer has to sign off the bond certificate and mail it in. This system is known as the Book-Based System. The physical preparation and retention of a certificate is known as the Certificate-Based System.

Bond Issuers

Government of Canada Debt securities issued by the federal government are considered to be of the highest quality and to be safer than those of any other Canadian borrower. With its broad taxing powers, the government is unlikely to fail to pay interest on or to redeem the "Canadas," as Government of Canada bonds are often called. Since the federal government's need for borrowed money has declined in recent years, fewer "Canadas" have been issued. They are, as a result, very marketable. In addition to its own bonds, the Government of Canada guarantees bonds issued by various Crown corporations. Although the federal government also issues Canada Savings Bonds, these investments are more like savings certificates than bonds; they will therefore be considered separately (see "Canada Savings Bonds," later in this chapter).

Provincial Governments The provinces also issue bonds in their own right; as well, they guarantee the bond issues of those commissions, hydro-electric corporations, and school boards under their jurisdiction. As previously mentioned, provincial bonds are usually considered to be a notch or two below the "Canadas" in security. Quebec and Ontario are currently the largest bond issuers in Canada.

Municipalities Local governments issue debentures to pay for costly but long-lasting public projects such as streets, waterworks, schools, and hospitals. By issuing bonds, the municipality can spread the cost over a number of years. The provinces usually exert some regulatory control over the borrowing done by their municipalities, a fact that may be a comfort to investors. Because municipal debentures do not trade as frequently as the more senior provincial and federal debentures do, they are generally less marketable. The quality of a municipality's securities depends on its tax base: municipalities with a broader range of industries are preferable to single-industry towns or regions. The bond-rating agencies usually rank municipal debentures below provincial and federal issues, but generalizing is difficult because the budgets of some large Canadian cities exceed those of the smallest provinces.

Corporations When long-term funding is needed, corporations issue a variety of bonds and debentures; a few types will be mentioned here. If a corporation's credit rating is high enough, unsecured debentures may be issued; otherwise, corporate bonds must be backed by some type of security. As a loan that is secured by property, a **mortgage bond** is similar to any mortgage. But because corporations borrow such large sums, each such loan is divided into smaller units, enabling a number of investors to be involved. Property that is put up as security will be used to compensate bondholders if the corporation should default. Among mortgage bonds, as with home mortgages, there are first-mortgage bonds and second-mortgage bonds; the "first" and "second" designations indicate the order in which creditors would rank in the case of compensation claims.

If a corporation has neither a high-enough credit rating to borrow with unsecured debentures nor any property to offer as security, it may issue **collateral trust bonds**, which are secured with financial assets held by the company, such as bonds and stocks.

Special Features

Bonds and debentures are often issued with special characteristics. They may be callable, convertible, extendible, or retractable. Some of these features are intended to make an issue more attractive to investors.

Callable Some bond certificates state that the issuer can recall the bond before the maturity date; such instruments are known as callable bonds. When borrowers wish to reserve the right to pay off bond debt before maturity, they issue **callable bonds**. The call or redemption feature usually includes an agreement to give the bondholder a month's notice of the intention to call them in. The issuer may agree to pay the owner somewhat more than the bond's face value as compensation for the early recall, although the Government of Canada usually does not do so. Bonds are assumed to be non-callable unless otherwise designated. With a call feature, the initiative remains with the issuer; bondholders do not have the option of redeeming a callable bond whenever they wish. Unless the bond is called by the issuer, investors who want to sell a callable bond must either find a buyer or wait until the maturity date. Personal Finance in Action Box 9.4, "A Bond Redemption," illustrates the recall of a bond issue.

Personal FINANCE in action 9.4

A Bond Redemption

Brenda, recently widowed, knew little about investing, having devoted her life to raising her three children and doing charitable work. At a bereavement group meeting, she had met a widower who had worked on the bond desk at a major investment house. On his advice she had invested in an Aliant Telecom Inc (formerly the Maritime Telegraph and Telephone Company) bond because of its high yield of 10.45 percent and the company's excellent reputation. Last week she received the following notice:

■ On March 1, 2006, the company will redeem all of its outstanding 10.45 percent, First Mortgage Bonds, Series AD, due March 1, 2013.

■ The redemption price will be equal to 101.00 percent of the $50 million principal amount.

■ Bondholders will receive the regular semi-annual interest payment on March 1, 2006.*

When she asked the widower why the company was doing this he said because interest rates had dropped so much since the bond was issued it could refinance a new issue at much less cost.

* **www.bce.ca/en/news/releases/aliant/2006/01/30/73301.html** (accessed February 8, 2006).

Convertible Bonds with a clause that gives the bondholder the option of exchanging the security for a specified number of the issuing company's common shares are called **convertible bonds**. The terms of the conversion, which are established when the bonds are issued, do not change. This feature gives the holder of a debt security the possibility of capital gain. The investor would profit if, in the future, the price of the borrowing company's common stock should rise above the set conversion price. The option of converting to common stock may help support the price of a bond, which might otherwise drop. The terms of one series of convertible debentures are shown in Personal Finance in Action Box 9.5, "Conversion Terms."

Extendible Sometimes bonds or debentures with short maturities carry an extendible feature. This feature of **extendible bonds** allows the bondholder to extend the maturity date, perhaps for 10 years, at the same or a slightly higher interest rate.

Retractable Long-term bonds that carry an option permitting the holder to shorten the maturity are called **retractable bonds**. This feature may attract investors who are willing to accept a slightly lower interest rate in exchange for this flexibility.

Floating Rate A **floating interest rate bond** is issued during a period of rapidly changing interest rates. The interest rate on such bonds is periodically adjusted in relation to the treasury bill rate. With this feature, neither the lender nor the borrower is locked into a set interest rate. Which of the parties—that is, the lender or the borrower—benefits in the long run depends on which way interest rates move. The price of floating rate bonds fluctuates very little, but their rate normally varies every six months.

Sinking Fund Provision Many debt securities carry a **sinking fund** provision, meaning that the issuer will be setting aside sums of money each year to provide for their redemption.

Personal FINANCE in action 9.5

Conversion Terms

Imhran and Faisal had worked for two years at the Royal Bank's call centre. In the process they learned a lot about banking, but they had become bored with their jobs. They decided it would be more interesting and more lucrative if they became Certified Financial Analysts. With this in mind, they enrolled in the Canadian Securities Course offered at their local college. When the course reached the section on Investment Products: Fixed Income Securities, they learned about bonds and debentures and were given the following example:

On October 31, 2005, Provident Energy Trust announced a public offering of $150 000 000

extendible, convertible, unsecured, subordinated debentures with an interest rate of 6.50 percent, payable semi-annually on April 30 and October 31. (An unsecured debenture is a loan that is not secured, or backed, by any collateral or asset. A subordinated debenture is unsecured debt that ranks below secured debt in its claim on assets and earnings.) The debentures are convertible into units of the Provident Energy Trust, at the holder's option, at a price of $14.75 per trust unit at any time prior to the close of business on the maturity date, April 30, 2011.

These funds are held in trust by a trustee—usually a trust company—until needed. A sinking fund provision is useful to the corporation as a way of reducing debt, but not particularly helpful to the investor, who may not want to have the bonds recalled before maturity.

Buying and Selling Bonds As mentioned, there is no bricks-and-mortar bond exchange. Yet the bond market in Canada is the main source of borrowing for governments as well as for the corporate sector. Buying bonds in both the primary (new issue) and secondary (those previously released) bond markets is dominated by investment dealers, insurance companies, and pension and mutual fund companies. New issues are advertised within the financial industry and sold by underwriters to interested parties, without the bidding process that takes place in the stock market. Investment dealers have lists of all available bonds on their computers along with all the relevant details. They buy new issues both for their own portfolios and also in order to sell some to their clients.

Spread in Bond Prices

Consider the following bond quotation:

Bell Canada 7.0 percent due 24 September 2007, bid 106.472, ask 107.472.

Until you are familiar with bond quotations, this little paragraph may not mean much to you. Here's what it says in English: Bell Canada is issuing a $1000 bond that may be either sold to a broker for $1064.72 or purchased for $1074.72.

The spread between these two prices represents the broker's commission. The amount of the spread depends on both the trading activity in a particular bond and the size of the transaction. If a certain issue of bonds trades thinly, the broker may have more difficulty finding a buyer or seller and thus may take a larger spread. Investors who place large bond orders are able to negotiate a smaller spread per bond than a small investor can. The minimum spread is generally around $10.

Small investors may buy individual bonds from their dealers. They can also participate easily in the bond market by buying units of bond funds. Each fund company has a number of such funds, and the MER (Management Expense Ratio, see Chapter 10) is usually lower than that for equity funds.

Suppose you are holding a bond that will not mature for many years, but you need the cash now. In this situation, you must find a buyer for your bond. Bonds are bought and sold on the **bond market** or "over the counter." When you, the investor, inform your broker that you have a bond to sell, your broker, in turn, sends this information to other brokers, one of whom may have a client who is interested in buying that very bond. Alternatively, an investment dealer may purchase the bond from you. In the distribution of bonds, investment dealers may act either as principals or as agents. They are said to be acting *as principals* when they buy bonds for resale to the public. Conversely, they are said to be acting *as agents* when, rather than buying the bonds for their own account, they just try to link would-be buyers with would-be sellers.

Commission is not charged on bonds; instead, investment dealers add their profit to the buying or selling price. The difference between the base price and the dealer's marked-up price is sometimes called the **spread**. The spread is greater for bonds that are less frequently traded and for small orders of bonds (see the boxed feature "Spread in Bond Prices" for an example).

Bond Price Fluctuation   When a bond is issued, the interest rate is fixed for the entire term, which may be 10, 20, or more years. But economic conditions generally cause interest rates to change during that period. This fluctuation creates a problem for anyone who wishes, for instance, to sell a bond that is paying 5 percent when rates on other, more-recently issued debt securities are closer to 10 percent. To interest a purchaser, the seller will have to lower the price of the bond below par—a process known as selling it **at a discount**. Likewise, if interest rates have fallen since this bond was issued, it can be sold for a price greater than par—or sold **at a premium**.

Yield to Maturity   In the financial world, **yield** usually means the annual return from an investment expressed as a percentage of its market price. In the case of bonds, the time value of future interest and the time value of the principal payments are taken into account. Payments received in the near future are worth more to the investor than those received in the uncertain, distant future. A precise calculation of bond yield to maturity takes into account the present value of interest payments and the present value of the principal repayment at maturity. Bond traders use a complex formula to make this calculation. The simple method used in the Personal Finance in Action Box 9.6, "Bond Prices and Yields," serves to show how the nominal interest rate and the potential capital gain or loss can influence the yield. (The results from calculations made using this method will be somewhat different from those found in bond yield quotations, since here we have made no adjustment for the time value effect.)

If you hold a bond until maturity, you can expect to receive the bond's face value, regardless of the price you paid for it. But if you sell the bond prior to maturity, you may experience either a capital gain or a capital loss. So when buying a bond, you must take into account the possibility of capital gain or loss, in addition to the amount of interest the bond will pay.

Accrued Interest   Bond interest is paid on fixed dates, usually every six months from the date of issue. This situation presents problems for people who buy and sell bonds, who may transfer ownership at any time. Whoever owns the bond on the interest payment date will receive six months' interest, but this person may have held the bond for only two months. The

Bond Prices and Yields

Danielle received a $20 000 Government of Canada bond as part of her divorce settlement from Andrew. It pays 5 percent interest and matures on June 1, 2010. Now that her son and daughter have left home, she is considering using the money as a down payment on a cottage on a nearby lake. She thinks this will encourage her children and grandchildren to visit her. She learns that if she sells the bond, she will make a capital gain of $2101. Interest rates have come down since she acquired the bond, and each $1000 bond is now worth $1110.05. If she keeps the bond, but does not want to pay capital gains tax, she will continue to earn interest of $1000 per year.

Paolo bought a Domtar bond for $21 499 with the money from his early retirement buy-out. The yield he will earn on this bond can be determined in the following way:

Face value	$20 000
Purchase price	$21 494
Nominal rate of interest	5%
Maturity date	April 15, 2015
Time to maturity	9.3 years
Date of purchase	November 29, 2005

The average annual return from this bond, if held to maturity, will consist of the interest paid on the bond minus the capital loss.

Annual interest	$1000
Capital loss over 11 years	$1494
Average annual capital loss	$1494/9.3 = $160.65
Total average annual return	$1000 − $160.65 = $839.35

$$\text{Annual yield to maturity} = \frac{\text{aver. annual return} \times 100}{\text{purchase price}}$$

$$= \frac{\$839.35 \times 100}{\$21\ 494}$$

$$= 3.91\%$$

Why is Paolo's yield to maturity less than Danielle's?

seller should not lose four months' interest because the bond was sold to someone else. The solution is to charge the buyer **accrued interest**, which is the amount that is owing but that has not yet been paid. Bonds are therefore sold at a certain price plus accrued interest. The buyer pays the seller for the interest due to date and recovers that amount in the next interest payment. Personal Finance in Action Box 9.7, "Accrued Interest," clarifies this process.

Bond Quotations Financial papers do not provide as much information about bond quotations as they do about stock prices because of the difficulty of collecting these data; bond trades are not concentrated on a few exchanges in the way that stock transactions are. Bond quotations may be found in *The Financial Post* or in the "Report on Business" section of each Monday's *Globe and Mail*. In these quotations, bond prices are given in hundreds, and bonds from the same issuer are distinguished by the interest rate and the maturity date. Therefore, the quote "8 percent Canadas of 1 June 2027" means that this issue of Government of Canada bonds

Personal FINANCE in action 9.7

Accrued Interest

Moriath bought a $1000 Government of Canada bond on February 3, 2006. It matures on June 1, 2025, and has a nominal rate of interest of 9 percent. However, since this rate was much higher than the current rate, she had to pay a premium of $62.04 per hundred, or $620.40, for a total cost of $1620.40, and will only receive interest of 5.554 percent (9 percent divided by $162.04). The bond pays interest every June 1, and when Moriath bought the bond, she learned that she had to pay accrued interest to the previous owner. At the time of purchase, eight months' interest was owed. She therefore had to pay $60.00 in interest ($1000 × 0.094 × 8/12). On June 1, she will receive four months' interest of $30.00.

carries an interest rate of 8 percent and will mature on June 1, 2027. The quotation will also give a recent price at which these bonds have traded, and the yield to maturity (see Table 9.4).

Strip Bonds

The **strip bond** is another fixed income security. A bond is stripped of its interest payments, and the stripped bond and the interest, or coupon belonging to the bond,[5] are sold separately. Both are sold at a discount. During the term to maturity, the bond minus its interest pays no interest, but at maturity, the holder receives the full face value. The interest the holder receives will be the difference between the discounted purchase price and the matured value. Such bonds, minus their coupons, are widely held in tax-sheltered retirement accounts where the interest is not taxed until the accounts are wound up. They are not popular outside such accounts because the interest earned must be declared each year but is not actually received until the bond matures.

The holder of the coupon, also purchased at a discount, receives the interest, or coupon rate, on the scheduled interest payment dates. Coupons are also popular in retirement accounts because small amounts, as low as pennies, can be invested, with maturities ranging from six months to 10 years, or more. This allows an investor to create a ladder with different interest rates in order to benefit from rate increases.

As with regular bonds, strip bonds and their underlying bonds trade in the over-the-counter market. The market for the latter is more liquid than that for the strips.

TABLE 9.4   BOND QUOTATIONS, FEBRUARY 3, 2006

ISSUER	MATURITY	COUPON	BID	ASK	BID YIELD	BID ASK
Canada	June 1, 2033	5.750	$124.65	$124.81	4.22	4.21
BC	Sept. 8, 2023	8.00	$140.99	$141.55	4.58	4.54
Saskatchewan	Dec. 3, 2012	5.250	$105.71	$105.97	4.27	4.23
Bell	May 1, 2024	6.550	None*	$110.54		5.72
Canadian Tire	April 13, 2028	6.250	None	$105.32		5.82
Coca-Cola						
Canada	March 11, 2009	5.85	$104.19	$104.43	4.39	4.31

*There were no bids for either the Bell or Canadian Tire bonds.

SOURCE: The *Globe and Mail*, February 4, 2006.

[5]In the past, bonds came with interest coupons attached. These were clipped and deposited at a bank when the interest payment was due. Coupons no longer exist, but bond interest is often referred to as the coupon rate.

TABLE 9.5   MARKET PRICE VOLATILITY

	MARKET PRICE	MARKET YIELD	PRICE (WHEN RATE DROPS TO 5%)	%PRICE CHANGE	PRICE (WHEN RATE RISES TO 7%)	%PRICE CHANGE
6% 5-Year Bond	$100.00	6.00%	$104.38	+4.38%	$95.84	−4.16%
5-Year Strip Bond	$74.41	6.00%	$78.12	+4.99	$70.89	−4.73%

SOURCE: Investment Dealers Association of Canada, "Strip Bonds and Strip Bond Packages."

The strip bond market is also more volatile than the regular bond market because no interest is paid on the strip before maturity, and the holder is therefore unable to reinvest interest payments at the new rates before maturity. An example of such volatility can be seen in Table 9.5.

Dealers usually pool the strip bond funds and give a deposit receipt or certificate. These go by a variety of names, depending on who issues them: examples include TIGRs (Treasury Investment Growth Receipts, stripped US treasuries, or US government debt, with a fixed income and varying maturities), Cougars, and Sentinels. In the latter case, the investor has a share in a pool of coupons or residuals that are held in trust. These certificates are registered in the name of the investor, who may sell them at any time on the secondary market. The sale price, which changes with general interest rates, will generally fluctuate more than bond prices. The purchase price of strip bonds reflects current interest rates and the time value of money, or the time the investor has to wait to receive the yield. The market offers investors discounted coupons that mature every six months.

Taxation of Bond Yield

Bond yield consists of interest income and the possibility of capital gain or loss if the bond is traded before maturity. Interest and capital gains are taxed differently. Interest is added to taxable income and taxed accordingly. Only 50 percent of a capital gain is taxed (see Personal Finance in Action Box 9.8, "What Has Happened to Our Income?").

The differential tax treatment of interest and capital gain provides an incentive for some investors to prefer to receive their bond return in the form of capital gain rather than in interest. The yield from stripped bonds is considered by Canada Revenue Taxation to be interest, not capital gain; for this reason, such bonds are often selected as a component in self-administered RRSP accounts, where the return is tax-sheltered. If strip bonds are not held inside a tax shelter, accrued interest must be reported annually, even if it is not received.

Canada Savings Bonds

Although they are called bonds, **Canada Savings Bonds** (CSBs) are actually very different from bonds and debentures. They are more like savings certificates. Since they cannot be traded but can only be redeemed, their value does not fluctuate. Canada Savings Bonds developed from Victory bonds, which were issued between 1940 and 1944 to help Canada fight World War II. Although they were an important part of the federal government's borrowing for over 50 years, they have become less so in recent years as the government's need for funds has declined.

Personal FINANCE in action 9.8

What Has Happened to Our Income?

Jan and Paul took early retirement in 1985 when they were 55. At the time, all of their savings were in bonds and GICs, earning interest at an average rate of 10 percent per year. This arrangement seemed excellent at the time they retired. But in the early years of the twenty-first century, interest rates dropped to their lowest levels in 30 years. For example, the highest rate they could get on their GICs was 3.75 percent. As a result, the couple's income had seriously declined. Jan and Paul now wondered whether they could continue to support themselves in the future.

When they retired, they owned $500 000 in GICs and government bonds. These securities had provided them with a healthy income of $50 000 a year, quite adequate in 1985. However, by 2006, since they had left their money in GICs, they were only earning $18 750 a year and felt financially stressed. Jan and Paul became very worried. Their friend Vince, a financial planner they had known since their university days, told them that to increase their capital and have a healthier financial future, they should invest in common stocks. Banks and utilities were his favourites: they pay good dividends, and their shares tend to increase in value. While capital gains are never guaranteed, Vince pointed out that bank stocks had been excellent performers in recent years because of Canada's low inflation. The stock of one bank he liked had tripled in four years. The economy was healthy and both inflation and interest rates were low. In addition, because of the favourable treatment of dividend income by Revenue Canada, Jan and Paul would pay less income tax. Whatever capital gains they made would not be taxed until they sold their investments. Vince suggested that they not sell these stocks unless absolutely necessary, since stocks perform best over the long term. He also pointed out that unless they switch a large portion of their investments to stocks, the purchasing power of their capital would decrease in value as time passed, as a result of inflation.

Features

A new series of CSBs goes on sale on October 1 each year. In the past, those sold directly, versus those sold through the payroll deduction plan, were only available for a few weeks. This changed recently. The bonds are now sold each year from October 1 to April 1. CSBs may be bought at any bank, trust company, credit union, or investment dealer. They may also be purchased through a payroll deduction plan. No commission is charged when CSBs are bought or redeemed. They may be redeemed for their face value on any business day and are thus very liquid. If redeemed within three months of their purchase, however, no interest is paid.

Canada Savings Bonds are considered low-risk investments because they always retain their face value. They have proven to be very popular with Canadians, especially the young. The interest paid is so low, however, that they have lost much of their appeal. Series 100, for example, issued in 2005–2006, only paid 2 percent in the first year. Interest for subsequent years will be announced later, when the future of interest on fixed income investments becomes clearer. While 2 percent may be low, it is an improvement on the 1.30 percent paid on the Series 76 and 77 bonds issued in 2002. The risk, therefore, when one buys a CSB is that the purchasing power of the funds invested will decline. This will surely happen if they are kept for any length of time. This risk is compounded when one realizes that the interest paid on the bonds is taxed at the highest possible level. Many seniors who have seen their income from CSBs and GICs seriously decline have turned instead to the higher-yielding income and royalty trusts.

CSBs may only be purchased by citizens of Canada. Regular interest bonds are available in denominations of $300, $500, $1000, $5000, and $10 000. They pay interest each November 1. Compound interest bonds, for which interest is reinvested annually, may be purchased for as little as $100, in addition to the denominations of the regular bonds. The maximum amount of each series that may be purchased is $500 000 for each type of registration. If someone wished, therefore, she could have $500 000 in her own name, $500 000 registered jointly, and the same amount registered in an RRSP.

As can be seen, CSBs do not have the features normally associated with bonds. They cannot be traded. They may only be redeemed, that is, returned to the Bank of Canada for cancellation, not sold to another party. The price does not fluctuate but remains constant. The rate of interest is not announced for the term of the issue, only the first year.

Canada Premium Bonds

Of greater interest to risk-averse investors than CSBs are the **Canada Premium Bonds**. (See Personal Finance in Action Box 9.9, "Canada Savings Bonds, Premium Bonds, or Common Shares," for an example of a choice between CSBs, premium bonds, and common stock.) They are also issued once a year by the Bank of Canada but may only be redeemed on the anniversary of their issue and for 30 days thereafter. They are not really bonds, either, but they do pay higher interest.

Personal FINANCE in action 9.9

The Investment Decision: CSBs, Premium Bonds, or Common Shares

Aramanta was now 30 years old. She had been working since she was 22, when she had graduated from college. Single, she had saved quite a sum of money, most of which she had put into Canada Savings Bonds, as her parents recommended. They had moved to Canada from Venezuela and were very conservative with their investments.

Aramanta had her doubts about CSBs. A quick search on the internet told her that the current bonds were only paying 2.00 percent. While viewing the Government of Canada site, she noticed that Premium Bonds were paying 2.50 percent, also not very exciting. Recently, she had read that Stephen Jarislowsky, who ran an investment management firm in Montreal, had been highly critical of bonds and said that investors were far better off with good dividend-paying stocks. In addition to the dividend income, he pointed out, stocks also had the potential for capital gains.

After further research, Aramanta decided to buy shares in Great-West Life, a leading insurance company that does business in Canada, the United States, and Europe, because of the following:

■ In February 2006, one share cost $29.49. In 1997, one share had been worth $9.63, which meant it had appreciated by 32.66 percent.

■ Neither of the two bonds would increase in value.

■ The dividend was .84 per share.

■ The yield was 2.85 percent, but because of the strange way dividends are taxed, is actually 3.648 percent [dividend per share = .84 plus gross-up of (45% × 0.378) = $1.218 – dividend tax credit of (19% × 0.23) = .988], considerably better than the bonds.

For example, series P 50, which matures in 2016, declared the following rates for the first three years:

- Year 1, 2006 2.50 percent
- Year 2, 2007 3.25 percent
- Year 3, 2008 4.00 percent

The rate for the three years, with interest compounded annually, is 3.24 percent. The rates for the following eight years will be announced once the Bank of Canada has a clear idea of what interest rates will be like in the future.

Income Tax

Before 1991, holders of compound interest bonds were allowed to choose one of two possible ways of reporting interest: (i) as received (that is, on a cash basis) or (ii) as earned (that is, on a receivable basis). As a result of revisions to the *Income Tax Act*, interest on bonds purchased since 1990 must be reported annually, whether or not it has been received.

Savings Bonds Versus Other Bonds

Despite their name, Canada Savings Bonds lack many of the attributes of bonds. Instead, think of them as a type of savings certificate. The unique features of CSBs are listed below:

(a) **Sale**—They are sold directly to investors, are not traded on the bond market, are not transferable, and carry no commission charges.
(b) **Eligibility**—Distribution is limited to Canadian residents.
(c) **Redemption**—Face value is available on any business day.
(d) **Denominations**—CSBs are available in smaller denominations than other bonds.
(e) **Types**—There are two types: regular interest bonds (interest mailed annually) and compound interest bonds (interest paid at redemption or maturity).
(f) **Annual interest**—Interest is paid each November on regular interest CSBs. The income must be reported annually.

Summary

- Term deposits, now rare, are deposits accepted by a financial institution for a short term at specified interest rates. Guaranteed Investment Certificates (GICs) are fixed income investments that guarantee the return of principal. Deposit insurance comes with certain forms of debt including bank accounts, GICs, T-bills, CSBs, and Canada Premium bonds. It is provided by the Canada Deposit Insurance Corporation and guarantees the money deposited in this way. Chequing accounts have no, or very low, interest but allow cheques to be written; the exact number varies by both account and institution. Ladder GICs in a portfolio mature at different times to take advantage of higher interest rates.
- The money market is the market for fixed income securities of less than one year. A money market fund is a mutual fund that allows small investors to participate in the money market. Treasury bills (T-bills) are short-term debt securities sold at a discount by the Bank of Canada. Commercial paper is short-term debt issued by a corporation. Bankers' acceptances are short-term promissory notes. Bearer-deposit notes are bankers' acceptances issued by a bank.

■ Asset-backed securities (ABSs) are bonds supported or backed by a pool of assets. Collateral trust bonds are the same as ABSs. Mortgage-backed securities are similar to ABSs. They are backed by a pool of residential mortgages, and the investor receives a payment each month comprising both interest and principal.

■ Bonds are debt securities issued for more than one year in order to raise capital. Debentures are unsecured debt securities. Unsecured debentures are not backed or secured by any assets. Subordinated debentures are unsecured bonds that only receive interest after secured bonds. Compounding is the frequency with which interest payments are added to a debt security to become part of the capital. Interest rate is the return paid to the holder of a debt security by the issuer.

■ Underwriters are securities dealers who agree to buy some or all of a new bond issue to resell to their clients. Par value is the face value, or issuing value, of a bond. Once bonds are sold the value fluctuates. Bond ratings tell investors the credit quality, or risk, of bonds. Junk bonds are very risky and have the worst credit rating.

■ The bond market is an invisible market that links parties in the investment industry by communications. Callable bonds may be redeemed by the issuer prior to maturity. Convertible bonds allow the holder to convert a bond into shares or units of the issuing company. Extendible bonds allow the holder to extend the maturity date at the same interest rate. Retractable bonds may be redeemed by the holder prior to maturity. Floating-rate debentures have interest rates that fluctuate because they are tied to a money market index. Sinking funds allow the bond issuer to redeem a certain percentage of bonds each year with funds set aside for this purpose.

■ Term is the length of time between the date a bond is issued and when it matures. Spread is the difference between the price an investment dealer pays for a bond issue and what it sells it for. Yield is the percentage return on debt instruments. It fluctuates on bonds. As the price of a bond goes up, the yield falls, and vice versa. Accrued interest is interest owed to a bondholder who sells a bond before the date of an interest payment. The interest is accrued from the date of the last payment to the sale date. Strip bonds are separated from their coupons (interest) and sold at a discount.

■ Canada Savings Bonds (CSBs) are not bonds but savings certificates sold by the Bank of Canada. Canada Premium Bonds are like CSBs but with a higher rate of interest.

Key Terms

accrued interest (p. 283)	Canada Savings Bonds (p. 285)
asset-backed securities (p. 273)	collateral trust bonds (p. 279)
at a discount (p. 282)	commercial paper (p. 270)
at a premium (p. 282)	convertible bonds (p. 280)
bankers' acceptances (p. 270)	debentures (p. 274)
bearer bonds (p. 277)	deposit insurance (p. 269)
bearer-deposit notes (p. 270)	extendible bonds (p. 280)
bonds (p. 274)	floating interest rate bond (p. 280)
bond market (p. 282)	floating-rate debentures (p. 273)
bond ratings (p. 275)	guaranteed investment
callable bonds (p. 279)	certificate (GIC) (p.268)
Canada Premium Bonds (p. 287)	junk bonds (p. 277)

ladder GICs *(p. 268)*	sinking fund *(p. 280)*
money market *(p. 270)*	spread *(p. 282)*
money market fund *(p. 271)*	strip bond *(p. 284)*
mortgage bond *(p. 279)*	term deposits *(p. 266)*
mortgage-backed securities *(p 273)*	treasury bills *(p. 271)*
par value *(p. 274)*	underwriters *(p. 274)*
retractable bonds *(p. 280)*	yield *(p. 282)*

Problems

1. On January 31, 2006, *The Globe and Mail* reported the following information about interest rates and yields:

	Bank Rate
Bank of Canada (overnight rate)	3.5%
Prime	5.25%
	Canadian Yields
one-month commercial paper	3.55%
three-month treasury bills	3.54%
three-month commercial paper	3.68%
six-month treasury bills	3.67%
30-year Canada bonds	4.25%

Look in a financial section of a recent newspaper or on the internet to find current rates and revise, if necessary.

(a) What is meant by the overnight rate? The prime?

(b) If the rates have changed, try to determine why.

(c) What is the difference between commercial paper and treasury bills?

(d) Why is the rate for three-month commercial paper higher than that for three-month T-bills?

(e) Who sells commercial paper? How much money is required to buy some?

(f) Why is the prime so much higher than the overnight rate?

 2. Go to **www.finpipe.com/tradebnds.htm** and answer the following:

(a) How do bonds trade?

(b) What must an investment company have if it wishes to trade in bonds?

(c) How do bond dealers make money?

(d) Who are the major bond investors?

(e) How large might a bond trade be?

(f) What is meant by a basis point?

3. Go to **www.answers.com/topic/michael-milken** and answer the following:

   (a) Who was Michael Milken?
   (b) What was his salary in 1986 and 1987?
   (c) How did he finance corporate takeovers?
   (d) What was his punishment?

4. The following bond quotations were in the paper recently:

   ■ Consumers Gas 7.60%, October 29, 2026 at $129.65 to yield 5.24%.
   ■ Prince Edward Island 4.6505%, November 19, 2037 at $97.24 to yield 4.82%.

   (a) When these bonds were issued, what would they have cost an investor?
   (b) Are they now selling at a premium or at a discount? Why?
   (c) What would your yield to maturity be if you bought the first bond on October 29, 2006, and the second on November 19, 2006?
   (d) Why are the yields not the same as the coupon rates?

5. (a) Compare the features of a Canada Savings Bond with those of a regular bond.
   (b) What is the maximum amount that anyone can put into one issue of a CSB?
   (c) If you had this kind of money, would you use it to buy a CSB?
   (d) Is there a better return on other fixed income investments?

6. Which bonds, issued in Canada, have the highest credit rating and the lowest? Why do you think this is so?

7. Explain the following bond features: callable; convertible; extendible; retractable. If you wanted to invest in a bond, which of these features would you want the bond to have?

8. Explain what is meant by the bond spread.

9. Explain the purpose of the Canada Deposit Insurance Corporation? Which of the following are insured by it? What is the limit of the coverage?

   (a) corporate bonds
   (b) savings accounts
   (c) mortgage-backed securities
   (d) strip bonds
   (e) GICs
   (f) chequing accounts
   (g) money market funds

10. (a) Explain what is meant by the money market.
    (b) Who participates in this market, and where is it located?
    (c) What securities are traded in the money market?

11. (a) Should the newer kinds of GICs, which are linked to stock market indices, be included in a chapter on debt securities?
    (b) How do they differ from other investments mentioned in this chapter?

12. (a) What is the advantage of a strip bond over a regular bond for investors of an advanced age?

(b) What is the difference between the two parts of the strip?

(c) Which of the following is similar to the capital portion of the strip: CSBs; GICs; T- bills; mortgage-backed securities?

13. You are a 25-year-old investor with a good income and no dependents (and no plan to acquire any dependents). You can therefore invest a large sum of money. Would you put this money into CSBs, GICs, or high-yielding common stock with excellent growth potential? Explain with reference to interest, dividends, and capital gains.

14. Assume that on February 10, 2006, you bought a $1000 Bell Canada 6.550 percent bond maturing on May 01, 2029.

(a) How much accrued interest would you have paid?

(b) Why did you have to pay this? To whom?

(c) If you bought this bond for $108.97 per hundred, what would your capital gain or loss be at maturity?

15. Use your computer to search for *Junk Bonds—The Sexiest Investment*.

(a) Why are such bonds alluring even when they are dangerous?

(b) Why are they dangerous?

(c) What kind of rating do they receive?

(d) What category does the author put them in? Do you think this is justified?

16. Moody's Investors Service rates the performance of corporations. The ratings determine the interest rates corporations must offer if they want to raise money through the sale of bonds. Go to **www.moodys.com**, Moody's website. You will need to create a user name and password to access their ratings information. There is no charge.

(a) Find out what the following credit ratings mean: Aaa, Aa, A, Baa, Ba, B, Caa, Ca, and C.

(b) Go to Quick Search and find out what rating Moody's gave to Bombardier, Suncor Energy, Air Canada, and Thomson.

(c) Find out what corporate developments caused Moody's to give such poor ratings to Bombardier and Air Canada. This information can be found by clicking on the Research Links under the ratings data for each corporation.

17. Moody's, and the ratings similar companies give, can make a great difference to the cost of raising money. Suncor, for example, recently issued a bond maturing in 2011 with a yield of 4.08 percent. A recent Bombardier's bond offering matures in 2026 and yields 8.02 percent. The length of this bond is partly responsible, but the poor credit rating is the main reason for the high interest Bombardier had to pay. How much more does Bombardier have to pay per year on a $100-million loan as a result of the Moody's rating? How will this affect the company's long-term growth?

References

BOOKS

Altman, Edward I. *Bankruptcy, Credit Risk and High Junk Bond Yields*. Edinburgh: Blackwell Publishers, 2001.

Altman, Edward I., and Scott A. Nammacher. *Investing in Junk Bonds: Inside the High Yield Debt Market*. Toronto: McGraw-Hill Ryerson, 2002.

Babson, Roger Ward. *The New Method of Investing Money: Economic Facts for Corporations and Investors*. Toronto: Books for Business, 2001.

Barnhill, Theodore, Mark Shenkman, and William Maxwell. *High Bond Yields: Market Structure, Valuation and Portfolio Strategies*. Toronto: McGraw-Hill Ryerson, 1999.

Brandes, Michael V. *Naked Guide to Bonds: What You Need to Know—Stripped Down to the Basics*. Toronto: Wiley & Sons, 2003.

Canadian Bankers Association. *The Interest in Your Life*. Toronto: Canadian Bankers Association, 1998.

Choudry, Moorad. *The Bond and Money Markets: Strategy, Trading, Analysis*. Oxford, UK: Butterworth-Heinemann, 2003.

Choudry, Moorad. *Introduction to Bond Markets*. Toronto: Wiley & Sons, 2006.

Crescenzi, Anthony. *The Strategic Bond Investor: Strategies & Tools to Unlock the Power of the Bond Market*. Toronto: McGraw-Hill Ryerson, 2002.

Fabozzi, Frank J. *Handbook of Fixed Income Securities*. 6th Edition. Toronto: McGraw-Hill Ryerson, 2000.

Fabozzi, Frank J. *Bond Markets: Analysis and Strategies*. 5th Edition. Toronto: Pearson, 2004.

Homer, Sydney, and Martin L. Leibowitz. *Inside the Yield Book: The Classic That Created the Science of Bond Analysis*. Princeton, NJ: Bloomberg, 2004.

Investment Dealers Association of Canada. *An Introduction To Bonds*. Toronto: IDAOC.

Investment Dealers Association of Canada. *A Question and Answer Guide to Bond Investing*. Toronto: IDAOC.

Investment Dealers Association of Canada. *Strip Bonds and Strip Bond Packages: Information Statement*. Toronto: IDAOC, 1998.

Moyer, Stephen G. *Distressed Debt Strategies: Strategies for Speculative Investors*. Toronto: McGraw-Hill Ryerson, 2004.

Phillips, George A. *Convertible Bond Markets*. New York: Palgrave, 1997.

Platt, Harlan D. *The First Junk Bond: A Corporate Boom and Bust*. Frederick, MD: Beard Books, 2002.

Richelson, Hildy, and Stan Richelson. *The Money-Making Guide to Bonds: Straightforward Strategies for Picking the Right Bonds and Bond Funds*. Princeton, NJ: Bloomberg Press, 2002.

Scott, David. *David Scott's Guide to Investing in Bonds*. Washington: Houghton Mifflin, 2004.

Shelmo, Michael. *Bond Market Rules: 50 Investing Axioms to Master Bond for Income or Trading*. Cambridge MA: Harvard Business School, 2000.

Standard and Poor's Stock and Bond Guide 2003. New York: McGraw-Hill Professional, 2003.

Thau, Annette. *The Bond Book: Everything Investors Need to Know About Treasuries, Municipals, GNMAS, Corporates, Zeros, Bond Funds, Money Market Funds, and More*. Toronto: McGraw-Hill Ryerson, 2001.

Tuckham, Bruce. *Fixed Income Securities: Tools for Today's Markets*. Toronto: Wiley & Sons, 2002.

Wengroff, Jake. *E-Bonds: An Introduction to the Online Bond Market*. Toronto: Wiley & Sons, 2002.

Wright, Sharon Salzgiver. *Getting Started in Bonds*. Toronto: Wiley & Sons, 2003.

Yago, Glenn, and Susanne Trimbath. *Beyond Junk Bonds: Expanding High Yield Markets*. Toronto: Oxford University Press, 2003.

PERIODICALS

The Financial Post. Toronto: *The National Post*, 300–1450 Don Mills Road, Don Mills, ON M3B 3R5. **www.nationalpost.com**

MoneySense: For Canadians Who Want More. Markham: *MoneySense*, P.O. Box 851, STN. Main, Markham, ON L3P 9Z9. **www.moneysense.ca**

Report on Business. Toronto: *The Globe and Mail*. 444 Front Street West, Toronto, ON M5V 2S9. **www.globeandmail.com**

Weekly Financial Statistics. Ottawa: Bank of Canada. **www.bankofcanada.ca/en** (go to Publications and Research).

Personal Finance on the Web

The Bank of Canada
www.bankofcanada.ca Gives current market rates and financial statistics.

Bank of Montreal
www.bmo.com This site has a lot of useful financial information.

BondLessons.com
www.bondlessons.com/course.html

Canada Deposit Insurance Corporation
www.cdic.ca

Canadian Bankers Association
www.cba.ca

Canadian Capital Markets Association
www.ccma-acmc.ca This site was established to improve the operation of Canadian capital markets.

The Canadian Depository for Securities Limited
www.cds.ca

Canadian Financial Network
www.canadianfinance.com This site provides access to valuable resources.

Canadian Western Bank Group
www.cwbank.com

CIBC World Markets
www.cibc.com

E*Trade Canada
 www.etrade.ca This site has information on strip bonds.

Department of Finance
 www.fin.gc.ca This site has information of value to investors.

Dominion Bond Rating Service Limited
 www.dbrs.com

Foundmoney.com
 www.foundmoney.com This site helps people to find forgotten bank accounts.

Industry Canada
 www.strategis.gc.ca This site has useful statistical information.

Investors Association of Canada
 www.iac.ca

Moody's Investors Service
 www.moodys.com

Royal Bank Financial Group
 www.royalbank.com

Scotiabank
 www.scotiabank.ca

Standard & Poor's
 www.standardandpoors.com Standard & Poor's is a major bond-rating company.

Statistics Canada
 www.statcan.ca

TD Bank Financial Group
 www.td.com

chapter **10**

Stocks, Mutual Funds, and Other Investments

"Why not invest your assets in the companies you really like? As Mae West said, 'Too much of a good thing can be wonderful.'"

Warren Buffet

Learning Objectives

Understanding the concepts discussed in this chapter should help you to become a wiser investor.

After studying this chapter, you should be able to:

1. Understand the rewards of stock market investing.

2. Interpret stock quotations in the daily press.

3. Identify the characteristics of common and preferred shares.

4. Understand the many terms associated with stock market investing.

5. Explain the features of the various kinds of mutual funds.

6. Assess the pros and cons of mutual fund investing.

7. Understand the different tax treatment of interest, dividend, and capital gains income.

8. Understand the investment risk and the value of diversification as a means of reducing this risk.

9. Explain the pros and cons of alternative ways to invest.

Introduction

This chapter introduces you to the fascinating and sometimes confusing world of investing in stocks and mutual funds. You will learn how stocks are bought and sold, and about the differences between common and preferred shares. You will also learn about the many features and types of mutual funds. This chapter should help you understand articles in the financial press, books about investing, the many investment newsletters available, and other information you may encounter on the internet or on television broadcasts about investing. You will not learn how to evaluate the quality of stocks and other types of investments; this complex subject is one that you must research on your own. Making wise decisions in this field depends on a number of constantly changing factors, including the economy's general health, the management of companies you might be interested in, events in the global economy, and the luck and skill of mutual fund managers. You will also learn about other ways to invest, including works of art, fine wines, and real estate. As with stocks, all come with risks, and these will be explained.

Investing in the Stock Market

You should not invest in stocks if you cannot afford to lose the invested money. Investing in publicly traded shares is too uncertain an activity to risk money that you may need. While share prices generally rise over the long term, the investment world can sometimes be like a minefield to both the experienced and the novice investor. It has not been uncommon, for example, to see the book value of an individual's fortune wiped out because share prices declined drastically and unexpectedly within just a few hours. Share prices have, of course, often rebounded just as dramatically. But such a rebound cannot be counted on; stock prices may remain depressed for long periods. As mentioned in Chapter 8, investing in stocks comes with no guarantee either of capital or of income. No one can predict when an event may occur in some remote corner of the world that may cause investors to panic. All investments come with risk. Stocks and mutual funds are no exception. But there are various degrees of risk. When investing, you should look for investments that match your own tolerance for risk.

Capitalization

The value of a company's outstanding shares is known as its **capitalization**. Traditionally, companies are divided into small-cap, mid-cap, and large-cap. The two larger categories are composed of older, established companies that often pay dividends. Small-cap shares usually don't pay dividends, since earnings are reinvested in the company for future growth. The capitalization distinction, however, is not an accurate one. Small-cap companies usually have a capitalization of less than $1 billion (but some have more); mid-cap, several billion; and large-cap, many billions. Analysts often expect shares of the first two categories to grow faster than those of the large-cap companies (that is why they recommend them). Large-caps have already grown and may have reached a point where no more suitable companies are left to purchase. This is not necessarily the case, however, as owners of resource-based stocks have recently found out.

Australia's BHP Billiton, the world's biggest mining company, for example, with a market capitalization in August 2005 of US $95.3 billion,[1] continues to grow. In February 2002 it

---

[1]Basic Points, August 18, 2005, BMO Nesbitt Burns.

acquired (along with Anglo American and Glencore International) Colombian coal mine Intercor from Exxon Mobil. In August of 2002 it acquired 18 blocks (for oil and gas production) in the outer continental shelf of the western Gulf of Mexico from the US Department of the Interior. In June 2005, it purchased 90.59% of Australian company WMC Resources, a miner of bauxite, copper, gold, nickel, and cobalt.

QLT Pharmaceutical, a mid-cap stock listed below, on the other hand, which once had a bright future and was forecast to grow significantly, now faces strong competition from another company that makes a similar product and has been downgraded by most analysts.[2]

Examples of the three categories follow:[3]

Small-Cap

Company	Capitalization	Dividend
Aur Resources, a mining company	$772 million	0
Optimal Group, manufacturer of industrial products	$487 million	0
FNX Mining	$703 million	0

Mid-Cap

Centurian Energy	$1054 billion	0
Reitmans, a clothing chain	$1181 billion	.48
QLT, a biopharmaceutical company	$976 million	0

Large-Cap

Rogers Communications Inc.	$5580 billion	.10
Teck Cominco, a mining company	$3847 billion	.80
Shoppers Drug Mart	$6744 billion	.40

Comparative Returns

Historically, the return from an investment in stocks has been greater than the return from an investment in bonds and other fixed-income securities. This is often referred to as the *equity risk premium*, the extra return an investor gets to compensate for the market risk of investing in stocks. In Canada this premium has averaged 4.5 percent over fixed income investments from 1900–2000.[4] In future, this premium is expected to increase because of low inflation and the corresponding low rates of interest earned by fixed income products. A low rate of inflation is usually good for stocks but not for interest rates. In September 2005, for

[2]Merger Squeezes QLT Profit Forecast, **www.globetechnology.com/servlet/ArticleNews/gtsearch/TGAM/ 20050224/RQLTREP24/Search/11/11/200/sortdate/10/management**.

[3]**www.globeinvestor.com/series/top1000/tables/market/2004**.

[4]Richard Guay, Equity Premium and Risk in a Global Economy, 5th Risk Management Conference, *Canadian Investment Review*, August 2003.

example, the interest on GICs with a five-year term averaged 3.71 percent,[5] a return not difficult to beat with good quality, high-yielding stocks.

Price Volatility

Even though stocks have been more profitable over the long term than investing in debt securities, fluctuations in stock prices can be a drawback. Stock prices are affected by business cycles that may last for years. During a business cycle, business activity tends to expand and then contract, causing stock prices to move up and then down. It is normal for stock prices to fluctuate, but the result can be low liquidity for the investor, who cannot be sure of selling without a loss on any given day. But genuine investors (as opposed to speculators: see Chapter 8's "Investing Versus Speculating" section), view stocks as relatively long-term investments, carefully choosing when to buy and when to sell.

Dividend Discount Model

The theory behind the **dividend discount model** (DDM) is that a stock's true or intrinsic value is what investors will earn in dividends. It only works for dividend-paying stocks. Expressed in another way, using the *time value of money*, the DDM says that a stock is worth the *present value* of its future dividends.

To find a stock's intrinsic value (P) using the DDM, you need to determine the dividends it will earn in the future. Since dividend forecasts may be wrong, a risk factor (r) must be included. The formula for the DDM is

$$P = \frac{Div}{r}$$

Enbridge is a major Canadian company whose dividends have grown by an average of 10 percent per year for 50 years. As of September 2005, it paid a dividend per year of $1.00 per share. Using a risk factor of 3 percent we can find the stock's intrinsic value using the above formula.

$$P = \frac{1.00}{.03} = 33.33$$

Enbridge shares closed on September 2, 2005, at $35.93.

For an online calculator go to **www.moneychimp.com/articles/valuation/dcf.htm**.

Need for Knowledge

To invest successfully in the stock market, you need to become reasonably well-informed. Two common problems arise when investors fail to understand price volatility and the breadth of choice within the stock market. Inexperienced investors may become pessimistic when stock prices are low and be reluctant to invest in the market. Conversely, rising prices lead to optimism; thus, these people often decide to buy just as the market reaches a high level. Later, when stock prices fall (as they invariably do), the

---

[5]Bank of Montreal, **www.bmoinvestorline.com** (accessed September 27, 2005).

inexperienced investor may panic and sell, vowing never to invest in the market again. Unfortunately, you cannot make money by buying high and selling low. These people have made the mistake of viewing stocks as short-term investments. Another difficulty arises for those with limited knowledge of investment alternatives. They may feel that their choices are restricted either to depositing their funds in low-yielding debt securities (see Chapter 8) or to speculating in the stock market. They fail to realize that many intermediate possibilities exist.

Stock Analysis

The major concerns of all investors are the direction of stock exchange indices and the performance of the individual stocks in their portfolios. In order to determine the latter, investment analysts have devised a number of different methods. One method, **quantitative analysis**, is based on information included in a company's financial statements. Another, **qualitative analysis**, is much more subjective and looks at such things as the skill of top managers. (A combination of these two is often referred to as fundamental analysis.) A third, **technical analysis**, looks at past performance of a stock in conjunction with overall market performance in order to try to detect a recurring pattern.

Shares in Nortel Networks were once very popular. The company was a high-tech heavy, and its shares were held by many shareholders and mutual and pension funds. Its share price was quoted frequently. At one point in 2000 when technology stocks were hot, Nortel stock was worth $124.50 per share. In the run-up to this price, the stock attracted many buyers, some of them new to investing. Then, like the shares of many technology stocks, its price plummeted, reaching a low of $0.67. By April 2003, it was trading in the $3.00 range. Following are analyses of Nortel using the above methods:

Quantitative (As of March 28, 2003)

	2001	2002	2003E	2004E
Earnings per share	–$1.00	–$0.35	–$0.05	$0.05
Revenue ($ millions)	17.511	10.500	9.00	9.500
Price/earnings			n.a.	43.1
Price: February 28, 2003:	$3.00			
Target Price:	$3.00			
52-week high:	$9.88			
52-week low:	$0.67			

The stock has rallied from its lows and is rated Market Perform. (Market Perform is not an enthusiastic rating. Dealers will not recommend the stock but suggest you keep it if you already own it.)

Qualitative While the company lost a number of key employees in 2002, current management has performed well, reducing long-term debt by close to US $500 million. The company should end 2003 with over US $2.0 billion in cash.

Technical (as of March 28, 2003) Nortel shares have rallied from the lows of 2002 and are fairly valued at $3.20. The stock is rated Market Perform.

Stock Trading

Stock Exchange

A **stock exchange** is an organized marketplace for buying and selling shares in corporations. Businesses that require working capital can obtain it by selling shares to investors—who, by purchasing the shares, become part owners of the corporation. Companies that have undergone this process are called publicly owned corporations. A new offering of shares may be put on the market when a business is new or whenever the company requires additional capital. After the new offering has been sold, the shares usually begin trading in the secondary market, where they change owners frequently. Investors cannot sell their shares back to the corporation whenever they wish. For instance, if you own some shares in CP Ships and you no longer wish to keep them, you must find a buyer for them. Stockbrokers and stock exchanges exist to link would-be sellers and would-be buyers of securities, and to facilitate transactions between them.

Stocks may be traded either at a stock exchange or on the **over-the-counter market**, which is not a physical place but rather a communication system. Generally, stocks that do not meet the listing requirements for a major stock exchange (referred to as unlisted stocks) are traded on the over-the-counter market. On a stock exchange, only members can execute orders for clients. Each member of an exchange has purchased one of a limited number of seats or member trading permits that entitle their owners to trade securities that are listed on that exchange. A firm of investment dealers that wishes to trade on a certain stock exchange must either purchase one of these seats or work through a dealer who owns one.

Computer technologies have allowed exchanges to trade shares through an electronic communications system instead of the old manual auction method which required that buyers' and sellers' representatives be present on the exchange floor when trading takes place. The Toronto, Montreal, NASDAQ Canada,[6] and TSX Venture exchanges have computerized trading. (One person's introduction to the last of these is recounted in Personal Finance in Action Box 10.1, "The TSX Venture Exchange.") The New York Stock Exchange has a hybrid system combining both manual and electronic trading. Ten percent of the trading on the NYSE is done by an automated trading system, which processes an average of 170 million shares per day. The remainder is done in the traditional way. Unlike the manual system, however, the automated system has a limit of 3 million shares per order.

Another victim of the computer is the share certificate. In the past, anyone who purchased shares received an elaborately engraved certificate of share ownership in the mail. While this is still possible for those who wish to have them, the vast majority of shares are now held in **street form**. This means that all the shares owned by a securities dealer's clients are registered in the dealer's name, and the dealer keeps a record for each client in its computer system. This approach is more convenient both for the investment dealer and for the dealer's clients. Now, when a client wishes to sell some shares, no certificate needs to be signed over to the dealer. Instead, the shares are transferred from dealer to dealer via the computer—or simply from one file to another file, if both clients use the same dealer.

Whichever way a trade is executed, information about the transaction is transmitted immediately to the stock exchange's computer system and is therefore available to exchanges and investment dealers around the world. Investment dealers now make trades on their computers and can notify clients of the results at once. Once a trade has been made, the client in Canada has three business days to settle the account.

[6]NASDAQ Canada, a subsidiary of NASDAQ in New York, does not have an exchange. Operating out of Montreal and Vancouver, it has terminals in Canadian securities firms which give access to all stocks listed on the NASDAQ.

Personal FINANCE in action 10.1

The TSX Venture Exchange

After graduating with a degree in astronomy, Jacob couldn't find a job suited to his education and interests. Desperate for work, he took a job at a burger franchise. He soon realized that his co-workers had little ambition or skill, and it wasn't long before he was asked to manage the shop. His job paid him more than he needed to maintain his lifestyle. Realizing that leaving too much money in the bank was foolish, he decided to invest. On a field trip in high school he had learned about the TSX Venture Exchange and speculative investing. He decided to put some of his money in one of the stocks listed.

Checking the listings in the paper he noticed the word Anaconda. This intrigued him because he had been to Brazil and seen the powerful constrictor. The stock only cost 20 cents per share and at one point in the past year, had been 32. An internet search told him that the company's full name was Anaconda Gold Corp., and that it had properties in the Northwest Territories, Newfoundland and Labrador, Nevada, and Ontario. While it had a loss of close to $300 000 the previous year, it had assets of over $2 500 000. He decided to take a risk it and bought 2000 shares. This cost $400 plus $25 for the online commission. If the price dropped a cent or two, he would buy more.

Trading Quantities

Just as "one dozen" is the basic unit for buying eggs, shares can be purchased in convenient quantities known as **board lots**. Board lots make trading easier because it is difficult to match buy and sell orders for odd numbers of shares. The number in a board lot is related to the share price, as shown below, but most shares are priced to sell in board lots of 100.

Price of Shares	Number in a Board Lot
Under 10 cents	1000
From 10 to 99 cents	500
From $1 to under $99	100
$100 and over	10

When fewer shares than a board lot are traded, they are referred to as an **odd lot**. Since it is harder to find buyers or sellers for odd lots, the price may be somewhat higher or the trade less quickly executed than those for board lots.

Kinds of Orders

Various kinds of orders may be placed with a broker. A **market order** is executed immediately at the best available price. Any order without a specific price is handled as a market order; the trader is responsible for getting the best price. An **open order** specifies a price; the order then remains open until it is either executed (because the share price reached the specified amount) or cancelled. If you want to buy a specific stock, but only if its price falls to a certain level, you give your broker an open order, which will be executed only if and when that price is reached. A **stop loss order** works in reverse, giving your broker the authority to sell your shares if their price falls to a named level. A stop loss order is used to ensure that the shares will be sold at a set price should prices fall, but makes it unnecessary to sell if the price keeps rising.

Cash and Margin Accounts, Leverage, and Short Selling

Investment dealers have two basic types of accounts: cash accounts and margin accounts. A *cash account* is just what it says. A client buys a security with cash and must settle the account within three days. When the client buys *on margin*, he or she buys on credit by borrowing part of the purchase price of the security from the dealer. Each dealer has a margin rate, which is a percentage of the market value of the security purchased. The more valuable the security, the higher the percentage. This money (the margin) is paid by the client and deposited in his or her margin account. The balance of the purchase price is the dealer's money. The security purchased is held as collateral. The interest charged to the client is based on the rate charged to the dealer when it borrows from a bank.

Buying on margin allows a client to use **leverage** to increase the value of his or her portfolio. This can be very risky. In a bull market it allows a client to increase the value of his assets more quickly than if he or she did not borrow, but in a bear market the loss is exaggerated because of the loan. The greater the leverage, the greater the potential for gain or for loss.

Example A: Stock Price Rises

Client's Money	*Dealer's Money*	*Stock's value*	*Value Rises 50%*
$10 000	$10 000	$20 000	$30 000

The client pays dealer $10 000 and makes $10 000. If the client had not borrowed $10 000, the gain would have been only $5000.

Example B: Stock Price Falls

Client's Money	*Dealer's Money*	*Value of Security*	*Value Falls 50%*
$10 000	$10 000	$20 000	$10 000

When the stock's price drops the dealer will make a *margin call*. The client, whose margin account is now worth nothing, will have to pay the dealer $10 000 or sell the security to do so. After selling and paying the dealer, the client has nothing left. If the client had only invested $10 000, the loss would have been $5 000, instead of $10 000.

Buying on margin is an example of using *leverage* to increase the size of one's investment portfolio. In a rising market it can help the investor make sizable gains, but in a falling market the losses can be very large. Such a tactic is not recommended for investors who can't sleep at night if the market drops.

Short selling also uses leverage. When an investor thinks the market is going to fall he or she borrows a stock from an investment dealer and sells it at the current price. When the price drops, the stock is sold and the dealer paid. If, instead, the stock rises in price, the investor is out the initial price of the stock as well as the amount of the gain. Companies whose shares are being sold short are listed regularly in the financial press. Some investors use this information to try to increase the size of their portfolios.

Stockbrokers

Stockbrokers—or registered representatives, as they are often called—may be classified as either full-service brokers or discount brokers. **Full-service brokers** charge higher commission rates, but also offer advice, research reports on companies, and other information. By contrast, **discount brokers** charge less than full-service brokers do but may offer very little, if any, information.

Brokerage Commissions

The fee schedule of a major full-service Canadian investment dealer is shown below. However, a minimum commission of $50.00 applies to all orders placed over the telephone. Commissions on orders over $250 000 are negotiable.

Stock Price	Commission
$0.00 − $0.245	2.50%
$0.25 − $1.00	$35 + 1/2 cent per share
$1.01 − $2.00	$35 + 2 cents per share
$2.01 − $5.00	$35 + 3 cents per share
$5.01 − $10.00	$35 + 4 cents per share
$10.01 − $20.00	$35 + 5 cents per share
$20.01 and over	$35 + 6 cents per share

Stockbrokers charge a **commission** for arranging either a sale or a purchase of securities. Each firm sets its own fee schedule, usually on a sliding scale, with lower rates per share for larger orders. If you plan to place a small order, you should inquire about the minimum commission charge, which is about $100.

Transactions involving large sums of money are carried out by verbal agreement, depending solely on trust. The client simply telephones an order to the broker, who then executes it. Consequently, a broker will not conduct business for a client until an account has been opened. Doing so usually involves a meeting between the client and the broker to discuss the investor's objectives and financial status. The broker may also check with the credit bureau (see Chapter 14) to verify the client's creditworthiness.

Insider Trading

One assumes when dealing with investment professionals that they are above reproach. A sense of trust must exist between the client and his or her investment dealer or advisor. If a client does not trust his or her investment dealer, for whatever reason, or feels uneasy with the proffered advice, the client should look elsewhere. While the large majority of investment professionals are honest, the financial industry, by its very nature, is likely to attract some shady characters who try to make money at their clients' expense or resort to taking advantage of their privileged position to enrich themselves.

One of the more insidious examples of the latter is **insider trading**. This happens, according to the RCMP, "when privileged, non-public information is used to trade on securities or commodities markets. It may include the purchase or sale of shares prior to the disclosure of a corporate news release or the purchase or sale of shares on the basis of information that would never be disclosed to shareholders."[7]

Insider trading is illegal. Corporate officers owning 10 percent or more of a company's stock must report their trades to regulators such as the Ontario Securities Commission. The OSC then publishes this information every Friday afternoon on the website of the System for Electronic Exposure by Insiders (SEDI).[8]

[7] www.rcmp.ca/scams/insider_trading_e.htm.
[8] www.sedi.ca.

Insiders know more about their company than most people, and investors may be able to profit from this knowledge. Stocks bought by insiders often beat the market[9] (usually by an average of 5 percent over a 12-month period), and presumably they are sold before a company's stock drops.

Stock Quotations

Considerable information about the previous day's stock trades appears in the financial press. Stock quotations give the price range within which the stock traded, the share price at the closing of the exchange, and how many shares were traded. In addition, the stock's high and low prices for the past year and the amount of the most recent dividend are usually included. (The income from a stock is known as a **dividend.**) Some newspapers provide even more information in their weekly summaries. Newspapers differ somewhat in the way they present stock quotations; see the box "Reading Stock Quotations" for a representative example. Some newspapers quote bid and ask prices. The **bid price** is what a buyer is willing to pay, and the **ask price** is what the seller is willing to accept. Unless buyer and seller can reach an agreement, there will be no transaction. Stock prices are quoted in dollar amounts, except in the case of those that are trading for less than $5; these are quoted in cents. Those with prices around $3 or less are often referred to as **penny stocks.**

Stock Classifications: Defensive, Blue Chip, Cyclical

A major concern of investors is what will happen to their securities in the event of a major bear market, or drop in share prices. Each investor has a different tolerance for risk. Some can't tolerate any risk at all, often shunning stocks for GICs and then seeing the value of their estate decline. Risk-averse stock owners want the least risky stocks. This usually means *defensive* or **blue chip** stocks that should hold up better in a market downturn. These stocks are often in industries with good products or services, for which there is a strong demand and a history of solid earnings. Bell Canada (BCE) is often referred to as blue chip.

Other investors, those willing to risk the fallout from a serious market decline, often cringe at the thought of owning BCE, sometimes described as a stock for widows and orphans. They shun defensive stocks and may turn instead to growth-oriented stocks or those referred to as cyclical. **Cyclical stocks** often have a history of erratic earnings because demand for their products rises and falls more frequently than that for defensive stocks. They are often in commodities but may also be in manufacturing. The North American auto industry, for example, entered a period of retrenchment in 2004 to 2005 as a result of stiff competition from Japanese cars. The only way they seemed to be able to sell cars was by offering customers huge "employee discounts."

Stock Exchange Indices

Every day, some stocks go up while others fall. The overall behaviour of the market can be learned by watching the performance of a **stock exchange index**. Such an index is a statistical measurement of the percentage change in the prices of a select group of common stocks. Changes in an index give an indication of the overall performance of the stock market and how investors in general feel.

[9]Hasan Nejat Seyhun, *Investment Intelligence from Insider Trading.*

Reading Stock Quotations

On September 24, 2005, Royal Bank common stock was quoted in *The Globe and Mail* as follows:

365 day high	low	Stock	Sym	Div	Hi/bid	Low/ ask	Chg	Vol(h)	Yld	Shr pro	P/E ratio
84.14	59.27	Royal Bank	RY	2.56	84.14	83	+ 0.98	12 704	3.05	5.22	16.1

Reading from left to right, this means that in the past year, common shares of the Royal Bank traded between a high of $84.14 and a low of $59.27. The stock is referred to by the symbol RY in stock quotation pages and by stock exchanges. (The bank has many preferred shares with different symbols.) The stock pays a dividend of $2.56 per share per year. The day before, those selling the stock were asking $84.14 per share while those wanting to buy it were offering $83.00. The price closed up 0.98 and 12 704 000 shares were traded. The stock yields 3.05 percent and earned $5.22 per share over the last 12 months. The stock's price/earnings ratio (stock price divided by the earnings per share for the past 12 months) is 16/1.

S&P/TSX Indices

There are many stock market indices. The Toronto Stock Exchange, Canada's major exchange, has 21. The most widely followed is the *S&P/TSX Composite Index*, which replaced the TSE 300 Composite Index on May 1, 2002. This index tracks the performance of Canada's largest publicly traded companies and is divided into 10 economic sectors and 24 industry groups. In addition there are 20 other indices. These are listed below. They allow investors interested in, for example, an energy stock, to compare its record with that of other energy stocks.

The value of the S&P/TSX Composite Index, on a specific day, is calculated using the following formula:

$$\text{Index value} = \frac{Aggregate\ Quoted\ Market\ Value}{Base\ Value} \times 1000$$

The Aggregate Quoted Market Value = the current market price × total shares − control blocks. The QMV is available from the TSX at marketdata@tse.com.

The Base Value = $38.0021 million, which is the Aggregate Quoted Market Value Weighted Average for 1975.

The other **S&P/TSX Indices**:

S&P/TSX Capped Composite Index
S&P/TSX 60 Index
S&P/TSX 60 Capped Index
S&P/TSX MidCap
S&P/TSX SmallCap
S&P/TSX Capped Consumer Discretionary Index
S&P/TSX Capped Consumer Staples Index
S&P/TSX Capped Diversified Metals & Mining Index
S&P/TSX Capped Energy Index
S&P/TSX Capped Financials Index

S&P/TSX Capped Gold Index
S&P/TSX Capped Health Care Index
S&P/TSX Capped Industrials Index
S&P/TSX Capped Information Technology Index
S&P/TSX Capped Materials Index
S&P/TSX Capped Real Estate Index
S&P/TSX Capped Telecommunication Services Index
S&P/TSX Capped Utilities Index
S&P/TSX Capped Income Trust Index
S&P/TSX Venture Composite Index

The TSX Venture Exchange is Canada's public venture, or risk, capital marketplace. It provides a way for new companies to raise capital in a regulated marketplace. Stocks listed on it are very risky because they have little (or no) track record and are sold on the expectation (always risky) of potential growth.

There is an even riskier market for *penny stocks*, the stocks of companies just starting out. Penny stocks are not sold in a regulated market such as that provided by the TSX, but in the *over-the-counter market*, made up of investment dealers who trade in these securities for their clients or for themselves.

The Dow Jones Industrial Average is the world's most-watched stock market index. Several others—for example, the Standard and Poor's 500—are also popular, but the Dow symbolizes stock trading for investors globally. The 30 stocks that make up the DJIA include some of the largest and most successful US companies; names like Coca-Cola, Walt Disney Co., Exxon, and GE are recognized worldwide. Coke has been one of the stellar performers on the Dow and provides the unexciting but solid growth that investors like Warren Buffet look for. On September 27, 1990, for example, the share price (adjusted for stock splits) was $8.37. On September 27, 2005, the price was $48.90. In 2005 it also paid a dividend of $1.12 per share.

Fluctuations in the DJIA can be misleading. Since the average is calculated by adding the prices of the 30 stocks and then dividing that sum (usually by 4), the more-expensive stocks receive a higher weighting. With so few stocks in the index, dramatic fluctuations occasionally occur. A major change in a heavily weighted stock can skew the average, affecting it far more than changes in the broader market really warrant. On the other hand, the Dow may underperform the market as a whole, since it comprises only blue chip stocks, which are usually less volatile than others.

The S&P/TSX Composite Index, like all stock indices, fluctuates frequently. This is more obvious if a shorter period is covered than the one in Figure 10.1. As this graph shows, though, over a long period the stock market generally rises. As can be seen, "bear markets" (the common term for markets in which price trends are travelling downward over a considerable period; the opposite situation is called a "bull market") eventually recover. The message for investors therefore seems clear: do not be overly concerned by periodic bear markets. The best advice from some of the world's most successful investors is to buy and hold. Since nobody can consistently outguess the market, your wisest approach is to become fully invested and then to ignore the periodic declines in the stock market indices. Over the long term, your investments should gain as the entire market rises.

Day Traders

Changes in technology, combined with relatively recent rapid increases in the prices of technology shares, have resulted in a new breed of investor, the **day trader**. Day traders profit from rapid fluctuations in the stock market during the day. As other investors try to do, day traders buy when stock prices are low and sell when the prices rise. They can also make

FIGURE 10.1   S&P/TSX COMPOSITE INDEX YEARLY CLOSE, 1925–2004

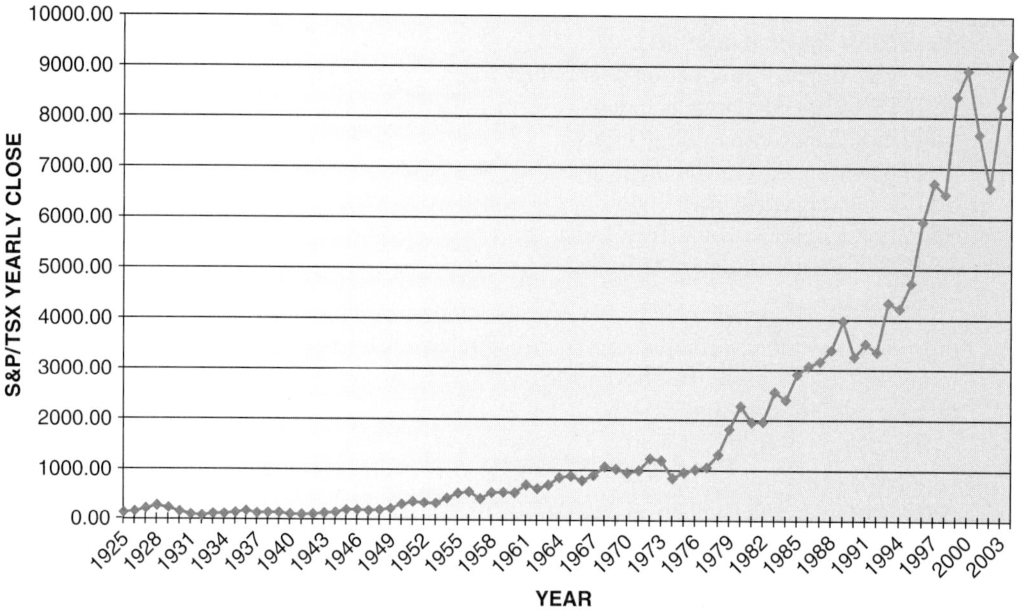

SOURCE: Econstats.

money by selling short when the market falls. Unlike other investors, however, day traders must close or sell all positions by the end of the day. This can be done in a split second on the internet. With the rapid rise in the prices of tech stocks like the dot-coms in 1999–2000, many day traders made a great deal of money. Such behaviour, it should be noted, is extremely risky because stock market volatility can be dramatic and unpredictable, and prices can drop just as quickly as they can rise. No one should "finance" day trading with the money he or she needs for survival in order to become a day trader. Each successful trade also results in a capital gain and therefore an increase in income tax.

Common Shares

Corporations, especially large ones, have many owners who provide capital for the business. These owners, or shareholders, may hold either common or preferred shares. Common shareholders take a greater risk; their investments may gain or lose more than the investments of preferred shareholders. Owners of preferred shares usually accept a smaller voice in the management of the enterprise in exchange for greater safety of principal and assurance of income. We will examine the characteristics of **common shares** first.

Characteristics of Common Shares

An investment in common stock has two attributes that differentiate it from a debt security: (i) equity (ownership), with its associated rights, and (ii) uncertainty of return. Common shareholders become part owners in a corporation. As such, they enjoy certain rights, which include the following:

(a) a vote at annual meetings,

(b) an opportunity to share in the company's profit (dividends or capital gain),

(c) regular financial statements from the company,

(d) a claim on the company's assets in case of dissolution.

Today, quarterly statements and press releases, which were traditionally mailed to all shareholders, are sent only to those who request them; this approach helps with cost control (always a concern, since lowering a firm's costs contributes to increasing its profitability). Shareholders must notify the company each year if they wish to remain on the mailing list. Most companies will now send statements electronically if you prefer. All publicly owned corporations also post their financial reports and other related information on the internet for the perusal of shareholders and other interested persons, who can print out and keep the information they find most useful. Quarterly reports are also usually published in the press.

Most voting at annual meetings is done by proxy, since relatively few shareholders attend in person. Traditionally, proxies were sent in by mail. Now, in both Canada and the United States, shareholders may register their votes either by mail, telephone, or online. The convenient, efficient Proxy Vote Canada Service has proven very popular with shareholders.

Some companies offer several types of common shares. These may be designated Class A or Class B. Holders of Class B shares typically have fewer rights. They may not have any voting rights at all, or they may be allowed to vote only in certain circumstances. Such shares may not be distinguishable from normal shares in the newspaper, but an investment dealer can identify them for you.

Buying common stock represents a decision to give up some measure of safety in favour of prospects for greater return. As mentioned earlier, an equity investment carries neither a promise that your capital will be returned to you nor a guarantee that your investment will earn income. When a company does well, its shareholders benefit; but when it does poorly, some or all of each shareholder's investment can be lost. Remember Nortel! Fortunately, a shareholder has a limited liability for the corporation's losses; if the firm goes bankrupt, each shareholder's maximum loss is limited to the funds that he or she has invested.

Rights and Warrants

Sometimes shareholders are offered **rights**, which are privileges that allow them to buy additional shares directly from the company. Rights can be an effective way for a firm to raise more capital while also offering the shareholder the chance to obtain more shares (often at a price below what is being paid on the open market) without paying commission. The recipient of rights has the choice either of exercising them to buy more shares or of selling the rights on the market. There is usually a short period during which rights may be exercised before they expire and become valueless.

The term **warrant** has more than one application: most commonly, it refers to a certificate that can be attached to bonds and to new issues of common or preferred shares to make them more appealing to investors. A warrant allows the owner to buy shares of the issuing company at a set price within a specified period of time (see Personal Finance in Action Box 10.2, "Warrants"). Warrants do not usually expire as quickly as rights; but like rights, they may be detached and sold separately.

Investment Terms Used with Stocks

The Price/Earnings Ratio Considered an important investment tool, the **price/earnings ratio** (P/E ratio) is used to help determine a stock's value. It is obtained by dividing the market price per share by the earnings per share and indicates how much investors are willing to pay for

Personal FINANCE in action 10.2

Warrants

In February 2003, Pan American Silver and Corner Bay Silver merged. Under the terms of the merger agreement, each Corner Bay share was exchanged for 0.3846 common shares of Pan American plus 0.1923 Pan American *warrants*. As a result, Ariel, who owned 100 shares of Corner Bay, received 38 shares of Pan American and 19 warrants. Each whole warrant can be used to buy one share of Pan American for $12.00 over a five-year period. Between April 2002 and April 2003, shares in Pan American traded between $7.16 and $15.00.

Personal FINANCE in action 10.3

Managed Money

Hans took early retirement from his job at Nortel. A computer engineer, he had made a fortune dabbling in tech stocks before they fell from grace in 2000. For peace of mind he has opened a wrap account. For an annual fee of 1.5 percent of his $2 000 000 portfolio, he gets exceptional advice and unlimited trades.

each dollar of earnings. It is thought to be a sign of a share's market potential but, at best, is an imperfect tool.

Nortel, once the darling of the Canadian investment community, is an indication of just how imperfect. At the height of the speculative high-tech boom in 2000, Nortel had a price per share of $124.50 and a P/E ratio of 125. While it was thought by the market (investors) and financial journalists to have good growth potential, some seasoned investors considered it very risky, hence the high P/E ratio. The latter were eventually proven right when the dot.com bubble burst in 2001 and Nortel's share price plunged and kept plunging until reaching a low of $0.69 by October 2002. By July 2005 it had regained a fraction of its former value, selling on the TSX for $3.40 per share, but because the company reported no earnings in 2004, only a loss, the stock had no P/E ratio.

What Is the P/E Ratio Supposed to Mean?

The higher the P/E ratio, the more investors are willing to pay for each dollar of expected earnings. A high P/E ratio also indicates that a company is expected to grow. It is also, as in the case of Nortel, a sign that the stock is more risky. Stocks with low P/E ratios are thought to have only low or moderate growth potential. They may also be the ones that pay good dividends, while so-called growth stocks usually pay little or nothing at all. In July 2005, for example, BCE, with a dividend payout of 4.46 percent—one of the highest in Canada—had a P/E ratio of 17.92. CIBC, with a relatively high dividend of 3.51 percent, had a P/E ratio of 13.20. Both are considered to be among the least speculative stocks with only moderate growth potential, the kind of stocks considered suitable for conservative investors. Barrick Gold, much more speculative, paid a dividend of 0.94 percent and had a P/E ratio of 166.8. It stood a better chance of rising or falling significantly than either Bell Canada or CIBC.

Some analysts suggest comparing a stock's P/E ratio with those of other companies in the same industry before deciding whether or not to buy the stock. If all other things are equal (recent earnings, future earnings potential, management's track record) and the P/E ratio of company A is lower than that of company B, then one would be foolish to buy the shares of company B. However, it is difficult to compare companies, even similar ones. Unpredictable random events such as the death or resignation of the CEO, a strike, or the cancellation of a big order may harm a company's earning potential and make the P/E ratio meaningless.

Par Value/No Par Value Traditionally, the price at which a stock was issued was known as its **par value**. Today, most stocks have *no par value* (NPV), and the market determines their price. A no par value stock can trade at any price.

Closing Tick If the market has a positive *closing tick*, then the number of stocks whose closing prices are higher than previous trades is greater than the number whose closing prices are lower. A positive closing tick indicates investors were in a buying mood. Individual stocks have their own closing ticks.

Preferred Shares

Characteristics of Preferred Shares

In addition to common stock, companies often issue a class of shares called **preferred shares**, which represent limited ownership in a corporation. Investors may choose preferred shares over common shares because the former involve lower risk and greater assurance of income. (In recent years, however, the number of preferred issues has decreased. Such offerings are more expensive for a company because the dividends paid are not treated as a tax-deductible expense.) Because such a broad spectrum of both common and preferred shares exists, it is possible to find common shares that are less risky than some preferred shares. Nevertheless, if the company prospers, its common shares typically rise in price more than its preferred shares do. Most preferred shares promise a certain rate of return—in contrast to common shares, which have no set dividend rate. Issues of preferred shares can vary considerably, but in general their characteristics may be summarized as follows:

(a) part ownership in the company,

(b) no voting rights,

(c) a set dividend rate,

(d) a risk level that is lower than that of the company's common shares.

When a company experiences financial difficulties, its first obligation is to pay interest on its bonds; second, it must pay dividends on any preferred shares. Only then can dividends be declared on the common shares. This arrangement puts the security of preferred shareholders midway between that of bondholders and that of common shareholders. Investors will regard any company that does not pay dividends on its preferred shares with disfavour. If a company closes down, bondholders (who are creditors, not owners) have claims on assets that take precedence over those of both preferred and common shareholders.

Stock Splits

The liquidity of an investment is a major concern of investors. When an investor wants to sell a stock, the more liquid it is, the better. As stocks increase in value, the theory goes, they become less liquid because investors will not be as willing to spend $50 for a share as they are $25.

Therefore, if a share price has risen for a long period of time, the company may decide to split it. With a **stock split**, there will be more shares available, and their price will be more appealing and will continue to rise. This sounds reasonable, and many companies do split their shares after extended runs. However, the activity of the stock market is motivated by fear and greed. When the latter takes over it does not seem to matter how high a stock's price has risen. A good example were the shares of communication giant Nortel, which went over $120 in 2000. This didn't stop investors from buying as greed replaced logic.

Whether or not a stock split is of value to investors depends on many factors. These include the performance of the market, the health of the industry to which the company belongs, the management of the company, its future prospects, and any number of other variables. After a stock is split, its price may continue to rise, or it may not. Stock splits do not come with guarantees.

Special Features

Issues of preferred shares often carry features that are intended to attract investors. Preferred shares may be cumulative, redeemable, retractable, or convertible.

Cumulative Most Canadian preferred shares are **cumulative preferred shares**, meaning that if the company does not pay the dividends that are due each quarter, the unpaid dividends accumulate in arrears. (See the boxed feature "BCE Inc. Series AC Preferred Shares" for an example of a cumulative preferred share.) All arrears of cumulative preferred shares must be paid before any common dividends are paid. Whenever the company's financial condition improves, dividends in arrears are paid to the current shareholders without any interest for the period they were in arrears. In stock quotations, companies with dividends in arrears are shown with an "r" or some equivalent designation. The existence of unpaid dividends usually causes the shares' market price to drop.

Dividends on non-cumulative preferred shares are not paid automatically; instead, these must be "declared" each quarter by the board of directors. If the board decides not to declare a dividend in some particular quarter, the shareholder has no future claim.

Redeemable **Redeemable (callable) preferred shares** give the issuer the right to redeem them at a future date. Like callable bonds, redeemable preferred shares may be called in by the company at its discretion, usually at a price slightly higher than the par value.

Sometimes redeemable preferred shares come with a **purchase fund** (also known as a **sinking fund**) included in their terms. Under such an arrangement, the company agrees to buy or redeem a certain number of preferred shares in the market if the trading price reaches or drops below a specified level. If the fund cannot buy enough shares, no redemption takes place.

Retractable If the shareholder has the right to sell the shares back to the company at a specific date, those shares are called **retractable preferred shares**. The option to exercise this privilege belongs to the shareholder. This contrasts with the redeemability feature, under which only the issuing company has the right to call in shares.

Convertible **Convertible preferred shares** give the investor the option of converting the shares into other stock of the company—often common stock—at a specified price and within a certain period. The shareholder thus has the opportunity to decide at a later date which type of stock—common or preferred—will be more beneficial to hold.

BCE Inc. Series AC Preferred Shares

Issued in February 2003, these shares had the following features:

Par Value $25.00

Cumulative

Convertible into Cumulative Redeemable First Preferred Shares on March 1, 2008 and every five years thereafter.

Redeemable on March 1, 2008, or on March 1 in every fifth year thereafter for $25.00 plus accrued and unpaid dividends.

A dividend of $1.385 per year for the five-year period ending March 1, 2008. For each subsequent five-year period, the shares will be entitled to a fixed cumulative preferred cash dividend to be determined by BCE Inc.

Investment Return

Investors in the stock market expect a return on their capital in one or more forms: cash dividends, stock dividends, or capital gain. The return from ownership of common shares will be examined first; then we will look at that of preferred shares.

Common Share Dividends

Unlike interest on debt securities, common stock dividends are neither promised in advance nor paid automatically. The corporation's board of directors decides whether a dividend will be paid, when it will be paid, and how large the dividend will be. As may be expected, the amount paid out in dividends varies with the company's profitability. At times, the directors may decide not to declare any dividend at all because of (i) low profits in the past quarter, (ii) a decision to invest most of the profits back into the business, or (iii) the need to conserve cash flow. When dividends are declared, they are usually paid every quarter.

The **yield** *per share*, an important factor in deciding which stocks to buy for income, is determined by dividing the dividend by the stock price. As the price of a stock increases, the yield declines if the dividend is not increased. However, the gain in a stock's price (capital gain) may be greater than the yield provided by the dividend, at which point an investor may choose to sell the stock since the tax on capital gains is less, for high-income investors, than the tax on dividends.

Three Canadian companies with a history of rewarding their shareholders with good dividends are Bell Canada Enterprises (BCE), the Bank of Nova Scotia (BNS), and Rothmans (ROC). Their share prices and dividends per share as of September 2, 2005 were as follows: BCE, $31.60 and $1.32; BNS, $40.75 and $1.36; ROC, $25.35 and $1.20.

Their yields:

$$\text{BCE } \frac{1.32}{31.60} = 4.18\% \quad \text{BNS } \frac{1.36}{40.75} = 3.34\%$$

$$\text{ROC } \frac{1.20}{25.35} = 4.73\%$$

Some companies—particularly younger, more growth-oriented firms—do not issue dividends. Instead, they reinvest any earnings in the company, with a view to helping it grow.

Personal FINANCE in action 10.4

Dividend Notice

At his broker's suggestion, Klaus bought some Class A shares in Brascan, a major Canadian company, with interests in real estate, power generation, finance, and resources. On February 12, 2003, the directors of Brascan declared the following dividends:

	Record Date	Payment Date	Dividend
Class A Voting	May 1	May 31	$0.25
Class A Preferred	March 15	March 31	$0.180 31

In addition, as Klaus's broker expected, the shares had risen in value since he had bought them.

Growth companies exist in a broad range of industries. For example, one company that has adopted this approach is Gildan Activewear Inc., a Montreal company best known for its T-shirts, which are sold as "blanks" to firms who add their own designs and logos. Others, like Vancouver's QLT, may be involved in research in science and technology (QLT is developing light-activated drugs to be used in the treatment of cancer). Shares in these and other young companies are more speculative, and therefore riskier, than are shares in more established, dividend-paying companies. They are purchased for the prospect of capital gains, rather than for any current income they might provide.

Since common shares are continually trading, there must be a way to determine who is entitled to receive a dividend cheque. Whenever a dividend is declared, a record date is set to determine ownership. For instance, notices often appear in the financial press stating that a dividend will be paid to **shareholders of record**, or those who owned shares at the close of business, as of a certain date (see Personal Finance in Action Box 10.4, "Dividend Notice"). This date may be set two weeks before the payment date, thereby giving the company time to prepare dividend cheques. During this two-week interval, the stock will continue to trade, but the corporation will send dividends only to those who were shareholders on the dividend record date.

The stock exchange sets a date, known as the ex-dividend date, on or after which the stock sells **ex-dividend**, or without a dividend for that quarter. During this time, the shares' sellers, not its buyers, receive the dividend. For example, if you purchase 100 shares of Noranda that are trading ex-dividend, you would not receive the next dividend; the shares' seller would. From the buyer's viewpoint, the advantage of ex-dividend shares is that they cost less than usual; the price of a share drops right after a dividend is paid, since there will be no further dividends for at least three months.

Stock Dividends Instead of cash dividends, companies may offer shareholders new shares in the company, known as **stock dividends**. Such new shares are allotted in proportion to the number of shares already held by each shareholder. Recipients of stock dividends may add them to the shares already owned or sell them on the market. The tax treatment of stock dividends is the same as that of cash dividends.

Automatic Dividend Reinvestment Plans Some major companies have **automatic dividend reinvestment plans**, known as DRIPs, whereby dividends are not paid in cash but instead are reinvested in more of the firm's stock. This can be arranged directly with the company, without a broker's assistance. One advantage for the investor is not having to pay commission on the new shares; another is the possibility of purchasing new shares below the current market price. Such plans are not only a useful way to increase net worth with little effort; they are also a disciplined way of reinvesting dividend income, rather than spending it.

Dividend Reinvestment Plans

Companies with **dividend reinvestment plans** that aren't automatic also allow investors to make extra payments to their plans without charge. Shares purchased in this fashion are usually sold at the market price, though some may be sold at a discount. There is also usually a limit to how much money may be contributed in this way. As with the reinvestment of dividend payments, the purchase of fractional shares is allowed with extra payments. No certificates are issued. A record of all transactions is kept in the companies' computers.

As of September 1, 2005, the following companies and investment trusts had DRIPs. The number changes periodically. For a list of stocks with such plans, go to **www.bmoinvestorline.com/FAQs/FAQ_DRIP.html** and click on *eligible securities* under the *"What is a Dividend Reinvestment Plan?"* heading.

- Aberdeen Asia-Pacific Income Investment Company
- Alcan
- Aliant
- BPI Global Opportunities 11 Fund
- Brascan
- Caldwell Partners
- Canadian Imperial Bank of Commerce
- Canadian Real Estate Investment Trust
- Caribbean Utilities Company
- Dofasco
- Enbridge
- Enbridge Income Fund
- Enerplus Resources Fund
- Falconbridge
- H & R Real Estate Investment Trust
- Homburg Invest Inc.
- Hudson's Bay
- Imperial Oil
- Mandate National Mortgage Corp.

- MDS Inc.
- Nexen
- Noranda
- Norbord
- Onex
- Pacific Coast Mortgage Investment Corp.
- Plazacorp Retail Properties
- Potash Corp. of Saskatchewan
- Retirement Residences Real Estate Investment Trust
- Riocan Real Estate Investment Trust
- Summit Real Estate Investment Trust
- Terasen
- TD Bank
- Torstar
- TransAlta Corp.
- TransAlta Power
- Tri-White Corp.
- Viceroy Homes

Preferred Share Dividends

Investors who buy a new issue of preferred shares pay the face or **par value**. After the initial offering has been sold, the shares trade in the market, where the price may fluctuate. Preferred share dividends are expressed either as a percentage of the par value or as a specified amount per share.

Interest rates declined so dramatically in the 1990s that it was not uncommon to see preferred shares issued at $20 and yielding 10 percent selling for much higher than their face value. Investors were willing to pay a premium for the high interest rate. When rates decline in this fashion, companies often redeem their high-yielding shares; they can then raise more money if necessary by offering new issues at lower yields.

Preferred shares are identified in newspaper stock quotations by the letters "pf" or "PR." For example, Bell Canada's preferred ("p") shares are labelled "BCEpfP" in one newspaper and "BCE.PR.P" in another. Despite the different labels they're using, both newspapers are referring to the same stock.

Further evidence that these are preferred shares can be found by looking at the dividend yields, which are higher for preferred shares than for common shares.

Capital Gains

Most investors in common stock are looking for capital gains (also known as capital appreciation) in addition to dividends—or, in the case of growth stocks, in lieu of dividends. They hope ultimately to sell each share at a higher price than they originally paid for it, but they must also face the possibility of a capital loss. Capital gain (loss) is calculated as follows:

$$\begin{matrix} \text{Total receipts} \\ \text{from sale} \end{matrix} - \left(\begin{matrix} \text{Selling} \\ \text{commission} \end{matrix} + \begin{matrix} \text{Purchase} \\ \text{cost} \end{matrix} \right) = \begin{matrix} \text{Capital} \\ \text{gain (loss)} \end{matrix}$$

The term **growth stocks** is usually applied to shares from companies that are thought to have very good prospects for increasing their business and thus their profits. As mentioned above, under "Common Share Dividends," growth companies tend to invest any profits back into the business instead of paying large dividends to shareholders. Investors who choose growth stocks are hoping that the shares' price will eventually rise, so that they can make a capital gain. If you want current income and low or moderate risk, do not choose growth stocks.

Investment Funds

Some people experience two obstacles to investing in the stock market. One is the management effort required. The other is the impossibility of achieving an appropriate level of diversity within a small portfolio. One solution to both problems involves investing in pooled funds, known collectively as **investment funds**. Such funds gather together the moneys of many investors; investment fund companies then, in turn, hire professional managers to invest the pooled funds in a portfolio comprising many securities. Each investor acquires units in the investment fund, rather than shares in the individual companies whose securities make up the fund's portfolio (see Figure 10.2). The fund itself owns the shares it buys on its unit holders' behalf. The investor pays fees to the investment funds company to make the investment decisions; in return, the investor receives whatever interest, dividends, or capital gain the securities held by the fund collectively earn.

Closed-End and Open-End Funds

Investment funds fall into one of two classes: (i) closed-end funds or (ii) open-end funds (see Figure 10.3). **Closed-end investment funds** issue a fixed number of units. After the initial offering, anyone who wishes to invest in a closed-end fund must find someone who has units

FIGURE 10.2 BUYING AN INVESTMENT FUND

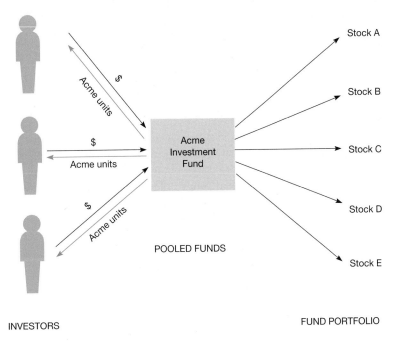

INVESTORS   POOLED FUNDS   FUND PORTFOLIO

FIGURE 10.3 CLOSED-END AND OPEN-END FUNDS

1. CLOSED-END FUND

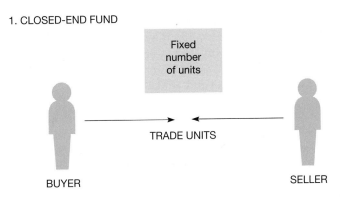

2. OPEN-END FUND—MUTUAL FUND

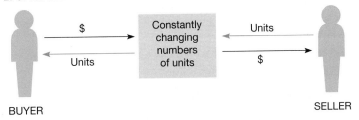

to sell. In September 2005, 198 closed-end funds traded on the S&P/TSX. Information on them may be found in the Saturday edition of *The Globe and Mail* in a special section, Fund Asset Values. These include the Aberdeen Asia-Pacific Fund and the Brompton Equal Weight Income Fund. To buy or sell such a fund, you must pay the usual broker's commission, but there are no front-end or back-end loading fees as are often charged by open-end mutual funds. The management expense ratio for such funds is also much smaller. The Brompton fund, for example, charges 0.45 percent of net asset value.

Open-end investment funds, commonly known as **mutual funds**, are much more numerous than closed-end funds. These funds do not have a fixed number of units; they will accept as much money as investors wish to put into them. Therefore, the total assets in a mutual fund portfolio are constantly changing; thus, such funds are referred to as open-ended. Investors buy units directly from the mutual funds company, which usually promises to redeem them at any time. Mutual funds differ from closed-end funds and from both common and preferred stock in that mutual fund units are never sold to one investor by another investor. A mutual fund, then, is an ever-changing common pool of funds that belongs to many investors, who have arranged for professional managers to invest in a portfolio on their behalf.

Exchange Traded Funds

Exchange Traded Funds (ETFs) are *closed-end* mutual funds that trade on a stock exchange, unlike regular mutual funds that do not trade. Also, unlike most mutual funds, ETFs are only passively, not actively, managed. Changes in the portfolios are usually only made when a company's stock is added to or deleted from the index tracked by the fund. Because of this characteristic, the MER for ETFs is much lower than that for mutual funds. The average MER for ETFs traded in Canada is 0.17 percent, while that for equity mutual funds is 2.29%.

The ETF is an asset class that is becoming increasingly popular because of its low MER and because, as a result of the bull market, investors with ETFs in their portfolios have experienced good returns. In 2000 only 30 ETFs traded on stock exchanges in Canada and the US. Today, there are over 100 with assets over $200 billion.

In Canada, ETFs are offered by TD Asset Management and Barclays Global Investors. As of June 30, 2005, TD had four Index Funds while Barclays[10] had 12.

TD ETFs are linked to the S&P/TSX Composite Index. The leading TD fund, the S&P/TSX Composite (Ticker symbol TTF-T) has an MER of .25%. It holds shares of the companies that make up the S&P/TSX Composite Index in the same proportion as they are in the index.

Barclays' funds are called iUnits. One example is the iUnits S&P/TSX 60 Index Fund, which invests in shares of the 60 companies that comprise the S&P/TSX 60 Index. It has an MER of 0.17 percent. Another, the iUnits S&P/TSX Capped REIT Index Fund, invests in real estate income trusts, or REITs, and has an MER of 0.55 percent.

For those wishing similar exposure to developing markets, Barclays recently started an emerging markets ETF. Known as MSCI Emerging Markets iShares, they trade on the American Stock Exchange. This ETF has an MER of 0.75 percent and is tied to the MSCI[11] Emerging Markets Free Index, which provides exposure to 26 developing economies including the booming Chinese and Indian markets.

This chapter's Women Take Charge follows one woman's introduction to ETFs.

---

[10]Barclays manages over 74 billion pounds of its clients' funds.

[11]MSCI stands for Morgan Stanley Capital International. Morgan Stanley is the largest investment bank in the US.

Women take CHARGE 10.1

Irene has graduated from university and found a steady job. She has built up an "emergency fund" by investing in term deposits and Canada Savings Bonds. These investments provide security and liquidity, but Irene would now like to explore alternatives that might provide a higher return.

Irene has decided to explore exchange traded funds (ETFs) as a possibility for getting into the stock market. Irene has done some research on ETFs through the internet and books written on the subject. She has discovered that an ETF enables her to invest in a diversified set of assets and thus spread the risk. The ETF is purchased from a broker, and a commission is paid just as if the person were buying a stock. Thus, front and back "loads" are avoided as with some traditional mutual funds. A very appealing feature of the ETF is that the management expense ratio (MER) tends to be lower than that for a mutual fund. The lower MER could make quite a difference in the value of Irene's investment over the long term. The stocks in an ETF index fund are the same as in the index being tracked. The manager of the ETF does not have to be as actively involved in selecting stocks. This is known as passive investing. For example, the iUnits S&P/TSE 60 holds the shares of 60 of Canada's largest companies, and the value of the S&P/TSE 60 closely follows the performance of these 60 companies.

When Irene decides to sell her ETFs, she can set a limit price because the ETF trades like a stock. With a mutual fund, you may have to decide to redeem shares at an unknown price since the redemption price is set once a day. An ETF is said to be more tax-efficient because there is not a lot of trading done within the fund to generate capital gains that are taxed.

Irene is impressed with the benefits offered by ETFs and would like to make some purchases. Upon researching which ETF to buy, she finds there are many options available. There are ETFs specializing in bonds such as the iUnits Government of Canada five-year Bond Fund. There are funds specializing in sectors of the economy such as the iUnits S&P/TSE Canadian Gold Index Fund and the iUnits S&P/TSE Canadian Financials Index Fund.

To attract global-minded investors, some ETFs, such as the MSCI South Korea Index, specialize in particular countries. The iShares MSCI EAFE Index Fund is a broader index covering Europe, Australasia, and the Far East.

Although she has discovered there are many benefits to having an ETF in her investment portfolio, Irene is also aware of the risk, as indices move both up and down. She has put aside an emergency fund and is looking at the long term, so she feels confident she can handle the risk.

Net Asset Value per Share

The value of an investment fund's individual shares, which is called the **net asset value per share** (NAVPS), is based on the net worth of the fund's total portfolio on any given date. The NAVPS is calculated by subtracting liabilities and management costs from the estimated value of the total portfolio, and then dividing the answer by the number of outstanding units. The calculation is as follows:

$$\text{Net asset value of portfolio} = \text{Total fund value of portfolio} - \left(\text{Liabilities} + \text{Management charges}\right)$$

$$\text{Net asset value per share} = \frac{\text{Net asset value of portfolio}}{\text{Total number of shares outstanding}}$$

The net asset value per share of a mutual fund is determined frequently (daily for most funds, but weekly or quarterly in some cases) and published regularly in the financial papers. While mutual funds are bought and sold at their NAVPS, closed-end funds trade on the stock market at prices that may be either at a premium or at a discount to their net asset value; the price depends on the demand for the shares. For instance, Central Fund of Canada, with a net asset value per share of $5.77, may be trading at $6.85 (that is, at a premium) on the same day that Aberdeen Asia Pacific, with a NAVPS of $9.80, is trading at $8.45 (or at a discount). The NAVPSs of closed-end funds are published occasionally in the financial papers.

Mutual Funds

Types of Mutual Funds

At the end of 2004 there were 1915 different mutual funds in Canada with assets of just under $500 billion. This money was invested in 48.7 million different accounts managed by 80 mutual fund companies.[12] Funds fall into different categories, each with different goals and approaches; the categories are described briefly below and are summarized in Table 10.1. There is probably a fund to suit the needs of every investor, from the most conservative to the most venturesome.

TABLE 10.1   CLASSIFICATION OF MUTUAL FUNDS

CATEGORY	DESCRIPTION
1. Money market funds	Invested in treasury bills, commercial paper, and short-term government bonds.
2. Mortgage funds	Invested in mortgages.
3. Bond funds	Invested in bonds.
4. Dividend funds	Invested in preferred shares and in good-quality common shares.
5. Balanced funds	Invested in both common shares and fixed income investments.
6. Asset allocation funds	Similar to balanced funds, but the shift between asset classes is more frequent.
7. Equity funds	Invested in common shares for the purpose of capital gains.
8. Specialty funds	Invested in common shares either in one specific industry or in one geographic location.
9. Global funds	Invested in markets outside Canada that are considered to have the best chance of gain.
10. Real estate funds	Invested in real estate companies for the purposes of gain.
11. Ethical funds	Invested in companies that do not make goods considered immoral or harmful to people, to animals, or to the environment.
12. Segregated funds	Sold by insurance companies as an alternative to the other types of mutual funds. Such funds are kept separate from all other funds controlled by the insurance company (see Chapter 6).
13. Labour-sponsored (venture capital) funds	For investors who are interested in long-term capital gain. Invested in companies that organized labour views as likely to help the economy grow (e.g., by creating jobs). Investors receive a federal tax credit.

[12]The Investment Funds Institute of Canada.

Money Market Funds The goal of a money market fund is income and liquidity. Income is usually distributed to unit holders each month, either as cash or as new units. As a result, there is no chance for capital gain.

Mortgage Funds The objective of a mortgage fund is income combined with safety. Since the mortgage terms are for five years or less, such funds are not very volatile, and thus they are considered less risky than bond funds.

Bond Funds A bond fund also has safety and income as goals, but because bond prices can fluctuate, investors in such funds may also have capital gains or losses. Such funds invest in high-yielding government and corporate bonds.

Dividend Funds Because the income from a dividend fund is paid in dividends, investors receive a dividend tax credit. And since they invest in stocks, these funds may also have capital gains or losses.

Balanced Funds A balanced fund seeks a combination of safety, income, and capital appreciation. Fixed income securities provide the stability, while common stocks provide income and the chance for capital gains.

Asset Allocation Funds Managers of asset allocation funds shift the weighting of their investments between equity, money market, and fixed income securities, with a view to maximizing the advantage to their investors by, for example, responding to what is happening with interest rates. Some such fund managers use computer models to determine the best moment for changing the asset allocation. Note, however, that whenever the assets in such a fund are reallocated, unit holders must pay tax on any capital gain.

Equity Funds While an equity fund's managers may purchase fixed-income securities for purposes of income and liquidity, most of the money in such a fund is invested in common shares. As a result, the values of equity fund units tend to fluctuate.

Specialty Funds The purpose of a specialty fund is capital gain. To achieve this goal, the specialty fund's managers invest in the shares of companies in one particular industry (such as high-tech companies) or in one geographical area, such as Latin America. The idea is to invest in a rapidly growing industry or area or in one that is viewed as being about to take off. As a result of this investment strategy, specialty funds are often more speculative than equity funds.

Global Funds A global fund is a type of specialty fund that invests in those global markets seen as best suited to the fund's objectives—which always involve growth and long-term capital gains. These funds do not specialize in a single geographic area; instead, they concentrate on emerging markets located anywhere in the world. Some global fund managers invest in bonds; others concentrate on equities; and still others aim to create a balanced fund.

Real Estate Funds A real estate fund's managers are interested in long-term growth; to achieve this result, they invest in income-producing real estate (that is, land and/or buildings that are rented to others at a profit, such as an apartment building, a shopping centre, or an office building).

Ethical Funds

An ethical fund is designed to appeal to people who are averse to investing in firms that produce socially and morally offensive products (such as tobacco or alcohol) or products that harm the environment; such funds concentrate instead on companies whose products are above reproach. They also invest in firms that have reputations for good employee relations.

Segregated Funds

As described in Chapter 6 (under "Segregated Funds"), segregated funds have a variety of objectives. Some invest in equities, while others choose bonds, and others aim for a balanced approach. In this way, they are like other mutual funds. The difference is that segregated funds are sold only by insurance companies and come with a guarantee of principal when the fund matures.

Labour-Sponsored (Venture Capital) Funds

A venture capital fund is one that is sponsored by organized labour (i.e., a trade union); its interests lie in long-term gain. Such funds invest in small and mid-sized companies to help promote economic growth and jobs. Investors who buy units in a venture capital fund receive a tax credit.

Risk Levels

Before investing in a particular mutual fund, you can estimate its risk level by examining the type of securities held in its portfolio and by comparing its past performance with that of others from the same fund category. The financial press rates mutual funds according to their risk or volatility based on the stability of the rates of return of the stocks in the fund's portfolio. The various financial papers use somewhat different measures of volatility, which are explained in the report each paper publishes on mutual funds. For instance, *The Globe and Mail*'s "Report on Business" section reports volatility on a scale of 1 (low) to 10 (high). Volatility data show how a fund's monthly return has fluctuated in recent years, compared with that of other funds within the same category. When one category of funds is compared against another, money market funds are usually at the low end of the scale, while growth funds are at the high end. High-variability funds make great gains when the stock market is rising—but conversely, they lose rapidly in a falling market. Low-risk funds will neither make nor lose as much money.

Fees

The fees charged for investing in mutual funds not only vary considerably among funds but have also become increasingly difficult for investors to assess. The sales commissions charged when shares are either purchased or redeemed are made quite explicit. But annual fees for management and other expenses tend to be less well-explained.

Acquisition Fees

A sales fee that is imposed when you purchase mutual fund units is called an **acquisition fee** or a **front-end loading charge;** such charges may range from 1 to 5 percent of the amount you are investing. This type of fee tends to be higher for funds managed by companies that hire their sales force directly. Independent brokers, who handle the funds of many companies, may be willing to negotiate a lower commission fee.

Redemption Fees

Another way of covering sales commissions is to charge a **redemption fee** or **rear-end loading charge,** which is paid when you withdraw money from the fund. Redemption fees may be a set amount per transaction (e.g., $15 to $25), or they may be calculated as a percentage (e.g., 1 to 8 percent) of either your initial investment or your holding's current market value. Redemption fees often have a sliding-scale structure: the longer you hold the funds, the lower the redemption fee you will pay when you do withdraw money. After nine years or so, the fee may fall to zero. Some investors are attracted by redemption fees as a way of postponing costs. But you should not select a mutual fund only by the timing of its fees; you will need to consider other factors, such as risk and performance, as well. Nevertheless, the length of time you expect to hold your shares is an important consideration when choosing between a front-load fund and a back-load fund.

No-Load Funds Funds that do not charge sales fees are called **no-load funds**. Be careful, though: such funds may simply disguise their fees. Some supposedly no-load funds impose a "distribution fee" of 1 percent a year, which is added to the management fee for the first few years as a way of compensating salespeople. Genuine no-load funds, most of which have no sales force, use other methods of finding investors, such as advertising, direct mail, and arrangements with stockbrokers. Sometimes, a system of reciprocal commissions will be arranged, whereby mutual funds managers who need the services of stockbrokers will agree to send business to a particular broker—who, in return, will promote sales of that particular mutual fund. In such instances, the investor pays no sales fee but may receive somewhat biased advice.

Management Fees Management fees represent a significant cost for both closed-end and mutual funds. While acquisition and redemption fees are visible, management fees are less so. Charges of between 1 and 3 percent a year are deducted directly from the fund's assets before the return to investors is calculated. Management fees cover a variety of costs, including investment advice, annual reports, legal services, brokerage commissions, sales commissions, and the federal goods and services tax (GST). A useful means of comparing the management fees of various funds is the **expense ratio**. This ratio, expressed as a percentage, is an annual ratio of all fees (excluding sales fees) and expenses to the fund's average net assets. A cursory examination of newspaper reports on mutual funds indicates how widely funds vary in their expense ratios, even within a similar group of funds. Some of the factors that affect fund expense ratios are the marketing and distribution costs of a fund, and whether or not the fund pays trailer fees. Some funds pay their agents annual commissions, called **trailer fees**, in addition to the initial sales commission. A broker receives trailer fees on an ongoing basis as encouragement to continue to provide services to the client. The **management expense ratio** (MER) is usually between 2 and 3 percent in Canada.

Buying Mutual Funds

Buying units in a mutual fund is easy. When you want to invest, you either contact the fund company directly or contact a mutual funds agent, and indicate how much money you wish to invest. Your cost will be the net asset value per unit plus any sales fees (see Personal Finance in Action Box 10.5, "Investing in a Mutual Fund"). Likewise, when you want to sell mutual fund units, you need only inform one of the fund's representatives. You will receive the current net asset value per unit less any exit fees.

Personal FINANCE in action 10.5

Investing in a Mutual Fund

Tulia was a very busy woman. Her job at one of the world's largest consumer products companies kept her busy most evenings and weekends. This didn't bother her because she loved the work and found it stimulating. Her job paid very well and she soon had surplus cash, which she decided should be invested. Realizing that she could not actively manage any investments she might make, she decided to check out some mutual funds. The things that mattered most to her were the fees the funds charged, the return she might expect to see, and the reliability of the fund. She decided to see what the chartered banks had to offer and then compare the results, assuming she had made an investment of $5000 in each of three funds five years ago.

Bank A	Bank B	Bank C
No minimum investment	$500 minimum investment	$1000 minimum investment
MER: 1.3%	MER: 1.45%	MER: 1.55%
Front/rear loading fees: 0	Front/rear loading fees: 0	Front/rear loading fees: 0
5-year average annual return 7.71%	5-year average annual return 11.8%	5-year average annual return 13.7%
$5000 invested	$5000 invested	$5000 invested
Value at end of 5 years: $6967.21	Value at end of 5 years: $8118.26	Value at end of 5 years: $8787.20

She realized that past performance was no guarantee of future performance, a caveat all funds stress, but concluded that Bank C's fund was the one she would invest in. Even with the highest MER, it had turned in the best performance.

Because the market is very competitive and many agents are anxious to sell mutual fund units, you must consider your choices carefully. As a guide, here are four steps to take when you are thinking of investing in mutual funds (each will be discussed in further detail below):

(a) Determine your objectives for this investment.
(b) Find a fund that matches your objectives.
(c) Investigate the fees that will be charged.
(d) Analyze the past performance of several possible funds.

Objectives   The names of mutual funds often indicate their different objectives—for example, growth, income, dividend, and money market funds. You can find more information about a fund's objectives in its prospectus, which lists the securities currently held in the portfolio. Since many mutual fund companies operate a number of funds with different objectives, you can contact a few companies, state your objectives, and request the prospectuses of any appropriate funds. You will find the web addresses of mutual fund companies in the "Personal Finance on the Web" section at the end of this chapter.

Fees The various fees already described can have a significant effect on the gains you will make from your mutual fund investment. Compare the fees (both obvious and hidden) carefully before choosing a fund.

Performance Information about a mutual fund's past performance can be useful to prospective mutual fund buyers. How does this fund's historical return compare with those of similar funds? The financial papers publish regular surveys of mutual fund performance over a number of years. The yield figures are based on annual compound rates of return, assuming that dividends and capital gain are reinvested in the fund. But the reported returns exclude direct charges, such as acquisition or redemption fees. Hidden fees for management costs have been taken into account, but you must also consider the effect of sales fees on reported investment return. Of course, past performance is not a sure indication of future success; still, it is one factor that is worth considering.

Advantages and Disadvantages To conclude this discussion of mutual funds, we will summarize the four advantages and the four disadvantages of such investment vehicles. The advantages of mutual funds are as follows:

(a) professional management,

(b) the wide variety of funds available,

(c) the opportunity to diversify,

(d) the units' marketability.

Mutual funds may also present disadvantages for investors; generalizing is difficult, though, because of the great variety of funds. The following factors do not apply to all funds, but the list suggests the matters you might wish to consider:

(a) low liquidity,

(b) high fees,

(c) the long-term nature of the investment,

(d) the variable skill of fund managers.

Equity mutual funds are low in liquidity because their unit values fluctuate as the whole stock market rises and falls. The optimum time for selling your units may therefore not coincide with your need for funds. The substantial fees attached to mutual funds may, at least in the short term, reduce the net yield on your investment. With the exception of money market funds, most mutual funds make for poor short-term investments; they are best selected with a view to remaining invested over the long term. And, of course, the success of a particular fund depends greatly on the skill of its managers.

Wrap Accounts

To reduce the confusion caused by the great variety of mutual fund accounts and by the complexities of the funds' elaborate fee structures, the investment industry has developed a new product. Known as a **wrap account**, this investment vehicle has the maintenance-free appeal of a mutual fund, along with some added benefits. A wrap account features none of the front-end or rear-end load charges that many mutual fund investors find so confusing. In addition, no commission is charged on each transaction (as is the case with equities). Instead, wrap account clients are charged an annual management fee, which ranges from 1 percent to 3.5 percent of the amount invested; and unlike standard mutual fund fees, this charge is tax deductible. To open a wrap, you need a minimum investment of at least $100 000. For your management fee, however, you do get individual service from a professional asset manager, and you will have more input into how your funds are invested than is possible with a mutual fund.

Investment Risk

Types of Risk

All investments are exposed to some degree of risk, but the kind of risk varies with the type of investment. It is essential that you be aware of and be willing to accept the risks associated with any investment you are considering. As explained in Chapter 8 (under "Investment Risks") investors face risks caused by (i) inflation, which causes the value of cash and that of debt securities to fall; (ii) interest rates, which have differential effects on various investments; (iii) the stock market, where the demand for a security rises and falls; and (iv) the poor performance or outright failure of a particular business. When you own stocks, your investment is subject to three kinds of risk: market risk, business risk, and interest rate risks.

Market Risk An asset may lose favour among investors because of factors other than either the company's profitability or the prevailing economic conditions. The price of an equity asset also depends on demand in a stock market that is variable. It is normal for stock prices to fluctuate for many reasons, some of which may be unrelated to earnings or dividend changes. Since a great deal of emotion is associated with stock ownership, irrational factors influence prices. It is therefore extremely difficult to predict the direction or magnitude of change in stock prices in the short run; over the long run, however, stock prices have produced real gains (that is, gains in excess of inflation).

Business Risk Although the business in which you have invested could fail totally, the more likely risk is that the firm's earnings could decline. Lower earnings often result in lower dividends and a drop in the security's price. You also risk paying too much for a stock. One example many Canadians will not soon forget concerned the price of gold. On the morning of November 14, 1997, gold's price per ounce fell to US $299.25. In January 1997, gold had been valued at over US $380 an ounce. Its price had not dropped below US $300 since February 1985. Because this price decrease meant that some gold producers would have a difficult time making money, their share prices fell accordingly. Shares of Agnico Eagle, a Canadian gold mine, for example, that had been worth $20.25 a year earlier fell to $7.05 at this news. By April 24, 1998, however, the per-ounce price of gold in Europe had rebounded to US $314. This did not mean that the US $380 price was again within reach, but at least the prospects for some gold producers were no longer quite so grim. Agnico Eagle shares, reflecting the more positive outlook, closed at $10.25 that day. Shares of Barrick Gold, a major producer, whose value had plunged to $25.80 on November 14, had climbed to $33 by April 24.

   The reality every investor has to face is that no one, not even the shrewdest investment professional, knows when share prices will rise or fall. You could conceivably find two opposite forecasts for the same stock on the same day in the same newspaper. That is just the nature of the market: investing is a very imprecise business. At any given time, some analysts will be bullish (that is, they will believe that market prices will continue to travel generally upward, perhaps with minor "corrections," for a considerable time to come) and others will be bearish (that is, they will expect market prices to fall). As already mentioned, the best investment advice is to buy and hold stocks in good companies. When you do this, you avoid the market's periodic ups and downs in the market and will likely come out ahead, since stocks generally rise over the long term. Practise patience, and operate with a long-term investment horizon.

Interest Rate Risk Rising interest rates, which are beneficial for people who have invested in debt securities, are not helpful for shareholders. High interest rates restrict business activity and tend to affect both profits and share prices adversely. When interest rates are low, people decide to buy cars and houses, and businesses borrow to expand. This increased activity is reflected in rising stock prices.

Risk Reduction

Since there is no way to pick investments that will do well under all circumstances or to avoid experiencing a certain number of bad results, the rational approach is to take steps to reduce the risk you are exposed to. Some risk will always remain because the future may not turn out as we expect. Some people are more averse to risk than others—that is, they are less comfortable with uncertainty. The most risk-averse people are uneasy with any but the most secure fixed-income investments. They prefer certainty to the possibility of greater yield.

Knowing that it is impossible to avoid all risk, wise investors decide on an acceptable risk level and then try to spread this risk by diversification. Diversification can be applied at several levels: to the investor's total portfolio, and to individual elements within it. For example, a portfolio might be balanced between debt investments and equity investments. Within both the debt portion and the equity portion, however, further diversity is possible as well as desirable. A well-constructed stock portfolio, for instance, does not concentrate solely on any one sector. Instead of holding shares in, say, only oil companies, some portfolios would also have shares in transportation, utilities, or industrial products sectors. A diversified portfolio increases the odds that while some securities will not do as well as you hope, others will do better than expected, thereby balancing out the portfolio's performance on the whole. In a well-balanced portfolio, the overall risk will be less than the risk associated with any particular investment. Diversity reduces risk by allowing successes in one sector to offset poor performance in another, since individual companies react in different ways to economic and other conditions.

But like nearly any good thing, even diversification can be carried to a problematic extreme. No one investor can effectively monitor a portfolio that contains too many kinds of assets. For a small stock portfolio, six to ten stocks may be appropriate. A workable guideline is until your investments exceed $50 000 (excluding the value of your residence), you should limit any given asset to roughly 10 percent of the total. People with a larger net worth may be able to handle 20 securities.

Beta

Beta is a term used to help determine a stock's risk by comparing its historic price volatility with that of the S&P/TSX Composite Index. The market has a beta of 1, and the beta for stocks ranges from 0.5 to 2. Stocks with a history of volatility (risk), such as the shares of resource-based companies, will have a beta higher than 1, while those with a less volatile history will have a beta lower than 1. According to investment theory, during a bull market, riskier stocks with higher betas will rise more than more defensive stocks with lower betas, and vice versa during a bear market.

The problem with using beta as a tool to determine a stock's risk is that it is based on the assumption that a stock's history and market history will be repeated. These are assumptions it may be financially dangerous to make. One recent example concerns the stocks of Canada's resource-based companies, the historic hewers of wood and drawers of water. They did very well in 2005, partly as a result of takeovers and expected takeovers and strong growth in China and India. According to past history, once such stocks have risen it is time to sell and lock in the gains before the inevitable happens and they drop in price. Resource-based stocks are classified as cyclical because of their volatility.

Many analysts are forecasting that the economies of the Asian giants will continue to grow and that therefore, their demand for Canada's resources will not slow down, at least not as soon as other, more bearish analysts speculate. We have reached a point because of the growth in the world's two largest countries where analysts are now referring to *super cycles*, meaning the cyclical demand for natural resources continues much longer than usual. It may, or may not. This is one of the conundrums associated with investing. No one knows what will happen.

Tax on Investment Income

Investment income may come in the form of interest, dividends, or capital gains. These three types of income are taxed at different rates.

1. Interest income is taxed at the same rate as one's salary.
2. Only 50 percent of capital gains must be included as income.
3. Dividend income is taxed in a strange way.

A new Canadian government was elected in 2005. In the 2006 budget it changed the way dividends are taxed. For 2006, dividends from Canadian corporations are *grossed-up* (increased) by 45 percent. Therefore, if a person receives dividends of $1000, $1450 must be reported as income. From this, however, a *dividend tax credit* of 19 percent of the grossed-up amount is deducted from the taxes payable.

Dividends received	$1000
Gross-up ($1000 × 1.45)	$1450
Dividend tax credit (19 × $1450)	$275.50

The credit of $275.50 is then deducted from taxable income.

This change reduced the tax on dividends as can be seen from Table 10.2.

Because of the dividend tax credit, there is a significant difference in after-tax income between dividends and interest income, as can be seen from Table 10.3. Interest income is taxed at the same rate as income from wages and salaries.

TABLE 10.2 FEDERAL TAX ON DIVIDENDS, 2005–2006

	2005	2006
Top marginal tax rate	29%	29%
Dividend gross-up	1.25%	1.45%
Dividend tax credit	16.6%	27.5%
Federal tax	19.6%	14.5%

TABLE 10.3	DIVIDEND AND INTEREST RATE COMPARISON				
Dividend Yield	2%	3%	4%	5%	6%
Interest Equivalent	2.56%	3.84%	5.12%	6.40%	7.68%

Alternative Ways to Invest

Cash Management Account / Asset Allocation Account

A recent addition to the services offered by some investment dealers is the **cash management account (CMA)**. For a minimum balance ranging from as low as $25 000 to as high as $250 000, clients can have all of their financial needs handled through their broker. CMAs allow clients to combine bank accounts, investment accounts, and credit-card accounts. Using their ABM card, customers can pay bills, write cheques, and even borrow on margin to purchase securities. In addition, the interest rates on CMA deposits are high and the annual fee low, usually about $200.

Split Shares

Another new product available to investors is the **split share**. A new company is created (let's call ours The Company) that purchases shares of a number of companies, usually in the same sector or industry. The Company's shares, in this example, trade at $46.00 and pay a dividend of $1.20 per share for a yield of 2.6 percent.

The Company then splits the shares into two types of shares, a preferred for investors wary of risk and desirous of income and a capital share for investors who want growth. In this example, the preferred share is valued at $25.00 and the capital share at $21.00. The dividend of $1.20 is paid to the preferred shareholder, providing a yield of 4.8 percent.

The capital share benefits from any capital appreciation of the underlying basket of stocks. It also benefits from a *leverage* feature not available to investors who own regular common stock. If the market value of the shares held by The Company rises to $55.00, all the gain (19.56 percent) goes to the capital share, which is now worth $30.00 (21 + 9), an increase of 42.85 percent. Should the share price of The Company decline by 19.56 percent, however, the capital share would only be worth $12.00, a decline of 42.85 percent.

Split shares mature in either five or seven years. At that time the preferred shareholder gets the lesser of, in the case of this example, (i) $25 or (ii) the market value of the portfolio. The capital shareholder gets what is leftover.

As of September 2005, 29 cyclical split shares were listed on the S&P/TSX, as Table 10.4 shows.[13]

Equity Derivatives

No discussion of stocks and mutual funds would be complete without some mention of **equity derivatives**, which have received considerable publicity in the financial press. While these instruments have been used mainly by institutional investors, they also show

---

[13]S&P/TSX Financial Split Share Corporations.

TABLE 10.4   CYCLICAL SPLIT SHARES LISTED ON THE S&P/TSX

COMPANY NAME	SHARES	QUOTED MARKET VALUE
5Banc, Split Inc.	FBS.A, FBS.PR.A	86 492 589
AIC Diversified Canada Split Corp.	ADC, ADC.PR.A	47 811 457
Allbanc Split Corp.	ABK.A, ABK.PR.C	83 527 197
B Split II Corp.	BXN, BXN.PR.A	52 690 264
Big 8 Split Inc.	BIG.A, BIG.PR.A	173 633 460
BMONT Split Corp.	BMT, BMT.PR.A	88 068 750
BNN Split Corp.	BNA. PR.A, BNA.PR.B	215 700 000
BNS Split Corp.	BSN, BSN.PR.A	21 854 747
Brompton Equity Split Corp.	BE, BE.PR.A	80 387 265
Canadian Life Companies Split Corp.	LFE, LFE.PR.A	220 835 275
Cyclical Split NT Corp.	CYC, CYC.PR.A	35 923 691
Dividend 15 Split Corp.	DFN, DFN.PR.A	214 200 000
Financial 15 Split Corp.	FTN, FTN.PR.A	284 272 000
Financial 15 Split Corp. II	FFN, FFN.PR.A	165 088 000
Global 45 Split Crop.	GFV, GFV.PR.A.	42 262 830
Global Resource Split Corp.	GSX, GSX.PR.A	67 722 407
Global Telecom Split Share Corp.	GT.A, GT.PR.A	34 100 875
Lifeco Split Corporation Inc.	LSC, LSC.PR.A	73 698 414
MCM Split Share Corp.	MUH.A, MUH.PR.A	120 798 447
Mulvihill Pro-AMS RSP Split Share Corp.	SPL.A, SPL.B	54 500 659
R Split II Corp.	RBT, RBT.PR.A	60 509 882
Sixty Split Corp.	SXT, SXT.PR.A	225 845 584
SNP Health Split Corp.	SNH.U, SNH.PR.U	84 129 267
SNP Split Corp.	SNP.U, SNP.PR.U	170 146 039
Split Yield Corporation	YLD, YLD.PR.A, YLD.PR.B	47 672 978
TD Split Inc.	TDS, TDS.PR.A	111 112 656
Thirty-Five Split Corp.	TFS, TFS.PR.A	53 650 679
US Finanical 15 Split Corp.	FTU, FTU.PR.A	110 223 750
World Finanical Split Corp.	WFS, WFS.PR.A	404 332 500

up in the portfolios of private or retail investors with a fondness for risk. They are not for the faint of heart.

An option to buy the underlying security is a call. An option to sell is called a put. Call options increase in value as the security on which they are derived rises in value. Holders of calls are bullish. A put option increases in value when the market falls. Holders of puts are bearish. Those who sell options are said to be writing an option. Those who buy options are called holders. (They are both investors but the term "investor" is not used in this case.)

Bearish investors (those who expect the market to fall) will be sellers of call options or buyers of put options. Those with contracts to sell call options are obligated to sell the shares from which the call is derived at a specified price before a specified time. Those with contracts to buy put options are obligated to buy the shares from which the put is derived at a specified price before a specified time. If they have speculated correctly, the market will have fallen and they will come out ahead in both cases.

Hedge Funds

Also known as *alternative strategies funds*, **hedge funds** are another form of derivative invest-ment. Hedge fund managers apply a variety of investment strategies to try to retain asset value and reduce the risk of loss. The easiest strategy to understand is the long/short equity fund. Hedge fund managers buy stocks considered cheap, planning to hold them until they rise in value and, in the process, make money for their clients. This is known as *going long* and is the traditional method of hedge fund investing. At the same time, managers sell securities that the fund does not own, by borrowing them from investment dealers, with the intention of buying the securities back when their price falls, and then paying the broker and making money on the difference. This tactic is known as **selling short**. Since the market must go either up or down, the fund is "hedged" and its risk of loss reduced. More complicated are funds known as *fund of funds*. Such funds use a variety of fund managers applying vastly dif-ferent strategies and very sophisticated methods. These may include *leverage*, *arbitrage*, *options*, *futures*, *cash*, and *swaps*, as well as short selling. These funds should only be consid-ered by those who fully understand the strategies used.

Originally, only an investor with over $1 million to invest could invest in hedge funds. Now, in Canada, those with as little as $50 000 may do so, though most funds require from $100 000 to $150 000. In spite of the name and the concept of wealth protection, such funds can be very risky. They can and do lose money. The negative side of such funds is exemplified by Long Term Capital Management, a US hedge fund with assets of over US $120 billion. Disaster struck this fund in 1998 when the Russian government devalued the ruble and stopped paying interest on its debt. The fund was bailed out by a consortium of 14 firms as a result of a deal organized by the Federal Reserve Bank. In spite of the bailout, fund investors lost a great deal of money. In April 2003 there was US $600 billion invested in hedge funds worldwide. Little is known about them because, unlike conventional mutual funds, they are not allowed to advertise.

Arbitrage

Securities trade on different exchanges. Many Canadian stocks, for example, trade on both the TSX and the New York Stock Exchange. Because of the exchange rate between the Canadian and American dollars, there may be a slight difference in the price per share traded on the two exchanges if converted from one currency to the other. When there is, hedge fund managers may simultaneously buy shares on the exchange with the lower price and sell them on the exchange with the higher price. Known as **arbitrage**, this may not seem very lucrative for the small investor, but it can make a significant difference when millions of dollars are involved.

Swaps

The **swap**, an obligation by two parties to exchange payments over a specific time at a pre-arranged rate, has been used since 1981. It includes commodity swaps, currency swaps, equity swaps, and interest rate swaps. The most common are *interest rate swaps*, which are agreements between two parties to make interest payments to each other periodically on pre-arranged dates. One party pays a fixed rate of interest agreed upon before the swap is made. The other is a floating rate player whose interest rate is determined by market forces. The notational[14] amount, on which the interest is paid, does not change hands.

---

[14]Notational money is simply a notation in a bank ledger.

The *currency swap* allows a hedge fund to reduce the costs of borrowing in both domestic and foreign markets. When currency is swapped, payments denominated in one currency are exchanged for those denominated in another currency at some future date. Payments are based on a *notational principal sum* (a notation in the fund's books) whose value is fixed before the swap is made. At maturity, a final payment is made based on the change in value of the notational principal amount.[15]

Income Trusts

Also known as *flow-through entities*, **income trusts** (ITs) are relatively new and have very quickly become an important addition to the list of products available to investors. In 2000, Income Trusts had a market value of $18 billion. By 2004, this had grown to $118 billion. ITs are derived from mature businesses with a regular flow of income. The underlying business creates a trust. Units in the trust are offered to investors in the same way as a new category of shares, through a prospectus. Once sold, the units are listed on a stock exchange and trade like stocks. With the proceeds the trust buys the equity and debt of the host company.

Income generated by the trust "flows through" to unitholders. Tax is not paid by the trust or by the business from which it is derived—unlike income from a corporation that is taxed both in the hands of the corporation and by the shareholder. (The dividend tax credit is an attempt to resolve this anomaly.) Instead, tax is paid by the unitholders. This income may be distributed as dividends or as capital gains. In addition, the trust may pay out more money than the trust earns. These extra payments are considered a return of capital and reduce the amount of the unitholder's cost base.

There are four categories of income trusts: business trusts, real estate investment trusts, natural resource trusts, and public utilities trusts. They have become popular, particularly with older investors, because they are tax-efficient and have high yields, at a time when interest rates are unusually low.

A *business trust* is based on businesses in industry, manufacturing, or services. The number of businesses converting to trusts has been constantly expanding.[16] They include coal and sugar distributors and those involved in retail sales, food sales and processing, chemicals, and refrigerated warehouses.

A *real estate investment trust* (REIT) is a trust that invests in income-producing properties, often in shopping centres, that generate regular distributions of cash. Income distributions are relatively constant because of the rental income paid to the trust. Such trusts allow investors to invest in real estate without the problems associated with ownership such as liquidity. In addition to REITS that invest only in shopping malls, there are those that invest only in apartment buildings, industrial properties, hotels, and nursing homes.

Resource trusts are based on businesses active in Canada's resource-based economy, including those that produce minerals, coal, oil, natural gas, and forest products. One variety

[15]For more detailed information on swaps refer to Francesca Taylor, *Mastering Derivatives Markets: A Step-by-Step Guide to the Products, Applications and Risk*, Second Edition.

[16]In the fall of 2005, the Finance Department indicated that it may change the tax-privileged status of ITs. It also put a halt to the creation of new trusts. These announcements cast a large shadow over ITs and caused some panic among older investors. The minority Conservative government, elected in January 2006, announced that it may change the way dividends are taxed in order to make corporate shares more competitive with income trusts. In November 2006, the Minister of Finance announced that the tax advantage enjoyed by trusts will end in 2011. From then on they will have to pay tax. The amount of money available for payment to investors will, therefore, decline.

is the oil and gas income trust, where the underlying business is in the production and distribution of oil and natural gas.

Unlike the income generated by REITS, that generated by the resource trust often varies because of the ebb and flow of commodity prices. And again unlike the REIT, the income stream from a resource trust may eventually run out as the ore body or supply of gas and oil runs out, unless some funds are kept back by the trust to purchase further properties.

The *Utility Trust* is usually based on businesses involved in the generation of electricity from various sources or in the operation of telecommunications. The income paid to unitholders of such trusts is relatively stable.

For a current list of income trusts, go to **www.tsx.com** and click on Sector Profiles and then Exchange Traded Funds and Structured Products.

Foreign Exchange: The Currency Market

No book on personal finance would be complete without some mention of the **foreign exchange market**. While not mentioned in the financial news nearly as often as the stock markets or the mutual funds market, the market in currencies is larger and therefore more important than either. The trade in currencies averages about US $1.5 trillion per day. The value of stocks traded on the New York Stock Exchange, the world's most important, by comparison, averages only about US $30 billion per day.[17]

Most of the trade in currencies is done to make money and serves no useful purpose. Some is business-related, as when corporations convert money earned in a foreign market into their domestic currencies or buy currencies to hedge against unexpected currency price fluctuations. Some foreign exchange trade is carried out by governments as part of their countries' monetary policies. The Canadian government, for example, may sell US dollars and buy Canadian dollars to try to stop the decline in value of the Canadian dollar. Individuals also participate in the market when they buy foreign currencies in anticipation of travel to other countries.

But the vast majority of transactions in the currency market are conducted by traders. As with the market in stocks, traders may either buy long or sell short. If someone expects a currency to rise in value, he or she can buy it and then sell when the price is higher. This is known as having a long position. Someone selling short expects a currency to decline in value. This trader sells the currency she or he does not have and buys it when the value actually falls, settling the account and making a profit in the process.

As can be guessed, the currency market is highly speculative and not for those who would be just as happy with a Canada Savings Bond. Like the bond market, there is no physical foreign exchange market. The currency market is known as the inter-dealer market, where transactions are carried out by traders over the telephone or electronically, with price changes known immediately. Over 85 percent of the currencies traded are *hard* currencies, that is, major currencies like the yen, the US dollar, the euro, or the British pound. These are all currencies of democratic countries with stable governments and therefore less risky than the currencies of developing and Third World countries.

Even though more secure, the trade in the currencies of democratic countries is still subject to rapid fluctuations caused by any of the major economic or political events that may occur. At the merest hint of bad news, traders will sell the currency of one country and

[17]Bank for International Settlements.

buy that of another. If interest rates in the United States are cut, for example, traders may sell US dollars and buy a currency with stable or rising rates. Such trading can cause significant changes in a country's currency and may cause political turmoil.

Collectibles

Wine   Books on investing often recommend collecting fine wines. As with other things of value such as works of art, fine and rare wines often appreciate in value. The impression of rare wines being sold at exorbitant prices has been enhanced by news stories emanating from legendary auction houses such as Sotheby's and Christie's. In Canada it has been impossible for collectors of wines to resell them. The liquor boards in most provinces have a monopoly in the sale of wine. In Ontario, however, it is now possible for an investor to sell wines at auction. Ritchies,[18] an auction house in Toronto, in conjunction with Vintages, the fine and rare wines division of the Liquor Control Board of Ontario, now conducts an annual auction. The wines sold are not available elsewhere. They are purchased by collectors, hoteliers and restaurateurs. Estimated sale prices at a recent auction ranged from $100 to $2000 a bottle. The first auction in 2002 sold over $2 400 000 worth of wine. No similar auction is held anywhere else in Canada.

As with auctions of other goods, Ritchie's charges a commission to sell wine. The amount charged is a percentage of the wine's value. This is determined as follows:

- 10 percent on lots (a lot may be one or more bottles) priced over $7500.
- 15 percent on lots priced between $ 2501 and $7500.
- 20 percent on lots priced up to $2500.

The seller is also charged an insurance fee of 1 percent of the lot's value.

Fine Art   When stock markets fall, affluent investors, looking for something of more stable value, often turn to art. They believe that if they buy quality paintings or sculpture, the values will increase and compensate them for the decline in value of their other investments. This may or may not happen. What one collector may regard as priceless, another may consider junk. Today's masterpiece may also become tomorrow's embarrassment if its price falls. The reverse, of course, can and does happen, as anyone with some knowledge of the history of art is aware.

The market for fine art is much less structured than that for stocks. The stock market lets investors know instantly what their shares are worth at any particular moment. It also provides an orderly mechanism to assist buyers and sellers in making trouble-free transactions easily, by telephone, or with the click of a mouse. In addition, it lets them know how much action there is in a particular stock and whether market sentiment is positive or negative. To make a transaction, buyers pay a commission whether they buy online or from a full-service broker.

There is also no "art market" comparable to a stock market. Collectors must go to an auction house, such as Ritchie's, that regularly has fine art auctions. These are not held every business day, as are the auction markets for stocks. Therefore, the collector or investor has no way of knowing what his/her work of art is worth. In addition, there is no

[18]www.ritchies.com/abo.cfm.

accurate pricing mechanism for works of art. Prices for artists' work are not quoted daily as they are for stocks. When auction houses have sales, their experts can only estimate what a painting will sell for. A work by Group of Seven painter A. Y. Jackson, for example, may be expected to sell for between $500 000 and $600 000. It may sell in this price range or some price higher or lower. A painting by Franklin Carmichael, estimated to sell at between $700 000 and $800 000 at Waddington's, another Toronto auction house, sold for $915 000 on December 3, 2002.[19] No one, not even the most sophisticated art expert, can predict for certain what a work of art will sell for. The buyer of the Carmichael may find, if he or she tries to sell the painting in a few years' time, that it may be worth much more, or it may be worth much less. It is a good idea therefore, when buying art, to buy only works you enjoy looking at. If you like them, they may be priceless to you even though no one else agrees with you.

Commissions for selling art are the same as those for selling wine. At 10 percent, the commission on the Carmichael was $91 500. Commissions on the sale of stock vary. One investment dealer charges the following:

■ For web or automated telephone banking, the charge is $25 on orders up to 1000 shares of any value.

■ For orders placed through a representative on shares worth $20.01 and over the charge is $35 plus six cents a share. Assuming an order for 1000 shares at $50 per share, the charge would be $35 plus $60, or $95.

■ Full-service commissions are based on the number of shares, the price per share and what commission the investment dealer is willing to accept. For very large orders these are negotiable. The dealer wants his client to be satisfied.

Coins and Stamps   Many people collect coins and stamps. Rare ones do appreciate in value. Both may be purchased in person or online. There are numerous dealers who have regular sales, often once a month. There are also online auction houses such as eBay. However, as with fine art, there is no "coin market" or "stamp market" comparable to the stock market. The pricing and sale of both is not structured. Collectors and investors have no way of knowing what items may be worth until they try to buy or sell them. Prices are not quoted in the press. Dealers will appraise collections and recommend prices, which may or may not be accurate. Stock prices are quoted throughout every trading day. It is therefore much easier for the investor in stocks to know the value of her/his portfolio. Investors who collect stamps or art should appreciate them for their historical interest rather than what value they might command at auction.[20]

Investing in Rental Accommodation

People unfamiliar with or distrustful of the stock market, mutual funds, and other traditional investments often invest in rental housing. Housing is considered a good investment, in theory, because prices for houses often increase. Therefore, in addition to the rent

[19]**www.waddingtons.ca** (accessed January 22, 2004).

[20]All Nations Stamp and Coin, **www.downtownstamps.bc.ca**, has an auction each week.

received, the homeowner should make a capital gain, which will be realized when the house is sold.

As with all types of investment, there are both pros and cons to investing in **rental accommodation,** but mostly cons. On the plus side, such an investment should provide the investor with a steady stream of income, not a bad thing in this age of uncertainty. This income, however, is treated like interest income and taxed at the highest rate.

Buying rental property has risks, like all other forms of investment. While the property's price may appreciate, this is by no means a certainty. House prices rise and fall like those for every other commodity. While they generally increase over the long term, the increase may be a long time in coming; it will depend on the community in which the property is located and the area of that community. Housing tends to increase in value faster in large centres. A beautiful house in a one-industry town where that industry is closing may only decrease in value. In addition to population size, price increases also depend not just on the quality of the house itself but on the condition and appearance of the residential community where the house is located and whether it is close to such things as schools, shops, and parks.

In a period of deflation when there is an excess supply of goods, the prices of all big-ticket items, including housing, often fall in value. This happens because consumers postpone their buying of expensive, non-essential goods, believing prices will fall further. This adds to the risk of investing in rental housing as a source of capital gains. Deflation occurred in 2003–2004 when technological changes resulted in an improvement in productivity. Recent examples of the economy's response were the rebates and interest-free loans on new car purchases.

The biggest disincentive for investing in rental housing as a source of income, however, is that rent increases, in all provinces except Alberta, are limited to a very low percentage. These range from 1 percent in Quebec to 2.9 percent in Ontario. (Highly rated corporate bonds should have higher yields and are easier to sell.) Landlords may apply to be allowed to charge a higher increase, but the process is time-consuming and the desired increase is by no means guaranteed. The various provincial acts and bodies regulating rent increases are as follows:

Newfoundland and Labrador: *Residential Tenancies Act*

Prince Edward Island: *Rental of Residential Property Act*

New Brunswick: *Residential Rent Review Act*

Nova Scotia: *Rent Review Act*

Quebec: *Régie du Logement*

Ontario: *Ontario Rental Housing Tribunal*

Manitoba: *Residential Tenancies Act*

Saskatchewan: *Residential Tenancies Act*

British Columbia: *Residential Tenancy Act*

In Alberta, where the *Landlord and Tenant Act* governs rental accommodation, there is no limit to the amount by which rents may be increased. For rents longer than one month, however, increases are only allowed after 180 days have passed since the last increase.

Housing must also be maintained if it is to keep its value. The handyman or woman may find this enjoyable and maintaining the property can become a hobby. For others it can be a chore. Property taxes may be deducted as a cost from rent as can expenses incurred in the upkeep of the property. Mortgage payments, should a loan be used to make the purchase, may not be so deducted.

Summary

- Capitalization refers to the value of a company's outstanding shares. Supporters of the dividend discount model believe that a stock's true value is what investors will earn in dividends.

- Comparative returns refer to the difference in returns or earnings between equities and fixed income securities.

- Stock exchanges are regulated marketplaces where securities are traded. The S&P/TSX Indices are the Toronto Stock Exchange indices that track the performance of securities traded on that exchange.

- Common shares are issued by a corporation to raise capital. They trade on stock exchanges and may pay dividends. Preferred shares are less risky than common shares, pay higher dividends but have less potential for gain. Beta helps to determine the risk of a stock by comparing its price volatility with that of the S&P/TSX Composite.

- Investors with cash accounts are expected to settle their accounts in three days. Margin accounts allow an investor to borrow money from a dealer. Leverage is the use of borrowed money to increase one's capital. Short selling is the sale of borrowed shares that are expected to drop in value; when this happens, they will be bought and the loan repaid.

- Insider trading refers to the use of privileged information to make investment gains.

- Stock analysis refers to the various methods used to determine a stock's value. Stock quotations refer to a stock's bid price and also its asking price. Stock classifications refer to the categorization of stocks into either defensive, blue chip, or cyclical. Yield is determined by dividing a stock's dividend by its price. The price/earnings ratio divides the market price of a share by the earnings per share.

- Split shares are the result of the creation of a new share, which is split into both preferred and capital shares that trade separately. Split shares is also a term referring to shares that are split into smaller denominations per share.

- Commissions are the fees an investment dealer earns after buying or selling securities. Investment returns are the gains from investing. Dividend reinvestment plans allow investors to have their dividends invested in new shares.

- Investment funds are another term for mutual funds. Mutual funds are pools of assets in which investors may buy units and benefit from the performance of a large number of securities. Closed-end funds do not issue new shares once the initial offering has been sold. Exchange traded funds are closed-end mutual funds that trade on exchanges. Wrap accounts are accounts managed by a broker for a fee.

- Investment risk refers to the danger involved in investing.

- Derivatives are securities whose value is derived from the performance of an underlying security. Hedge funds use a variety of investment strategies to preserve investors' capital.

- Arbitrage involves the buying and selling of the same shares on different exchanges at the same time when there is a slight difference in the price per share. Swaps are a contract between two parties to exchange payment over a specific period at a pre-determined rate. Income trusts are investment trusts that hold income-producing assets.

- Foreign exchange refers to the buying of foreign currencies in the expectation of making a gain from currency fluctuations.

- Collectibles are things people invest in other than securities; they include wine, coins, stamps, and works of art. Investing in rental accommodation is another alternative to security investments.

Key Terms

acquisition fee (front-end loading charge) *(p. 322)*

arbitrage *(p. 331)*

ask price *(p. 305)*

automatic dividend reinvestment plans *(p. 314)*

beta *(p. 327)*

blue chip *(p. 305)*

bid price *(p. 305)*

board lots *(p. 302)*

capitalization *(p. 297)*

cash management account (CMA) *(p. 329)*

closed-end investment funds *(p. 316)*

collectibles *(p. 334)*

commissions *(p. 304)*

common shares *(p. 308)*

comparative returns *(p. 298)*

convertible preferred shares *(p. 312)*

cumulative preferred shares *(p. 312)*

cyclical stocks *(p. 305)*

day trader *(p. 307)*

discount brokers *(p. 303)*

dividend *(p. 305)*

dividend discount model *(p. 299)*

dividend reinvestment plans *(p. 315)*

equity derivatives *(p. 329)*

exchange traded funds *(p. 318)*

ex-dividend *(p. 314)*

expense ratio *(p. 323)*

foreign exchange market *(p. 333)*

full-service brokers *(p. 303)*

growth stocks *(p. 316)*

hedge funds *(p. 331)*

income trusts *(p. 332)*

insider trading *(p. 304)*

investment funds *(p. 316)*

investment returns *(p. 313)*

investment risk *(p. 326)*

leverage *(p. 303)*

management expense ratio *(p. 323)*

market order *(p. 302)*

mutual funds *(p. 318)*

net asset value per share *(p. 319)*

no-load funds *(p. 323)*

odd lot *(p. 302)*

open-end investment funds *(p. 318)*

open order *(p. 302)*

over-the-counter market *(p. 301)*

par value *(p. 311, 315)*

penny stocks *(p. 305)*

preferred shares *(p. 311)*

price/earnings ratio *(p. 309)*

qualitative analysis *(p. 300)*

quantitative analysis *(p. 300)*

redeemable preferred shares *(p. 312)*

redemption fee (rear-end loading charge) *(p. 322)*

rental accommodation *(p. 336)*

retractable (callable) preferred shares *(p. 312)*

rights *(p. 309)*

shareholders of record *(p. 314)*

short selling *(p. 303, 331)*

S&P/TSX Indices *(p. 306)*

sinking fund (purchase fund) *(p. 312)*

split share *(p. 329)*

stock analysis *(p. 300)*

stock classifications *(p. 305)*

stock dividends *(p. 314)*

stock exchange *(p. 301)*

stock exchange index *(p. 305)*

stock quotations *(p. 305)*

stock split *(p. 311)*	technical analysis *(p. 300)*
stop loss order *(p. 302)*	trailer fees *(p. 323)*
street form *(p. 301)*	warrant *(p. 309)*
swap *(p. 331)*	wrap account *(p. 325)*
tax on investment income *(p. 328)*	yield *(p. 313)*

Problems

1. Use stock quotations from a recent newspaper to answer the following questions. Look at the legend (usually at the top of the relevant page or section in the newspaper) for an explanation of the footnotes.

   (a) How much was the most recent dividend per share, in annual terms, on Noranda common stock? On Bell Canada/BCE Inc.?

   (b) Try to find an example of a preferred share for which the dividend is in arrears.

   (c) Look at the volume figures and find a stock that traded very actively.

   (d) Find a quotation for stock warrants. (It may be indicated by a "w" after the name of the corporation.)

   (e) Examine the quotations for Bank of Montreal preferred shares to find out how many issues are listed.

   (f) Look for a stock that has issued stock dividends recently.

2. Are these statements true or false?

   (a) Insider trading is legal in Canada.

   (b) The MER on ETFs is usually lower than that on regular mutual funds.

   (c) Leverage is probably not an investing technique that a person who only buys CSBs would want to hear about.

   (d) Selling short is one of the least risky ways to invest.

   (e) If a client wants to buy shares on margin, the dealer will only let him or her invest in blue chip securities.

   (f) Risky stocks always have a high beta.

   (g) The equity-risk-premium is a reward earned by the investor in stocks.

   (h) There are markets for most items considered to be collectibles.

   (i) Blue chip stocks are not popular with risk-averse investors.

   (j) The NYSE is the only North American exchange that has an electronic trading system.

   (k) Large-cap companies are too big and bureaucratic to successfully take over smaller companies.

 3. What to invest in is a question that confronts investors of all backgrounds, ages, and financial means. Stocks have long been a favourite. Historically, they have been proven to deliver better returns over the long run than bonds and other fixed-income securities. With the collapse of shares in technology companies in 2000 and the ensuing bear market in the US and Canada, however, many investors lost faith in the markets. The bear mauled stock prices to such an extent that many investors hunted for something considered to be

safer. One interesting alternative was the hedge fund. This newer investment was considered a good means of protecting investors from the vagaries of the stock market.

To determine if this assumption is true, at least for one such fund, compare the performance since April 2003 of one hedge fund, the AGF Managed Futures fund, with that of the TD S&P/TSX Composite ETF, which tracks the performance of the S&P/TSX 300 Composite Index. Assume that $2000 has been invested. This is the minimum investment required for the AGF fund.

AGF Managed Futures
Minimum investment: $2000
Management fee: 3.00

TD S&P/TSX Composite ETF
Management fee: .25
Quarterly dividend paid in cash.

Information on these funds may be found at the following URLs:
www.agf.com/t2scr/static/app/fundview/public/en/fund794.jsp
http://investdb.theglobeandmail.com/invest/investSQL/
gx.company_prof?company_id=200907

(a) How much is the investment in each fund worth today?

(b) Was the hedge fund a better investment?

(c) Have stock markets been bearish or bullish since 2003?

4. Compare the yield on a five-year GIC with the yield on shares of the TD Bank. Should a 10-year old who wants to save for college put the money from her paper route in the GIC or in shares of the bank and enroll in the bank's dividend reinvestment plan? Explain your answer.

5. Use the dividend discount model to determine the intrinsic value of the following Canadian companies: Brookfield Asset Management, Falconbridge, Power Financial, Thomson, Great-West Life. Assume a risk factor of 3 percent. How do their current values compare with their intrinsic values?

 6. Go to **www.tsx.com** and click on Sector Profiles, etc. and then Income Trusts.

(a) What is the largest category of Income Trusts?

(b) How many REITs are there?

(c) Which REIT has the largest quoted market value?

(d) What is one share of this Income Trust worth?

(e) What is its P/E ratio? Does this make it a good buy?

(f) What is its yield?

(g) Compare its yield with that of Primaris Reit, a similar kind of REIT. Which is higher?

(h) Click on REI.UN and PMZ.UN.

(i) Download the free annual reports.

(j) Compare asset sizes and net income/earnings.

(k) Which REIT has the best property portfolio?

(l) Why is the yield on Primaris higher?

7. A survey of mutual funds published in the financial press is shown below.

Mutual Funds

A. AGF Canadian Growth Equity
B. Altamira Balanced
C. Fidelity Canadian Asset Allocation
D. TD Canadian Equity

	A.	B.	C.	D.
Rates of Return				
1 month	−6.75	−0.167	−1.60	−2.05
1 year	−24.46	−12.61	−8.40	−21.37
3 years	−11.21	−7.06	−2.22	−8.58
5 years	2.71	0.24	2.33	−0.28
Assets	$707.39 million	$57.36 million	$5.65 billion	$1.55 billion
Sales Fee	Optional	No load	Optional	No load
MER	2.99%	2.20%	2.49%	2.27%
Volatility	0.96	0.80	0.980	0.73

MER, the acronym for management expense ratio, is the annual fee charged to the fund by the fund manager. Volatility refers to the variability in a fund's monthly rate of return over three years compared with all other funds listed. The volatility of the stock market is considered to be 1.00. The lower the number, the more stable the monthly rate of return. Optional means that investors may select a front-end load and pay a fee when they purchase the units or pay a fee when the units are redeemed.

Rates of return take management fees and expenses into consideration.

Source: **globefund.com** Accessed on April 14, 2003.

(a) Which fund has the largest amount of money invested?

(b) Does there appear to be any relationship between the MER, the fees, and the volatility?

(c) How much is the management paid to manage these funds? Which fund charges the most? Does the high fee result in a better performance?

(d) Is past performance a good indicator of how a fund will do all of the time?

(e) Are the funds that do not charge either a front-end or a back-end fee better funds in which to invest from a performance point of view?

8. AGF, AIM TRIMARK, CI Funds, Fidelity, and Templeton are mutual fund companies operating in Canada. Their websites are as follows:

www.agf.com

www.aimfunds.ca

www.cifunds.com

www.fidelity.ca

www.templeton.ca

Find out the size of the following funds, what MERs they have, and what this worked out to in dollar terms for the fund managers in 2003. Find out as well what front-end or rear-end fees these funds have. Then research the past five-year history of one of these funds. Do you feel that its performance justifies these fees and charges?

AGF Canadian Dividend Fund

BPI Canadian Resource Fund

Fidelity Far East Fund

Templeton Growth Fund

Trimark Canadian Fund

9. Shares of Canadian companies Bank of Montreal, Brookfield Asset Management, Teck Cominco, Manufacturers Life, and Thomson trade on both the TSX and the NYSE. List the closing prices of these shares on the NYSE. Convert the closing prices on the TSX to US currency. Could an investor make money using arbitrage on any of these shares on this particular day?

10. List the pros and cons of investing in real estate.

11. Which do you think is a riskier investment, shares in mining giant Teck Cominco or bottles of highly priced French wines? Explain your answer.

12. Explain the difficulties facing investors in fine art.

13. If you had a salary of $40 000 a year, what would be the best type of investment income for you to earn?

References

BOOKS AND ARTICLES

Altamira. *Solutions for Successful Investing Workbook*. Prepared by a leading mutual fund company, this workbook may be downloaded from the following website:**www.altamira.com/altamira_en/education-tools/mutual+fund+basics/investor+profile.htm**.

Atkinson, Howard J., and Donna Green. *The New Investment Frontier III: A Guide to Exchange Traded Funds for Canadians*. Toronto: Insomniac Press, 2005.

Anderson, Hugh. *Bulls and Bears: Winning in the Stock Market in Good Times and Bad*. Toronto: Penguin, 1997.

Anderson, Hugh. *Investing for Income*. Toronto: Penguin, 1997.

Anderson, Hugh. *Second Wave: On-line Investing in the New Era for Canadians*. Toronto: Warwick, 2003.

Armstrong, Christopher. *Blue Skies and Boiler Rooms: Buying and Selling Securities in Canada, 1870–1940*. Toronto: University of Toronto Press, 1997.

Beck, Peter, and Miklos Nagy. *Hedge Funds for Canadian: New Investment Strategies for Winning in Any Market*. Toronto: Wiley, 2003.

Canadian Securities Institute. *How to Invest in Canadian Securities*. Scarborough: Prentice Hall, 1994.

Carlos, Miguelito. *Stock Market Discoveries: Avoiding Pitfalls [and] Learning Secret Investing Strategies*. Richmond, BC: Carlos, 1996.

Carrick, Rob. *The Online Investor's Companion*. Toronto: Wiley, 2002.

Carroll, Jim, and Rick Broadhead. *Mutual Funds and RRSPs Online: A Financial Guide for Every Canadian*. Scarborough: Prentice Hall, 1997.

Carter, Ted E. *Successful Stock Market Speculation: A Speculator's Manual*. Calgary, Alberta: Mistaya, 1991.

Chand, Ranga. *Ranga Chand's Getting Started with Mutual Funds*. Toronto: Stoddart, 1995.

Chandler, Beverly. *Investing with Hedge Fund Giants: Perform with the Market's Power Players*. Edinburgh: Prentice Hall, 2002.

Chevreau, Jonathan, Stephen Kangas, and John Platt. *The Financial Post Smart Funds 1998: A Fund Family Approach to Mutual Funds*. Toronto: Key Porter Books, 1997.

Chevreau, Jonathan, Michael Ellis, and Kelly Rogers. *The Wealthy Boomer: Life After Mutual Funds. Low Cost Alternatives in Managed Money*. Toronto: Key Porter Books, 1998.

Choudry, Moorad, Didier Jounnas, Richard Pereira, and Rod Piennar. *Capital Market Instruments Analysis and Valuation*. Toronto: Prentice Hall, 2002.

Cooper, Sherry. *The Cooper Files. A Practical Guide to Your Financial Future*. Toronto: Key Porter Books, 1999.

Croft, Richard. *A Beginner's Guide to Investing: A Practical Guide to Putting Your Money to Work for You*. Toronto: HarperCollins, 1997.

Croft, Richard, and Eric Kirzner. *The Fundline Advisor*. Toronto: HarperCollins, 1997.

Dagys, Andrew. *Common Sense Investing in Real Estate Investment Trusts*. Scarborough: Prentice Hall, 1998.

Ellmen, Eugene. *Canadian Ethical Money Guide: The Best RRSPs, Mutual Funds, and Stocks for Ethical Investors*. Toronto: Lorimer, annual.

Friedland, Seymour, and Steven G. Kelman. *Investment Strategies: How to Create Your Own and Make It Work for You*. Toronto: Penguin, 1996.

Gerlach, Douglas, James Gravelle, and Tom McFeat. *The Complete Idiot's Guide to Online Investing for Canadians*. Scarborough: Alpha Books, 1999.

Heady, Christy, and Stephen Nelson. *The Complete Idiot's Guide to Making Money in the Canadian Stock Market*. Scarborough: Prentice Hall, 1997.

Heinzl, Mark J. *Stop Buying Mutual Funds: Easy Ways to Beat the Pros Investing on Your Own*. Toronto: John Wiley & Sons, Inc., 1999.

Howell, Sydney, Andrew Stark, David Newton, Dean Paxon, Mustafa Cavus, José Pereira, Kanak Patel. *Real Options: Evaluating Corporate Opportunities in a Dynamic World*. Edinburgh: Prentice Hall, 2001.

Jaeger, Lars. *Managing Risk in Alternative Investment Strategies: Successful Investing in Hedge Funds and Managed Futures*. Edinburgh: Prentice Hall, 2002.

Kan, Joe, ed. *Handbook of Canadian Security Analysis: A Guide to Evaluating the Industry Sectors of the Market, From Bay Street's Top Analysts*. Toronto: John Wiley & Sons, Inc., 1997.

Kelman, Stephen G., Ned Goodman, and Jonathan Goodman. *Investing in Gold: How to Buy It, How to Profit from It*. Toronto: Key Porter Books, 1992.

Kennedy, Gail. *You're Worth It! Investment Strategies for Women.* Etobicoke, ON: Raintree, 1995.

Kim, Charles. *Swift Trader: Perfecting the Art of Day Trading.* Toronto: Prentice Hall, 2000.

Koch, Edward T., Debra DeSalvo, and James Langton. *The Complete Idiot's Guide to Investing Like a Pro for Canadians.* Scarborough: Alpha Books, 1999.

Lassonde, Pierre. *The Gold Book: The Complete Investment Guide to Precious Metals.* Toronto: Penguin, 1994.

Macbeth, Hilliard. *A Canadian Guide to Investment Traps and How to Avoid Them.* Scarborough: Prentice Hall, 1999.

Maude, Timothy J. *The Internet Investor: A Practical and Time-Saving Guide to Finding Financial Information on the Internet.* Toronto: HarperCollins, 1997.

Orman, Suze. *The Courage to Be Rich: Creating a Life of Material and Spiritual Abundance.* New York: Riverhead Books, 1999.

Otar, Cemil. *Commission Free Investing: The Handbook of Canadian DRIPs and SPPs.* Etobicoke, ON: Uphill, 1997.

Pape, Gordon, and Eric Kirzner. *Gordon Pape's 2004 Buyer's Guide to Mutual Funds.* Toronto: Penguin, 2004.

Penman, Stephen H. *Financial Statement Analysis and Security Valuation.* New York: McGraw Hill-Irwin, 2002.

Pring, Martin. *Technical Analysis Explained.* Toronto: McGraw Hill-Ryerson, 2002.

Sander, Jennifer Basye, Anne Boutin, and Janice Biehn. *The Complete Idiot's Guide to Investing for Women in Canada.* Scarborough: Alpha Books, 2000.

Schwartz, Martin "Buzzy." *Pit Bull: Lessons from Wall Street's Champion Trader.* New York: HarperCollins, 1998.

Sease, Douglas, and John Prestbo. *Barron's Guide to Making Investment Decisions.* Paramus, NJ: Prentice Hall, 1999.

Sharpe, William F., Gordon J. Alexander, and David John Fowler. *Investments.* Toronto: Prentice Hall, 1996.

Stanley, Thomas J., and William D. Danko. *The Millionaire Next Door: The Surprising Secrets of America's Wealthy.* Atlanta: Longstreet Press, 1996.

Stenner, Gordon, and William Annett. *Stenner on Mutual Funds: The Complete and Authoritative Guide to Mutual Fund Investment in Canada.* Toronto: HarperCollins, 1999.

Stewart, Samuel Black. *It's That Easy: A Proven Strategy for the Individual Investor.* Toronto: Copp Clark, 1995.

Stiles, Paul. *Riding the Bull: My Year in the Madness at Merrill Lynch.* Toronto: Random House, 1998.

Tadich, Alexander. *Rampaging Bulls: Outfox Promoters at Their Own Game on Any Penny Stock.* Calgary: Elan, 1995.

Taylor, Francesca. *Mastering Derivatives Markets.* Second Edition. Edinburgh: Prentice Hall, 2000.

Wise, Michael H. *Canadian Asset Allocation Strategies.* Calgary: WiseWords, 1993.

Woods, Shirley E. *Through the Money Labyrinth. A Canadian Broker Guides You to Stock Market Success.* Toronto: John Wiley & Sons, Inc., 1994.

PERIODICALS

The Canadian Speculator
www.speckstock.com

Financial Post. The National Post. 1–800–668–7678 toll-free or 416–383–2300 in the Toronto area.

Lombardi Publishing, 905–760–9929, publishes the following newsletters:

Explosive Mine Stocks

Micro-Cap Reporter

NASDAQ Advisor

Pennies to Millions

Penny Stock Reporter

Small-Cap Growth Stocks

MPL Communications Inc., 133 Richmond Street West, Toronto, ON M5H 3M8, publishes the following newsletters. It may be reached toll-free at 1–800–804–8846, or 416–869–1177 in the Toronto area or by fax at 416–869–0456.

Canadian Mutual Fund Advisor

The Blue Book of CBS Stock Reports

The FundLetter

Investor's Digest

The Investment Reporter

The MoneyLetter

Money Reporter

Report on Business. The Globe and Mail. 416–585–5000.

The Successful Investor
www.thesuccessfulinvestor.com

Personal Finance on the Web

MUTUAL FUND COMPANIES

AGF Management
　www.agf.com

AIM Trimark
　www.aimfunds.ca

Altamira Investment Services
　www.altamira.com

Assante
　www.assante.com

C.I. Funds
　www.cifunds.com

Dynamic Funds
www.dynamic.ca

Fidelity Investments
www.fidelity.ca

First Canadian Funds (Bank of Montreal)
www.bmo.com/mutualfunds

Franklin Templeton Investments
www.templeton.ca/ca

GrowthWorks
www.growthworks.ca/funds/canadian

Guardian Mutual Funds
www.ggof.com

Mackenzie Financial Corporation
www.mackenziefinancial.com

Mutual Fund Dealers Association of Canada
www.mfda.ca

RBC Funds
www.rbcfunds.com

Saxon Mutual Funds
www.saxonfunds.com

Scotia Mutual Funds
www.scotiabank.com

Scudder Funds of Canada
www.scudder.ca

Talvest Fund Management
www.talvest.com

TD Canada Trust
www.tdcanadatrust.com

FULL-SERVICE BROKERS

These firms sell a complete range of investment products, including mutual funds.

BMO Nesbitt Burns
www.bmonesbittburns.com

CIBC Wood Gundy
www.cibc.com

National Bank Financial
www.nbf.ca

Phillips, Hager & North
www.phn.ca

RBC Dominion Securities
www.rbcinvestments.com/ds

ScotiaMcLeod
  www.scotiamcleod.com

DISCOUNT BROKERS

Bank of Montreal: InvestorLine
  www.investorline.com

CIBC Investor's Edge Discount Brokerage
  www.investorsedge.cibc.com

E*Trade Canada
  www.canada.etrade.com

HSBC InvestDirect Canada
  http://investdirect.hsbc.ca

QuesTrade
  www.questrade.com

RBC Action Direct
  www.actiondirect.com

TD Waterhouse
  www.tdwaterhouse.ca

Trade Freedom
  www.tradefreedom.com/splash

HEDGE FUNDS

Canadian Hedge Fund Research and Analysis
  www.hedge.ca

Canadian Hedge Watch
  http://canadianhedgewatch.com

Derivatives Institute
  www.d-x.ca

Managed Funds Association
  www.mfainfo.org

Tremont Capital Management, Inc.
  www.tremontadvisers.com

OTHER USEFUL SOURCES

Bloomberg.com
  www.bloomberg.com Provides a wealth of financial information.

Ontario Securities Commission
  www.osc.gov.on.ca

Canadian Securities Institute
  www.csi.ca

The Canadian Shareowner Group
  www.shareowner.com

Chicago Board of Options Exchange
www.cboe.com

Chicago Board of Trade
www.cbot.com One of the few sites that provides information on futures.

Chicago Mercantile Exchange
www.cme.com A major commodities exchange where futures contracts are traded.

CNN Money
www.money.cnn.com Provides quotations from the various US stock markets.

DayTraders
www.daytraders.com Provides a full list of day-trader websites.

Fortune
www.cnn.com/magazines/fortune A leading American business magazine famous for creating the "Fortune 500" rating system for US corporations.

Fund Monitor
www.fundmonitor.com

The Globe and Mail's "Report on Business"
www.globeandmail.ca Considered one of Canada's leading sources of financial news; *The Globe and Mail's* "Report on Business" is always of interest to investors. *The Report on Business Magazine*, published once a month, contains in-depth articles on related subjects.

Gordon Pape's Buildingwealth. ca
www.gordonpape.com Through his books and radio broadcasts, Gordon Pape has become one of Canada's best-known investment commentators. This site gives his opinions of the many mutual funds available.

The Investment Funds Institute of Canada
www.ific.ca IFIC publishes many booklets on mutual funds, which are available free of charge.

Morningstar.ca
www.morningstar.ca Filled with information on mutual funds.

Proxy Vote Canada
www.proxyvotecanada.com

Quicken
www.intuit.com Allows you to obtain current stock and mutual fund values.

Quote.com
www.quote.com Provides quotes on stocks, bonds, mutual funds, and commodity futures. Also offers company profiles and access to stock exchange information.

Rogers Yahoo! Finance
http://ca.finance.yahoo.com Considered by many to be the best free site on the internet.

StockSmart
www.stocksmart.com Lets investors set up an alert so that they are notified by e-mail or pager if a stock price drops below a certain level.

Toronto Stock Exchange
   www.tsx.com

The Wall Street Journal
   http://online.wsj.com/public Widely viewed as the leading financial newspaper in the United States, the *Journal* is considered essential reading by many investors. It provides online stock quotes.

chapter **11**

Wills and Powers of Attorney

"Life levels all men; death reveals the eminent."

George Bernard Shaw
Playwright, *Man and Superman (1903)*

"Either he is dead or my watch has stopped."

Groucho Marx
Actor and comedian, *A Day at the Races (1937)*

Learning Objectives

Understanding the concepts discussed in this chapter should help you become a wiser planner.

After studying this chapter, you should be able to:

1. *Explain how wills fit into comprehensive financial planning.*

2. *Differentiate among the responsibilities involved in drawing a will, witnessing a will, and acting as executor of an estate.*

3. *Compare the effects of the existence of a valid will and no will (intestacy) on the settling of an estate.*

4. *Identify two situations in which assets are not distributed by a will.*

5. *Explain the purpose of probate.*

6. *Explain the distribution of an estate in the case of intestacy.*

7. *Evaluate the legal position of dependents who are not provided for in the will.*

8. *Distinguish between the following pairs of terms: testator and testatrix; executor and administrator; bequest (or legacy) and beneficiary (or legatee); codicil and holograph will; joint tenancy and tenancy in common.*

9. *Explain the following terms: letters of administration, letters probate, preferential share, testamentary trust, and power of attorney.*

10. *Differentiate among the various types of powers of attorney and their roles in managing for others.*

11. *Explain how the transfer of ownership of assets underlies most of the formalities associated with wills and with the settling of estates.*

Introduction

The general discussion of financial planning in Chapter 1 focused on the maximization of resources during one's lifetime. Persons with assets also need to provide for the distribution of their estate after death, but estate planning is often postponed because there is no sense of urgency. Ultimately, regardless of how we face it, we have to face our ultimate demise, our mortality. Unfortunately, those who die leaving no legal statement covering how they wish to dispose of their possessions and assets often create difficulties for the surviving family members. In such cases, as we shall see, provincial laws direct how the estate is distributed.

A will provides an orderly procedure for changing the ownership of assets after a death, indicating which assets should be transferred to which people. When a person dies without a will, that person's assets are distributed according to the law of the province, which may or may not coincide with the desires of the deceased. A comprehensive financial plan thus includes a will that will ensure the orderly transfer of assets at death.

Some of the general procedures and terminology associated with wills and estates are introduced in this chapter. Although they may seem confusing at first, there is a logic in the process that, once identified, makes it quite understandable.

After death, the person named to act in your place—your executor—gets the power to do so from the will. Often the will is submitted to a special court to verify that it is valid. Then the executor makes a list of the assets of the deceased, pays the bills, and distributes the estate according to the will. Much of the legal formality associated with wills is concerned with transferring the ownership of assets from the deceased to other people after paying debts and taxes.

There has been an increasing concern about the management of an individual's assets while that individual is still alive and about the appropriate use of powers of attorney. These powerful documents enable one person to manage the affairs of another person. As well, Ontario's Power of Attorney for Personal Care or "living will" is discussed, along with the likely future of the laws governing the control of an individual's estate while the person is still living but possibly incapable of making financial or personal-care decisions for him or herself.

Need for a Will

What Is a Will?

A **will** is a legal document that gives someone the power to act as your financial representative after your death and directs how your assets should be distributed. The person named in the will to act as your agent is called an **executor** if a man, and an **executrix** if a woman. A will has no effect or power during your lifetime; while you are alive, you can change your will as often as you wish, give away the possessions listed in your will, or write new wills. A will takes effect when the person who signs the will (the **testator** if a man and the **testatrix** if a woman) dies.

Who Needs a Will?

Most adults should have a will for two reasons: it ensures that their estate is distributed according to their wishes after their death; and because the will names an executor, it simplifies the handling of the estate. Most people have a larger estate than they realize because they tend to forget about those assets that do not form part of their estate until they die, such as the proceeds from privately purchased life insurance, the lump-sum death benefit from the

Canada Pension Plan, group life insurance plans in connection with their employment, registered retirement savings plans, and credits in company pension plans. All of these assets become part of your estate at death, even though some may not be accessible during your lifetime.

Legal Capacity to Make a Will

To make a valid will, the testator must meet the following criteria:

(a) He or she must have reached the age of majority (17 in Newfoundland; 18 in Alberta, Manitoba, Ontario, Quebec, Prince Edward Island, and Saskatchewan; 19 in New Brunswick, the Northwest Territories, Nova Scotia, Nunavut, British Columbia, and the Yukon). A person is permitted to make a legal will before reaching the age of majority only if he or she is married or is a member of the military.

(b) He or she must be of sound mind—i.e., he or she must understand what is being done. People who are mentally unfit may not meet this requirement. This is a particular concern with those who may have some degree of senility, or with regard to anyone who is undergoing psychiatric treatment. If the will is contested (disputed before a court) after such a person's death, and it can be shown that the person was not of sound mind when signing it, the will may be considered invalid.

(c) He or she must be free of undue influence by another person. If a will is signed under conditions of coercion or persuasion, there may be a basis for contesting it.

Drawing up a Will

How to Begin

First, take stock of possessions, assets, and any other moneys that would form part of your estate. Next, decide how you want to allocate this estate. If you take this list to a lawyer, or advocat in Quebec, along with the name of your executor, a will can be drafted for you. The lawyer's role is to translate your wishes into legal language and to suggest ways of allowing for various contingencies that you may not have considered, such as naming an alternative executor, including a common-disaster clause in case husband and wife are killed in the same accident, and allowing for children who have not yet been born.

It is not essential that a will be drawn up by a lawyer. The law does not require any special format, or legal words, or even typing. You can write a will in your own words, use a standard form bought at a stationery store, or even use software specifically designed for will preparation. However, if you are not experienced in writing wills, your choice of words may not make your intentions perfectly clear, and you may forget important clauses. Lawyers charge nominal fees for drawing up a will, and it is worthwhile to have the assistance of such a professional.

What to Include in a Will

A will usually includes the following information:

(a) the domicile (or home) of the testator,

(b) a statement that previous wills made by the testator are revoked,

(c) a direction to pay funeral expenses, debts, and taxes before distributing the estate,

(d) possible specific bequests (or legacies) of certain possessions or moneys to named persons,

(e) a clause that covers how to dispose of the residue of the estate (e.g., naming one or more persons as **residual legatees** to receive any balance remaining after debts, taxes, and specific bequests),

(f) the appointment of an executor and possibly an alternative executor,

(g) the naming of a guardian if the testator has any minor children,

(h) possibly, a common-disaster clause to cover such situations as the death of a couple as a result of one event.

A person who benefits from a will is called a **beneficiary**, and an asset or possession left to this person is called a **bequest** (or **legacy**); if it is real property, it is called a **devise**.

Guardians for Children

A guardian for children is often designated in a will, but the testator does not have the final word on this decision. After the death of their parents, the court appoints a guardian for the children; in many cases, of course, the guardian named in the will is appointed by the court if that person is agreeable and able to act. You cannot bequeath a human being; only possessions and property may form part of an estate and be distributed according to the wishes you express in your will. Not being bound by the terms of a will, the court has the flexibility to make the most appropriate decision about the guardianship of children after the death of their parents. (See Personal Finance in Action Box 11.1, "Mike and Tara Had Wills.")

Can the Family Be Disinherited?

Contrary to the hopes of some children, there is no legal requirement that a person must leave his or her estate to family members. However, if a spouse or children who were financially

---

Personal FINANCE in action 11.1

Mike and Tara Had Wills

Shortly after Mike and Tara married, they prudently went to Mike's parents' lawyer and had their wills drawn up. They ensured that each would be the sole beneficiary of the other's estate as well as the executor of the estate. No arrangements were discussed regarding their funerals or future children. The lawyer advised them that since they had no children as yet, there was no need to accommodate them in the will until they were born. Mike and Tara planned to postpone starting a family until they were more secure in their careers.

Later, after moving to a new city and acquiring their first house, Mike and Tara had their dream family—a boy and a girl. Life was busy and their wills remained in their hometown with their lawyer, a matter to be dealt with when they had more time.

Tragedy struck when an automobile accident took the lives of Mike and Tara. Because they had both died, there was no executor to manage their estate. And because their wills had not been updated, there were no legal guardians for their children (ages one and three). With the two sets of grandparents disagreeing over who should raise the children, the responsibility for the children had to be brought before a judge.

Now the grandparents had to demonstrate their capacity to care the best for each of the children. Age, skills, time, health, and other factors all became matters of discussion and debate.

dependent on the deceased at the time of the latter's death are disinherited, these survivors may have a basis for contesting the will under provincial legislation. If they can show that they have financial needs, and that the deceased did financially care for them, the court may award them a share of the estate. The relevant acts are as follows:

Alberta, Newfoundland	*Family Relief Act*
British Columbia	*Wills Act* and *Wills Variation Act*
Manitoba	*Dependents Relief Act* and *Marital Property Act*
New Brunswick	*Wills Act* and *Provision for Dependents Act*
Nova Scotia	*Family Maintenance Act*
Ontario	*Succession Law Reform Act*
Quebec	*Civil Code*
Prince Edward Island	*Dependents of a Deceased Person Relief Act*
Saskatchewan and the Territories	*Dependents' Relief Act*

Provisions in family law acts regarding the division of family property (after family breakup or the death of one of the spouses) can affect the spouse's share of an estate. For instance, under the *Ontario Family Law Act* of 1986, a spouse may choose either (i) the provisions accorded to him or her under the will or (ii) a half-share of the net family property calculated according to this legislation. Certain property of the deceased, such as a prior inheritance, may be excluded from net family property. This legislation has implications for wills written before 1986. For instance, a will that leaves an estate in trust for a spouse during that person's lifetime, with the balance going to a third party after the spouse's death, may be put aside if the spouse elects to take half the net family property. If there is no will, the family will have to take the share outlined later in this chapter.

Signing and Witnessing a Will

A will must be signed at its end almost simultaneously by the testator and by two witnesses; all three signers must be present together. By their signatures, the witnesses attest that they watched the testator sign this will, but they need not read the will or know the contents. It is advisable that neither a spouse nor a person who is to benefit from a will serve as a witness to that will. Ignoring this suggestion could mean that any gift to that person would be declared void. Check provincial legislation on this point.

A person named in a will as executor may also be, and often is, a beneficiary. For instance, if a man names his wife as executrix and leaves his estate to her, this choice should present no difficulty.

How to Choose an Executor

When selecting an executor, consider the person's age, willingness to handle your business, and capability of doing so. It is wise to appoint an executor who may be expected to survive you. Often close relatives are appointed executors, but in cases involving large and complex estates, a trust company may be appointed either sole executor or joint executor with a family member. If, for instance, the testator believes that managing the estate may be a burden for the survivor, the spouse may be appointed a **co-executor** with a trust company. Such arrangements allow the spouse to be involved in settling the estate and aware of what is being done without taking the sole responsibility. However, few trust companies are very interested in small estates because of the limited revenue generated compared with the amount of work required to settle the estate.

An executor named in a will is not bound to accept this appointment and may refuse if unable or disinclined; therefore, it is wise to ask the nominee before naming him or her in the will. The executor need not see the will, but he or she would no doubt appreciate knowing where the document is kept. More than one executor can be named to act as co-executors, although for small estates this can be an unnecessary complication. Requiring the signatures of several people to implement each action when settling an estate can cause inconvenience. However, it is wise to name an alternative executor—someone who would act if the person originally selected is unwilling or unable to act, or has died.

The executor can be reimbursed by the estate for the time and effort spent enforcing the will. The amount varies and there is no set rate, but it can be agreed upon by the beneficiaries or ultimately the courts will set a "fair and reasonable" fee. If selected to be an executor, remember, you are personally responsible for all outcomes.

Where to Keep a Will

A will should be kept in a spot that is safe but easy for the survivors to find. The main alternatives are to leave it with a trust company or a lawyer (to be kept in the company's or the lawyer's vault) or to put it in a safety-deposit box. There is only one signed copy of a will, but an unsigned duplicate could be kept at home with other personal papers.

Disposing of Small Personal Possessions

People often change their minds about which relative should receive the grandfather clock or the antique rocker, but it may be inconvenient and expensive to have a new will drawn to accommodate each change. One solution is to attach a memorandum to the will listing such possessions and who should receive each. The list can easily be changed because it is not part of the will; as long as there is harmony in the family about the distribution of possessions, the executor is likely to follow these instructions. However, remember that such a memorandum carries no legal weight; thus, if the will were contested, this list might not be followed. Although it has no legal weight, it is wise to refer to the memorandum within the will.

Instructions About Funeral Arrangements

Funeral or memorial instructions need not be included in a will because after an individual's death, that person's body belongs to his or her next of kin, who will decide on its disposition. Also it is quite common that the funeral is completed prior to the will even being read.

In most cases, though, relatives try to follow the wishes of the deceased. Such instructions can therefore be filed with the will if desired, but it is important to ensure that others know about the instructions; otherwise, they may not be found until it is too late to act on them. This matter is of particular interest when a prepaid funeral has been arranged or when the deceased has died far from home.

Marriage and Wills

Usually a will made before marriage is rendered void by the event of marriage, unless the spouse elects in writing to uphold it after the testator's death. To avoid having to make a will on your wedding day, you may write a "will in contemplation of marriage," which takes effect after the marriage. Such a document states that it was written in contemplation of marriage and names the expected spouse.

Revoking or Altering a Will

While you are alive, you can alter your will or make a new one as often as you wish, because the document has no power until after your death. A will may be cancelled or **revoked** by (i) destroying it, (ii) writing a new will that expressly states that previous wills are revoked, or (iii) getting married. You can change your will after it has been drafted but not yet signed, as long as each alteration is signed and witnessed. To alter an existing will without writing a new one, you must add a codicil. Although it is really a separate document, a **codicil** is merely a postscript to a will. It must contain a reference to the will to which it is appended and must be dated, signed, and witnessed.

Some lawyers believe that it is better to rewrite a will than to add a codicil. However, if there could be any doubt about the testator's mental capacity at the time the new will is being made, it might be better to add a codicil. Better that the codicil alone should fail than that the entire will should be declared invalid.

The Holograph Will

A will entirely in the handwriting of the testator, dated and signed but not witnessed, is called a **holograph will**. Such documents are valid in some provinces (e.g., in Ontario, if the will was written after 1978; in Quebec; in New Brunswick; and in Saskatchewan). Note that a will prepared using a stationery-store form on which the testator fills in the blanks is not a holograph will; this type of will must therefore be properly witnessed. Holograph wills are not valid in British Columbia, Nova Scotia, or Prince Edward Island, all of which require that the testator's signature be witnessed. An example of a holograph will is shown in Figure 11.1.

FIGURE 11.1   MRS. HASTINGS'S HOLOGRAPH WILL

For Winston

In case I should be taken before Cedric R.M. Hastings

July 30, 1933

If my brother, Winston, should outlive me, there are a few things that I wish he would attend to, viz:-

If my Husband, Cedric Hastings, outlives me and there is any of my property left, please see that he is provided for.

I should like to see my personal property, such as the family silver, bedding, and my trinkets, brooches, etc., divided among my nieces Camille, Mabel, and Beatrice. Likewise, the furniture that was mine at the time of our marriage. I should like Cedric to have the gold (Howard) watch that Dad gave me. The books and pictures are left for Winston to dispose of as he sees fit. If there are any items that Cedric particularly wished to keep, please see that he has them.

Rebecca Maud Hastings

Settling an Estate with a Will

Finding the Will

After a death, the first and perhaps most obvious step in settling the estate involves finding the most recent will. A thorough search of the deceased's home, safety-deposit boxes, and appropriate lawyers' offices must be conducted before concluding that there is no will.

Duties of the Executor

A will usually names one or more persons to act as executors—that is, as the personal financial representatives of the deceased. The executor is charged with a variety of duties, many of which are listed below:

(a) applies for the death certificate;

(b) arranges for the funeral;

(c) secures and takes control of the assets of the estate;

(d) ensures the assets are protected by insurance;

(e) makes claims for life insurance benefits;

(f) identifies and pays for the necessary expenses to be paid out of the estate, such as the funeral, bills, mortgage and rent payments, taxes, and support payments;

(g) files outstanding income tax returns including one for the year of the death;

(h) files the final income tax and requests clearance from the Canada Revenue Agency;

(i) potentially initiates probate of the will;

(j) communicates with the beneficiaries of the will;

(k) applies for any relevant death benefits such as CPP or other pensions;

(l) manages investments including any cash that is to be distributed at a later date;

(m) disposes of any personal or household items that have not been left to anyone in particular;

(n) if necessary, advertises for creditors.

Source: Intuit Will Expert. C. 2002.

In situations where (i) no executor was named, (ii) the named executor either is deceased or is unable or unwilling to act, or (iii) the deceased has died without a will, someone with a financial interest in the estate must apply to the appropriate Surrogate Court for **Letters of Administration**, which appoint an administrator to act for the deceased. The **Surrogate Court** is the provincial court that arbitrates matters relating to wills and to the settling of estates. Once appointed, an **administrator** has the same duties and responsibilities as an executor. The only difference between an executor, who is named by a will, and an administrator, who is given authority by the Surrogate Court, is in the manner of his or her appointment and in the possible requirement that the administrator be bonded. A bond, equivalent to the value of the estate, can be posted by paying a fee to a bonding company to ensure that the administrator is trustworthy in carrying out his or her duties. Bonding, of course, represents an additional cost to the estate. Clearly, having an administrator appointed means additional steps before the settling of the estate can begin. In Quebec, should there be no executor named or should the named person prove unwilling or unable to act, the settling of the estate falls to the heirs and legatees.

Proving the Will

A will is submitted to the Surrogate Court for **probate**, a process whereby the Court verifies the authenticity of the will and the appointment of the executor. The confirming document is called **Letters Probate**. In the subsequent steps of assembling the assets and paying the taxes, the Letters Probate are used to support the authority of the executor to conduct these transactions.

Some wills are not probated, especially when the estate is small and uncomplicated. The legal transfer of the ownership of assets from the name of the deceased to the name(s) of the heir(s), the crucial task in settling an estate, is sometimes accomplished without probate. However, the financial institutions involved require adequate documentation if there are no Letters Probate.

Administering the Estate in Trust

After the testator's death, the property included in the will comes under the authority and control of the executor, whose duty it is to implement the provisions of the will. An executor usually engages a lawyer, delegating to this person certain tasks involved in fulfilling the legal formalities connected with the estate. Final responsibility, however, rests with the executor. The extent of the executor's task depends on the complexity of the deceased's estate and on whether or not the estate was left in good order.

Assembling the Assets   Once the executor's or administrator's authority to proceed has been established, the next task is to compile an inventory of the deceased's assets and liabilities. In the process of doing so, the executor informs all financial institutions holding these assets that the testator has died. The executor opens a trust account, into which funds belonging to the deceased may be deposited temporarily. This account is needed in order to handle the estate's business, including the payment of bills and the final distribution of the estate to the beneficiaries.

Paying the Debts   Once the financial institutions that hold accounts in the name of the deceased are given proof that the person has died and that the executor is empowered by the will to act, funds are usually released. While the estate is being settled, the assets may be generating income in the form of interest, dividends, rent, or profit, or any combination thereof. For income tax purposes, the executor must keep a record of the income received by the estate during the time it was held in trust.

Before the estate can be distributed, all debts must be paid, with taxes and funeral expenses taking first priority. There are no longer any succession duties or estate taxes in Canada, but there are probate taxes, which vary by province. Should the debts of the deceased exceed the assets, the executor must devise a way to distribute what there is among the creditors, perhaps on a pro rata basis, usually a negotiated solution.

The executor has to pay any income tax that is due on (i) any income the deceased received from January 1 of the year in which the person died until the date of his or her death, and (ii) any income generated by the estate between the date of death and the date of distribution. An executor should contact the local office of CRA Taxation for instructions about income tax for deceased persons and their estates. Essentially, the first task is to complete an income tax return for the portion of the year during which the deceased was alive. The executor must pay whatever income tax is owing from the estate funds that are being held in trust. Just before the estate is distributed, another income tax return must be completed; this return reports any estate income and must be accompanied by payment of the appropriate tax. This process is summarized in Figure 11.2.

FIGURE 11.2   INCOME TAX RETURNS FOR DECEASED PERSONS

Return I	Return II
INCOME RECEIVED WHILE THE PERSON WAS ALIVE	INCOME RECEIVED BY THE ESTATE WHILE IT WAS HELD IN TRUST
January 1 until date of death	Date of death until the estate is distributed

Personal FINANCE in action 11.2

Marcelo and Lizbeth came to Canada with a strong work ethic and the desire to provide for their family. It came as somewhat of a surprise to them, when they were approaching their seventies, to realize that after 30 years their net worth was rapidly approaching $1 million in RRIFs and other financial assets. Their prudent savings and effective investment strategies throughout the bull market of the 1990s had set them up quite comfortably, far beyond their wildest dreams of 30 years earlier.

When the two of them sat down to try to arrange their wills it became obvious to them that there was a significant opportunity for them to make reasonable donations to their favourite charities and help out their children and their young families. But first they needed some tax advice. Some friends said to postpone any gifts till they died, others to give the money now so they could witness the impact of their generosity.

Ultimately, they decided to gift some money to their children now, while the two boys were establishing their businesses. Selling some of their investments at this time would mean that some capital gains would be experienced now. By not leaving a large capital gain for the estate to pay taxes on, they will avoid a large liability for the boys to manage as co-executors for their parents' estates, potentially long after the boys' need for the money will have passed.

At the same time the will had a stipulation that the shares in RIM, purchased when the company first went public, would be donated to the two charities Marcelo and Lizbeth had considered most important, providing a major tax credit that could reduce the significant tax liabilities that the estate would incur upon their death.

The family heirlooms were specifically bequeathed to children and grandchildren so that there would be no debate when the disbursement of the estate took place. Only by being well-organized did the two of them feel comfortable when they took off on their long-planned trip back to the home they had left. It was nice the boys knew where everything was and what was to happen if anything did go wrong.

Recording the Accounts The executor is responsible for maintaining a record of accounts showing all receipts and disbursements, but this task may be delegated to a lawyer. Beneficiaries with questions may wish to see the accounts, and if there is concern about the misuse of funds, the court may require that the accounts be submitted for inspection, a process known as **passing the accounts**.

Distributing the Estate

When the executor has paid the deceased's debts, filed an income tax return, and paid the legal fees, the estate may be distributed to the beneficiaries according to the will. In some instances, it may be necessary to sell certain assets in order to pay the debts and make the distribution; other assets may be transferred to new owners. Whether all assets must be converted into cash or whether some may be transferred in their present form depends both on the instructions in the will and on the wishes of the beneficiaries.

In some cases, the executor may have to sell property in order to divide the estate among several people. For instance, if the estate's chief asset is a house and there are three beneficiaries, the house could be sold and the proceeds divided, or one of the heirs could buy the house by paying the other beneficiaries their shares. In cases where dividing the asset is not necessary, the executor may simply transfer ownership of the property.

The demands on the executor at this stage depend on the estate's complexity. A lawyer can help with the legal formalities of transferring various forms of property. The assistance of a lawyer or trust company can speed up the whole process and enable quicker distribution of the estate to the beneficiaries. Still, the executor has a normally accepted "executor's year" in which to do his or her job.

Fees for Settling an Estate Settling an estate involves two sets of fees: one for the services of a lawyer and one for those of the executor. Lawyers prepare applications for probate, and there is usually a Surrogate Court tariff setting the fee (not including disbursements) that a lawyer may charge for handling an estate of average complexity—for example, $5 per $1000 of value for the first $50 000 and $15 per $1000 of value over $50 000.

Because executors are personally responsible for all the other work involved in settling the estate, they are entitled to a fee based on the estate's complexity and on the time and effort they have expended. This fee is usually around 4 to 5 percent of the estate's value. The actual amount or rate of pay can be stated in the will. If the executrix wants the lawyer to do her work, the lawyer charges the executrix, who pays the lawyer from the moneys due to her as executrix. If more than one executor is involved, the fee is divided between them. Frequently, family members act as executors without taking any fees from the estate.

Legal fees depend on the amount of work the lawyer has to do for the estate. Such fees may be based either on the time the lawyer spends or on a percentage of the assets. The executor should discuss the fee schedule with the lawyer before work on the estate begins. Legal fees can be reduced if the executor decides to do some tasks, such as assembling the assets and paying debts. These fees are paid from the estate funds that are being held in trust before the distribution of the estate.

Settling an Estate Without a Will

It is not uncommon to discover that a deceased person has left no will. Many people—even those who are fond of talking about their wills and about their plans for disposing of their possessions—have never made a will at all. We tend to postpone this task, thinking that it is not an urgent matter. Also, we are reluctant to contemplate our mortality. However, before concluding that no will was left, a thorough search must be done.

If the deceased's relatives believe that a will existed at some time, but it cannot be found, the will is presumed to have been revoked unless evidence can be discovered to the contrary. Should a will be found subsequent to the distribution of the estate, altering the distribution may prove very difficult or even impossible.

Naming the Administrator

If you die without a will, or **intestate**, someone with a financial interest in your estate must apply to the court to be appointed administrator of your estate. If family members do not do so, a creditor (for example, the funeral director) may press for action. This application includes an inventory of the estate's assets and debts, a list of close relatives, and an affidavit stating that the deceased left no will. As previously mentioned, the applicant may also be asked to post a **bond of indemnity** with the court so that the estate is protected should the administrator prove to be dishonest. If the administrator absconds with the assets or dissipates the estate and fails to render a true accounting to the court, beneficiaries can call on the bond of indemnity to protect their financial interests. A fee also must be paid to the Surrogate Court. After the applicant receives the Letters of Administration, he or she can begin to settle the estate.

Will But No Executor If a will is found but no executor is prepared to act, someone must apply to the court for Letters of Administration and the appointment of an administrator. Such a situation is referred to as an **administration with will annexed**.

The Administration

The administrator carries out the same duties as an executor does, but he or she may be required to withhold distribution of the assets of the estate until one year after the deceased's death, unless there has been an advertisement for creditors. This requirement does not apply to an executor, but it is often done anyway, for convenience and for the protection of the executor: an executor can be held personally liable if the estate is distributed to beneficiaries without prior repayment of debts. The one-year waiting period is one way to ensure that all creditors are informed of the death and have an opportunity to submit any outstanding bills.

Distributing the Intestacy

When there is no will (an *intestacy*), the estate is distributed according to the provisions of the appropriate provincial law. An outline of some rules regarding intestacy is shown in Table 11.1. For greater accuracy and completeness, you should consult the appropriate provincial statute. You may note a reference to **preferential shares** in this table, which means that the spouse gets a specified share before any other beneficiary. For example, if the spouse's preferential share is $50 000, this must be paid to the spouse before anyone else gets anything. If the estate is less than $50 000, then the spouse gets it all. (For an example, see Personal Finance in Action Box 11.3, "Brent Left No Will," on page 365.)

Consanguinity There is a method of classifying relatives according to the nearness of their relationship to the deceased. To illustrate how the system works, an abbreviated table of **consanguinity** (blood relationships) is shown in Table 11.2. Relatives beyond the nuclear family are grouped in classes. Should the deceased die intestate leaving no spouse or children, the estate may be divided equally among the next-of-kin in the class closest in blood relation. If there are no relatives in Class I, the estate is divided equally among all those in Class II. When there is even one relative in a class, that person gets the whole estate, and the distribution does not continue to the next class. If the deceased leaves grandchildren, but no living children, the estate goes to the grandchildren through a process called **representation** because they receive their parents' share.

Common-Law and Same-Sex Spouses The status of common-law and same-sex spouses is changing to generally recognize these partners as spouses and to be treated the some as married partners. It is necessary to monitor provincial and federal rulings on this

TABLE 11.1 PROVINCIAL LEGISLATION REGARDING INTESTATE SUCCESSION

Although legislation governing intestate succession varies from province to province to territory, there are a number of aspects that are the same in all 13 jurisdictions. Similarities will be outlined first, with differences listed below.

(I) GENERAL RULES FOR INTESTATE SUCCESSION

If the deceased left	the estate goes
spouse, no children	all to the spouse
spouse and 1 child*	preferential share to spouse; excess split 50/50 between spouse and child
spouse and 2 or more children*	preferential share to spouse; excess split 1/3 to spouse and 2/3 shared equally among children
no spouse, but children	all to children, shared equally
no spouse	all to parents or children
no spouse, children, or parents	all to brothers and sisters
no relatives	all to the government

(II) INTESTATE SUCCESSION AND VARIATONS FROM GENERAL RULES

Province	Relevant Legislation	Variations from General Rules
Alberta	Intestate Succession Act	• spouse's preferential share is $40 000
British Columbia	Estate Administration Act (Pt. 10)	• spouse's preferential share is $65 000
Manitoba	Intestate Succession Act	• spouse's preferential share is $50 000 • spouse gets 1/2 excess regardless of number of children
New Brunswick	Devolution of Estates Act	• spouse receives all joint (matrimonial property), then 1/3 goes to the spouse, 2/3 to the children
Newfoundland and Labrador	Intestate Succession Act	• no preferential share to spouse, see above rules
Northwest Territories	Intestate Succession Act	• spouse's preferential share is $50 000; if one child, spouse receives 1/2 of remainder and balance equally to child; if more than one child, spouse receives $50 000 plus 1/3 and other 2/3 is split among children
Nova Scotia	Intestate Succession Act	• spouse's preferential share is $50 000, plus 1/2 to spouse if one child or 1/3 to spouse and balance equally to children
Nunavut	Intestate Succession Act	• spouse's preferential share is $50 000; if one child, spouse receives $50 000 and 1/2 of remainder and balance equally among children; if more than one child, spouse receives $50 000 plus 1/3 and other 2/3 is split among children
Ontario	Succession Law Reform Act	• spouse's preferential share is $200 000, set by order of Lieutenant Governor in Council

TABLE 11.1 PROVINCIAL LEGISLATION REGARDING INTESTATE SUCCESSION (CONTINUED)

Prince Edward Island	*Probate Act*	• spouse shares equally with any children
Quebec	*Civil Code of Quebec*	• no preferential share to spouse • spouse gets 1/3 of estate; children get 2/3
Saskatchewan	*Intestate Succession Act*	• spouse's preferential share is $100 000
Yukon	*Estate Succession Act*	• spouse's preferential share is $75 000; if one child, spouse receives 1/2 of remainder and balance to the child; if more than one child, spouse receives $75 000 plus 1/3 and other 2/3 is split among children

* Predeceased children are "represented" by their surviving children.

matter. While the Canada Pension Plan, as well as some other pension plans (such as RRSPs and RRIFs), may provide benefits to all spouses, some provincial statutes consider them to be legal spouses in cases of intestacy. Therefore, it is difficult to generalize about their rights. At the time of writing, most common-law spouses do receive a share of an intestacy but may go to court to argue for a different portion because of financial dependency. Of course, if there is a will, a common-law spouse can be named a beneficiary.

Stepchildren With the increasing number of blended families due to divorce and remarriage, the legal status of stepchildren is a growing concern. In the case of marriage, all spouses have the same legal rights before the law, whether or not either spouse has been previously married. This is not so for stepchildren. The difficulty is that stepchildren are not considered "children" of the stepparent, especially if the biological parent of the same gender is still alive. Only if the stepparent names the stepchildren in his or her will, will they inherit; otherwise, they will likely be excluded as beneficiaries. Conversely, if one partner of the new couple dies and leaves his or her estate to the surviving spouse with no other beneficiaries, then the surviving spouse will inherit. When the surviving spouse dies, his or her estate will pass to his or her children, which may totally exclude the children of the previously deceased spouse. This is why widowed seniors particularly require a will. When the will is drawn up, the desired beneficiaries are named, thus ensuring that the deceased's wishes are followed and the beneficiaries do inherit. Grand-stepchildren also require naming, even if their parent is named a child.

TABLE 11.2 ABBREVIATED TABLE OF CONSANGUINITY

Beyond children, all blood relatives are ranked in numbered classes as follows:

Class I	father, mother, brother, sister
Class II	grandmother, grandfather
Class III	great-grandmother, great-grandfather, nephew, niece, uncle, aunt
Class IV	great-great-grandfather, great-great-grandmother, great-nephew, great-niece, first cousin, great-uncle, great-aunt
Class V	great-great-uncle, great-great-aunt, first cousin once removed, etc.

Personal FINANCE in action 11.3

Brent Left No Will

Brent, like many people in their seventies, had a will at one time, which in his case gave all of his possessions upon his death to his wife, and the will stipulated that if she died before he did, the assets were to be equally distributed to their three children. The three children were to manage the estate as joint executors. As most plans go, this did not happen: Brent's wife died before he did, and he inherited her estate.

Six months after his wife's death, Brent met another single older person who was also recently widowed. Margaret had three adult children of her own from her previous marriage. None of the six children felt very strongly about this new partnership, which resulted in Brent and Margaret's getting married a year later.

Two years later Brent suffered a stroke, and Margaret was burdened with his care, but only for a short while, as he died a few months afterwards, still in hospital and never able to manage his own affairs after the stroke. Now came the time to distribute Brent's estate, but his will had not been updated after his remarriage. Under Ontario law, all of the estate, valued at $150 000, was to go to his new widow, who unfortunately died shortly after Brent.

This event meant that both estates, that is, Brent's and Margaret's, would go to Margaret's children. This made Brent's children even more upset as many of their mother's possessions that they expected to receive were now the property of Margaret's children, who had never even known their mother.

Transferring the Ownership of Assets

The main purpose of settling an estate is to transfer the ownership of assets from the deceased to designated beneficiaries, and the various formalities are necessary in order to ensure that this transfer is done correctly. The diagram in Figure 11.3 summarizes the transfer of the ownership from the deceased to the executor (administrator) in trust, and finally to the beneficiaries.

Estate Assets Not Distributed by the Will

There are two situations in which the deceased's assets go directly to a beneficiary, independently of the will, *by contract* and *at law*. Certain financial assets—such as life insurance, annuities, RRSPs, and RRIFs—may have a designated beneficiary who was named in the contract by the deceased during his or her lifetime. On proof of death, the financial institution

FIGURE 11.3   TRANSFER OF THE DECEASED'S ASSETS

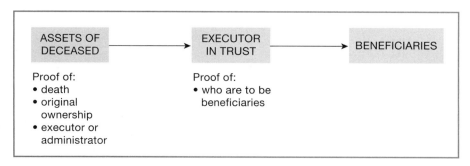

that holds these assets automatically transfers ownership to the beneficiary; the will is not involved. If the named beneficiary has predeceased the testator, the assets are generally paid into the estate unless an alternative beneficiary was named.

Other assets that are not distributed by the will are those held in **joint tenancy**, a situation that confers the right of survivorship. For instance, if a couple has a joint bank account, the wife, through right of survivorship, becomes the sole owner of the account when her husband dies. Real property such as a house held in joint tenancy is handled similarly. Note that joint tenancy is not the same as **tenancy in common**. In the latter instance, each owns an undivided share of the asset. If a couple owns the family house as tenants in common, and one partner dies, only half the value of the house forms part of the deceased's estate; the other half continues to belong to the survivor. However, if the house was held in joint tenancy, ownership of the house passes to the survivor. (Joint tenancy and tenancy in common are the subjects of this chapter's Women Take Charge.)

Frequently with elderly relatives, bank accounts are jointly held to enable the children to manage their parents' money. This also reduces the costs of probate. Tenancy in common is more likely to be arranged or favoured in remarriage situations to ensure that each set of children inherits.

Testamentary Trusts

A will may state that particular assets or property are to be held in trust for some person or persons. Such an arrangement is called a **testamentary trust** because the trust is established by a will; in contrast, a **living trust** becomes operative during the lifetime of the person who established it. A testamentary trust must be managed by an appointed trustee. Usually the trustee (and perhaps an alternative) is named in the will. Trust companies specialize in this

Women take CHARGE 11.1

Janet and her husband, Dan, owned their home and savings accounts as joint tenants. Because joint tenancy offers the "right of survivorship," the jointly held assets passed on to Janet fairly easily. Probate fees were avoided as well. Dan had named Janet as the beneficiary on his life insurance policies and RRSP. The insurance proceeds were tax-free and helped Janet to cover expenses. As the spouse, Janet was able to roll over Dan's RRSP into her own RRSP without immediate taxation.

Janet invested some of her savings and insurance proceeds in the stock market and made some gains. She is considering making her adult, married daughter a joint tenant of these stocks. Assets held in joint tenancy do not go into the estate. Janet and her daughter would each be able to receive one-half of the income and increase in the value of the shares. Janet's financial advisor tells her that such a transfer would result in a "deemed disposition" of the shares.

Janet was surprised to learn she would be responsible for tax on the capital gains related to the shares transferred to her daughter.

Joint tenancy can present problems when all of the joint tenants must give permission to sell an asset held in joint tenancy. If Janet and her daughter held recreational land as joint tenants, each would have to give permission to sell. Creditor and spousal rights with respect to the new joint tenant should also be considered in joint tenancy arrangements. Janet can obtain more information on these issues from her financial advisor before finalizing any joint-tenancy arrangements.

If Janet remarries, it will be necessary to make a new will. Janet and her new spouse should consider holding assets as "tenants in common." Then Janet's portion of the assets would pass into her estate and be distributed by the direction of her will. There would be no right of survivorship for the assets held as tenants in common.

service and have trust departments that offer advice in planning the trust. The company acts as trustee when the trust becomes operative. When trust companies are involved in planning an estate, with or without a trust, they usually insist that the company be named executor or co-executor of the will. If there is to be a trust, the company may be named the trustee. Trust companies, of course, charge a fee for managing assets on someone's behalf. In fact all trustees, whether they are corporations or individuals, are entitled to charge a fee, subject to review by the court. In some situations, the executor may also be the trustee, and he or she may decide to appoint someone to carry out the management of the trust property. In such a case, the executor retains ultimate responsibility.

It is wise to select a trustee who does not have a conflict of interest. As an example, suppose that Jane has been named the trustee of funds for her disabled brother, John. The will states that the income from the estate is to be used for John, and that after his death the balance of the estate goes to Jane. There can be a conflict of interest in such a situation; by restricting the money available for her brother, Jane may inherit a larger estate. A trustee, however, is obliged to be even-handed in dealing with the interests of beneficiaries. Consideration must be given to the life interest of one beneficiary as well as to the ultimate interest of the other.

LEGAL ISSUES

Contesting a Will

The will is the last set of wishes that an individual has established for distribution of his or her assets after death. But what if a person, usually a relative, feels that he or she should be a beneficiary of the estate but has been left out or should have received a different share from that provided for?

The individual challenging the will must meet one of two broad criteria to challenge the will in court and have the allocation of the estate meet new criteria. The *first* group of people that could make a claim would be any financial dependents. The *second* group would be those who are attempting to prove that the deceased was not of sound mind and hence the will being contested was established without capacity and therefore void. This would be a similar situation to the recent case in California where an elderly man in his eighties bequeathed a major portion of his estate to his recent wife of *Playboy* fame.

(a) What group(s) of people do you think would be most likely overlooked in a will but may have a valid claim on the estate?

(b) What is meant by the term "capacity"?

(c) Frequently when a new will is contested, what is the new beneficiary accused of doing concerning the deceased?

(d) In your opinion, where should the law stand in such a case as the one mentioned above? What if the case did not involve an estate of hundreds of millions of dollars?

Power of Attorney

Another aspect of financial planning involves providing for the possibility that you may become incapacitated through accident, age, or illness. As has been explained in this chapter, there is a process for handling the affairs of a deceased person. An incompetent person presents different problems. Unless the client has a legally appointed representative, the officers of financial institutions have no choice but to follow the client's instructions, regardless of his or her competency level. Family members are helpless to intervene unless a power of attorney has previously been signed or unless they initiate the slow, painful court process of having the person ruled mentally incompetent and naming a legal representative. In some situations, a joint bank account for depositing income and paying expenses may be a practical and informal alternative, at least for a time.

A **power of attorney** is a legal document that names someone to handle your finances under certain conditions. It is a wise precaution to assign power of attorney to a trusted person who can handle your financial affairs if necessary. It is also advisable to name an alternative, in case your first choice is unable to act. There are various ways to make a power of attorney restrictive enough so that you do not lose control of your affairs prematurely. For instance, the family lawyer can keep the document and can be instructed to release it only when two doctors have stated in writing that the person can no longer handle his or her own affairs. Such an arrangement should of course be discussed clearly with your lawyer and your physician.

It is easier, cheaper, and less cumbersome for the family if a power of attorney is signed when the individual is capable. Several additional safeguards are built into the more complex court process of determining incompetence. The person named by the court to manage assets must submit regular detailed reports to the court for approval. Should the individual who has been declared incompetent die, the power of attorney dies as well, and the will comes into force.

In 1996, Ontario enacted the *Substitute Decisions Act of 1992* and the *Health Care Consent Act*, both of which addressed the area of "living wills." Residents of Ontario can now legally specify the level of medical care they wish to receive in the event that a serious injury or illness leaves them incapacitated. This may be done by issuing specific instructions to their medical caregivers or, more frequently, by assigning a trusted family member or friend to make what he or she considers to be appropriate decisions regarding their personal care. Known as the **power of attorney for personal care** (the generic name is **personal care directive**), this document is similar to the power of attorney for financial matters described earlier but is limited to making decisions about the level and costs of the personal and health care that will be given to an incapacitated person. In some jurisdictions this directive may extend beyond care issues but not to financial matters, such as lifestyle.

A point that is of major concern to all parties involves knowing when this power of attorney comes into force. When does a person cease to have the ability to make his or her own decisions about the desirable level of physical care? The legislation has established limits on the professions that can decide an individual's ability, but this matter remains one of some contention among health care practitioners and medical ethicists. While Ontario residents must be 18 in order to decide financial matters for themselves, the law enables anyone older than 16 to decide on his or her own health care. This area of law is rapidly evolving and will probably take many years to establish firm standards, so anyone considering a personal care directive would be wise to discuss the matter with both his or her lawyer (who will draw up the document) and the attorney, agent, or substitute decision-maker whom he or she plans to appoint with the document.

Summary

- A will is a legal document giving someone the authority to act as one's agent upon one's death; it provides directions of disposal for one's assets. The executor/executrix is the individual named in a will to act as agent for the deceased. A co-executor is one of two or more executors jointly responsible for the estate. A testator/testatrix is a signatory of the will.

- A beneficiary is a person benefiting from a will. A residual legatee is someone to receive the proceeds of the estate after the debts and bequests are disposed of. A bequest (legacy) is the assignment of an asset or possession to a beneficiary in a will. A devise is real property left to a beneficiary in a will.

- To revoke a will is to cancel it. A codicil is a postscript to a will. A holographic will is unwitnessed and hand-written by the testator/testatrix.

- A Letter of Administration appoints an administrator for a deceased person in place of an executor. Surrogate Court is the provincial court that arbitrates matters of wills and estates. An administrator is an agent for the deceased as appointed by the court. Probate is a process whereby the court verifies the will. A letter probate is a confirming document from the court appointing the executor. Passing the accounts is where the court inspects the accounts of the executor.

- Intestate is the state of a person who dies without a will. A bond of indemnity is posted by a person applying to be the administrator of an estate. Administration with will annexed occurs when there is a will but no executor, resulting in the appointment of an administrator. A preferential share usually occurs when a spouse receives a share of the estate prior to any other beneficiary. Consanguinity refers to the level of closeness of blood relatives. Representation occurs when grandchildren receive their parents' share of a grandparent's estate.

- Joint tenancy confers the right of ownership to the surviving tenant. With tenancy in common, each tenant owns an undivided share of the asset.

- A testamentary trust is a trust set up for a beneficiary as laid out in the will and does not take effect until the testator's death. A living trust is a set of assets or property held for a beneficiary while the establisher is still alive.

- A power of attorney is a legal document naming a person to manage a person's financial matters while he or she is alive. A power of attorney for personal care, or personal care directive, appoints a person to make decisions limited to health matters for the signatory.

Key Terms

administration with will annexed (p. 361)

administrator (p. 357)

beneficiary (p. 353)

bequest (legacy) (p. 353)

bond of indemnity (p. 361)

codicil (p. 356)

co-executor (p. 354)

consanguinity (p. 361)

devise (p. 353)

executor (p. 351)

executrix (p. 351)

holograph will (p. 356)

intestate (p. 360)

joint tenancy (p. 365)

Letters of Administration (p. 357)

Letters Probate (p. 358)

living trust (p. 365)

passing the accounts (p. 359)

personal care directive (p. 367)

power of attorney (p. 367)

power of attorney for personal care (p. 367)

preferential shares (p. 361)

probate (p. 358)

representation (p. 361)

residual legatee (p. 353)

revoke (p. 356)

Surrogate Court (p. 357)

tenancy in common (p. 365)

testamentary trust *(p. 365)*   testatrix *(p. 351)*

testator *(p. 351)*   will *(p. 351)*

Problems

1. **A Case of Intestacy**

   When he died, Eugene Markotic was living with his common-law wife, Mrs. Anna Pavlicek, and her children, and was operating a successful pig-raising business with the help of Anna's son, Larry. Because Mr. Markotic left no will, there was much uncertainty about who should look after his affairs, including the growing pigs. Mr. Markotic was divorced and had no children of his own, and his parents were deceased; by the rules of intestacy, the collateral relatives (in this case, his three brothers) would be the heirs. It was agreed that one brother, Tom, would apply to be the administrator of the estate.

   Initially, Mr. Markotic's affairs appeared quite straightforward. He left two rented barns full of pigs, a truck, some supplies and equipment, personal belongings, and a bank account. But a search of his apartment revealed seven burlap bags of personal papers dating from the late 1940s. Tom found that his brother had held two mortgages, several bank accounts, stocks, bonds, and two life insurance policies with named beneficiaries—in one case his deceased mother and in the other his divorced wife.

   Mr. Markotic had lived with Mrs. Pavlicek for a number of years, treating her family as his own. However, Mr. Markotic's brothers did not approve of this situation and had kept their distance. Gradually it was revealed that Mr. Markotic had had plans for the disposition of his estate but had not put them in writing. He had often mentioned making Larry a partner in the business, and he had always meant to change his life insurance policies to name Anna as beneficiary, and also to cancel the mortgage he had held for her daughter and son-in-law. His lawyer had known about his intention to make a will that would name one brother as executor and recipient of 60 percent of the estate, and that would divide the remaining 40 percent so that half would go to Anna and the other half would be split between the other two brothers. Unfortunately, he died before making a will; as a result, his plans could not be implemented.

   (a) Would probate be involved in settling Mr. Markotic's estate?

   (b) Since Mr. Markotic did not leave a will, what steps would be necessary to have Tom appointed to handle his estate?

   (c) Would there be any additional costs or delays incurred because Mr. Markotic did not name an executor?

   (d) Who would receive the benefits of the two life insurance policies?

   (e) In your province, what is the name of the law that specifies how Mr. Markotic's estate would be distributed?

   (f) Assume that this situation had occurred in your province; estimate the share that Anna Pavlicek would receive under the intestacy law.

   (g) Make a list of things that would probably have turned out better if Mr. Markotic had written a will.

(h) Do you think the common-law wife should investigate the possibility of making a claim as a dependent? What law would be involved?

(i) Does Larry Pavlicek have a basis for contesting the distribution of this estate?

2. **Wills of All Sorts**

When Mrs. Hastings died in 1972 at the age of 94, her family began to search for her will. Someone remembered that there had been a letter in her brother's desk for years, with instructions to open it after her death. That turned out to be the holograph will reproduced in Figure 11.1. The search did not end there, however, because someone thought that Mrs. Hastings had once said something about keeping her will at a certain bank. A search of several banks revealed some Canada Savings Bonds, a life insurance policy belonging to her husband, and his will.

After the funeral, a careful search of her room uncovered a second will, which had been drawn by a lawyer in 1939 (Figure 11.4). Mrs. Hastings had made some revisions to this will nine years later, cutting out certain sections and pasting in changes. Finally, the matron of the nursing home where Mrs. Hastings had been living just before her death produced yet another will, which was on a stationery store form (Figure 11.5). This last will was the most recent, and it was submitted for probate.

(a) When Mrs. Hastings died, her holograph will, written in 1933, would have been valid in Quebec if she had not written later wills. Would it be acceptable now in British Columbia or Ontario?

(b) What is your opinion of the way Mrs. Hastings revised her second will? Do you think the entire will would be valid, or only a part of it? If your will needed revision, how would you do it?

(c) Changes occurred during Mrs. Hastings's long life, and some personal possessions listed in her various wills were disposed of before she died. In your opinion, how might this matter of designating the distribution of personal possessions be handled?

(d) How many executors did Mrs. Hastings name in her third will? Were they to act as co-executors, or were some of them alternatives in case the others were unable or unwilling to act? How many executors and alternatives would you suggest that she needed for a very small estate?

3. John Vander Kamp died, leaving an estate estimated at approximately $235 000. There was no will, but he did have a wife and three children under age 15 plus his parents. John's share of the farm that he jointly owned with his father was $125 000.

(a) How would his estate be distributed if he died in your province?

(b) There was also a mortgage life insurance policy on the farm mortgage. What happens to this money and the farm ownership?

(c) The $150 000 life insurance John owned had also stated his wife as the beneficiary. What happens to this money?

(d) If John and his father owned the farm as tenants in common, what would happen to his ownership of the farm?

FIGURE 11.4 ■ MRS. HASTINGS' SECOND WILL

ON THIS twenty-first day of the month in February, in the year one thousand nine hundred and thirty-nine, at the Village of Rockport, County of Crompton, District of St. Francis, and Province of Quebec:

Before the undersigned Witnesses, Catherine Ross, Advocate, and Mary Goodman, Accountant, both of the Village of Rockport, said County, District, and Province,

CAME AND APPEARED

REBECCA M. HASTINGS (née Cassells), of the Township of Smithton, said District and Province, who, being of sound mind, memory, and understanding, has declared the following to be her Last Will and Testament:

1. I commend my soul to Almighty God.

2. Hereby revoking any and all former Wills, I hereby will, devise and bequeath any and all property, real and personal, which I now own, or may own or possess at the time of my death, in the following manner:

November 25, 1948

If my good and faithful husband, Cedric Hastings, outlives me, I wish what property is left to be used for his benefit as my dear brother Winston Cassells sees fit. Also that the Sun Life Insurance money be used for Cedric's benefit.

I should like a double tombstone erected for both of us, whenever seems most suitable, the cost thereof to come out of our estate. I wish Cedric to have my large trunk and the best black suitcase. Also Dad's gold "Howard" watch. Will Winston and Camille please be my executors?

3. I desire my niece Camille H. Cassells to have the Blue and White bedspread woven by her grandmother. And my niece Mabel Cassells to have the White bedspread with "Theresa A. Green" woven thereon. And to my niece Beatrice Cassells the silk quilt.

4. I desire my furniture, books, pictures, silverware, and household effects generally, to be divided among my three nieces, Camille, Mabel, and Beatrice Cassells abovementioned, as my Executrix may see fit.

After due reading of this Will by the Testatrix, she has signed the same in the presence of the Witnesses, who have also signed in her presence and in the presence of each other.

WITNESSES   *Rebecca M. Hastings*
<u>   </u>

Catherine Ross
<u>   </u>

FIGURE 11.5   MRS. HASTINGS' LAST WILL

THIS IS THE LAST WILL AND TESTAMENT OF ME, Rebecca Maud Cassells Hastings, at present residing at Eliza Gregson Home, in the Township of Smithton, in the District of St. Francis, retired.

I hereby revoke all former wills and testamentary dispositions heretofore made by me.

I NOMINATE AND APPOINT my brother, Winston Charles Cassells, farmer, residing on Rural Route 4, Crompton, Quebec, and my nieces, Camille Cassells, teacher, residing in Perth, Ontario, and Mabel Cassells, nurse, residing in Toronto, Ontario, and the survivor of them, to be the Executors and Trustees of this, my Will.

I GIVE, DEVISE, AND BEQUEATH all the Real and Personal estate of which I shall die possessed or entitled to unto my said Executors and Trustees hereinbefore named, in Trust for the purposes following:

Firstly, to pay my just debts. Secondly, to pay the expenses of my burial, which I wish to have undertaken by L.O. Cass and Son, Ltd., funeral directors, of Crompton, Que. Thirdly, to provide for the erection of a modest headstone over the grave of my husband and myself, and to cover all testamentary expenses. Fourthly, to pay to Eliza Gregson Home in the Township of Smithton, Que., whatever may be required for the maintenance of my husband, Mr. Cedric Hastings, during his lifetime. Fifthly, to divide among my nieces, Camille Cassells and Mabel Cassells (aforementioned) and Beatrice (Mrs. B.M. Thomas), my pictures, trinkets, and personal things. All the rest and residue of my estate, both Real and Personal, I GIVE, DEVISE AND BEQUEATH unto Eliza Gregson Home in the Township of Smithton in the Province of Quebec absolutely.

With full power and authority to my Executors and Trustees to sell and dispose of all or any part of my Real or Personal estate, where necessary, for the carrying out of the purpose of this my will, and to execute any and all documents that may be necessary for so doing.

IN WITNESS WHEREOF I have subscribed these presents at Eliza Gregson Home in the Township of Smithton, this 14th day of September, Nineteen hundred and sixty-five.

SIGNED published and declared by the above-named
testatrix as and for her last Will and Testament in
the presence of us both present at the same time,
who at her request and in her presence have
hereunto subscribed our names as witnesses.   Rebecca M. Hastings

(Witnesses)

Name	Terry Petrie	Name	Miss Betty McDonald
Address	290 Oba St. Sherbrooke	Address	Eliza Gregson Home

4. Marie, who lived common-law for 15 years, tells the following story:

Intestacy and Common-Law Spouses

My common-law husband was a wonderful man, but although I tried and tried to get him to make a will, he said that he considered wills to be meaningless pieces of paper. As the years went by, I worried less about this and concentrated on planning our future together. I never gave up my well-paying job because we needed the money. We pooled our finances to pay current expenses as we raised his three daughters, bought a house, and established a retirement fund.

Suddenly, my husband died, leaving me not only grief-stricken but also penniless. Now I am living alone in a nearly empty apartment with very few of the lovely things we had over the years. Our house is for sale, and the antique furniture that I collected as a hobby has been distributed among my husband's grasping family, who never approved of our relationship. I never thought my stepchildren would show such disloyalty to their father by doing things he never would have wanted.

(a) What can a common-law wife like Marie do to protect her financial security?

(b) Do you think she has a strong case for contesting the distribution of this estate?

(c) If a person dies without a will in your province, does that person's common-law spouse automatically get a preferential share? Does the length of time the couple lived common-law make any difference?

5. Mrs. DeMelo has a dependent daughter who is severely handicapped and has a limited capacity to handle financial affairs. Mrs. DeMelo's will leaves her estate in equal shares to her daughter and to her son, but she is wondering whether she should revise her will to establish a testamentary trust for the daughter. Because her son is financially independent and her daughter is not, Mrs. DeMelo proposes leaving her total estate in trust for her daughter, with the residue to go to her son after her daughter's death.

(a) List some factors that should be considered in deciding whether to leave the estate in trust for the daughter.

(b) Do you think a testamentary trust would be a wise approach in this case?

(c) Do you see a potential conflict of interest for the son if he is made a trustee?

6. Mr. Schwartz left a will stating that his estate was to be divided equally among three of his four children. His youngest son, Leon, now 32, with whom he had been on bad terms for some years, was left out of the will. Does the fact that Leon was the only child excluded from the will form a good basis for him to contest the will?

7. (a) Why does an executor need a trust account?

(b) The main task of an executor is to assemble the assets of the deceased and distribute them to the designated beneficiaries. Why is there so much formality associated with transferring the assets?

(c) If the beneficiaries of a will suspect that an executor is not acting in their best interests, what can they do to check on this?

8. When Mrs. Mears died, her will appointed her two daughters, both now in their seventies as co-executors. One daughter was suffering from Alzheimer's disease, and the other lived a couple of days' travel away. Given that one of the executors may not be capable to administer the estate and the other daughter may decline the task due to

the significant travelling required, how will the estate be settled? Do both daughters have to act to fulfill the will's requirements?

9. Maisie had often talked about how she would leave her estate, but after her death no will could be found. As a result, her estate had to be treated as an intestacy and was administered by her cousin John. Maisie's estate included the following assets:

- cash and deposits of $26 000,
- a house, valued at $185 000, which she had owned as a tenant in common with her estranged husband,
- Canada Savings Bonds, worth $5000,
- a car, valued at $8000,
- a life insurance policy with a face value of $38 000, which named her husband as beneficiary,
- a $136 000 RRIF,
- a pension plan credit of $6849.

In addition to her estranged, but never legally divorced, husband, Maisie left a mentally disabled daughter and an elderly mother.

(a) Make a list of the assets that would form part of Maisie's estate.

(b) Using the rules for intestacy for your province, show how this estate would be divided.

(c) Might there be a reason for applying to the Surrogate Court for a change in this division to favour the mentally disabled daughter? What information about the family would you need to know in order to determine whether such a case could be made?

(d) If the husband wanted the house, would it have to be sold or could it go directly to him?

10. In your own situation, list your assets and determine how the assets would be distributed, according to your provincial laws. Is this what you would want to happen? Would there be a need for probate proceedings? Who is likely to be the administrator or executor?

11. Proceed to the Living Will Registry's website at **www.livingwills.com** and find the four tests to assess competency. Who (are) is the most likely person(s) to determine competency? What do you think is his/her/their legal responsibility and to whom?

12. Proceed to the website for your province or territory and determine if there is a law for a form of a personal care directive.

(a) Are you old enough to enact a power or attorney (or whatever terminology is used)?

(b) What criteria must be met to be an attorney for someone?

(c) For yourself, what conditions would you desire to have met before someone could use the POA?

(d) Discuss this measure with your classmates.

(e) Is there consensus?

(f) What factors are common?

(g) What factors cause differing conditional measures? And are there any commonalities?

(h) Do other members of your family have these POAs?

13. What are the preferred disbursements in your jurisdiction when a person dies intestate?

14. What characteristics would you look for in an attorney for personal care?

References

BOOKS AND ARTICLES

Cestnick, Tim. *Winning the Estate Planning Game, Estate Planning Strategies for Canadians*. Toronto: Pearson Education Canada Inc., 2001. A regular *Globe and Mail* contributor in tax and financial planning provides insight into wills, trusts, succession planning, and life insurance matters.

Deloitte and Touche. *Canadian Guide to Personal Financial Management*. Toronto: Prentice-Hall Canada, annual. A team of accountants provides guidance on a broad range of topics, including planning finances, estimating insurance needs, managing risk, and determining investment needs. Instructions and the necessary forms for making plans are also included.

Foster, Sandra E. *You Can't Take It with You*. Fourth Edition. Toronto: John Wiley & Sons Inc., 2002. A current Canadian perspective on death and the transactions surrounding estate disbursements.

Gray, Douglas, and John Budd. *The Canadian Guide to Will & Estate Planning*. Second Edition. Toronto: McGraw-Hill Ryerson, 2001. A practical guide from two experts on a complex and critical set of issues.

Kruzeniski, Ronald, and Jane E. Gordon. *Will/Probate Procedure for Manitoba and Saskatchewan*. Fourth Edition. Vancouver: International Self-Counsel Press, 1990. A basic explanation of the terminology and procedures involved in drawing or probating a will.

Life Underwriters Association of Canada. *Elements of Estate Planning, 1994 Edition*. Toronto: Life Underwriters Association of Canada, 1994. An academic book used in the life insurance industry to help agents deal with clients who require estate-planning services.

Olkovich, Edward. *The Complete Idiot's Guide to Estate Planning in Six Simple Steps for Canadians*. Toronto: Pearson Education Canada Inc., 2002. Another in the popular line of how-to books that is practical for individuals who wish to take control of their own estate and protect their beneficiaries.

Spenceley, Robert. *Estate Administration in Ontario*. Toronto: CCH Canada Limited, 1996. A professional reference for estate administrators.

Personal Finance on the Web

Living Wills Registry (Canada)
www.livingwills.com This site discusses and registers information regarding powers of attorney and related matters.

Wills and Estate Planning
www.preplannet.com This site provides information regarding the pre-arrangement of funerals and basic information regarding wills and estates. There are some links to legal firms and other government authorities regarding tax, especially for Quebec.

Credit

"Remember that credit is money."

"Remember that time is money."

Benjamin Franklin,

"Advice to a Young Tradesman," (1748)

This section presents a thorough discussion of consumer and mortgage credit. Following the convention of treating mortgage credit separately from consumer credit, Chapter 12 discusses home mortgages. Chapter 13 discusses trends in the use of consumer credit in Canada, consumer loans and vendor credit, some of the institutions that provide credit, and the terminology they use and also provides some samples of the contracts used by lenders. These samples will help familiarize you with the contracts and help you understand these documents.

Chapter 14 explains credit reporting and debt collection proceedings, which can confuse most people. That chapter also discusses an unpleasant topic: the options and strategies available for debtors who find themselves overcommitted.

chapter 12

Home Mortgages

"*Making an offer to buy a home is not something most people do on a regular basis. The process is usually stressful and exciting all at the same time. Buyers need to remember to keep their emotions in check and keep in mind that this is a big investment; making a rash decision may come back to haunt you!*"

Andy MacDonald
(MortgageBroker Inc., http://mortgagesincanada.com)

Learning Objectives

Understanding the concepts discussed in this chapter should help you better understand mortgages.

After studying this chapter, you should be able to:

1. Explain the opportunity costs in buying a house.

2. Compare the costs and benefits of the various means of mortgage funding.

3. Explain the differences between a conventional mortgage and an insured mortgage.

4. Explain how lenders determine whether a potential borrower qualifies for a loan.

5. Calculate the size of loan for which an applicant is eligible.

6. Distinguish between equal instalments of principal and blended payments.

7. Calculate the interest and principal in a mortgage payment.

8. Identify the components in a mortgage contract.

9. Explain how the total cost of buying a house is determined.

10. Understand the many terms associated with mortgages, including mortgage term, amortization period, and open and closed mortgages.

11. Explain how a reverse mortgage can provide an income to the homeowner.

12. Explain the relationship between the National Housing Act, the Canada Mortgage and Housing Corporation, and lenders in the mortgage business.

13. Explain the following terms: gross debt service, total debt service,

closing costs, closing date, appraisal, mortgage discharge, interest penalty, prepayment privilege, capital gain, commitment period, equity, maturity date, amortization, mortgage broker, equity of redemption, high-ratio mortgage, non-money income, preapproved mortgage, interest adjustment date, and interest-rate differential.

Introduction

Owning a home is probably the goal of most Canadians. Because of the cost involved, the decision to buy a home is the most important financial decision anyone can make. The cost of a new car, the other major purchase in the lives of most people (unless one is looking at a Rolls Royce, or a similarly priced car), pales in comparison with the cost of a house. The decision to buy "the house of one's dreams" can also be very daunting, not just because of the great cost involved but also because the location of a house is often just as important as the house itself. The decision about where to buy, therefore, can be just as challenging as choosing the right house. A house in a nice neighbourhood and one that is close to schools, parks, and shopping should appreciate in value. A house that is not so well-situated will likely increase in value as well, but probably more slowly. Buying a home is also a daunting experience because of the process involved and the language or terminology of real estate and mortgages. To most people, the world of financing the purchase of a home is a strange one. This chapter will help to clarify the process by explaining what is involved so that buying a home becomes a pleasurable rather than a frightening experience.

Buying or Renting: Which Is Better?

A Look at the Options

As with many financial decisions, the choice between buying or renting is not an easy one to make. There is no right or wrong answer. The decision depends on the individual and his or her particular financial and social circumstances. Many Canadians today are very mobile, moving from one community to another frequently as their jobs or personal situations dictate. For such people, home ownership is probably foolish. In addition to the large cost of a house, a homebuyer ends up paying many fees including appraisal fees, legal fees, home inspection fees, and real estate commissions. This heavy outlay of expenses suggests that one should only buy a house if one is planning to stay in a community for an extended period of time. The longer one stays the better, as far as personal finances are concerned. There are also major costs in selling a home, including legal fees and real estate commissions. Also, while any gain in the value of a house is not taxed when the house is sold, the gain may only come slowly. In fact, houses may decline in value when the economy slows and unemployment rises. So selling, moving, and buying on a frequent basis is often a recipe for financial distress for the individual unless one is very lucky. And wise financial planning should not be based on luck.

The choice between buying or renting also involves other factors that should not be ignored. Renting is similar to leasing a car. When the rental or lease is over, the renter/tenant walks away without any further financial commitment. For the money paid in rent, the tenant has nothing left but memories when the lease expires. But, for the duration of the lease, the tenant has care-free accommodation. During this time, the apartment or condominium building is maintained by the superintendent, and the property taxes are paid by the property's owner without the tenant needing to give these matters a second thought. Renting, therefore, can be a wise decision for those who would find home maintenance a chore, as well as for those who move often. For it is a foolish homeowner who neglects routine property maintenance and then sees his or her investment decline in value.

With the purchase of a house, however, should come the pride of ownership, with all that this implies. Many people find great pleasure in planting a flower garden and growing fruits and vegetables. (There is also a financial saving in growing your own produce.) They may also enjoy the tasks that always face the homeowner, from mowing the lawn to painting the living room. And, for the cost of the home, usually involving a mortgage, the homeowner has accommodation and an investment that should appreciate in value.

Purchasing a house does come with an **opportunity cost**, however. Just because the opportunity cost cannot be seen and is difficult to quantify, it should, nonetheless, be considered. The opportunity cost is that the money invested in the house cannot be used for anything else. (You cannot buy a yacht for sailing on the Great Lakes, go on the Mediterranean cruise you had your heart set on, or make any other investments if you use all of your savings as a down payment.) And, while a house is considered an investment, money invested in something else may increase more quickly. (Shares in Canadian Western Bank, for example, increased over 300 percent in 10 years.) Neither does a house provide an income as other investments do. When a house is sold, the resulting capital gains are not taxed, but the gains only come in the future. Many elderly homeowners find themselves with a valuable home but very little other income. If they sell their house to use money from the sale to live on, then they still must find another place in which to live. For all of these reasons, the decision to buy a house is not an easy one to make.

Which Is Better Financially?

Are you better off financially buying or renting? Realistically, this question is impossible to answer definitively because there are too many variables involved. You would have to make numerous assumptions, any one of which, or all, could turn out to be wrong. Obviously, at the start, renting is cheaper because the only expense is your rent. On the other hand, buying entails a down payment and all of the other associated expenses (to be discussed later in the chapter). Some funds also need to be set aside for taxes and routine maintenance. In addition, there are the monthly payments to consider. Buying, and also maintaining, a house is a very costly endeavour.

If you can afford to buy but choose to rent, what will you do with the money you save? If you spend it, you will be worse off. If you invest wisely, your estate may grow faster than the equity you would have had in the house. However, no one knows what will happen to investments of any kind. Your investments may decline in value. So may the value of your house. The values of all investments rise and fall with the ebb and flow of economic activity. The best answer to the question, therefore, is the choice that would bring greater satisfaction to the individual. Financial choices have a psychological aspect as well as a monetary one. The former has no monetary value, but as the investor who cannot sleep at night when the market drops can testify, worry hurts. Stress kills. Whichever choice results in the least worry is the right one, whether it is right financially or not.

Real Estate: Is There a Housing Bubble?

Real estate prices soared between 2002 and 2005. They went up by 10 percent in 2005 alone. There were several reasons for this, which economists refer to as fundamentals. These include the following:

- Interest rates were at historic lows. The last time they were as low was in the 1960s. The Bank Rate in January 2001 stood at 5.75 percent. By January 2002 it had dropped to 2.25 percent. From there it began a slow climb upwards but had only reached 3.50 percent by December 2005.
- Housing was considered cheap. The cost of paying for a home had dropped to 30 percent of household income.
- The bull market in stocks that took place at the same time had produced some very wealthy people who bid up housing prices.
- The baby boomers (anyone born between 1947 and 1964) inherited considerable sums and also went looking for expensive homes.

The combination of these factors pushed housing prices in some centres to great heights, sometimes resulting in bidding wars. For example, a house listed in Toronto in 2002 for $669 000 ended up selling for $900 000.[1] Similar "wars" took place across the country with varying degrees of lunacy.

What happened in Calgary is typical of many Canadian cities. The trend in this city can be seen in Table 12.1. The forecast for 2006 was that the average would increase to $260 000.[2]

It was Vancouver, however, that experienced the most rapid increase. Just how rapid can be seen in Figure 12.1, which covers the period from 1980 to 2005. Midway through 2001 prices began to escalate and have continued to do so. The increase began with the decline in mortgage rates coinciding with the drop in the bank rate. The condominium market in the city has recently been the hottest real estate in the country. This trend fuels speculation that the city, if not the country, is in the midst of a real estate bubble.[3]

Have these factors caused a housing bubble in Canada? Are prices artificially high? Will the bubble burst and destroy the fortunes of huge numbers of Canadians? The risk of such a thing happening is low.[4] Inflation remained low. The core Consumer Price Index, as reported by the Bank of Canada, stood at 2.6 percent in October 2005. Mortgage rates were also low and were expected to remain so. One bank posted the rates shown in Table 12.2.

What happened in Vancouver is not likely to be duplicated elsewhere. Available land is at a premium in that city. As long as the factors that have caused the boom in prices continue, there is no reason to expect a significant drop in housing prices, even in Vancouver.

TABLE 12.1 AVERAGE RESALE HOUSING PRICES IN CALGARY

2001	2002	2003	2004	2005
$182 090	$198 058	$211 155	$221 900	$232 000

[1] Katherine Macklem. "Did Someone Say Bubble?" *Maclean's*, May 10, 2004.
[2] Calgary Housing Gains Seen Leading Country in 2006, *CBC News*, December 1, 2005.
[3] **www.discovervancouver.com/forum/topic.asp**.
[4] TD Economics, Housing Bubble Watch, November 29, 2005.

FIGURE 12.1 REAL ESTATE BOARD OF GREATER VANCOUVER AVERAGE PRICE GRAPH
JANUARY 1980 TO SEPTEMBER 2005

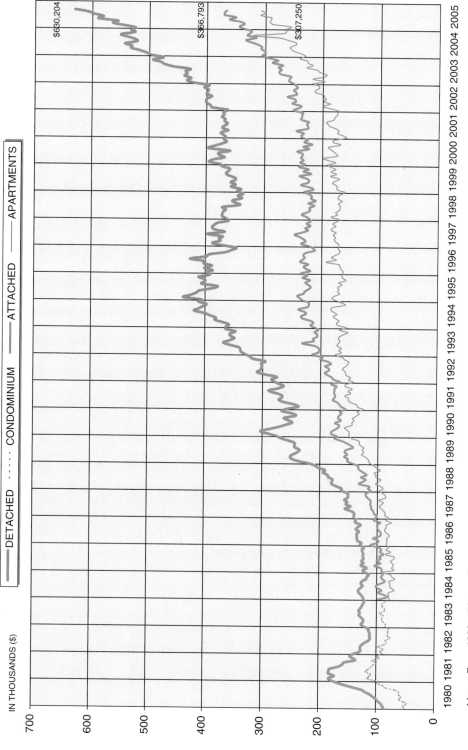

IN THOUSANDS ($)

— DETACHED   ····· CONDOMINIUM   — ATTACHED   — APARTMENTS

$630,204

$366,793

$307,250

700 600 500 400 300 200 100 0

1980 1981 1982 1983 1984 1985 1986 1987 1988 1989 1990 1991 1992 1993 1994 1995 1996 1997 1998 1999 2000 2001 2002 2003 2004 2005

NOTE: From 1980–1984 condominium averages were not *separated into attached & apartment.*

SOURCE: Real Estate Board of Greater Vancouver, courtesy Eileen Day, Manager of Communications.

TABLE 12.2   MORTGAGE RATES AT BANK OF MONTREAL, DECEMBER 2005

FIXED RATE		VARIABLE RATE	
6 month convertible	5.050%	6 year flexible below prime	4.625%
6 month open	7.490%	3 year open	5.000%
1 year closed	4.550%	5 year protected	4.900%
1 year open	7.250%		
2 year closed	4.950%		
3 year closed	5.340%		
4 year closed	5.490%		
5 year closed	5.590%		
6 year closed	5.990%		
7 year closed	6.600%		
10 year closed	6.600%		
18 year closed	8.250%		

SOURCE: Bank of Montreal, December 5, 2005.

What House Can I Afford?

The decision to buy a home, as has been said, is the most important financial decision the new homebuyer will likely ever make. Often, the decision will be based, not on the house you like the best, but on the house you can afford. The mortgage officer at the bank may tell you that you qualify for a mortgage three times your annual salary, but this is not necessarily what you can afford. Affordability, like opportunity cost, is not something that can easily be quantified. It will vary between two people with the same salary. People who don't eat out a lot or spend a lot on entertainment or costly winter vacations can afford a more expensive home than those who do. To start with, they are likely to have saved more money and can therefore afford a larger down payment. Before buying a house, the prospective homeowner needs to consider how large a down payment she can make without causing undue stress. She must then also determine how much she can afford to spend on gas, hydro, water, property taxes, and a mortgage before negotiating the mortgage. (See personal Finance in Action Box 12.1, "Barbara and the Elusive Condo," for an account of one person's decision-making process.)

Personal FINANCE in action 12.1

Barbara and the Elusive Condo

Barbara had rented an apartment since graduating from college six years ago. Her friends had done the same but were now buying houses and suggested she buy a home, too, while mortgage rates were low. They had all been saving for just such a purpose. Barbara had an RRSP worth $78 000 but

agreed with her friends that a house would be a better investment. Any increase in the price would be tax-free if she sold it, a bonus that would not be available when she collapsed her RRSP.

She decided to sell some of the bonds in her plan that had risen in value and use $20 000

continued

under the Homebuyers' Plan (see Chapter 6) for a down payment. She had read in the newspaper that a condominium selling for $190 000 was available in a nearby building that she liked. It had a number of features that were lacking in her apartment, including a pool, an exercise room, and a security guard at the entrance. With her $20 000 she could make a down payment of 10.5 percent. Her bank said she could have a five-year closed mortgage for 5.44 percent, which she could just afford (she tried other banks but could not get a better deal). However, when she called the realtor whose number accompanied the ad, she was told that the condo had sold quickly for more than the asking price. The realtor also said that this sort of thing had become the norm lately. All condos were going very fast and there were none listed now for less than $200 000. Since that was more than the amount Barbara could afford, she decided to continue renting for the time being.

The Canada Mortgage and Housing Corporation has prepared some guidelines on affordability for people who want to buy a new home with a down payment of 5 percent. These guidelines are shown in Table 12.3 and are based on the following assumptions: interest of 8 percent; average Canadian property taxes and heating costs; the amount of mortgage that the average person would qualify for, based on a gross debt service of 32 percent. (The term "gross debt service" is explained later in this chapter.) This chapter's Women Take Charge feature outlines some of the CMHC's many services to homebuyers.

Women take CHARGE 12.1

Home ownership has been a lifelong dream of Maxine's, but she is not able to afford the 25 percent down payment required by a conventional mortgage. Fortunately, the Canada Mortgage and Housing Corporation (CMHC) is there to help make the home ownership dream a reality.

Maxine will seek out a CMHC-approved lender to help her obtain a CMHC-insured mortgage with a down payment as low as 5 percent. The lender is willing to take on such a high-ratio mortgage because the CMHC provides mortgage insurance for the lender, who will pass on the cost of the premium to Maxine. She can decide to pay the premium in a lump sum or as part of the monthly payments on the mortgage. Because the insurance provided by the CMHC lessens the risk of holding the mortgage, the lender may also be able to offer a lower rate of interest than would be found on an uninsured mortgage, making the monthly payments affordable to Maxine.

In 2006, the CMHC undertook a pilot project to test the feasibility of a 30-year mortgage, as opposed to a 25-year term. Although there is a premium surcharge for the longer mortgage, the monthly payment would be reduced and become more affordable to some homebuyers.

The CMHC also rewards energy-efficient homes with a premium reduction and sponsors programs that help with refinancing and renovating homes. Maxine should consult the CMHC about secured lines of credit, title protection, and mortgage transferability.

After moving into her new house, Maxine can get valuable information from the CMHC website on home maintenance. With the help of the CMHC, Maxine was able to get an early start on home ownership. Such an investment will help her keep up with inflation, as home prices tend to increase over the long term. When she sells her home, she can again get advice from the CMHC website. The capital gain on the sale of her principal residence will be tax-free.

TABLE 12.3 THE HOME YOU CAN AFFORD: INCOME, HOME PRICE, AND DOWN PAYMENT GUIDE

HOUSEHOLD INCOME	5% DOWN PAYMENT	MAXIMUM HOME PRICE	10% DOWN PAYMENT	MAXIMUM HOME PRICE	25% DOWN PAYMENT	MAXIMUM HOME PRICE
$25 000	$3 000	$60 000	$6 300	$63 000	$18 900	$75 600
$30 000	$3 900	$78 000	$8 200	$82 000	$24 700	$98 800
$35 000	$4 800	$96 000	$10 100	$101 000	$30 300	$121 200
$40 000	$5 700	$114 000	$12 000	$120 000	$36 000	$144 000
$45 000	$6 600	$132 000	$13 900	$139 000	$41 700	$166 800
$50 000	$7 500	$150 000	$15 800	$158 000	$47 400	$189 600
$60 000	$9 300	$186 000	$19 600	$196 000	$58 800	$235 200
$70 000	$11 050	$221 000	$23 400	$234 000	$70 100	$280 400
$80 000	$12 500	$250 000	$27 200	$272 000	$81 500	$326 000
$90 000	$14 400	$288 000	$31 000	$310 000	$92 800	$371 200
$100 000	$16 275	$325 500	$34 800	$348 000	$104 300	$417 200

Figures are rounded to the nearest $100.

SOURCE: Canada Mortgage and Housing Corporation (CMHC). All rights reserved. Reproduced with the consent of CMHC. All other uses and reproductions of this material are expressly prohibited.

Mortgage or RRSP?

Another mortgage-related question, which is not easy to answer but is frequently asked, concerns RRSPs. If a homeowner has some extra money, should he or she put this money into RRSPs or reduce the mortgage? Again, no one can be sure which of these choices is the best financially. As usual, there are too many variables involved and too many assumptions that must be made before one can say with any degree of certainty which choice will be better. One cannot predict the future course of interest rates or the direction of the stock market. (Analysts' opinions on these issues are frequently quite diverse, and their predictions often wrong.) All we really know for certain is that money invested in both an RRSP and a house compounds tax-free. But tax must be paid when funds are withdrawn from an RRSP, while there is no tax on the gain from the sale of a house. See Personal Finance in Action Box 12.2, "Reducing the Mortgage or Adding to the RRSP," for an example of a choice between mortgage reduction and adding to an RRSP.

Financing a Home

Most people who buy homes or other real estate need credit to finance the purchase, but because the loan is likely to be large and the repayment period long, the borrowing process is somewhat more complex than for the usual personal loan. To obtain such a large loan, the buyer must pledge security of some significance—usually the property being purchased.

When real estate (immovable property) is used to secure a loan, the borrower signs a contract called a **mortgage**—not to be confused with a chattel mortgage (discussed in Chapter 13, under "Security for Loans"), which is used for movable goods. The mortgage contract refers to the borrower as the **mortgagor** because this person gives the mortgage to the lender, who in turn becomes the **mortgagee**—that is, the one who receives the mortgage as security for the loan. Sometimes chargor and chargee, respectively, are alternatives to these terms. The gradual repayment of a mortgage by periodic payments of principal and interest is

Personal FINANCE in action 12.2

Reducing the Mortgage or Adding to the RRSP?

Laurie, who is 35, received a Christmas bonus of $5000 from her employer. This bonus was offered because the company's new product line was so successful. Her manager told her there was no guarantee it would happen again. Laurie wondered whether she should put the money into her RRSP or make a prepayment on her mortgage. Friends at work were of no help. Some had said one thing, others another. Some had told her to do both. Since she was confused, she decided to ask her financial advisor Mary, who worked for Broad and Strong Financial Consultants, a division of Sherman & Sterling, the world's largest mutual fund company. This is what Mary advised:

■ Make a prepayment on your mortgage.

■ The future of all investments is uncertain. Reducing the size of your mortgage saves you money, which we know for certain. While you would get a tax reduction by adding to your RRSP, your marginal tax rate is not high to start with.

■ Funds invested in an RRSP are taxed when they are withdrawn. There is no tax on any gain in the value of your house. Your house should grow in value because it is attractive and in a good area. When you have reached 69, you can sell your house if you wish, invest the proceeds to provide a pension, and then move into an apartment.

Personal FINANCE in action 12.3

Buying a House

Theo and Sarah are ready to buy a house. They have enough money to make a down payment on what they consider an ideal house, but the process of negotiating a mortgage frightens them. They have never owned a house or borrowed money, and do not know what questions to ask their banker. The banker simplifies things by asking the following questions:

Do you think interest rates will rise?

Do you want to pay down the mortgage quickly?

Do you want financial stability?

Theo and Sarah are unsure about the future of interest rates but recently read that they are on the way up, so answered yes to all three questions. The banker says this simplifies things because it means that they should choose a fixed-rate mortgage with an amortization period of less than 25 years. This will mean stability if interest rates rise. It also means that they can renegotiate without penalty and will have lower interest rate costs because of the shorter amortization period.

referred to as **amortizing** the debt. (See Personal Finance in Action Box 12.3, "Buying a House," and Personal Finance in Action Box 12.8, "Interest and Principal Payments.")

Mortgage Debt Most of the total debt of households is mortgage debt, although the pattern varies somewhat with income level, occupation, marital status, and number of children. It is perhaps not surprising to find that, regardless of income level, mortgage debt represents the largest component of total family debt. There appears to be a tendency for mortgage debt to represent a larger proportion of total debt among higher-income households, which can afford more-expensive houses and may also have vacation homes.

In 2004, mortgage debt was 68.7 percent of total household debt, which averaged $66 800 per family.[5] This was a decline from the high of 74.5 percent in 1993.[6] The decline was helped by the drop in mortgage rates and the growth in household income.

Equity in Real Estate

Equity, which in this context refers to the value that the owner has in a property, can be estimated by finding a fair market price and then subtracting the outstanding mortgage debt. If house prices fall, equity falls too, as people who live in areas that have experienced severe economic downturns have discovered.

Types of Mortgages

First and Second Mortgages

A particular property may have more than one mortgage on it; the multiple mortgages will be ranked as first, second, and so on, according to the order in which they were recorded at the local Registry Office. If the first mortgage on a property is discharged, the second

[5]Vanier Institute of the Family, Average Household Debt Greater Than Annual Disposable Income, January 27, 2005.
[6]CMHC, 2005 Report on the State of Canada's Housing.

mortgage automatically becomes the first mortgage. This does not happen often, though, because first mortgages are usually for larger sums and longer terms than second mortgages.

What distinguishes a first mortgage from a second mortgage is its priority ranking in claims against the property. In the event that the buyer defaults on the mortgage payments and the property must be taken back and sold, the holder of the **first mortgage** has first claim on the proceeds from the sale. Only after this has been paid will the claims of the holder of the **second mortgage** be settled. If there are insufficient funds to pay all claims, the second mortgagee might have to accept a loss. Second mortgages are therefore considered to be riskier than first mortgages, and consequently carry higher interest rates.

From the homeowner's perspective, the number of mortgages on the property is not as important as the amount of equity he or she has in the property. For instance, on a property valued at $200 000, the owner's equity of $30 000 would be the same (i) with a first mortgage of $150 000 and a second mortgage of $20 000, or (ii) with a first mortgage of $160 000 and a second mortgage of $10 000. The interest rate paid on the second mortgage depends on the owner's equity. From the lender's point of view, if the first and second mortgages combined are less than 75 percent of the appraised value (that is, the owner's equity is 25 percent), the second mortgage is nearly as secure as the first; the interest rate should reflect this.

Security for the Lender

Mortgage money may be obtained either privately or from financial institutions such as banks, trust companies, and credit unions. Because a mortgage is a large loan, the lender must have assurance that it is a sound investment. To protect the lender, the mortgagor must either make a sizable down payment or have the mortgage insured. When the down payment is less than 25 percent of the property's value, the buyer's equity might not be enough to cover costs if, in the case of default, the lender had to take back the property and sell it. When the buyer cannot provide a down payment of at least 25 percent of the property's value, an institutional mortgagee will not offer a loan without mortgage insurance.

Mortgage insurance covers the risk to the lender that the borrower will default on the loan. The Canada Mortgage and Housing Corporation (CMHC), a Crown corporation, provides full loan insurance to mortgage lenders. The CMHC reimburses the lender for loss in cases of default—but correspondingly imposes a number of restrictions on the granting of the mortgage, as will be explained later (under "Qualifying for a Mortgage").

Mortgage Default

The most common reason for a mortgage to be in default is when the mortgagor fails to make the repayments agreed to in the contract. In addition there may be a failure to pay the property taxes, maintain the property, or properly insure the property.

The most common cause of mortgage default in 2004 was personal bankruptcy (29.5 percent). Some of the other causes included being financially overextended or stressed (18 percent), a drop in income (10 percent), and separation or divorce (9.5 percent).[7]

Conventional Mortgages

A **conventional mortgage** is a loan where the property being purchased is given as security. It is the cheapest mortgage because it does not have to be insured against default and may have a

[7]www.themortgageguide.ca.

Karl and His Inability to Make Mortgage Payments

Karl worked for Abitibi Consolidated in Kenora, Ontario. He had moved there five years ago with his partner, Denise. Denise worked part-time at the local A&W. They had bought a house, only a three-minute drive from the mill, for $75 000 with a down payment of $3 750. They had taken out a mortgage for the balance, $71 250, and now owed $70 000 to the bank. The mortgage rate was 7.50 percent and the monthly payments were $437. On December 15, the head office of Abitibi announced that it was closing the mill and laying off all the employees. Karl was earning $41 000 a year at the mill and had no other source of income. Denise made $7.45 an hour but rarely got more than 10 hours of work a week. They could no longer make their mortgage payments. Unless Ken could find another job quickly—highly unlikely in Kenora at that time—they would have to sell their house and move.

fixed or variable rate. The mortgagor has to pay to have the property evaluated by an independent appraiser and is also responsible for paying the legal fees required to register the mortgage.

Conventional mortgages usually require a down payment of 25 percent, though often a larger percentage is needed. They are not insured by the Canada Mortgage and Housing Corporation (CMHC). If the mortgagor defaults, the mortgagee forecloses (seizes the property) and sells it to recover the money lent (a prospect that one young couple face in Personal Finance in Action Box 12.4, "Karl and His Inability to Make Mortgage Payments"). Foreclosure will take place in one of two ways, either by a **power of sale** or a **judicial sale.** The former is initiated by the sending of a notice to the borrower and to the owner of the property. A judicial sale begins with a lawsuit against the borrower.

The foreclosure process varies slightly from province to province. Power of sale is used in Newfoundland, New Brunswick, Prince Edward Island, and Ontario. The other provinces, with the exception of Nova Scotia, use judicial sale. In Nova Scotia, the foreclosure process is called order of foreclosure, sale and possession, which involves the court. Under a power of sale, once the redemption period is over and the borrower is still in default, the property can be sold. The property may be sold by auction, privately, or by tender. The usual practice is to list the property with a real estate agent. The judicial sale process varies from province to province. In British Columbia, the court must approve the purchase price, the terms of the sale, and also the amount of the realtor's commission.

Insured Mortgages

Insured mortgages are approved by the Canada Mortgage and Housing Corporation (CMHC) or by Genworth Financial Canada (formerly GE Capital Mortgage Insurance). A mortgage must be insured when the loan is for more than 75 percent of the cost of the house. Eligible borrowers are those who plan to buy a house in Canada and to make it their principal residence.

First-time homebuyers may purchase a home with insurance for as little as 5 percent down. Without this insurance, many Canadians would not be able to buy a home because the down payment would be considerably higher.

Homeowner mortgage loan insurance premiums are calculated according to the loan-to-value ratio. These are shown in Table 12.4. Borrowers may qualify for a refund of 10 percent on their loan insurance premium for energy-efficient homes.

TABLE 12.4 INSURED MORTGAGE PREMIUMS

FINANCING REQUIRED	PREMIUM % OF LOAN AMOUNT
From 75% to 80%	1.00%
From 80% to 85%	1.75%
From 85% to 90%	2.00%
From 90% to 95%	2.75%

SOURCE: www.cmhc-schl.gc.ca/en.

An insured first mortgage that is equal to a high proportion of the house's cost is called a **high-ratio mortgage.** Those who take out such a mortgage used to have to pay an application fee. This was recently cancelled by the CMHC. There is still a premium to be paid, however, which ranges from a low of 1.00 percent to a high of 3.25 percent of the size of the loan.

Finding a Mortgage

There are a number of ways to obtain a mortgage. It may be possible to arrange a private mortgage with a relative or other individual who has money to lend. In such a case, a lawyer would draw up a contract stating terms that are agreeable to both borrower and lender. Most mortgages, however, are obtained from financial institutions: banks, trust companies, and credit unions.

Occasionally, it is possible to arrange a **seller** or **vendor take-back mortgage,** where the vendor, and not a financial institution, finances the mortgage. The vendor lends the borrower the money. There is often a benefit to the buyer in this situation because the interest may be lower than the current market rate. The title of the property is then transferred to the buyer, who makes payments directly to the vendor. An example follows:

(a) The house has a value of $250 000.
(b) The vendor has a mortgage on the house for $140 000.
(c) The buyer assumes this mortgage.
(d) The buyer gives the vendor a down payment of $60 000.
(e) The vendor lends the outstanding $80 000.

Assumption of an Existing Mortgage

At times it is advantageous to take over a mortgage that already exists on the property. If the vendor has a mortgage with four years remaining in the term, and that mortgage has a lower interest rate than that currently available for a new mortgage, the buyer may wish to take over the vendor's mortgage. The buyer should investigate whether the mortgagee's approval is required for such a transfer and if so, whether that approval can be obtained. Mortgage contracts vary in this regard. If an existing mortgage is assumed, the buyer replaces the original mortgagor by taking responsibility for the agreements in the mortgage contract; in case of default, the original borrower may still be bound by the personal covenant, which is the promise to repay the debt. In practice, when the purchaser has been approved to assume the existing mortgage, the vendor often obtains a written release of this covenant from the lender as protection from this contingency.

Mortgage Brokers

A **mortgage broker** finds a lender for the homebuyer who needs a mortgage. No fee is charged clients with good credit ratings. The broker is paid a referral fee by the lender. Those with poor credit ratings for whom it is difficult to find a lender will be charged a fee.

Ninety percent of mortgage brokers belong to the Canadian Institute of Mortgage Brokers and Lenders, the only national organization. It has a strict code of ethics, which ensures professionalism and prohibits discrimination. Its brokers promise to get clients the best mortgage rates, to help them find the best house for their needs, and to lead them through the often-confusing mortgage market. The organization helps consumers find a broker in their community with a "Find a CIMBL Member" feature on its website (see **www.cimbl.ca**).

Qualifying for a Mortgage

The rules and procedures that govern the mortgage-granting process originate from three sources: (i) legislation, both federal and provincial, (ii) insurers' requirements for high-ratio mortgages, and (iii) the policies of each financial institution. Two basic criteria for determining whether or not to grant a mortgage relate to the quality of the property as security and the borrower's creditworthiness.

The Property

Before agreeing to arrange a mortgage on a property, a lender will have it appraised to determine its **lending value (appraised value)**—that is, the value assigned to the property by the lender's appraiser, which is not necessarily the same as the selling price. It is conceivable that a buyer may be prepared to pay $300 000 for a much-desired property that the lender considers to be worth $286 000. In such a case, the mortgage loan is based on the lending value, not the selling price.

The CMHC has rules that vary from time to time and from place to place, relating to the proportion of the value of the property that may be lent for an insured mortgage. The CMHC has placed ceilings on loans of 95 percent. These range from $125 000 to $300 000, depending on the property's location. For example, in the Ontario counties of London, St. Thomas, Middlesex, and Elgin, the ceiling is $250 000.[8]

The Borrower

A potential lender will want a full report on the buyer's credit history, as well as complete details about the buyer's income, assets, and debts. The applicant will be asked to provide a statement from an employer, verifying the current income and employment history of the applicant and his or her spouse, and a statement from a banker about funds available for a down payment.

From these facts, the lender will calculate two ratios to determine the client's capacity to handle the proposed mortgage: the gross debt service and total debt service. **Gross debt service** (sometimes abbreviated GDS) is the percentage of the buyer's annual gross income needed to cover the mortgage payments and the municipal taxes (and sometimes also heating costs). If a condominium is to be purchased, 50 percent of the condominium fee is

---

[8]http://realtors.mls.ca/London/cmhc.htm.

usually included in the calculation. Lenders have guidelines, which change from time to time, about the maximum gross debt service that is acceptable to them; it may range from 25 percent to 32 percent.

A quick way to determine the maximum mortgage that you can afford is to find 30 percent (or whatever the ratio is) of your gross annual income, subtract the estimated annual property taxes, and divide by 12. The resulting amount is the monthly payment that you can presumably afford for principal and interest. For a given interest rate and amortization period, the size of the loan can be found from an amortization table.

Another measure of capacity to handle a mortgage is **total debt service** (TDS), that is, the percentage of annual income needed to cover mortgage payments, taxes, heating costs, and consumer debt payments. This number should not exceed 37 percent to 38 percent of annual income, or 40 percent if heating costs are included. Lenders may use this rule for any type of mortgage, conventional or insured. (For an example of how one couple would calculate their GDS and TDS, as well as the largest mortgage for which they will be eligible, see Personal Finance in Action Box 12.5, "Gross and Total Debt Service.")

Personal FINANCE in action 12.5

Gross and Total Debt Service

The Ghoris have three questions about financing the house they would like to buy: (i) How much is the gross debt service? (ii) How much is the total debt service? (iii) What is the largest mortgage they can afford?

In order to find the answers to these questions, they make the following assumptions:

- Combined incomes — $120 000
- Property taxes — $4000/year
- Heating costs — $ 5000/year
- Mortgage — $200 000
- Interest — 6.000%
- Amortization period — 10 years
- Payments — $1000/month; $12 000/year
- Consumer debt — $5000/year
- Lender's maximum TDS — 38%

1. How much will the gross debt service (GDS) be?

$$GDS = \frac{payments/yr. + taxes/yr. + heating/yr.}{gross\ annual\ income} \times 100$$

$$= \frac{\$12\ 000 + \$4000 + \$5000}{\$120\ 000} \times 100$$

$$= \frac{\$12\ 000}{\$120\ 000} \times 100$$

$$= 17.5\%$$

2. How much will the total debt service (TDS) be?

$$TDS = \frac{payments/yr. + taxes + heating + consumer\ debt}{gross\ annual\ income} \times 100$$

$$= \frac{\$12\ 000 + \$4000 + \$5000 + \$5000}{\$120\ 000} \times 100$$

continued

$$= \frac{\$26\ 000}{\$120\ 000} \times 100$$

$$= 21.67\%$$

3. **What is the largest mortgage for which the Ghoris are eligible?**

Their TDS is much less than the lender's maximum. They wonder how large a mortgage they could get if their TDS were 38 percent.

$$\frac{\text{Payments} + \text{taxes} + \text{heating} + \text{consumer debt}}{\text{gross annual income}} + \times 100 = \text{TDS}$$

$$\text{Payments} + (\text{taxes} + \text{heating} + \text{consumer debt}) = \frac{\text{TDS} \times \text{gross income}}{100}$$

$$\text{Payments} = \frac{\text{TDS} \times \text{gross income}}{100} - (\text{taxes} + \text{heating} + \text{consumer debt})$$

$$= 38 \times \frac{\$120\ 000}{100} - (\$4000 + \$5000 + \$5000)$$

$$= \$45\ 600 - \$14\ 000$$

$$= \$31\ 600 \text{ per year (or \$2633.33 a month)}$$

With a TDS of 38 percent, the monthly payment would be $2633.33. The next step is to find the principal of such a loan. Table 12.5 shows the monthly payment per $1000 for mortgages at various rates. At 6.00 percent, and with a 10-year amortization period, the monthly payment per $1000 is $11.06. Multiply this amount by the number of thousands of dollars in the principal to find the monthly payment. The formula is as follows:

$$\text{Monthly payment} = \frac{\text{principal}}{\$1000} \times \text{payment per \$1000 (\$11.06)}$$

Rewriting the formula,

$$\text{Principal} = \frac{\text{monthly payment} \times \$1000}{\$11.06}$$

Assuming monthly payments of $2633.33,

$$\text{Principal} = \frac{\$2633.33 \times \$1000}{\$11.06}$$

$$= \$238\ 095$$

Based on a total debt service ratio of 38 percent, the Ghoris would be eligible for a maximum mortgage of $238 095.

In addition to gross debt service and total debt service, a third requirement for most mortgages is that the buyer should have enough personal funds to make a down payment that represents some minimum proportion of the selling price. For a conventional mortgage, this would be 25 percent; for a high-ratio mortgage, it might be as little as 5 percent. If the total available funds for a down payment combined with the maximum mortgage are less than the price of the house, a second mortgage might be a consideration. However, the cost of servicing the second mortgage would have to be included in the gross and total debt service ratios. In qualifying purchasers for a mortgage, some conservative lenders may wish to satisfy themselves that the down payment actually comes from the borrower's own resources and not from a gift or an undisclosed loan. To this end, the lender may require evidence of the source of the funds, such as the history of a savings account. (The impact of these sorts of considerations is demonstrated in Personal Finance in Action Box 12.6, "Tulia Obtains a Mortgage Without Having to Make a Down Payment.")

TABLE 12.5   MONTHLY PAYMENTS REQUIRED TO AMORTIZE A $1000 LOAN, INTEREST COMPOUNDED SEMI-ANNUALLY

NOMINAL INTEREST RATE	AMORTIZATION PERIOD (YEARS)						
	5	10	15	20	25	30	35
%	(DOLLARS PER THOUSAND)						
6	19.30	11.06	8.40	7.12	6.40	5.94	5.65
6 1/4	19.41	11.19	8.53	7.26	6.55	6.10	5.82
6 1/2	19.53	11.31	8.66	7.40	6.62	6.26	5.98
6 3/4	19.64	11.43	8.80	7.55	6.85	6.42	6.15
7	19.75	11.56	8.93	7.69	7.00	6.59	6.32
7 1/4	19.87	11.68	9.07	7.84	7.16	6.75	6.49
7 1/2	19.98	11.81	9.20	7.99	7.32	6.91	6.66
7 3/4	20.10	11.94	9.34	8.13	7.47	7.08	6.83
8	20.21	12.06	9.48	8.28	7.63	7.25	7.01
8 1/4	20.33	12.19	9.62	8.43	7.79	7.42	7.18
8 1/2	20.44	12.32	9.76	8.58	7.95	7.58	7.36
8 3/4	20.56	12.45	9.90	8.74	8.12	7.76	7.54
9	20.68	12.58	10.05	8.90	8.25	7.93	7.72
9 1/4	20.08	12.71	10.19	9.05	8.45	8.11	7.90
9 1/2	20.92	12.84	10.34	9.21	8.62	8.28	8.08
9 3/4	21.04	12.98	10.48	9.36	8.78	8.46	8.26
10	21.15	13.11	10.63	9.52	8.95	8.63	8.45
10 1/4	21.27	13.24	10.77	9.68	9.12	8.81	8.63
10 1/2	21.39	13.37	10.92	9.84	9.29	8.99	8.81
10 3/4	21.51	13.51	11.07	10.00	9.46	9.17	9.00
11	21.63	13.64	11.22	10.16	9.63	9.34	9.18
11 1/4	21.74	13.78	11.37	10.32	9.80	9.52	9.37
11 1/2	21.86	13.91	11.52	10.49	9.98	9.71	9.56
11 3/4	21.98	14.05	11.67	10.65	10.15	9.89	9.74
12	22.10	14.19	11.82	10.81	10.32	10.07	9.93
12 1/4	22.22	14.32	11.97	10.98	10.50	20.25	10.12
12 1/2	22.34	14.46	12.13	11.15	10.68	10.43	10.31
12 3/4	22.46	14.60	12.28	11.31	10.85	10.62	10.50
13	22.59	14.74	12.44	11.48	11.03	10.08	10.69
13 1/4	22.71	14.22	12.59	11.65	11.21	10.99	10.88
13 1/2	22.83	15.02	12.75	11.82	11.39	11.17	11.07
13 3/4	22.95	15.16	12.90	11.99	11.56	11.36	11.26

Tulia Obtains a Mortgage Without Having to Make a Down Payment

Tulia rented an apartment in Calgary for $750 a month. She decided it was time to own her own house but did not have enough savings for a down payment. She was often financially stretched, as it was, to pay her rent. She found an online mortgage service that said she could obtain a mortgage for 100 percent of the value of a house with no money down if she had a good credit rating and had had the same job for two years. She had been a library assistant for six years and had never had any financial problems. Her credit rating was excellent. All she needed was a suitable house. During weekends she went to look at houses listed for sale in the newspaper. After several weeks she saw a new listing, a bungalow for $179 000. It was just what she wanted and was within walking distance of the library. She decided to apply online and was told that all she would have to pay were her legal costs and an appraisal fee. She was able to get a mortgage for 100 percent of the house's value for five years at 5.26 percent. She could just manage the payments if she sold her car.

The Mortgage Contract

Equity of Redemption

In the mortgage document, the mortgagor (the borrower) agrees to transfer the ownership of the property to the mortgagee (a financial institution or an individual lender) as security for the loan until such time as it is repaid. The mortgagor receives a copy of the signed mortgage; the mortgagee retains the original. The mortgage leaves the mortgagor with an interest in the property, called the **equity of redemption**, which is the right to redeem the property and have the ownership transferred back when the mortgage is discharged. The document states that the mortgagor will retain possession of the property and may enjoy the use of it, but must take good care of it and keep it insured, with the mortgagee as joint beneficiary of the insurance policy. If there is a fire while the mortgage is outstanding, the insurance money will be paid to the mortgagee, who will then decide what to do about the repairs.

The exchanges involved when using real property as security for loans are summarized in Figure 12.2. The purchaser briefly acquires title to and possession of the property, but on giving the first mortgage, legal title is surrendered to the first mortgagee; the mortgagor retains the equity of redemption. If the mortgagor gives a second mortgage on this property, the equity of redemption is transferred to the second mortgagee as security.

The Contract

The essential features of a mortgage are as follows:

(a) a description of the property,

(b) identification of the mortgagor and the mortgagee,

FIGURE 12.2 EXCHANGES WHEN REAL PROPERTY IS SECURITY FOR A LOAN

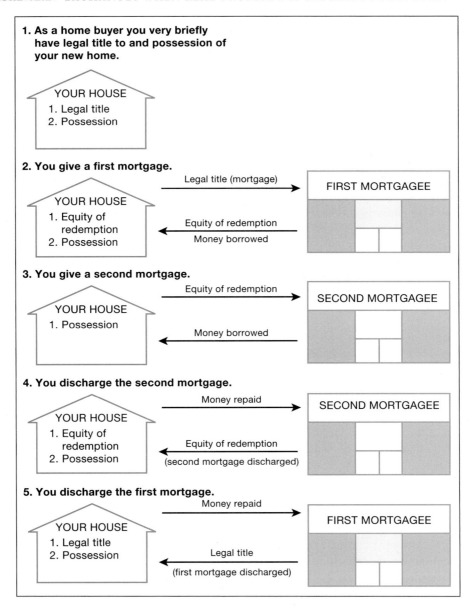

1. As a home buyer you very briefly have legal title to and possession of your new home.

YOUR HOUSE
1. Legal title
2. Possession

2. You give a first mortgage.

YOUR HOUSE
1. Equity of redemption
2. Possession

Legal title (mortgage) → FIRST MORTGAGEE

Equity of redemption
Money borrowed

3. You give a second mortgage.

YOUR HOUSE
1. Possession

Equity of redemption → SECOND MORTGAGEE

Money borrowed

4. You discharge the second mortgage.

YOUR HOUSE
1. Equity of redemption
2. Possession

Money repaid → SECOND MORTGAGEE

Equity of redemption
(second mortgage discharged)

5. You discharge the first mortgage.

YOUR HOUSE
1. Legal title
2. Possession

Money repaid → FIRST MORTGAGEE

Legal title
(first mortgage discharged)

(c) specification of the amount of the mortgage and the terms of repayment,

(d) an agreement that the mortgagor will give a charge on the property to the mortgagee but will keep the right of possession and the right to redeem the property when the mortgage is discharged,

(e) certain promises or covenants.

Some lenders give the borrower a mortgage contract written in legal language as well as a version in plain English.

Mortgage Covenants

Apart from the main contract, every mortgage contains a number of **covenants**, or binding promises made by the borrower (the mortgagor). Particularly important is the personal covenant, which is the mortgagor's promise to pay principal and interest. This convenant is described as personal because having obtained it, the mortgagee can then sue the mortgagor personally to obtain repayment in full or to recover any payments that are in arrears. The mortgagee can also take a number of other actions to recover the loan (see "Breach of Mortgage Contract" below).

Taxes Other covenants bind the mortgagor to pay the taxes, to insure the property, and to maintain it in good repair. It is important to the mortgagee that taxes be paid on time because taxes are a prior claim on property, taking precedence over a first mortgage. If taxes are allowed to fall into arrears, the mortgagee's security may be impaired, as in the case of a property being sold to pay for taxes. Some lenders require that the mortgagor pay one-twelfth of the annual taxes with each monthly mortgage payment, in order to build up a fund to pay the taxes when they become due. This approach saves the mortgagee the annual bother of finding out whether the taxes have been paid. Interest on this tax fund may or may not be credited to the mortgagor, depending on the agreement. Penalties for inadvertent late payment of taxes by the lender are usually debited to the borrower's account.

Property Insurance Before mortgage money is advanced, the mortgagor (the borrower) may be required to insure the property against fire and other possible risks, and to have the policy made in favour of the mortgagee. The insurance policy will be endorsed to ensure that the insurer knows about the mortgagee's interest in the property.

Sale of Mortgages

A person or institution who holds a mortgage (a mortgagee) sometimes decides to have the cash at once instead of receiving a monthly income stream for the term of the mortgage. The mortgagee can sell the mortgage without asking the mortgagor's permission, although the mortagee would inform the mortgagor of the transaction. Mortgages may be sold at their face value, or for more or less than their face value (i.e., at a premium or at a discount), depending on interest rates at the time. (Refer to Chapter 9 to review how changing interest rates affect the price of a security.) For the mortgagor, one of the risks of assuming a vendor take-back mortgage is that if the vendor sells the mortgage, the purchaser (the mortgagor) will have to deal with an additional person or institution. This is the principal reason why all of the terms of the loan should be written into the mortgage document.

Breach of Mortgage Contract

If the mortgagor fails to carry out any of the promises agreed to in the mortgage contract, this failure is considered a default. A mortgagor in default may be subject to a variety of penalties. The mortgage contract stipulates that the mortgagor must (i) make payments on time, (ii) pay the taxes, (iii) keep the property insured, (iv) keep the property in good condition, and (v) not sell the property without the mortgagee's written approval.

If you ever find it impossible to make a mortgage payment on time, contact the mortgagee immediately to search for a solution to the problem before it gets worse. Under these circumstances, the mortgagor is usually liable for late interest charges, which would be added to the outstanding principal and thus cause interest to be paid on interest. A mortgagee has a number of options to force a defaulting mortgagor to pay: these may include taking possession of the property, suing the borrower under the personal covenant, exercising the acceleration clause, selling the property, and foreclosure. Before beginning any of these actions, the mortgagee would notify the mortgagor of the mortgagee's intentions, giving the mortgagor an opportunity to take some preventive steps if desired.

Discharge of Mortgages

When a mortgage has been repaid in full, steps are taken to obtain a legal **mortgage discharge** and to transfer the property ownership to the mortgagor. Either the mortgagor or the lawyer will take a signed statement, which indicates that the debt has been paid, from the mortgagee to the local land registry or (in Ontario) Land Titles office. For a small fee, the claim against the property is removed and the title is cleared.

At the end of 2005, the big five Canadian chartered banks charged the following amounts to discharge mortgages:[9]

- Bank of Montreal $200.00
- CIBC $225.00
- Royal Bank $250.00
- Scotiabank $180.00
- TD Canada Trust $200.00

Mortgage Repayment

Term and Amortization Period

Repaying a mortgage can take as long as 25 or 30 years. The time allowed for completely repaying a mortgage, which is established when the mortgage is arranged, is called the **amortization period**. The length of time before the lender can demand repayment of all the outstanding principal is the **mortgage term**. In most cases, the interest rate and the monthly payments are fixed for the term. Although it has not always been so, mortgage terms are now usually much shorter than amortization periods. At the end of the term, or at the **maturity date**, the lender can legally demand full payment for all the outstanding balance; usually, though, the lender will offer to renew the mortgage at the prevailing rate. There have been times in the past when the term and amortization period were the same, but in recent years the high variability in interest rates has made lenders less likely to offer mortgages with interest rates that are fixed for 20 to 25 years. (See Personal Finance in Action Box 12.7, "Reducing the Amortization Period.")

There is considerable variety in the mortgage terms available. Canada's major chartered banks offered the following terms in December 2005:

- Bank of Montreal: from 6 months up to 18 years
- CIBC: from 6 months up to 10 years
- Royal Bank: from 1 year up to 25 years
- Scotiabank: from 1 year up to 7 years
- TD Canada Trust: from 6 months up to 10 years

[9]**www.thestar.com** (December 21, 2005).

Personal FINANCE in action 12.7

Reducing the Amortization Period

It was time for Sue to renew her mortgage. She still had $100 000 standing on her mortgage. She made an appointment to see her bank manager. The manager told her she could pay off her mortgage faster if she agreed to reduce the amortization. (The manager gave as an example interest of 8 percent.)

Interest Rate per Annum	
Compounded Half-yearly	8%
Monthly Payment, 15-year Amortization	$948.16
Monthly Payment, 25-year Amortization	$763.31
Difference per Month	$184.95
Total Savings	$58 299.80

Sue agreed to make the change. What she knew nothing about at the time, because she was not the least bit handy around the house, was that the boards on her back porch were rotting and her roof was leaking above the guest bedroom. When her friend Raymond pointed these problems out to her, she found that there wasn't enough money in her bank account to have the repairs done.

Methods of Repayment

Mortgage loans may be repaid in a number of ways, as long as an agreement can be reached between the mortgagor and the mortgagee. Since it is not practicable for most people to repay an entire mortgage with interest in a lump sum, most mortgages are amortized—that is, the debt is extinguished by making regular payments of interest and principal over a period of time.

Two methods of repayment will be explained here: (i) equal instalments of principal and (ii) blended payments. The difference between them is in the proportions of interest and principal in each payment, as illustrated in Figure 12.3. Each horizontal bar represents one payment and shows the way that the payment is divided between principal and interest. (These diagrams illustrate the proportions in a general way only; an exact plot of blended payments would result in a curved line rather than a straight one dividing interest and principal.) As will be explained below, if a mortgage is repaid with equal instalments of principal, the amount of interest owing declines, making succeeding payments smaller. By contrast, if all payments are the same amount, as is the case with blended payments, the proportions of interest and principal of each payment will vary over the repayment period.

Equal Instalments of Principal

In this repayment schedule, the principal is repaid at a constant rate, but each consecutive payment becomes smaller because, as the principal owing is reduced, the interest due also decreases (see Table 12.6 and Figure 12.3). This arrangement is used for various payment intervals—for instance, annually, semi-annually, or quarterly—but seldom monthly. Mortgages with equal instalments of principal are much less common than those with blended payments.

FIGURE 12.3   PROPORTIONS OF PRINCIPAL AND INTEREST PER PAYMENT, EQUAL
INSTALMENTS OF PRINCIPAL, AND EQUAL BLENDED PAYMENTS

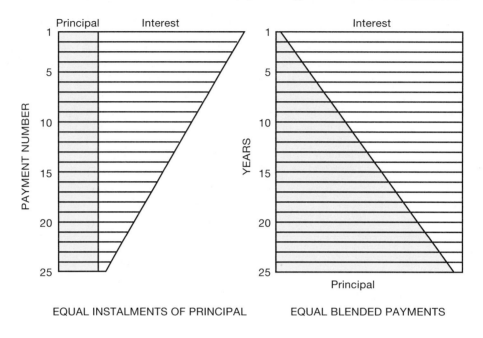

EQUAL INSTALMENTS OF PRINCIPAL   EQUAL BLENDED PAYMENTS

TABLE 12.6   MORTGAGE REPAYMENT SCHEDULE, EQUAL INSTALMENTS
OF PRINCIPAL

PRINCIPAL	$100 000
TERM	20 YEARS
INTEREST	9% ANNUALLY ON OUTSTANDING BALANCE
ANNUAL PAYMENT	$5000 PLUS INTEREST

Payment Number	Payment to consist of		Total Payment	Balance Outstanding
	Principal	Interest		
1	$5 000	$9 000	$14 000	$95 000
2	5 000	8 550	13 550	90 000
3	5 000	8 100	13 100	85 000
4	5 000	7 650	12 660	84 000
5	5 000	7 200	12 200	75 000
6	5 000	6 750	11 750	70 000
7	5 000	6 300	11 300	65 000
8	5 000	5 850	10 850	60 000
...	...	...	...	...
19	5 000	900	5 900	5 000
20	5 000	450	5 450	nil

Total interest paid in 20 years = $94 500

Equal Blended Payments

Repaying a loan in equal instalments of principal is quite easy to understand, but this method is not widely used because of the very large unequal payments. Most people prefer to repay loans with smaller and more frequent regular payments that fit more easily into their budgets. To accomplish this, the arithmetic becomes somewhat complicated. Essentially, each payment will include one month's interest on the total outstanding balance. The remainder of the payment is applied to reduce the principal. As the principal owing slowly drops each month, the interest component declines, allowing more of each payment to be applied to reduce the principal, as is illustrated in Figure 12.3 and Table 12.7.

Calculating the Repayment Schedule for Equal Blended Payments The procedure for calculating the repayment schedule for mortgages is identical to that used for instalment loans as described in Chapter 7. The steps in calculating the interest and principal components in each payment are reviewed in the box titled "Calculations for Blended Payments."

Renewing a Mortgage

If a mortgage has a term of five years and an amortization period of 25, the contract must be renewed every five years. When the term is up, the outstanding balance on the principal is due and must be repaid or renegotiated for another term. For most people a loan must be renegotiated for another term. The mortgage can be renewed with the same lender or transferred to another. Transferring may result, in addition to better rates, in better service and more flexible repayment options. However, it also may result in more

TABLE 12.7 PORTION OF MORTGAGE REPAYMENT SCHEDULE, EQUAL BLENDED PAYMENTS

PRINCIPAL	$ 100 000			
INTEREST RATE	9 PERCENT COMPOUNDED SEMI-ANNUALLY			
AMORTIZATION PERIOD	20 YEARS			
MONTHLY PAYMENT	$889.20			

Payment Number	Monthly Payment	Principal Portion	Interest Portion	Balance Outstanding
First Year				
1	$889.20	$152.89	$736.31	$99 847.11
6	889.20	158.60	730.60	99 065.60
12	889.20	165.74	723.46	98 089.14
Final Year				
230	889.20	820.33	68.87	8 533.49
239	889.20	876.32	12.88	873.33

Total interest = $113 392.30

legal and appraisal fees.[10] The borrower needs to search out this information before deciding to change lenders.

At the end of a term, when the total outstanding balance becomes due, there is an opportunity to reduce the principal before renegotiating the mortgage. As illustrated in the boxed examples included throughout this chapter, any reduction in principal will result in considerable interest savings over the long run.

Calculations for Blended Payments

MORTGAGE TERMS:

Principal	$120 000
Interest rate	7.25%
Compounding	semi-annual
Amortization period	25 years
Term	5 years
Monthly payment	$859.20
	(see Table 12.5)
Interest factor	.005 952 3834

(a) **Amount of monthly payment:**

Consult an amortization table (Table 12.5) to find the monthly payment for a loan of $1000, at 7.25 percent, for 25 years. Calculate the monthly mortgage payments for a loan of $120 000.

$$\text{Monthly payment} = \frac{\text{principal}}{\$1000} \times \text{payment/\$1000 [7.25\%] (Table 12.5)}$$

$$= \frac{\$120\ 000}{\$1000} \times 7.16$$

$$= \$120 \times 7.16$$

$$= \$859.20$$

(b) **Interest at end of first month:**

Interest for one month	=	outstanding principal	×	appropriate interest factor
	=	$120 000	×	0.005 952 3834
	=	$714.29		

(c) **Principal component of the first month's payment:**

Repayment of principal	=	monthly payment	−	interest for one month
	=	$859.20	−	$714.28
	=	$144.92		

(d) **Principal outstanding after first payment:**

Principal outstanding	=	principal owing before payment	−	payment on principal
	=	$120 000	−	$144.92
	=	$119 855.08		

continued

[10]At the time of writing (December 2005), only CIBC offered to pay all legal and appraisal fees when a mortgage was transferred from another financial institution.

(e) **Second month's interest:**

Interest for 1 month	=	outstanding principal	×	appropriate interest factor
	=	$119 855.08	×	0.005 952 3834
	=	$713.42		

(f) **Mortgage schedule for the first six months:**

PAYMENT NUMBER	DATE OF PAYMENT	MONTHLY PAYMENT	INTEREST PORTION	PRINCIPAL PORTION	OUTSTANDING BALANCE
1	June 1	$859.20	$714.28	$144.92	$119 855.08
2	July 1	859.20	713.41	145.79	119 709.31
3	August 1	859.20	712.55	146.65	119 562.70
4	September 1	859.20	711.68	147.52	119 415.10
5	October 1	859.20	710.80	148.40	119 266.70
6	November 1	859.20	709.92	149.28	119 117.50

Prepayment of Principal

The difference between repayment and prepayment is that **repayment** means following the mortgage schedule in extinguishing the loan, while **prepayment** is a way of accelerating the reduction of the principal during the term. A mortgagor may wish to repay a mortgage faster than the original schedule, make lump-sum payments to reduce the principal, or discharge the mortgage when selling the property. (Steffan, whose situation is summarized in Personal Finance in Action Box 12.8, should consider these options.) But whether the mortgagor may actually take any of these actions will depend on the terms established under the original mortgage contract.

Open and Closed Mortgages

There tends to be some confusion about open and closed mortgages because of the degrees of openness and the fact that few are completely closed. A fully open mortgage permits

---

Personal FINANCE in action 12.8

Interest and Principal Payments

Steffan was able to make a down payment of 5 percent on a $200 000 house. His mortgage was amortized over 25 years with an initial term of five years. The interest on the mortgage was at 7.30 percent compounded semi-annually. His payments were $1366.17 monthly. This seemed a lot to Steffan, who had little knowledge of mortgages. He was surprised to find that after the initial five years he will have paid $81 970.20, but that only $16 370.68 of this money will be applied to reduce the principal of his $190 000 loan.

prepayments without restriction or penalty; as well, the loan may be paid off completely at any time. A totally closed mortgage, on the other hand, permits no prepayments. In practice, most so-called closed mortgages permit some prepayments without penalty under certain conditions, and mortgages referred to as open may actually be only partly open. Some mortgage contracts permit limited amounts to be prepaid at specified times, while others are more liberal. In summary, prepayment may be totally unrestricted, or mortgagees may restrict either the amount of prepayment allowed or the timing of the prepayment.

Prepayment Penalties

When you make a prepayment, the lender may charge a fee called a prepayment penalty. Having to pay a penalty to make a prepayment of principal is not unusual. The fee is based on the rationale that the mortgagee has invested money in this mortgage, expecting to receive a regular income and is therefore inconvenienced by having to reinvest unexpected repayments.

The penalty charged will be determined by the terms of the mortgage agreement. It is usually based on three months' interest or the *interest rate differential*—whichever is greater using the following formulas:

(a) the three months' interest formula:

$$\text{Amount of prepayment} \times \frac{\text{interest rate}}{12 \text{ months}} \times 3 \text{ months}$$

(b) the interest rate differential formula:

$$\text{Amount of the prepayment} \times \frac{\text{the mortgage rate} - \text{the current rate} \times \text{months left in term}}{12 \text{ months}}$$

Since mortgage lenders change their policies about prepayment from time to time, it is important to find out the prepayment opportunities being offered by competing lenders. Regardless of what a lending officer may tell you, you must read a mortgage contract carefully to find out exactly what the prepayment conditions are. There may be a requirement not only to give the lender notice of intention to repay, but also to pay a penalty.

When prepayments are made, it is common practice for the lender to make no change in the size of the monthly payments, thus shortening the time that the loan will be outstanding. The reduced amortization period will result in less total interest.

To calculate the savings in making a prepayment, use an amortization schedule that shows the principal and interest components of each payment. A prepayment eliminates a number of payments from the schedule, thus reducing both principal and interest for the mortgagor. Consequently, the mortgage will be repaid in less time than originally expected. (See Personal Finance in Action Box 12.9, "Costs and Benefits of a Prepayment.")

Prepayment *Without* Penalties

Competition among banks for mortgage customers has resulted in various prepayment features. Several banks now allow customers to increase their mortgage payments without fees or penalties. The exact amount is the bank's choice. Usually a bank allows an increase of no

Costs and Benefits of a Prepayment

The Changs, who had a CMHC-insured mortgage for $100 000 at 9 percent, amortized over 20 years, were in a position to repay an additional $11 000 two years after the mortgage had started. The mortgage contract stated that they could make a prepayment of 10 percent of the original loan at the end of the second year with a penalty of three months' interest. In their case, the maximum prepayment would be calculated as follows:

$$\text{Amount of the prepayment} \times \frac{\text{interest rate}}{12 \text{ months}} \times 3$$

$$\$ 10\ 000 \times \frac{0.09}{12} \times 3 = \$225.00$$

What are some of the costs and benefits of making this prepayment?

Costs

(a) *Penalty of three months' interest* = $225

(b) *Forgone interest on prepayment*: The Changs had a choice of either leaving the $10 000 invested to earn interest or using it to reduce the principal outstanding on the mortgage. Assuming they could have earned 6 percent interest on $10 000 for 18 years (the time remaining in their amortization period), what is the opportunity cost of this prepayment?

A well-diversified stock portfolio should easily average returns of over 6 percent for 18 years. The S&P/TSX Composite, and its predecessor the TSE 300, for example, was up 369.61 percent in the past 21 years, for an average gain of 17.60 percent.[11]

$10 000, invested at 6 percent and compounded annually for 18 years, would grow as follows:

Future value = principal × compound value of $1 [6%, 18 years]
= $10 000 × 2.85
= $28 500

Interest Component = $28 500 − $10 000
= $18 500

Assuming a 30 percent average income tax rate:

Income tax = $18 500 × 0.30
= $5550

After-tax income = $18 500 − 5550
= $12 950

Total Cost = $225 + 12 950
= $13 175

Benefits

(a) *Reduction in total mortgage interest*:
Using an amortization schedule, the balance outstanding on the Changs' mortgage is as follows:

Balance outstanding:
After payment #24 = $96 002.43
After prepayment = $96 002.43 − $10 000
= $85 002.43
After payment #70 = $86 063.18

Interest = accumulated interest at payment #70 − accumulated interest at payment #24
= $48 307.28 − 17 343.27
= $30 964.01

(b) *Reduction in time*:
Number of payments eliminated = 70 − 24
= 46

Mortgage discharge is nearer by 46 months (3 years, 10 months).

Conclusion:

The results will, of course, vary with the interest rates on mortgage loans and deposits, and with the mortgagor's marginal tax rate. In this case, looking at after-tax dollars, the prepayment would have saved the Changs $30 964, compared with a potential investment return of $13 175, and their mortgage would be discharged nearly four years sooner. In this example, no allowance was made for the opportunity to invest the interest savings resulting from the prepayment.

What are some other factors you would want to consider in making a decision to prepay or not?

[11]Courtesy BMO Nesbitt Burns, January 9, 2006.

more than 10 percent and usually only once every 12 months. If the borrower wishes, he or she can continue paying the increased payments for the duration of the term. Prepaying in this fashion is an excellent idea, if the funds are not needed to maintain the house, because the extra money is used to reduce the principal, thereby shortening the amortization period. Some banks may allow prepayment for a slightly higher rate. Without the higher rate, a three-month penalty is charged. Still other banks do not offer prepayment options or do offer them and without a penalty.

Cash-Back

At the time of writing, four of the major chartered banks offered a **cash-back** feature that appeals to many borrowers. The details differ, but the principle is the same. Borrowers are offered cash on some fixed-rate mortgages based on the interest rate and the term. The money may be used in a variety of ways. Three of the banks will allow it to be used for anything, including the paying down of the principal. One bank specifies that it can be used for anything but the reduction of the principal. In all cases, the larger the mortgage and the longer the term, the greater the cash-back. The money is also tax-free. Those who decline this feature are offered a lower effective annual rate.

Following are the cash-back features offered by one lender:

■ 5 percent cash-back to help pay for things like renovations, furniture, a vacation, down payment, or closing costs;

■ available on 5-, 7-, or 10-year terms at a fixed interest rate;

■ approval obtainable online;

■ interest rate guaranteed for 120 days on a purchase and for 60 days when transferring or refinancing;

■ mortgage payable weekly, biweekly, monthly, semi-monthly, or accelerated weekly or biweekly to speed mortgage pay-off;

■ up to 20 percent of the principal payable each year;

■ payment amount may be increased by up to 25 percent each year;

■ one payment allowed to be missed each year.[12]

Total Interest

Not infrequently, the total interest paid during the life of a mortgage greatly exceeds the purchase price of the house. For example, a mortgage of $80 000 at 10 percent for 25 years would result in total interest charges of $134 677. Three influential and interrelated factors that affect total interest are (i) the principal, (ii) the interest rate, and (iii) the amortization period. If it is possible to reduce any of these factors, the total interest will be decreased. (You may wish to refer to Chapter 7 to review the method of calculating total interest.)

The first opportunity to reduce total interest is when the mortgage is being arranged. If you can lower the principal of the loan by making a larger down payment, you will pay less total interest (see Figure 12.4). A second factor is the interest rate. Finding a loan at a lower rate will be to your advantage. What might appear to be quite a small difference in interest

---

[12]President's Choice Financial, operated by CIBC.

FIGURE 12.4 TOTAL COST OF A HOUSE, VARYING DOWN PAYMENT AND
AMORTIZATION PERIOD (PURCHASE PRICE AND INTEREST RATE
HELD CONSTANT)

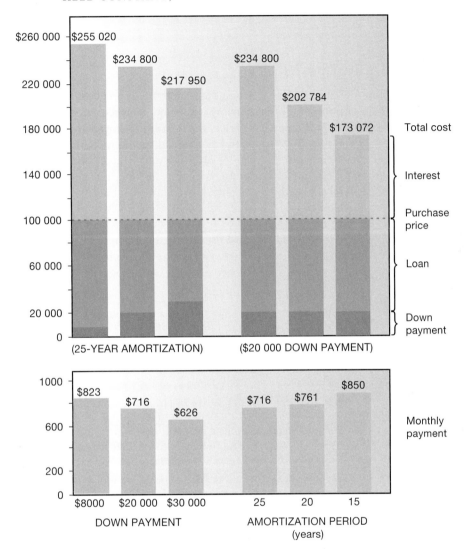

rates can have a significant effect on the total interest. Using the example in the previous
paragraph, a 0.25 percent reduction in interest rate on the $80 000 loan would mean $4026
less in total interest. Finally, the shorter the amortization period, the less total interest, as
illustrated in Figure 12.4; it is, of course, necessary to make larger monthly payments to
accomplish this.

Closing Costs

When a property is purchased, the agreement to purchase is often signed some time before
the date for closing the deal. When the **closing date** arrives, the buyer must pay (i) the seller
for the property; (ii) the lawyer for services and disbursements, such as registration of the

transaction at the registry or Land Titles office; (iii) taxes (where applicable), such as land transfer or property purchase tax, goods and services tax, and provincial sales tax; and (iv) adjustment costs. With or without a mortgage, you can always expect to have to pay closing costs when property is purchased.

Statement of Adjustments

Some time before the closing date for the house purchase, the lawyer sends the buyer a **statement of adjustments**, which sets forth the accounts between buyer and seller relating to this sale. It includes the purchase price, the deposit, and property taxes, as well as, possibly, insurance and fuel. Since the vendor has been paying property taxes and insurance, the buyer must reimburse the vendor for any prepaid taxes and insurance when ownership changes. For example, if a house is bought in June, the insurance may have been paid until September and the taxes until November. The buyer would pay the vendor three months' insurance and five months' taxes. Sometimes there is fuel oil in the tank to be paid for.

The new property must be insured against fire, as noted in the mortgage contract. At this stage, the buyer can decide whether to take over the vendor's property insurance policy, convert a previous policy to fit this new property, or take out a new one.

Legal Fees and Taxes

The lawyer's bill usually includes fees for services and any expenses paid on the buyer's behalf, such as fees for title searches and for the registration of various documents, as well as any federal or provincial taxes. The lawyer's fee itself depends on the complexity of the transaction and on the local guidelines for such fees.

Seven Canadian provinces now charge a fee on real estate transactions known as a **land transfer tax**, a **property transfer tax**, or a **deed transfer tax**. These taxes are applied on a graduated scale as shown below for 2005. The three territories have no such taxes.

British Columbia:	1% on the first $200 000
	2% on the amount above $200 000
Alberta:	No tax
Saskatchewan:	No tax
Manitoba:	0% on the first $30 000
	0.5% on the next $60 000 up to $90 000
	1.0% on the value between $90 000 and $150 000
	1.5% on the value between $150 000 and $200 000
	2% on the amount above $200 000
Ontario:	0.5% on the value up to $55 000
	1% on the value between $55 000 and $250 000
	1.5% on the value between $250 000 and $400 000
	0.5% on the amount above $400 000
Quebec:	.5% on the first $50 000
	1.0% on the value from $50 000 to $250 000
	1.5% on the value in excess of $250 000
New Brunswick:	0.25% of the assessed value

Nova Scotia:	Deed transfer tax rates are set by the municipalities. They range from 0.5% to 1.5% of the property's value. For example, in Windsor the tax is 0.5%, while in Halifax it is 1.5%.

Prince Edward Island: Previously, the province had no property transfer tax. In May 2005 the government passed the *Real Property Transfer Tax Act*. Now 1% is charged on either the sale price or the property's assessed value, whichever is greater.

There are numerous exceptions, including these:

- no tax payable if the value, determined by either method, is less than $30 000,
- no tax payable if the purchaser is a first-time home buyer,
- no tax payable if the property is transferred to a family for $1.00.

Newfoundland
and Labrador: No tax

A copy of an up-to-date land survey is usually required by all lenders. The vendor or the vendor's mortgagee may provide a copy of the survey. Otherwise, the purchaser may be liable for significant surveyor fees in conjunction with placing a new mortgage on the property.

The federal goods and services tax (GST)—along with any relevant provincial sales tax—is applied to some aspects of property purchases (e.g., mortgage insurance, legal fees, and certain disbursements), adding to closing costs.

A list of other possible costs follows.

Other Costs the Mortgagor May Encounter[13]

A. The Up-Front Costs
- Mortgage loan insurance application fee and premium
- Appraisal fee, which can cost between $250 and $350
- A deposit, which can be as much as 5 percent of the purchase price (This eventually becomes part of the down payment.)
- A down payment (The exact amount depends on whether the mortgage is high-ratio or conventional.)
- Estoppel certificate fee[14]
- A home inspection fee, which can cost over $200
- A land transfer tax
- Title insurance in case of defects in the title to the property
- Property insurance
- A land survey, which can cost up to $2000
- A water quality inspection if the property has a well

[13]Canada Mortgage and Housing Corporation.
[14]A document issued by a mortgagor, mortgagee, or condominium that sets out certain conditions. It is not used in Quebec.

B. Other Costs That May Be Incurred

- New appliances
- Gardening tools
- Snow removal equipment
- Materials needed to redecorate the house
- Moving expenses
- Fees to hook up utilities
- Renovation expenses

Life Insurance and Mortgages

If they so wish, a homebuyer may arrange a life insurance policy with a decreasing term with his or her own insurance company in order to provide enough funds to discharge the mortgage in the event of his or her death. Initially, the value of the life insurance policy will be approximately the same as the amount of the mortgage loan, with periodic reductions in value to roughly correspond to the declining debt on the property. If the person whose life is insured dies before the mortgage is fully repaid, the beneficiary of the life insurance will have some funds to discharge the mortgage debt, but he or she is not obligated to do so.

Some lenders maintain group policies covering the lives of a number of borrowers and therefore offer mortgage life insurance as part of the mortgage package. If this coverage is selected, a deceased mortgagor's survivors have no choice in how to use the insurance money, since the policy is not a personal one. In such cases, the insurer repays the outstanding balance on the mortgage directly to the lender. If the incomes of two people purchasing a residence are required for debt servicing, it is important to determine whether the policy covers the lives of both wage earners. If not, purchasing additional private life insurance may be prudent. In any event, it is always wise to compare the cost of optional group life insurance offered by the mortgagee with that of similar coverage available in the open marketplace.

Decreasing term insurance is sometimes called mortgage life insurance, but it should not be confused with the mortgage insurance that lenders use to cover the risk of losing their money if the borrower defaults. The latter type of insurance is mandatory for CMHC-insured mortgages.

The Mortgage Market

Buying a new house is usually a very exciting time, one of the most exciting that any individual or couple experiences. Home ownership brings with it a sense of pride that, as far as our lives as consumers are concerned, is rarely equalled. In the excitement of looking for a home to buy, choosing the right mortgage, while very important, is often given a lesser priority than finding a house. This is a mistake because the mortgage market offers an array of features the careful consumer will find interesting and worthwhile. The first thing someone shopping for a mortgage may notice is that the rates offered by competing financial institutions are often very similar. This can be seen in Table 12.8.

Rates have to be similar because for anyone with a computer this information is only a mouse-click away. Therefore, lenders usually offer a variety of other features to attract customers. Some of these are listed below, along with other relevant information.

(a) **Preapproved Mortgage**. Every financial institution in the mortgage business has a **preapproved mortgage**. The details will differ from customer to customer, but such

TABLE 12.8 A COMPARISON OF CLOSED FIXED-RATE MORTGAGES

LENDER	1 YEAR	2 YEARS	3 YEARS	4 YEARS	5 YEARS	7 YEARS	10 YEARS
BMO	4.80%	4.95%	5.34%	5.49%	5.59%	6.60%	7.35%
Scotiabank	5.75%	5.90%	6.00%	6.15%	6.30%	6.95%	
CIBC	5.70%	5.95%	6.05%	6.20–%	6.30%	7.45%	7.65%
Royal	5.80%	5.90%	5.95%	6.20%	6.30%	7.15%	7.25%
TD Canada Trust	5.90%	5.95%	6.00%	6.05%	6.305%	6.60%	7.05%

SOURCE: www.canadamortgage.com/RatesShow/ShowRates.cfm (December 30, 2005).

a mortgage is arranged before a house is bought. Preapproval gives customers peace of mind. They know when looking for a house just what they can afford. The five big banks all have preapproved or prearranged rates. But the guaranteed period differs. One bank has a 60-day guarantee, three have 90-day guarantees, and one guarantees its rate for 120 days. In what is already a stressful situation, such a guarantee reduces the pressure to buy when interest rates are rising quickly. A prearranged mortgage is often conditional upon an appraisal of the property. Even with a prearranged mortgage, there is nothing to stop customers from looking for a lower rate of interest.

(b) **Open Mortgage.** With an **open mortgage**, the principal can be prepaid without incurring a penalty. There are, however, a number of different "open mortgages," some not as open as others. Some allow prepayment at any time but charge a penalty for the privilege. Others allow a percentage of the mortgage to be prepaid without a penalty, say 15 percent, but the rest of the mortgage is closed. The best kind of open mortgage allows prepayment at any time without a fee or penalty. Potential borrowers need to clarify just what kind of open mortgage is being offered.

(c) **Convertible Mortgage.** Borrowers may opt for a short-term or a long-term mortgage. Interest rates are lower with the former (that is why people like them), but a **convertible mortgage** allows the borrower to switch to a longer-term mortgage, which becomes an advantage in a period of rapidly rising rates. If one had to wait until the term expired on a short-term mortgage in order to switch, rates might be considerably higher.

(d) **Fixed-Rate Mortgage.** The interest rate is set for a specific term, from 6 months to 25 years, and cannot be renegotiated. Interest is calculated semi-annually.

(e) **Variable Rate Mortgage.** As the name implies, with the **variable rate mortgage** the rate varies. With such a mortgage, one never knows what will happen. Rates may rise or fall, but one cannot know for sure when they would do so. This uncertainty can be unsettling. When rates fall, the principal is reduced faster. When they rise, the reverse happens, and a higher proportion of the payment is interest. The variable rate is determined by the bank's prime rate. This, in turn, is determined by the Bank of Canada's overnight rate, the setting of which is part of Canada's overall monetary policy and macroeconomic strategy. Some lenders have an added feature, the "rate stopper" or "rate capper," which allows the borrower to put a cap or maximum on the variable rate if interest rates start to rise.

The prime rate in January 2006 was 5 percent, up slightly from the previous few years. Variable rate five-year mortgages were available from all the major banks at prime, or slightly below prime.

(f) **Closed Mortgage**. The **closed mortgage** allows for no flexibility. The interest rate stays the same for the duration of the term. The advantage of such a mortgage is that the rate is lower than those for open or convertible mortgages.

(g) **Discount Mortgage**. In order to attract mortgage customers (because unused money earns no revenue), Canada's banks may offer mortgages with rates of interest that are at a discount to the posted rate. At the time of writing, three of the major banks (CIBC, BMO, and TD Canada Trust) openly advertised their discount or better-than-posted rates. While the other two may have them, it is not obvious. The most innovative was TD Canada Trust, which offered a discount rate for the first year of a fixed-rate mortgage. For the balance of the term, the rate was guaranteed to be less than the fixed rate when the mortgage was first approved.

(h) **High-Ratio Mortgage**. A **high-ratio mortgage** is one where the mortgagor has a down payment of less than 25 percent of the purchase price of the house.

(i) **Conventional Mortgage.** If the down payment is at least 25 percent of the value of the house, the mortgage is considered a **conventional mortgage**.

(j) **Bridge Financing**. Required when the purchase of a new home is completed before the sale of the old home and the homebuyer lacks the funds to pay for the new house, **bridge financing** is a short-term loan for the value of the house being sold, not the house being bought. It is paid back when the sale is closed. A new mortgage and a down payment cover the difference in prices between the old and the new houses.

(k) **Loan-to-Value**. The **loan-to-value** is the ratio between the value of the mortgage and the value of the property. A mortgage of $200 000 on a house worth $250 000 has an 80 percent loan-to-value ratio.

(l) **Interest Adjustment**. **Interest adjustments** are charged when borrowers have to pay interest from the date the money is needed to pay for the house to the date the mortgage starts.

(m) **Early Renewal**. This feature allows the borrower to renew a mortgage before the term is up, usually at any time during the last year. Early renewal is valuable if interest rates are expected to rise or if they have fallen since the mortgage was negotiated.

(n) **Portable Mortgage**. This mortgage allows the borrower to sell a house and take the mortgage to a new house. With such a feature, the mortgagor can take out a long-term loan when rates are low and take the mortgage and its low rate from house to house.

(o) **Assumable Mortgage**. This mortgage allows the purchaser to take over the seller's mortgage. This is of value to the purchaser when the assumed mortgage has an interest rate less than current rates. Before a mortgage can be assumed, the lender must give permission to do so.

(p) **Shortening the Amortization Period**. The amortization period is usually 25 years. Borrowers can ask for a shorter amortization. While this requires larger payments, it results in lower interest costs and results in considerable savings in the long run. One way of shortening the amortization is to ask for compounding to be done more frequently. The important thing is not to make the payments too onerous.

(q) **Skipping Payments**. Some lenders now allow the mortgagor to periodically skip payments if all payments are up to date. While there is no fee, the unpaid interest is added to the principal. Therefore, skipping payments means that it takes longer to pay off the mortgage.

(r) **Comparison Shopping**. Comparing mortgages offered by different financial institutions is essential for the prospective homebuyer. In the past, comparison shopping required a great deal of time and legwork. Technology has made the task simpler. The computer allows prospective homebuyers to do their comparison shopping at home and gives them an advantage over the lenders. They can decide what features most appeal to them at their leisure and without pressure. It is also very easy to find the interest rates offered by competing firms on their websites and to compare the rates using one of the many tables available online. Comparision shopping and technology have made selecting a mortgage much easier. Borrowers can even apply for mortgages online and avoid the inconvenience of having to travel to a financial institution.

(s) **Offer to Purchase**. This legally binding document must include all the terms and conditions of the sale agreed to by the homebuyer and the vendor. The most obvious are the purchase price, all of the financial details of the mortgage, as well as the closing date, the date of occupancy, and any conditions that must be met such as the sale of an existing house. It should also include a list of the items the vendor is leaving behind such as curtains, appliances, and lamp fixtures (chattel).

(t) **Homebuyers' Plan**. Under the **Homebuyers' Plan**, first-time homebuyers may withdraw $20 000 from their RRSPs to help purchase a house. This will certainly help with the purchase of a house, but the plan does have some negative features. The withdrawn money is no longer tax-sheltered and loses the benefit of tax-free compounding. The money must also be repaid in full over 15 years at the rate of 1/15 each year. Anyone who finds it difficult to make a down payment without resorting to withdrawing funds from an RRSP may find the repayment requirement just as difficult. Any money not repaid in a given year must be included as income on Line 129 of the tax return. If the tax owing on this income is not paid, there is a late-filing penalty of 5 percent. This interest, however, is compounded daily. Therefore, 5 percent is equivalent to an effective annual rate of 5.126 percent.

$$i = \frac{0.05}{365} \qquad\qquad f = (1.000\ 136\ 986)^{365} - 1$$

$$= 0.000\ 136\ 986 \qquad\qquad = 5.126$$

In addition, there is a fine of 1 percent of the balance of tax owing per month that the payment is late. Anyone considering withdrawing money from an RRSP to buy a house should think very carefully about the consequences of not being able to repay the money. See Personal Finance in Action Box 12.10, "Financing a Home Through the Homebuyers' Plan," for some other considerations relevant to this plan.

(u) **Canada Mortgage and Housing Corporation**. The federal government established the Canada Mortgage and Housing Corporation in 1946 to help returning World War II veterans obtain housing. It now provides **mortgage loan insurance** to lower-income Canadians in the housing market who cannot afford the 25-percent down payment required by financial institutions. Instead, a house can be purchased, under this plan, with a down payment of as little as 5 percent of the value of the house. Mortgage loan insurance was introduced in 1954. Since that time, the CMHC claims it has helped one-third of Canadians buy homes.

(v) **Mortgage-Backed Securities**. A means of increasing the amount of money in the mortgage market, **mortgage-backed securities** (MBSs) are a fixed-income investment insured by CMHC. MBS certificates may be purchased for as little as $1000. The yield varies, but it is higher than that paid on government bonds. Those who buy MBSs are indirectly lending money to homebuyers. The funds from their purchases are added to the pool of money available to the mortgagors. People who buy MBSs receive blended payments of principal and interest from mortgagors.

Many terms of MBS are available, from six months to 25 years. There are four categories: single-family dwellings; multi-family dwellings; social housing such as seniors' residences and co-ops; and mixed dwellings, which can be any combination of the other categories. Since the program began in the 1980s, $27 billion has been invested in MBSs. They may be purchased at banks, trust companies, and investment dealers.

Personal FINANCE in action 12.10

Financing a Home Through the Homebuyers' Plan

Darlene and Henry are both in their mid-thirties. They are self-employed with their own rug-cleaning business. Since they have no company pensions, both have been putting as much of their savings as they could afford into their RRSPs since they started their business 10 years ago. Darlene's RRSP has grown to $160 000 and Henry's to $140 000. Up until now, they have rented a beautiful apartment for $2000 a month. Recently, they began to think they should buy a house. Their friends were all happily housed, and they were envious of the extra space their homes provided. Last weekend, they went to an open house in a new subdivision and saw a house they could not resist. The listing price was $450 000. To finance the purchase, they plan to do the following:

■ Use $75 000 in GICs.

■ Withdraw $20 000 each from RRSPs.*

■ Take out a 25-year mortgage at a fixed rate of 10 percent, compounded monthly, to pay the balance of $335 000.

First, they need to calculate the monthly mortgage payment by using the following formula, where i is the interest rate and n is the number of payments:

$$\$335\,000 = \text{monthly payment} \left(1 - \frac{(1 + i)^{-n}}{i}\right) \qquad n = 300$$

$$i = \frac{0.1}{12} = .00833$$

$$\$335\,000 = \text{monthly payment} \left(1 - \frac{(1.0083)^{-300}}{.0083}\right)$$

$$\$335\,000 = \text{monthly payment} \times 110.3895$$

$$\frac{\$335\,000}{110.3895} = \$3\,034.708$$

$$\text{Monthly payment} = \$3034.71$$

Therefore, their monthly payments will be $3034.708. The interest they will pay over the 25-year period is $575 412.40. The total principal and interest they will pay is $910 412.40.

Was this house worth the cost? Assuming a conservative annual increase of 4 percent, which is much less than recent increases, we can use the following formula to calculate the house's future value:

$$\begin{aligned} \text{Future value} &= P(1 + i)^n \\ &= 450\,000(1.04)^{25} \\ &= \$1\,199\,626.349 \end{aligned}$$

If the house grows in value by less than 3 percent per year, they will end up spending more than they paid. If their home's value grows by more than 3 percent, their gain will be significantly more.

They should, of course, consider the opportunity costs before they buy the house. What would the money in their RRSPs be worth if they did not withdraw it, leaving it to be compounded tax-free?

continued

We will assume that Darlene and Henry leave the money in their plans. It will therefore grow for 34 years. We will assume the money compounds at 3 percent per year. This rate, of course, could be wrong. Using the formula for future value:

$$FV = \$40\ 000(1 + i)^n$$
$$FV = (1 + 0.03)^{34} \qquad\qquad FV = \$40\ 000 \times 2.731905295 = \$109\ 276.21$$

The \$40 000 would grow to \$109 276.21 by the time each of them reaches 69.

What would happen to their GIC funds if they do not buy the house? We have to make too many assumptions to predict accurately. Would the money be spent or invested? If invested, in what? The money is not tax-sheltered and would therefore be taxed. All we can say for certain is that if invested wisely, the money should be worth more than it was when the house was purchased.

* First-time homebuyers are allowed to withdraw \$20 000 from their RRSPs.

Personal FINANCE in action 12.11

Negotiations

Tally was fascinated by mortgages and their ability to allow someone with little money to acquire the house of his or her dreams. In her finance class at college, she absorbed every bit of information she could and also searched in the library for more information. After working for several years, Tally had had enough of paying rent and decided to buy a condo. When she was ready to negotiate, she prepared the following questions for potential mortgagees (lenders):

■ What types of mortgages do you have?
■ What terms are you offering?

■ What are your rates?
■ Do you offer a discount on your posted rates?
■ What are your payment options?
■ How large a down payment do you require?
■ Will you require a credit rating?
■ Will you help to pay my legal costs?
■ Will you pay to have the property appraised?
■ Is there a penalty for skipping a payment?

Comparison Shopping for a Mortgage

Personal Finance in Action Box 12.11, "Negotiations," shows how one well-informed person approached the problem of how to choose a mortgage. You can use the following chart to record the information you gather when comparison shopping.

Item	Lender		
	1	2	3
Interest rates			
First mortgage			
Second mortgage			
Fixed for term or variable			

Frequency of payment

      Monthly, biweekly, or weekly   _____

      Flexibility   _____

Charges

      Appraisal fee   _____

      Application fee   _____

Qualification guidelines

      GDS   _____

      TDS   _____

Prepayment privileges

      Amount   _____

      Time   _____

      Penalty   _____

Item	**Lender**		
	1	2	3
Flexibility			
Renewal conditions			
Fee			
Time before maturity			

    After you select a mortgage, it is important to insist that any special features be written into the mortgage contract.

Reverse Mortgages

The investment world at the start of the twenty-first century gave some senior citizens cause for concern. Stock markets were down. As a result, their portfolios were probably worth much less than they were in the 1990s. Interest rates were also lower than they had been for over a generation. This meant that seniors who relied on fixed income investments for security found their income plummeting like a waterfall. At the same time, caused partially by these low rates, housing prices rose. Many seniors therefore found themselves in the unusual situation of owning expensive real estate but being relatively cash poor. For some, the idea of the **reverse mortgage** was a dream come true.

    Reverse mortgages have been around since 1986. They are only available to homeowners who are 60 years of age or older and live in a geographical area served by the **Canadian Home Income Plan** (CHIP). The exempted areas include the three territories and some parts of rural Canada. Reverse mortgages allow the equity tied up in the family home to be turned into cash without the burden or emotional stress of selling the home. In the process, the owner's equity in the home decreases (this is why they are called reverse mortgages), as the amount owed on the reverse mortgage increases. Homeowners can receive from $20 000 to $500 000. The exact amount is based on a percentage (from 10 to 40 percent) of the home's appraised value. Whether or not the loan is approved will depend in addition on the ages of the homeowners, the house's value and location, and the kind of dwelling. The loan becomes due when the property is sold or the owner dies. No payments of interest or principal are necessary before then. Interest rates for a reverse mortgage at the time of writing were as follows:

- 6 months   6.95%
- 1 year   7.70%
- 3 years   8.25%

A big selling point in the literature on reverse mortgages is that the recipients pay no tax on the money. This is because it is only a loan and on loans, no taxes are ever paid.

The reverse mortgage has appealed to some seniors. (See Personal Finance in Action Box 12.12, "Wulin and the Reverse Mortgage," for one example.) In Canada, reverse mortgages are only available through CHIP. Before CHIP agrees to lend money, it requires prospective customers to do a number of things, all of which cost money, including the following.

(a) The home's value must be determined, at a cost of from $150 to $400, by a Canadian Residential Appraiser.

(b) Legal advice, the cost of which will vary, must be obtained so that the customer understands the implications of the plan.

(c) The property's title must be searched and other fees, costing around $1200, must be paid.

Personal FINANCE in action 12.12

Wulin and the Reverse Mortgage

Haibin and Wulin came to Canada from Hong Kong when he was 55 and she was 43. Their families were very wealthy and they brought enough money with them to buy a house for $500 000. Haibin soon got a job teaching advanced computer courses at the local community college. Wulin's English was too poor for her to find a good job, and she ended up serving food in a Chinese fast-food restaurant.

Haibin took early retirement at 60. They soon realized that his pension was too small for them to do much of anything but stay in their home. Their families could not send them any money because of government restrictions, and they had no other source of income apart from Wulin's part-time job. A friend told them about

CHIP, so they applied and obtained a reverse mortgage for $168 990.00 with interest of 8.25 percent.

After 15 years Haibin died. Wulin, who was only 58, wanted to sell the house and buy something smaller close to where her friends from Hong Kong lived. But she soon found out that the reverse mortgage loan with interest had grown to $554 982.74. If she sold the house, she would still owe $54 982.74. It suddenly dawned on her that it would have been far better if she and Haibin had sold their home upon his retirement and moved into something smaller. There would have been no tax on any appreciated value in the house and they would have had enough money to do many of the things on their wish list.

Anyone who wants to leave an estate to his or her children or other heirs will not find a reverse mortgage attractive. For those who don't have heirs and do not care if they accumulate debt, the reverse mortgage may be the ideal solution to the cash shortage problem. However, there are other, less expensive, ways to borrow money. CHIP charges interest of two to three points higher than the banks' prime rate.[15] An alternative,

---

[15] When the prime was 5 percent, CHIP's interest was 8.25 percent.

therefore, is to get a line of credit with the house as equity. This credit can ease the financial woe caused by the decline in investment income. Another alternative is to sell the house when the market is high and buy a smaller, more manageable house. This will free up some cash, which can be spent or invested to provide income, and also, potentially, leave an estate.

Summary

- The mortgagor is the borrower; the mortgagee is the lender. Amortization is the time period, usually 25 years, during which a mortgage is paid off. Home equity refers to the market value of a home minus the amount of the outstanding mortgage.

- Mortgage brokers help the homebuyer find a lender. Appraised value is the lending value. A first mortgage is the mortgage that is registered first against a property and which must be paid off first when the property is sold; second mortgages are granted on properties on which there are already mortgages. Mortgage insurance protects lenders against loss if a mortgage is not repaid. An insured mortgage is required when the amount of the loan is greater than 75 percent of the cost of the house. A conventional mortgage is one where the property is given as security. A high-ratio mortgage is one where the down payment is less than 25 percent of the appraised value or purchase price. With a vendor-take-back mortgage, the vendor, or seller of the property, and not a finance company, finances the mortgage. Payments are made directly to the vendor.

- The mortgage term is the length of time a lender will lend funds to the mortgagor. During the term, the interest rate remains the same. Prime rate is the interest rate on which financial institutions base their other interest rates.

- Terms range from six months to 18 years. The maturity date is when the term expires. Mortgage default occurs when the mortgagor fails to make the repayments agreed to in the mortgage contract. Foreclosure is the way the mortgagee acquires a property in the event of a default. Judicial sale is a way the mortgagee can foreclose on a property should the mortgagor default. Power of sale is another way the mortgagee can foreclose should the mortgagor default.

- Gross debt service is the percentage of total household income necessary to cover the monthly payments. Total debt service is the percentage of the mortgagor's total income needed to pay all the costs associated with the house and all other debts.

- Equity of redemption is the right of the mortgagor to redeem the property and have the ownership transferred back once the mortgage is discharged. A covenant is a binding promise made by the mortgagor. Mortgage discharge transfers ownership of the property to the mortgagor once the mortgage is paid off.

- Prepayment allows the mortgagor to prepay some of the principal. A penalty may be charged. Equal blended payments is the most common way of repaying a mortgage; it applies differing proportions to interest and principal as the term progresses. Some financial institutions allow the borrower to skip payments without a penalty.

- A statement of adjustments tells the buyer what costs are payable on completion of the sale. These can include legal fees and property transfer taxes, which are fees charged by some provinces when property changes hands.

- Preapproved mortgages are arranged before a house is bought. Open mortgages may be repaid at any time. Closed mortgages have the interest rate locked in for the duration of the term. Convertible mortgages allow borrowers to switch from a short-term to a long-term mortgage. With a variable rate mortgage, the interest rate fluctuates as rates in the economy change; when the rate falls, more of the principal is paid off. Discount mortgages have interest rates below the posted rate. Bridge financing is necessary when the purchase of the new home is completed before the sale of the old home. Loan-to-value is the ratio between the value of the mortgage and the value of the property. To attract customers banks often sweeten their mortgage deals by giving new mortgagors cash ("cash-back"), which can be used for a variety of purposes.

- Comparison shopping is comparing the rates and terms offered by various financial institutions. The offer to purchase is a legally binding document that includes all terms agreed to by both the buyer and the seller. The Homebuyers' Plan is a means by which first-time homebuyers can use funds in their RRSPs to help purchase a house. The Canada Mortgage and Housing Corporation (CMHC) is Canada's national housing agency. Mortgage-backed securities, designed to attract investment money to the mortgage market, consist of a pool of residential mortgages insured by CMHC.

- Reverse mortgages allow cash-strapped homeowners to use some of the equity in their homes. The Canadian Home Income Plan (CHIP) offers reverse mortgages.

Key Terms

amortization period (p. 398)
amortizing (p. 387)
bridge financing (p. 412)
Canadian Home Income Plan (p. 416)
cash-back (p. 406)
closed mortgage (p. 412)
closing date (p. 407)
covenant (p. 397)
conventional mortgage (p. 388, 412)
convertible mortgage (p. 411)
deed transfer tax (p. 408)
equity (p. 387)
equity of redemption (p. 395)
first mortgage (p. 388)
foreclosure (p. 398)
gross debt service (p. 391)
high-ratio mortgage (p. 390, 412)
Homebuyers' Plan (p. 413)
insured mortgage (p. 389)
interest adjustment (p. 412)

judicial sale (p. 389)
land transfer tax (p. 408)
lending or appraised value (p. 391)
loan-to-value (p. 412)
maturity date (p. 398)
mortgage (p. 386)
mortgage-backed securities (p. 413)
mortgage broker (p. 391)
mortgage discharge (p. 398)
mortgage insurance (p. 388)
mortgage loan insurance (p. 413)
mortgage term (p. 398)
mortgagee (p. 386)
mortgagor (p. 386)
open mortgage (p. 411)
opportunity cost (p. 380)
power of sale (p. 389)
preapproved mortgage (p. 410)
prepayment (p. 403)
property transfer tax (p. 408)

repayment *(p. 403)*   total debt service *(p. 391)*

reverse mortgage *(p. 416)*   variable rate mortgage *(p. 411)*

second mortgage *(p. 388)*   vendor seller take-back mortgage

statement of adjustments *(p. 408)*   *(p. 390)*

Problems

1. You want to buy a house in Ontario that lists for $125 000, and you can make the minimum down payment of 5 percent. What will you have to pay in fees and charges? There could be other charges as well, such as utility fees.

   (a) Land Transfer Tax of 1 percent

   (b) Treasurer of Ontario to register transfer: 2 percent of Land Transfer Tax

   (c) Mortgage insurance premium of 3 percent (Premiums range from 0.5 percent to 3.75 percent.)

   (d) Application for insurance of $75 (Fees range from $75 to $235.)

   (e) 7 percent GST, minus rebate of 2.5 percent on homes costing less than $450 000

   (f) Appraisal fee of $200

   (g) Legal fees of $750

   (h) Moving costs: $100/hour for van and three men, six hours minimum

   (i) Home inspection fee of $150

   (j) Certification of water quality and quantity: $50 (highly recommended)

   (k) Property taxes of $500

   (l) Land survey: $250

2. Ken needs a mortgage of $200 000. His bank gives him the following two choices:

   (a) The 4-percent cash-back option. He can get 4 percent of the mortgage value in cash, which he can use for any purpose. For this privilege, he will be charged the posted rate of 6.25 percent for five years. Assume he takes the $8000 cash and applies it to reduce the mortgage principal.

   (b) Without the cash-back option, the bank will charge him the discounted rate of 5.19 percent for five years.

   Which choice should Ken accept, assuming a mortgage term of 20 years? Use the following formula,

   $$\text{Principal} = \text{Payment}\ \frac{\left[1 - (1 + i)\right]^{-n}}{i}$$

   to find the payment per month. Then subtract the payment for option (b) from that for option (a), and multiply by 240.

3. Charmaine and Barbara had $180 000 outstanding on their mortgage. They were locked into a closed mortgage for 10 years, had eight years left on the term, and were paying a fixed rate of 9 percent. Recently, interest rates had dropped to their lowest level in a generation and they wanted to renegotiate and get a lower rate at 7.350 percent. Their financial institution said they could do this but would have to pay a penalty of three months' interest. Should they do it?

(a) Using the following formula where A equals the outstanding balance and B equals the rate of interest, calculate this penalty.

$$A \times \frac{B}{12} \times 3 = penalty$$

(b) Was the penalty worth it? To find out, go to **www.fiscalagents.com/toolbox/index.shtml#tb4** and calculate the difference the change in rates will make. How much principal and interest would they have paid at nine percent? How does this compare with what they will pay at the new rate of 7.350 percent?

4. Go to **www.chip.ca** Click on Am I Eligible? Assuming you are 60 and own your own home, fill in the application. Select Single Family Detached. Estimate the market value of your home at $200 000. You have paid off your mortgage and have no other loans outstanding.

How much are you eligible for? What is the range of the amount you qualify for?

Click on Future Equity Calculator. Assume that your home appreciates by three percent annually. Click on ABCs of CHIP. What interest rate will you be charged for three years?

Now go to any chartered bank site and find out what rate is charged to open a line of credit. Would you need the same amount you can get from CHIP? If you were really short of cash would you go to CHIP, or to your bank?

5. Sergio and Frank live in Calgary. They each recently inherited $100 000 from their grandfather. Sergio invested his money in a Canadian equity growth fund, which had grown by an average of 12.14 percent compounded over the past 10 years, and rented a one-bedroom apartment, with appliances included, for $1750 a month. His income is $75 000 per year. Assume that his fund continues to grow by this much.

(a) How much will his $100 000 be worth in 10 years?

(b) How much tax will he pay on the gain each year? He has no other investment income.

(c) Assume that his rent increases by 3 percent per year. How much rent will he have paid in total over 10 years?

Also assume that Sergio's new furniture cost him $5000.

Frank decided to use his money as a down payment on a $350 000, two-bedroom house and took out a $250 000 closed fixed-rate mortgage at 7.350 percent for 10 years. To do so, he had to pay numerous charges and fees, including an appraisal fee, a property survey, and legal fees, which totaled $3500.

Housing had appreciated in Calgary by an average of 5 percent over the past 10 years. Assume that it will continue to do so.

(a) How much will Frank have paid on his mortgage in 10 years?

(b) How much will his house be worth in 10 years?

Frank's property taxes average $6 000 per year, and his utilities average $700 a month. His appliances (washer and dryer, stove, and refrigerator) cost him $2500, and new furniture cost $10 000.

Frank sells his house after 10 years. Which of the two brothers' investments is worth more?

Their First House

After a lengthy search, Tiep and Vinh finally locate a house they really like. Its $145 000 asking price seems reasonable. They recognize that the house will require redecorating as soon as possible in two downstairs rooms, and that they will have to buy major appliances. Property taxes were $1350 last year; heating costs for the same period amounted to $550. They offer to purchase the house for $135 000, on the condition that they can arrange adequate financing.

The bank's mortgage officer inquires about the family income and about how much money they have available as a down payment. Tiep explains that his annual income is $48 000, and Vinh's part-time earnings come to $18 900; their

only debt is for their car, and payments on that loan cost $280 a month. They have saved $16 000 for a down payment.

The mortgage officer calculates their gross debt service and their total debt service for a mortgage of $119 000 at 8.75 percent to be amortized over 25 years, and suggests that they apply for a CMHC-insured mortgage. They are told that the application will cost $100 and that an appraiser will look at the house they want to buy and will determine its lending value. The appraisal fee will be $150.

In a few days' time, they learn that the house has a lending value of $132 500 and that they are eligible for a $119 000 mortgage.

6. (a) List the criteria that the lender probably uses to determine the eligibility of (i) Vinh and Tiep, and (ii) the property.

(b) Would this couple be eligible for a conventional mortgage?

(c) How much would the monthly payments be on this mortgage?

(d) Calculate the couple's gross debt service and the total debt service.

(e) Work out the interest and principal components of the first payment.

(f) How much total interest will this couple pay over 25 years, assuming that interest rates do not change and that the couple makes no prepayments?

(g) How much would the total interest cost be reduced if they could get a mortgage for half a percent (0.5 percent) less?

(h) How much interest could they save by amortizing this mortgage over 20 years instead of 25 years?

(i) Use the chart below to estimate some of the costs (in addition to the down payment and mortgage) that Tiep and Vinh will probably encounter as they complete the house purchase and move from their apartment. What is the grand total?

SOME COSTS ASSOCIATED WITH HOME BUYING

Note: The numbers used here are estimates. Find out current costs.

Mortgage Fees   **Totals**
  Appraisal fee $ _____
  Mortgage insurance fee (added to mortgage; assume 2%) $ _____ $ _____

Statement of Adjustments
  Tax adjustments (allow 6 months) $ _____
  Fire insurance $ 600.00
  Fuel oil (part of a tank) $ 300.00 $ _____

Goods and Services Tax (if applicable)	$ _____	
Lawyer's Account		
Disbursements by lawyer for land transfer tax (if applicable)	$ _____	
Deed registration	$ 75.00	
Legal fees	$ 1000.00	$ _____
Moving and Related Costs		
Moving (two men and a truck for 5 hrs. @ $60/hr.)	$ _____	$ _____
Connection of utilities		
Telephone	$ 58.50	
Cable TV	$ 34.42	
Electricity	$ 48.50	
Others	$ 25.00	$ _____
Appliances, Repairs		
Purchase of major appliances	$ 2900.00	
Decorating supplies	$ 600.00	
Repairs	$ 1000.00	$ _____
Grand Total	_____	$ _____

What are some other costs that might be anticipated but that are not included here?

7. Rheal withdrew $20 000 from his RRSP under the Homebuyers' Plan to help purchase his new home in Richmond Hill, Ontario. He earned a good salary as a web designer and fully expected to be able to repay the money as required. However, unfortunately for him, a new office manager was appointed who knew little about the complicated software he was using. She complained to him and then to her superiors in Calgary that he was too slow and lazy. After three months of pressure from her to speed up his work, which was not possible, he was fired. This meant that he could not make the first repayment to his RRSP.

   (a) How much will his penalty be if a full year goes by before he can repay the 1/15 of the balance owing?

   (b) What will happen if he remains unemployed for four years and is unable to make any repayments to his RRSP? To find out, go to **www.cra-arc.gc.ca/tax/individu-als/topics/rrsp/hbp/repayments/howmuch-e.html**.

8. The Valenzuelas' offer to purchase a house has been accepted. Now they are considering ways of financing it. The purchase price is $187 000, and they have $18 000 for a down payment. They are considering the following alternatives:

Down payment	First mortgage	Second mortgage
(i) $18 000	$169 000 @ 9%, 25 yrs.	none
(ii) $18 000	$169 000 @ 9%, 20 yrs.	none
(iii) $10 000	$169 000 @ 9%, 25 yrs.	$8000 @ 10% for 5 yrs. ($169.19/mo.)

   (a) Which of these alternatives would result in the lowest monthly cost?
   (b) Which of these alternatives would result in the lowest total interest?
   (c) What are some factors the Valenzuelas should consider when making their choice?

9. Answers to questions concerning money are often complicated. Because of uncertainties associated with interest rates, there may be no perfect answer. You must decide

whether to put the maximum you are allowed into your RRSP or use the money to reduce the principal on your mortgage, which you can do without penalty.

(a) What are the financial benefits of adding to your RRSP? The disadvantages?

(b) What are the benefits of paying off your mortgage faster than expected? Are there any potential disadvantages?

10. Answer true or false.

(a) Mortgage payments over a 25-year amortization period are greater than the initial value of the house because of what is known as the "present value of money."

(b) Everyone can obtain a mortgage even without the money needed for a down payment.

(c) Houses always appreciate in value.

(d) Insured mortgages are only available from CMHC.

(e) You will be charged a fee for taking out a high-ratio mortgage.

(f) There is a refund of 15 percent on CMHC insurance for energy-efficient homes.

(g) With a conventional mortgage the mortgagor must give the property being purchased as security.

(h) In recent years divorce was the major cause of mortgage default.

(i) Consumers with good credit ratings are not charged a fee by a mortgage broker who finds them suitable housing.

11. How much will the GDS be for someone with the following income and expenses?

Gross annual income	$80 000
Mortgage payments per year	$8 000
Property taxes per year	$3 000
Heating per year	$4 000

12. How much will the above person's TDS be if she has an outstanding credit card balance of $4000 but no other debts?

13. What property or land transfer tax will be paid in each of the Canadian provinces and territories by someone buying a $600 000 home? This is not this person's first home.

14. A very small percentage of eligible Canadians have applied for and obtained a reverse mortgage from CHIP. Suggest reasons that a great many more seniors do not avail themselves of this service.

15. Go to **www.canadamortgage.com** and click on Compare Rates. Assume you are a first-time homebuyer.

(a) Compare the rates for a closed mortgage and a one-year open mortgage. Would you select an open mortgage or take a 10-year closed mortgage?

(b) For a 10-year closed mortgage, compare the following features at the Bank of Montreal, the CIBC, and President's Choice (which has the lowest interest):

■ rate commitment

■ payment options

■ amortization options

■ portability

■ pre-payment options: monthly OR annually

Which of these three choices is best in the long run? Why?

16. The website in Problem 15 invites you to apply online. Click on Apply Online. This leads you to Pioneer West Acceptance. Now go to **www.tdcanadatrust.com/mortgages/index.jsp**, the mortgage website for TD Canada Trust, and find their online application feature. Compare the Pioneer West and TD Canada Trust apply-online application forms.

    (a) How do the two forms differ?

    (b) Which requires the most information?

    (c) Which company seems most credible?

    (d) Which provides the most interest rate information?

17. (a) Why must someone looking for the perfect mortgage ask very detailed questions when told her or his mortgage is open?

    (b) Would you want to have a fixed rate or a variable rate mortgage? Explain.

    (c) Why does someone who has sold his house often require bridge financing?

    (d) What has likely prompted banks to offer discount mortgages?

    (e) Explain why shortening the amortization period is not always a good idea.

18. Define the following terms:

    (a) posted rate

    (b) bridge financing

    (c) loan-to-value

    (d) mortgage-backed securities

    (e) judicial sale

    (f) second mortgage

    (g) mortgagee

    (h) lending value

    (i) equity of redemption

    (j) mortgage covenant

    (k) amortization

    (l) mortgage discharge

    (m) opportunity cost

19. A popular feature in the United States is the *interest-only mortgage*. For the first five years the mortgagor pays interest only at a fixed interest rate. Beginning in the sixth year, the sixty-first month, the unpaid principal is fully amortized for 25 years with blended principal and interest payments. Is this a good idea? Find out by doing the following:

    (a) Go to **www.interestonlyloans.com/interest_only_mortgage_calculator.html** and calculate the monthly payment on a $200 000 mortgage at 7 percent. How much will have been paid in five years?

    (b) Now go to **www.bankrate.com/goocan/mortgage-calculator.asp** and calculate the payment on the $200 000 at 7 percent amortized over 25 years. How much will have been paid in interest and principal? Add this to what has already been paid in interest. How much will have been paid in total?

    (c) Now calculate what would have been paid if both interest and principal had been paid over 25 years.

References

BOOKS AND OTHER RESOURCES

Barry, Dave. *Homes and Other Black Holes.* Toronto: Random House, 1995.

British Columbia Mortgage Practice Manual. Vancouver: Continuing Legal Education Society of B.C., 2005.

Canada Mortgage and Housing Library. **www.cmhc-schl.gc.ca/en/index.cfm**. Click Library, Library Catalogue, Access Library Catalogue, and Search for Mortgages.

Carr, Nancy. *Reverse Mortgages: Let the Seniors Beware.* **www.wednesday-night.com/reverse-mortgages.asp** (2003).

Donahue, D. J., P. D. Quinn, and Danny Grandfilli. *Real Estate Practice in Ontario.* 6th Edition. Toronto: Lexis Nexis, 2003.

Eldred, Gary W. *106 Mortgage Secrets All Homebuyers Must Learn—But Lenders Don't Tell.* Toronto: Wiley, 2003.

Eldred, Gary W. *106 Common Mistakes Homebuyers Make (and How to Avoid Them).* 4th Edition. Toronto: Wiley, 2005.

Fletcher, June. *House Poor. Pumped Up Prices, Rising Rates, and Mortgages on Steroids: How to Survive the Coming Housing Crisis.* Toronto: Collins, 2005.

Garton-Good, Julie. *All About Mortgages: Insider Tips for Financing and Refinancing Your Home.* Chicago: Dearborn Trade Publishing, 1999.

Glink, Ilyce R. *100 Questions Every First-Time Home Buyer Should Ask.* Toronto: Random House, 2005.

Gray, Douglas A. *Mortgages Made Easy: The All-Canadian Guide to Home Financing.* 2nd Edition. Toronto: Wiley, 2006.

Guttentag, Jack. *The Mortgage Encyclopedia: An Authoritative Guide to Mortgage Programs, Practices, Prices and Pitfalls.* Toronto: McGraw-Hill Ryerson, 2004.

Home Fund Line of Credit. Mississauga: Credit Union Central of Ontario.

Irwin, Robert, and David L. Ganz: *How to Get an Instant Mortgage.* Toronto: Wiley, 1997.

Irwin, Robert. *Home Closing Checklist.* Toronto: McGraw-Hill Ryerson, 2004.

Irwin, Robert. *Tips and Traps When Buying a Condo, Co-op, or Townhouse.* Toronto: McGraw-Hill Ryerson, 1999.

Irwin, Robert. *How to Buy a Home When You Can't Afford It.* Toronto: McGraw-Hill Ryerson, 2002.

Irwin, Robert. *Robert Irwin's Power Tips for Buying a House For Less.* 1st Edition. Toronto: McGraw-Hill Ryerson, 2000.

Johnson, Randy. *How to Save Thousands of Dollars on Your Home Mortgage.* 2nd Edition. Toronto: Wiley, 2002.

Just the Faqs: Answers to Common Questions About Reverse Mortgages. The NRMLA Consumer Guide to Reverse Mortgages. National Reverse Mortgage Lenders Association. **www.reversemortgage.org**.

Kerr, Margaret, and JoAnn Kurtz. *Buying, Owning, and Selling Your Home in Canada.* 2nd Edition. Toronto: Wiley, 2001.

Lyons, Sarah Glendon, and John E. Lucas. *Reverse Mortgages for Dummies.* Toronto: Wiley, 2005.

Marshall, Clifford, and Stephen S. Soloman. *Canadian Mortgage Payments*. New York: Barron's Educational Series, 1993.

Miller, Peter G. *The Common-Sense Mortgage*. Toronto: McGraw-Hill Ryerson, 1999.

Mortgage Amortization Schedules. North York, Ontario: Computofacts.

Mortgage Insurance: What to Consider Before You Buy. Revised Edition. Dartmouth, Nova Scotia: True Help Financial Planning, 2005.

Mortgage Wise: A Guide for Home Buyers. Toronto: Canadian Bankers Association.

O'Hara, Shelly, and Bruce McDougal. *The Complete Idiot's Guide to Buying and Selling a Home in Canada*. Toronto: Prentice Hall, 2000.

Pokorny, Jennifer A. *Pocket Idiot's Guide: Reverse Mortgages*. Toronto: Penguin, 2005.

"Reverse Mortgages Explained." *CBC Marketplace*, April 11, 2000.

Shankman, Martin M., and Warren Boroson. *How to Buy a House with No (or Little) Money Down*. 3rd Edition. Toronto: Wiley, 2002.

Silverstein, Alan. *The Perfect Mortgage: Cutting the Cost of Home Ownership*. Toronto: Stoddart, 1995.

Silverstein, Alan. *Hidden Profits in Your Mortgage: The Smart Move to Home Ownership*. Toronto: Stoddart, 1995.

Silverstein, Alan. *The Perfect Mortgage: A Book No Home Buyer Can Do Without*. Toronto: Stoddart, 1989.

Silverstein, Alan. *Save!: Alan Silverstein's Guide to Mortgage Payment Tables*. Toronto: Stoddart, 1993.

Sinclair, Clayton, and June Yee. *Have Your Home and Money Too: The Canadian Guide to Home Equity Management. Reverse Mortgages and Other Housing Options*. Toronto: Wiley, 1999.

Traub, Walter M. *Falconbridge on Mortgages*. 5th Edition. Toronto: Emond Montgomery Publications, 2002.

Tymstra, Cornelis. *Flying Toasters and the Mortgage Maze*. Calgary: Temeron Books, 1998.

Tyson, Eric. *Home Buying for Dummies*. 3rd Edition. Toronto: Wiley, 2006.

Tyson, Eric and Roy Brown. *Mortgages for Dummies*. 2nd Edition. Toronto: Wiley, 2004.

Walma, Mark A. *Advanced Residential Real Estate Transactions*. Toronto: Emond Montgomery Publications, 2003.

Personal Finance on the Web

Bankrate.com Canada
   www.bankrate.com/goocan/rate/calc_home.asp

Canada Mortgage Brokers
   www.truenorthmortgage.ca

Canada Mortgages.ca
   www.canadamortgages.ca No-fee discount mortgages coast to coast.

Canada Mortgage.com
   www.canadamortgage.com Mortgages online.

Canada Mortgage and Housing Corporation (CMHC)
  www.cmhc-schl.gc.ca A useful site.

Canada Wide Mortgages
  www.canadawidemortgages.com

Canadian Home Builders' Association
  www.chba.ca

Canadian Home Income Plan
  www.chip.ca The site for reverse mortgages. 1-800-522-2447

Canadian Institute of Mortgage Brokers and Lenders
  www.cimbl.ca A link to the mortgage industry.

The Canadian Real Estate Association
  www.crea.ca

Canadian Real Estate Resources
  www.homebuyingrealestate.com/Canada/Canada.htm

The Catalyst. The website of P. J. Wade, author of *Have Your Home and Money Too.*
  www.thecatalyst.com

Financial Consumer Agency of Canada
  www.fcac-acfc.gc.ca/eng

Genworth Financial Canada
  www.genworth.ca

Insurance Bureau of Canada
  www.ibc.ca

Invis
  www.invis.ca A mortgage broker

MLS Online
  www.mls.ca Contains all multiple-listed properties in Canada.

Mortgage Brokers Canada
  www.mortgagebrokerscanada.ca

The Mortgage Centre
  www.mortgagecentre.com

Mortgage Consultant
  www.mortgageconsultant.com

Mortgage for Less
  www.mortgageforless.com Another site for mortgages that are available online.

Mortgage Made Easy
  www.mortgage-made-easy.com Everything you need to know about mortgages.

National Reverse Mortgage Lenders Association
  www.reversemortgage.org The American version of CHIP.

Pro Link Mortgage Inc.
  www.prolinkmortgages.com

Western Canada Mortgage
www.westerncanadamortgage.com

Where Can We Buy and Sell a House On-line?
http://where-can-we-buy-and-sell-a-house-online.com

Yourmortgage.ca
www.yourmortgage.ca/ B.C.'s mortgage source

CANADIAN FINANCIAL INSTITUTIONS

Bank of Montreal
www.bmo.com

Canadian Imperial Bank of Commerce
www.cibc.com

Canadian Western Bank Group
www.cwbank.com

Citizens Bank of Canada
www.citizensbank.ca

Laurentian Bank of Canada
www.lbcdirect.laurentianbank.ca

National Bank Financial
www.nbfinancial.com

RBC Royal Bank
www.royalbank.com

Scotiabank
www.scotiabank.com

TD Canada Trust
www.tdcanadatrust.com

Consumer Credit and Loans

Learning Objectives

Understanding the concepts discussed in this chapter should help you become a wiser borrower.

After studying this chapter, you should be able to:

1. Explain some of the trends in the use of consumer credit.

2. Formulate generalizations that apply at the household level about relations between the following variables: income and the probability of having consumer debt; income and average consumer debt; stage in the life cycle and incidence of consumer debt; and age and average consumer debt.

3. Examine four major reasons for using credit.

4. Distinguish between enforcement of security and other ways of collecting debts.

5. Explain how a promissory note, wage assignment, chattel mortgage, and lien differ from one another and identify a situation where each might be used.

6. Ascertain the following by examining a chattel mortgage: the security pledged, the repayment conditions, the penalties for late payments, and the conditions under which a creditor may enforce security and the means that may be used.

7. Compare the costs of various types of consumer loans and suggest reasons for the interest rate spread.

8. Distinguish among debit cards, charge cards, credit cards, conditional sales contracts/agreements, and chattel mortgages.

9. Explain the main provisions of the legislation regarding the following matters: disclosure of information about credit transactions; supervision of itinerant sellers; repossession of goods when the borrower defaults; advertising credit; and unsolicited credit cards and unsolicited goods.

Introduction

To set the foundation for the discussion of consumer credit, we will first examine some information on the amount and types of consumer credit used in Canada. We will also look at some national data and micro surveys of households with respect to consumer credit. This chapter also discusses consumer loans, with a focus on how consumers arrange for a loan from a financial institution (as opposed to point-of-sale-credit, which is arranged when an item or service is purchased). In the former situation, the purchase is separate from the arranging of the loan. We will briefly discuss debit cards, and finally we will review some issues and problems that concern credit users; in particular, we will provide sample credit contracts that will help you understand such documents.

What Is Credit?

Credit and Debt

Every borrowing transaction involves two actors. The lender (the creditor) supplies money for a loan in exchange for a credit, and views the transaction in terms of the amount of credit that has been extended. The borrower (the debtor) receives the money and views the transaction as an accumulation of debt. That which is *consumer debt* to you, the borrower/debtor, is *consumer credit* to the lender/creditor. Information about this transaction may be reported either as debt or as credit, depending on the reporter's perspective. Although it is really the same phenomenon, data obtained from households about their borrowing are usually reported as consumer debt, while statistics gathered from lenders are referred to as consumer credit. This chapter examines both kinds of data.

The debtor in a credit/debt transaction accepts a commitment to repay the debt at some time in the future, and thus must be prepared to give up future purchasing power in order to have extra resources available at present. In deciding that it is more important to have extra funds now than to wait until the money can be saved, the debtor should realize that a cost of using credit is the commitment of future income to interest payments; these funds will not be available for other uses. The borrower/debtor promises to repay not only the principal (that is, the sum borrowed) but also the interest (that is, the charge for borrowing). Thus, the lender/creditor holds a claim that the borrower/debtor will repay interest and principal as promised.

It is conventional to distinguish between consumer debt and mortgage debt: **total debt** is the sum of these two. **Consumer debt** is defined as all the personal debt incurred by households, excluding mortgage debt or business debt. **Mortgage debt** is any debt that is secured by real property, such as buildings and land. To summarize:

Consumer debt + mortgage debt = total debt of households

However, mortgage debt generally involves much larger amounts and much longer terms than consumer debt does. So actually combining statistics about mortgage debt and consumer debt would obscure trends in consumer debt. From the household's perspective, mortgage debt can be viewed as the ongoing cost of housing—a regular expense—in contrast to short-term debt. Also, borrowing to invest in property can be an effective way to accumulate assets, but borrowing for current consumption is not. For a discussion of mortgages, refer back to Chapter 12.

National Consumer Credit Data

Sources of Information

Lenders are required to report regularly to Statistics Canada about the amount of credit they have extended; when gathered together, these data are called the **total consumer credit outstanding**. These statistics, collected at the national level (macro data), show the amounts of credit held by various lenders, but they provide no information about individual borrowers. Still, macro data are quite useful for giving a picture of national trends. Such data were not available before 1951; the shift toward collecting them probably indicates the increasing significance of consumer credit in our society.

How Much Credit Do We Use?

You may have heard that Canadians now use more consumer credit than ever before. To verify this statement, examine the trends in the total consumer credit outstanding since 1970 (Figure 13.1). Clearly, the increase in total credit outstanding over this time span has been dramatic. Look at one decade at a time to find when the rate of increase (slope of the line) changed significantly. What are some possible explanations for the great increase in the use of consumer credit? It may be that (i) the population grew rapidly and thus more credit was needed in Canada, or (ii) the prices of goods rose substantially, necessitating larger loans, or (iii) each person used more credit. We will examine primarily the population change factor.

Population Changes   The data shown in Figure 13.1 make no allowance for any changes in Canada's population. To correct this problem, we can divide each year's total

FIGURE 13.1   TOTAL CONSUMER CREDIT OUTSTANDING, CANADA, 1970–2005

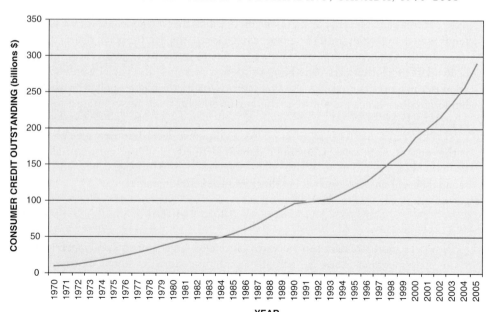

SOURCE: Statistics Canada, Canadian Economic Observer, Historical Supplement, 2002/2003, Catalogue No. 11–210, table 36, p. 97. Bank of Canada, Weekly Financial Statistics, March 28, 2005, BFS Table E2.

FIGURE 13.2 CONSUMER CREDIT OUTSTANDING PER CAPITA, CANADA, 1970–1998 (IN CURRENT AND CONSTANT 1970 DOLLARS)

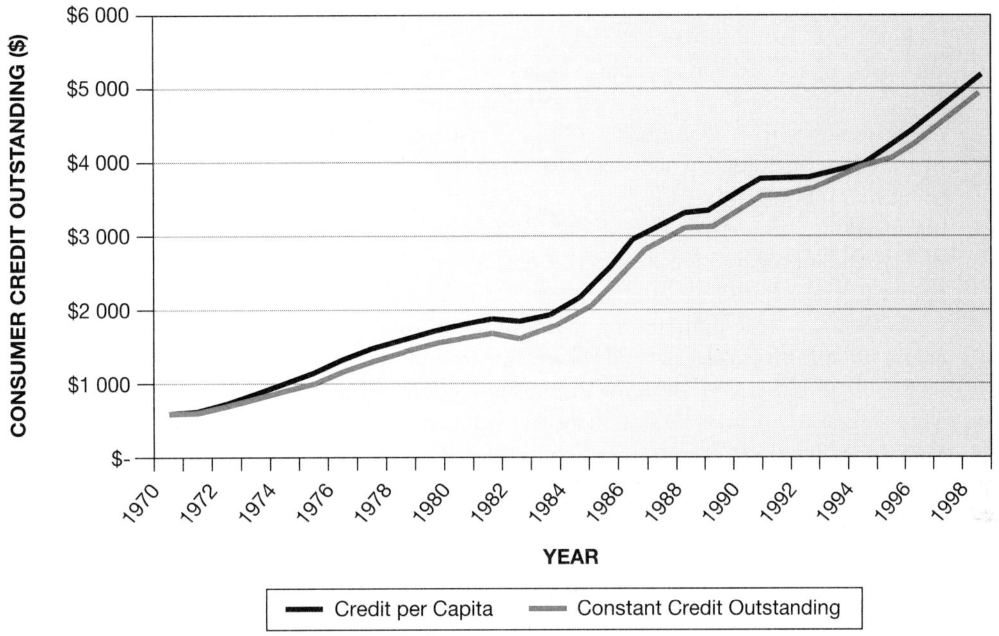

SOURCE: Data from *Bank of Canada Review* (Ottawa: Bank of Canada), Winter 1980/81, Table 50, p. S100; Winter 1989/90, Table E2, p. S72; Winter 1993/94, Table E2, p. S48; Winter 1997/98, Table E2, p. S50; *Weekly Financial Statistics* (Ottawa: Bank of Canada), February 16, 2001, Table E2, p. 13.

credit figure by Canada's population for that year. If you graphed the corresponding data, the result is shown in Figure 13.2. Examine the line in Figure 13.2 showing the amounts of consumer credit outstanding per capita. The slope of this line generally matches that in Figure 13.1, indicating about the same rate of increase. Apparently, then, the rapid increase in total consumer credit outstanding cannot be explained by a change in Canada's population.

Inflation Perhaps rising prices caused people to use increasing amounts of consumer credit. For example, as the prices of cars rose, the size of each car loan necessarily increased. Thus, inflated prices increased loan amounts, rather than more people buying more cars. To check whether the rapidly rising amounts of consumer credit were caused by inflation, we must adjust the credit outstanding per capita to reflect changes in consumer prices. The statistical procedure for doing so involves converting the values that were in **current dollars** (that is, the dollar amounts recorded in each year) into **constant dollars** (which estimate the values if prices had remained constant). The numbers plotted in Figure 13.1 reflect current dollars, but these may be converted to constant dollars by using the following formula:

$$\frac{\text{Value in current dollars in Year X}}{\text{Consumer Price Index in Year X}} \times 100 = \frac{\text{Constant \$}}{\text{in Year X}}$$

This conversion is a way of eliminating, statistically, the effect of changes in prices. In other words, if consumer prices had remained unchanged since 1971, the amount of consumer credit extended would be approximately that shown in constant dollars in Figure 13.2.

If the increase in outstanding consumer credit had been entirely due to population changes and rising prices, the constant dollar line in Figure 13.2, which has been corrected to reflect both, would be perfectly horizontal. Since instead it shows a rising trend, we can conclude from these data that regardless of any changes in population or in consumer prices, Canadians' use of consumer credit did increase during the years in question. Much of the difference between the two lines in Figure 13.2 can be attributed to the effects of inflation; as prices of goods and services rose, so did the amounts borrowed.

These data clearly show that the recessions of 1982–83 and 1991–92 were turning points in Canadians' use of consumer credit. The slowdown in the economy, escalating interest rates, and high unemployment combined during each of those periods to create uncertainty and a natural reluctance to incur more debt. Many people who already had debts found it very difficult to maintain their payment schedules, and bankruptcies were common. For a while, attitudes toward using consumer debt became more cautious. How long did these effects last? To answer this question, we need only look at what happened to the trend from 1982 through 1990, and at what the trend has been since 1992.

By 1985, Canadians had begun once again to increase their use of consumer credit, and the trend resumed its climb—slowly at first, and then more rapidly between 1987 and 1990. Predictably, the 1990–92 recession resulted in another downturn in outstanding consumer credit. But in 1994, the trend had returned to its previous steady ascent.

Debt Burden/Personal Use

Another way of analyzing the use of consumer credit involves relating it to income levels. If people commit about the same proportion of income to repaying debts year after year, their burden of debt does not change, even though the actual level of debt rises. **Debt burden** is often measured as a ratio of debt or credit to income. Continuing to use macro data, we will now compare the ratio of total consumer credit outstanding to total personal income in each of the years since 1970. (**Personal disposable income** is defined as all the income received by Canadians after income tax was paid.)

Debt burden, which was less than 10 percent in 1951, had by 1980 more than doubled, to 22 percent; it then declined for a few years before rising again (Figure 13.3). To understand debt burden, consider what was happening to family incomes in the same period. After World War II Canadians' **real incomes** (adjusted for inflation) increased substantially, leaving most families with more **discretionary income**, which is income left over after paying for such necessities as food, clothing, and shelter. This new prosperity made it possible to buy more consumer durables (items that are expected to last for some time, such as appliances or stereos) and recreational goods, which at the time were the types of items most frequently bought on credit. People's steadily rising incomes made repaying their debts easier because incomes tended to increase annually while most debt contracts remain fixed for several years. Thus, the combination of fixed debt commitments and rising incomes was beneficial for borrowers. But in times of slower economic growth, wise people reduce their debt burden. By 1990, the ratio of debt to income had dropped somewhat. After the recession of the early nineties, the debt burden began once again to increase steadily each year.

FIGURE 13.3 RATIO OF TOTAL CONSUMER CREDIT OUTSTANDING TO PERSONAL DISPOSABLE INCOME, CANADA, 1970–2005

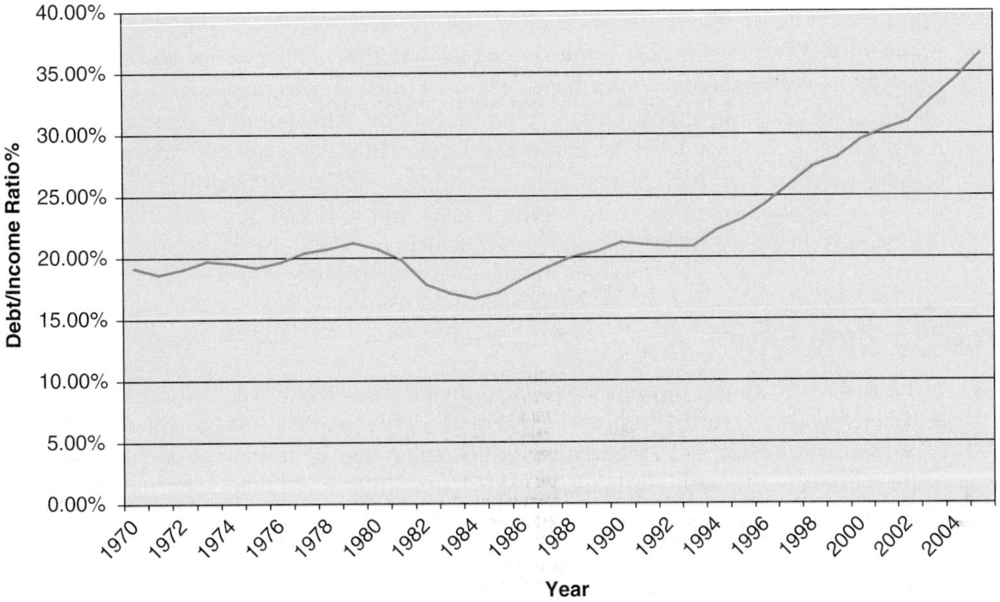

SOURCE: Adapted from the Statistics Canada publication Canadian Economic Observer, Historical Statistical Supplement, 2004–2005, Catalogue 11-210, July 2005, Table 2, page 9 and Table 36, page 104.

Consumer Debt Use at the Household Level

Thus far, we have been examining macro statistics that give a general picture of credit use in Canada over a number of years. Another source of information about credit or debt is micro data, obtained by interviewing householders. Statistics Canada conducts occasional surveys of consumer debt. Asking people about their debts, incomes, and other variables allows researchers to explore the relationships, if any, between debt levels and other characteristics such as income, age, education, and occupation. Let us examine the connections between the consumer debt and both income and age, based on studies conducted in the past by Statistics Canada.

When reviewing research reports, make sure you know exactly how a particular study defines credit and debt. Although debt is generally classified as either consumer debt or mortgage debt, somewhat different terms are used in Statistics Canada household surveys, where "personal debt" refers to all non-mortgage debt. For our purposes, we will consider personal debt and consumer debt to be the same.

Income and Consumer Debt

Are people with higher incomes more likely to incur consumer debt than those with lower incomes? Low-income families may wish to use credit but are usually denied it because they lack the ability to repay their debts. Previous Statistics Canada studies (as mentioned above) allow us to generalize that if 1984 patterns have remained unchanged, a household's probability of having consumer debt increases with the household's income.

Stage in the Life Cycle and Consumer Debt

Is a person's stage in the life cycle (or age) associated with the probability of having certain kinds of debt? A curvilinear relation (which reflects an increasing, then decreasing, probability of two events or variables occurring together) between age and the incidence (probability) of personal and mortgage debt was clearly shown in past studies. People who are 35 to 44 years old appear most likely to have both kinds of debt (this age group also has the highest average levels of consumer debt), while those over 65 appear most likely to have neither. This pattern is consistent with people's needs at different stages in the life cycle. Younger families start buying houses and collecting household durables; by retirement, they have usually discharged these debts.

Debt/Income Ratio

So far we have seen how income and stage in the life cycle (that is, age) affect the likelihood that households will carry consumer debt. Another way to analyze the use of consumer debt is to look at the ratio of consumer debt to income—that is, to look at debt burden. Here again, no recent data are available, but past researchers have found that middle-income households have a higher propensity for incurring a heavy debt burden. This pattern is quite understandable, considering that the heads of low-income families are often very young or very old, and are therefore not usually seen as good candidates for consumer credit. People with high incomes, while they are heavy users of credit, have incomes that are large enough to make the burden manageable.

Why Do We Use Credit?

People no doubt use credit for many reasons, but most can be classified into four main categories. We use credit (i) for convenience; (ii) to obtain something before we have saved enough to pay for it; (iii) to bridge the gap when our income is insufficient, infrequent, or irregular; and occasionally (iv) to consolidate debts. Each of these reasons may have costs as well as benefits.

Convenience

Many of us find it very handy to use a credit card instead of carrying cash, as well as to pay a number of bills using just one cheque (to the credit card company). As long as you pay the outstanding amount monthly, a credit card is an interest-free convenience. Some charge accounts require you to pay your total bill each month, but others, such as bank credit cards and retail revolving accounts, offer you a choice: you may pay all or only a portion of the debt. Having this option makes it quite easy to let bills accumulate, and the interest rates charged on unpaid balances are usually high. A credit card also tends to encourage impulsive shopping; having to pay in cash is a more effective restraint.

Immediacy

As advertisers eagerly point out, credit allows us to have things immediately and pay later. Offering credit is a very successful way to sell high-priced goods and services: buyers need not consider whether they can afford the selling price, but merely whether they can manage the monthly payments. Each individual must decide whether or not credit's benefits outweigh its costs. Sometimes, the chance to have a good or service immediately can be worth the cost. When you take into account the costs of being without a car or certain equipment, you may discover monetary benefits in using credit.

But most of the benefits of using credit for this reason are not monetary. Many of us find it very appealing to have something we want as soon as we see it, but whether the resulting satisfaction offsets the cost must be a personal decision. Some people find it almost impossible to save enough to accumulate the purchase price of certain expensive items; using credit is thus the only way they can acquire such things. In such instances, credit becomes a form of forced saving, albeit an expensive one.

Two costs of using credit to obtain immediate satisfaction are (i) the interest to be paid, and (ii) the loss of financial flexibility. Interest is a direct monetary cost that varies directly according to the time taken to repay the debt. Another cost—which can be very significant, although it may be less visible—is the cost in flexibility of having committed some future income to debt repayment. When you use credit, you are accepting an obligation to make future payments; those payments may curtail your freedom to spend in other ways. If something happens to your income stream—if, for example, you become ill or lose your job— debt payments can become a substantial burden. If unexpected emergencies occur, you will have less money available for large expenses. When you buy consumer durables or vehicles on credit, you must consider not only the flexibility cost but also whether you will be able to handle the recurring expenses of operating and maintaining the item you are buying.

To Bridge the Gap

People who have an irregular income (such as many self-employed people) may require loans in order to pay regular expenses until the arrival of their next income cheque. Until a sufficient reserve fund is built up, loans that will bridge this gap may be necessary. Even with a regular income, people sometimes find themselves without enough money to cover reasonable needs. When your income prospects appear good, you may consider it worthwhile to incur debt to furnish your first home, to support a growing family, or to obtain an education.

Consolidation Loans

When their bills and debts exceed their income, some people borrow enough to repay all outstanding debts. With a consolidation loan, they then owe one large amount to one lender for a longer time. Such loans may reduce the financial pressure temporarily, but this approach tends to lock people into continual debt. We will discuss this topic in more detail in Chapter 14, under "Alternatives for the Overcommitted Debtor."

Inflation

In inflationary periods, borrowers tend to benefit at the expense of lenders. As prices rise and incomes tend to increase, a borrower pays back loans that have fixed payments. This makes it comparatively easy to handle debt. The lender, on the other hand, is paid back in dollars that will buy less than when they were lent. Another aspect of very rapid inflation is the advantage to the borrower of being able to make a purchase before the price goes up any further. Under such conditions, it may be quite rational to use credit rather than to accumulate savings. But using credit may leave you vulnerable if economic conditions change, as they did for Canada in the early 1980s and the early 1990s.

The Two Forms of Consumer Credit

As mentioned earlier, we can classify consumer credit transactions according to the source of the funds. You may obtain a **consumer loan** from a financial institution. Alternatively, you may arrange for financing to be extended at the time you make a purchase; this approach (which may involve a credit card, a charge card, or a conditional sales contract) is known as **point-of-sale credit**. We will discuss consumer loans next; later, we will examine point-of-sale credit (sometimes called vendor credit), as well as debit cards.

Major Consumer Lenders

Funds can be borrowed from a number of places, but four types of financial institutions are particularly active in providing consumer loans: banks, credit unions, trust companies, and small loans companies. You may also borrow against the cash value of your life insurance if you happen to own the right kind of policy—see Chapter 5, especially the sections "Policy Loan" and "Collateral for a Loan" under the heading "Uses for the Cash Reserves." (Other possible sources of borrowed funds, which will not be discussed here, are family, friends, pawnbrokers, and loan sharks.)

Market Shares

Earlier in this chapter, we saw that the long-term trend in Canada has been an increase in the use of consumer credit. We will now examine how the consumer credit market is shared by various creditors. In Figure 13.4, each bar represents all the consumer credit outstanding in Canada in a given year; the divisions within the bar show how the business was divided among major lenders. These data include both consumer loans and point-of-sale credit (both of which are explained in detail later in this chapter); since some creditors offer both, the data are difficult to separate. Bank consumer lending, which includes personal loans and credit cards, represents a mixture of loan and point-of-sale credit.

As Figure 13.4 clearly shows, significant changes in market shares occurred during the latter half of the century. The most striking shift involves the banks' steadily increasing role as the major creditors; they have taken market share from retail trade, as well as from sales finance and small loans companies. Credit unions slightly increased their share of the consumer credit business, while life insurance policy loans showed a decline. Trust companies, which entered the consumer credit business more recently than the other types of institutions, gained an increasing market share. We will review the major consumer lenders and think about possible reasons for the changes.

Financial Institutions

At one time banks, credit unions, trust companies, and small loans companies were distinctly different in their structures and in the services they provided, but now the trend is toward greater similarity. Legislative changes have removed many of the barriers that once kept banks, brokers, trust companies, and insurers operating independent and different businesses. Although consumers may find that little has changed on the surface, behind the scenes things are very different. Banks have bought much of the brokerage industry, have become active in mutual funds, are dominating the trust business, and are trying to

FIGURE 13.4 SHARE OF TOTAL CONSUMER CREDIT OUTSTANDING BY SOURCE, CANADA, 1970–2005

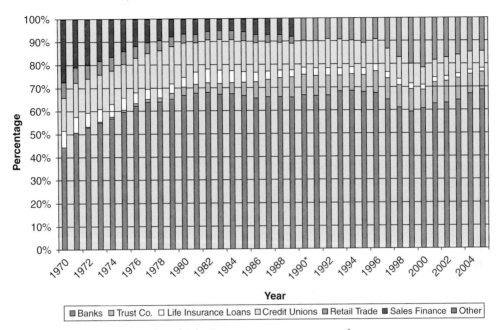

*After 1990, The Retail Trade and Sales Finance categories were merged.

SOURCE: Data from *Bank of Canada Review* (Ottawa: Bank of Canada), various issues; adapted in part from the Statistics Canada publication Canada Year Book, Catalogue 11-402, various years.

get into the life insurance industry. What does all this change mean for consumers? For one thing, there is less competition in the marketplace, which is now dominated by a few giant companies. Whether these changes will affect service and prices remains to be seen, but the possibility that they would do so was frequently considered when the proposed mergers were denied in 1999. At the time of writing, the proposals appear to be ready to be reintroduced.

In the present period of rapid change, it is difficult to find clear distinctions among financial institutions. Soon, we may go to just one place to do our banking, buy insurance, order mutual funds, and set up trusts. Credit unions have changed, too, but so far they have not merged with other financial institutions.

Banks

The chartered banks, many of which have large systems of branch offices, borrow from depositors in order to lend to those who need money. They charge enough interest on the money they lend so that they are, in turn, able to pay interest to their creditors (the depositors). The difference between the interest rate charged on loans and the interest rate paid on deposits, which is called the **spread**, covers the bank's operating costs and also provides profit for the bank's shareholders. Chartered banks are regulated by the federal *Bank Act*, which is revised about once a decade. Until its 1967 revision, the *Act* restricted banks in their consumer loan activity. Afterward, banks became very active in consumer loans (see Figure 13.4). Although they once concentrated on banking, chartered banks are now Canada's most powerful financial institutions.

Trust Companies

Trust companies, which have been active in Canada since the latter part of the nineteenth century, provide financial and trustee services to individuals and corporations. A **trustee**, which may be a person or a trust company, manages the financial affairs of others—either during their lifetime or after death. Some people stipulate in their wills (see Chapter 11) that a trust fund must be set up on their death; they name a person or trust company as trustee to handle the funds. In Canada, trust companies have been the only corporations that may act as trustees. Previously, banks and other financial institutions were not permitted to conduct **fiduciary** business—that is, to act as trustees—but this distinction has been loosened somewhat as many banks own trust companies.

Trust companies have certain advantages over individuals who are acting as trustees: a company can provide continuous service over a long period of time. A trust company's expertise may be invaluable with a complex trust that involves large sums of money. In exchange for their services, trust companies charge an annual fee—usually a percentage of the capital being managed. For individuals, trust companies handle both **living trusts**, which have been established by people who are still alive, and **testamentary trusts**, which are created by a will, on a person's death. A large part of a trust company's business involves acting as a trustee for other corporations in handling pension funds, bond issues, and the like.

A trust company's charter does not limit it to fiduciary business, so trust companies are active financial intermediaries, taking in deposits and making loans of various kinds. Generally, only the larger trust companies are in the consumer loan business, but mortgage lending is a different matter. In recent years, trust and mortgage loan companies have provided significant amounts of mortgage funds. As many small trust companies are bought by larger ones or by banks, we see fewer and larger trust companies dominating the scene. The survivors compete directly with the banks in the services they offer, even with the banks that own them.

Small Loans Companies

Many small loans companies and money lenders are affiliated with other financial institutions; this is especially true of sales finance companies. It is not uncommon for a firm to operate both a small loans company and a sales finance business from the same premises; because of this close affiliation, the statistics of such businesses are often combined. The principal distinction is that small loans companies and money lenders make cash loans, while sales finance companies buy credit contracts arranged by retailers commonly when there are no payments for an extended time period. The cost of credit at a small loans company tends to be high, reflecting such factors as their willingness to accept higher-risk borrowers, the cost of processing small loans, and the fact that they themselves are not deposit-taking institutions but must instead borrow from other sources in order to have money to lend. Before 1975, such firms had a significant share of the consumer credit business, but that share subsequently diminished (see Figure 13.4). As a result, there are fewer small loans companies or sales finance companies in business these days.

Life Insurance Policy Loans

Loans may be made against life insurance policies that have a cash surrender value, such as whole life policies, but not against term policies or against most group policies, which have no cash value. It takes two or three years for a policy's cash surrender value to build up enough to make the policyholder eligible for a loan. The policy's cash value grows each year that the policy is in force, and the amounts are shown in the policy. Generally, policies permit about 90 percent to 100 percent of the cash value to be borrowed.

The interest rate on life insurance policy loans is usually lower than that available from other commercial sources. Before 1968, the maximum loan rate was 6 percent, but policies written since that time have not been so restricted; the usual practice now is not to state a lending rate in the policy. There is no difficulty in obtaining the loan because the policyholder is borrowing from the cash value of his or her own policy. Nor is there a time limit for repaying the loan; any interest that is due will automatically be added to the loan. A loan on a policy does not invalidate life insurance coverage. When the policyholder dies, the policy remains intact, but any outstanding debt is subtracted from the payment to the beneficiary. The terms of the loan are stated in the life insurance policy. Look at the sample life insurance policy in Chapter 5 (see Appendix 5A, "A Sample Life Insurance Policy") to find out what the terms are for a policy loan.

As a share of all consumer credit outstanding in Canada, life insurance policy loans are not very significant; in fact, they have been decreasing. In 1955, policy loans represented less than 9 percent of all consumer credit, but by 1997 this share was down to 3 percent. Some possible reasons for this change are (i) that the demand for consumer credit has increased at a much faster rate than the purchase of life insurance has, (ii) that more life insurance without cash value is being sold now than previously, and (iii) loans are readily available elsewhere. It is quicker and simpler to charge things on a credit card than to negotiate a life insurance loan. Life insurance companies do not especially promote policy loans, and many people have so little understanding of their life insurance coverage that they may not be aware of this source of credit.

Credit Unions

The financial co-operatives in the consumer lending and saving business are the **credit unions**, originally created to offer services to low-income families whose only other option was to borrow from a loan shark. By pooling the funds of savers, a credit union allows money to be lent at reasonable rates to those who need to borrow, resulting in an arrangement that is advantageous both to savers (who receive dividends from the interest paid on the loans) and to borrowers. Early credit unions were small; their members knew one another, and personal needs received careful attention. A debt to one's credit union was seen as a personal obligation to friends or associates, so social pressure to repay loans was strong and losses were thus minimized. But sadly, the growth of credit unions has meant a shift in the attitudes of some borrowers, who now default on loans nearly as often as people who borrow from other kinds of financial institutions.

The credit union movement began in 1847 when Friedrich Raiffeisen, who was a mayor and a lay preacher, became concerned about the peasants of southern Germany, who were hopelessly in debt following a series of crop failures. The only sources of loans available to them were banks, which required gilt-edged security, or loan sharks, who exacted punitive interest rates. Raiffeisen was instrumental in establishing credit societies, using the small savings of members to create funds that could be borrowed by others. By the time Raiffeisen died, in 1888, 423 credit unions were flourishing in Germany.

As the twentieth century dawned, Alphonse Desjardins of Lévis, Quebec, a legislative reporter, noted the high rates being charged by money lenders to the region's poor people. Using some of Raiffeisen's ideas, Desjardins started La Caisse Populaire de Lévis with an initial membership of 80 people and assets of $26. This venture met a widespread need so successfully that credit unions were organized in many Quebec parishes. As the credit union idea spread, first from Lévis to Boston, and then to Nova Scotia, Saskatchewan, and across the continent, people adapted it to meet local requirements. Few credit unions were established in Ontario before 1945, when the move toward industrial credit unions began.

Common Bond

To do business with a credit union, you must be a member of the co-operative. Moreover, legislation requires that a credit union's members share a **common bond**: they may all work for the same company; belong to the same church or synagogue, labour union, or volunteer organization; or live in the same community or on the same military base. Potential members must meet the common bond requirement; they must also buy a share in the credit union, which may cost as little as $5. Recently, as a result of mergers, larger credit unions with residential common bonds have replaced small credit unions with very specific common bonds (such as place of employment or church membership).

Member Involvement

As part of a non-profit co-operative, a credit union's members have a say in its operation through the elected board of directors, which determines general policy and either handles operating decisions or delegates them to a paid manager. The credit union's net earnings are returned to members, whether those members are borrowers or depositors or both, in a variety of ways, such as dividends on the share accounts, higher interest rates on deposits, lower charges for loans, or additional services.

Provincial Differences

In Canada, the credit union movement is strongest in Quebec (where over 60 percent of the population are members) and in Saskatchewan (where more than half of the population are members). In most other provinces, credit union members represent less than a third of the population. The Quebec credit unions, or *caisses populaires*, have nearly half of all the Canadian credit union assets. Saskatchewan and Quebec far out-rank the other provinces in credit union assets per capita.

Network

All credit unions are linked into regional, provincial, and national networks. Starting at the top, the World Council of Credit Unions comprises national associations such as the Credit Union Central of Canada. In Canada, the three-tiered structure consists of provincial chapters or centrals, regional groupings within the province, and local credit unions. This arrangement leaves credit unions with a great deal of local autonomy but with connections to the larger organization. Local credit unions, with their separate boards of directors, are more independent from the larger umbrella organizations than are the branches of large banks with respect to the banks' head offices. Nevertheless, there is a move to coordinate services so that a member of one credit union can conduct business at another credit union.

The provincial centrals offer important assistance to credit unions, including investing their surplus funds or lending them additional money; supplying legal assistance, lobbying power, and educational services; and helping them save money through central purchasing of supplies. Deposit insurance, which is very important to savers, is arranged through the provincial centrals.

Security

Borrowers at credit unions may be asked to provide several forms of security. For example, they may be required to maintain the equivalent of 10 percent of the outstanding balance on their loans in a deposit account; in addition, they may be expected to sign a

FIGURE 13.5 NUMBER OF CREDIT UNIONS IN CANADA, 1947–1995

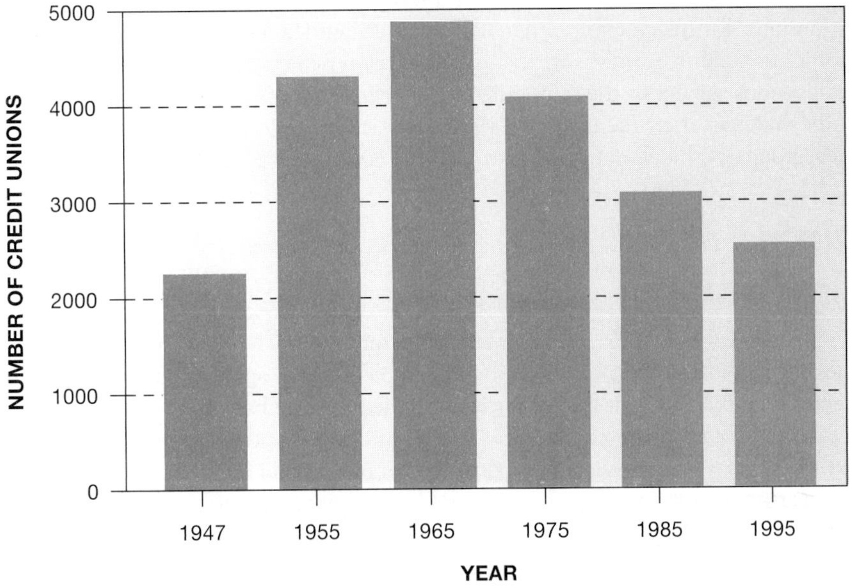

SOURCE: Adapted from the Statistics Canada publication *Canada Year Book*, Catalogue 11-402, various years, 1948–49 (p.1051),1961, Table 18 (p.1130), 1962, Table 18 (p.1108), 1972, Table 17 (p.1245), 1990, Table 18.14 (p.18-6), 1997.

promissory note, a wage assignment, and, if appropriate, a chattel mortgage. In some instances a co-signer may be required. These terms will all be explained later in this chapter under "Security for Loans."

Numbers of Credit Unions Historically, most credit unions were operated by volunteers in premises that were often rent-free. These small amateur operations were low-cost and intimate, but eventually they became unable to compete with the larger-scale and more-professional activities of banks and trust companies. As a consequence, many small credit unions merged to form fewer, larger unions, hiring staff to run them and making them into more efficient and impersonal institutions. Figure 13.5 illustrates the pattern of change in the numbers of credit union locals, showing the gradual growth of credit unions in the early years, their rapid expansion during the 1950s and 1960s, and the effects of the mergers beginning in the 1970s. According to the credit unions' national trade association, Credit Union Central of Canada, there were 1802 affiliated credit unions in Canada in 2005, as well as 1663 other credit unions and *caisses populaires*.

Services Credit unions vary considerably in size and in the range of services they provide. All receive deposits and make loans, but some also offer a variety of deposit accounts and savings vehicles, chequing services, mortgage loans, and automatic tellers. The larger credit unions have become quite competitive with banks and trust companies in interest rates and services offered.

As larger credit unions were created, volunteer staff were replaced with paid professional managers, loans officers, and independent auditors. Such changes were necessary if credit unions were to compete with other financial institutions. Interestingly, credit unions were the first financial institutions to offer such innovations as weekly-payment mortgages and daily interest savings accounts, and to explore the use of debit cards (see the "Debit Cards" section later in this chapter, under "Economic Significance"). To increase the competition among financial institutions, British Columbia revised its *Financial Institutions Act*, making credit unions subject to the same rules as other institutions and giving them the right to sell equity shares to their members. In 1992, the Credit Union Central of Canada introduced a new group of ethical mutual funds across the country.

Obtaining a Loan
Applying for a Loan

The procedure for obtaining a loan is about the same at any lender. The credit manager (sometimes called a loans officer) will ask you to complete a loan application form that requires considerable detail about your past financial activities. On the basis of this and other information that may be obtained in a credit report, the loans officer decides whether or not to approve the loan. (Chapter 14 discusses credit reports, credit bureaus, and how lenders evaluate a customer's creditworthiness.) If the decision is favourable, the next step is to settle the main **terms of the loan**: the principal to be lent, the interest rate, the length of time to repay, and the security required. The date by which the loan must be completely repaid is known as the **maturity date**, and the maximum length of time that the loan is to be outstanding is called the **term of the loan**. (Notice the distinction between the "terms" of the loan and the "term" of the loan.)

Types of Loans

The kinds of loans available to individuals at financial institutions differ in their terms and conditions. Interest rates depend on the risk level represented by the borrower and on the services provided. Some arrangements provide funds on an ongoing basis; others are contracts drawn up for a specific instalment loan. Examples of the types of ongoing loans are (i) a line of credit, (ii) overdraft protection, and (iii) cash advances on a bank credit card. All of these give the borrower advance permission to borrow within set limits if the need arises. The advantage of these arrangements is that the funds are available to you if you need them, but you pay no interest charges if you do not use them. At other times, a sum may be borrowed for a specific purpose with a set repayment schedule; examples of such arrangements include (i) a demand loan or (ii) an instalment loan.

Personal Line of Credit Banks, trust companies, and credit unions may offer their creditworthy customers a personal line of credit as a convenient substitute for personal loans. A personal line of credit is a flexible way to use credit; the financial institution makes funds available to you up to a set limit, whenever you need the money. You pay no interest charge until you use some or all of the available funds.

Once your line-of-credit application has been approved, the financial institution supplies you with a line of credit up to a specified maximum amount. You will usually be required to make a minimum monthly payment in addition to paying interest on any outstanding monthly balance. Your line of credit could involve an amount as low as $2500 or $5000; payments must generally cover at least 3 percent to 5 percent of the outstanding balance. The interest rate on a line of credit is related to the prime rate (defined below, under "Demand Loan") and is adjusted monthly. Sometimes you can arrange a line of credit that requires interest payments only. If you are eligible for one, a line of credit may cost less than a personal loan.

Overdraft Protection The difference between a personal line of credit and overdraft protection may be blurred by some financial institutions. Overdraft protection, which is available at banks, trust companies, and credit unions, allows deposit accounts to become overdrawn to a set limit—for instance, $1000. The overdraft becomes a loan that is subject to interest rates as high as or higher than those charged on credit card loans. The rates on a personal line of credit may be 6 percent to 7 percent lower than those on overdraft protection; clearly, then, it is worthwhile to check the rates.

Credit Card Cash Advances Anyone with a credit card issued by a financial institution (bank, credit union, trust company) has the option of obtaining a loan, called a cash advance, without making a special application each time funds are needed. The original contract and the previously established loan limit cover the situation. Interest, calculated daily, begins at once—usually at rates that are higher than those charged for either a line of credit or a personal loan.

Demand Loan Rather than choosing flexible credit, customers with a good credit rating may arrange for a demand loan by signing an agreement to repay the loan in full at a certain date, with interest due monthly. The lender has the right to recall a demand loan at any time. Holders of demand loans often renegotiate them at maturity. Interest charges will be set slightly above the prime rate and will fluctuate according to the prevailing rate. The **prime rate** is the lowest interest rate that financial institutions charge: offered to their best corporate customers, the prime rate also serves as a guide for setting other interest rates. (Thus, you may be charged "prime plus two," meaning that you will pay interest set at two percentage points higher than the prime rate. So if the prime rate is 6 percent, you will pay 8 percent.)

Instalment Loans Instalment loans usually have a set interest rate, a maturity date, a repayment schedule, and certain security requirements, as will be explained shortly under "Security for Loans." The contract you will sign varies with the kind of security you are pledging. Personal Finance in Action Box 13.1, "Applying for a Personal Loan," illustrates part of the decision-making process for one couple who are applying for an instalment loan.

Personal FINANCE in action 13.1

Applying for a Personal Loan

Sarah and Devon want to buy a sailboat. When they apply at their bank for a $10 000 personal instalment loan for this purpose, they know that they will need to list outstanding balances on several credit and charge cards, but they also know that their credit ratings are well-established. After the loans officer hears about their debts—$1100 to MasterCard, $500 to American Express, and $950 to Sears—she strongly recommends that they consolidate these debts into one bank loan, so that they will have only one payment to make. The bank will be happy to lend them the $10 000 they are asking for—and, in addition, enough to pay off all their other debts.

Sarah and Devon are not keen to consolidate their credit card debt with the bank loan, but they have the impression that the bank will look more favourably at their loan application if they agree to do so.

What factors should they consider before deciding to consolidate their debts?

Security for Loans

Lenders must consider the risk of not being repaid and take steps to minimize the consequences. Some lenders do so by accepting as borrowers only those who appear to be good risks; others lend to a wider range of people but ask each borrower for certain assurances. It is common practice to require a borrower to sign documents that give the lender permission in advance to take over specified possessions or assets belonging to the borrower if the latter fails to make all payments as agreed. These various claims on the borrower, which are arranged when the loan is taken out, are referred to as the security for the loan.

Security and Collateral Distinguishing clearly between security and collateral can be difficult. It may help to consider security as a claim or right that the borrower has voluntarily assigned to the lender in order to reduce the lender's risk. The term **collateral** applies only to tangible assets that are used as security, such as financial assets or durable goods. So the signature of a guarantor or co-signer is a form of security for the lender, but because the signature is not a tangible object, it is not collateral. Promises may have some security value, but they do not qualify as collateral.

Fully and Partly Secured Loans

Loans may be fully or partly secured. If the borrower signs over to the lender assets that are equal in value to the total loan, that loan is said to be **fully secured**. Naturally, very few consumer loans are fully secured because people who have enough assets to do so would probably buy the goods for cash. But requesting a fully secured loan can occasionally be a reasonable decision. For instance, if you need funds for only a few months, you might prefer to use your assets as security rather than to sell the assets so that you can pay in cash. If the assets in question are already invested and are producing a higher yield than would be possible in the current market, you might be wiser to retain the assets and instead take a short-term loan. When you use bonds or similar financial assets as security for a loan, you can expect to be charged a very favourable interest rate because the lender is taking no risk at all.

More often, loans are only **partly secured** because borrowers rarely have sufficient assets to obtain a fully secured loan. A car buyer may use the car as security for the car loan, but this debt is not fully secured because cars and certain other durables depreciate faster than loans are repaid.

Signature Loans

A borrower who is considered to present little risk to the lender may be asked for nothing more than a signature on a **promissory note**, which is an unconditional promise to repay the loan. Such a loan, also called a signature loan, is considered by the lender to be unsecured. In other words, if the borrower does not repay the loan as promised, the lender has nothing of value belonging to the borrower that can be liquidated to pay the debt. The legal contract used for a signature loan is the promissory note, which, as noted above, is simply a promise to repay the loan. Figure 13.6 shows a sample promissory note used for a personal loan.

FIGURE 13.6 PERSONAL LOAN PROMISSORY NOTE

Reproduced with the permission of the Bank of Montreal.

Many people are not eligible for signature loans, and even those who are may instead choose the greater flexibility offered by a personal line of credit. If you are a long-time customer of a financial institution, and if its credit managers judge your character and credit record to be exemplary, you may be permitted a signature loan with no other security; otherwise, like most borrowers, you will probably be required to provide a tangible form of security in addition to your promise. For this reason, promissory notes are often incorporated into more complex credit contracts of the sort we will discuss below. Four frequently used forms of security for loans are (i) co-signers, (ii) future wages, (iii) financial assets, and (iv) durable goods.

Co-signers

A lender may require that the borrower find another person to sign the loan agreement. By signing, the **co-signer** (also called the guarantor) is agreeing to repay any outstanding balance on the loan if the borrower fails to do so. People sometimes agree to co-sign loans as a gesture of friendship, without fully realizing the commitment they are making. The extent of their responsibility becomes evident to them only when the lender requires them to make restitution on behalf of the friend or relative who cannot repay or who has disappeared without repaying the loan. People who can't be found are referred to in the credit business as skips.

FIGURE 13.7 ASSIGNMENT OF WAGES

ASSIGNMENT OF WAGES

TO: ..Guelph...and..Wellington.................. CREDIT UNION LIMITED
(hereinafter called the "Credit Union")

I..
(Name of Assignor)

for Valuable Consideration hereby assign, transfer and set over unto the Credit Union, (i) 20 per cent of all wages, (as defined in the Wages Act of Ontario), but excluding any amount that an employer is required by law to deduct from any such wages and (ii) all other monies owing to me, or hereafter to become owing to me by my employer: ....

....

or any other person, firm, corporation or entity by whom I may be hereafter employed.

AND I HEREBY AUTHORIZE AND DIRECT my said employer or any future employer to pay the said 20 per cent of all such wages and all such other monies to the Credit Union, and I hereby irrevocably authorize the Credit Union to take all proceedings which may be proper and necessary for the recovery of any amount or amounts above assigned and to give receipts for same, or any part thereof, in my name and I hereby release and discharge my said employers and each of them from all liability to me for or on account of any or all monies paid in accordance with the terms hereof. Nothing herein shall prevent the Credit Union from exercising any other right of recovery available in law of any amount lawfully owing to the Credit Union in excess of the amounts assigned above.

THIS ASSIGNMENT OF WAGES is irrevocable by the Assignor, and shall remain a valid and enforceable security in respect of all debts owing by the Assignor to the Credit Union until delivery of notice in writing signed by the Credit Union to the contrary.

Signed, Sealed and Delivered this .... day of ...., ...

.... at .... Ontario in the presence of:

Witness

....
(Signature of Assignor)

(FORM # 021923)

Rev. 10/98 31

Reproduced with the permission of the Guelph and Wellington Credit Union.

Future Wages

Sometimes borrowers sign an agreement that if they do not maintain the repayment schedule, the lender has permission to collect a portion of their wages directly from their employers. This type of contract is called a **wage assignment**. To protect borrowers from certain abuses of this system that occurred in the past, the use of wage assignments has been curtailed. For instance, in Ontario, credit unions are the only creditors that are permitted to use wage assignments. Figure 13.7 shows a sample wage assignment. By signing this document, the borrower is voluntarily agreeing that if he or she does not repay the debt, the Guelph and Wellington Credit Union may collect a percent of his or her wages—in this case, net wages, after the standard payroll deductions for income tax and CPP—directly from the employer until the loan is repaid. (Whether the percent figure is based on gross or net wages varies according to jurisdiction.)

In practice, the credit union would not enforce a wage assignment until other, less drastic collection measures had failed. The debtor would also be informed that the wage assignment was about to be enforced, giving him or her time either to repay the debt or to petition for a reduction in the amount of wages to be taken. (Note that a wage assignment differs from the wage garnishment discussed in Chapter 14 under "Debt Collection": a wage garnishment requires a court order, while a wage assignment—as a contract that is signed in advance by the borrower—can be initiated by a credit union as a result of its own internal decision.) Either the credit union's loans officer or its board of directors decides when and whether to enforce a wage assignment; they may also grant an exemption or reduction if the borrower's situation seems to warrant doing so.

Financial Assets

To secure a loan, a lender may require a borrower to lodge in the lender's possession some form of **collateral**, such as bonds, stock certificates, life insurance policies, or deposits. These types of collateral are financial assets that can be readily converted to cash, which is what the lender will do if the borrower fails to maintain the terms of the loan agreement. With each form of collateral offered, the borrower will be asked to sign an appropriate agreement giving the lender the power to realize these assets if the borrower defaults on the loan. Different types of contracts are used, depending on the nature of the asset being pledged.

A borrower who has a life insurance policy with an adequate cash surrender value may assign the policy to a lender as security for a loan. This process was discussed in Chapter 5, under "Collateral for a Loan" in the "Uses for the Cash Reserves" section. Essentially it means that the policy is held by the lender until the debt is cleared, but the policyholder must continue to pay the premiums. If the borrower defaults on the loan, the lender can cash in the policy.

Durable Goods

When consumer durables such as vehicles, appliances, and furniture are bought with credit, the articles themselves are usually offered as security. If you obtain a loan from a bank, a credit union, a small loans company, or a trust company, you will be required to sign a **chattel mortgage** or **security interest**, a document that transfers ownership of the goods to the lender (Figure 13.8). Note that the term **chattel** applies to movable goods, but not to land or buildings (which are called real property); the latter are used as security in home mortgages (see Chapter 12). As the borrower, you have possession and full use of the goods, but through the chattel mortgage you are agreeing to maintain them in good condition and in most cases to insure them.

During the term of the chattel mortgage, which is the time until the debt is repaid, you do not have the right to sell the pledged goods without the lender's permission. If you default on the loan, the lender has your written prior permission to repossess and sell the goods. In some provinces—Ontario, for instance—the creditor (the lender) may also have the right to sue for any balance outstanding if the proceeds from the sale of the repossessed goods are insufficient to extinguish the debt. Elsewhere (in British Columbia, Alberta, and Newfoundland and Labrador), there has been a trend toward "seize or sue" laws, which give the creditor the option of either repossessing the goods or suing the debtor, but not both.

It is important to take careful note that chattel mortgages are the contracts used by lenders when taking the title to goods as security. Vendors of goods, who already have title to the goods they are selling, are in a position to retain the title until the total cost is paid; for these transactions a different contract, called a conditional sales contract, is used. If you default on one of these agreements, the vendor will enforce security by repossessing the goods (see "Enforcing Security" and "Conditional Sales Contracts," later in this chapter).

Lien

In popular usage, the term **lien** is often used as a synonym for a chattel mortgage, but there is a distinction in law. A lien is a claim registered against certain property, generally in cases

FIGURE 13.8 SECURITY AGREEMENT

SECURITY AGREEMENT - CONSUMER CREDIT

DATE:_____

ACCOUNT NO.:_____

TO: _____ (the "Credit Union")
(Name of Credit Union)

FROM: _____   AND: _____
(Surname)   (First Name)   (Middle Initial)   (Surname)   (First Name)   (Middle Initial)

Date of Birth: _____ (Day) _____ (Month) _____ (Year)   Date of Birth: _____ (Day) _____ (Month) _____ (Year)

_____   _____
(Number and Street)   (Number and Street)

_____ _____ _____   _____ _____ _____
(City, Town)   (Province)   (Postal Code)   (City, Town)   (Province)   (Postal Code)

(Collectively referred to hereinafter as the "Debtor")

1. Security Interest

The Debtor for valuable consideration hereby assigns, transfers, sets over, mortgages, charges and grants to the Credit Union a security interest in the following motor vehicle(s):

Make	Year	Model	Style	Vehicle Identification Number	Colour	Ontario Plate Number

and the property, if any, described in Schedule A attached hereto and any and all substitutions or replacements thereof, increases, additions or accessions thereto and any interest of the Debtor therein (all of which shall hereinafter be referred to as the "Collateral").

In this Agreement, any reference to the word "Collateral" shall, unless the context otherwise requires, refer to "Collateral or any part thereof". In this Agreement, the word "Collateral" shall include the proceeds thereof. Until default, the Debtor may have possession of the Collateral and enjoy the same subject to the terms hereof.

2. Obligations Secured

The fixed and specific mortgages, charges and security interests granted hereby:

(CHECK AND INITIAL AS APPROPRIATE)

☐ (a) secure payment to the Credit Union of all debts and liabilities, present or future, direct or indirect, absolute or contingent, matured or not, at any time owing by the Debtor to the Credit Union or remaining unpaid by the Debtor to the Credit Union, whether arising from dealings between the Credit Union and the Debtor or from other dealings or proceedings by which the Credit Union may be or become in any manner whatever a creditor of the Debtor and wherever incurred, and in any currency, and whether incurred by the Debtor alone or with another or others and whether as principal or surety, including expenses under paragraph 5 of this Agreement and all interest, commissions, legal and other costs, charges and expenses (all of the foregoing being herein called, and included in, the "Obligations");

☐ (b) secure payment to the Credit Union of the principal amount of $_____ and interest on the unpaid principal amount at the rate of _____% per year calculated daily and payable monthly, as well after as before maturity, default and judgment and interest on overdue interest at the rate aforesaid (the principal amount and accrued and unpaid interest being herein called, and included in, the "Obligations");

3. Representations and Warranties

The Debtor represents and warrants as follows:

(a) the Debtor is, or is to become, the beneficial owner of the Collateral;

(b) the Collateral is, or will be when acquired, free and clear of all security interests, mortgages, hypothecs, charges, liens, encumbrances, taxes and assessments; and

(c) the Debtor's name, address and the date of birth shown at the beginning of this agreement are correct.

4. Covenants

The Debtor hereby agrees that:

(a) Maintain, Use, etc. - the Debtor shall diligently maintain, use and operate the Collateral in a proper and efficient manner so as to preserve and protect the Collateral and the earnings, incomes, rents, issues and profits thereof;

(b) Insurance - the Debtor shall cause all of the Collateral to be properly insured and kept insured with reputable insurers against loss or damage by fire or other hazards and shall maintain such insurance with loss if any payable to the Credit Union and shall deliver to the Credit Union evidence of such insurance satisfactory to the Credit Union and if the Debtor fails to obtain satisfactory insurance, the Credit Union shall have the right to obtain it at the Debtor's expense;

(c) Rent, Taxes, etc. - The Debtor shall pay all rents, taxes, rates, levies, assessments and government fees or dues lawfully levied, assessed or imposed in respect of the Collateral or any part thereof as and when the same shall become due and payable, and shall exhibit to the Credit Union, when required, the receipts and vouchers establishing such payments;

(d) Observe Law - the Debtor shall duly observe and conform to all valid requirements of any governmental authority relative to any of the Collateral and all covenants, terms and conditions upon or under which the Collateral is held;

(e) Information - the Debtor shall furnish to the Credit Union such information with respect to the Collateral and the insurance thereon as the Credit Union may from time to time

Page 1 of 2
(Form O.L.-D 1922/7-95)

---

continued

where the goods or services provided cannot be seized. For example, if a contractor has already paved a driveway, but payment is now overdue, the creditor may register a lien against the house. This claim against the property would have to be settled before the owner could ever obtain a clear title (so a lien on the house prevents its owner from selling the

FIGURE 13.8 ■ SECURITY AGREEMENT (CONTINUED)

require and the Credit Union may examine and inspect the Collateral at any time upon reasonable notice.

(f) Other Encumbrances - the Debtor shall not, without the prior consent in writing of the Credit Union, create any security interest, mortgage, hypothec, charge, lien or other encumbrance upon the Collateral of any part thereof;

(g) Defend Title - the Debtor shall defend the title to the Collateral against all persons and shall, upon demand by the Credit Union furnish further assurance of title and further security for the Obligations and execute any written instruments or do any other acts necessary, to make effective the purposes and provisions of this Agreement;

(h) Dealings with the Collateral - the Debtor shall not sell, exchange, assign or lease or otherwise dispose of the Collateral or any interest therein without the prior written consent of the Credit Union;

(i) Motor Vehicle - the Debtor shall, if any part of the Collateral is a motor vehicle, not remove the motor vehicle from the Province of Ontario; and

(j) Change of Name - the Debtor shall not change its name.

5. Immediate Possession

Upon failure by the Debtor to perform any of the agreements described in paragraph 4 hereof, the Credit Union is authorized and has the option to take immediate possession of the Collateral and, whether it has taken possession or not, to perform any of the agreements in any manner deemed proper by the Credit Union, without waiving any rights to enforce this Agreement. The expenses (including the cost of any insurance and the amount of taxes or other charges and reasonable solicitors' costs and legal expenses) incurred by the Credit Union in respect of the custody, preservation, use or operation of the Collateral shall be repaid forthwith by the Debtor to the Credit Union immediately after they are incurred, shall bear interest at the rate of 20% per annum and the repayment of such expenses and interest thereon shall be secured by this Agreement.

6. Events of Default

At the option of the Credit Union, the Obligations shall immediately become due and payable in full upon the happening of any of the following events:

(a) if the Debtor shall fail to pay or perform when due any of the Obligations;

(b) if the Debtor shall fail to perform any provisions of this Agreement or of any other agreement to which the Debtor and the Credit Union are parties;

(c) if any of the representations and warranties herein is or becomes incorrect in any respect at any time;

(d) if the Debtor or any guarantor of any of the Obligations dies, commits an act of bankruptcy, assigns or is petitioned into bankruptcy, becomes insolvent, or proposes a compromise or arrangement to its creditors;

(e) if any execution, sequestration or any other process of any court beomes enforceable against the Debtor or any guarantor of any of the Obligations or if any distress or analogous process is levied upon the Collateral or any part thereof;

(f) if the Credit Union in good faith believes that the prospect of payment or performance of any of the Obligations is impaired.

7. Remedies

If pursuant to paragraph 6 hereof, the Credit Union declares that the Obligations shall immediately become due and payable in full, the Debtor and the Credit Union shall have, in addition to any other rights and remedies provided by law, the rights and remedies of a debtor and a secured party respectively under the Personal Property Security Act, 1989 and those provided by this Agreement. The Credit Union may take immediate possession of the Collateral and enforce any rights of the Debtor in respect of the Collateral by any manner permitted by law and may require the Debtor to assemble and deliver the Collateral or make the Collateral available to the Credit Union at a reasonably convenient place designated by the Credit Union. The Credit Union may take proceedings in any court of competent jurisdiction to sell, lease or otherwise dispose of the whole or any part of the Collateral at public auction, by public tender or by private sale, either for cash or upon credit, at such time and upon such terms and conditions as the receiver may determine.

Page 2 of 2
(Form O.L.-D 1922/7-95)

DATE: _____

ACCOUNT NO.: _____

TO: _____
(Name of Credit Union)

FROM: _____
(Surname)   (First Name)   (Middle Initial)

8. Expenses

Any proceeds of any disposition of any of the Collateral may be applied by the Credit Union to the payment of expenses incurred in connection with the retaking, holding, repairing, processing, preparing for disposition and disposing of the Collateral (including solicitors' fees and legal expenses and any other expenses), and any balance of such proceeds may be applied by the Credit Union towards the payment of the Obligations in such order of application as the Credit Union may from time to time effect. All such expenses and all amounts borrowed on the security of the Collateral under paragraph 7 hereof shall bear interest at 20% per annum and shall be Obligations under this Agreement. If the disposition of the Collateral fails to satisfy the Obligations and the expenses incurred by the Credit Union, the Debtor shall be liable to pay for any deficiency on demand.

9. Miscellaneous

The Debtor and the Credit Union further agree that:

(a) the Debtor shall not be discharged by any extension of time, additional advances, renewals and extensions, the taking of further security, releasing security, extinguishment of mortgages or charges or the security interest as to all or any part of the Collateral, or any other act except a release or discharge of the mortgages or charges or security interest upon the payment in full of the Obligations including charges, expenses, fees, costs and interest;

(b) any failure by the Credit Union to exercise any right set out in this Agreement shall not constitute a waiver thereof; nothing in this Agreement or in the Obligations shall preclude any other remedy by action or otherwise for the enforcement of this Agreement or the payment or performance in full of the Obligations secured by this Agreement;

(c) all rights of the Credit Union hereunder shall be assignable and in any action brought by an assignee to enforce such rights, the Debtor shall not assert against the assignee any claim or defence which the Debtor now has or may hereafter have against the Credit Union;

(d) the Debtor agrees that all proceeds of the Collateral shall be held in trust by the Debtor for the Credit Union;

(e) all rights of the Credit Union hereunder shall enure to the benefit of its successors and assigns and all obligations of the Debtor hereunder shall bind the Debtor, his heirs, executors, administrators, successors and assigns;

(f) if more than one person executes this Agreement as Debtor, their obligations under this Agreement shall be joint and several;

(g) this Agreement shall be governed in all respects by the laws of the Province of Ontario;

(h) the Debtor hereby acknowledges receipt of an executed copy of this Agreement; and

(i) this Agreement shall become effective when it is signed by the Debtor.

SIGNED, SEALED AND DELIVERED as of the date first above written.

_____) _____ (seal)
Witness   ) Debtor

_____) _____ (seal)
) Debtor

SOURCE: Reproduced with the permission of the Guelph and Wellington Credit Union.

house without paying off the debt represented by the lien). If a service station has not been paid for repairing a car, a mechanic's lien can be registered against the car. The proprietor of the garage would then have the right to keep the car until the debt is satisfied—or, if the default continues, to sell the car.

Cost of Borrowing

Insurance

When you sign a credit contract, you assume not only the responsibility of repaying the debt, but also the risk that something will happen to make it impossible or difficult for you to carry out this intent. Unexpected illness, unemployment, disability, or death may disrupt a payment schedule. Insurance can protect against two of these risks—death or disability.

Credit Life Insurance Lenders often require that their consumer loans be life-insured. The lender arranges for this coverage by having a group life insurance policy that covers the lives of its borrowers against the risk that any given borrower will die before his or her debts have been repaid. This insurance on the life of the borrower is often called credit life insurance. When an insured borrower dies, the insurance company pays the lender the outstanding balance due on the debt. The borrower's estate does not receive anything, but the survivors may be relieved that the debt has been paid.

Some lenders automatically include credit life insurance without an additional charge; others offer it as an option with a specific cost. Either way, the borrower ultimately pays for this service. Even if it is optional, you might give some thought to whether purchasing it would make sense. When a borrower with an outstanding debt dies without credit life insurance, the balance of the debt becomes a charge on the debtor's estate; this charge must be paid before any funds are distributed to the heirs. If the estate is adequate, such a situation may cause no difficulty; but if the family has many needs and few assets, a large debt could create hardship for the survivors.

Disability Insurance Not all lenders offer disability insurance, but credit unions often do. For an additional fee, disability insurance covers the borrower for the risk of being unable to make payments because of a personal disability. It is important to find out the conditions of such insurance as well as what it will cost. How does the insurance company define disability? How long must one be disabled before the insurance will take effect? If the borrower meets the criteria for disability, the insurance company will assume responsibility for the debt payments as long as the disability lasts.

Interest Charges

The cost of borrowing depends on the lender's cost of money (how much it costs the lender to acquire the funds it lends), the lender's assessment of the risk that the loan might not be repaid, and the services offered by the lender. Deposit-taking institutions, which have a ready supply of funds to lend, can charge lower rates than small loans companies, which must borrow the funds they plan to lend. To cover their costs, banks, trust companies, and credit unions allow a spread of between 1 percent and 3 percent between the interest rate they pay to depositors and the interest rate they charge borrowers.

When you submit a loan application, the creditor assesses the degree of risk involved in lending money to you. Some lenders—notably small loans companies, which will lend to higher-risk borrowers—charge higher rates aimed at covering their losses on bad debts. Most lenders establish the level of risk they will accept and then refuse loans to those who do not qualify.

Interest Rates At present, financial institutions vary little in the rates they charge for the same type of loan; but there are significant differences in the rates charged for different types of loans.

Enforcement of Security

In Arrears

When a debtor does not adhere to the repayment schedule originally agreed on, the account is first considered to be **in arrears (delinquent)** because the payments are somewhat behind. But if the borrower contacts the lender and explains the problem, it is usually possible to make some adjustments. If the borrower is ill or unemployed, the lender may agree either to freeze the loan payments or to allow the borrower to pay only interest until able to begin making full payments again. An account that is in arrears, provided that the situation does not last too long, is not as serious a blot on the debtor's credit record as an account that is in default.

In Default

The difference between an account in arrears and one in default is largely a matter of degree. In both cases, the borrower has not maintained the regular payment schedule. An account is **in default** if payments are hopelessly behind and if the lender is having no success in collecting the debt. Such an account may be turned over for collection to a special department within the firm or to an outside collection agency. Default has a negative effect on your credit record. Lenders' leniency varies; in recessionary times, creditors may take action more quickly than in periods of prosperity and high employment.

Enforcing Security

When a debtor defaults, the lender is in a position to **enforce security**—that is, to realize funds from whatever the borrower put up for security before the loan was granted. If there was a co-signer, the lender will first try to collect from that person, using various degrees of pressure. If the creditor is a credit union, a decision may be made to exercise the wage-assignment, which means directing the debtor's employer to deduct up to 20 percent of the debtor's wages due on each payday and to send the amount to the creditor. If financial assets—such as bonds, stocks, deposits, and life insurance—were used as security, the lender can now convert these into cash to cover as much of the debt as possible. If consumer durables were the security, the lender can repossess them and offer them for sale.

Enforcement of security is limited to whatever the particular credit contract specifies; it means taking only those steps necessary to obtain funds from goods, assets, or co-signers, according to the pledges made when the loan was initially arranged. At this stage, the creditor cannot seize goods unless they were listed as security in the credit contract. A creditor may choose not to enforce his or her security, especially in the case of chattel mortgages or conditional sales contracts, if the pledged goods have been in use for some time. Whether exercised or not, the possibility of repossession serves as a powerful threat to debtors.

Enforcement of Security Versus Court Action
There is a distinction between enforcing security and using the courts to collect debts. In the first instance, the lender exercises a right given by the borrower when the loan was arranged; as explained above, the creditor can take any of the steps specified in the contract without resorting to the courts. If the creditor does not realize enough from the sale of the pledged assets, or decides not to enforce

security, the creditor can sue the debtor in the appropriate court. The court will determine the validity of the creditor's claim on the debtor and will decide how much is owed to the creditor. If the creditor wins the case, there are ways to coerce the debtor to make payment. Court collection of debts is discussed in Chapter 14, under the heading "Using the Courts to Collect Debts."

Regulations and Policies

Consumer credit practices are governed by federal laws and by provincial statutes, as well as by the policies of lenders. It may be difficult at first to distinguish between government regulations and commercial policies. Laws can be changed only by legislatures, and regulations can be changed only by an order-in- council; but lender policies can be altered much more readily and are therefore often modified in response to the pressures of competition. For instance, determining acceptable levels of risk or deciding when a loan is in default are based on a firm's policy.

Federal Regulation

The power to regulate consumer credit is shared between the federal and provincial governments. The federal government has jurisdiction over banks, promissory notes, bills of exchange, interest, and bankruptcy. In general, there is no legislated ceiling on interest rates on consumer loans. The *Small Loans Act* does state that charging more than the criminal rate of interest, which is 60 percent, is an indictable offence.

Provincial Regulation

All provinces have consumer credit laws requiring that borrowers be informed about the cost of credit. The cost of credit must be expressed both as an annual rate and as a total dollar cost. Also, all provinces have an *Unconscionable Transactions Relief Act*, which permits a debtor to apply to court for a review of a loan contract. If the court finds, after considering the circumstances, that the cost of the loan is excessive and the contract harsh and unconscionable, the transaction may be reopened and all or part of the contract set aside. There is more about the regulation of consumer credit later in this chapter (see "Credit Regulation").

Point-of-Sale Credit

As mentioned earlier (under "The Two Forms of Consumer Credit"), consumer loans are not the only type of consumer credit. Rather than having to apply for a consumer loan from a financial institution, you can often arrange to have credit at the retailer from which you make a purchase. Credit cards, charge cards, and conditional sales contracts are three types of retail credit.

Economic Significance

Canadian society depends on credit for much economic activity; the studies discussed earlier in the chapter (see the sections "National Consumer Credit Data" and "Consumer Debt Use at the Household Level") show clearly that our use of consumer credit has accelerated quite rapidly. In recent times, we have come to depend quite heavily on credit cards: approximately two-thirds of Canadians have at least one credit card, and it is not at all uncommon to have

FIGURE 13.9 DOLLAR TRANSACTIONS USING MASTERCARD AND VISA, CANADA, 1977–2005 (IN CURRENT DOLLARS)

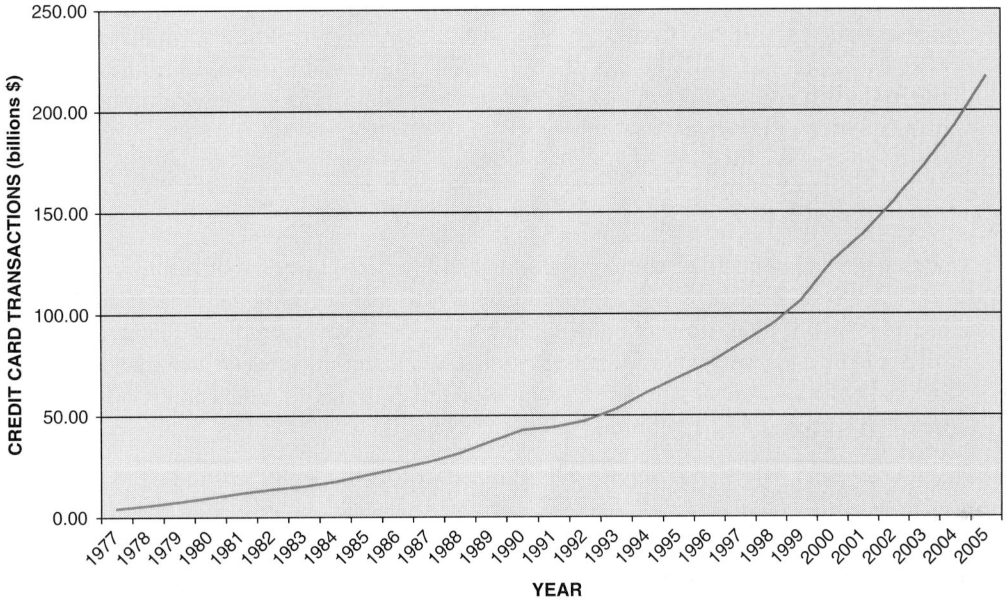

SOURCE: Canadian Bankers Association website, **www.cba.ca**, Credit Card Statistics Visa and Mastercard, DB 38 Public, March 2006.

more than one. This trend toward greater use of consumer credit cards is reflected in the increasing value of sales charged to cards issued by Visa and MasterCard between 1977 and 2002 (Figure 13.9). In 28 years, sales increased about 20 times; even when converted to constant dollars, sales have risen around 10 times. During this same period, the number of MasterCard and Visa cards in circulation more than quadrupled, to about 50 million cards. The Canadian credit card market is dominated by these two cards: together, they account for more than 50 percent of all the credit cards in circulation and for 75 percent of the total outstanding balances on credit cards.

Debit Cards

Although debit cards are not used for credit, they are included in this chapter to prevent confusion with credit cards. A **debit card**, also called a payment card, differs from a credit card in that the costs of any purchases are immediately deducted from the cardholder's chequing or savings account at the time of purchase. Some debit cards may be attached to a line of credit to handle overdrafts. Debit cards may also be used to access the cardholder's banking accounts at automatic teller machines.

Credit unions initiated the use of debit cards, most often at the local level. Other financial institutions, especially banks, have established a nationwide electronic system that allows their customers to pay for goods and services without using either cash or a cheque. With this electronic payments system in place, you can now use a plastic card to instantly debit your bank account for the week's groceries right at the supermarket's checkout counter, the gas station for your fill-up, and even at some restaurants. These cards are widely accepted because paying by debit is easy to do, but as with all other cards, the risk of loss to unscrupulous persons is a concern. So, if you use a debit card, protecting your personal identifier, or security number, at all times is important, especially when using your card at an automated teller or when paying a bill. Businesses also benefit from this system as the money is immediately transferred to their accounts, earning interest or paying down loans. As banks charge businesses to make deposits, they prefer that the transactions be electronic, and hence the banks will frequently extend a discount to those using electronic services rather than the manual systems of the past.

Point-of-Sale Credit Arrangements

Whenever you obtain credit in connection with a purchase, you are obtaining point-of-sale credit (or vendor credit)—in contrast to loan credit, which is obtained separately from purchases. We will focus on three of the most common kinds of point-of-sale credit: charge cards, credit cards, and conditional sales. Note the distinction between a **charge card**, which is based on an account that requires payment in full each month, and a **credit card**, which is based on an account that permits instalment payments.

Charge Cards

Charge cards are provided for short-term credit (about a month), primarily by oil companies and by travel and entertainment clubs, such as American Express or Diner's. Such a charge account requires full payment within a specified **grace period**—the number of days after the statement date before a late-payment penalty becomes effective. The grace period varies, but may range from 21 days to 45 days. After that, late payments will attract a penalty at a fairly high rate of interest.

Credit Cards

Revolving Accounts Credit cards are used for **revolving charge accounts**, so named because it is possible to continue charging purchases to the account as long as a portion of the bill is paid each month. There are two major types of credit cards: (i) those issued by banks, trust companies, credit unions, and other financial institutions (often called "bank cards") and (ii) those issued by retailers. Credit card accounts at financial institutions differ from retailers' credit card accounts in two respects. In the former case, the institution is providing a loan, while in the latter, the institution is selling goods. The two types of account also differ in the way that credit charges are calculated.

To open a revolving charge account (referred to in legislative documents as **variable credit**), you must complete an application form similar to the one in Figure 13.10 or one on the internet. The institution's credit department evaluates the information provided in the application and sometimes obtains your credit report from the credit bureau (explained in Chapter 14). On the basis of your current financial situation and previous credit record, the credit manager assesses your creditworthiness and establishes a ceiling on the amount of credit that you may have outstanding at any one time. See Personal Finance in Action Box 13.2, "Ivana Considers Using a Line of Credit."

Once you have opened the account, you may make credit purchases within the set limit. You will receive monthly statements reporting the account's status, including the minimum payment you are required to make that month, your outstanding balance, and how much credit you still have available. Whenever your balance reaches the account's established limit, you are supposed to stop using the card until the debt has been reduced. In some instances, though, the credit card issuer may simply increase the

FIGURE 13.10 CREDIT CARD APPLICATION

DETACH HERE AND MAIL TODAY

Request your TD Visa Card today!

MARKETING CODE: M P A 0 0 1

CHECK ONE:

☐ TD Green* Visa Card GRO ☐ TD Emerald* Visa Card EMN ☐ TD U.S. Dollar Advantage* Visa Card USI

Please Tell Us About Yourself

SALES I.D. | SALES BRANCH | BRANCH TRANSIT

☐ Mr. ☐ Mrs. ☐ Miss ☐ Ms. ☐ Dr.

Last Name | First Name | Initial(s) | Social Insurance No. (Optional)

Home Address (Own ☐ Rent ☐ Live with parents ☐ Other ☐) | Apt. No. | Telephone

City | Province | Postal Code | How Long? Yrs. / Mths.

Previous Address (if less than 2 years at current address) | City | Province | Postal Code | How Long? Yrs. / Mths.

Date of Birth M / D / Y | $ Monthly Rent / Mortgage | Preferred Language ☐ English ☐ French | Mother's Maiden Name (for security purposes)

Please Tell Us About Your Job and/or Other Income

Employer Name and Address | Occupation | How Long? Yrs. / Mths. | Current Gross Monthly Income

Current Business Phone No. | Previous Employer (if less than 2 years with current employer) | How Long? Yrs. / Mths.

Other Monthly Income / Source | Do you currently have a banking relationship with TD Canada Trust? ☐ Yes ☐ No (e.g. Bank Account, Mortgage, Investment, Loan, Visa card)

Please Tell Us About the Co-Applicant

Last Name | First Name | Initial(s) | Social Insurance No. (Optional) | Date of Birth M / D / Y

Employer Name and Address | Occupation | How Long? Yrs. / Mths.

Current Gross Monthly Income | Business Telephone | Home Telephone

Please Complete Your Options

Credit Limit Requested $________

Current TD Visa Card Account Number

☐ I'll keep my current TD Visa Card, if I am eligible for the additional credit **OR,**
☐ Cancel my current Card, transferring the balance (and if possible, Green Machine* access) to my new TD Visa Card

If you wish to access your TD Canada Trust accounts, please see your branch after you receive your Card.

Please Sign Below and Return

On this form, the words *"you"*, *"your"* and *"yours"* mean the Applicant and Co-Applicant, if applicable. The words *"we"*, *"us"* and *"our"* mean the TD Bank Financial Group††. The word *"Information"* means your personal information (except health information). It includes Information provided to us by you, including through the products and services you use, and obtained from others with your consent. You agree as follows: (a) you certify all of the above Information to be true and complete. You represent that you are presently current with all of your creditors, there are no liens or judgments against you personally or professionally and you are not now nor have you ever been bankrupt or had any part of an account written off by a creditor as not collectible; (b) you request the TD Visa* Card(s) (the "Card(s)") be issued to you as indicated above, and renewals or replacements thereof from time to time; (c) you will read and be bound by our Visa/Chargex† Cardholder Agreement (the "Agreement") that you will receive with your Card(s); (d) each of you is a Cardholder for the purpose of the Agreement; (e) each of you is jointly and severally (individually and collectively) liable for all obligations (including repayment) under the Agreement; (f) use of the Card(s) by any one of you shall evidence receipt and your agreement to the terms of the Agreement; (g) **How We Use Information** – We may use Information: to establish and serve you as our customer(s); to determine whether any products or services of the TD Bank Financial Group are suitable for you and offer them to you; or when required or permitted by law. If you provide us with your Social Insurance Number (SIN), we may use it to verify your identity and to keep your Information separate from that of other customers with a similar name, including Information obtained through the credit approval process. We may share Information within the TD Bank Financial Group, where permitted by law; and (h) **Collection and Use of Credit Information – We may obtain Information about you from parties outside the TD Bank Financial Group, including through a credit check, and verify Information with them.** You authorize those parties to give us the Information. We may disclose Information to: other lenders and credit bureaus – this helps establish your credit history and supports the credit approval process; any authorized user for whom you request a Supplementary Card and suppliers of services that you receive as an included benefit with the Card or that you request in order for the supplier to establish and serve you as a user of that service.

You may obtain our privacy code – "Protecting Your Privacy" – or review your options for refusing or withdrawing this consent, including your option not to be contacted about offers of products or services, by contacting your branch or calling us at 1-866-567-8888.

APPLICABLE IN THE PROVINCE OF QUEBEC ONLY: It is the express wish of the parties that this Agreement and any directly or indirectly related documents be drawn up in English. Les parties ont exprimé la volonté expresse que cette convention et tous les documents s'y rattachant directement ou indirectement soient rédigés en anglais.

* Visa International Service Association/TD Canada Trust, licensed user of Mark.
† TD Canada Trust, licensed user of Mark.

†† The TD Bank Financial Group means The Toronto-Dominion Bank and its affiliates, who provide deposit, investment, loan, securities, trust, insurance and other products or services.

Your Signature X ____ Date Month / Day / Year | Co-Applicant's Signature X ____ Date Month / Day / Year

875 Highland Rd. W. 0395
KITCHENER, ON N2N 2Y2

SOURCE: TD Canada Trust, reproduced with permission.

limit, without consulting the cardholder; the new credit limit will just be shown on the next statement.

Grace Period Most credit card issuers offer the cardholder a certain number of days after the statement date, called a grace period, in which to make full payment without interest charges. Some low-interest-rate accounts, however, have no grace period. Generally, bank, trust company, and credit union accounts have a grace period of 21 days, while retailer accounts offer between 21 days and 30 days. There is no grace period on amounts carried over from previous months, or on cash advances.

Personal FINANCE in action 13.2

Ivana Considers Using a Line of Credit

When Ivana moved to a new city for a job promotion, she had to set up new banking arrangements. Transferring her credit card and chequing account from the branch at her bank to another branch was no problem. The bank officer did, however, offer her a line of credit that would be tied into the credit card and provide unsecured credit up to $15 000 whenever she needed the money. At the same time, the account would be linked to her chequing account and debit card, so that any time the account was overdrawn, the money would be automatically advanced for a transaction fee of $3. This arrangement sounded excellent to Ivana, as there was significant travel involved in her new position, and she frequently found banking difficult to conduct when far from home.

The interest rate on the line of credit would be the same as her credit card for balances under $2500 and prime plus 3 percent for any balances over $2500. However, any advances would be charged interest from the date of the advance and not from the date of the statement. To make matters even more complicated, the whole banking arrangement would be accessible via the internet or over the telephone. In this way Ivana could pay bills or make transfers from wherever the job demanded her presence. The convenience was enticing, but Ivana was concerned about the increased availability of such a large amount of credit, the interest charges, and the possibility of losing her access card and someone else running up a large balance for which she would be responsible.

Cash Advances Credit cards issued by financial institutions permit cash advances, within limits, as well as retail purchases. These advances are treated as small daily loans, with daily interest charged from the date on which the funds are advanced.

Comparative Interest Rates It is instructive to compare the relation between the Bank Rate (defined in Chapter 9) and the rates charged on retail and bank cards between 1981 and 2001 (Figure 13.11). During most of that time, there was a substantial spread between credit card rates and the Bank Rate; note that interest rates for retail cards were the highest and the most infrequently adjusted. One reason for high interest rates on credit cards is the substantial risk associated with them; credit card issuers lose millions of dollars each year through uncollectible debts and fraudulent use of these cards.

Note also that credit card rates changed slowly in response to changes in the Bank Rate. Two contributing factors that make credit card rates "sticky" are (i) the requirement that issuers give their cardholders at least a month's notice (six months in some provinces) of a change and (ii) the large fixed costs of running a credit card operation. Before concluding that it will cost more to use a retail card than to use a bank card for instalment credit, you should examine the different methods of calculating interest charges, which will be demonstrated later in this chapter (see "Interest Charges").

Lost or Stolen Credit Cards If a credit card is lost or stolen, the owner's responsibility tends to vary with the policy of the company issuing the card. In Alberta, Manitoba, or Quebec, however, cardholders have no legal obligation for any debts incurred after they have notified the company of the loss. If any bills are charged after the loss and before notification, the cardholder's responsibility in Alberta and Manitoba is limited to about $50. All banks limit the cardholder's liability to $50 after notification. Some firms offer insurance protection against lost or stolen credit cards in return for an annual fee.

FIGURE 13.11 THE BANK OF CANADA RATE AND CREDIT CARD INTEREST RATES

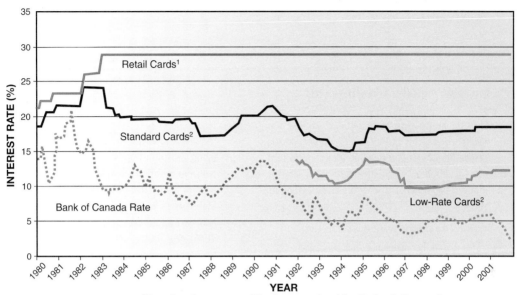

[1]Based on the average of the Sears card and the Hudson's Bay card.
[2]Based on the average of the six major banks (for purchases).

SOURCE: The Bank of Canada Rate Changes and Credit Card Interest Rates from "Credit Cards and You," Spring 2003, © Financial Consumer Agency of Canada. Reproduced with the permission of the Minister of Public Works and Government Services Canada, 2003.

Premium Credit Cards Nowadays, you can get more than credit with a credit card. For an additional fee, it is possible to have a kind of super credit card, called a premium card, that provides such features as a higher credit limit, travel insurance, guaranteed hotel reservations, collision insurance on rental cars, health insurance, a credit card registry, airline points, and travellers' cheques. To determine whether or not you would

Lost and Stolen Credit Cards

In 1991, of the roughly 25 million bank credit cards then in use in Canada, more than 600 000 were reported lost or stolen. Of the 37 000 that were used fraudulently, 8000 were taken from an unattended purse, jacket, or locker, and 6000 from automobiles. Some were stolen from lockers at recreational facilities, and about 5000 lost cards were left behind in restaurants and bars. A few cards are also pilfered from the mail every year.

Before reporting a card as lost, it is wise to check with family members. When a credit card is reported as lost or stolen and someone uses it, this becomes a criminal matter. If a family member should inadvertently use your lost card, you may be surprised to find yourself caught up in the justice system.

By 2005 there were over 56 million bank credit cards in use in Canada and over 1.25 million were lost or stolen. The banks wrote off over $168 million in 2005 due to fraudulent use at merchants and unapproved users of credit cards.

benefit from having such a card, you must evaluate your need for these additional services in relation to the extra cost involved. The annual fee may be in the range of $100 to $150.

Do You Need a Credit Card?

Consumer and Corporate Affairs Canada has developed a set of questions to help you decide (i) whether or not you need a certain credit card and (ii) whether you can afford it. A slightly adapted version of these questions appears below.

(a) Why do you want this credit card?

(b) What inconveniences are you experiencing by not having this credit card?

(c) When and why would you use this credit card rather than cash, a debit card, a cheque, a personal line of credit, or your existing credit card(s)?

(d) What types of purchases would you be making with this credit card, and how often would you be using it?

(e) How much new credit do you feel you require, and why?

(f) What portion of your current average monthly expenses is related to the use of existing credit cards?

(g) How would the use of this credit card affect your monthly expenses?

(h) Would you expect to pay your monthly balance in full? If not, what repayment schedule would you meet?

(i) Can you afford new debt, and how will you budget for it?

(j) Should you be trying instead to cut back on your use of credit cards?

Conditional Sales Contracts/Agreements

For the sale of high-priced items—such as vehicles, appliances, and furniture—that are paid for in instalments, the retailer may use a conditional sales contract rather than a revolving charge account in order to increase the vendor's security in case of default. With a credit card sale, the vendor has no security claim on the merchandise purchased; instead, the vendor has only the borrower's signature with a promise to repay. A **conditional sales contract** (sometimes referred to as a conditional sales agreement), however, permits the creditor to retain title of the goods until they are paid for, with the option of repossessing them if the buyer defaults. For more information, see the heading "Conditional Sales Contracts" later in this chapter.

Rates for Point-of-Sale Credit

There is no regulation of the rates charged either on revolving charge accounts or on conditional sales because it is expected that competition among creditors will keep rates in line with other forms of consumer credit. At present, a comparison between lenders shows interest rates to be about the same for similar forms of credit. There is, however, variation among types of credit at any given source (Figure 13.12). Although the interest rates move up and down, the relationship among rates for different types of credit remains fairly stable.

FIGURE 13.12 CREDIT AND CHARGE CARD INTEREST RATES, CANADA, 1992

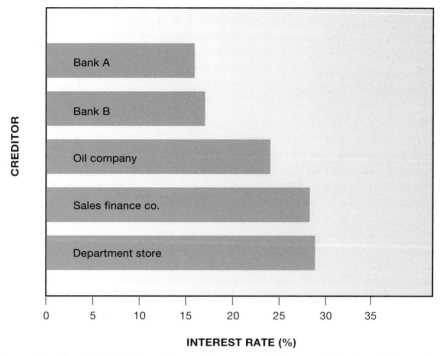

SOURCE: Data from *Credit Card Costs* (Ottawa: Consumer and Corporate Affairs Canada, September 1992). Reproduced with the permission of the Minister of Public Works and Government Services, 2004.

Credit and Charge Card Costs

Holders of credit cards may be charged for two types of costs: (i) transaction or annual fees and (ii) interest. Each will be examined in turn.

Transaction or Annual Fees

Some financial institutions, such as banks, trust companies, and credit unions, may impose either an annual fee (between $8 and $15) or a transaction fee (15 cents per transaction). Travel and entertainment cards (which, as we have seen, are charge cards, not credit cards) have much higher annual fees, perhaps in the range of $30 to $55 for a basic card, with additional fees charged for some of the optional services. As mentioned earlier, fees for premium cards typically run much higher, sometimes totaling well over $150 per year. Retailers usually do not charge fees for their credit cards. With this much variation in costs, it is worthwhile to check out the fees before applying for a credit card.

Interest Charges

Interest charges are not a concern for the 50 percent of credit cardholders who pay their total outstanding balance each month, but they are of some significance to the rest of us. Two important factors affect interest costs on partial or instalment payments: (i) how often interest

Women take CHARGE 13.1

Crystal had received her first credit card. She found it useful when shopping because she could make purchases without paying in cash. This was not only convenient but enabled her to spend money she did not currently have.

Crystal co-signed a loan for $500 as a supportive gesture for a friend. When the friend moved away without paying the loan, Crystal was held responsible for the $500, which depleted her cash resources. Thus the credit card enabled her to make purchases even though she was low on funds. When the credit card bill came due, she did not have the money to make the required payment. She was shocked to learn that the effective annual rate of interest on her credit card was over 19 percent. The fine print showed that the interest rate on the credit card was 1.5% per month. After compounding, the effective annual rate was 19.56 percent ($1.015^{12} - 1 = 19.56\%$). It took several months for Crystal to finally pay off the credit card debt. The interest paid could have been money saved to earn interest. Instead she was paying interest out.

The credit card experience prompted Crystal to take inventory of the way she was handling her finances. She started to keep a record of her expenditures and found that while some of the expenses were necessary, others were not. She prepared a budget to serve as a guideline for prudent management of her resources. Crystal saved enough to eliminate the credit card debt.

Crystal has put use of the credit card on hold. She has arranged with her bank to set up a line of credit to handle emergency needs. The line of credit charges a lower interest rate than the credit card issuer. Now that Crystal is again debt-free, she has decided to "pay herself first" and contribute 10 percent of her monthly paycheque to a savings account.

is calculated and (ii) timing, or when the interest charges are applied. Lenders can change their methods of calculating interest at any time, making it difficult to generalize about these matters. The essential point of this section is to make you aware that methods of determining interest charges can be quite complex and that consumer information about these charges is often hard both to obtain and to understand. (This chapter's Women Take Charge recounts the steps one woman took to repair the financial damage stemming from her confusion about her credit card rate.)

Frequency of Interest Calculation Banks, trust companies, and credit unions calculate interest on the daily outstanding balance. For example, suppose you use a bank card to charge three purchases that are posted to your account on March 2, March 12, and March 23, respectively, and you make a partial payment after receiving the first statement. Daily interest charges on Purchase A begin March 2; those on Purchase B begin March 12, and those on Purchase C begin March 23. This approach makes it virtually impossible for cardholders to figure out the interest charges on bank cards. Retailers, on the other hand, are more apt to charge interest on the monthly balances.

Timing of Application of Interest Charges When you receive a credit card statement, you have the option of (i) paying the balance in full without interest, or (ii) making a partial payment. If you choose the latter option, you may be surprised to find that some financial institutions charge interest for three periods: (i) from the date the credit card office posts the transaction to the next statement date, (ii) from one statement date to the next, and (iii) from the second statement date to the payment date (called **residual interest**). The amount of residual interest due appears on the second statement.

Retailers, on the other hand, generally charge interest on a monthly basis, starting from the statement date, not from the purchase date (except in Quebec, where all interest must be calculated daily). Usually, retailers do not charge residual interest; interest charges apply only to the balance outstanding after partial payment is made, accruing from the previous statement date. One example of such complexity is described in Personal Finance in Action Box 13.3, "Gina's Charge Accounts," and is illustrated in Figure 13.13. However, by changing the assumptions about the proportion of the debt repaid each month, a different result may be obtained. The point of this example is to illustrate the complexity involved in interest charges on credit cards rather than to present a model that is generally applicable.

Effect of Substantial Payment If your partial payment represents 50 percent or more of the balance you owe, credit card issuers differ in when they apply interest charges. Retailers usually subtract the partial payment from the outstanding balance before calculating the new interest charges. Financial institutions, however, calculate interest on the previous total balance and then subtract the partial payment. When the partial payment is less than 50 percent of the balance, retailers do not subtract the payment before calculating the interest.

Personal FINANCE in action 13.3

Gina's Charge Accounts

Soon after she starts her first job, Gina applies for and is given two credit cards—a bank card and a department store card. She makes purchases using each card that are posted to her accounts on March 2, 12, and 23. Soon after the end of the month, statements arrive from both the bank and the retailer: both statements are dated March 30.

When Gina settles down to pay a batch of bills on April 11, she knows that if she pays these credit card bills in full, there will be no interest charges. But she is a bit short of funds at the moment, so she decides to pay only half of each bill. Each statement indicates the minimum payment due, but neither shows any interest charges.

In May, new statements (both dated April 30) arrive for both credit cards, showing how much she has paid and how much interest has accrued.

Gina knows that there is a difference in interest rates (16.75 percent on the bank card and 28.8 percent on the store card), but she does not understand how the interest is calculated. After some investigation, she learns that the retailer has charged interest on the unpaid portion of her bill for the month between statement dates. On the other hand, the bank card's interest charges began from the date her purchases were posted. Moreover, each charge is divided into three periods—(i) from the posting date to the statement date, (ii) from one statement date to the next, and (iii) from the second statement date to the payment date (residual interest)—as shown in Figure 13.13. After her partial payment on April 11, the bank charged her interest on the new balance.

On May 13, Gina pays the total outstanding balance shown on each of her April 30 statements. Although she has not charged any other purchases to her bank card in the meantime, she is surprised to find another interest charge on the May 30 statement. That charge, she learns, represents residual interest for the period between April 30 (the last statement date) and May 13 (the payment date).

continued

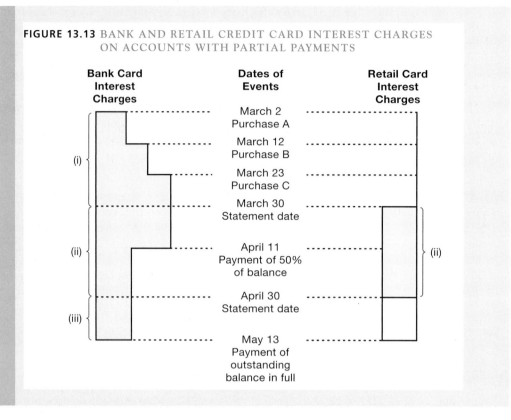

FIGURE 13.13 BANK AND RETAIL CREDIT CARD INTEREST CHARGES ON ACCOUNTS WITH PARTIAL PAYMENTS

Nominal and Effective Interest Rates Nominal interest rates on revolving charge accounts can vary significantly; recently the range extended from 16.75 percent to 28.8 percent. (Recall from Chapter 7 that the nominal interest rate is the quoted rate, but that this rate may not be the same as the more significant effective rate—that is, the real rate of interest.) Unfortunately, the complex calculation methods make it quite difficult to compare effective annual interest rates on credit cards.

Conditional Sales Contracts

When you examine the sample contract in Figure 13.14, you will notice that a conditional sales contract is quite similar to a chattel mortgage. Both state the terms of the credit agreement, describe the security pledged, and specify the penalties for failing to honour the contract's terms. The main difference is that the former document is a sales agreement rather than a loan agreement. The vendor retains title to the goods until complete payment has been received, reserving the right to repossess the pledged goods if the buyer does not make payments as scheduled.

Acceleration Clause

A statement indicating that the lender can demand immediate payment of the total outstanding debt if the borrower is late with one or more payments, or does anything else that makes the lender feel "insecure," is called an **acceleration clause**. Such a clause is often included in credit agreements for the benefit of the lender. By making the total balance due at once, the lender positions itself to initiate court proceedings to collect the debt, rather than having to wait for each monthly instalment to become in arrears.

FIGURE 13.14 CONDITIONAL SALE CONTRACT

CONDITIONAL SALE CONTRACT

SELLER: Keyboards Plus
Name

Address
Peterborough, Ont.
City Province P.C.

BUYER(S): [illegible signature] Trainski
Name(s)

Address
Peterborough, Ont.
City Province P.C.

Dear Customer:
We are writing this Contract in easy-to-read language because we want you to understand its terms. Please read your Contract carefully and feel free to ask us any questions you may have about it. We are using the words, *you, your* and *yours* to mean all persons signing the Contract as the Buyer. The words *we, us* and *our* refer to the Seller.

Contract Coverage: We sell and you buy the following Property and/or Services:

Description of Goods	Make	Model	Serial No.	Price
Piano	Yamaha	YH252	23Y3467	#3560

SEE REVERSE SIDE FOR TERMS OF THIS CONTRACT

Disclosure of your credit costs:

Cash Price	$ 3560.00
Less Trade-In	$ —
Net Cash Price	$ 3560.00
Provincial Sales Tax +GST	$ 534.00
Fees for Registration	$ 10.00
Total Cash Price	$ 4104.00
Cash Down Payment	$ 304.00
Amount Financed	$ 3800.00
Scheduled Finance Charge	$ 1216.18
Total Amount of Contract	$ 5016.18
Annual Percentage Rate 28.22 %	

Payment Schedule: Your payment schedule is 24 payments of $ 209.03, except the last which shall be the balance owing. Each payment shall be due on the first day of each month beginning June 1, 19 XX, or one month from the date of this Contract if not otherwise specified.

Date of Contract May 18th, 19 XX

Notice to Buyer: Do not sign this Contract before you read it, or if it contains any blank spaces.

1. Please note that in connection with this credit application a consumer report containing credit information or personal information may be obtained by the prospective creditor. If you so request the creditor will inform you of the name and address of the consumer reporting agency supplying the report. Any information obtained in connection with this credit application may be divulged to other credit grantors or to a consumer reporting agency. 2. When you sign this Contract, you acknowledge that you have read and agreed to all its terms. 3. Be sure and read the terms and conditions contained on the reverse side of this Contract as they are binding on you as well. 4. All copies must be individually signed in ink.

[illegible signature]
Seller's Signature

I hereby guaranty payment of the total of payments of this Contract:

Guarantor's Signature

You confirm receiving a completed copy of this Contract with disclosures of your credit costs.

[illegible signature] Trainski
Buyer 1's Signature

Paul Wong
Buyer 2's Signature

AP 24 ONT. Ed. 9/89

continued

FIGURE 13.14 CONDITIONAL SALE CONTRACT (CONTINUED)

TERMS AND CONDITIONS

1. Promise to Pay: You promise to pay the total amount of contract according to your payment schedule.

2. Interest Rate: The rate shown on the front page as Annual Percentage Rate shall be the rate agreed upon for the computation of pre-judgment and post-judgment interest and shall be used in the computation of any such interest by a Court of Justice when making an order or granting a judgment to enforce this contract.

3. Credit Statement: You certify that all statements in your credit statement are true and complete and were made for the purpose of obtaining credit.

4. Warranties: Unless you have been given a written warranty, there is no warranty on the goods purchased and no statements or promise made by any party shall be valid or binding.

5. Title: Title, and therefore legal ownership, to the goods which you have purchased by this Contract does not pass to you until payment in full of this Contract. You understand and acknowledge that the Seller, and any assignee of the Seller, retains a continuing security interest in the goods which you have purchased until payment in full of this Contract. Furthermore, you agree not to transfer possession or control of the property to any other person without first notifying us by registered mail of your intention to do so.

6. Location: You agree that the goods are to remain at the address indicated on the front of this Contract. If you wish to move the goods, you must notify us by registered mail before you do so. The registered letter can be sent to the same address where you send you payments. If you move from the address shown on the reverse side, you must notify us of your new address without delay.

7. Insurance: It is your obligation to keep the property insured against fire and theft. You acknowledge that any loss, injury or destruction of the property covered by this Contract does not relieve you of your obligation to pay the full amount owed on the Contract.

8. Default: You will be considered in default under the terms of this Contract if:

a) you fail to make any payment on time;
b) you fail to meet any promise you have made in this Contract;
c) you become insolvent or bankrupt;

d) the property is lost or destroyed;
e) the property is seized in any legal proceeding.

9. Remember: *If you are in default under this Contract, we have certain legal remedies available to us. We may, at our election,*

a) *demand that the full balance owing be paid immediately;*
b) *take possession of the goods according to law;*
c) *commence legal proceedings for recovery of the balance owing.*

Where we have taken possesion of the goods, you will be sent the required notice which will explain how you may regain possession of the goods. If you do not do so, we will be entitled to dispose of the goods at a public or private sale, or at an auction. We may exercise our rights at any time. Where a deficiency has resulted from such a sale, we may commence legal proceedings for recovery of the deficiency, if permitted by law.

10. Additional Charges on Default: You agree to pay a delinquency charge of 5¢ per each $1.00 of any instalment which is not paid within 5 days after the instalment due date. You agree to pay interest at the same annual percentage rate as stated in this contract after maturity on any unpaid balance which remains.

11. Insufficient Funds Charge: In the event a cheque tendered for payment is returned for insufficient funds, we may collect a $10.00 charge as a reasonable charge for expenses incurred, over and above any other charges.

12. Refund: If you repay in full one month or more before the maturity date of this Contract, a portion of the Total Amount of Contract shall be refunded to you, calculated according to the Consumer Protection Act of Ontario and the regulations. We are entitled to retain an additional amount of $20 or one half of the refund, whichever is less. You are not entitled to the rebate if after deducting the amount we can retain, the rebate is less than two ($2.00) dollars.

13. Assignment: You understand that this Contract may be assigned by the Seller. The assignee will then be entitled to all the rights which the Seller may have had.

14. Applicable Law: Any part of this Contract which is contrary to the laws of any province shall not invalidate the other parts of this Contract.

THIS CONTRACT CONTAINS THE ENTIRE AGREEMENT BETWEEN THE PARTIES

Assignment of a Conditional Sales Contract to a Third Party

Signing a conditional sales contract gives you the chance to buy—and to begin enjoying the use of—a high-priced durable good sooner than you might otherwise have been able to afford it. Such contracts accomplish this by distributing the cost over a number of months or years. Retailers find that this approach encourages sales but also ties up working capital that they need to buy new stock. This difficulty is solved by sales finance companies and some banks, which make a business of buying conditional sales contracts from retailers—a transaction sometimes referred to as selling credit paper.

Careful examination of most conditional sales contracts may reveal a statement specifying that the contract may be assigned to a third party—a named financial institution. The blank contract forms that are often supplied to the retailer by the sales finance company may bear the name of that company. The arrangements made between retailers and sales finance companies vary, but the sales finance company usually buys the contract from the retailer for a sum equal to the item's purchase price; this makes it equivalent to a cash sale from the retailer's perspective. The purchaser now makes payments directly to the sales finance company that holds the contract.

The sales finance company makes its profit from the interest part of the contract. Depending on competition and economic conditions, the sales finance company may offer the retailer an additional premium, or it may charge a discount.

Credit Regulation

Historical Background

Consumer protection legislation began proliferating in the mid-1960s, continuing to expand until all provinces had enacted one or more laws that confirmed consumers' rights in credit transactions. This surge of legislative activity reflected the fact that the use of consumer credit had increased fairly gradually in the 1950s but had accelerated in the 1960s. But many consumers, having little expertise in the credit market, were at a disadvantage in their dealings with large corporate creditors. Consequently, provincial governments tried to come to the consumer's aid with consumer protection legislation.

Until the middle of the twentieth century, most credit transactions had been conducted between businesses, and both businesses were typically experienced in the credit market; except for informal charge accounts at the local store, few consumers ever entered the credit market. This pattern changed after 1950, with the advent of mass production of high-priced consumer durables that were merchandised on a "buy now, pay later" basis. Unsophisticated buyers, unversed in credit or contracts, entered the market, enlarging the demand for both the durables and the credit; but unfortunately many consumers signed contracts they did not understand, waiving rights they did not know they held.

Not surprisingly, some borrowers got into difficult situations for which they had no legal defence. Provincial legislatures responded by entrenching certain rights of consumers in law and by setting up ministries of consumer affairs to oversee the regulation of credit. The provinces' aims were laudable, but the ministries' budgets were rarely sufficient to provide help on the required scale. Although consumers acquired rights that lawyers and creditors knew about, most consumers remained unaware of these rights. The resources allocated either for public information or for law enforcement were insufficient. Consumers still benefited from the legislation, however, because lenders knew the rules and tried to follow them.

The different provincial statutes that regulate credit contain many similar provisions. The following very general discussion is limited to some of the highlights. For greater detail or precision, consult the relevant legislation in your province. In most provinces, the statute in question is called the *Consumer Protection Act*; in New Brunswick and Saskatchewan, the equivalent laws are called the *Cost of Credit Disclosure Act*; and Alberta's residents are protected by the *Consumer Credit Transactions Act*.

Disclosure of Credit Charges

One of the main achievements of the consumer protection legislation was to require creditors to disclose all the costs of credit, both as annual percentage rates and as total dollar amounts. Because of divided federal–provincial jurisdiction regarding the regulation of consumer credit (interest is a federal matter, while trade is a provincial one), there was uncertainty about exactly which costs of borrowing could be called interest. Consequently, the provincial acts generally avoid using the word interest, substituting a broader term—credit charges—instead. Disclosing the full cost of credit, both as an amount and as a rate (an approach referred to as "truth in lending" in the United States), is now mandatory in all provinces and states.

After the disclosure laws had been in effect for a number of years, some research was done to determine whether consumers using this information were aware of the true interest rates in comparison shopping for credit. Many borrowers were found to be generally insensitive to interest rates and more concerned with the size of their monthly payments. Apparently, users of consumer credit are often more interested in shopping for the purchase than in shopping for the financing.

For variable credit or revolving charge accounts, the disclosure requirements stipulate that the borrower must be told in advance what the interest rate will be and that after extending the credit, the lender must provide a statement showing the outstanding balances at the beginning and end of the statement period, the amounts and dates of each transaction, and the cost of borrowing expressed in dollar amounts.

When a conditional sales contract is used for a consumer purchase, it is subject to provincial consumer protection legislation regarding disclosure of credit charges and the content of the contract. The statutes covering conditional sales contracts may refer to them as a type of **executory contract**—that is, one in which both parties have made promises regarding future action, but have yet to act.

The rules for disclosure of credit costs apply to conditional sales contracts whether they are signed at the vendor's premises or in the customer's home. The method of calculating credit charges on conditional sales is set forth in the regulations that accompany the various provincial acts. The disclosure legislation contains a list of information that must be included in an executory contract (e.g., a conditional sales contract) if the total cost of the purchase, excluding credit charges, is above a specified amount—typically around $50. Essentially, the contract must contain the full name and address of both the buyer and the seller, a description of the goods being purchased, and details about the financial transaction.

Supervision of Itinerant Sellers

Do door-to-door sellers exert undue pressure on people to buy their products? Perhaps. At any rate, each province has legislation that allows consumers time to change their minds about contracts signed in their own homes. In fact, the consumer's right to cancel the agreement can apply to any sales contract signed at a location other than the company's place of business. The length of this "cooling-off" period varies from province to province, but within the specified time, a consumer may cancel the contract simply by informing the company of his or her intention to do so. This is best done by registered mail, but verbal notice is acceptable in some provinces. The date on the letter's postmark is usually considered to be the time the notice was received by the company. When calculating the cooling-off period, do not include Sundays and statutory holidays (i.e., a standard seven-day calendar week would comprise only six days—Monday through Saturday—that would count as part of the cooling-off period). If you cancel a conditional sales contract during the cooling-off period, you are expected to return any goods that you received and possibly to pay compensation for having had the use of them; the seller is expected to return any down payment. A summary of the relevant legislation by province is shown in Table 13.1.

Prepayment of Credit Contracts

Most creditors arrange the repayment of accounts by calculating the credit charges on the outstanding balance at the end of each month, as discussed in Chapter 7. Less frequently, a precomputed schedule of credit charges may be used. In both instances, the monthly payments are of equal size, comprising varying amounts of principal and interest. The difference is that the proportions of interest and principal are established in advance in the precomputed schedule, instead of being computed for each payment period. The monthly

TABLE 13.1   COOLING-OFF PERIODS BY PROVINCE

PROVINCE	LEGISLATION	LENGTH OF COOLING-OFF PERIOD	NOTIFICATION OF CANCELLATION
Newfoundland and Labrador	*Direct Sellers Act*	Within 10 days of date on which contract was signed.	Sent or delivered by means of proving the notice is sent, in which case it is deemed effective on the date it is sent.
Prince Edward Island	*Direct Sellers Act*	Within 7 days of date on which contract was signed.	In writing or by personal delivery, telegram, or registered mail to vendor's last known address. When sent by registered mail, it is deemed effective on the day after it is mailed.
Nova Scotia*	*Direct Sellers Licensing Act*	Within 10 days of date on which contract was signed.	Written or by personal delivery to direct seller or to one of the direct seller's sales representatives or by registered mail to address shown on contract, in which case it is deemed effective at time of mailing.
New Brunswick	*Direct Sellers Act*	Within 10 days of receiving a copy of the contract. Within 5 days of date on which contract was signed.	Written, to direct seller or to one of the direct seller's sales representatives or by personal delivery, fax, registered mail, or any other method that permits the purchaser to provide evidence of cancellation.
Quebec*	*Consumer Protection Act*	Not later than 10 days after buyer receives copy of contract.	By returning goods to vendor's address, by written notice, or by returning the contract.
Ontario*	*Consumer Protection Act*	Within 2 days after buyer receives duplicate original copy of contract.	Written, by personal delivery or by registered mail to address stated in contract, in which case it is deemed effective at time of mailing.
Manitoba*	*Consumer Protection Act*	Within 10 days of date on which contract was signed.	Written, by personal delivery by fax, or by registered mail to vendor, provided proof of date of cancellation is given when sent.
Saskatchewan	*Direct Sellers Act*	Within 10 days of date on which contract was signed.	Written, by personal delivery, fax, or registered mail to vendor's last known address. If sent other than by personal delivery, it is deemed effective on the date sent.

continued

TABLE 13.1   COOLING-OFF PERIODS BY PROVINCE   (CONTINUED)

PROVINCE	LEGISLATION	LENGTH OF COOLING-OFF PERIOD	NOTIFICATION OF CANCELLATION
Alberta	*Direct Sales Cancellation Act*	Not later than 4 days after date on which buyer receives copy of contract by personal delivery or by mail.	Written, by personal delivery or mailed to vendor named in contract. If no contract, notice sent to any address of sales representative known to buyer. Deemed effective at time of mailing.
British Columbia*	*Consumer Protection Act*	Not later than 7 days after date on which buyer receives copy of contract.	Written, by personal delivery or mailed to seller's address as stated in contract or to any address of seller known to buyer.

* In these provinces, legislation is effective only when the purchase exceeds a minimum dollar price.

In Manitoba and Nova Scotia, if the contract does not include rescission rights, the cooling-off period is 30 days after the goods or services were delivered.

All provinces, except Ontario and Quebec, provide for cancellation after longer periods if certain conditions are not met.

computation offers more flexibility to a borrower who may wish to repay the debt faster than scheduled. In such a case, the lender simply charges interest on whatever principal sum is outstanding at the end of the month, subtracts this amount from the payment, and uses the remainder to reduce the principal. (You may wish to review the section "Compound Interest on Instalment Loans" in Chapter 7.) Precomputed charges create more complexity if the borrower wishes to repay early; but since precomputed charges are becoming less common, we will not go into the details here.

Unsolicited Credit Cards and Goods

Provincial legislation sets limits on your responsibility for unsolicited goods or credit cards you may receive.

Unsolicited Credit Cards Five provinces prohibit the issuing of unsolicited credit cards (Table 13.2). Other provinces do not make it illegal to send out such cards, but they make it quite clear that if a credit card was not requested, the intended recipient has no legal responsibility for transactions made with it unless some indication of acceptance was made, such as signing the card and presenting it to a vendor.

Unsolicited Goods Prince Edward Island is the only province that prohibits sending unsolicited goods. In British Columbia, Newfoundland and Labrador, Nova Scotia, Ontario, and Saskatchewan, the recipient of unsolicited goods has no responsibility to return, pay for, or take any special care of such goods. But if residents of British Columbia or Saskatchewan acknowledge having received such goods (e.g., by signing for them—but even simply using an unsolicited credit card constitutes acknowledgment of having received it), they lose their immunity from responsibility.

TABLE 13.2   PROVINCIAL LAWS REGARDING UNSOLICITED CREDIT CARDS

THE LAW STATES THAT. . .	PROVINCES WHERE THIS LAW APPLIES
issuing of unsolicited credit cards is forbidden.	Alberta, Manitoba, New Brunswick, Prince Edward Island, Quebec
if an unsolicited credit card is received, the recipient has no legal obligation for transactions made with it, unless he or she writes to the card's issuer stating that he or she intends to accept it.	Alberta, British Columbia, Newfoundland and Labrador, Nova Scotia, Ontario, Saskatchewan
signing and using an unsolicited credit card is considered to be acceptance of responsibility for the card.	Alberta, Newfoundland and Labrador, Nova Scotia, Ontario
if an unsolicited credit card has not been accepted, the intended recipient has no responsibility if the card is lost or misused.	Alberta, British Columbia, Ontario, Newfoundland and Labrador, Nova Scotia, Saskatchewan

Advertising the Cost of Credit

All provinces regulate advertising the cost of credit. This became necessary because retailers and lenders had begun to deceive potential customers by advertising credit arrangements in such a way as to be misleading. For instance, an advertisement might have stated that there would be no down payment without telling the rest of the story. Lenders who advertise the cost of credit must indicate the cost of borrowing expressed as an annual percentage rate. If other information about the credit terms is to be advertised, lenders are required to present all relevant information, which includes the number of instalments, the amount of the down payment, and the size of each instalment.

Repossession of Secured Goods

If a debtor is in default, the creditor can usually seize the secured goods without a court judgment. However, provincial laws place some restrictions on this process. In practice, most creditors prefer to press for payment of the debt rather than become involved in the complications of repossession. Although threatening to repossess is a powerful weapon for encouraging borrowers to make payments, carrying out the threat is not worthwhile for creditors unless the pledged goods are of significant value. The creditor usually has the right to repossess the goods, sell them, and claim against the debtor for any balance not covered by the sale. But because some unscrupulous creditors would sell the goods at a lower price to friends and then sue the debtor for the difference, some provinces (Alberta, British Columbia, and Newfoundland and Labrador) have "seize or sue" laws that allow the creditor either to repossess secured goods or to sue, but not to do both.

Promissory Notes on Conditional Sales Contracts

A promissory note is not only an unconditional promise to repay a debt; it is also a negotiable instrument. Like a cheque, it can be endorsed and made payable to a third party. A promissory note is generally implied in a conditional sales contract, but when such a contract is sold, there are some restrictions to protect borrowers. A person who holds the usual type of promissory note can demand payment regardless of any responsibilities for delivery, quality of goods, and so on. But anyone who buys a conditional sales contract from a retailer shares responsibility with the retailer for ensuring that the obligations associated with the goods are met. The vendor and the third party, usually a sales finance company or a bank, share the responsibility for ensuring that the goods or services are satisfactory for the intended purpose.

Issues and Problems

Credit Cards

Need for Standardized Disclosure Despite the widespread use of credit cards, their costs are not well understood by many users. The available cards differ significantly in two kinds of costs: (i) non-interest costs (such as annual or transaction fees) and (ii) the terms and conditions associated with interest charges. To make rational choices, consumers must understand each credit card's terms and conditions. But the present state of information disclosure makes this level of understanding impossible. Although the nominal interest rates are readily available, they are not, as we have seen, an accurate basis for comparing costs.

Some of the information that card issuers do provide is not presented in an easily understandable form. For instance, many people believe that a partial payment will proportionately reduce the interest charges, but this is not the case with all credit cards. Consumers would be well served by having a standardized set of terms and conditions for calculating interest charges on credit cards, as is the case for consumer loans.

In 1987, in response to a demand for better information about credit card costs, Consumer and Corporate Affairs Canada began issuing a brief release called "Credit Card Costs" three times a year. It includes a chart comparing credit cards by fees, grace periods, interest rates, and the period to which interest charges apply. Contact the department if you wish to be on its mailing list for these updates.

Disputes with Retailers A complicating aspect of purchases made with bank cards is that if you need to dispute any goods or services you purchase with them, you must deal with a retailer who has already been reimbursed by your financial institution. The bank or other institution, which specifically states in your cardholder agreement that it takes no responsibility for merchandise or services you may purchase using its card, will not be interested in hearing about the dispute. While trying to resolve the dispute with the retailer, you must also keep your payments to the card's issuer up to date. Withholding payment for the disputed transaction will not help resolve the dispute; in fact, it will merely cause you further expense and trouble, since more credit charges will be added to the unpaid amount. Instead, you will need to handle the problem exactly as you would handle an unsatisfactory cash purchase.

Some consumers have faced a quite different problem. They have had the unfortunate experience of having a credit card rejected at the point of sale, despite a good payment record. The cause could be an employee error, or it could be that the card issuer's computer has detected unusual purchasing patterns of the sort that might reflect the use of a stolen card. When mix-ups like this occur, it is difficult to get the problem resolved in a store or hotel lobby. One alternative is to ensure that you always have another method of payment— such as cash, a debit card, or another credit card—available.

Credit Card Costs There is no restriction on the interest rates that issuers may charge on credit card debt. Legislators have apparently assumed that cardholders will be able to compare costs among various sources of credit and make rational choices based on the information they gather. An estimated 70 percent to 80 percent of cardholders pay interest charges at least some of the time. Banks claim that they need high interest rates to cover losses from fraud and default. Yet the delinquency rate on bank cards is only about 1.5 percent, compared with 2 percent on other bank personal loans.

Contracts

Two significant problems that consumers face when they sign credit contracts are their weak bargaining position and the difficulty of understanding the legal terminology used in the contracts. Chattel mortgages and conditional sales contracts are drawn up by lawyers who are hired to protect the creditors' interests, not those of consumers. As a borrower, your choices are limited: you can either accept the contract as it stands, or reject it and go elsewhere for credit. The salesperson or credit manager usually lacks the authority to renegotiate the credit contract's terms to suit you—and rarely understands the contract any better than you do. It is encouraging, however, to find that some creditors have started to rewrite their contracts in language that is much easier to understand.

Conditional sales contracts are quite similar to a chattel mortgage. Both state the terms of the credit agreement, describe the security pledged, and specify the penalties for failing to honour the contract's terms. The main difference is that the sales contract is an agreement where the vendor retains title to the goods until complete payment has been received and usually reserves the right to repossess the pledged goods if the buyer does not make payments as scheduled.

Summary

- Consumer debt is the personal debt of households excluding mortgages. Mortgage debt is any debt secured by real property. The sum of consumer and mortgage debt is referred to as the total debt. Total consumer credit outstanding equals reported outstanding debt to lending institutions by consumers.
- Current dollars are the value of recorded debt by lenders. Constant dollars are current dollars corrected for inflation, estimating constant prices. Debt burden is the ratio of debt to income. Personal disposable income is the total income received by people after income tax is paid. Real income reflects income after adjustment for inflation. Discretionary income is the amount of income left over after paying for food, clothing, and shelter.
- Consumer loans are usually obtained from a financial institution. Point-of-sale credit is usually obtained through credit cards, charge cards, or a conditional sales contract.
- Spread is the difference between the amount paid for deposits and loans. Living trusts are established while the donor is alive; testamentary trusts are established by a will.
- Credit unions are financial co-operatives owned by their members. By definition, the members of a credit union are bound together by a common bond, such as place of employment.
- Terms of the loan include amounts, rate, security, and length of time for repayment. In contrast, *term* of the loan is the maximum length of time the loan is to be outstanding. The maturity date is the day by which the loan is to be fully repaid. The prime rate is the lowest interest rate that financial institutions charge.
- A loan that is fully secured is one that has collateral equal to the value of the loan. A loan is partly secured when the collateral is less than the amount of the loan. A promissory note is an unconditional promise to repay the loan. A co-signer (guarantor) agrees to repay the loan should the borrower fail to do so. Wage assignment is an agreement that the lender may collect a portion of the borrower's wages to repay the loan. Tangible assets pledged to secure a loan are referred to as collateral. Movable goods are called chattel. A chattel mortgage (security interest) transfers ownership of the asset to the lender.

- Lien is a claim registered against the property of the borrower. A borrower is in arrears (delinquent) when he or she does not adhere to the terms of the repayment schedule, and in default when the payments are delinquent and there is no success in obtaining payment. To enforce security is to realize on the collateral pledged.
- Debit cards directly access the bank accounts of the holder. Charge cards generally require payment in full each month. Credit cards require minimum repayment each month.
- A credit card permitting continued use providing a minimum payment is regularly received is called a revolving charge account or variable credit. The grace period is the time permitted for the borrower to pay his or her credit off without interest charges applying. A conditional sales contract (agreement) permits the vendor to retain title of the asset until the asset is paid for.
- Residual interest is the amount of interest charged from a second statement date till payment is received. An acceleration clause in the conditional sales contract permits the lender to speed up repayment of the loan.
- An executory contract is another technical term for a conditional sales contract.

Key Terms

acceleration clause (p. 464)
charge card (p. 456)
chattel (p. 449)
chattel mortgage (security interest) (p. 449)
collateral (p. 446, 449)
common bond (p. 442)
conditional sales contract (agreement) (p. 460)
constant dollars (p. 433)
consumer debt (p. 431)
consumer loan (p. 438)
co-signer (p. 447)
credit card (p. 456)
credit unions (p. 441)
current dollars (p. 433)
debit card (p. 455)
debt burden (p. 434)
discretionary income (p. 434)
enforce security (p. 453)
executory contract (p. 468)
fiduciary (p. 440)
fully secured (loan) (p. 446)
grace period (p. 456)

in arrears (delinquent) (p. 453)
in default (p. 453)
lien (p. 449)
living trusts (p. 440)
maturity date (p. 444)
mortgage debt (p. 431)
partly secured (loan) (p. 446)
personal disposable income (p. 434)
point-of-sale credit (p. 438)
prime rate (p. 445)
promissory note (p. 446)
real incomes (p. 434)
residual interest (p. 462)
revolving charge account (p. 456)
spread (p. 439)
term of the loan (p. 444)
terms of the loan (p. 444)
testamentary trusts (p. 440)
total consumer credit outstanding (p. 432)
total debt (p. 431)
trustee (p. 440)
variable credit (p. 456)
wage assignment (p. 448)

CHAPTER 13 ■ Consumer Credit and Loans **475**

Problems

Note: You may need to consult the appropriate consumer protection legislation for your province to find the information needed to answer these questions.

1. What are the four reasons for using consumer credit suggested in the chapter? Are there any other reasons you can suggest? What, in your opinion, is the primary reason for using consumer credit?

2. Have you observed any difference between your parents' and your own generation's use of credit? Comment. Any differences between male and female?

3. What changes have you faced in your own use of credit? Have you increased your usage? And if so, to whom? What are or will be your monthly payment, term, and total expected payments when the loan comes due? (Hint: Don't forget any student loans.)

4. What are the responsibilities of a person who co-signs a loan?

5. (a) Why did the Dubois (see "Borrowing to Buy a Car" below) pay a lower rate of interest on the fully secured loan?

   (b) Was the loan for the car fully or partly secured? How can you tell?

   (c) The loans officer at the bank told the Dubois that credit life insurance would be included at no additional cost. Does that mean that if Peter or Chantal were to die, the other would receive some money from insurance? Explain.

Borrowing to Buy a Car

The Dubois have had two experiences with consumer loans. First they borrowed money from the bank to buy a washing machine. By using Chantal's Canada Savings Bonds as collateral, they were able to obtain a fully secured loan at a low interest rate.

A year later, Peter and Chantal realized that they needed a new car, but they knew that they could not pay cash for it. They thought about approaching the credit union in Brandon, Manitoba, where Peter worked, but since he had never joined it, he wasn't sure how their request would be received. Remembering how easy it had been to borrow at the bank, they went back for a larger loan. The loans officer asked them to sign a chattel mortgage on the car and gave them the loan.

   (d) There are real estate mortgages and chattel mortgages. What characteristics of the security that the Dubois pledged differentiate these mortgages?

   (e) Must the Dubois carry insurance on this car? Does it matter to the bank?

   (f) If the Dubois wish to trade in this car and get another before the debt is repaid, do they need to consult the bank, as long as they make their payments?

   (g) If the bank's loans officer had reservations about the ability of the Dubois to repay the loan on schedule, would she

   i. offer them a signature loan?

   ii. offer them a loan without credit life insurance?

   iii. require more security before making the loan?

6.   What factors would a loans officer consider if you or one of your friends walked into a bank today to apply for a loan? Would these factors change as you age 10, 20, or 30 years? What would you expect to happen to the interest rate you pay over the same periods of time?

7.   Shameem was frustrated because the lawn mower she purchased from Handy Appliances, using her Visa card, had been defective since she brought it home. She took it back to the store but was unable to get satisfaction there. When she first called the store, an employee of the store told her, "Bring it in and we'll look it over." But the store turned out to be only a sales outlet and to have no service personnel. The store suggested that she try the mower again, as it appeared to be in working order. Meanwhile, her Visa bill arrived. Since she was contesting the sale, she advised Visa that she would not pay the bill until she was either satisfied with the mower or provided with a replacement. In time, another Visa bill arrived: the mower remained on the bill, and now a credit charge for delayed payment had been added.

   (a)   Where can Shameem find out what her rights are in the dispute with Visa?

   (b)   What are these rights?

   (c)   What is your opinion of the situation? What would you recommend that Shameem do?

   (d)   What rights does Shameem have with the retailer?

   (e)   What interest rate would Shameem pay if she obtained a cash loan with her Visa card? How does this compare with the rates that banks charge for personal loans? (Refer to the business section of your newspaper or call a financial institution to gather the information you need before answering this question.)

8.   If you obtain a cash advance on your Visa card and repay it all when the bill arrives, will you pay any credit charges?

9.   Suppose that you and a friend each want to own a particular computer game so that you can play against each other via modem. You buy the appropriate software using your debit card, while your friend makes a parallel purchase using a credit card. What differences would there be between the two transactions?

10.   Proceed to any of the financial institution's websites listed below in "Personal Finance on the Web" and explore the consumer credit area.

   (a)   What credit facilities may you apply for?

   (b)   What are the terms of the credit card?

   (c)   What are the interest rates charged on the loan, line of credit, or credit card?

   (d)   What do you authorize the financial institution to do regarding your past?

   (e)   Are there any specific services for students available at the site?

   (f)   How comfortable do you feel placing your confidential information on the web?

   (g)   Would you use the web to apply for credit? Why or why not?

11.   Proceed to Consumer and Corporate Affairs Canada's website at **www.fcac-acfc.gc.ca/ eng/consumers/Quizzes/default.asp**. Proceed through the credit card quiz. How did you fare?

12.   Proceed further to the Credit Card Cost Calculator at **www.fcac-acfc.gc.ca/eng/ consumers/resource/calculator.asp**. What is the lowest rate you could pay for a cash advance of $500 regularly used? Is it worth it?

References

BOOKS

Beares, Paul. *Consumer Lending*. Third Edition. San Francisco: American Bankers Association, 1997. An industry-specific training manual from the lender's perspective.

Consumer and Corporate Affairs Canada. *Charge It: Credit Cards and the Canadian Consumer*. Ottawa: Consumer and Corporate Affairs Canada, 1989. Minutes and proceedings of a House of Commons Committee that reviewed the background regarding Canadians' problems with credit card costs, the extent of market competition, and current disclosure practices, and made proposals for legislation. Data in appendix.

Dymond, Mary Joy. *The Canadian Woman's Legal Guide*. Toronto: Doubleday, 1989. Includes a section on women and credit.

Graham, Terry, and Pamela Graham. *Credit Cure: A Guide to Improving Your Credit*. Aurora, CA: Credit Cure Publications, 1996. Two experienced lenders and credit bureau managers outline a step-by-step method for reviewing and improving your credit standing. Caution, however: since this is an American book, some of the authors' advice will not apply in Canada. Still, the general material is useful.

PERIODICALS

Canadian Commercial Law Guide. Don Mills, ON: CCH Canadian, Topical Law Reports. Subscription service in two volumes on federal and provincial laws regarding the sale of personal property and consumer protection.

Canadian Economic Observer. Ottawa: Supply and Services Canada, monthly. (Catalogue No. 11-010.) Published by Statistics Canada.

Credit Card Costs. Ottawa: Consumer and Corporate Affairs Canada, three times a year. Lists fees, interest rates, grace periods, and date from which interest is calculated by name of creditor. Free copy on request.

Personal Finance on the Web

Bank of Canada
www.bank-banque-canada.ca The resource centre and home for the institution that regulates our banks and influences interest rates and exchange rates. Includes many references for both historical and projected economic and financial perspectives.

Bank of Montreal
www.bmo.com Provides full exposure to all aspects of bank operations, including both personal and commercial banking. You can even apply for a MasterCard on the internet.

Canadian Bankers Association
www.cba.ca The website for the association representing all the banks of Canada offers informative and helpful guides to successful financial management.

Canadian Financial Network
www.canadianfinance.com Solid information regarding personal finance for Canadians with extensive links to other relevant sites.

Canadian Imperial Bank of Commerce
www.cibc.com Allows you to apply online for loans and credit cards; also provides numerous financial tools for such tasks as calculating your mortgage or applying for insurance.

Citizens Bank of Canada
>   **www.citizensbank.ca** This bank, owned by Vancity Credit Union, has no branches; it does all its business over the telephone or via the internet.

Credit Union Central of Canada
>   **www.cucentral.ca** This home of the majority of the credit unions in Canada assists in locating and speaking for over 500 credit unions in Canada.

Financial Consumer Agency of Canada
>   **www.fcac-acfc.gc.ca/eng/consumers/resource/default.asp** This branch of Industry Canada provides excellent tools and insights into the complexity of the financial industry of Canada. Many calculators are also available.

ING Bank of Canada
>   **www.ingdirect.ca** This international bank is making significant inroads into Canadian financial markets. It possesses no branches but has two offices in Toronto and Vancouver. The majority of its business is conducted via the internet or over the telephone.

RBC Royal Bank
>   **www.royalbank.ca** Incorporates all information on investments, mutual funds, loans, and so on, covering all facets of the bank's operation.

Scotiabank
>   **www.scotiabank.ca** A fully searchable site with significant information on most facets of financial planning.

TD Bank Financial Group
>   **www.tdbank.ca** Provides financial management tools and allows you to apply for loans, personal lines of credit, mortgages, and Visa credit cards.

TD Canada Trust
>   **www.tdcanadatrust.com** Includes the company's online banking service, from investment services to a list of automated teller locations.

Visa
>   **www.visa.com** Describes and offers worldwide services. Be aware, though, of "flagged" material that applies only in the United States.

chapter 14

Credit, Debt, and Bankruptcy

"Bankruptcies don't just occur when economic times are bad; they can hit any time a person runs into an unexpected bump in the financial road."
Douglas Hoyes, C. A., Trustee (Hoyes, Michalos and Associates, Kitchener, Ont.)

Learning Objectives

Understanding the concepts discussed in this chapter should help you become a smarter consumer.

After studying this chapter, you should be able to:

1. Outline the role of credit bureaus in the establishment of credit ratings and risk assessment.

2. Define consumer rights according to the relevant legislation.

3. Show how collection agencies assist creditors and how they are controlled by provincial legislation.

4. Discuss the ways in which debts may be collected without going to court as well as by suing a debtor.

5. Discuss the role of garnishments and execution orders in debt collection.

6. Distinguish between the various kinds of garnishment.

7. Define the various terms associated with credit reporting such as credit file, credit scoring, and third-party collection.

8. Identify six major causes of overindebtedness.

9. Discuss the process of negotiating with creditors and when doing so may be appropriate.

10. Explain the costs and benefits of a consolidation loan and the process of a debt repayment program.

11. List seven reasons for the high rate of consumer bankruptcies.

12. Distinguish between a consumer proposal and a bankruptcy.

13. Explain the duties of five actors in the insolvency process.

14. Outline the results of bankruptcy for both creditors and debtors.

15. Evaluate the possible benefits of a consumer proposal for an insolvent debtor.

16. Define the following terms: overindebtedness, debt management, bankrupt, and discharged bankrupt.

17. Identify six methods of consumer fraud.

Introduction

This chapter deals with the use and abuse of credit, with credit reporting, and with debt. It also deals with the roles of credit bureaus in the establishment of credit as well as with those of collection agencies in dealing with debt. It is a sad fact that many Canadians get into financial difficulties and have to declare bankruptcy. We will examine some of the causes of overindebtedness and what forces some people to become bankrupt. We will then look at what people who are in great debt can do to deal with the problem, including consumer proposals and bankruptcy.

Credit Reporting

When you apply for credit, the lender must estimate the probability that you will be able to repay the debt as scheduled. What does a lender need to know in order to predict your reliability and your capacity to repay this debt? The creditor starts by assessing your application for credit, in which you provide quite a bit of information about yourself—for instance, your residence, occupation, bank, salary, mortgage, and consumer debts (see Figure 13.10, "Credit Card Application"). In addition, the lender may want to know how you have handled previous credit transactions; such information can be obtained from the local credit bureau.

The Credit Bureau

A **credit bureau** is a business that sells information about credit transactions to its subscribers, who are mostly creditors and other businesses. The credit reporting business in Canada is currently dominated by a large multinational company and a few smaller ones that are in competition with each other.

Credit bureaus obtain funds by selling memberships to firms that extend credit—especially financial institutions and retailers—as well as to a variety of other businesses that need information on the credit histories of customers. Employers and landlords have an interest in subscribing to the credit bureau, as do life insurance companies; however, to become a member, each must have a legitimate business interest in such credit information.

Credit bureau subscribers pay an annual membership fee in addition to a charge for each credit report that they obtain. These days, most credit reports are transferred electronically from the credit bureau to the member, instead of by telephone as would have been the case in the past. Now, with electronic transmission of information, credit bureaus can easily send reports nearly anywhere in the world. The service contract signed by members binds them to using the information obtained from the credit bureau for strictly bona fide business purposes only. It also requires that they give the credit bureau any relevant credit information they have about their customers.

The Credit File

Anyone who has credit cards or charge accounts, has ever obtained a mortgage or another type of loan, has rented accommodation, or is connected to utilities such as telephone or hydro, probably has a **credit file** at a credit bureau. Most of the information in the file comes from three major sources: the individual, the individual's creditors, and public records. Each time you apply for credit, the facts supplied on the application form are transferred to your credit bureau file by the credit grantor when a credit report is drawn.

In addition, it is common practice for major credit grantors, such as bank credit card companies, large retailers, and financial institutions, to send their entire credit files to the credit bureau every month via computer. These computer files, which report the status of all their credit accounts, are electronically merged with those already in the credit bureau files. The information in a credit bureau file includes the account number, the outstanding balance, and whether payment has been made on time. Items of public record, such as chattel mortgages and conditional sales agreements registered with provincial authorities, and reports on court judgments or bankruptcies are obtained by the credit bureau and added to the files.

Since credit bureaus computerize their files, the bureaus can easily and quickly share information. For a sample credit report, visit **www.equifax.com/EFX_Canada** and click on "Consumer Information Centre" and "Your Credit Report."

Applying for Credit

Whether done in a store or online, applying for credit is remarkably simple. According to numerous department-store online application forms, it can be obtained in less than a minute. All the applicant needs is a valid Canadian address, an employer's name, and a reference from a company whose card he or she already has. In addition, the sites stress that a report from a credit bureau is essential, but how this is obtained in less than a minute is not clear.

To have a good credit rating, the applicant must have a history of paying bills on time. The credit bureau will make the information it has collected available to businesses, landlords, employers, or any organization questioning a person's credit history. There are few rules requiring a credit bureau to check the identification of those requesting credit information.

The requirements when applying for credit for the first time are slightly more rigorous. A good, steady job that provides an income greater than expenses is essential. It is also easier if the person has assets and good credit references. The latter can be obtained by opening a savings account and making regular deposits or by having a chequing account that is never overdrawn. Credit can also be established if hydro, gas, and telephone bills are paid on time. Applying for a store credit card is another way to start. These cards are easier to get because they have a lower credit limit.

Some of the qualifications are waived for students. The only requirements they must satisfy are Canadian residency and some income, often as little as $1200 per year.

Credit Rating

The decision regarding whether or not to extend credit is made by the credit grantor, not the credit bureau. Credit bureaus merely collect and sell information; they do not assess anyone's capacity to handle credit. In the interests of efficiency and of keeping costs down, large retail firms are coming to depend heavily on an automatic assessment system, called **credit scoring**, whereby points are given for certain characteristics. The weight given to these characteristics may vary somewhat from retail firm to retail firm—as well as from time to time, as the retail firm makes credit easier or harder to obtain. There is general agreement that the traditional three Cs—capacity, character, and collateral—play an important part. Higher scores are assigned to those who own property, who show stability in where they live and in their jobs, who possess several credit cards, who have paid past obligations on time, who do not write bad cheques, and who have a low debt/income ratio.

A credit score, produced by either **Equifax** or **TransUnion**, is known as a **FICO score**. Created by the American firm Fair Isaac & Company, a FICO score is determined by mathematical formulas calculated according to information contained in a person's Equifax credit history. Scores range from a low of 300 to a high of 850, with low scores indicating that the application for credit is a bad risk. FICO factors and their weighting are as follows:

- past payment history (35 percent): bankruptcies, late payments, past due accounts, and wage attachments
- amount of credit owing (30 percent): amount owed on accounts, proportion of balances to total credit limits
- length of time credit has been established (15 percent): time since accounts opened, time since account activity
- search for and acquisition of new credit (10 percent): number of recent credit inquiries and number of recently opened accounts
- types of credit established (10 percent): number of various types of accounts (credit cards, retail accounts, mortgage)

It should be pointed out that errors could be made in a person's credit history. It is therefore recommended that everyone obtain a credit report from time to time and correct any errors it may contain.

The distribution of FICO scores in Canada is shown in the following table:

TABLE 14.1   NATIONAL DISTRIBUTION OF FICO SCORES IN 2004

Up to 549	550–599	600–649	650–699	700–749	750–799	800–849	850+
4 percent	4 percent	6 percent	11 percent	19 percent	27 percent	24 percent	5 percent

SOURCE: Copyright © Fair Issac Corporation. Used with permission.

Lenders have programmed their computers to score the information on the application form quickly and to indicate whether the applicant is a good risk, a bad risk, or an uncertain risk. In the first two instances, the decision regarding whether to grant credit or not is fairly obvious and may be made without contacting the credit bureau. A firm may decide, for example, that all applicants whose scores rank in the top 10 percent to 15 percent will be considered good risks and will be automatically accepted, while the bottom 30 percent will be considered bad risks and will be automatically rejected. About half the applicants thus fall into the "uncertain" category. More information is needed about these applicants in order to reach a decision; credit bureau reports (which cost the credit grantor money) will then be drawn only for this group of people.

Since the assessment of your creditworthiness depends on the creditor, you may find that at any one time some lenders will grant credit while others will not. Obviously, this is more apt to be true if you fall into the uncertain category because creditors vary in the levels of risk they are willing to accept. Nevertheless, whether or not credit will be granted may be influenced by factors other than personal history. Lenders' policies are affected by conditions in the economy and by the situation in the lender's own business. Sometimes a lender has surplus funds and is very anxious to lend, but at other times scarce funds or poor economic conditions (such as high unemployment) may discourage lending.

The Consumer and the Credit Bureau

Many users of consumer credit are unaware that some of their financial transactions are on file at the credit bureau; in fact, they may never even have heard of the credit bureau. Often, they discover its existence only when there is a mix-up over their files or when they are refused credit. The policy of the Associated Credit Bureaus of Canada, and a legal requirement in all provinces, is that consumers be permitted to know what is in their files, if they ask.

Regulation of Credit Bureaus

All of the provinces and territories except for New Brunswick have laws that regulate consumer reporting agencies, including credit unions. The two basic concerns reflected in these laws are (i) the consumer's privacy with regard to credit information and (ii) the consumer's right not to suffer from inaccurate credit or personal information.

The penalties for breaking these laws can be quite steep. For example, in Ontario anyone found guilty of knowingly providing a consumer reporting agency with false information or contravening the act is liable to a fine of up to $50 000 or to imprisonment of up to one year, or both. A corporation committing a similar offence can be fined up to $250 000.[1] Governments obviously take the rights of consumers quite seriously.

Information in Files Provincial laws make a distinction between **consumer information** (which includes such details as name, address, age, occupation, residence, marital status, education, employment, estimated income, paying habits, debts, assets, and obligations) and **personal information** (which has little to do with financial transactions and includes, for example, character, reputation, and personal characteristics). Credit bureaus are restricted to consumer information only. Although the details differ, all of these acts limit the type of information that can be included in a consumer report; generally such reports must be restricted to consumer information. In addition, there are limits on the inclusion of detrimental information in a credit report. For example, in Ontario, the time limit for reporting that a bankruptcy occurred is seven years from the discharge date for the first bankruptcy. After two bankruptcies, the information is never deleted from a person's file. In Saskatchewan, no credit reporting agency may include information regarding any debt six years after the debt was paid, or if no payment was made, six years after the person first went into debt. In addition, any information harmful to the consumer may not be included unless it is voluntarily supplied. Disclosing other detrimental information that is more than seven years old is also prohibited. Restrictions are set on the situations in which consumer reporting agencies may make reports. Acceptable circumstances include being required to do so by a court order and receiving a request from a person or organization who is concerned with extending credit, with renting, with employment, or with insurance.

Permission for Credit Report Consumer reports, also known as credit reports, may not be requested unless a consumer either has given written consent or is sent written notice that the report was obtained. Ontario requires that notice be given before the report is obtained. In Saskatchewan, as in most provinces, consumers must give consent before a credit report is issued. A request for permission to obtain a report may be included in a credit application, as in Figure 12.10.

If you have not applied for credit, the credit bureau cannot give a credit report to a third party without informing you of the request and providing you with the third party's name and address.

[1] www.cbs.gov.on.ca/mcbs/english/56VMM5.htm.

Access to Own File As a consumer, you have the right to know what is in your credit bureau file. You can ask the local bureau to tell you what is in your record. If you find that the information there seems inaccurate, the agency must make every effort to verify the record and to correct any errors. (See Personal Finance in Action Box 14.1, "Sonya and Her Credit Report.")

Personal FINANCE in action 14.1

Sonya and Her Credit Report

Sonya's friend Darlene told her that she had recently applied to Equifax Canada for a current credit report. Much to her dismay it gave her a very bad credit rating. She found upon closer examination that most of the negative information related to things that she had never done. She always paid her bills on time—not, as the report said, never. It also indicated that she had recently applied for bankruptcy, which she had never done. Lastly, the report showed that she had been turned down for a mortgage because she was unemployed. Correcting these mistakes had taken some time and energy and she advised Sonya to ask for her credit report as soon as possible to ensure its accuracy.

Sonya did so immediately and was asked for the following information:

- her name, birthday, address, and SIN;
- a list of her credit accounts;
- what types of bank accounts she had and with what banks;
- whether she had a mortgage and with what company.

When she received the report it had no errors. It indicated that she always paid her bills on time, never wrote cheques for which there were insufficient funds, and had never been turned down for a mortgage. Lastly, it showed that Canadian Tire had asked for a copy of her credit report when she had recently filled out an application for a credit card.

Credit Reporting Legislation

Province or Territory	Title
British Columbia	*Business Practices and Consumer Protection Act*
Alberta	*Fair Trading Act*
Saskatchewan	*Credit Reporting Act*
Manitoba	*Consumer Protection Act*
Ontario	*Consumer Protection Act*
Quebec	*Consumer Protection Act*
New Brunswick	No act
Prince Edward Island	*Consumer Reporting Act*
Nova Scotia	*Consumer Protection Act*
Newfoundland and Labrador	*Consumer Protection Act*
Yukon	*Consumer Protection Act*
Northwest Territories	*Consumer Protection Act*
Nunavut	*Consumer Protection Act*

Other Credit Reporting Agencies

Although this chapter focuses primarily on credit bureaus, brief mention should be made of two other types of reporting agencies. **Information exchanges** are formed by groups of creditors, such as small loans companies and sales finance companies, to share information about their debtors as a way of preventing the occurrence of bad debts. Information exchanges and credit bureaus are interested in the same kinds of information, though they differ in their organizational structure. **Investigative agencies**, on the other hand, collect a wider range of information, including very personal data about family relations, addictions, and so on; they may even visit an individual's neighbours for opinions on his or her character. Private investigators formed their own group in 1999 to assist in the exchange of information. Every private investigator now belongs to CPIRC, the Canadian Private Investigators Resource Centre.

Debt Collection

When a debt is in arrears or in default, the creditor is initially concerned with retrieving the money owed as quickly and cheaply as possible, with minimal destruction of the debtor's goodwill. If the first phase of debt collection—notices and reminders—is unsuccessful, difficult-to-collect debts may be handled more aggressively. They may be referred to a special collection division of the creditor's firm or to an independent collection agency. Finally, the debtor may be sued in court.

Who Does the Collecting?

From among the various possible approaches, creditors will choose whichever debt collection procedure is suitable for them and seems most likely to be successful for the particular debt. Firms in the finance business, such as banks, small loans companies, or credit unions, tend to have collection facilities to collect their own overdue accounts. Large retailers also do much of their own collecting. Smaller companies, along with independent professionals, typically tend to turn delinquent accounts over to a collection agency. Some firms will pursue overdue accounts for a time, referring only the very difficult ones for further action. For simplicity, a distinction will be made between (i) a creditor's internal debt collection practices and (ii) third-party collecting.

Internal Collection Practices Collection practices vary, but it is usual to begin with polite reminder notices or telephone calls. At this stage, most overdue accounts are collected without resorting to harassment, and without even requiring much personal contact. Debtors who remain resistant will find the creditor's collection techniques becoming progressively more aggressive, since after a point, the creditor becomes more concerned with collecting the debt than with maintaining goodwill. Though the debt may eventually be written off in the accounts of the business, it may yet be possible to collect a portion of the debt by referring the matter to a lawyer or to an independent collection agency.

Collection Agencies

Hiring a collection agency to collect an overdue account is often referred to as **third-party collection**. A **collection agency** is a provincially licensed business that specializes in collecting overdue accounts for others. Its income depends on its success in collecting, since the collector typically retains between 30 percent and 50 percent of the amounts collected but earns no fees if unsuccessful. Not surprisingly, then, collection agencies are quite energetic in their efforts to collect.

In recent years, some collection agencies have started calling themselves "collection services" and have begun offering a wider range of services to creditors. A collection service might manage another company's credit approvals. Alternatively, a bank credit card company or a large utility might arrange for the collection services to send out the usual monthly statements to cardholders or households. The collector's computers are programmed to identify anyone who is more than one day late with a payment. This way, the collector can contact the creditor to ask whether a cheque has been sent. If payment is not on the way, collection procedures can then be put in place immediately. This approach saves money for the card company or utility since it means that receivables will be outstanding for a shorter time.

Third-Party Collection Practices
Since the collection agency's staff work on commission, they are under pressure to get funds coming in as soon as possible. As a result, they usually demand immediate receipt of the amount owed—or at least evidence that it will be coming very shortly. Failing that, they will threaten to sue the debtor. In practice, the collector will sue only if there is a good chance of getting a return—for instance, if they find that there are wages that may be garnisheed or assets that can be seized. Creditors who refer debts to collectors expect to recover an average of 20 percent to 25 percent of the funds in question within three months. Collectors who cannot meet this target will lose business to those who can.

Collection procedures often depend heavily on psychological tactics, particularly in the early stages, before the collector takes the debtor to court. Measures are chosen with the aim of intimidating debtors to some degree: for example, using legal-looking forms and letterheads, referring the debt to a lawyer or a collection agency, or making threats that may not be enforceable but that will go unchallenged by uninformed debtors. At any time, the debtor can slow down or stop the collection process by making some payments.

No technique—however persuasive or intimidating—will be effective if the debtor cannot be found. Nowadays, reporting networks of credit bureaus make it much more difficult for debtors to disappear. An alert is placed on the file of a missing debtor. Whenever or wherever that person next applies for credit, his or her credit history will be examined; the creditor making the inquiry will provide the applicant's most recent address, which will then be forwarded to the creditor who is looking for the defaulter. Not all defaulters skip deliberately; some have merely moved, forgetting to inform their creditors. (For another example, see Personal Finance in Action Box 14.2, "Irving and the Bailiffs.")

Enforcement of Security
Normally, a creditor will enforce any security considered worthwhile before beginning aggressive collection processes. When the creditor holds security in the form of assets, durables, or promise of future income, the creditor also has the debtor's prior permission to realize the value of the security in the case of default. But sometimes the realized value of the security is not sufficient to cover the balance owing, and alternative procedures are needed.

Regulation of Collection Agencies
All provinces and territories have legislation governing debt collection.[2] This legislation tries to protect debtors from harassment while at the same time providing a means for creditors to collect their debts. For example, collection agencies may only telephone at reasonable times and may not bother debtors while they are at work.

---

[2]See **www.bankruptcycanada.com**.

Personal FINANCE in action 14.2

Irving and the Bailiffs

Irving Schwartz, a physiotherapist, had lived in Southside (not its real name), a mid-sized city, for 20 years. He realized several years ago that another man in town had the same name. Numerous phone calls over the years from total strangers about things with which he was not familiar had convinced him of this. The other Schwartz—who, he found out by chance, was a teacher—even used the same bank. Irving discovered this when his account was debited incorrectly for $800. When he complained to the bank, the cancelled cheque was retrieved for him to see and he was able to prove it should have been drawn on another account.

Six months ago Irving bought a new 32″ plasma TV for just under $7000, paying for it with his credit card, which had a $9000 spending limit. One month ago he received a notice from Southside TV & Audio, where he had bought the TV, telling him that his account had been turned over to a collection agency because of his repeated failure to pay anything on the account. He had paid no attention, thinking it was a mistake since he had charged the TV. Then, more recently, he had received two phone calls from the collection agency asking when he would make a payment. He explained that he had paid for the TV and that the store had made a mistake. When he arrived home from work on Thursday, two men in uniform came to his door. They asked if he was Irving Schwartz, explaining that they were bailiffs and had an order to repossess his TV. They ignored his pleas of innocence, walked in, and took the television.

The *Criminal Code* of Canada prohibits indecent, threatening, or harassing telephone calls. This prohibition applies to all collection endeavours; thus, the consumer who is being pursued for payment by someone whose activities are not regulated under provincial legislation does have some recourse. The initiative for lodging a complaint with provincial authorities rests with the consumer. Another difficulty may arise in determining what constitutes harassment. The Canadian Human Rights Commission defines harassment as "any unwanted physical or verbal conduct that offends or humiliates." This includes threats and racist or sexist remarks.

Legislation Regulating Collection Agencies

Province or Territory	Legislation
British Columbia	*Business Practices and Consumer Protection Act*
Alberta	*Fair Debt Collection Practices Act*
Saskatchewan	*Collection Agents Act*
Manitoba	*Consumer Protection Act*
Ontario	*Consumer Protection, Collection Agencies,* and *Debt Collectors Acts*
Quebec	*Office of Consumer Protection*
New Brunswick, Prince Edward Island, and Nova Scotia	*Collection Agencies Act*
Newfoundland and Labrador	*Collections Act*
Yukon	*Consumers Protection Act*
Northwest Territories and Nunavut	*Consumer Protection Regulations*

Using the Courts to Collect Debts

As mentioned earlier, the creditor who has an account in default has the right to enforce security and use reasonable collection procedures. If these are not sufficient, the next alternative is to sue the debtor. The details of the procedure vary from province to province, but a general summary of the process will indicate the procedure for collecting debts through the courts in each province.

The creditor files a claim at the appropriate court (this depends on the amount of the claim), giving the names and addresses of both debtor and creditor, and the creditor's reasons for suing. The court clerk sends the claim and a summons to the debtor, who has three alternatives:

(a) try to settle the matter out of court (for instance, by repaying the debt),
(b) file a defence if there seem to be grounds for dispute, or
(c) do nothing.

When the debtor selects the first alternative, the debtor and creditor may reopen negotiations about payment of the debt; if they reach an agreement, the creditor drops the claim. Should the debtor choose the second alternative, he or she must file a defence in the same court within a specified number of days, stating his or her reasons for disputing the creditor's claim. Anyone who decides to ignore the summons may be surprised to discover that failure to file a defence may result in a judgment against the debtor by default.

When the debtor files a defence, there may be a trial to hear both sides of the matter. On the trial date, all witnesses, the creditor, the debtor, and any lawyers for either party appear before the judge. Small claims courts are meant to be informal courts where legal counsel is not required. After hearing both sides of the story, the judge announces the decision. On very small claims, no appeal may be permitted. The judge's decision or judgment has two possible outcomes: either the debtor does not owe the money and the case is dismissed, or the debtor does owe some or all of the money claimed by the creditor. In the latter instance, the debtor is responsible for paying the amount owing, which becomes a **judgment debt**.

Enforcement of Judgment   If the debtor either cannot or will not repay the debt, the creditor can attempt to enforce the judgment in one of several ways. The creditor may choose either to garnishee the debtor's wages or bank account or to seize some of the debtor's goods under an execution order.

Garnishments   Wages or bank accounts may be garnisheed to satisfy a judgment debt. A **wage garnishment** is a court order that instructs an employer to pay into the court's trust some percentage of the debtor's wages. (Note that the terms can be slightly confusing. The word garnish*ment* applies to the court order itself; the debtor named in that document is called a garnish*ee*. The act of garnishment can be referred to by either of two verbs: to **garnishee**—the form used in this book—or simply to garnish.) If a debtor has more than one garnishment order outstanding, the court will send them out one at a time. The debtor will not be taken by surprise but will receive a statement from the court that the creditor has requested a garnishment, with time to respond to the court. The debtor can plead for a reduction in the amount taken off his or her wages and can stop the garnishment if it can be shown that steps are being taken to handle the debt problems. Sometimes, when more than one creditor has obtained a judgment against a debtor, the court may divide the funds collected by each garnishment order among the creditors, rather than handle the claims sequentially.

Personal FINANCE in action 14.3

Bahadar and the Garnishment

Bahadar owned a furniture store in Surrey. He never sold anything on credit but decided to this one time when a friend of his brother's came into the store looking for some bedroom furniture. The man, who introduced himself as Rajindar, was soft-spoken and very sincere. He worked in a camera shop, and, though he had no money now, he would begin to pay Bahadar some of the $6500 owing as soon as he was paid at the end of the following week. Bahadar agreed to loan him the money because he was his brother's friend and also came from the same village in the Punjab as they did.

When the time came for Rajindar to start making payments, nothing happened. He did not show up at the store and did not return Bahadar's phone calls. When Bahadar's brother approached him, he was told to mind his own business.

At the end of three months, Bahadar sued Rajindar in the small claims court. The court heard his argument and Rajindar did not contradict him, saying everything was true but that he lacked the money to pay for the furniture. The judge issued a court order that Rajindar start paying Bahadar at the rate of $150 per week.

Bahadar was overjoyed, but he soon found that he was no better off than before because Rajindar still paid him nothing. He then decided to garnishee Rajindar's wages. To do so, he had to prepare an **affidavit**. This identified the court order issued against Rajindar and the amount he owed. Then he filed the affidavit and a garnisheeing order in the small court registry, naming Rajindar's employer, the Far Eastern Camera Shop, in the order. The court then garnisheed $500 of Rajindar's $3000 monthly salary. Bahadar delivered the order personally to the shop owner.

Garnishment is governed by a number of regulations, including some that exempt certain persons, some that exempt a portion of wages, and some that protect employees from being dismissed when their wages have been garnisheed. Income from social security programs— i.e., welfare, Employment Insurance, or Old Age Security—is exempt from garnishment. Provincial laws specify what proportion of wages may be garnisheed: 70 percent to 80 percent of gross wages may be *exempt* from garnishment, and that proportion can be increased if the debtor can persuade the court of need. An employer that receives a garnishment order may be inclined to dismiss the employee on the assumption that he or she is not very reliable. Provincial laws attempt to prevent this, but sometimes the real reason for dismissal is difficult to discern. Homeowners are occasionally surprised to receive garnishment orders for temporarily employed tradespeople who have outstanding judgment debts.

Under a **bank account garnishment**, money can be withdrawn from a debtor's bank account to satisfy a judgment debt. As with a wage garnishment, the process of garnishment is initiated through the court. One difference is that a bank garnishment order may result in 100 percent of an account to satisfy a debt. Bank account garnishments are sometimes used to collect debts from persons receiving welfare.

Demand on a Third Party A demand on a third party may be issued by the federal government for debts incurred against the federal government (such as income tax arrears and Employment Insurance benefit overpayments). The demand on a third party is like a garnishment in many ways, but it does not require a court judgment and it allows attachment (seizure) of a larger share of income. In the case of a self-employed individual, a demand on a third party may be issued against the person's bank account.

Family Court Garnishment Whenever payments on a maintenance order are not kept up to date, the family court can issue an attachment on wages, or **family court garnishment**, that has a continuing effect, similar to a demand on a third party. Again, these are circumstances under which the percentage of the person's wages that can be attached may exceed the limits set under provincial wage legislation. In Ontario, under the *Family Responsibility and Support Arrears Enforcement Act,* a garnishment can be issued for 50 percent of gross wages minus CPP, EI, union dues, and taxes. To apply for relief, the person must file a dispute with the courts and await a hearing. At the hearing, the judge decides whether or not to reduce the percentage garnisheed.

Execution Order A creditor who has obtained a favourable judgment has the right to seize and sell some of the debtor's property to satisfy the debt. In legal terms, this process is called **executing against the debtor's property**. The goods seized must be completely owned by the debtor, without liens or mortgages attached to them. Each province's *Execution Act* exempts certain possessions, such as essential household furnishings, from seizure.

Consumer Issues

Two issues of great concern to consumer credit users relate to (i) protecting the privacy of personal data and (ii) handling the credit records of married women.

Privacy of Personal Data

With the advance of computer technology and the increasing use of credit cards, bank machines, and the internet, protecting the privacy of personal data has become a major worry of consumer groups. There is considerable information available electronically about people who use the new technology. Just who has access to this data and how it is used are two of the questions that concerned Canadians have. Some still remember the guarantees made by the federal government about the privacy of SIN (Social Insurance Number) records. Only the Canada Revenue Agency was allowed access to SIN records. Now, of course, every financial institution, as well as Canada Revenue, have access, and possession of a SIN is essential for every Canadian.

Realizing the urgency of concerns about privacy, the federal government and most of the provinces have passed laws to control access to personal data. In 2000, the federal government passed the *Personal Information Protection and Electronic Documents Act* (PIPEDA). It came into effect on January 1, 2001. Initially, the *Act* only applied to organizations regulated by the federal government, including banks and telecommunications companies. Since 2004 it also applies "to all personal information collected, used or disclosed in the course of all commercial activity."[3] This, of course, includes the private sector.

The federal government also introduced the *Canadian Code of Practice for Consumer Protection in Electronic Commerce* in January 2003. This Code deals specifically with

[3]Industry Canada, "The Privacy Protection Guide," **www.strategis.gc.ca**. Accessed January 17, 2006. In addition, all provinces have passed privacy acts. Most of these acts, however, apply only to information gathered by government organizations. They do not cover information gathered and used by the private sector. The exception is Quebec, which has legislation covering both the public and private sectors. PIPEDA will not apply to Quebec or to other provinces that pass similar laws.

purchases made online, and it is "intended to establish benchmarks for good business practices for merchants conducting commercial activities with consumers."[4]

Credit Records of Married Women

In the past, when a woman married, a credit bureau combined her credit file with her husband's. Now that does not happen; if it does, a woman can ask to have a separate file set up. Any credit bureau normally maintains a separate file for each individual. When a couple co-signs a loan or mortgage, the information in the document is entered into both their credit files. Anyone who has any doubts about how his or her record is stored can make an appointment at the appropriate credit bureau to discuss the file. Some women make a special effort to develop an independent credit history by using credit in their own names, without a co-signer. A credit report cannot be drawn for the spouse of a person who is applying for credit unless the spouse also signs the application.

Overindebtedness: Why Does It Happen?

Overindebtedness

Overindebtedness is the condition of having more debts than one can or is willing to repay. An overindebted person is often found to have several accounts in arrears, with creditors and collectors actively pressing for payment. As we saw earlier in this chapter (under "Debt Collection"), reneging on a promise to a lender may prompt gentle reminders that lead to more urgent requests, possible enforcement of security, and eventual referral of the debt to a collection department or agency. If all these measures fail to obtain results, the lender may sue the debtor in court. A lender who wins a court case gains some additional ways of collecting a debt, such as garnisheeing wages or seizing property and possessions. Of course, at any stage of overindebtedness, the debtor can take the initiative by contacting the creditor and trying to negotiate a new arrangement, by consulting a credit counsellor for help in identifying possible solutions to debt problems, or by talking with a trustee in bankruptcy (or an administrator).

Why Debtors Default

There are different degrees of overindebtedness, just as there are many reasons for becoming overindebted. Some people are unable to repay their debts because of an unexpected loss of income, unforeseen large expenses, personal difficulties, poor financial management, or some similar reason. A few are unwilling to pay, either because of disputes with creditors or retailers or because of their own irresponsibility. Those with a small amount of overindebtedness and reasonable earning capacity have the potential to get their affairs under control, perhaps with some professional help (see this chapter's Women Take Charge). Others are too deeply in debt and have such limited capacity to repay that more drastic measures are necessary.

The causes of personal bankruptcy are many and often quite complex. Personal and lifestyle problems, sometimes compounded as a result of illiteracy, are frequently to blame. These problems may include one or more of the following:

(a) a poor education,
(b) the inability to socialize and form lasting, meaningful relationships,
(c) marrying or forming a relationship at a young age,

[4]Industry Canada, "Electronic Commerce Code," **www.strategis.gc.ca**. Accessed January 17, 2006.

Women take CHARGE 14.1

Susan just completed her post-secondary education and is faced with a debt of $20 000 in student loans. Susan would like to pay off her loans as soon as possible since interest started accruing after she graduated. Fortunately, Susan's higher education landed her a well-paying job.

During her years of post-secondary education, Susan elected to carry forward her tuition and education amounts. She can now claim these amounts on her tax return as a non-refundable tax credit. The tax savings can be used to pay down the student loans. Susan will claim a second non-refundable tax credit for the interest paid on her student loan during the tax year—another aid to paying off the loan.

Susan plans to handle her finances wisely. She will keep only one credit card and pay it off every month so as to avoid high interest charges. She will pay her phone bills and utility bills on time. An interest rate of 1.5 percent per month on unpaid balances is equivalent to an effective rate of 19.56 percent per year. Timely payment of bills will enhance her credit rating.

Susan has chosen a simple, healthy but interesting lifestyle to keep expenses down. She will get a bus pass to travel to and from work and around the city. She will rent an apartment. She will engage in volunteer activities such as helping low-income taxpayers file their income tax returns. This will give her an opportunity to apply knowledge gained in post-secondary finance courses. She will enjoy outdoor activities such as biking and hiking.

It won't take long for Susan to pay off her student loan. Once the loan is paid off, she will go ahead with plans for a savings and investment program that will enable her to purchase a new car and to travel.

Individuals with student loans who are not as foresighted as Susan may find themselves mired in a sea of debt. A student must wait seven years now before a student loan can be discharged by bankruptcy proceedings. Bankruptcy is damaging to one's credit rating and morale. Students finding themselves overwhelmed by debt should contact a credit counsellor for advice or the National Student Loans Service Center for information on getting interest rate relief.

(d) addiction,

(e) serious medical problems or disabilities,

(f) large student loans,

(g) loss of job and income.

A Poor Education   Children learn most of what they know about financial management from their parents. Unfortunately, many parents know very little about finance themselves and are therefore unable to properly prepare their children to face the economic world. This problem is often compounded by an incomplete education. Many young people thus enter the world functionally and financially illiterate. As a result, they may be unable to find a good job and may be forced to live at the margins of society. Many make poor use of consumer credit and soon find themselves in financial difficulty (see Personal Finance in Action Box 14.4, "It's Never Too Young to Start").

The problem of functional and financial illiteracy has become a major public issue. At one point the dropout rate across the country was as high as 25 percent.[5] It is a very serious problem in Ontario, where an estimated 45 000 students drop out of high school each year.

[5]*Dropping Out of High School: Definitions and Costs.* Federal Department of Human Resources and Skills Development, January 17, 2006.

Personal FINANCE in action 14.4

It's Never Too Young to Start

When Tommy was a small boy, every time his father bought him candies or an ice-cream cone, he wrote down the amount he spent in a notebook he always carried. When Tommy asked why he did this, his father said, "I need to know where my money goes. If I'm not careful, there won't be enough to pay for all of the things we need as a family." To help him understand that he should be careful with his money, Tommy's father gave him an allowance as soon as he was old enough to shop by himself. Tommy then had to tell his father at the end of each week just where his allowance went. He could do what he liked with the money, but he had to know where it went. He could also not get any more from his father if he ran out.

With a dropout rate of 30 percent of the graduating class, the government was so concerned that it decided to try and reverse the trend by denying dropouts the right to drive cars.[6]

The causes for students leaving school early are not clear but are expected to be low family incomes, poorly educated parents with a lack of interest in education, and basic illiteracy. For most, of course, the result is an inability to function satisfactorily in any way, not just financially.

The Inability to Socialize and Form Lasting, Meaningful Relationships

Broken homes and dysfunctional families have become quite common in Canada. Children from such a background, following the example of their parents, may never learn to properly socialize and form stable relationships. When families break up, they must maintain two homes instead of one. The extra financial burden on single parents can become unbearable. Consumer debt is often a result.

Marrying or Forming a Relationship at a Young Age People who marry or live together at a young age often lack the financial resources necessary to run a home. They may see credit as their only option for acquiring the furniture and appliances they need. Since their incomes are often low, the burden of debt can soon become intolerable. Financial pressures can then lead to the end of the relationship and further financial hardship.

Addiction Gambling has become a serious problem in Canada. Attracted by government-run lotteries and casinos, an increasing number of people are becoming addicted. In the mid-1990s, it was estimated that some three million Canadians were harmed by gambling, and since then the popularity of the "sport" has increased greatly. An Ontario study in 2001 found that 340 000 gamblers in the province had moderate or severe gambling problems, some so severe that an estimated 200 per year commit suicide.[7] Much of the distress is caused by the financial ruin associated with gambling addiction.

Shopping is also an addiction for some people. Because buying provides pleasure, it becomes an end in itself. Fuelled by the easy availability of credit, such shoppers can soon accumulate more debt than they can afford. See Personal Finance in Action Box 14.5, "Ramon and Maria and Their Shopping Addiction," for an example.

[6]*CBC News*, December 13, 2005.
[7]Canada Safety Council, December 17, 2004.

Personal FINANCE in action 14.5

Ramon and Maria and Their Shopping Addiction

Ramon and Maria had recently moved to Canada from the US, believing Canada to be a better place to raise their two sons. Maria was Canadian with a degree in business and had little trouble finding a good job. Ramon decided that he would enroll in the business program at the local college and then look for a job. They registered their sons, aged four and five, in the local Montessori school.

The problem for Ramon and Maria—a problem they had tried to ignore when they lived in the US—was that they were addicted to shopping. Their spending habits soon exceeded Maria's income as a marketing rep for a large multinational corporation. They had bought a nice house in a good neighbourhood with a mortgage of $200 000 and were faced with monthly payments of $1290.68. They could easily afford the mortgage payments, school fees for their sons that totaled $490 a month, and Ramon's tuition of $300 a month on Maria's net income of $4000 a month. What they couldn't afford were their shopping habits. Neither of them could resist shopping. Most weekends they spent at local malls buying things they did not need. Their house was soon stuffed with furniture and their clothes cupboards were so full they could not walk into them. They also had televisions, DVD players, and stereo equipment in every room, along with computers they never used. Their sons had the most expensive toys available and rarely played with them. They were only able to pay the minimum amounts on their

credit cards and neglected to pay their utility bills until the final notices came in the mail.

One month, when the bills were piling up and they could not pay the phone bill, their service was disconnected. They decided it was time to seek professional help. An office colleague of Maria's suggested they contact an addiction centre and ask for counselling. Ramon made an appointment for the following week and Maria took the day off from work, calling in sick. The centre gave them an assessment and scheduled an appointment for the following week to discuss the results. When they returned, they were told the following:

- You have no goals or purpose in life.
- You have no hobbies.
- You have no self-esteem and only feel good when you are shopping.

To help them overcome their addiction, the counsellor suggested they try some of the following:

- Cut up all but one of your credit cards and pay the bills off as fast as possible.
- Join a service club.
- Join a fitness centre and work out on weekends instead of shopping.
- Invite friends over on a regular basis.
- Join a book club.
- Try to deposit money in the bank each week.
- Plant a flower garden.

Serious Medical Problems or Disabilities Sometimes very ill people find themselves in debt because the cost of their medications, special treatments, or special equipment is so great. Those with disabilities may be unable to find jobs that pay well and may therefore end up in debt. Problems like these occur less often today than in the past as the barriers facing disabled people continue to come down.

Large Student Loans Many students require a loan to go to college or university. Paying off this debt is rarely difficult for those who ultimately graduate and find a full-time job. But for those who drop out or who fail to find appropriate employment after graduating (a common problem in the 1990s), such a debt can lead to bankruptcy.

Loss of Job and Income Unfortunately, expenses do not stop with the loss of employment. The recent and continuing waves of corporate and public downsizing in Canada have led to more debt and bankruptcy. Those who had debts before being laid off may find themselves in an impossible situation and see bankruptcy as the only solution.

Some Common Symptoms of Insolvency A number of symptoms are often found in cases of bankruptcy. These may include one or more of the following:

(a) The debtor does not understand what happened.
(b) The debtor does not know how to handle money.
(c) The debtor does not understand basic consumer credit concepts.
(d) The debtor has never saved money and does not understand the principle.
(e) The debtor does not make budgets and does not understand the concept.

LEGAL ISSUES

The Legitimization of Usury

Usury, the charging of excessive rates of interest, has long been illegal, not just in Canada but in most countries. For example, the Catholic church in the Middle Ages considered it a sin, and those who practised it, heretics. Martin Luther considered the lending of money at 5 percent usury, a crime that should be punished by hanging. Today, what used to be a domain of the mob and hidden from public scrutiny is being practised openly from one end of Canada to the other. The usurers, or loan sharks, no longer need to ply their trade in dark alleys or dingy basements but are allowed to operate openly in strip malls and on street corners beside dry cleaners and coffee shops.

Today's loan sharks, known as **lenders of last resort** (LLRs) or **payday lenders**, offer small, unsecured loans.[8] Cheques, postdated on the borrower's next payday, cover the loans. The Criminal Code allows lenders to charge up to 60 percent, in itself a usurious rate, but lenders of last resort charge much more. For example, one payday lender wanted to charge the writer $95.63 to borrow $500 for one month. Is this an example of usury?

$$i = prt \qquad 95.63 = 500 \times r \times 1 \qquad \frac{95.63}{500} = \frac{500r}{500} \qquad r = 0.19126$$

$$r = 0.19126 \times 12 = 2.295\% \qquad r = 229.5\%$$

In addition to the interest charged, LLRs may add a number of fees or charges to the cost of the loan. These include an administration fee—also known as a processing fee, a verification fee, or a convenience charge—which can range from 10 to 35 percent of the value of the loan. A broker's fee is charged when the payday lender acts as an intermediary between the customer and the real lender. Collection fees can be charged for any loans in default and borrowers who pay their loans back early may be charged an early repayment fee.[9] In the above example it is not clear what fees are charged. From the borrower's point of view they all amount to interest.

continued

---

[8]Credit card loans are also unsecured loans. That is why the interest charged on unpaid accounts is so high.
[9]Federal Consumer Agency of Canada, *The Cost of Payday Loans*.

Who patronizes such firms? Because the industry is worth approximately $2 billion a year,[10] a great many Canadians must be. They are not street people; to qualify for such a loan, and indeed any loan, a person needs a bank account in order to write a cheque and proof of employment. Those who pay these exorbitant rates must also be financially illiterate because overdraft protection at a chartered bank is 2 percent per month or 24 percent per year.

The growth of this industry raises some interesting questions:

1. **Discussion:** Since clients of the lenders of last resort have bank accounts and jobs, why do they not obtain overdraft protection from their banks?

2. **Research:** Why has the federal government, which has responsibility for banking, allowed this new form of usury to prosper?

3. **Research:** What does the Criminal Code of Canada say about the charging of such high interest rates? Go to **http://www.canlii.org/ca/sta/c-46/sec347.html**, which gives details of Section 347 of the *Criminal Code*.

Consumer Fraud: Scamming the Innocent

One issue that is closely related to personal debt and bankruptcy is **consumer fraud**. Countless thousands of Canadians are scammed or defrauded each year. Many lose money they can never recover. Some are so badly hurt that they go from relative prosperity to outright poverty, losing their life's savings in the process. Fraud artists prey upon the elderly and the vulnerable, the rich and the poor, the well-educated and the poorly educated, the well-informed and the ill-informed. The art of conning the innocent is well-refined and widely used. No one is immune.

How does one avoid being conned? The best way is to be as informed as possible and to question every "good idea" that comes along. There is a well-worn cliché: *If something sounds too good to be true, it probably is.* While hackneyed in the extreme, this saying should be repeated and never forgotten. Many who have forgotten its simple wisdom have come to grief. Even some who have remembered it have succumbed to fraud because it is often difficult to spot a skillful con.

There are a great many scams being perpetrated on Canadians. One of the most common, and one of the easiest to spot, is the **Nigerian letter scam**. Such scams may originate in other African countries, but all are similar to the Nigerian. The widespread use of the internet has made the list of potential victims much longer. Thousands can be reached at the click of the send button. The scam takes the form of a letter or email requesting that the recipient help a government official get some money (always a vast sum) out of the country. The recipient is asked to provide a bank account where the money can be deposited and pay a processing fee. In return, he or she is promised a percentage of the money. Often there are several processing fees required. Once the recipient is hooked, his or her bank account is drained of money. To prevent being taken in by such scams, the best advice is to never divulge your bank account information to anyone you don't know and trust and to never pay anything like a processing fee for something that sounds unbelievable. The exact number of people scammed in this way is not known because often the victims are too embarrassed to tell anyone.

Another popular **computer scam** is known as **phishing**. Unsuspecting people receive what look like emails from legitimate financial organizations and are asked to update and confirm

---

[10]**www.womentodaymagazine.com/money/paydayloan.html** (16k); accessed April 12, 2006.

their financial information such as bank account numbers and SINs. To fool the recipient, the email may link to what looks like a legitimate website. An example of a phishing email is shown below.

Sent: April 14, 2005 3:58 PM

To: Jane Doe

Subject: Security Update

Dear valued "Any Bank" client,

Recently there have been a large number of identify theft attempts targeting "Any Bank" customers. In order to safeguard your account we require that you confirm your Personal details. *This process is mandatory.*

Please click link below and submit the required information.

"Any Bank" Financial Group Login[11]

Failure to do so may result in a temporary cessation of your account services pending submission. Thank you for your prompt attention to this matter and your co-operation in helping us maintain the integrity of our customers' accounts.

"Any Bank" respects your privacy. Click here to read the "Any Bank" Privacy Policy Statement. Please do not reply to this e-mail, as this is an unmonitored alias.

© 2005 "Any Bank" Inc.[12]

One common and none-too-subtle scam promises, and may even guarantee, great investment returns. The scam involves "notifying" people in a variety of ways of how they can make a lot of money with almost no effort. The con artist is well-versed in psychology and understands basic human greed. The potential victims may be told "in confidence" of a guaranteed scheme that should not be revealed to anyone else. (*We are taking you into our confidence because we trust you.*) One version of this scam starts with sending a cassette (or CD). On this cassette, one can listen to a very refined and cultured voice (to lessen the victim's suspicions) read the details of an investment suggestion. The speaker is sometimes a member of an elite organization. For a fee of hundreds of dollars, the potential victim will be allowed to join the elite group and told the secret of how to become rich. The only thing the victim gets for the money, however, is membership in a phony organization. To avoid being taken in by such a scam, all one has to do is remember that no investment return can be guaranteed except that on a GIC or a similar investment.

A well-used and successful scam is to send out false bills or invoices. Many people receive a lot of bills and may not notice a false one when it is in the midst of a pile of legitimate bills. The phony bill is paid along with the proper ones. This scam has become less common with the advent of the internet and the ability to pay bills online. But it has been replaced by internet scams where the gullible may be told they have won a vacation. Such schemes bombard users of the internet. To receive the vacation, the potential victim must pay a fee. When the vacation materializes, the victim will find the accommodation is of an inferior nature to what was promised and other unexpected bills must be paid.

Another scam, similar to the above, tells victims they have won a prize. Notification may come by mail, telephone, or the internet. To receive the prize, the victim must pay something for shipping and handling and taxes. One of the commonest of such scams involves jewellery. Once the money has been paid and the jewellery arrives, the unsuspecting

---

[11]No bank site could be accessed. This was used for illustrative purposes.

[12]Reprinted with permission of Canadian Bankers Association.

victim finds it is worthless or virtually so. Calls or letters of complaint to the company go unanswered. Its telephone number will no longer be in use and no contact with company officials can be made.

A scam much like the phony invoice scam is used by bogus charities. People perpetrating this scam are relying on the kindness of Canadians who annually give many millions of dollars to charities. Potential victims may receive a notice that looks like it comes from a legitimate charity. This notice may thank them for last year's donation and ask for it to be repeated. The notice may also thank them for their pledge and ask for early payment. They may receive a telephone call from someone who sounds as if he or she is representing a real charity. The caller might use words like *heart, stroke, blind,* or *cancer.* Often the caller speaks so quickly that all the potential victim hears is the bait word. And all written communications look genuine. To avoid being stung by this kind of fraud, people who wish to donate to charity should select one or a few real charities and donate only to them.

This scam is also worked on a door-to-door basis. When the unsuspecting open their doors, they are greeted by someone reputed to be from a proper charity, and this person may even have phony name tags and receipts. Municipalities frequently warn their citizens about such scams. The best way to avoid being hurt is not to give money at the door unless you are absolutely certain that the person does represent a charity. Legitimate charities usually use neighbourhood residents who are known or recognized in their community.

The elderly are often hooked by someone going door to door acting as a salesperson for a home repair company. The homeowner will be told that her roof is in need of re-shingling, which can be done cheaply because the roofing company is in the neighbourhood offering special deals to seniors. A decision must be made quickly before the offer expires. Usually there is nothing wrong with the roof. If the homeowner agrees, some work may be done but it is often shoddy. A roof that did not leak may now do so. When the victim realizes he or she has been taken, the dubious company has left town and cannot be contacted. To avoid this scam, homeowners need to get several quotes for any major home repairs and renovations from established companies.

Alternatives for the Overcommitted Debtor

A creditor has a number of options to try to force a debtor to repay a debt, some of which may be quite unpleasant. What rights does the debtor have, and what steps can he or she take? If debt commitments exceed the debtor's capacity to repay them, the debtor's options include the following:

(a) negotiating new terms with creditors,
(b) obtaining a consolidation loan,
(c) seeking help from a credit counselling service,
(d) declaring insolvency and filing a consumer proposal,
(e) making an assignment in bankruptcy.

Unfortunately, whether from fear or ignorance, some overextended debtors do nothing at all, letting the situation worsen rapidly.

Negotiating with Creditors

If you ever become overindebted, talk to your creditors as soon as you realize that things are getting out of hand. Tell them what has happened, and ask what adjustments can be arranged. Creditors vastly prefer to see their money returned, even if its return is slightly delayed, rather than being forced to take strong measures. A particular institution's policies will determine which alternatives may be available to debtors who encounter financial difficulties. The creditor may offer to freeze the loan—that is, to accept no payments at all for a time. Additional interest payments may or may not be charged for this period, but the completion date for the credit contract will of course be moved forward.

Consolidation Loan

Some lenders offer consolidation loans to overcommitted debtors. A **consolidation loan** is a new loan that is used to discharge a number of existing debts; such loans are usually requested by a debtor who is unable to maintain previous repayment commitments. Advertisements often exhort credit users to borrow enough money to pay off all their debts and thus owe just one company. Unfortunately, this is not a perfect solution. Borrowing sufficient funds to cover all outstanding obligations and yet make smaller monthly payments than before has two predictable consequences: the new loan must be for a longer term, and the total interest charges may be increased. (See Personal Finance in Action Box 14.6, "Sophie and Françoise and Their Indebtedness.")

A consolidation loan may be a reasonable solution in some cases, but for many people it can be the beginning of a vicious cycle from which it is difficult to escape. Unfortunately, the smaller monthly payments tempt many debtors to take on even more debt; thus the problem worsens.

Before deciding on a consolidation loan, examine the interest rate that will be charged, comparing it with the rates on your existing obligations. It is unwise to transfer to a consolidation loan any debts that currently carry a lower interest rate or that are not interest-bearing. (Consolidation loans may carry quite high rates of interest because they are extended to people who are not very good credit risks.) Also, for any loan contract that is close to completion, the final payments consist mostly of principal and very little interest. If you prepay such a contract with funds from a consolidation loan and transfer the amount owing to the original creditor to the new creditor (i.e., the one who is extending the consolidation loan), you will significantly increase the amount of interest you pay.

During the recession of the early 1990s, banks became less eager to offer consolidation loans because of the high number of defaults on such loans. Some people were getting consolidation loans to lower their monthly debt payments but then running up more debt on their credit cards.

Credit Counselling

Another option for the overcommitted debtor involves approaching one of the government- or community-sponsored credit or debt counselling services that are found in many larger centres. Although their organizational structure varies from province to province, all such agencies have the same objective; many offer services without charge. They help clients find an appropriate solution to their financial problems; in some instances, this involves mediating between overindebted families and their creditors to alleviate the crisis and facilitate the eventual repayment of the debt. Credit counselling usually begins with an assessment interview, followed by a review of possible solutions.

Assessment Interview The credit counsellor begins by interviewing the debtor, along with his or her partner; obtaining detailed information about the family's financial situation allows the counsellor to consider what type of solution might be appropriate. This financial

Personal FINANCE in action 14.6

Sophie and Françoise and Their Indebtedness

Sophie and Françoise had a number of outstanding debts that were a constant drain on their finances. Sophie hadn't been able to find a job after graduating from college as a correctional service worker. Françoise had worked as a sous-chef at a large downtown hotel in Toronto, but when the hotel was taken over by a subsidiary of the Hilton hotel chain, she was declared surplus and laid off. Without a regular income they were now unable to make the required monthly payment of under $225 on their debts. These debts were as follows:

Creditor	Balance Outstanding	Interest Rate
Future Shop	$2 400.50	28.80%
Canadian Tire	$350.62	28.80%
BMO Mosaic Mastercard (no-fee option)	$923.47	18.50%
CIBC Classic Visa	$1 927.43	19.50%
Royal Bank Student Loans	$18 000.00	7.50%
Total	**$23 602.02**	

The young women knew little about credit. It had been easy to apply for and obtain their credit cards, but they paid no attention to the interest charges, assuming they were simply a cost that went with the convenience of using credit. But with Françoise losing her job, necessity made them take a closer look at their financial situation. They had managed to save $2000, but they had put this money in a chequing account so they could pay their bills. The account paid no interest. They were allowed 10 self-serve and four full-service transactions per month for a fee of $3.95 a month. The fee was waived if they kept at least $1000 in the account.

One day in the supermarket, they noticed a sign at the small bank branch that had just opened. It advertised, *"No-fee banking! Unlimited transactions!"* The young women entered the bank to learn more about this offer. They learned that they could open an account with these features, without a $1000 minimum deposit. The next day they closed their old account and opened a new one in the supermarket. They didn't have to pay a monthly fee and now had more flexibility with their meagre resources.

The problem of their outstanding debts remained. They explained their problem to the bank manager. She offered them a loan to consolidate their debts at a variable interest rate of prime plus 1.25 percent. Their low monthly payments would be $60 or 3 percent of the balance. The problem still remained that neither was working, but they were hopeful that one of them, at least, would soon find a job.

analysis includes a complete listing of income, living expenses, and debts. If the family's monthly income is sufficient to cover living expenses and debt obligations, the counsellor may discuss ways of improving their financial management so that the family can make their income stretch from one payday to the next. If there is a prospect of allocating a reasonable amount toward debt repayment, although less than the family's present commitment, a debt repayment plan may be developed. But if there is insufficient income to cover living expenses and partial debt payments, another solution may be needed, such as applying for insolvency protection under the *Bankruptcy and Insolvency Act*.

Debt Repayment Program The counsellor will work out with the family the amount that can be used to repay debts and allocate this amount among the family's creditors in proportion to each creditor's share of the total outstanding debt (pro rata). This process is a debt repayment program, also known as debt management or a prorate or a debt pooling plan. The creditor who is owed the largest part of the family's total debt will receive the largest share of any repayment. Once a debt repayment plan that is acceptable to both the debtors and the creditors is set up, the debtor signs a contract specifying the amount to be forwarded to the counselling agency on a regular basis. The agency, acting as a trustee, handles the distribution of the funds to the creditors.

The success of a debt repayment program depends on the family's ability to live within the budget drawn up in consultation with the counsellor, the stability of the family's circumstances, and the creditor's willingness to participate in the plan. Often creditors will co-operate because they prefer to accept reduced but regular payments instead of trying more collection procedures or writing the account off as a bad debt. If the family fails to maintain the agreed-upon payments, the agency will cancel the plan. Personal Finance in Action Box 14.7, "A Debt Repayment Plan," illustrates how a debt repayment program may be set up.

Personal FINANCE in action 14.7

A Debt Repayment Plan

Constant strife about bills has made life so unpleasant that Michael and Susan have decided to seek the help of a credit counselling service. With the counsellor's assistance, they begin for the first time to get a clear picture of their financial situation. When the counsellor asks them to list all their expenses and all their income, they are surprised at the result. They discover that their monthly living costs currently exceed their income before they make any consumer debt payments. The chart below shows that they are short $750 a month.

	Monthly Cash Flow
Total family take-home pay	$3 550
Living expenses (food, rent, hydro, gas, entertainment, etc.)	$2 900
Debt repayment	$1 400
Monthly expenses	$4 300
Monthly deficit	−$750

Michael and Susan are also surprised to learn how much their total debt is; they know that their loan balance at the credit union is low, but since they have never before added up the rest of what they owe, they hadn't realized how quickly their credit card debts were mounting up. When the counsellor goes over the monthly statements from their various credit cards with them, they get another surprise: the balances are increasing, despite their sporadic payments and recent purchasing restraints.

After carefully reviewing their financial affairs, the counsellor discusses several possible solutions with them, helping them analyze each one. Michael and Susan decide that they will go on an agency-administered debt repayment program. The counsellor explains that this approach will require them to reduce their living expenses, increase their income, or do both. They think that the potential for augmenting their income is low but feel that they can cut back on some of their expenses.

continued

For a start, they decide to reduce their gift-giving and forgo vacations until their situation improves. The effect of these changes on their deficit will be approximately $100 per month. They propose cutting their expenses a further $270 a month by dropping the premium channels from their TV cable package and reducing the number of restaurant and takeout meals they consume. Before encouraging them to make any more sacrifices, the counsellor suggests that they take some time to consider the implications of these modifications and to decide what other actions they might take.

When Susan and Michael return to the counselling agency a week later, they tell the counsellor that they are now saving $47 a month in telephone bills by eliminating unlimited long distance ($28.00), call display ($8.00), call waiting ($6.00), and phone care ($5.00). They will also save approximately $100 a month in babysitting expenses by eating out less. But they now realize that they were a little overzealous last week; they have since decided that even if they do not go away for vacations,

they will spend some extra money while they are off work—probably $200 a year. The counsellor, who also recognizes that such changes are easier to plan than to carry out, suggests that they allocate $650 per month toward repaying their consumer debt.

The counsellor confirms the outstanding balances with each creditor and is not surprised to find that the couple's debt is about $747 more than they have estimated—making the total debt $19 186. The counsellor's debt profile for this family shows the following list of creditors and amounts of debt, and the proportions of the total to be paid each month to each creditor.

Susan and Michael will require three and a half to four years to repay these debts; during that time, they must also refrain from assuming any new ones. If they successfully make the necessary lifestyle adjustments, they will probably eliminate their debt and become more effective financial managers. Unfortunately, some families cannot accept such a regimen, or their circumstances change and they do not complete the debt management program.

CREDITOR	REASON FOR DEBT	MONTHLY PAYMENT	CONFIRMED BALANCE	PERCENT OF TOTAL LOAN	PRORATE* PAYMENT
Credit union	Car	$295	$4 917	25.6	$166.40
The Bay	Stove, refrigerator, dishwasher, stereo	49	4 023	21.0	136.50
Zellers	Clothing, household goods, Christmas gifts	227	3 813	19.9	129.35
Sears	Washer, dryer, clothes, gifts, VCR	228	3 967	20.7	134.55
Visa	Car repairs, vacuum, cash advances, misc.	136	2 304	12.0	78.00
Esso	Gas		162	0.8	5.20
Total		$935	$19 186	100.0	$650.00

* To prorate is to distribute proportionally.

Consumer Proposals and Bankruptcy

Another solution to overindebtedness is to apply for insolvency protection under the federal *Bankruptcy and Insolvency Act*, either by filing a consumer proposal or by making an assignment in bankruptcy. These procedures are discussed in some detail in the following sections.

Bankruptcy and Insolvency

This discussion covers procedures that relate to consumers under 1985's federal *Bankruptcy and Insolvency Act*. The law allows for a formal process of declaring insolvency by filing either a consumer proposal or an assignment in bankruptcy; eventually, the debtor obtains a certificate indicating that the conditions of the consumer proposal have been met or declaring the debtor to have been **discharged from bankruptcy**. Declaring insolvency, the last resort of the overindebted, is much dreaded because of the social stigma attached to this drastic measure and because of its detrimental effect on the bankrupt's credit rating. But it may be the only alternative for families that do not have enough income to cover their regular living expenses and also repay their debts in full. A **consumer proposal** is a plan for paying creditors a portion of the total debt. **Bankruptcy** allows an insolvent debtor to obtain relief from a financial crisis, with any assets distributed in an orderly fashion among creditors. After the conditions of the proposal or bankruptcy are met, the insolvent debtor is free to start over. The bankruptcy process can be painful. The steps involved are explained in Personal Finance in Action Box 14.8, "Bankruptcy or Asset Liquidation?"

Personal FINANCE in action 14.8

Bankruptcy or Asset Liquidation?

When a credit counsellor encounters a family whose debts far exceed their ability to repay, a consumer proposal or an agency-administered debt management plan may not be possible options. Shanti is such a case. Until her separation from her alcoholic husband, Shanti managed to keep all the bills paid; the family lived well on a combined income of over $100 000. After the separation, she hoped that with her salary as an executive secretary and substantial support payments for the two young children, she would still be able to keep on top of her expenses. But her ex-husband lost his middle-management job a few months after the separation, and the sporadic support payments have now ceased.

Shanti is currently behind on the mortgage and owes the gas company for fuel; the bank is threatening to take her car; her credit cards and charge accounts are at their limit. She still owes money to the lawyer who handled her separation. The pressures from these financial problems sometimes make Shanti wonder if she and the children are really better off living apart from her abusive husband. It seems to her that things are always going wrong.

The situation that Shanti finds herself in is not uncommon in today's climate of frequent marriage and relationship breakdowns and employment instability. Expenses that are manageable on two incomes are not always manageable on one. Shanti is so angry at what she feels to be the injustice of her circumstances that it is hard for her to take any kind of objective look at her financial affairs. The counsellor tries to help Shanti focus on one problem at a time.

It soon becomes evident to both Shanti and the counsellor that keeping the house is not going to be possible; nor, on her income alone, will she be able to meet her other monthly debt commitments. The counsellor suggests two alternatives. Since Shanti is insolvent, bankruptcy is one possibility. Another option is to use the equity in her home, along with some valuable antiques, by selling them and offering her creditors a cash settlement from the proceeds. Neither solution is ideal. The credit counsellor also recommends that Shanti seek legal advice, particularly concerning her right to sell the house and the antiques.

Shanti is also encouraged to seek psychological counselling for herself and for the children concerning their feelings about the separation.

Bill C-55, an "Act to Amend the Bankruptcy and Insolvency Act," was passed by Parliament in November 2005. Under the act an insolvent person is allowed to receive payment for wages owing for the six months before the date of bankruptcy. In addition, all RRSPs and RRIFs are exempt from seizure except for contributions made in the 12 months prior to bankruptcy.

What Is Bankruptcy?

Declaring bankruptcy is a legal method of helping a person deal with a financial crisis. It allows someone to get free from the burden of debt and to start over again. Before you can declare bankruptcy, you must first be *insolvent*. This means that you owe at least $1000 and are unable to pay your creditors. Between 1990 and 2004 personal or consumer bankruptcies increased by 97 percent. In 2005, there were 78 739 personal bankruptcies, an increase of only 0.6 percent from 2004.[13] This modest increase was credited to the large number of full-time jobs that were created and the unusually low mortgage rates.[14]

The federal *Bankruptcy and Insolvency Act* currently offers more options for seriously indebted consumers than were previously available. Earlier legislation was designed for bankrupt businesses and was very out of date. Today, approximately 90 percent of all bankruptcies are consumer bankruptcies, not commercial bankruptcies.

The legislation was designed to respond to some of the needs of overindebted consumers with a more streamlined process and an emphasis on rehabilitation. It is based on the premise that the best that the insolvency system can do for society is to return bankrupts to the marketplace as better-informed and more responsible citizens, with an enhanced ability to contribute to the economy. Recovery of funds is actually less important. In most **consumer bankruptcies,** there are few assets (other than income tax refunds) to distribute, and there is little potential for repaying debts from income. A bankrupt's family tends to have an income that is only 40 percent of the Canadian average.

Personal bankruptcies are regulated by the federal *Bankruptcy and Insolvency Act*. This law was enacted in 1985 and has been amended several times since. All trustees in bankruptcy are licensed by the federal government and administer bankruptcies and consumer proposals. The *Act* provides for an Orderly Payment of Debts program. In some cases, this program is administered by the provinces. In Prince Edward Island, Nova Scotia, Alberta, Saskatchewan or British Columbia, people who live in financial distress may apply for a consolidation order. If approved, the order will detail the amount and the times when payments must be made to the court. The court will then make payments to creditors. Such an order allows debts to be paid off in three years and puts an end to the garnisheeing of wages and any harassment from creditors. Ontario has a similar process administered by the Small Claims Court. In Manitoba, for a fee, the Financial Counselling Services will help a person in financial difficulty develop a plan to manage his or her money.

Basics of the Insolvency Process

A hopelessly indebted person who applies for insolvency protection under the *Bankruptcy and Insolvency Act* now has a new option that was not available in the past—filing a consumer proposal.

---

[13]**BankruptcyCanada.com**, January 20, 2006.

[14]Office of the Superintendent of Bankruptcy Canada, Bankruptcy Statistics, 06/01/06.

Eligibility An applicant for a consumer proposal must be insolvent and must have less than $75 000 in debts (excluding a mortgage on the applicant's principal residence). To file for bankruptcy, a debtor must owe at least $1000.

Initiating the Process Insolvency proceedings are usually started when a debtor applies either to an administrator of consumer proposals or to a trustee in bankruptcy.

Insolvency Actors There are five main actors in the insolvency or bankruptcy drama:

(a) an **insolvent** person is someone "who is not bankrupt and who resides, carries on business or has property in Canada, whose liabilities to creditors provable as claims under the *Bankruptcy and Insolvency Act* amount to $1000,"[15] and who is not able to pay his or her bills.

(b) the **creditors**, who are all those who can prove a claim against the insolvent,

(c) the **official receiver**, the federal civil servant who oversees the insolvency process,

(d) the **trustee in bankruptcy**, a federally licensed official (usually a chartered accountant) who carries out the insolvency process,

(e) the **administrator of consumer proposals**, who has more limited powers than a trustee (trustees may handle both bankruptcies and consumer proposals, while administrators are limited to handling only consumer proposals and the related counselling).

In addition to those mentioned above, it is very likely that other members of society are aware of personal bankruptcies. If a bankrupt person has significant assets, a notice will be put in a newspaper telling creditors when they are to meet. With few assets, creditors are only told by mail. Filings for bankruptcy also become public documents to which anyone has access.

Responsibilities of the Debtor The insolvent person must reveal complete information about his or her assets, debts, and income and may be asked to meet the official receiver and answer questions under oath. If there is a meeting of creditors, the debtor is expected to be there to provide information. The debtor must attend several counselling sessions and submit regular statements about income and expenses. The debtor is expected to co-operate with the insolvency officials.

Responsibilities of the Creditors In bankruptcy cases, all creditors are invited to a meeting to consider the debtor's affairs and to confirm the trustee's appointment; creditors may also appoint inspectors to act as their agents in the bankruptcy process. But in a streamlined consumer bankruptcy process, some of these steps may be unnecessary. Finally, the creditors' agreement is necessary to discharge the insolvent person from bankruptcy. In the case of a consumer proposal, the creditors must accept the plan before it can be put into effect.

Duties of the Official Receiver The official receiver generally oversees the whole insolvency process, performing tasks that include receiving petitions or proposals from the trustee or the administrator, making decisions about holding creditors' meetings, and submitting applications to court.

[15]*Bankruptcy and Insolvency Act* (R.S. 1985), c. B-3, s. 2 (definitions).

Duties of the Trustee in Bankruptcy　When a person inquires about insolvency protection, the trustee investigates that person's financial situation by conducting an assessment interview and possibly by checking with creditors. The debtor decides whether to submit a consumer proposal (which is the option the trustee will normally advise taking wherever possible under the circumstances) or file for bankruptcy. If the debtor decides on a consumer proposal, the trustee changes hats, becoming an administrator of consumer proposals. Either a trustee or an administrator can handle the legally required counselling sessions and can prepare a consumer proposal, but only a trustee may look after the bankruptcy process.

Duties of the Administrator of Consumer Proposals　An administrator of consumer proposals may be a trustee in bankruptcy or another person appointed to this task. The administrator can provide counselling, conduct an assessment interview, help the debtor file a consumer proposal, and disburse funds to creditors. If, at the assessment interview, the debtor decides to file for bankruptcy, the client must be transferred to a trustee.

Costs of Insolvency　There are two types of bankruptcies. An estate of less than $10 000 is known as a summary bankruptcy. The fees for such a bankruptcy are as follows:

(a)　$100 filing fee,
(b)　$110 each for two mandatory counselling sessions,
(c)　trustee fee of 100 percent of the first $975,
(d)　trustee fee of 35 percent of the next $1025,
(e)　trustee fee of 50 percent of the amount above $2000.

For estates over $10 000, the rate is not fixed and it will depend on the size and complexity of the estate. The trustee may submit a statement for remuneration "not exceeding 7.5 percent of the amount remaining out of the realization of the property of the debtor after the claims of the secured creditors have been paid."[16] When this is not enough to cover their costs, trustees must go to court to get a judge's approval for payment.

Assets Exempt from Seizure

Each province exempts some assets from seizure by the trustee in bankruptcy. These vary considerably. Following are several examples:

British Columbia
Equity in a home equal to $9000, $12 000 in either Vancouver or Victoria.
Household goods equal to $4000.
A motor vehicle worth $5000.
Work tools worth $10 000.

Alberta
Food needed by the debtor over the next 12 months.
Clothing worth up to $4000.

Furniture and appliances up to a value of $4000.
Medical and dental aids.
If debtor is a farmer, 160 acres, if farmer lives on the land and farms it.
A home worth up to $40 000.
Property needed to earn a living up to a value of $10 000.
Farm equipment needed to earn a living if debtor is a farmer.
One motor vehicle worth up to $5000.

continued

[16]*Bankruptcy and Insolvency Act* (R.S. 1985), c. B-3, s. 39(2).

Ontario

Clothing, $5560.

Household goods, $11 300.

Tools of the trade, $10 000.

Farmers, $28 300.

Motor vehicle, $5650.

Nova Scotia

Necessary wearing apparel, household furnishings, and furniture.

Necessary food and fuel.

Necessary grain, seeds, cattle, hogs, fowl, sheep, and other livestock.

Necessary medical and dental aids.

Farm equipment, fishing nets, tools, and implements used in debtor's occupation, not exceeding $1000.

Household goods not exceeding $5000.

Motor vehicle not exceeding $3000, $6500 if needed for work.

Newfoundland and Labrador

Food required by debtor and dependants during the next 12 months.

Medical and dental aids required by debtor and dependants.

Domesticated animals kept as pets.

Fuel or heating as a necessity for the debtor and dependants.

Clothing of the debtor and dependants, worth $4000.

Appliances and household furnishings (washing machine, clothes dryer, "reasonably necessary" bedroom suites and bedding, oven and stovetop burners, "necessary" dishes and kitchen utensils, and "necessary" strollers, cribs and highchairs), of a value totaling $4 000.

Motor vehicle of the debtor, worth $2000.

Items of sentimental value to the debtor, of a value totaling $500.

The debtor's equity in the principal residence, $10 000.

Personal property used by and necessary for debtor to earn income from occupation, trade, business, or calling, $10 000.

Assets exempt from seizure under the *Federal Bankruptcy and Insolvency Act* are as follows:

- Household furnishings of $ 5000 or less, clothing, food, fuel.
- Motor vehicle worth $3000 or less.
- Tools of the trade, $10 000.
- Farmers, $28 300.
- Motor vehicle $5 650.[17]

Counselling Sessions

The legislation, with its focus on rehabilitation, offers the possibility of three counselling sessions. The first occurs when the overindebted person contacts a trustee or an administrator to discuss possible solutions to the insolvency problem. The administrator or trustee examines the debtor's whole financial situation and reviews possible alternatives. The second counselling session takes place a month or two after the filing of either a consumer proposal or an assignment in bankruptcy. At this session, the emphasis is on identifying the root causes of the financial difficulties and on finding ways to change the situation. Failure to attend the second counselling session results in a penalty: the debtor will not be eligible for an automatic discharge from bankruptcy. The third counselling session, which is optional, takes place within six months of filing a proposal or making an assignment. It is intended to provide the debtor and his or her family with further guidance in financial management or assistance with such personal problems as substance abuse, gambling, relationship difficulties, or compulsive shopping. The first counselling session is for individual debtors, but subsequent counselling may be done in groups.

[17]**BankruptcyCanada.com**, January 16, 2006.

The legislation requires that an administrator or trustee who agrees to assist an insolvent debtor must provide for at least two counselling sessions. The trustee or administrator can either do the counselling or delegate it to another qualified person. The counselling fees are paid out of the debtor's estate (i.e., his or her assets) before any distribution to creditors.

Consumer Proposals

As we have seen, a consumer proposal is a plan for reorganizing a debtor's personal financial affairs for presentation to his or her creditors. The debtor, with help from an administrator, prepares a plan for repaying all or part of the debt within five years. (See Personal Finance in Action Box 14.9, "Ariana Becomes Insolvent," for an example of how this works.) If the proposal is accepted by the court and the creditors, it becomes binding on the debtor and the creditors. Generally, a consumer proposal does not release a debtor from

Personal FINANCE in action 14.9

Ariana Becomes Insolvent

Ariana's family had moved to Canada from Jordan when she was 12. Now 18 and thoroughly Western, she balked at the restrictions placed upon her by her parents. Against her father's wishes she got a job as a waitress and moved into a small apartment so she could be on her own and make her own decisions.

Shortly after moving, financial reality struck. While in her parents' home she had had no expenses. Now she had to pay rent as well as hydro and phone bills, buy her groceries and clothing, and pay for a bus pass to get to work. It was not long before she was financially stretched to the limit. After paying her rent and buying groceries, she had little left for anything else. Bills began to accumulate and often went unpaid for months. Out of desperation she decided to cancel her telephone. While the phone bill was not that high, she could no longer afford it. The phone company reacted quickly. She was notified that according to her contract she would be charged the following:

- A termination charge of $100.
- The service fee and taxes for 30 days after the termination date.
- A service charge of $175.

Ariana was desperate. She could pay for none of the phone company's charges, or any of her other bills. She was too embarrassed to ask her father for help, knowing what his reaction would be. Her friend Natasha, whom she had met at the library, told her that her brother Phil was a trustee in bankruptcy in a nationwide accounting firm and offered to introduce Ariana to him before she ran into further difficulties.

When she met Phil and explained her situation, he told her that she was insolvent and, if she liked, he would act as an administrator to help solve her problems. She readily agreed. He explained that he would prepare a consumer proposal for her and asked her to see him again in three weeks. When she returned he told her that her finances were so bad that she would have to move back with her parents (at least temporarily) and with the money saved from not renting her apartment she could gradually pay off her debts. Unhappily, she agreed. Phil contacted all of her creditors, and while complaining at the length of time it would take for their accounts to be settled, they agreed. Ariana could now face the world without worry, but she planned to leave her parents' home again as soon as she could build up a healthy bank balance.

certain kinds of obligations, such as fines, penalties, alimony, maintenance agreements, or co-signer responsibilities. It does, however, protect the debtor from any claims for accelerated payments or discontinued service by public utilities; it nullifies the effect of any existing wage assignments; and it prohibits an employer from taking any disciplinary action because the employee has made a consumer proposal. If a person's creditors accept a consumer proposal, bankruptcy can be avoided; if they reject the proposal, an assignment in bankruptcy may follow.

Certificate of Performance When all the conditions of a consumer proposal have been met, the debtor receives a certificate to that effect.

Bankruptcy

The first step in bankruptcy is the assignment of all the debtor's assets to a licensed trustee. From this time until he or she is released from debts by the court, the debtor is an undischarged bankrupt. Next, the trustee will call a meeting of creditors. At this meeting, the appointment of the trustee is affirmed and instructions are given concerning the administration of the estate. The trustee then proceeds to liquidate the estate. All the debtor's property is available for payment of debts, except that which is exempt from execution or seizure under the laws of the debtor's province (see Personal Finance in Action Box 14.10 "The Bankruptcy Process"). All creditors must prove their claims against the estate; secured creditors will be paid first because they have a claim on specific assets. Any remaining assets are then distributed in a specified order, with payment for the cost of administering the bankruptcy taking precedence over other claims.

Personal FINANCE in action 14.10

The Bankruptcy Process

Brenda is in a financial mess. Since the break-up of her marriage, she has been unable to make ends meet. Her income, even though she is a full-time teacher, never seems to be enough. She has cut her expenses to the bone but still owes over $8000. Her creditors are becoming nastier with each passing month. At her friend Gail's suggestion, Brenda makes an appointment to talk with a trustee in bankruptcy. The trustee explains that bankruptcy would immediately stop the legal actions of her creditors and also help to eliminate most of her debts. Since she owes more than $1000, she does qualify for bankruptcy. The trustee explains the process, if she decides to file.

1. She might be examined by an official receiver to determine the cause of her bankruptcy.

2. She will have to attend a meeting of her creditors to tell them about the bankruptcy and confirm the appointment of the trustee.

3. She will have to attend two counselling sessions to assess her finances and discuss her problems.

4. Since this is Brenda's first bankruptcy, after she receives counselling, she will be eligible for an automatic discharge in nine months.

5. If the creditors make an objection, Brenda may have to attend a bankruptcy court. However, the trustee said the court will grant her an absolute discharge.

Discharge from Bankruptcy Once the debtor's existing assets have been distributed, the court may grant the bankrupt a discharge. This document releases the debtor from all claims of creditors except fines imposed by a court, money owed as a result of theft, items obtained by misrepresentation, liability for support or maintenance of spouse or child under an agreement or court order, damages awarded by a court for assault, and student loans. If there is no opposition from creditors, and if the counselling sessions have been attended, a first-time bankrupt is eligible for an automatic discharge nine months after declaring bankruptcy.

Complexities of Overindebtedness

Personal Finance in Action Box 14.11, "Debt Problems of a Blended Family," illustrates how family relations and financial matters can become interconnected. None of the alternatives identified appears to be a perfect solution, a situation that will force the family to look for the least costly option.

Personal FINANCE in action 14.11

Debt Problems of a Blended Family

When the letter carrier brings Robert a summons to appear in family court regarding arrears in his support payments, it is the last straw. He persuades Denise that they had better get some help.

Robert and Denise are obviously feeling very overburdened and stressed by their financial situation when they approach the credit counselling agency. They are seriously considering separating. In addition to their debt difficulties, Denise's recurring medical problem has flared up again, and the school principal has called about some serious problems Denise's son, Tim, was having at school. Denise has been missing a fair amount of work recently, and Robert's boss has told him to do something about his personal problems. It is apparent to the counsellor that the family needs relief from its financial problems soon.

The counsellor asks the couple to outline their family situation as necessary background for any new plans. Denise and Robert explain that they have been living common-law for several years and are caring for Denise's 12-year-old son from a previous marriage. Robert, who has also been married before, is required by a court order to pay $1200 per month to his ex-wife for the support of their three teenaged children. These children spend every other weekend, as well as much of the summer, with Denise and Robert. Both Robert and Denise resent having to make such large support payments; Denise feels as if she works for Robert's ex-wife. To make matters worse, Denise's ex-husband is $2400 behind in support payments to her, since he rarely sends his court-ordered $500-a-month payments.

When Robert and his wife separated two and a half years ago, he had to assume their debts of approximately $12 000 ($7000 for the car and $5000 on charge accounts) because she went on long-term social assistance.

Anxious to establish her own credit rating after her separation, Denise borrowed $5000 to buy a car; her elderly parents served as co-signers. Denise still owes about $3500 on that loan, and she also has another $2500 in credit card debt. Cash advances on Robert's credit cards and loans from her family have allowed them to keep up their commitments but have added a further $6500 to their debts.

Their resources for financial aid have been exhausted for months now; creditors have begun to call both Robert and Denise at work about

continued

their delinquent payments. Robert has received a summons to appear in family court regarding $1050 that he owes in support payments. The arrears accumulated when Denise was laid off earlier in the year. The only payments that are up to date are those related to the bank loan for which Denise's parents co-signed. Denise says

that she would starve before she would let her parents use their pension to pay that debt.

Before the counsellor can help this couple look at possible solutions to their problems, everyone needs to have a clearer picture of their financial position. The counsellor's assessment reveals the following:

BALANCE SHEET

Assets

Small bank account, two cars, household furnishings	$9 500	
Support arrears owed to Denise	2 400	
Total Assets		$11 900

Liabilities

Robert's old debts	$12 000	
Robert's support payments in arrears	1 050	
Denise's loan	3 500	
Robert's current debts	6 500	
Total Liabilities		$23 050
Net Worth		−$11 150

MONTHLY CASH FLOW

Income		$3 022
Expenses		
Net living expenses	2 286	
Robert's support payments	1 200	
Consumer debt payments		
Charge accounts, credit cards	675	
Bank loans	502	
Total Expenses		**$4 663**
Deficit		−$1 641

The counsellor helps the couple to look objectively at their situation, and together they draw up the following possible solutions:

1. **Both seek legal recourse regarding support payments that are in arrears.** Denise might be successful in obtaining a form of garnishment for current and future support payments as well as for those in arrears. This could increase the family's income by at least $300 a month. Robert could apply to the family court for a reduction in support payments, but it seems unlikely that a judge would be sympathetic to his situation.

2. **Find cheaper living accommodation.** Robert and Denise are renting a four–bedroom townhouse so that there will be space for Robert's children when they come to visit. They could reduce their housing expenses by at least $300 a month if they moved into a two-bedroom apartment. But they would then be very cramped when Robert's children came to stay.

3. **Consolidate their debts.** Charge account and credit card interest rates are usually higher than consumer loans. A consolidation loan might reduce their monthly debt load

continued

and the total amount owed. Unfortunately, since the couple currently has a negative net worth, it is doubtful that they could find a lender willing to give them a loan for the total owed.

4. **Arrange a debt repayment program.** This may be done through a governmental or social agency and would allow the couple to repay their debts with more manageable monthly payments, over a longer period of time. There are risks involved in this choice. If the pro rata share on Denise's bank loan were less than the contractual amount, the bank might ask Denise's parents to make up the deficit. Unless interest concessions are negotiated, though, the total debt could increase substantially through accrued interest charges. It is possible that a creditor might decide to exercise his or her rights to security and thus take possession of household chattels or of a car. And last, but not necessarily least, the family would have to make lifestyle changes to reduce living expenses. They would need to exert considerable self-discipline for approximately four years for the program to be a success.

5. **Declare bankruptcy.** This action would relieve the family of their monthly debt burden, with the exception of support arrears. But they would undoubtedly lose some of their possessions. There is also a stigma attached to bankruptcy; as well, having been bankrupt may limit the ability of an individual or family to get credit in the future. Denise's elderly parents would, no doubt, be forced to take over her bank loan if she were to file for bankruptcy.

What do you think they should do?

Summary

- Credit bureaus sell information about those who have credit to potential issuers of credit. Credit files are records of a person's credit history. Credit scoring is done by credit bureaus and is based on a person's credit history.

- Equifax is the largest credit rating agency in Canada, and TransUnion is another such agency. FICO scores, produced by these two agencies, are the common way of determining someone's credit worthiness.

- Debtors are people who owe others money, and creditors are those to whom they owe the money. Third-party collection is when a collection agency is hired to collect debts. Collection agencies are paid to collect overdue accounts. Garnishment is a court order instructing an employer to withhold a percentage of a debtor's wages. An execution order allows a creditor to seize and sell some of a debtor's property to pay off debts. An affidavit is a sworn statement that the facts in the case are true.

- Consumer fraud is an attempt, by various means, to separate unsuspecting people from their money. Computer scams are one method used to defraud unsuspecting consumers. The Nigerian letter scam is a sophisticated method of consumer fraud involving a plea by a stranger to help him or her get money out of an African country. Phishing is the use of counterfeit financial websites to obtain personal data from unsuspecting recipients of fraudulent emails.

- Overindebtedness means a person has more debts than he or she can repay. Insolvency is another term for having too little money to pay one's debts. Administrators counsel insolvent people to prevent bankruptcy. Consolidation loans allow the overindebted to pay off all of their debts with one major loan. Consumer proposals are organized plans to help resolve financial crises.

■ Bankruptcy is determined by a court and solves a financial crisis for an overly indebted person. The *Bankruptcy and Insolvency Act* is a federal law regulating insolvency and bankruptcy. Bill C-55 is a 2005 amendment to the *Act*. Consumer bankruptcy may be caused by any number of factors, including a poor education, an inability to socialize with others, marrying or forming a lasting relationship at too young an age, some form of addiction, medical problems, student loans, and job loss.

■ A trustee in bankruptcy is licensed to administer bankruptcies and consumer proposals. The discharge of bankruptcy relieves the bankrupt of debts that existed before the declaration of bankruptcy.

Key Terms

administrator of consumer
   proposals *(p. 505)*

affidavit *(p. 489)*

bank account garnishment
   (p. 489)

bankruptcy *(p. 503)*

Bill C-55 *(p. 504)*

collection agency *(p. 485)*

computer scam *(p. 496)*

consolidation loan *(p. 499)*

consumer bankruptcy *(p. 504)*

consumer fraud *(p. 496)*

consumer information *(p. 483)*

consumer proposal *(p. 503)*

credit bureau *(p. 480)*

credit file *(p. 481)*

credit scoring *(p. 481)*

creditors *(p. 505)*

discharge from bankruptcy *(p. 503)*

Equifax *(p. 482)*

executing against the debtor's
   property *(p. 490)*

family court garnishment *(p. 490)*

FICO score *(p. 482)*

garnishee *(p. 488)*

information exchanges *(p. 485)*

insolvent *(p. 505)*

investigative agencies *(p. 485)*

judgment debt *(p. 488)*

lenders of last resort *(p. 495)*

Nigerian letter scam *(p. 496)*

official receiver *(p. 505)*

overindebtedness *(p. 491)*

payday lenders *(p. 495)*

personal information *(p. 483)*

phishing *(p. 496)*

third-party collection *(p. 485)*

TransUnion *(p. 482)*

trustee in bankruptcy *(p. 505)*

wage garnishment *(p. 488)*

Problems

1. Answer true or false:

(a) Applying for credit is now more complicated because of the internet.

(b) A report from a credit bureau is no longer necessary to get credit.

(c) Credit bureaus follow strict guidelines for making credit information available.

(d) Students do not need any money or assets to obtain credit.

(e) Equifax is the only nationwide credit-granting agency.

(f)   Consumer consent is not necessary for a credit report to be issued.

(g)   All Canadians are governed by laws regulating credit unions.

(h)   It is now possible for collection agencies to pester debtors whenever and wherever they want.

(i)   A court order in favour of a creditor is a guarantee that a debtor will start to pay his or her debts.

2.   How is information in a credit report obtained? Why is such information often incorrect?

3.   Is credit too easily obtained?

4.   Explain what is meant by a FICO score. How is such a score determined? According to the scores of Canadians, is credit abuse a major problem in Canada?

5.   Refer to Personal Finance in Action Box 14.5, "Ramon and Maria and Their Shopping Addiction." What happened to Ramon and Maria is not uncommon. Who, or what, can be blamed, in addition to this couple's lifestyle, for this kind of behaviour?

6.   Go to **www11.hrsdc.gc.ca/en/cs/sp/hrsdc/arb/publications/research/2000–000063/ page07.shtml**, or search for the article "Dropping Out of High School." Identify the reasons given to explain why students drop out of school. Which of these could be a cause of financial illiteracy? Do you think Ontario's attempt to rectify this problem (identified in the article) will work?

7.   Analyze the reasons why debtors default. Which of these is the easiest for governments to prevent?

8.   Go to **www.olgc.ca/sitemap.jsp**, the site map of the Ontario Lottery and Gaming Corporation. Click on Where the Money Goes. How much of Ontario's gaming revenue was paid to the government?

Now go to **www.healthunit.org/adults/php_gambling.htm** and refer to Health Consequences. Do the revenues from gambling paid to Ontario justify the health consequences of problem gambling?

9.   How does someone find out about credit and the best way to use it?

10. Explain the steps a creditor can take to collect his debts.

11. Read **The Novice Counsellor** on the next page and answer the following questions:

(a)   Why is this family in a financial mess?

(b)   Were this family's problems caused by anything mentioned in this book? (See the section, "Why Debtors Default.")

(c)   Is there any way this family's situation could have been avoided?

12. Refer to Personal Finance in Action Box 14.11, "Debt Problems of a Blended Family."

(a)   Do you think this family should declare bankruptcy? What would be the advantages if they did?

(b)   Can the family afford the cost of bankruptcy?

(c)   Will the creditors get anything if the family goes bankrupt?

(d)   Will the family lose their household furnishings?

(e)   How will bankruptcy affect the family's credit rating if another loan is needed?

The Novice Counsellor

My first assignment in a student counselling practicum involved Glen and Maria. An administrator for the local housing authority wanted me to visit them because they had fallen behind in their rent payments. I made my first call at their house, confident that with a bit of help from me, this family would soon find itself able to cope with its financial problems.

When I arrived at their home at the appointed time, Maria was out shopping, but she returned within the hour. This friendly woman, in her mid-thirties, seemed most cooperative, telling me that her husband is employed at a local factory, that she works part-time at a nursing home, and that they have three children between the ages of 5 and 13. During this interview, I tried to determine the actual amount of their debts, but Maria remained very vague about the amounts.

My second visit was equally pleasant. Maria seemed to be making every attempt to answer my questions. Unfortunately, it appeared that she really did not know much about their financial situation. For example, she wasn't sure what her husband's usual take-home pay was. Still, we managed to estimate their main debts, which totaled about $14 000.

I was astonished to find two large TV sets in the middle of a rather poorly furnished living room. According to Maria, both units are quite new and in splendid working condition; they bought the first one about a year ago and the second one last month. "The man who sold them to us," Maria confided, "is a very good friend of ours. Whenever he gets a really good deal, he calls us and we go down and look at it. He is awfully nice about letting us pay for the televisions when we can."

When I looked at the contracts for their television sets, I realized that they were paying a substantial amount in credit charges. I mentioned this to Maria, who was very surprised; evidently she hadn't realized that her friend was charging them anything extra. She says that they are paying off the TVs fairly quickly because every so often they use Glen's whole paycheque for some of the television debt. I asked what they do about their other debts on these occasions, and Maria said that they often let hydro, rent, and telephone bills accumulate for a few months. As we talked about their debts, it became obvious to me that Maria had virtually no understanding of credit contracts or credit costs.

During the period of my visits to this household, Glen absolutely refused to meet me, although I was willing to stop by when he would be at home. I discovered that they have two cars—although Maria doesn't drive. The whole family enjoys going out to eat once or twice a week, and Glen usually meets a friend to have a few drinks at their club every week.

My visits ended without my ever meeting Maria's husband. Maria herself had stated repeatedly that unless Glen agrees to make some changes, there is very little that she can do. I later learned that they will probably be evicted from their low-rental townhouse. This experience has helped me to realize that solving financial problems is more complicated than I had thought; simply providing this family with information clearly will not change much about their situation. This particular couple does not seem eager to change, and until they become motivated to review their goals and values in the light of their actual resources, a counsellor cannot help them. This experience was obviously more beneficial for me than it was for the family I was "counselling."

(f) What could the family have done to avoid this predicament?

(g) Are there any other solutions to this family's financial problems that might have been addressed in another interview? Discuss.

13. Why might a debtor decide to file a consumer proposal instead of making an assignment in bankruptcy?

14. Go to **www.canadastudentdebt.ca/studentloansong.asp** and listen to "Broke! The Student Loan Song." How realistic are the lyrics?
    Click Watch the CBC Canada Now video.

    (a) How many former students had defaulted at this time?
    (b) How were they treated?
    (c) How much money was involved?
    (d) Should debt collectors be used to collect these loans?
    (e) How else could the debts be collected?

15. Review Personal Finance in Action boxes 14.4, 14.6, 14.7, and 14.8. Try to determine the cause of the indebtedness in each case.

16. Try to determine from the research available whether there is a connection between gambling and insolvency.

17. Contact the Ministry of Education in your province to find out whether any courses in personal finance are offered in the province's elementary or secondary schools. If there are such courses, find out what topics they cover.

18. Apply for a major credit card. On the application, indicate that you have never used credit before and have student debt. What is the result?

19. Displays of credit card applications are a common sight at colleges and universities every fall. Should students, who typically have either no income or only a very limited income, be given credit when they lack the financial resources to pay off their bills and will therefore incur high interest charges? Discuss.

20. Read the following bullets and then answer the questions.

    ■ Statistics Canada reported the following facts in its publication *The Daily* on September 2, 2004:

    Undergraduate tuition averaged $4172 for the 2004–05 academic year. Between1990–91 and 2002–03, tuition increased by an average of 8.1 percent per year, while inflation, as measured by the CPI, increased an average of 1.9 percent per year.

    ■ The Association of Canadian Community Colleges stated the following in its June 2001 *Position Paper*:

    Education is becoming unaffordable due to a conjunction of various factors, including system underfunding, decline in real family incomes, regional unemployment, erosion of financial aid programs, and rising costs to students. Those students who start poor end up poor by being subject to crippling debt loads and uncertain futures.

    ■ The Council of Ontario Universities, in a press release dated January 21, 2004, reported that full-time university enrollment in Ontario was 326 000, up 28.6 percent from 2001.

    ■ University enrollment in Canada in 2003–04 was 990 400, up 6.1 percent from the previous year. This was the sixth year in a row for a record high.[18]

[18]Statistics Canada, "University Enrolment," *The Daily*, October 11, 2005.

- The Association of Canadian Community Colleges[19] said that 900 000 full-time and 1.5 million part-time students attend Canada's colleges.

- The *Ontario University Graduate Survey, Highlights,* July 2005, reported the following information about graduates:

  In 2002, 96.4 percent were employed two years after graduation.
  After six months, 92.7 percent were employed.
  The average salary, two years after graduation, was $43 578.
  Two years after graduation, 83.5 percent were working in a field related to their education.

  (a) If post-secondary education is such a financial burden, as the media frequently report, how can the large enrollment in universities and colleges be explained?

  (b) Go to **www.cbc.ca/consumers/market/files/money/credit/numbers.html**, and click By the Numbers: Credit Stats and Facts (February 27, 2005). What, according to this article, was the average graduate student debt?

  (c) If students are this successful, should they complain about student debt?

  (d) If students benefit financially from their education, who should pay their debts?

  (e) Are students who started off poor likely to continue being so?

  (f) If this debt remains an insurmountable problem after several years of successful employment, who should take the blame?

21. One university advertises that it tries to connect students with the financial resources to meet their needs. It provides information about government aid, university loans, bursaries, and scholarships. It offers help in debt management and budget counselling. Check to see if your college or university offers the same service, and if it does, how many in the student body avail themselves of this service.

22. If students have to go deep in debt to pay for their post-secondary education, should they also apply for major credit cards with their high interest rates?

23. In 2003, the estimated total household debt in Canada was $731 billion. The average household debt in 2004 was $69 450. The total estimated personal savings in 2003 were $9.39 billion. The ratio of household debt to income in 2003 was 105.2 percent.[20]

    (a) How would you describe the financial health of Canadians?

    (b) If you were in a position to do so, would you lend money to the average household?

    (c) What are the implications of this situation for Canada's financial system?

    (d) Why is this debt problem not as big an issue as graduate student debt?

    (e) How do you think this situation developed?

24. Go to **www.hoyes.com/Gambling.htm** and answer the following:

    (a) What is the connection between gambling and addiction?

    (b) How does this affect everyone, gamblers and non-gamblers?

[19]Accessed January 23, 2006.
[20]CBC *Marketplace,* "By the Numbers: Credit Stats and Facts," February 27, 2005.

25. Consumer fraud has become a major problem for all Canadians, regardless of the level of worldliness and financial sophistication. Just how serious can be found out by a visit to the Phonebusters website at **www.phonebusters.com/english/index.html**.

    (a) Go to this site, click Recognize It, and make a list of the scams identified.

    (b) Click on Advanced Fee Letter and The 419 Coalition website. Explain how this example of consumer fraud works.

    (c) Why is it so successful at separating people from their money?

26. Go to the TransUnion website at **www.tuc.ca/TUCorp/home.asp**. Click on Personal Solutions and then Order Credit Report & Score. Select Option Two.

    (a) Order a copy of your credit report.

    (b) What information does TransUnion require?

    (c) Does any of this information include consumer information that relates to your financial affairs or credit history?
    Next, click on Fraud Victim Information and How can I avoid being the next victim?

    (d) What advice is given to help consumers protect themselves?

27. Go to Industry Canada's website at **http://strategis.gc.ca**. Then go to the Site Map. Click on C. Go to Credit Card Costs Calculator.

    (a) Click Yes (*I pay my bills by the due date*). List all of the cards that have no fees.

    (b) Click No. Click Continue. Answer the questions, according to your specific circumstances. If you don't use credit cards, make up some numbers. What is the range of interest rates for MasterCard, Visa, and American Express? Which card has the lowest rate? The highest?

References

BOOKS AND OTHER REFERENCES

Baker, Murray. *The Debt-Free Graduate: How to Survive College or University Without Going Broke*, Revised Edition. Toronto: HarperCollins, 1999.

Baker, Murray. *The Money-Runner*. Free newsletter. **http://debtfreegrad.com.**

Baugham, Richard. *The Friendly Banker*. Toronto: Insomniac Press, 1999.

Bennett, Frank. *Bennett on Creditors' and Debtors' Rights and Remedies*. 5th Edition. Toronto: Carswell, 2006.

Bennett, Frank. *Bennett on Bankruptcy*. 8th Edition. Toronto: CCH Canadian Limited, 2004.

Bennett, Frank. *Bennett on Collections*. 5th Edition. Toronto: Carswell, 2003.

Caher, James P., and John M. Caher. *Personal Bankruptcy Law for Dummies*, 2nd Edition. Toronto: Wiley, 2005.

Canadian Bankers Association Reports. *Safeguarding Your Money, Managing Money,* and *Getting Value for Your Service Fees*. Available free at 1-800-263-0231.

Canadian Consumer Handbook. Ottawa: Industry Canada, 2005.

Costa, Carol, and James R. Beaman. *Complete Idiot's Guide to Surviving Bankruptcy*. Toronto: Penguin, 2003.

Daskalof, Alexander. *Credit Card Debt: Reduce Your Financial Burden in Three Easy Steps*. Toronto: HarperCollins, 1999.

Department of Finance Canada. *Canada's Credit Unions and Caisses Populaires*. Department of Finance: Ottawa, 2003.

Fuhrman, John. *The Credit Diet: How to Shed Unwanted Debt and Achieve Fiscal Fitness*. Toronto: Wiley, 2002.

Industry Canada. *All About Bankruptcy Mediation*. Ottawa: Industry Canada, 1998.

Industry Canada. *Dealing with Debt: A Consumer's Guide*. Ottawa: Industry Canada, 1998.

KPMG. *Options Available, Personal Bankruptcy Process, Questions About Bankruptcy, Consumer Proposals, Credit Bureau & Collection Agency Information*. KPMG, a leading trustee in bankruptcy, has prepared a series of information bulletins that are available online at **www.personalbankruptcy.com.**

Lim, Sylvia. *Personal Budgeting Kit*. 2nd Edition. Vancouver, Self-Counsel Press, 2005.

O'Reilly, Miles D., and Steven G. Cloutier. *Advising Individual Debtors in Ontario*. Toronto: Carswell, 1995.

Pahl, Greg, Nancy Dunnan, with Warren Ladenheim. *The Unofficial Guide to Beating Debt*. Toronto: Wiley, 2000.

Public Legal Education Association of Saskatchewan, Saskatoon. Several very relevant booklets (*Buying Stuff, Consumer Contracts, Consumer Fraud, Consumer Wisdom, Debts and Credit, Warranties and Guarantees*) are available free and online at **www.plea.org/freepubs/ freepubs.htm** (as of November 2003). There are other similar associations in other provinces.

Personal Finance on the Web

BankruptcyCanada.com
www.bankruptcycanada.com

Bankruptcy Survival Guide
www.bankruptcysurvivalguide.com

CanadaStudentDebt.ca
www.canadastudentdebt.ca

Canadian Association of Insolvency and Restructuring Professionals
www.cairp.ca/English/index.html

The Canadian Code of Practice for Consumer Protection in Electronic Commerce.
http://strategis.ic.gc.ca/epic/internet/inoca-bc.nsf/en/ca01832e.html
Protect yourself against debit card fraud.

Canadian Financial Wellness Group
www.cfwgroup.ca/forum

Canadian Private Investigators Resource Centre (CPIRC)
www.cpirc.com

Canoe Money: Credit Card Rates
http://money.canoe.ca/rates/credit.html

Chartered Accountants of Canada
www.cica.ca

Credit Bureau Collections
www.cbcollections.com

Credit Bureau of Sudbury
www.porcupinecomputers.com/sudbury

Credit Counselling Canada
www.creditcounsellingcanada.ca

Credit Counselling Service of Toronto
www.creditcanada.com

Credit Counselling Society
www.nomoredebts.org

Credit Union Central of Canada
www.cucentral.ca

Debt 911 Network
www.bankruptcy-ont.com

Department of Justice Canada
http://laws.justice.gc.ca

Equifax Canada
www.equifax.ca

Financial Consumer Agency of Canada
www.fcac-acfc.gc.ca

Hoyes, Michalos & Associates Inc., Trustees in Bankruptcy
www.hoyes.com

Identity Guard
www.identityguard.ca

Industry Canada
http://strategis.ic.gc.ca/pics/ca/consumerprotection03.pdf

Insolvency Dictionary
www.sands-trustee.com/ab.htm

Insolvency Institute of Canada
www.insolvency.ca

Investigators Group
www.investigators-group.com

Ontario Ministry of Government Services
www.mgs.gov.on.ca

Ontario Wages Act
www.canlii.org/on/laws/sta/w-1

Phonebusters
www.phonebusters.com/english/index.html

Superintendent of Bankruptcy
   www.strategis.ic.gc.ca/epic/internet/inbsf-osb.nsf/en/home

TransUnion Canada
   www.transunion.ca

Trust CanLaw: How to Check Your Credit Rating
   www.canlaw.com/credit/credit.htm

Index